Alfred Döblin
Monsters, Cyborgs and Berliners 1900-1933

# LEGENDA

LEGENDA is the Modern Humanities Research Association's book imprint for new research in the Humanities. Founded in 1995 by Malcolm Bowie and others within the University of Oxford, Legenda has always been a collaborative publishing enterprise, directly governed by scholars. The Modern Humanities Research Association (MHRA) joined this collaboration in 1998, became half-owner in 2004, in partnership with Maney Publishing and then Routledge, and has since 2016 been sole owner. Titles range from medieval texts to contemporary cinema and form a widely comparative view of the modern humanities, including works on Arabic, Catalan, English, French, German, Greek, Italian, Portuguese, Russian, Spanish, and Yiddish literature. Editorial boards and committees of more than 60 leading academic specialists work in collaboration with bodies such as the Society for French Studies, the British Comparative Literature Association and the Association of Hispanists of Great Britain & Ireland.

The MHRA encourages and promotes advanced study and research in the field of the modern humanities, especially modern European languages and literature, including English, and also cinema. It aims to break down the barriers between scholars working in different disciplines and to maintain the unity of humanistic scholarship. The Association fulfils this purpose through the publication of journals, bibliographies, monographs, critical editions, and the MHRA Style Guide, and by making grants in support of research. Membership is open to all who work in the Humanities, whether independent or in a University post, and the participation of younger colleagues entering the field is especially welcomed.

ALSO PUBLISHED BY THE ASSOCIATION

*Critical Texts*
*Tudor and Stuart Translations* • *New Translations* • *European Translations*
*MHRA Library of Medieval Welsh Literature*

*MHRA Bibliographies*
*Publications of the Modern Humanities Research Association*

*The Annual Bibliography of English Language & Literature*
*Austrian Studies*
*Modern Language Review*
*Portuguese Studies*
*The Slavonic and East European Review*
*Working Papers in the Humanities*
*The Yearbook of English Studies*

www.mhra.org.uk
www.legendabooks.com

# GERMANIC LITERATURES

*Editorial Committee*
Chair: Professor Ritchie Robertson (University of Oxford)
Dr Barbara Burns (Glasgow University)
Professor Jane Fenoulhet (University College London)
Professor Anne Fuchs (University College Dublin)
Dr Jakob Stougaard-Nielsen (University College London)
Professor Annette Volfing (University of Oxford)
Professor Susanne Kord (University College London)
Professor John Zilcosky (University of Toronto)

Germanic Literatures includes monographs and essay collections on literature originally written not only in German, but also in Dutch and the Scandinavian languages. Within the German-speaking area, it seeks also to publish studies of other national literatures such as those of Austria and Switzerland. The chronological scope of the series extends from the early Middle Ages down to the present day.

APPEARING IN THIS SERIES

11. *E.T.A. Hoffmann's Orient*, by Joanna Neilly
12. *Structures of Subjugation in Dutch Literature*, by Judit Gera
13. *Isak Dinesen Reading Søren Kierkegaard: On Christianity, Seduction, Gender, and Repetition*, by Mads Bunch
14. *Yvan Goll: The Thwarted Pursuit of the Whole*, by Robert Vilain
15. *Foreign Parts: German and Austrian Actors on the British Stage 1933–1960*, by Richard Dove
16. *Paul Celan's Unfinished Poetics*, by Thomas C. Connolly
17. *Encounters with Albion: Britain and the British in Texts by Jewish Refugees from Nazism*, by Anthony Grenville
18. *The Law of Poetry: Studies in Hölderlin's Poetics*, by Charles Lewis
19. *Georg Hermann: A Writer's Life*, by John Craig-Sharples
20. *Alfred Döblin: Monsters, Cyborgs and Berliners 1900–1933*, by Robert Craig
21. *Confrontational Readings: Literary Neo-Avant-Gardes in Dutch and German*, edited by Inge Arteel, Lars Bernaerts and Olivier Couder
22. *Poetry, Painting, Park: Goethe and Claude Lorrain*, by Franz R. Kempf
23. *Childhood, Memory, and the Nation: Young Lives under Nazism in Contemporary German Culture*, by Alexandra Lloyd

*Managing Editor*
Dr Graham Nelson, 41 Wellington Square, Oxford OX1 2JF, UK
www.legendabooks.com

# Alfred Döblin

## *Monsters, Cyborgs and Berliners 1900-1933*

Robert Craig

Germanic Literatures 20
Modern Humanities Research Association
2021

Published by Legenda
an imprint of the Modern Humanities Research Association
Salisbury House, Station Road, Cambridge CB1 2LA

ISBN 978-1-78188-926-8 (HB)
ISBN 978-1-78188-927-5 (PB)

First published 2021

*All rights reserved. No part of this publication may be reproduced or disseminated or transmitted in any form or by any means, electronic, mechanical, photocopying, recording or otherwise, or stored in any retrieval system, or otherwise used in any manner whatsoever without written permission of the copyright owner, except in accordance with the provisions of the Copyright, Designs and Patents Act 1988, or under the terms of a licence permitting restricted copying issued in the UK by the Copyright Licensing Agency Ltd, Saffron House, 6–10 Kirby Street, London EC1N 8TS, England, or in the USA by the Copyright Clearance Center, 222 Rosewood Drive, Danvers MA 01923. Application for the written permission of the copyright owner to reproduce any part of this publication must be made by email to legenda@mhra.org.uk.*

*Disclaimer: Statements of fact and opinion contained in this book are those of the author and not of the editors or the Modern Humanities Research Association. The publisher makes no representation, express or implied, in respect of the accuracy of the material in this book and cannot accept any legal responsibility or liability for any errors or omissions that may be made.*

*Trademark notice: Product or corporate names may be trademarks or registered trademarks, and are used only for identification and explanation without intent to infringe.*

© *Modern Humanities Research Association 2021*

*Copy-Editor: Dr Nigel Hope*

# CONTENTS

| | | |
|---|---|---|
| | *Acknowledgements* | ix |
| | *Abbreviations* | xi |
| | *Note on Editions, Translations and Permissions* | xii |
| | Introduction | 1 |
| 1 | The Hermeneutics of Guilt: Döblin's Short Prose | 19 |
| 2 | Another Time, Another Place: *Die drei Sprünge des Wang-lun* | 56 |
| 3 | Of Cyborgs and Other Monsters: *Berge Meere und Giganten* | 91 |
| 4 | After the Deluge: The Anthropology and Nature-Philosophy | 127 |
| 5 | A Creaturely Carnival: *Berlin Alexanderplatz* | 156 |
| | Conclusion: Redemption after All? | 181 |
| | *Bibliography* | 188 |
| | *Index* | 201 |

*For my parents*

# ACKNOWLEDGEMENTS

This book was made possible through the generous support of numerous individuals and institutions. I would firstly like to thank David Midgley, who first sparked my fascination with all things Döblin and supervised the Cambridge PhD thesis on which the study is based. At every stage of my doctoral research he gave so generously of his time and expertise, asked the right questions at the right times, and — often imperceptibly — helped to clarify ideas even I didn't know I had. Without his support and advice, there would certainly be no book.

It is with great pleasure and gratitude that I acknowledge the Arts & Humanities Research Council, which fully funded both my MPhil and subsequent PhD, and also made substantial contributions towards research and travel expenses. Trinity Hall, Cambridge, proved an immensely supportive and friendly environment in which to research and write, along with providing a number of small grants and awards. The Tiarks Fund of the German Department was also forthcoming with support; and a generous travel grant from the American German Studies Association enabled me to present at their 2016 conference. Whether in Cambridge, London, Chicago, San Diego, or elsewhere, a trickle of fascinating papers, well-placed questions, and impromptu coffee break conversations shaped both thesis and book in many happy ways. The monograph itself came to fruition under the shadow of the tortuous Brexit process, and it's with gratitude and not a little sadness that I acknowledge the Erasmus study grant which enabled me to spend a semester conducting doctoral research at the Friedrich Schlegel Graduiertenschule at the Freie Universität in Berlin.

Many individuals played important roles in the development of this project. Martin Boden's inspiring teaching first ignited my love of the German language in the early 2000s. Martin Ruehl, Neil Kenny and the late Philip Ford fostered my interest in European intellectual history as an undergraduate at Cambridge; Michael Minden, Andrew Webber and Sarah Colvin have been the sources of fascinating conversations and fresh perspectives on German modernism; and Peter Hutchinson deserves a special mention for all his advice and encouragement over the years, not to mention the bookcase-bending gifts of innumerable books. After my move there in January 2017, the Institute for English and American Studies at the University of Bamberg has provided a congenial and enriching backdrop against which to complete the study; and I would especially like to thank Christa Jansohn for allowing me the space and time to do so.

My PhD examiners, Martin Ruehl and Ritchie Robertson, helped make the viva a genuinely enjoyable experience, while asking questions and making suggestions that proved invaluable as the thesis gradually became the book. As the Germanic

Literatures series editor at Legenda, Ritchie Robertson subsequently guided the project to completion with remarkable efficiency, patience and good humour. Graham Nelson and Nigel Hope have made the 'business end' of things both straightforward and surprisingly pleasant.

Finally, and on a more personal note, I would like to thank many wonderful friends from all over the world for countless moments of moral support and light relief over the past few years. Many people deserve a mention, but a few names really do stand out. The journey would have been a great deal harder without Gerard Corvin, Sarah Lebrecht, Matt Craig, Allen and Edwina Swann, Ruthie Tilt, Erica Wickerson, Nikolai Beland, Sarah Becker, Ben Rossner, Rahel Eisenmann and Hanyi Du. And last but absolutely not least, my parents: their unstinting support, in every way, shape and form, has been indispensable throughout. I dedicate this book to them.

R.C., Bamberg, May 2021

# ABBREVIATIONS

On account of their frequency, references to Döblin's individual works will be parenthesized and provided 'in-text', in the form of the appropriate abbreviation, followed by page number(s). For example: '...' (BA 145, 148). Throughout the text I use the following set of abbreviations; the full details of each volume can be found in the Bibliography.

| | |
|---|---|
| AzL | *Aufsätze zur Literatur* |
| BA | *Berlin Alexanderplatz* |
| BMG | *Berge Meere und Giganten* |
| *Briefe*, I | *Briefe*, I |
| *Gedächtnisstörungen* | *Gedächtnisstörungen bei der Korsakoffschen Psychose* |
| IN | *Das Ich über der Natur* |
| KS I–IV | *Kleine Schriften, I–IV* |
| *Manas* | *Manas: Epische Dichtung* |
| RP | *Reise in Polen* |
| SÄPL | *Schriften zu Ästhetik, Poetik und Literatur* |
| SE | *Die Ermordung einer Butterblume: Sämtliche Erzählungen* |
| SLW | *Schriften zu Leben und Werk* |
| SPG | *Schriften zur Politik und Gesellschaft* |
| SR | *Schicksalsreise: Bericht und Bekenntnis* |
| SV | *Der schwarze Vorhang* |
| UD | *Unser Dasein* |
| W | *Wallenstein* |
| WL | *Die drei Sprünge des Wang-lun* |
| WuV | *Wissen und Verändern!* |

# NOTE ON EDITIONS, TRANSLATIONS AND PERMISSIONS

The edition used here is Alfred Döblin, *Ausgewählte Werke in Einzelbänden* [*Selected Works in Individual Volumes*], ed. by Walter Muschg, Anthony W. Riley, and Christina Alten (Olten, Solothurn, Düsseldorf and Zurich: Walter, 1960–2007). This remains the standard scholarly edition of Döblin's works, despite the emergence of a new edition with S. Fischer (Frankfurt am Main), published from 2008 onwards. Not included in the *Ausgewählte Werke* are Döblin's doctoral dissertation, *Gedächtnisstörungen bei der Korsakoffschen Psychose*, and his essay on nature-philosophy of 1927, *Das Ich über der Natur*, both of which were published as stand-alone volumes. All translations of Döblin's works are my own, and for ease of reading, the English translation is given first, followed by the German in square brackets. In order to avoid excessive clutter, I have provided the German original in instances of especial significance and interest to my argument. Unless otherwise indicated, translations of other primary texts, philosophical works and secondary texts are my own; any use of existing, published translations is clearly indicated in both the footnotes and the Bibliography. My own translation does not necessarily imply any criticism of the available alternatives.

Parts of Chapter 3 appeared in an earlier form in the volume *Internationales Alfred-Döblin-Kolloquium Cambridge 2017: Natur, Technik und das (Post-)Humane in den Schriften Alfred Döblins*, ed. by Steffan Davies and David Midgley, *Jahrbuch für Internationale Germanistik*, Series A, 133 (Bern: Lang, 2019). Chapter 5 is a substantially expanded version of my chapter in *Biological Discourses: The Language of Science and Literature around 1900*, ed. by Ina Linge and myself (Oxford: Lang, 2017). I am very grateful to Peter Lang for granting me permission to reproduce revised material from both pieces here.

The cover image is a slightly cropped reproduction of the painting *Die Nacht* [*The Night*] (1918-19), by Max Beckmann. I would like to thank the Kunstsammlung Nordrhein-Westfalen (Düsseldorf), as well as the bpk-Bildagentur (Berlin), for permission to reproduce it.

# INTRODUCTION

Er wird Sie beunruhigen; er wird Ihre Träume beschweren; Sie werden zu schlucken haben; er wird Ihnen nicht schmecken; unverdaulich ist er, auch unbekömmlich. Den Leser wird er ändern. Wer sich selbst genügt, sei vor Döblin gewarnt.[1]

[He will unsettle you; he will haunt your dreams. You'll have to swallow; you won't like his taste; he's indigestible, unwholesome as well. He'll change his reader. If you're satisfied with yourself, beware of Döblin.]

A literary health warning could hardly be more categorical than that. Alfred Döblin is a risky and unsettling prospect, Günter Grass told his audience at the close of his anniversary tribute to his late 'teacher' in 1967. And yet, a decade after his death, now was the time to return to the vast novels and rediscover a unique contribution to literary modernism: a strangely anti-canonical author who spent his literary career up to his exile in 1933, as Grass put it, moving relentlessly from book to book, essay to essay, and one philosophical and aesthetic 'position' to the next. As the literary scene of the Federal Republic was searching for a more radical voice after the conservatism of the Adenauer years, the call to rediscover Döblin was a timely one.[2] Following his return to Europe from American exile in 1945, the author of the literary sensation *Berlin Alexanderplatz* had found himself largely forgotten. Döblin was a wartime convert to Catholicism — a surprise in itself for a Jewish socialist — who fell uneasily between irreconcilable camps. He was far too Catholic for the progressive Left, and too much of an anarchist for the Catholics, as Grass drily had it. In an even more intractable sense, Döblin felt himself profoundly at odds with a damaged society propped up by the bureaucratic and cultural remnants of National Socialism.[3] There were certainly exceptions to the forgetfulness and indifference, as both his autobiography *Schicksalsreise* [*Destiny's Journey*] (1949), and *Hamlet oder Die lange Nacht nimmt ein Ende* [*Tales of a Long Night*] (1956), attracted some critical acclaim. But the landscapes and preoccupations of the post-war years were far removed from those of Weimar Berlin, his last German home and the site of his greatest success.[4]

Rather than a postponed funeral oration for a stranded returnee, Grass's address was a plea to re-tread the idiosyncratic paths of this literary 'visionary' of the pre-war years, as he described him. 'Where is the author?', he asked of a modernist who had claimed in 1928 that he kept his work as a doctor demarcated from his literary persona (SLW 103–05), and whose fictional worlds added further layers of obfuscation: should we look for him in the post-apocalyptic utopias of free love in *Berge Meere und Giganten* [*Mountains, Oceans and Giants*], in Berlin's steamy abattoirs, or even at the altar of his eventual conversion in 1941?[5] However, Grass's search also drew attention to an experimental literary praxis that saw the sovereignty of the author, and the subject *tout court*, obscure itself behind the fragmented and reassembled languages and materials of the epic novels. In the face of Döblin's own contradictions, the question of his authorial identity is perhaps all the more striking in retrospect for its resonances with Roland Barthes's path-breaking essay of the same year as the address, *La mort de l'auteur* [*The Death of the Author*] (1967).[6] Barthes's radical challenge to interpretations on the basis of authorial intentionality chimed with the work of an author who throughout his career rejected any straightforward sense of hermeneutic mastery over his own works. Central to Grass's health warning was his sense of an epic writing grounded in a loss of sovereign control: here was a radical and often shocking literary output which, in reshaping the possibilities of the modern epic work, also began to rethink the contours of the modern subject itself. And in the spirit of Barthes, the traces of his influence lived on both explicitly and implicitly. Bertolt Brecht claimed, in his retrospective review of 1943–44, that no one had so profoundly shaped his own theory and practice of epic theatre.[7] Such authors as Hans Henny Jahnn, Erich Kästner, Irmgard Keun and Klaus Mann, among others, also found a creative impetus in Döblin's experimental configurations of the modern epic novel. Grass's own novels, notably *Hundejahre* [*Dog Years*] (1963) and *Die Rättin* [*The Rat*] (1986), show his teacher's intertextual fingerprints; and Rainer Werner Fassbinder's avowed obsession with *Berlin Alexanderplatz* was the starting point of his decision to make a fourteen-part television miniseries out of it.[8]

If Döblin's own cultural status has long since acquired something of the 'writer's writer', not least on account of the difficulty of his fiction, his rewards for readers are now more accessible and more widely recognized than ever before. Fittingly for an author whose works range widely across cultural boundaries, new English translations of the city masterpiece and the short stories have found a fascinated reception among critics and readers alike.[9]

This book is neither a retelling of the life nor a study of the influence. Instead, it takes as its starting point Grass's temptation to follow the traces: not the phantasmic presence of Döblin the author as such, but rather the deconstructions and reconfigurations of the human subject in his works before 1933. In his most famous literary manifesto, the 'Berliner Programm', he called on his fellow novelists to give up both their sovereignty over the text and any aesthetic and epistemic claim over their characters' inner lives and motivations. 'Let's get away from the human being!' ['Los vom Menschen!'] (SÄPL 123) was a daring enough suggestion for 1913; and it is all the more interesting for us today, as we grapple with delineations and definitions of the posthuman as both a cultural idea and a socio-political reality. In that light, I want to investigate how Döblin's literary works, his poetics, his nature-philosophy and his anthropology offered a pioneering and highly distinctive literary response to the crises of the human subject in literary modernism. Entering the literary scene in the earliest years of the twentieth century, Döblin was aware of working in a cultural environment intensely conscious of the strangeness of the subject to itself, and the alienness of the nature of which it was a part. Against an intellectual backdrop strongly shaped during his school years by Schopenhauer, Nietzsche and

Spinoza (SLW 289), this study takes as its particular focus the multifarious ways in which his work up to 1933 engaged with the question of the human subject's, and humankind's, relationship with nature.

More explicitly than perhaps any of his German-language contemporaries, Döblin found his central literary theme in this relationship, which comes to the fore in his work in myriad forms. The self wrestles with its own body and sexuality in the short stories and novellas. Döblin's historical fiction conceives both individuals and masses as natural forces in themselves, while sharply pointing up the problems and paradoxes of precisely that; and *Die drei Sprünge des Wang-lun* [*The Three Leaps of Wang-lun*] (1915) is as much a meditation on our reconcilability with nature as it is a negotiation with the political possibilities of pacifism. His science fiction *Berge Meere und Giganten*, of 1924, stages a tellurian struggle between man and the natural world, while his mature works of anthropology and nature-philosophy seek ways of rethinking and reconciling the two. Perhaps most unexpectedly, *Berlin Alexanderplatz* (1929) offers us a Weimar cityscape, and a beleaguered protagonist, just as much a part of 'nature' as the Icelandic volcanoes that the European city-states of the distant future smash open, and the icecaps that they melt. Döblin's conception of nature evolves in complex ways over the course of his pre-exile career, and it is entwined with an equally complex and evolving sense of the self. A central purpose of this study is to delineate that multifaceted relationship; and by doing so, it also argues for Döblin's deep and urgent relevance to contemporary debates over human identity, posthumanism, and the ways in which both relate to a looming climate catastrophe. The language of physiological response in Grass's address — 'indigestible', 'unwholesome' — testifies to a writer who still productively unsettles our sense of our entwinement with both body and material world.

## Shifting Contours

The concept of nature's proximity to the human, combined with its otherness to us, took on radical new dimensions around the turn of the nineteenth century. Writing about the philosophical and scientific forebears and contexts of European modernism, Richard Sheppard has highlighted a 'paradigm shift' in ways of understanding reality, pointing to the end of a 'logocentric' conception of reality fundamental to both 'classical modernity and the liberal humanist epoch'. This paradigm found many of its formative intellectual origins in the Renaissance, and it reached its zenith in the Enlightenment's doctrines of human emancipation.[10] But in connection to that, Western culture's deep-rooted Judaeo-Christian beliefs in teleological progress and redemption were also crumbling away.

These sets of ideologies had met a radical challenge in the shape of Charles Darwin's theory of natural selection, which was first articulated in *On the Origin of Species* (1859), and which entered the German (and European) consciousness in large part through the work of Ernst Haeckel. Such best-selling works as *Natürliche Schöpfungsgeschichte* [*The History of Creation*] (1868), and *Die Welträthsel* [*The Riddle of the Universe*] (1899) offered monistic reconstructions of Darwin, grounded in a German

Romantic tradition reaching back to the spiritualist, and originally Spinozist, idea of *deus sive natura* (God and nature as one).[11] Aspects of Darwinian thought also mixed with the ateleological pessimism of Arthur Schopenhauer's philosophy of the Will and Eduard von Hartmann's conception of 'the Unconscious'. Building on these inheritances, Friedrich Nietzsche and Sigmund Freud were finding new ways of conceiving the embodied self through their unique combinations of scientific and literary methods. In relation to a resurgence of interest in Schopenhauer and Nietzsche in the 1890s, Ritchie Robertson highlights a 'turn-of-the-century model of life as powerful unconscious striving'.[12] In short, the rational subject was sovereign neither over the rest of nature nor even himself. The masculine reflexive pronoun is significant; and in a characteristically patriarchal formulation of one of the central premises of psychoanalysis in an essay of 1917, 'Eine Schwierigkeit in der Psychoanalyse' ['A Difficulty in the Path of Psycho-Analysis'], Freud argued that the 'ego' ['Ich'] is no longer even 'master [...] in his own house' [*Herr* [...] *in seinem eigenen Haus*'].[13] From a different disciplinary perspective the physicist and philosopher Ernst Mach had reduced the human subject to a disparate bunch of sensations, against the backdrop of a physics of flux and radical indeterminacy.[14]

In different ways, then, the intellectual culture of early modernism was witnessing a shift in notions of 'humanness' in view of its deep continuities with the animal kingdom on the one hand, and the metaphysical flux of nature at large on the other. Robertson views the various reconfigurations of the self to be found in the work of German modernist writers as points through which these multifarious energies and forces crossed.[15] Even in a literary culture steeped in the latest scientific and philosophical developments, Döblin's active philosophical interests, combined with an exceptional degree of theoretical self-reflexivity, marks him out as a particularly important interlocutor. His thinking was the product of a climate in search of an all-unifying *Weltanschauung*, a metaphysics that might remain grounded in empirical perception and circumvent the pitfall of theism.[16] This search took place within a constellation of philosophical responses to a perceived loss of any unifying metaphysical vision after a nineteenth century dominated by the rise of the natural sciences and the pervasive influence of forms of positivism.[17] And yet, in the wake of Schopenhauer and Nietzsche, German writers and thinkers were becoming ever more acutely conscious of the contradictions of the human condition as both an integral part of nature and yet alienated from it.[18]

With his revaluation of the body and its impulses and instincts, Nietzsche became a particularly significant sparring partner for Döblin, and the inspiration (and irritant) behind some of his earliest writing. Two essays dated from his time as a medical student in Berlin: 'Der Wille zur Macht als Erkenntnis bei Friedrich Nietzsche' ['The Will to Power as Cognition in Friedrich Nietzsche'] was written in 1902, and 'Zu Nietzsches Morallehre' ['On Nietzsche's Theories of Morality'] in 1903, although the pieces were not published until 1978. As Mirjana Stancic has pointed out, from today's perspective Döblin's arguments offer less a philosophically viable interpretation of Nietzsche than an insight into his own metaphysical orientations.[19] He objects fundamentally to what he sees as Nietzsche's reduction of moral judgments to the level of psychological phenomena, along with a more general rooting of morality in biology. Furthermore, he considers the 'Übermensch' to be a travesty of Darwinian evolutionary thought. On his reading, Nietzsche recasts the human being's constitutive moral 'striving' as the 'vehicle' for evolution: the 'moral' individual should actively appropriate the evolutionary process as the 'executor of his will' ['Vollstreckerin seines Willens'] (KS 1, 44), with the ultimate goal of a superiority conceived in terms of a 'heightened intensity of life, power itself' ['erhöhte Lebensintensität, "Macht"'] (46). In short, the triumph of biological strength over weakness, with its deterministic hereditary and racial factors, is elevated to a normative moral principle (41–44).

Döblin's distaste at this elision is a revealing indicator of his own sense of mankind's relationship with the rest of the natural world: it is, perversely, an article of post-monotheistic religious dogma to suggest that man's greater evolutionary 'differentiation' dictates that he 'rules' over an earth whose species diversify not according to various degrees of strength and richness of life, but rather through the adaptation of anatomy to environment (47–49). The backdrop to all this is a critique of Nietzsche as embodying the endpoint of a positivistic belief in the epistemological supremacy of the natural sciences (19–20). Scepticism and dogmatism collapse into one another, as 'spirit' or 'mind' ['Geist'] is seen as utterly reducible to nature's materiality (23). The only metaphysical principles remaining are — to Döblin's mind — the anthropocentric myths of the 'Übermensch' and the eternal recurrence of the same (52).

This supposed exposure of Nietzsche as a metaphysician by other means testifies to Döblin's passionate conviction that the metaphysical should not be reduced in any straightforward sense to the realm of the observable and empirical. I will discuss the interactions between his fiction and his medical interests in Chapter 1; but his own later remarks about his choice to train as a doctor offer some telling insights into his preoccupations at the outset of his writing career. In an essay of 1938, 'Persönliches und Unpersönliches' ['Things personal and impersonal'], he admitted that his interests as a medical student had not been in bones, joints or intestines, but rather 'what holds the world together in its innermost being' ['was die Welt im Innersten zusammenhält'] (SLW 239–40). With a nod to Goethe's *Faust*, Döblin is suggesting that the relationship between the physiological and the psychical should be understood through an immanent metaphysical principle, rather than subjected to the dissecting 'mastery' of empirical science.[20] This will carry significant implications as we consider the complex relationship between Döblin's medical and writerly vocations. Perhaps just as significantly, though, we can also see emerging a way of conceiving and figuring the natural world that resists our epistemological, clinical or technological domination of it.

As David Midgley has shown, Döblin's search for an all-encompassing vision was offset by his fascination with 'the look and feel of empirical reality' and the 'material phenomena of human experience':[21] in short, the irreducible *qualia* that make it up. This closely associated him with a recent and contemporary movement in German and French intellectual culture known as 'life philosophy' ['Lebensphilosophie'].

Under the influence of Schopenhauer and Nietzsche, as well as the German Idealists, the philosophers Wilhelm Dilthey, Henri Bergson and Georg Simmel aimed to reconceive life itself as a 'creative process', constituted through a continuity of mental experiences and grasped not primarily by reason, but rather through intuition.[22] In a markedly more positive vein than Schopenhauer's philosophy of the Will, their overlapping metaphysics aimed to unify contradictory propositions about the phenomenon of life — aporias of subject and object, and natural cycles of creation and dissolution. While there is no hard evidence that Döblin directly read these thinkers,[23] I will discuss the highly illuminating parallels that can be found in Chapter 4, and points of commonality can be mapped out throughout his literary, philosophical and aesthetic writings. In the duologue of music philosophy *Gespräche mit Kalypso: Über die Musik* [*Conversations with Calypso: On Music*], first published in the Expressionist magazine *Der Sturm* [*The Storm*] in 1910 and an important propaedeutic to the later aesthetics, he reinterpreted music as the auditory 'mirror' of a transient world caught between flux and form, and indeterminacy and determinacy, as well as an art form that embodied the ineluctable meaning and meaningfulness of human experience itself (SÄPL 62–65, 106–07). There is a remarkable crossover here with Bergson's understanding of music as a mirror of human identity *in* memory, in his *Essais sur les données immédiates de la conscience* (1889), which appeared in German translation as *Zeit und Freiheit* [*Time and Free Will*] in 1911.[24] But we also hear the echoes of Schopenhauer's Will and Nietzsche's justification of the world as an aesthetic phenomenon alone in *Die Geburt der Tragödie* [*The Birth of Tragedy*] (1872).[25]

In a retrospective essay of 1932, Döblin would admit that the same era often brought very similar ideas into being in very different places (SLW 217). This hint of an anxiety of influence was a tacit concession to the impact of contemporary thinkers and writers on his work, conscious and unconscious, and explicit and implicit; and it also spoke to the sheer range of his repertoire, from contemporary biology and philosophy, through the nature-philosophy of the German Romantics and the pantheism of Spinoza, and all the way back to the ancient philosophies of Daoism and Buddhism. Through an array of cultural and intellectual prisms, he figures human life as caught between energies of formation and dissolution, creation and destruction. In his pre-exile work, he also moves progressively away from the notion, beloved of modernism, of the 'self' as an irredeemably fragmented fiction. I may live in a strange and 'terrible' world that is constantly 'flowing away from me and disintegrating' ['eine schrecklich fließende, verderbende Welt'], as we read in 1933; and yet the phenomenon of the human being is dignified by the very fact that it 'is' (UD 54–55).

This paradox of meaning and meaninglessness, rolled into one and mutually inextricable, comes to define what it means to be human both within and apart from nature; and Döblin's works generate their peculiar energy in no small part by both negating and affirming the intrinsic value of corporeal existence at one and the same time. As one regular reviewer, Ferdinand Lion, put it with some archness in 1928, he could be read as both a 'world-affirming Buddhist' ['weltbejahender Buddhist'] and a 'Daoist of the soul' ['Taoist der Seele'].[26]

## Rethinking Nature, Reconstructing the Self

Döblin was, in short, working with and within a set of philosophical traditions rooted in a broadly shared understanding of the flux and fluidity underlying human existence; but over the course of his pre-exile career, he was also developing his own complex dialectics of mind and matter, nature and culture, and nature and technology. In certain important respects, this dialectical thinking anticipates the arguments developed by the Marxist sociologists Theodor W. Adorno and Max Horkheimer in *Dialektik der Aufklärung* [*Dialectic of Enlightenment*] (1947); and even when not explicitly invoked, the about-turns, switchbacks and innate contradictions of this seminal text inform many of my readings. Drawing upon the example of Homer's *Odyssey*, they argue that human beings have, since their evolutionary beginnings, faced a choice between their own 'subjection to nature' and the 'subjection of nature to the self' ['ihrer Unterwerfung unter Natur oder der Natur unter das Selbst'].[27] While the illustration is a schematic one, the sight of Odysseus stopping his men's ears and lashing himself to the mast in order to resist the sirens' song encapsulates the central paradox: any mastery over nature is utterly tied up with both mastery of the self and domination of other human beings.[28] The alternative can hardly be contemplated, as it would entail the disintegration and destruction of subject and society; and yet a liberal-humanist ideal of autonomy and freedom is reduced to little more than an ideological myth.

The implications of this dialectic run both deeper and faster than its stylized presentation here might suggest. 'Nature' is never merely something 'out there', to be mastered, manipulated or aestheticized,[29] but also that amorphous 'Other' lurking within human beings and their societies. It is a slippery and polyvalent cover-all for our evolved bodies, our impulses (individual and collective), and the world that surrounds and sustains us. In contrast to the fetishization of 'Nature' as an aesthetic object, or else as a placeholder which 'wavers in between the divine and the material' — between post-Burkean 'substance' and post-Kantian 'essence' — the environmental philosopher Timothy Morton recasts nature in literally environmental terms, as something that is always intensely historical and discursive, and inseparable from ideologies of self and society.[30] It re-emerges as a kind of non-thing that is uncannily and destructively 'there' rather than sublimely 'over there'. Not only that, but it also remains irreducible to ideologies of either essentialism or social constructivism.[31]

I suggest that the self-consciously inter-discursive character and texture of Döblin's work embodies something of that recalcitrance, and that he is a uniquely compelling literary example precisely because his works shot through with 'otherness' in all its guises. His narratives and essays are criss-crossed with myriad motifs and discourses — mythical, philosophical and scientific — which circle around the dialectical relationship between the self and its bodily and material Others; but the fragmentariness of his writing in form and content reflects both the fragmentation of that relationship, and the mediation between autonomy, heteronomy and heterogeneity that constitutes it.

Ever since Grass's address, there has been a growing critical fascination with this otherness, in all its forms, at the heart of Döblin's works. Traditional accounts of his creative development have been all too willing to map out a linear trajectory towards a 'reconstruction' of the modern self, and to suggest that Döblin ends up redeeming his early fascinations with psychopathology and natural destructiveness through the reinvented and suspiciously well-behaved Franz Biberkopf at the close of *Berlin Alexanderplatz*. Klaus Müller-Salget's sense of a redemptive 'refounding of the self' ['Neubegründung des Ich'] in *Berlin Alexanderplatz*, in contrast to Franz Biberkopf's 'bad' individualism, now seems a capitulation to an ideology of conformist civic selfhood;[32] but subsequent critics, too, have developed aspects of this idea, albeit in more nuanced forms. Otto Keller's contribution of 1980, for example, traces Biberkopf's circuitous movement, through a text replete with mythical and Old Testament motifs, towards an acceptance of the logic of self-sacrifice. In turn, Birgit Hoock has situated Döblin at an aesthetic threshold between modernism's yearning for a reinvested sense of metaphysical wholeness, and reconciliation with nature, and the dissolution and negation of that possibility in postmodernism.[33] Döblin's own aversion to any straightforward suggestion that 'the subject' might be redeemed is encapsulated in his own account in the retrospective essay 'Epilog' (1948). 'Sacrifice' ['Opfer'] is certainly the central theme of his great Berlin novel; but he accepts that while he has broken and reassembled — redeemed — his protagonist on the surface, he has not quite managed to break him down on the inside. The author's own disquiet at an incomplete job, even the whiff of a bourgeois cop-out, is faint but unmistakable (SLW 296).[34]

Given the perhaps unavoidable ideological colouring of such hermeneutical approaches to Döblin, more recent work has turned to focus on the cross-discursive textures of the prose. Specifically, the neologism of 'fact-fantasy' ['Tatsachenphantasie'], which is the centrepiece of the early manifesto of poetics and aesthetics, the 'Berliner Programm' (1913), has become a particular focal point (SÄPL 123). This oxymoron refers most directly to the capacity of the poetic imagination to combine and recombine the raw data — the 'facts' — of sensory and mental experience in unexpected new constellations, without smoothing them down with the help of psychological reconstructions. More broadly, however, it has come to evoke the manner in which Döblin constructs his narratives from the epistemological 'data' of other discourses and orders of knowledge.

In a seminal study of 1995, Wolfgang Schäffner offered a reassessment of his works that found its starting point in Döblin's call in the 'Programm' to 'learn from psychiatry' (SÄPL 120–21). In part, Schäffner was attempting to re-read his works in the light of Döblin's clinical training in psychiatry; but in an extension of Foucault's historical critiques and analyses in *Folie et déraison* [*Madness and Civilization*] (1961), he also viewed 'psychiatry' more broadly as symptomatic of the construction of discourses in modernity with a view to defining norms and pathologies, and excluding aberrancies.[35] A relatively recent collaborative volume has read 'Tatsachenphantasie' as embodying the experimental orientations of his works as sites at which multiple discourses of scientific 'fact' (medical, technological, historiographical) are brought into play and figuratively reworked. Julia Genz and Yvonne Wübben notably show how Döblin's most famous early stories, 'Die

Tänzerin und der Leib' ['The Dancer and the Body'] and 'Die Ermordung einer Butterblume' ['The Murder of a Buttercup'], problematize even the pathological self by bringing modes of psychoanalytic and psychiatric diagnosis into play with each other within mythic spaces.[36] In a similarly epistemological vein, Eva Horn's article of 2003 entirely broke with teleological interpretations of *Berlin Alexanderplatz* to highlight its role as a kind of aesthetic-experimental arena for the converging and conflicting epistemological claims of modernity.[37]

In recent years in particular, Döblin's works have been the site of intensive philological archaeology, with a view to excavating his materials and the sources of his ideas. Gabriele Sander's archival work, as evident in her critical editions of *Berge Meere und Giganten* (2006) and *Die drei Sprünge des Wang-lun* (2007), has profoundly enriched our understanding of 'Tatsachenphantasie' by revealing the combination of encyclopaedic seriousness and poetic licence with which Döblin reworked his 'knowledge'. Sander's research has inspired and been accompanied by a resurgence of interest in the colonial and postcolonial dimensions and dynamics of the novels, most notably in relation to the functions of his cultural reappropriations; and alongside the broader question of the relationship between 'Literatur' and 'Wissen', the theme of Döblin's interculturality plays a significant role in the compendious *Döblin-Handbuch* of 2016.[38] His works 'let other discourses in', thus revealing modernity in all its multifacetedness, as Steffan Davies and Ernest Schonfield have succinctly put it.[39] This porousness unsettles any sense of a modern self in relationship with a body or a nature that is safely demarcated from it.

We might broadly divide these sets of critical approaches between the 'hermeneutical' and the 'epistemological', while recognizing their many points of overlap. But my submission is that neither approach, perhaps even in combination, can do full justice to works which persistently ironize and relativize their constitutive materials, while leaving in their wakes tantalizing traces of 'meaning'. I hope to show that a sensitive reading of Döblin must remain resolutely irreducible to any one line of interpretation, while also holding out against a kind of zero-sum game of interplaying discourses and motifs. As the historical fiction of an eighteenth-century rebellion against the Qing Dynasty, *Die drei Sprünge des Wang-lun* seems to culminate in the failure of both the Daoist doctrine of *wu wei* (literally 'without action') and the military force that it paradoxically requires in order to endure. Indeed, Wang-lun's martyrdom is portrayed as an insignificant submission to the masses, as he and his comrades burn to death without so much as an affirming moment of tragic witness. But the novel closes in a different direction: the wife of the Emperor's field commander, mourning her dead children and vowing revenge on Wang-lun beyond the grave, asks herself, 'Be still, be still, do not resist, can I do that?' ['Stille sein, nicht widerstreben, kann ich es denn?'], in a meditation on *wu wei* (495). Her question mediates passivity through agency, and negation through affirmation; and the existential possibility of the non-resisting subject is left open even as the corpses of the dead rebels rot in the streets and return to the earth. This small example is a highly revealing one, as I discuss at greater length in Chapter 2. In Döblin's imagined world of militarized *Realpolitik*, the possibility of *wu wei* is mooted one final time — along with the hope for a form of humanness reconstituted beyond the endless cycles of violent action and counter-action.

These almost negligible shards of hope, I want to argue, are discernible in Döblin's work from the outset of his career. In accounting for this elusive yearning for a different kind of place and another time, I am guided by Charles Taylor's conception of the 'epiphanies' of modernism in his seminal study of subjectivity, *Sources of the Self* (1989). Taylor reminds us of the collapse of representative forms of mimesis in Symbolism and modernism, defining the function of art in these traditions as bringing us 'into the presence of something which is otherwise inaccessible' and 'infinitely remote'.[40] Central to this is the notion that the work of art refracts a world of which it is an integral part, as opposed to reflecting a supposedly 'objective' reality. This is an originally Romantic conception of aesthetic truth grounded in the notion of it as expressive rather than propositional or predicative. As Martin Heidegger, one of phenomenology's most original thinkers and a beneficiary of the Romantic intellectual tradition, wrote in his controversial essay 'Der Ursprung des Kunstwerkes' ['The Origin of the Work of Art'], art 'works', as it were, through a dialectic of disclosure and hiddenness, and concealing and revealing.[41] For Taylor, the artistic visions of modernism, profoundly shaped as they were by Schopenhauer and Nietzsche, produced not a positive image of reconciliation with nature, but a cluster of far less comfortable revelations. The destructibility of the human subject, whether through the crushing violence of society or in the alien flux of nature, gave rise to forms of aesthetic expression that could only motion towards a different kind of world through a process of relentless negation; and this negation necessarily involves a form of complicity, an imitation of the very conditions it is opposing.[42] With an unprecedented intensity, modernist art and literature blurs the boundaries between form and content, between itself as an autonomous aesthetic product and its heterogeneous materials and discourses; and this blurring is so complete that 'we cannot separate what is manifested from the medium which we have created to reveal it'.[43] For Adorno, the work of art is torn between the illusion of its own autonomy — its existence in and for itself — and an attraction to its own contents, materials, and their histories.[44]

Döblin's texts creatively work through their constitutive discourses and motifs, and in so doing, I suggest that they leave behind them the faint memory, or promise, of reconciliation in the face of violence and fragmentation: in other words, the aesthetic trace (even the faint memory) of a harmony of body and mind, self and nature. Fragments and snippets of other discourses arise from and sink back into his narratives, just as they emerge from and collapse back into one another. In short, it is in the spaces between its aesthetic and non-aesthetic materials that art does its work, obliquely hinting at the possibility of better relationships with an amorphous 'thing' that is always *in excess* of our structures and apparatuses of knowledge and power. Art for Adorno remains 'the promise of happiness, which is broken' ['das Versprechen des Glücks, das gebrochen wird'].[45] I identify this ineliminable promise in Döblin's works as their 'hermeneutic remnant', a term that attempts to evoke their truth-value both in, and in spite of, their formal dissipation and fragmentation.

Without slipping back into fallacies of authorial intention in respect of art's truth-value,[46] the concept of epiphany is so fruitful partly because it corresponds to Döblin's own developing sense of what he was trying to do as an author. Towards the end of the work on *Berlin Alexanderplatz* in 1929, he published the essay 'Der Bau des epischen Werks' ['The Construction of the Epic Work'].[47] Here he lays out his theory of the epic work, distinguishing it from the Realist novel in the sense that it does not narrate contingent stories about and for individuals, but rather probes surface realities in order to expose 'the *exemplary nature of the events and the characters*' ['das *Exemplarische des Vorgangs und der Figuren*'] (SÄPL 218).[48] While this programmatic theory of the epic is, necessarily, never quite equal to the achievements of the works themselves, what it does offer is a keen sense of their aesthetic truth-value, their 'Wahrheit', beneath or beyond the level of mundane reality (219). It is the job of the epic work both to 'know' ['erkennen'] and 'to bring into being' ['erzeugen'] (221). Just as it brings new combinations and constellations into existence, the epic work performs an important philosophical function in disclosing something that might otherwise have lurked beneath the surface, hidden from view. It is by its very definition epiphanic, and an important purpose of my arguments will be to work out the aesthetic, ethical and even political implications of that.

Remapping the Journey

This insight had a long backstory to it, and my study will trace a distinctive combination of continuity and evolution over the three decades before Döblin's flight into exile. Human impotence in the face of both natural forces and anonymous social and political masses is one of the central themes of the early stories and novels. As Döblin argued in 1948, *Die drei Sprünge des Wang-lun* characterized both 'nature' and 'society' as a 'crushingly heavy iron tank' ['tonnenschwere[r] eiserne[r] Tank'], which indifferently rolled over Wang-lun and his allies (SLW 291; cf. 308). Reading along the grain of his own assessment, we can certainly identify the emergence of a dialectical reconception of the individual human beings from deep within the masses (SLW 308–13); and as I shall show, this figuration of individuality comes to fruition in *Berlin Alexanderplatz* and *Unser Dasein*. Accompanying the innovations of the literary texts, in turn, was an extensive process of philosophical reflection: as Döblin put it in 1932, each of his stories and novels worked through an existing conceptual position, only to unsettle it, supersede it and lay the ground for something new (SLW 216). In that light, this book will take a roughly chronological approach, and it will draw upon a selection of very different kinds of writing, whether literary, theoretical or philosophical.

There are three broad reasons for my choice of texts. The focus on works published before 1933 relates primarily to the deep biographical and intellectual caesura of exile. Döblin's painful personal experience, initially in France and, from autumn 1940 onwards, in the United States, was a significant factor behind his conversion to Catholicism in 1941. This religious turn grew out of his preoccupations as a writer and thinker, and it irrevocably shaped the works that were to follow,[49] thus marking a distinct thematic and tonal shift from what had gone before. The second factor behind my selection is Döblin's sheer variety as a writer. His own plea for the philosophical import of the epic work reflects on the dialogue that he wanted to stimulate *across* boundaries of form and genre, and I will consider how his relatively little-read philosophical, anthropological and medical texts shed light on his literary achievements, and vice versa. It is only by bringing different lenses to bear that he achieves his highly original and distinctive insights into the reconfigured place of the self in modernity.

Brecht suggested in a letter to the author of October 1928 that his novels were uniquely capable of giving voice to the new world-view of a dehumanizing capitalism and a crumbling bourgeoisie: Döblin discomfited his readers and upset their assumptions, and Brecht wanted to do the same kind of thing in the theatre.[50] In his review of *Berlin Alexanderplatz*, Walter Benjamin, too, hailed the epic 'possibilities' opened up by Döblin's breaking apart the old structures and styles of the bourgeois novel with a bewildering array of languages, discourses, and — quite literally, given his propensity to paste newspaper headlines and bus timetables into his manuscripts — materials.[51] Arguing alongside Brecht and Benjamin, I see his writing as opening up new possibilities of form and genre, but also figuring different ways of thinking humanness and being human.

With that scope in mind, Döblin's thematic breadth has necessitated some big omissions. I have focused on major works that I believe have the most to say about the dialectic of nature and the self that so preoccupied him. As a grotesque and strangely disjointed 'comic' counterpart and follow-up to *Wang-lun*, the early Berlin novel, *Wadzeks Kampf mit der Dampfturbine* (1915) has, I suggest, relatively little to add to its widely acclaimed half-brother and is not discussed here. (In reflection of a general consensus, David Dollenmayer offers a largely critical assessment in his chapter, 'The Advent of Döblinism: *Die drei Sprünge des Wang-lun* and *Wadzeks Kampf mit der Dampfturbine*', in *A Companion to the Works of Alfred Döblin*, ed. by Roland Dollinger and others (Rochester, NY: Camden House, 2004), pp. 55-74 (especially pp. 55 and 70). Although I treat questions of history and memory in Chapter 2, Döblin's path-breaking contributions to the tradition of the historical novel also remain largely unexplored here. In his recent work on *Wallenstein* (1920), Döblin's expansive exploration of the Thirty Years War, Steffan Davies has shown how the novel represents a new way of 'writing history'. In contrast to the supposedly interpretable and reconstructible histories of the nineteenth-century historical novel, Döblin's extraordinary mixture of fact, half-truth and myth gives rise to a vibrant reconfiguration of history and historicity as something chaotic, unordered and irreducible to any single perspective; and yet, as Davies argues, the central antagonism between the imaginatively minded Ferdinand II and his 'hard-headed' military commander Wallenstein also reflects Döblin's sense of the epic work as mediating fruitfully between the truth claims of 'fact' and those of 'fiction', even fantasy.[52] Döblin's novella *Die beiden Freundinnen und ihr Giftmord* [*The Two Girlfriends and their Murder by Poisoning*], published in 1924, deploys a kind of 'Tatsachenphantasie' from within the very different genre of true-crime fiction.[53] Given the complexity of current debates over these genres, and their relatively oblique relationship to my principal theme, both works have been bracketed out of my discussions here. Nonetheless, a number of Döblin's more obscure texts, along with the work of both contemporaries and kindred spirits from other times, enter my readings at resonant points.

My title is intended as a snapshot of the array of worlds and beings we will visit and encounter. Monsters there are in plenty, from the sadistic Johannes, and the hallucinatory buttercup of Michael Fischer's nightmare, through to the prehistoric creatures that emerge from beneath the melted Greenland icecap in *Berge Meere und Giganten*. Cyborgs are harder to spot, but they are here, too, if not quite in the forms to which we may have grown accustomed. And the denizens of Döblin's home city, by virtue of their epic ordinariness, may tell us almost as much about ourselves as they do about their own febrile time and place. Just as his monsters embody the ultimate uncontrollability of the world of which we are a part, so his cyborgs and Berliners might offer us at least two ways of making sense of our place in it. Nature, simultaneously a thing and a slippery non-thing, will take both conventional and surprising forms in this study.

Chapter 1 explores the short prose, focusing predominantly on stories from the collection *Die Ermordung einer Butterblume* (1912), but with a sideways nod to the shocking early short novel *Der schwarze Vorhang* [*The Black Curtain*], written in 1902–03. These Expressionist miniatures mediate between the psychiatric, the psychoanalytic and the mythic in their portrayal of a cast of bizarre and, in some cases, pathological characters from the margins of *fin-de-siècle* society. Ranging from a modernist reworking of Romantic *Liebestod* to two finely wrought medical case-study narratives, 'Die Ermordung einer Butterblume' ['The Murder of a Buttercup'] and 'Die Tänzerin under Leib' ['The Dancer and the Body'], they creatively negotiate the intricate intertwining of the subject and nature, and self and body. Situating the latter 'case studies' in close relation to so-called 'Willenskultur', or the 'culture of the will', which Michael Cowan has identified as an ideological undercurrent within German Expressionism,[54] I argue that they represent the mind's failure to achieve sovereign control over the body. Working with Freud and Adorno, my argument is that Döblin critiques the dualistic belief that any such control can be achieved; and that this critique challenges the dualisms that still structure much current thinking about relationships between mind and matter in the medical humanities. Even in the face of crumbling mental sovereignty and bodily contortion, the stories stake their ethical claims in their hints of reconciliation.

The second chapter turns to *Die drei Sprünge des Wang-lun* (1915), which uses a Chinese setting as the backdrop against which to explore possibilities of pacifism. In line with other democratically minded Expressionist writers, Döblin draws upon the thought of Daoism, and specifically the doctrine of *wu wei*, which entails a pacifist philosophy and comportment of non-resistance. Arguing in dialogue with Benjamin and Brecht, I read the novel as an incisive and original contribution to radical political critique. It exposes the dangers inherent in utopian and revolutionary thinking by repeatedly undercutting its own social and political ideals. But the formal innovations of Döblin's novel, in turn, expose the chinks in the armour of the social and political status quo, and we are left with the question of whether a meaningful change might in fact be envisioned after all.

The 'Chinese novel' is notable for its portrayals of the affinities between mankind and the natural world, and it suggests that real change, if it is ever to materialize, must go hand in hand with a new kind of ecological thinking. In that spirit, the study then moves forward to the science fiction epic *Berge Meere und Giganten* (1924), which I re-examine through the filter of contemporary ecocriticism. By bringing humanity to its vanishing points in war and anthropogenic natural catastrophe, the novel critiques configurations of technology and biopower that have spun dangerously out of control. Reading Döblin in counterpoint to later pictures of dystopian futures — particularly Aldous Huxley's *Brave New World* (1932) and J. G. Ballard's *The Drowned World* (1962) — I suggest that he brings modern humanity and its residual ideologies of humanism to a point of no return. But through his fantastical reworkings of myriad mythological, ethnographic and scientific materials, Döblin opens up posthuman possibilities in the shape of what I call the 'natural cyborg': a way of rethinking ourselves as hybrids of nature, culture and technology. While refusing to promise anything that looks like substantive and sustainable utopia, this concept of hybridity might at least lay the foundations for a less damaging form of coexistence, both with nature and with one other. Monsters, in short, must give way to cyborgs.

Chapter 4 narrows the optic in its focus on the human subject. Working from the tentative posthumanism emergent in the science fiction, it focuses on Döblin's hybrid essay of anthropology and nature-philosophy, *Unser Dasein* [*Our Existence*], which he began to draft in 1928 and published in 1933. In spite of Döblin's careerlong coyness in specifying his exact sources of inspiration, I probe a fascinating convergence between his own anthropology, recent movements in *Lebensphilosophie* and the life sciences, and the ground-breaking phenomenology of Heidegger's *Sein und Zeit* [*Being and Time*] (1927). This constellation of ideas unlocks a powerful new way of thinking the modern self in terms of a co-creating hybridity of *Leib* and *Seele*, and self and world. The idea of 'metaphor' emerges here as the aesthetic facet of Döblin's anthropology: a crystallization of the meaning that is inextricable from the nature which, in turn, is both an uncanny part of us and insuperably 'other' than us.

Finally, we travel to Döblin's home territory, the Alexanderplatz, where we will re-read his experimental masterpiece through this prism of hybridity. In contrast to recent attempts to read Döblin's Berlin simply as a proto-postmodern maelstrom of discourses and repetitions, I suggest that the novel in fact sows the seeds of a new 'creaturely' hermeneutics of modern urban life by illuminating the traces of nature in the joints of the self and the joints of the city: the alterity that persistently undermines our claims to sovereign subjectivity, and our pretences to 'know' and determine who we are and what we are a part of. Weimar Berlin is both an urban and a natural space where meanings and established truths are relentlessly fragmented and reconstituted. We now know what became of that vibrant but fragile ecosystem, and *Berlin Alexanderplatz* rumbles with the sounds of right-wing populism and masculine violence, alongside its trams and advertising jingles. But there were (and are) always alternatives for thinking and being, and as this study aims to show, Döblin is nothing if not a writer of other paths and possibilities.

## Notes to the Introduction

1. Günter Grass, 'Über meinen Lehrer Döblin', in Grass, *Werkausgabe in zehn Bänden*, ed. by Volker Neuhaus (Darmstadt & Neuwied: Luchterhand, 1987), IX: *Essays, Reden, Briefe, Kommentare*, ed. by Daniela Hermes (1987), pp. 236–55 (p. 255).
2. Ibid., p. 236. See Gabriele Sander, *Alfred Döblin* (Stuttgart: Reclam, 2001), especially pp. 80–81; on the broader literary scene, see Moray McGowan, 'German Writing in the West (1945–1990)', in *The Cambridge History of German Literature*, ed. by Helen Watanabe-O'Kelly (Cambridge: Cambridge University Press, 1997), pp. 440–506 (pp. 451–55).
3. Grass, *Werkausgabe*, IX, 255; see also Sander, *Alfred Döblin*, pp. 75–76 and 90–91.
4. For a compact account of Döblin's literary fortunes during his lifetime, see Gabriele Sander, 'Rezeption zu Lebzeiten', in *Döblin-Handbuch: Leben — Werk — Wirkung*, ed. by Sabina Becker (Stuttgart: Metzler, 2016), pp. 2–4.
5. Grass, *Werkausgabe*, IX, 236 and 238.
6. See Roland Barthes, *The Death of the Author*, reproduced in Barthes, *Image — Music — Text*, ed. and trans. by Stephen Heath (London: Fontana, 1977), pp. 142–48.
7. Bertolt Brecht, 'Über Alfred Döblin', in Brecht, *Werke: Große kommentierte Berliner und Frankfurter Ausgabe*, 30 vols, ed. by Werner Hecht, Jan Knopf, Werner Mittenzwei and Klaus-Detlef Müller (Berlin and Weimar: Aufbau-Verlag, 1993), XXIII: *Schriften III: 1942–1956*, ed. by Barbara Wallburg, p. 23.
8. See here Gabriele Sander, 'Literarische Wirkungsgeschichte', in *Döblin-Handbuch*, ed. by Becker, pp. 9–11. For an extensive discussion of Fassbinder's miniseries of 1980, in relation to the novel, see Andrew J. Webber, *Berlin in the Twentieth Century: A Cultural Topography* (Cambridge: Cambridge University Press, 2008), especially pp. 216–26.
9. See, for example, Adam Thirlwell, 'An Explosion of Pure Fact', *The New York Review of Books*, 25 October 2018 <https://www.nybooks.com/articles/2018/10/25/berlin-alexanderplatz-explosion-pure-fact/> [accessed 21 November 2019].
10. Richard Sheppard, *Modernism — Dada — Postmodernism* (Evanston, IL: Northwestern University Press, 2000), p. 34.
11. See Robert J. Richards, *The Tragic Sense of Life: Ernst Haeckel and the Struggle over Evolutionary Thought* (Chicago, IL: University of Chicago Press, 2008), pp. 8–9; and Wolfgang Riedel, *'Homo Natura': Literarische Anthropologie um 1900* (Berlin: De Gruyter, 1996), p. 78.
12. See Ritchie Robertson, 'Modernism and the Self: 1890–1924', in *Philosophy and German Literature, 1700–1990*, ed. by Nicholas Saul (Cambridge: Cambridge University Press, 2002), pp. 150–96 (p. 151).
13. Sigmund Freud, 'Eine Schwierigkeit in der Psychoanalyse', in *Gesammelte Werke* [henceforth *GW*], ed. by Anna Freud and others, 18 vols (London: Imago, 1991), XII: *Werke aus den Jahren 1917–1920*, p. 11. The emphasis is in the original.
14. On the intellectual and aesthetic impact of developments in subatomic physics and astrophysics, in particular, on High European modernism, see Sheppard, pp. 35–38.
15. See Robertson, 'Modernism and the Self', p. 151.
16. See David Midgley, '"Creative Evolution": Bergson's Critique of Science and its Reception in the German-Speaking World', in *The Evolution of Literature: Legacies of Darwin in European Cultures*, ed. by Nicholas Saul and Simon J. James (Amsterdam: Rodopi, 2011), pp. 283–99 (pp. 283–84).
17. See Riedel, *'Homo Natura'*, pp. 47 and 52–53; cf. Birgit Hoock, *Modernität als Paradox: Der Begriff der 'Moderne' und seine Anwendung auf das Werk Alfred Döblins (bis 1933)* (Tübingen: Niemeyer, 1997), pp. 33–51.
18. See here Terry Eagleton, *The Ideology of the Aesthetic* (Oxford: Blackwell, 1990), p. 161.
19. Mirjana Stancic, 'Auseinandersetzung mit Friedrich Nietzsche', in *Döblin-Handbuch*, ed. by Becker, pp. 273–75 (p. 275).
20. Johann Wolfgang von Goethe, *Werke: Hamburger Ausgabe in 14 Bänden*, ed. by Erich Trunz, 10th edn (Munich: Beck, 1973–76), III: *Dramatische Dichtungen: Erster Band. Faust*, 382–83 (p. 20); cf. here David Midgley, 'Metaphysical Speculation and the Fascination of the Real: On the Connections between Döblin's Philosophical Writing and his Major Fiction before *Berlin*

Alexanderplatz', in *Alfred Döblin: Paradigms of Modernism*, ed. by Steffan Davies and Ernest Schonfield (Berlin: De Gruyter, 2009), pp. 7–27 (p. 13).
21. Midgley, 'Metaphysical Speculation', p. 27.
22. David Midgley, 'After Materialism: Reflections of Idealism in *Lebensphilosophie*: Dilthey, Bergson and Simmel', in *The Impact of Idealism*, ed. by Nicholas Boyle, Liz Disley and John Walker, 4 vols (Cambridge: Cambridge University Press, 2013), II: *Historical, Social, and Political Thought: The Legacy of Post-Kantian Thought*, pp. 161–85 (p. 161).
23. It is notoriously difficult to pin down Döblin's biographical engagements with the diffuse movement of *Lebensphilosophie*: see Ursula Elm, *Literatur als 'Lebensanschauung': Zum ideengeschichtlichen Hintergrund von Alfred Döblins 'Berlin Alexanderplatz'* (Bielefeld: Aisthesis, 1991), p. 12.
24. Henri Bergson, *Essai sur les données immédiates de la conscience*, 8th edn (Paris: Alcan, 1911), p. 76.
25. Friedrich Nietzsche, *Sämtliche Werke: Kritische Gesamtausgabe*, ed. by Giorgio Colli and Mazzino Montinari (Berlin: De Gruyter, 1967–) [henceforth *KG*], III.1: *Die Geburt der Tragödie/ Unzeitgemäße Betrachtungen I–III* (1972), p. 43; Nietzsche, *The Birth of Tragedy and Other Writings*, ed. by Raymond Geuss and Ronald Speirs (Cambridge: Cambridge University Press, 1999), p. 33. The emphasis is in the original.
26. Ferdinand Lion, 'Das Werk Alfred Döblins: Zum fünfzigsten Geburtstag des Dichters am 10. August 1928', *Neue Rundschau*, 39.2 (1928), 161–73 (p. 169).
27. Max Horkheimer and Theodor W. Adorno, *Dialektik der Aufklärung*, in Adorno, *Gesammelte Schriften*, ed. by Rolf Tiedemann and others, 20 vols (Frankfurt a.M.: Suhrkamp, 1970–2003) [henceforth *GS*], III: *Dialektik der Aufklärung: Philosophische Fragmente*, p. 49; Horkheimer and Adorno, *Dialectic of Enlightenment*, trans. by John Cumming (London: Verso, 1997), p. 32.
28. See Horkheimer and Adorno, *Dialectic of Enlightenment*, pp. 32–42. For a cogent discussion of this paradox, see Simon Jarvis, *Adorno: A Critical Introduction* (Cambridge: Polity, 1998), pp. 27–28.
29. See here Timothy Morton's critique of the ways in which Nature has been idealized in ecological writing since the Romantics, in his *Ecology without Nature: Rethinking Environmental Aesthetics* (Cambridge, MA: Harvard University Press, 2007), especially pp. 2–8.
30. Ibid., pp. 16–17 and 21.
31. In her influential study of 1995, *What is Nature?*, the philosopher Kate Soper could still justly characterize opposed movements in environmental philosophy and eco-criticism in terms of a 'nature-endorsing' approach convinced of the ultimate reconcilability of humankind and the natural world, and a 'nature-sceptical approach' bent on deconstructing 'nature' and 'the natural' as ideological edifices encrusted with society's prevailing power relations: see Soper, *What is Nature? Culture, Politics and the Non-Human* (Oxford: Blackwell, 1995), pp. 4 and 98.
32. Klaus Müller-Salget, *Alfred Döblin: Werk und Entwicklung* (Bonn: Bouvier, 1972), p. 324.
33. See, for example, Otto Keller, *Döblins Montageroman als Epos der Moderne* (Munich: Fink, 1980), especially pp. 177–96; Erwin Kobel, *Alfred Döblin: Erzählkunst im Umbruch* (New York: De Gruyter, 1985), pp. 280–88; and Birgit Hoock, *Modernität als Paradox: Der Begriff der 'Moderne' und seine Anwendung auf das Werk Alfred Döblins (bis 1933)* (Tübingen: Niemeyer, 1997), pp. 242–59.
34. That sense of disquiet echoes Walter Benjamin's argument, in his famous review of 1930, that Biberkopf's reinsertion into the city as a psychologically stabilized and socially responsible factory watchman represented the final stage, the final outpost, of the 'old bourgeois Bildungsroman': see Walter Benjamin, *Gesammelte Schriften*, ed. by Rolf Tiedemann and Hermann Schweppenhäuser, 7 vols (Frankfurt a.M.: Suhrkamp, 1972) [henceforth *GS*], III: *Kritiken und Rezensionen*, p. 236.
35. See Wolfgang Schäffner, *Die Ordnung des Wahns: Zur Poetologie psychiatrischen Wissens bei Alfred Döblin* (Munich: Fink, 1995), pp. 10–12.
36. See Julia Genz, 'Döblins Schreibweise der Evokation und Aussparung: Psychoanalytische und psychiatrische Diskurse in *Die Tänzerin und der Leib*', in *Internationales Alfred-Döblin-Kolloquium Emmendingen 2007: 'Tatsachenphantasie': Alfred Döblins Poetik des Wissens in Kontext der Moderne*, ed. by Sabina Becker und Robert Krause (Bern: Lang, 2008), pp. 69–82; and Yvonne Wübben, 'Tatsachenphantasien: Alfred Döblins *Die Ermordung einer Butterblume* im Kontext von Experimentalpsychologie und psychiatrischer Krankheitslehre', ibid., pp. 84–99 (especially pp. 96–99).

37. Eva Horn, 'Literary Research: Narration and the Epistemology of the Human Sciences in Alfred Döblin', *Modern Language Notes*, 118 (2003), 719–39 <http://dx.doi.org/10.1353/mln.2003.0057>.
38. See, for example, Markus Joch, 'Der Platz des irdischen Friedens. Sommer 1912 [sic]: Alfred Döblin beginnt die Arbeit am *Wang-lun*', in *Mit Deutschland um die Welt: Eine Kulturgeschichte des Fremden in der Kolonialzeit*, ed. by Alexander Honold and Klaus R. Scherpe (Stuttgart: Metzler, 2004), pp. 415–21; Oliver Jahraus, 'Chinoiserien, Chinawaren, chinesischer Roman: Döblins "Die drei Sprünge des Wang-lun" mit einem Seitenblick auf Bertoluccis "Der letzte Kaiser"', in *Alfred Döblin: Neufassung*, ed. by Sabina Kyora, *Text + Kritik: Zeitschrift für Literatur*, 13/14 (2018), 66–77; and Marion Brandt, 'Interkulturalität', in *Döblin-Handbuch*, ed. by Becker, pp. 343–46.
39. Steffan Davies and Ernest Schonfield, 'Introduction', in *Alfred Döblin: Paradigms of Modernism*, ed. by Davies and Schonfield (Berlin: De Gruyter, 2009), pp. 1–6 (p. 6).
40. Charles Taylor, *Sources of the Self: The Making of the Modern Identity* (Cambridge: Cambridge University Press, 1989), pp. 419 and 478.
41. Martin Heidegger, *Holzwege*, 8th edn (Frankfurt a.M.: Klostermann, 2003), pp. 37–38 and 51.
42. Taylor, *Sources of the Self*, especially pp. 477–82.
43. Ibid., p. 429.
44. See Theodor W. Adorno, *Ästhetische Theorie*, in Adorno, GS, VII: *Ästhetische Theorie*, p. 18.
45. Ibid., p. 205.
46. For a nuanced discussion of the complex relationship between art's 'meaning' and its creator's 'intention', in the context of Adorno's aesthetic theory, see Jarvis, pp. 101–02.
47. The essay was an extended version of a lecture he gave to over a thousand students on 10 December 1928 at the Friedrich-Wilhelms-Universität in Berlin: see Sander, *Alfred Döblin*, pp. 38–39.
48. The emphasis is in the original.
49. See Friedrich Emde, *Alfred Döblin: Sein Weg zum Christentum* (Tübingen: Narr, 1999), especially pp. 311–12.
50. Brecht, *Werke*, XXVIII: *Briefe I*, ed. by Günter Glaeser, pp. 315–16.
51. See Benjamin, GW, III, 232.
52. See Steffan Davies, 'Writing History: Why *Ferdinand der Andere* is called *Wallenstein*', in *Alfred Döblin: Paradigms of Modernism*, ed. by Davies and Schonfield, pp. 121–43 (especially pp. 121–22 and 128–29).
53. See, for example, Hania Siebenpfeiffer, 'Dokumentarische Erzählung: *Die beiden Freundinnen und ihr Giftmord* (1924)', in *Döblin-Handbuch*, ed. by Becker, pp. 93–97.
54. See Michael J. Cowan, *Cult of the Will: Nervousness and German Modernity* (University Park: Pennsylvania State University Press, 2008).

CHAPTER 1

# The Hermeneutics of Guilt: Döblin's Short Prose

When *Die Ermordung einer Butterblume* was published as a collection in November 1912, its critical reception signalled the emergence of a significant but unusual talent. Clearly his own man, doing something beyond the kens of Realism and Naturalism, Döblin was developing a unique capacity to unsettle, confuse and disturb. The short stories were acclaimed, admittedly still within narrow literary circles, as an extraordinary curiosity shop whose mediations of the natural through the fantastical criss-crossed unusual and unexpected aesthetic territories. Often not knowing quite where to find a foothold, reviewers highlighted the absurdities, the non-sequiturs, and the moments of horror, disgust and abjection pervading the pieces. In a breathless response straight after publication, Max Jungnickel situated them both beyond the pale of the rational and outside any recognizable hermeneutical precedents. Here were stories that demanded to be greeted with a 'fiery dithyramb' ['einem feurigen Dythirambus'] (sic).[1] Döblin's preoccupation with death, the macabre and the Gothic — the shadow sides to the everyday vignettes out of which many of his narratives grew — grabbed the attention of one reviewer after another.[2]

His eclecticism made a powerful impression, too. The collection opens with the tale of a Brazilian family man who renounces the strictures of his bourgeois existence to drown himself off the coast at Ostend, with a macabre twist. In another piece, a queen and her Prince Consort throw off the mannered artifices of courtly life with their own *Liebestod*. The legend of Bluebeard gets a proto-psychedelic makeover. A canoness's flirtations with Death stir a mixture of prudishness and prurience; and in a similar key, a dancer's body becomes the site of clinical discipline and control. The title story is the darkly comic case study of a small-time Freiburg businessman whose obsessive repression of his unruly body, mind over matter, eventually leads him back into his own black forest of madness.

But if the stories themselves played host to bizarre twists and turns and misfits from the social margins, they did not come out of the blue. Döblin's contribution to literary Expressionism had been marked by oddities of character and plot, but it was also shaped by the interplay between his literary and medical vocations. His first novel, *Jagende Rosse* [*Rushing Steeds*], was written while he was still in school and first appeared posthumously. Two early stories, 'Erwachen' and 'Adonis', never saw the light of day despite probably being prepared for print. Emerging in the course of 1902–3 and inflected in part, as Wilfried Schoeller suggests, by the young author's own sexual inexperience,[3] *Der schwarze Vorhang* [*The Black Curtain*] was the story of the erotic perversions of its loner-protagonist Johannes. His sexuality vacillates between things and people, and love and hatred, as he embarks on a sadomasochistic relationship with a passive female lover, Irene. This culminates in a bizarre *Lustmord* and self-immolation: aspects of Magnus Hirschfeld's strongly gendered analysis of sadism and masochism, with which Döblin was familiar, come to life in the garish colours of early Expressionism.[4] But his negotiations with the natural force of the libido, in its vacillations between man and nature, mark out a broader thematic touchstone for his early fiction. In a rather pretentious covering letter to Axel Juncker's publishing house in April 1904, he described the novel as a psychologized story of eros. It would show how 'the love drive presses the 'hero' out of his natural state of isolation, how it leads him to plant, animal, male friend, and finally to his "heroine" and her murder' ['[der Liebestrieb] aus der natürlichen Isolierung den "Helden" herausdrängt, ihn zu Pflanze, Tier, Freund, schließlich zur "Heldin" und zum Mord an ihr führt'] (*Briefe*, I, 23).

Juncker's reader, one Rainer Maria Rilke, was left bemused by the relentless violence of this curiously plotless narrative. The novel was serialized in *Der Sturm* in 1912, but it was only in 1919 that it appeared as a book with S. Fischer Verlag.[5] Nonetheless, Döblin's association with the musician, critic and prolific literary patron Herwarth Walden led him into involvement with an important corner of Berlin's literary, artistic and theatrical avant-garde. Written between 1903 and 1911, almost all the short stories in the *Ermordung* collection appeared either in *Das Magazin* or *Der Sturm*, both edited by Walden and the latter one of the flagships of literary Expressionism after its launch in 1910. In spite of a personal and professional distance from the bohemian culture of the Berlin Expressionists, he garnered a name for himself as a significant representative of Expressionist prose, a reputation underscored by fifty-three literary and critical contributions to *Der Sturm* by 1913.[6]

This early work overlapped in complex ways with his clinical work as a medical doctor. His motivations for studying medicine, as he admitted in 1938, apparently had less to do with an intrinsic passion for bones, muscular spasms and mechanisms of urine secretion, than a lively interest in the metaphysical vistas that the exactitude of clinical observation seemed to open up (SLW 239–40). Contrary to a long-standing assumption that he specialized in psychiatry at an early stage as a medical student, his training in Berlin (1900–1904) and Freiburg (1904–05) was relatively broad-based, as Christina Althen has recently shown.[7] A varied palette in Berlin, which included lectures in philosophy and classics, nonetheless prepared him for a certain degree of specialization as he completed his doctoral dissertation on chronic memory loss due to Korsakoff syndrome in Freiburg in 1905 under the supervision of the psychiatrist Alfred Erich Hoche. Even more than other doctor-poets of his generation, notably Gottfried Benn and Hans Carossa, who viewed medicine primarily as a day job, Döblin strove for a creative dialogue between the two 'halves' of his professional existence, the medical and the writerly, while at the same time underlining their fractious cultural differences.[8] His medical training added a unique ingredient to his literary and philosophical repertoires, giving his early fiction an air of fine-grained clinical observation; but there were also stylistic affinities with the characteristic parataxis and asyndeton of the early Expressionist aesthetic, along with its externalization of inner emotional excesses.[9] In my discussion of *Wang-lun*, I will consider in detail the exhortation, in the 'Berliner Programm', that authors should 'learn from psychiatry' (SÄPL 120). In keeping with an Expressionist and early modernist fascination with madness as a symbol, or anti-symbol, of social and cultural marginality,[10] Döblin's own work at the psychiatric coalface made for *sui generis* portrayals of mental and bodily abnormalities and extremities.

It was through representations of abnormality that he began to dissect and problematize the fraught relationship between body and mind, and between the self and nature in its myriad forms. And yet the stories also reached further than that. Of persistent interest to Döblin's first readers, and significant to my argument here, is the peculiar dialectic at play in the early short prose between the supposedly 'real', the mythical and the mad; and a particular source of fascination is the question how to interpret miniature narratives which lurch from mundane worlds described in naturalistic terms to places populated by mythic and ghoulish forms and creatures. The *Hamburgischer Correspondent* marvelled at an imagination which 'fashions from the simplest things the strangest, most bizarre happenings' ['macht aus den einfachsten Dingen die seltsamsten, wunderlichsten Ereignisse'], overlaying them with variegated shades of mythical and metaphysical truth.[11] Writing in the *Zentralblatt für Kinderheilkunde* [*Principal Journal of Paediatrics*, of all titles], another reviewer compared Döblin's mythical and mystical inspirations and inflections to those of Benn and Georg Heym.[12]

These narratives fuse an almost neurotic exactness of description with events, feelings and atmospheres that inhabit the borderlands of the unconscious, the mythical and the mystical. In their oscillations between surface appearance and metaphysical depths, internal psychical processes and highly stylized gestures and behaviours, they mark an important creative transition into a radically experimental modernism. Arguing strongly against a traditional critical scepticism about their intrinsic aesthetic value, I suggest that they anticipate in miniature the themes, styles and stylistic shifts of the later epic works.[13] There is a characteristic Expressionist preoccupation, bordering on an obsession, with strange specimens from the margins of Wilhelmine life: the loner, the madman, the neurotic, the hysteric, the pervert. Döblin's most famous creation, the war veteran and rapist Franz Biberkopf, finds his forebears here. The condensed form of the short story mirrors the compacted style and structure of the psychiatric case study; and in this mimicry, his narratives criss-cross the ambiguous borders between knowledge ['Wissen'] and aesthetics, medical science and literature, and madness and normality. As recent scholarship has recognized, they open up experimental spaces,[14] in which discourses and motifs by turns relativize and intensify each other's effects.

But there is also a recognizable line of continuity from his fractured early poetics to the mythopoeic departures of 'Der Bau des epischen Werks'. In a continuation of the interplay of 'reality' and 'truth' that I considered in the Introduction, Döblin describes the job of the epic writer as that of penetrating the uneven and often chaotic surface of empirical reality ['der realen Sphäre'] in a paradoxical bid to reach a 'superreal sphere' ['überreale Sphäre']: what he describes as 'the sphere of a new truth and a very particular kind of reality' ['die Sphäre einer neuen Wahrheit und einer ganz besonderen Realität'] (SÄPL 223). This mediation between the real and the mythic sets us a hermeneutical puzzle. Inasmuch as his imagery feeds upon, and is continuous with, the stories' concrete, corporeal or psychiatric realities, it remains irreducible to a decipherable set of meanings. Midgley has rightly suggested that the stories 'hold the promise of revealing a higher meaning behind human experience, but at the same time their imagery resists translation into such a scheme of thinking'.[15] But I want to go further by arguing that the stories' particular aesthetic and ethical value resides precisely in a negative mode of disclosure. They express truths that skirt the edges of representation, and these disclosures raise far-reaching questions about what kind of meaning we might expect to find at the fragmentary sites of early modernism.

In this light, my argument strikes out in a markedly different direction from existing discussions of the early prose. These pieces are not simply the literary correlate to a backdrop of monistic philosophy,[16] nor are they simply readable as epistemological and aesthetic playgrounds. Instead, I suggest that the stories creatively work through their criss-crossing discourses and motifs, whether mythic, psychiatric or psychoanalytic; and in so doing, they leave behind them the hint of reconciliation: in other words, the aesthetic trace (even memory) of a harmony of body and mind, and the human being and nature, in the face of dissolution and fragmentation. We are repeatedly brought up short, our expectations confounded by Döblin's turns into the absurd, the mad, or the mythical. What these shifts leave in their wake is a hermeneutic remnant, an elusive residue of a dignified form of bodily existence.[17]

That hint is a red thread running through stories which *prima facie* seem to have relatively little in common. From multiple angles, Döblin's stories deconstruct modes of thinking that oppose and hierarchize mind and matter, or man and nature. As Michael Cowan has shown, the so-called 'culture of the will' ['Willenskultur'] of *fin-de-siècle* and early twentieth-century German culture was working to this end by revalorizing individual human agency in the face of the passive and nervous body. The effective mastery of spirit over body, and mind over matter, was to be both conceived and enabled through the centralizing power of the will.[18] In the wake of Nietzsche's vitalistic revalidation of the will, this dialectic shaped a shift in body-cultural thinking, both through Expressionism's emphasis on the will's creative agency (in supposed contrast to its passive Impressionistic predecessors), and also through a revalidation of dance, music and sport education as a means of reinforcing willpower over a pliant and compliant body precisely by means of the body.[19] Working in dialogue with these strains of thought, not least in 'Die Tänzerin und der Leib' and 'Die Ermordung einer Butterblume', Döblin radically undermines any attempt to establish and stabilize a hierarchy of mind and matter, and the human and the natural, showing these poles instead to be irreducibly and qualitatively interdependent.

I begin my chapter by following the vagaries of 'Die Segelfahrt' ['The Boat Trip'], bringing both 'Die Verwandlung' ['The Metamorphosis'] and 'Der Ritter Blaubart' ['Bluebeard the Knight'] into dialogue as stories which, in working through their mythopoeic modes, bring into lurid focus the relationship between the human and the natural. The figurations of *Liebestod* in the first two narratives draw on a far darker imagining in *Der schwarze Vorhang*, where Johannes's closing immolation of himself and Irene is a striking negation of Romantic ideals of union and reconciliation. A fresh reading of 'Das Stiftsfräulein und der Tod' ['The Canoness and Death'], a cousin to the early novel in its almost obsessive gaze at scenes of abjection and self-loathing, will then bring me to the collection's acknowledged flagships: the famous case study narratives of 'Die Ermordung einer Butterblume' ['The Murder of a Buttercup'] and 'Die Tänzerin und der Leib' ['The Dancer and the Body']. Against a backdrop of guilt, I end by revisiting the unjustly overlooked piece 'Die Flucht aus dem Himmel' ['The Flight from Heaven'], first published in 1920: a story which, for all its hostility to a Judaeo-Christianity, offers us the faint hint of what poetic redemption might at least *begin* to mean in this fragmented universe.

## Ambiguous *Liebestod*

My discussion will end up in heaven, but it begins on the coast of Belgium. 'Die Segelfahrt' is the story of a married Brazilian man, known to us only as Copetta, who has left his homeland and travelled to Europe, in what is suggested to be a desperate search for happiness. The decision was linked to his sudden realization that he had turned forty-eight: an allusion to a Wilhelmine-era mid-life crisis, perhaps, but also the poignantly personal motif of a father rashly abandoning his patriarchal responsibilities.[20] He has whiled away a decadent four months in Paris, contracted a suitably decadent illness (pneumonia), and after a hospital stay set out for the seaside resort of Ostend. The momentary glimpses of a woman in her mid-thirties precipitate his impulsive decision to pass on his card, before ridding himself of the traces of his married life in a private orgy of destruction. He invites her in writing to join him the following morning for a boat trip; she signs off her acceptance as 'L.'; and having sailed out to sea, he drowns himself in front of her. His act is premeditated, as he has already sent a telegram to the authorities (SE 13), but we are left entirely in the dark concerning either protagonist's motives. As Copetta disappears into the waves, so does any vestige of a linear hermeneutic; and the narrative shifts into an uncanny circularity and repetition as L. matches Copetta's footsteps a year later and heads down into the sea in a *Liebestod*-like embrace with his grotesquely resurrected corpse.

The story's laconic economy of gesture, and its divestment of any sense or prospect of unitary selfhood, brings the naturalistic and the mythic into play with each other, both suggesting and in the same motion withholding meaning. The twist to Döblin's fragmentary characterizations lies in their inviting the reader to play the psychologist, or even the psychiatrist, in attempting to divine motivations in the complete absence of dialogue, while suggesting the snapshots of gesture and movement to be entirely contingent. There are fleeting hints of some indeterminate yearning: on his stroll along the promenade, Copetta casts the occasional happy glance over the grey-green water as his 'yellow-brown bloated face twitched' ['sein gelbbraunes schwammiges Gesicht zuckte'] (SE 9). At the same time, this is clearly a man trying to conceal himself, even a text trying to cover its own tracks. As the noonday sun 'flows' over his shirtfront, Copetta sighs at the thought that his own gaze might be casting shadows. The source of distraction, a woman, sporadically flickers in and out of the field of vision. She 'glided past him for a second time now; rust-red hair beneath a broad white hat. [...] A grey glance from a clever, no longer youthful face shied away from him' ['glitt zum zweiten Male an ihm vorüber; rostfarbenes Haar unter breitrandigem weißen Hut. [...] Ein grauer Blick aus einem klugen nicht jungen Gesicht wich vor ihm zurück'] (10). In the filmic, non-causal moments of narrative description, Copetta's motivations seem to elude him just as much as they elude us. Having passed on his visiting card, he asks himself what the point of it actually was; and the same woman hovers between seeming entirely contingent on the one hand, and uncannily talismanic on the other, as it occurs to him that she has passed by him on three separate occasions already (10–11).

'Die Segelfahrt' blurs distinctions between the subjective and the objective, the inner and outer, and the abstract and concrete, in moments of naturalistic description that seem to border on moments of seemingly mythic significance. In gazes that take on a weirdly concrete or corporeal form, the figures become continuous with their surroundings. Traces of nature are anthropomorphized in an anticipation of the vitalistic 'living totality' ['lebendige[] Totalität'] which, according to the 'Berliner Programm', modern prose must strive to capture (SÄPL 120). In counterpoint to the quixotic arbitrariness of Copetta's actions and gestures, his surroundings are inscribed with meaningful patterns of circularity, repetition and return. The relentless ['unablässig'] rolling and roaring of the sea, which 'swelled up again and again, always swelled back' ['schwoll wieder an, schwoll immer wieder ab'] (SE 9), is echoed in subtly changing permutations (10, 15). Smuggled into the text under the cover of physiological exactitude, in turn, are glimpses of an alien yet agential universe, as we read of Copetta raising his eyes from the thin sand 'pulling away under his feet' ['[e]r hob den Blick von dem dünnen Sande, der unter seinen Füßen wegzog'] (10). Even his outburst of violence, in which he destroys his wedding ring and pictures of his children and scatters this sand over the floor of his hotel room, is both chaotic and at the same time intensely meaningful: a casting-off of domesticity and a symbolic return to nature (11). In the fabric of the prose we can find a combination of mythic suggestiveness, an observational precision, and the loose ends of the psychiatric case study.[21] And as Mirjana Stancic argues, there is also the hint of exotic otherness in a Brazilian man escaping European bourgeois strictures.[22]

The eponymous boat trip promises some form of resolution and in the same motion reduces meaning to nothingness, a literal vanishing point. In an analogue of the reader's experience, L. herself has failed to read a man bent on renouncing the world. She tries to kiss him, but he refuses. She searches in vain for his mouth and neck, she fingers his chest. But in the ultimate gesture of self-submission, Copetta, wordless to the last, instead simply lies back on the waves and literally lets himself be carried away (13). Döblin's figuration of dissolution here ironizes itself by figuring the dissolution of any hermeneutic whatsoever: we are left in the indeterminate space between a Romantic (*mutatis mutandis*, Freudian) yearning for death on the one hand, and the mental chaos of madness on the other. As I discussed in my Introduction, one of Döblin's most important philosophical interlocutors was Nietzsche,[23] and the resonances here, though indirect, are unmistakable.

Copetta's disappearance echoes Nietzsche's eulogy of tragic art — most consummately, music — as helping us to contemplate in symbolic form the Dionysiac universality of the all-pervasive *Wille*. What Nietzsche celebrates in music is what he calls the 'tragic myth' ['tragische[r] Mythus'], a 'symbolic' truth that speaks both in and through the moment of individual destruction vicariously witnessed in tragedy. He directly links a metaphysical joy in the tragic to the negation of the tragic hero, in other words, to a vicariously lived-out return to a nature figured as 'the primal mother, eternally creative beneath the surface of incessantly changing appearances, eternally forcing life into existence'.[24] But this moment of intensely experienced presence is relativized in a return to a nexus of disappearance and absence. Perfect presence amounts to complete absence: having renounced his empty bourgeois existence, and surrendered both literally and figuratively to the elements, Copetta has 'nothing to his back, nothing in front of him', in Erwin Kobel's words.[25] His return to nature symbolically affirms the mythic wisdom of Silenus, namely that '"the very best thing is utterly beyond your reach: not to have been born, not to *be*, to be *nothing*. However, the second best thing for you is: to die soon"'.[26] And yet, Copetta's 'closed gaze' ['verschlossene[r] Blick'], as he murmurs indistinctly and heads down (13), suggests that death itself — and even madness — together symbolically mark the silent limit points at which every narrative, and every piece of folk philosophy, as Nietzsche describes it, breaks down.

What emerges in the uncanny turn is a negative parable that finds its meaning at the discursively irreducible site of the body. The contemporary 'return' of the uncanny drew upon what Andrew Webber has identified as a 'Gothic revival' at the turn of the nineteenth century, a literary and cultural current which would set the scene for Otto Rank's 1914 treatise, *Der Doppelgänger*, and Freud's essay of 1919, 'Das Unheimliche' ['The Uncanny']. The repetitions that echo throughout 'Die Segelfahrt' speak to the ambiguities expounded by Freud, not least in relation to the *Doppelgänger*-like splitting of the modern subject between self and other, and between identity and non-identity. Tied up with this dynamic is an ominous pattern of repetition;[27] and in an uncannily similar vein, L. reacts to Copetta's rejection of her, and his subsequent watery suicide, with a rash of repetitions. Having precisely repeated her own actions on the boat in a paroxysm of gestures, she heads to Paris, where she surrenders herself to all takers as a prostitute (SE 13), before returning to Ostend in Copetta's footsteps a year later. A reiteration of the story's shadow motif suggests a flirtation with the idea of renouncing all individuated bodily traces, of becoming a nothing, a *Nichts*. In a modulation of the *Doppelgänger* motif, L. 'played with her shadow falling black before her, danced for it on the street, whistling, thumbed her nose at it' ['spielte mit ihrem Schatten, der schwarz vor ihr hinfiel, tanzte ihm pfeifend auf offenem Weg etwas vor, machte ihm lange Nasen'] (16). And accompanying all this is an oscillation between 'homesickness' ['Heimweh'] and 'bliss' ['Seligkeit'] (15): a metonymic yearning for home, for sure, but also a duality that resonates with Freud's metapsychological speculation in *Jenseits des Lustprinzips* [*Beyond the Pleasure Principle*] (1920) that the ultimate requirement and goal of organic life may lie in the restoration of an earlier, more primal state of affairs: the return to the 'home' of the womb doubles as a metonym for nature itself, the latter a symbol for the former.[28]

Copetta is waiting for her out there. What is unsettling about the *dénouement* is its *stretto*-like suggestion of a climactic finale, bringing a moment of psychopathological collapse into proximity with myth. Döblin's notion of the mythic symbol straddles the border between the metonymic and the metaphoric in the sense that it both immanently generates *and* reflects meaning. Looking back on his abiding attachment to a form of natural theology in his 'Epilog' of 1948, Döblin reflects on a career-long passion for the intransigent and incommensurable stuff of sensory existence (SLW 289, 318). Tied up with his abiding mistrust of the traditional configuration of metaphor (SÄPL 122) is his self-characterization as a *Dichter* in an expressive tradition of plastic imagery and symbolism running from Goethe to Thomas Mann.[29] As L. sails out to sea, a dark form looms large and hauls itself into the boat. Copetta has swollen beyond recognition. In a metonymic continuum with the sea itself, thin white sand (another repetition) and mussels trickle and flow from his shoulders and sleeves (SE 16). This is a discursive interplay between the mythic and the mad, blurring the border between literary symbol and hallucinatory symptom. In an externalization of the ever-repressed urge in the individual body towards self-dissolution, the revenant channels literary Expressionism's Gothic undercurrent.[30]

For Helga Stegemann, Copetta represents a perfect *unio mystica* with natural forces, and the communion of the figures symbolizes a Dionysian affirmation, a yes-saying to nature, to pain, to death and decomposition. In a distinctly cinematic finale, his face becomes young, hers young and youthful, their mouths fuse and their eyes gaze into each other under closed lids. Certainly, there are resonances with Nietzsche's ground-breaking avowal, in *Die Geburt der Tragödie*, that both human existence and the world itself are justified only as an 'aesthetic phenomenon' ['*aesthetisches Phänomen*']:[31] L.'s eyes, grey on the metonymic Ostend seafront, now radiate yearningly, and the story's recurrent locus of the gaze intersects with figurations of luminosity, as the flashing midday sun of the story's start modulates into the dazzling white moonlight that opens its *dénouement*. But any literary reflection of vitalism, as Stegemann would have it, falters in the face of L's terror at awkwardly being a body that ineluctably *matters* in an indifferent universe. She 'broke out into a furious sobbing [...] she could no longer hear her own angry cries under the storm's singing and whistling' ['brach in ein wütendes Schluchzen aus [...] sie hörte ihr eigenes entsetztes Rufen nicht unter dem Singen und Flöten des Sturmes'] (16–17).

The story sets up a twist on the Romantic motif of the *Liebestod*, which in various guises became a recurrent point of fascination for Döblin. There are echoes of this dynamic in the musician's terror at drowning at the end of *Gespräche mit Kalypso*, and Franz Biberkopf's rape of Ida in *Berlin Alexanderplatz* draws upon a related semantic field of dissolution into nature (BA 39–40). But there is another parallel with Johannes's sadistic sexual murder of Irene in *Der schwarze Vorhang*. In a portrayal that inverts and rejects Nietzsche's myth of the self-renewing 'Übermensch',[32] we are confronted with a windowless monad both lost in the existential solitude of his own intense crisis of language (SV 160), and equally devoid of any yearned-for reconciliation with an Other of any kind. In one of the narrative's disorienting shifts between self-pitying inner monologue and free indirect discourse, we are told that 'I'm too poor for loneliness, I'm nothing but desire and love' ['[z]u arm für die Einsamkeit bin ich, nur Begierde und Liebe bin ich'] (SV 142); but in a modulation on what Freud memorably figures as the ambivalent status of the death drive *between* the forces of erotic love and hatred,[33] eroticism is triangulated destructively with violence. He was created for destruction, his love nothing more than a 'predatory' emptiness that 'grasps for plenitude' ['griff räuberisch nach Fülle'] (SV 142). As we read in a grim repetition, 'Liebe' amounts to possessing the living Other even beyond the borders of life and death ['ein Lebendes, eine Menschenseele auf Tod und Leben zu besitzen'] (SV 159); and in answer to the masochistic Irene's desire for her own murder, Johannes obliges with a vampiric bite and immolates himself with her. Any sense of erotic reunion in death is negated in the ugly, writhing forms of the final moments. A flame shoots up from the twitching bodies, as his white hands smother her contorted mouth. In pointed contrast to the German Romantic sense of death as serving the endurance of life — the infinite embodied in the finite — we hear Johannes's words (or thoughts) in the realization that 'life is dead, stiff as a corpse' ['[t]ot ist das Leben, leichenstarr das Leben'] (SV 204).[34]

What distinguishes the subtler and far more tightly controlled 'Segelfahrt' is the sense that the story gives us of human existence irreducible to the opposing forces of *Eros* and *Thanatos*, of living and self-preservation and death. The closing *mythos* of the story, L.'s embrace with Copetta's corpse, leaves behind it a fleshly remainder that resists schematization. In *Ästhetische Theorie*, Adorno describes the (Kantian) sublime in terms of an indeterminate trembling between freedom on the one hand and the insuperable forces of nature on the other;[35] and we catch the hint of that here, in the trembling between the meaningful, the meaninglessness and the absurd: the corpse's black eyes questioningly meet L.'s, then negate the gaze as they look straight past her in another suggestive loose end (SE 17). The closing salvoes are ambiguously conclusive, insisting on their own mysteriousness through the exchangeability of subject and object in the description of the water's overwhelming force:

> Eine Wassermasse, stark wie Eisen, schickte das unermeßliche graugrüne Meer heran. Die trug sie, mit der Handbewegung eines Riesen an die jagenden Wolken herauf. Die purpurne Finsternis schlug über sie. Sie wirbelten hinunter in das tobende Meer. (SE 17)

[The unfathomable grey-green sea sent a mass of water, strong as iron, surging towards them. With a giant's hand, it lifted them up into the racing clouds. The purple blackness closed over them. They swirled down into the raging sea.]

The narrative's suggestion of the case study of a woman's suicide, its vibration with psychopathology in the face of an observational prose at once terse and extravagant, undercuts the story's resolution in this *unio mystica*. As we shall see on broader canvases in the novels, there is a mismatch between the observational directness of the writing itself, and the flickers of animism in the nature it invokes. The architectonic of the parable reasserts itself as Copetta's 'intoxicated, open gaze' ['berauschte[r], aufgeschlossene[r] Blick'] contrasts pointedly with its earlier 'verschlossene[r]' counterpart (17, 13); and the final union seems positively to symbolize the *ideal* of some kind of reconciliation with nature. But as the blackness snaps shut over L. and the revenant, we are left to ponder that alienating choice of 'wirbeln' in the final sentence, capturing as it does a final moment of destructive union between nature and the wordless protagonists. In the shadow of *Der schwarze Vorhang*'s irreconcilables, it seems that this parable of reconciliation finds negative expression (Taylor's 'epiphany') at the liminal site between the individual body and an all-dissolving nature.

The tensions of that in-between space play out in a minor key in 'Die Verwandlung' ['The Metamorphosis']. This is another negative modernist parable with the dream-like combination of concreteness and an abstract sense of weightlessness that would come to the fore a few years later in Kafka's fictions. The Queen and her Prince Consort lead a restless and dissatisfied married life, hardly soothed by the arrival of their first child; and the ensuing narrative tracks a relationship of curated, courtly appearances, which gradually come apart at the seams. The culmination is a turn into a different register of existence (or rather non-existence) entirely. Probably written in the spring of 1911, the story borders on the confessional: the dedication to Erna Reiss speaks to the turbulent backstory of Döblin's own reluctant engagement to her in February of that year.[36] Made at the insistence of his parents, the arrangement stood in the way of his sexual relations with the nurse Frieda Kunke, who — as it would transpire — was pregnant with his son. Bodo was born in October, and Döblin kept up periodic if furtive contact until the end of his life. Still, his sense of having done Frieda an injustice was to become a lasting source of guilt, one acutely compounded by Erna's own admission that she had had an abortion after Döblin had expressed his own doubts about their engagement in a letter.[37]

'Die Verwandlung' acquires an added melancholy, I suggest, if we can find the remnant of the author in it: after Barthes, certainly not as the centre of a miniature *roman à clef*, but rather a point of crossover between the text and indelible traces of personal history. Both look for sexual gratification elsewhere, the 'wild Queen' in Count Hagen, the court poet, whom she had already welcomed into her chambers before her wedding, and the Prince Consort in 'the lap of a delicate, black-haired maid of court with shining eyes' ['den Schoß eines schmächtigen, schwarzen Hoffräuleins mit strahlenden Augen'] (31); and the narrative has them find a febrile *modus vivendi* through which they can more or less accommodate their dalliances. As the story progresses through wordless gesture and body language, together with the fragmentary divulgence of inner realities, the artifice and aestheticism of court life become unsustainable. Count Hagen is violently dismissed by the queen before disappearing from court; the maid drowns herself after setting light to her room; and the story closes with an attempt at reconciliation.

Döblin's use of gesture, in a series of filmic jump cuts in the narrative, makes for a discontinuous string of snapshots Moments of connection and identification appear and evaporate. Dressed in elaborate courtly garb, the royal couple keep up appearances as they glide naturally down the palace corridors and touch foreheads in the Queen's quarters before an abrupt cut to the Prince Consort's room. The act of undressing in front of the mirror hints at a dialectic between a reflected sense of self, and the alienating artifice and otherness of that construct. The Prince Consort is shocked at his wigless hair and sleeves that cling fast to his arms; but even after casting off his 'strange' garments, he fingers his face and 'his' uniform as if to make sure that 'he' is really there. There is a self-conscious attempt both to reassure himself of his own presence and identity and, in the same motion, hide from himself: 'he sometimes brushed his hand over his face, his head, tore at the high collar of his uniform, tried to hide his arms under the table; he felt as if he was wearing a mask' ['[e]r fuhr manchmal mit der Hand über sein Gesicht, seinen Kopf, riß an seinem hohen Uniformkragen, suchte die Arme unter den Tisch zu verstecken; kam sich maskiert vor'] (34).

The story's personal connection leaves its dark trace as this confected performance belies the guilt of the past. As both of them walk along the palace corridor after the disappearance of their respective lovers, without their courtly masks, they seem incapable of casting the past off as they might a strange garment. In a Gothic twist, we read that 'from the eyes of the severe queen gleamed the black wildness of the dead' ['[a]us den Augen der strengen Königin leuchtete die schwarze Wildheit der Toten'] (36). An extraordinary personal barb juts out of Döblin's narrative in the shape of the Queen's expressed desire, as she symbolically cuts herself, to have her child killed, whom she enigmatically dubs 'not mine' and 'a living lie' ['nicht meines [...] eine lebende Lüge'] (37).

The story resolves itself in irresolution. On the island of their self-imposed exile, the protagonists try in vain to find a moment of physical and spiritual union, and the attempts at reciprocity interplay with the mollifying calmness of the sea itself (38). The final twist is a turn from the metonymic into the metaphorical, and the literal into the mythical, as the couple try to achieve a final presence in disappearance and absence.[38] In an image of apartness reminiscent of the wordless strolls in the palace, and suggestive of the vestiges of sovereignty, a round sceptre and a golden crown float side by side on the water's glittering surface (39). As with Franz Kafka's short stories, we encounter what looks like a parable: a story that seems to hope for resolution in a reconciled existence where we might be both historical and free of the unatonable shame of being historical, that is, of simply *being* in space and time. That hope, however, remains ambiguous in a closing image that reads not as an aestheticization of reunion, but rather as a question suspended in silence.

## Psychoanalytic Dynamics

I have already sounded out the striking resonances between Döblin's prose and the more speculative aspects of Freud's metapsychological theories, and these will now briefly be placed in a biographical and clinical context. As Ingrid Maaß has shown, his interactions with psychoanalysis are rooted in a combination of psychiatric knowledge, his use of Freud's writings, and his eventual identification in the 1920s as a critically minded practitioner.[39] However, he was still largely unshaped by Freud's theories when working on his dissertation on psychiatry under the supervision of Hoche, whose antipathy towards Freud is well documented, and who is amusingly sent up in the account of Franz Biberkopf's treatment in the psychiatric clinic at Buch in *Berlin Alexanderplatz*.[40] During his doctoral research, Döblin had become dissatisfied with the lack of an effective aetiology in Hoche's symptom-descriptive approach, which significantly limited a doctor's diagnostic capacities in response to the insufficiencies of contemporary neurology's anatomical approach to mapping the brain.[41]

While he recognized the inadequacy of an approach to mental illness focused on physiology and brain anatomy, Döblin also rejected any attempt to reduce mental illness to psychological causes.[42] As he would argue in his 1914 essay 'Leib und Seele' ['Body and Soul'], the relationship between mind and body remained irreducible to psychiatry's explanative apparatus (KS 1, 163–64). Döblin's sense of these limitations led him to adopt a more psychologically oriented approach in his writings on psychiatry, following his move first to the large psychiatric institution in the Berlin suburb of Buch in 1906, and then to the hospital 'Am Urban' in Kreuzberg in 1908. This increasingly entailed the close observation and recording of his patients' facial expressions and gestures, as well as their own self-narratives of their afflictions, however full of contradictions and dead-ends these were; and this approach, in its turn, was to feed into his empathetic narrative portrayals of mental afflictions, not least in the case of Franz Biberkopf.[43] Döblin's article of 1909, 'Aufmerksamkeitsstörungen bei Hysterie' ['Attention Disorders in Hysteria'], drew not only on his discussions with Berlin psychiatrists, but also a critical reading of Freud's *Zur Psychopathologie des Alltagslebens* [*On the Psychopathology of Everyday Life*] of 1901. By 1909, Döblin had left clinical psychiatry behind for more psychological approaches, while also employing the symptom-descriptive approach adopted by Emil Kraepelin. In 1911, he opened a practice for working-class patients, shifting his attention towards a combination of internal medicine and, increasingly, psychoanalysis.[44] After a process of training analysis at the hands of Ernst Simmel in 1919, he stated at the close of 1921 that he was now 'doing' psychoanalysis — even if, as Veronika Fuechtner points out, it was slightly unclear if he meant this as a patient or as a doctor.[45] Nonetheless, Döblin's involvement with the Berlin Psychoanalytic Institute was complemented by a vigorous exchange of ideas and approaches with the clinic's analysts.[46]

This is the broad clinical backdrop against which we should read Döblin's later reservations about the 'lyricism' in Freud's metapsychological writings, and it informs his growing, if qualified, sense of the value of psychoanalysis as a therapeutic approach with its roots in literature. In a December 1922 review of *Jenseits des Lustprinzips*, Döblin would describe Freud's arguments, with their Haeckelian linking of ontogeny and phylogeny, as extremely 'gripping' and 'stimulating' speculation (KS II, 183). Although he clearly admires what he calls the essay's 'lyrical depth' ['lyrische Tiefe'] (186), Döblin sees little *clinical* justification for Freud's extrapolation from the persistence of ancient drives and impulses in the individual human being: an individual striving for an earlier, stimulus-free state of reincorporation into nature, which reflects the species' phylogenetic origins (185).

What this shows is that he was intent on preserving the integrity of his own clinical territory as a doctor in the face of overly speculative or poetic ideas; and that sense of demarcation needs to qualify any use of Freudian theory to interpret the stories. His essay 'Psychoanalyse von heute' ['The Psychoanalysis of Today'], published in 1923, was a review of the International Psychoanalytic Congress, which Döblin had attended the previous year in Berlin. He spoke approvingly of Freud's own dictum that "established medicine and psychoanalysis are working in each other's directions, like two tunnels: one day the breakthrough will happen" ["[d]ie eigentliche Medizin und die Psychoanalyse arbeiten sich wie zwei Tunnels entgegen: eines Tages wird der Durchschlag erfolgen"] (KS II, 262). In an engaged and sympathetic discussion of the triadic economy of the ego, the super-ego and the id, as elaborated in *Das Ich und das Es* [*The Ego and the Id*] of 1923,[47] Döblin singles out Freud's earlier distinctions between the conscious, the pre-conscious and the unconscious as an eminently useful way of dividing up the psyche, grounded in empirical observation (KS II, 264). But in a follow-up article, 'Praxis der Psychoanalyse' ['The Practice of Psychoanalysis'], he calls passionately for a focus on the clinical rather than the arcanely philosophical (KS II, 273); and in his short piece 'Arzt und Dichter' ['Doctor and Poet'], published in 1927, he would claim — rather disingenuously — that Freud had told him nothing ground-breakingly new (SLW 93): a suggestion, as Fuechtner puts it, that Döblin and other clinicians 'were already working with concepts akin to those of Freud before they were labelled Freudian'.[48]

Of particular interest here is Döblin's growing recognition of the non-essentialist and heuristic character of psychoanalysis, as well as its detachability from Freud himself. He recognized that it was developing into an eminently adaptable toolkit, rather than a definitive scientific or hermeneutic 'key' for ailments that could be reduced to neither body nor mind. The philosophical flipside to this sense of approximation was the keen recognition, in both Freud's and Döblin's works, of the human being's evolutionary position as a hybrid of nature and culture. In Chapter 4, I will discuss Döblin's comprehensive exploration of our lives as 'part and counterpart of nature' ['Stück und Gegenstück der Natur'] in *Unser Dasein*. However, against a similar philosophical grounding in Schopenhauer and Nietzsche, Freud's metapsychological works, notably *Jenseits des Lustprinzips* and *Das Ich und das Es*, illuminated the biological and metaphysical undercurrents already pulsing through the short stories: the tension, with its modern roots in the thought of the Romantics, between human emancipation from nature and our helpless entwinement with it; and between our unconscious desires for either libidinal union or destruction.⁴⁹ These intersections between the thinkers do not map neatly onto Freud's theories, nor are they vitiated by Döblin's own later, clinical scepticism. Rather, they bring into sharp focus a discursive cross-section, at which motifs and dynamics of description, both mythical and scientific, overlap, constitute and even reshape each other.

## Death and Dishonour

'Der Ritter Blaubart' is such an interesting illustration of this because it exposes that point of undefinability, while also offering us a route into a reading of the more intimate portrayals of bodily guilt and shame in the collection. On a first reading we seem to encounter a cluttered montage of the Bluebeard legend, a mythically inflected Mariology, and the Grimm Brothers' Low German story 'Von dem Fischer un syner Fru' ['The Fisherman and His Wife'], the fable of a woman, Ilsebill, whose ever more rapacious requests of a golden flounder — through the intermediary of her husband — eventually land them back in the hovel where they began.⁵⁰ Döblin's complex amalgamation begins with the Baron Paolo di Selvi, a model of machismo, who ends up buying a stretch of coastal land whose austere but mysterious beauty recalls the Frisian panoramas of Theodor Storm's novella *Der Schimmelreiter* [*The Rider on the White Horse*] (1888).⁵¹ A traumatic encounter with an indeterminate abomination out on the coastal heath inexplicably prompts him to move out of the local town and build an elaborate residence for himself there. A wife is to follow, of course, but after two of them end up dead in mysterious circumstances, and the exhumations exonerate him, the socialite withdraws from all local contact. Ilsebill then appears, and her curiosity about the infamous baron and his castle seems to set the cycle in motion yet again, promising yet another dead female body.

In her study of the Bluebeard motif in German literature, Mererid Puw Davies has justifiably argued that Döblin's variant breaks with Charles Perrault's inherently subversive source text of 1697. *La Barbe bleue* spells out a happy ending which is remarkable for being '*material* and *immediate*', the curiosity of Bluebeard's last wife providing the catalyst for a transgressive and utopian usurpation of patriarchal authority. In Perrault's version, the wife both overthrows Bluebeard's violent patriarchal regime and redistributes the bloody murderer's fortune among her family. By contrast, Döblin's text seems to take as its tragic focus the male protagonist's 'autistic and frightened subjectivity'. His castle becomes a well-worn figure for his beleaguered psyche, and the eventual dissolution of Ilsebill into the landscape — a sacrificial punishment for her namesake's insatiable curiosity — reduces the feminine to little more than an extension of the natural, thus forestalling any end to a sexual and mythic cycle of violence.⁵² However, I argue that this reworking *does* in fact prove tacitly subversive by playing out the motifs through which we negotiate our fraught relationship with nature, before leaving unreduced the remnants of both the human and its Other within the text: what seems to be a zero-sum conflict between man and nature ends up leaving behind it an awkward, indissoluble remainder.

The narrative orbits around two absent centres, which provide the foci for the story's ambiguous *dénouement*, and in turn represent switching points between intersecting motifs and 'narrative idioms'.[53] The cause of the baron's body-and-soul beholdenness to the rumoured sea monster, the jellyfish, remains obscure; but so too does the rumour itself, tied up as it is with the local folklore. The setting is, tellingly, a symbolic no man's land from which 'both sea and earth turned away' ['Meer und Erde wandten sich von ihr ab'] (SE 68). The story's blurring of the real and the symbolic, suggested in the hints of nature's agency, is crystallized in an old peasant's belief in an evil monster that resides in the cliff and, like the Minotaur, periodically demands human flesh. In a metafictional twist he tells Ilsebill that although the whole thing might sound like a tall tale, it is in fact true (76). It was upon returning on horseback from a business trip in the local town that the baron had his narratively absent encounter with this monster, and was found lying unconscious on the cliff, his body covered in mud and seaweed, and his face 'strangely swollen, glowing hot, blistered, as if it had been burned' ['eigentümlich geschwollen, glühend, mit Bläschen, wie verbrannt'] in an echo of Copetta's uncanny revenant (69).

No one knows exactly what happened; or at least, that is what we are told in an excursus into the community's collective unconscious which is paralleled in the baron's own obliviousness. Nonetheless, the suggestion of an unnameable violence resurfaces in his subsequent symptoms of trauma. The castle's locked room, into which nature penetrates in the guise of a white cliff spur (73), emerges as the story's second absent centre. In contrast to the blood-drenched abattoir of Perrault's murder scene, Döblin offers us a narrative limit point. Ilsebill almost echoes the baron's declaration of ignorance in the self-reassurance that absolutely nothing had happened to her, after spending a night in the room up against the rock, civilization's outer limit against the sea monster's abode. The cliff itself 'shimmered like a playful fancy' ['schimmerte wie ein spielerischer, phantastischer Einfall'] (74). A recurrent motif of light illuminates the uncanniness of coming up against the indeterminate suture between I and the Other, culture and nature, and the real and the mythical; and the uneasy literal-symbolic ambiguity of 'Einfall' ('incidence' of light, but also 'idea' or 'notion') discloses the antagonisms within these pairings.

There are certainly traces of cultural misogyny to the libidinal forces that are shown to act upon Bluebeard from both within and without: the peasant claims that he would have been long since free from the creature's malign sway were it not for the promiscuity and ungodliness of his wives (76). But these figurations paradoxically show how far the dialectical interplay between the self and its unnameable Other stubbornly refuses any kind of reduction to a binary psychocultural relationship between masculine self and feminine nature. Indeed, 'Der Ritter Blaubart' concludes much less in a *stretto* than in an unfurling of motifs, which problematize the suggestion of a misogynistic resolution in the baron's exoneration. The interaction between nature and the psyche is marked here by a blurring of boundaries between inner and outer, and between the 'real' and the symbolic, an obfuscation that extends right to the limits of symbolization.

*Berlin Alexanderplatz*'s motif of the horseman — a figure for the illusory sovereignty of the masculine ego — is prefigured here, too, in the sinister sight of the 'conquering' ['eroberungssicher'] baron riding on a black stallion (SE 68), as well as in the traces left behind on the dead body of his second wife, who one morning is found in a black riding habit, a shroud covering her proud white face (70–71).[54] The baron's bringing his horses under control (73) partakes of a figuration of the hierarchy of body and mind that reaches from Plato to Freud's horseman analogy in *Das Ich und das Es*, an illustration of the precarious relationship between the beleaguered ego and the id: through the sublimated energies of the id, as the locus of the passions, this rider must 'tame the superior strength of the horse' ['die überlegene Kraft des Pferdes zügeln'], as Freud puts it here.[55] In contrast to Paolo's pathologically civilized repression of his wilder side, Ilsebill's greens, whites and blues speak to a promised reconciliation and erotic reunion with nature (73); but after she is told of the existence of the sea monster, her behaviour takes a startlingly erratic turn. Lost in a Dionysian dance with the poet assigned to distract her, she exults in the projection of herself as a wild animal desperate to break out of her prison (76). As things run their mad course, it seems mythically fated that the dramatic emergence of the jellyfish from the cliff, and the diluvial breaking of the corporeal spell on the baron, should be exactly mirrored in Ilsebill's propitiatory dissolution.

But the plethora of motifs at play reminds us of the proximity of erotic reunion and annihilatory sacrifice, and that dynamic undermines any attempt at a schematic reading. In *Jenseits*, as we have seen, Freud would invoke Nirvana as the final goal of an organic striving for a return to Nature; and tied up with this motif is an ambivalent relationship between love and hatred within sexuality, a dialectic of the *Lebenstriebe* and the *Todestriebe* which triangulated eroticism with violence.[56] This constitutive tension finds expression here in a different idiom. The jellyfish is described as a 'Meduse', a scientific term that carries with it the mythic connotations of unharnessed female sexuality. In a different vein again, 'Meduse' also bears the imprint, as Midgley has suggested, of Wilhelm Bölsche's interweaving of myth, literature and evolutionary biology in the popular-scientific bestseller *Das Liebesleben in der Natur* [*Love-Life in Nature*] (1898–1903). In this epic reworking of Darwin's narrative of natural selection, he describes a natural world pervaded by a force of destruction, procreation and endless regeneration: an idea that drew both him and Freud, from very different orientations, into a shared Schopenhauerian inheritance.[57] Bölsche viewed the evolution of organic life as embodying the self-development of a universal principle of love. It was a 'universal history of love' ['Weltgeschichte der Liebe'], culminating in humanity as creation's teleological endpoint.[58] As Bölsche argued, sexual love was evolution's driving force, the continuum that phylogenetically linked primitive life forms, notably and prominently including the jellyfish, to the rapturous erotic communions and (transcending that) the religious and artistic creations of human beings.[59] In figurative affinity with what Nicholas Saul has described in this connection as 'that quintessentially *fin-de-siècle* sense of oceanic oneness of self and universe',[60] Döblin's Medusa biologically and mythically fuses the antagonists of destructive horror and beauty.

Sure enough, as the cliff is burst asunder, the ultimate Other — the hitherto invisible jellyfish — finally rips into the narrative. In another confluence of nature's harmony and danger, an all-enveloping 'paralyzing sweetness' is juxtaposed with Ilsebill's 'mortal fear' ['Todesangst'], a dynamic which, following her disappearance, shades over into the baron's dedication to the Virgin Mary — that corporeal, and therefore, natural bearer of the divine whose iconography was a source of persistent fascination for Döblin — of her own sublime gift of deathly fear mixed with love (SE 78–79). For all its bizarreness, then, the story culminates in another portrayal of human existence caught both individually and collectively in a flux between antagonistic and symbiotic energies; but sedimented in this discursive play is, again, the remainder of bodily existence, an indelible *thisness* that prevents the story from slotting into a single schema, whether vitalistic, misogynistic, or both.

> Ilsebill wanderte auf den Berg. Und wie sie zwischen den Bäumen ging, trat der Nebel in den Wald. Aus einem Baume, an dem sie betete und ihr Kreuz aufhing, trat ein feiner, feiner Rauch, der süßer als Flieder duftete. Er legte sich um die wandernde Ilsebill, so daß sie eingehüllt war in die Falten eines weiten, duftenden Mantels. [...] Rascher und rascher lief sie, aber sie stürzte bei jedem Schritt:'Ich möchte doch leben. Ach, liebe Mutter Gottes, laß mich doch die Blumen noch sehen, laß mich doch die Vöglein sehen'. [...] Ihre Lippen blaßten. Sie wurde dünner und dünner. Seufzend löste sie sich auf und verschwand in dem feinen Nebel, der über die Birken zog. (SE 78)
>
> [Ilsebill wandered up onto the hill. And as she walked among the trees, a mist came into the forest. She stopped at one tree to pray and hang up her cross, and out of it came a fine, fine smoke sweeter than lilacs. It enveloped Ilsebill as she moved, such that she was wrapped in the folds of a white, fragrant mantle. [...] She ran faster and faster, but she fell at every step: 'But I want to live. Oh, beloved mother of God, let me still see the flowers, let me still see the birds.' [...] Her lips went pale. She became thinner and thinner. Sighing, she dissolved and disappeared into the delicate mist that drifted over the birch trees.]

Nature's reaffirmation of itself brings us full circle back to the opening of the story, whose memory of a landscape untouched by humanity anticipates the sprawling natural histories of *Berge Meere und Giganten*. As both metonymies of the natural world and bearers of the divine, the mist and the smoke take on an almost animistic colouring that is suggestive of the organic aesthetics of *Jugendstil*.[61] Nature is animated in strange new configurations: 'from the sea there came a thundering and a bursting. A huge spring flood, a grey wall a mile wide, broke through the dams and dikes, spilled rolling and foaming all over the accursed plains' ['vom Meere her kam ein Donnern und Bersten. Eine Springflut, eine meilenweite graue Wand durchbrach die Dämme und Deiche, setzte rollend und schäumend über die verwunschene Ebene'] (78). This explosion, with its distinct echoes of nature's Realist and very *real* reassertion in the tragic bursting of the dyke at the end of *Der Schimmelreiter*,[62] seems to embody a mythic revenge for Ilsebill's own flirtations with chaos ('crazy, yes she was crazy, a corpse in a living body' ['[w]ahnsinnig, ja wahnsinnig wäre sie, eine Leiche bei lebendigem Leibe']) (76); but rather like L. in 'Die Segelfahrt', her exclamations of despair individualize her as a terrified body in the face of an external and internal nature that is losing its contours. The unredeemed absurdity of it all blurs the figurative boundaries between inner and outer, the particular and the universal, and the body and nature. The jellyfish brings us down into the unlovely but crucial subject matter of bodily history. Ilsebill bitterly laments her mythically sanctioned reabsorption. Her plea for life is a despairing claim to *thisness*, which subversively juts out of the fabric of a closed mythical and propitiatory circle.[63] In one final departure from Perrault, and in a strangely alienating final turn back into historical Realism, we learn that the baron himself was killed many years later in a skirmish in Central America (79). Döblin's story denies us either consolation or catharsis, but the residues of its protagonists speak to the disjointed presence of the individual — along with its awkward claim to life and meaning — in the wake of both jellyfish and deluge.

'Das Stiftsfräulein und der Tod', the first story in the collection to be published (in *Das Magazin* in January 1908), trains its queasy gaze on the individual body as a troubled hybrid of mind and matter, and death as its radically unrepresentable limit point. In tandem with that, though, it is also a parable about the intensely personal nature of our own 'narratives' towards our final ends. The story sets in motion a dynamic of corporeal and spiritual imbalance, and eroticism gone bad, in the form of a nun's lustful fear of death: a combination of flirtation and mortification which brings the collection to a close that is as creepy as it is grotesque. Walking alongside the dark waters among the trees outside the abbey (an Expressionist premonition of the echoes of Jeremiah in *Berlin Alexanderplatz*), it suddenly dawns on her — without any elaboration — that her end is coming. The terse 'I have to die, I have to die' ['[i]ch muß sterben, ich muß sterben'] (SE 104) reveals a panicked desire to reclaim agency and self-presence — in the face of inevitable absence — through a desire for self-submission redolent of Copetta. This utterance follows directly on from a rash attempt to reclaim a sense of presence by stopping the uncannily anthropomorphized clocks. Even time itself, that fleeting marker of persistent absence, is embodied.

The story's endgame pushes these tensions to their outermost limits by enacting the interplay of sexuality and death. The nun's gestures express both a pathological luring and a fearful warding-off of the figure she addresses in flirtatious love letters as 'my dear strict master, Death' ['meinen lieben strengen Herrn, den Tod'] (108); and this is a quirk which bubbles to the surface as she 'left a small spot next to her, which she hesitantly covered up with her arm, then she removed it, replaced it, it was a game' ['ließ einen kleinen Platz neben sich, den sie zögernd mit dem Arm bedeckte, dann nahm sie ihn wieder weg, legte ihn wieder herüber, es war ein Spiel'] (108). A tersely observational aesthetic again shades over into something of symbolic moment; and the nun's flirtatious game — you can have me, no you can't — finds its consummating image in the final, burlesque image of Death swinging himself into the empty spot in the bed next to her. What is intriguing here is not just symbolic illustration of a sexualized welcoming of death, but also the anticipation of the dynamics of the game of *fort-da* with which Freud sets up his discussion of the repetition compulsion in *Jenseits*.

Like the jellyfish, Death breaks into the narrative as a figuration of unmasterable otherness, responding to the nun's advances by sadistically murdering her; and Stephanie Catani has rightly underlined Döblin's violent break with a *fin-de-siècle* beautification of death as a site of transfiguration.[64] The logic of *fort-da* involves both the constitution and preservation of the self in the face of the desired Other, and the constitution of signification in an interplay between presence and absence, and between identity and non-identity. Through a re-enactment of disappearance and return, Freud's child achieves individuation, that is, he provisionally defers the instinctual gratification of being in communion with the maternal body, and in the same motion 'compensates' himself for this loss.[65] In the very different context of war neuroses, we also find in *fort-da* a repetition-compulsion that attempts both retroactively to master traumatic stimuli and to safeguard the individual's bodily 'narrative' towards death.[66] Despite Döblin's own later scepticism at the speculative complexion of Freud's metapsychology, this hint of symptomatic yet symbolic *fort-da* in 'Das Stiftsfräulein' adumbrates the obscurity that shrouds the limits of discourse at the edge of death.

Anticipating the arrival of her master, the nun experiences a rejuvenation that provokes whispered condemnation throughout the convent, and her blue blouse, white gloves and freshly cut roses suggest preparation for a tryst, if not something more. But in its sheer directness and concreteness, the eventual meeting spells not reconciliation, but brutal negation. At the end of a series of reiterated gestures of welcoming and rejecting, her death is criss-crossed with gestures of repetition. The voyeurism suggested, or even invited, by Ernst Ludwig Kirchner's accompanying woodcut illustrations makes the final figurative murder even more alienating:

> Sie schlief ein. Wachte im Finstern auf. Wuchtige Schritte im Zimmer. Das Bett krachte. Mit einem Satz schwang sich der Tod neben sie ins Bett. Da war ein Platz frei. Er griff nach ihren Knieen. Sie stieß um sich. Wie ein Bauernlümmel schlug er mit flacher Hand auf ihre Schultern. Da fiel die geballte Faust auf ihre Brust, den Leib, den Leib, und wieder auf den Leib. Ihre Lippen flehten. Ein Würgen kam. Die Zunge fiel in den Rachen zurück. Sie streckte sich. (SE 110)
>
> [She fell asleep. Woke up in the dark. Heavy footsteps in her room. The bed cracked. In a single leap, Death swung himself into bed next to her. There was a spot free. He grabbed at her knees. She tried to fight him off. Like a country peasant he struck her shoulders with the flat of his hand. His clenched fist fell on her chest, her body, her body, and her body once again. Her lips pleaded, a retching came. Her tongue rolled back in her throat. She stretched out.]

Sadism and masochism enter into the same space in a meaningless finale of sex and violence;[67] and the characterization of the nun's last end as both a rape and a murder at the hands of Death — another *Lustmord*[68] — makes our ignorance of the real cause even more jarring. The 'Herr' drags the nun out of the window by her 'cold little hands' ['an ihren kalten Händchen'] (110). Of her abject final moments, we read that 'a retching came. Her tongue rolled back in her throat. She stretched out' ['[e]in Würgen kam. Die Zunge fiel in den Rachen zurück. Sie streckte sich'] (SE 110). The grotesqueness of these descriptions highlights both the personal unrepresentability of death and its symbolic emptiness, that is, the culmination of our narratives in nothingness. The translatability of 'Herr' as both 'master' and 'Lord' adds a further layer of irony, as this particular Lord comes quite literally as a thief in the night, in a suggestive nod to I Thessalonians 5. 2.

In a similar vein to 'Die Segelfahrt' and 'Der Ritter Blaubart', Döblin's parable promises something that at least *looks* like meaning, in the form of a yearned-for reconciliation and redemption, before withholding both; and the ultimate act of withholding, in the form of the disappearing female corpse, brings the collection as a whole to an abrupt close. I now turn to examine this tension more closely as it plays out at the interfaces of body and mind in 'Die Ermordung einer Butterblume' and 'Die Tänzerin und der Leib'.

**Narrative Collapse**

As a way of making sense of the collection's flagship stories, I want to set them very briefly in dialogue with Adorno's theory of mimesis, a concept that transcends traditional definitions of artistic imitation, and which also sheds powerful light on the anthropological tensions of man and nature delineated in Freud's metapsychology. While Platonic and Aristotelian concepts of mimesis as imitation have fundamentally shaped the debate around aesthetic representation in Western intellectual culture,[69] my interest here is in the anthropological turn that the concept took in the twentieth century through the work of Benjamin and, in particular, Adorno. In such essays as 'Über das mimetische Vermögen' ['On the Mimetic Faculty'] and 'Lehre vom Ähnlichen' ['Doctrine of the Similar'] (1933), Benjamin traced mimesis back to the beginnings of human language itself, reading it as the marker of our evolutionary-biological tendency to imitate and, through that, to establish pre-linguistic connections with the natural world around us.[70] In close affinity, Adorno's concept of mimesis speaks in its most elemental form to a creaturely mode of being: one that was originally keyed to our evolutionary instincts for self-preservation in the face of nature's violence and chaos. We protected ourselves, and warded off nature's threats, by mimicking them; and this mimicry underpinned the prehistoric and pre-religious rites of the shaman.[71]

As Adorno delineates the concept in *Dialektik der Aufklärung*, the emergence of the unitary subject in 'enlightened' modernity was predicated on the elimination of a fear of uncontrollable nature through the repression of these primal mimetic impulses.[72] Integral to the emergence of an autonomous and unitary subject, distinct and ultimately alienated from nature, was a form of internalized violence: an attempt to eliminate the incommensurable in the quest for an elusive state of identity and stability.[73] As the remnant of our primal imitative urges, mimesis finds its last refuge from a violent and coercive world in a promise of uniqueness and non-identity, a promise that is integral to what Adorno calls art's 'semblance quality' ['Scheincharakter'].[74] The keynote argument of *Ästhetische Theorie* (1970), his uncompleted posthumous masterpiece, is that each true work of art is inherently utopian by virtue of its oblique portrait of reconciliation between the mind and body, and — by extension — the 'human' and the 'natural'. As a 'semblance of non-semblance' ['Schein der Scheinlosigkeit'], art presents us with the illusionary promise (or memory) of a world in which people, animals and things *might* be able to 'be themselves', without fear of violence or coercion, in their unique 'here and now'. And as a vehicle of mimesis, art is the last representative and reminder of undamaged life in the midst of modernity's profoundly damaged natural and social fabric.[75]

I will consider this utopian aspect of mimesis in more detail in the next chapter. But its dynamics are illuminating for the short stories for two closely related reasons. Firstly, they help us to think through the aesthetic effects of the stories' portrayals of radical imbalance and disappointed (or deferred) reconciliation. Our mimetic impulses remain torn between a fear of nature's destructive power, and the supposed bliss of disappearing into that nature. This tension draws the concept into unmistakable proximity with Freud's death drive.[76] Secondly, the work of art recapitulates and mirrors our own mimetic impulses. Although seemingly autonomous, it is shot through with the recalcitrant materials of society, history and nature, 'that which strives against it' ['das ihr Widerstrebende'], which it must formally integrate.[77] If only at one remove, it embodies its creators' repressed desire anonymously to disappear back into those Others. 'Die Ermordung einer Butterblume' and 'Die Tänzerin und der Leib' present us with two protagonists desperate to take control of unruly bodies and, with that, to assume sovereignty over their own narratives. Integral to both stories is not merely an acute sense of disharmony, but also the reflection of that imbalance and disorientation in their criss-crossing discourses and motifs: these narratives combine aesthetic and non-aesthetic contents and materials in their finest details. From the perspectives of both protagonist and reader, the stories show bids for narrative and interpretative sovereignty gone irreversibly wrong.

In 'Die Ermordung', the *petit bourgeois* Freiburg businessman Michael Fischer accidentally decapitates a buttercup when his walking stick becomes caught in some undergrowth on the edge of the Black Forest. After watching a Doppelgänger of himself murder the flower, his imagination runs away with itself. What begins as a puerile private joke — being found out and hunted down — escalates rapidly into a paranoid bid to track down the mutilated buttercup, whom he has posthumously christened Ellen, and to cover up her remains. Torn between his fury at the dead flower, a frantic fear of the consequences and a polymorphously perverse excitement, he imagines himself hunted down by a mythically vengeful forest, seemingly in league with the local village community. A mythic logic of substitution and atonement sets in. Fischer sets up a private business account for Ellen and offers her food and drink *in absentia* at each mealtime. He descends into near-suicidal despair, unable to expiate his egregious crime, and weeps bitterly for the first time since his childhood, when he has the idea of contractually tricking the flower by planting a surrogate daughter with the legal code's paragraph on debt compensation inscribed in charcoal on the plant pot. His happiness at a new-found freedom from legal obligation is consummated when, one evening, his cleaning lady admits to accidentally knocking the plant pot off its little table and sweeping its contents into the bin. Contractually released from his debt, and seemingly now at liberty to massacre as many flowers as he wants, he duly does precisely that, before vanishing into the darkness of the forest.

This bizarrely compelling allegory of mind and matter finds its austere counterpart in the pubescent female dancer of 'Die Tänzerin und der Leib'. Ella, we learn, was destined for dancing from the age of eleven because it suited an eccentric temperament that was oriented towards control and self-contortion. Her choreographic discipline is an embodiment of early twentieth-century ideologies of dance education as an aesthetic exercise in strengthening the force of the will by means of the body. Indeed, as Cowan has argued, the 'Jaques-Dalcroze Method' of music, dance and rhythmical gymnastics, pioneered by the Swiss composer Émile Jaques-Dalcroze in 1911 at his educational institute in the Dresden suburb of Hellerau, saw one of its central goals as the controlled direction of the body through the bodily performances of music and dance.[78] At the age of nineteen, Ella succumbs to an indeterminate consumptive illness and is taken to hospital, in an ironic play on the *fin-de-siècle* motif of the *femme fragile*: the slight, androgynous form, pale face and oversized dark eyes make for a melancholic parody of consumption.[79] But this is a very different aesthetic space from that of transfiguration in death, integral as this was to consumption's idealized figuration. Ella's loss of the ability to speak in hospital is a succinct expression of the inseparability of human meaning and corporeality. The story's endgame plays out through an unravelling of meticulously executed aesthetic control, as she stitches the embroidered image of a violent suicide before committing it for real.

'Die Ermordung' opens with a picture of neurotic self-control, as Fischer obsessively counts his steps up to a hundred and back again (SE 56). His carefree unleashing of violence against weeds and flowers is the flipside of a buttoned-up neurotic who also slaps his apprentices when they do not swat the office flies quickly enough and present them to him in strict order of size (57). Ella's choreographic disciplining of her unruly body in 'Die Tänzerin' also reflects her desire for control over her personal narrative as an embodied subject. To quote Döblin's excursus on music philosophy, *Gespräche mit Kalypso* (1910), she subscribes to the contemporary notion of dance as an aesthetic exercise in 'the subjugation of the body to the will' ['die Unterjochung des Leibes unter den Willen'] (SÄPL 75–76). Her story's austere compactness mimics the sublimated violence of her aesthetic play, as she persists in harshly disciplining a body which takes on a life of its own: we are struck by the pointed militarism, barely disguised desire, and literal creepiness in the observation that 'she crept carefully and patiently down into her toes, her ankles, her knees [...] she greedily attacked her slender shoulders and the curve of her thin arms, kept vigilant watch over the play of this taut body' ['sie schlich sich behutsam und geduldig in die Zehen, die Knöchel, die Kniee ein [...] überfiel habgierig die schmalen Schultern und die Biegung der schlanken Arme, wachte lauernd über dem Spiel des straffen Leibes'] (SE 18). 'Habgierig' hints at the body's tacit complicity in this assault on itself.

We can begin to make sense of these drives for corporeal control if we set

Döblin's disturbed protagonists in the context of 'Willenskultur'. As I have already suggested, this represented a multifaceted cultural, pedagogical and therapeutic endeavour to bolster the resources of willpower, and to affirm its agency over a nervous or aboulic body.[80] The discourse of nervousness, neurasthenia and aboulia was in large part the cultural product of a rapidly industrializing modern society whose speed and mechanization was shattering any residual sense of unitary subjective experience and subjective narrative.[81] Fischer tells himself that he is 'made nervous' by the over-stimulations of the city (57), and his wilful bid for self-control manifests itself in his stuttering, mechanistic attempts to centralize his body ('he wanted to bring these little horses under control. [...] A sharp jab in the flanks would tame them') '[d]iese Pferdchen wollte er bald kirren. [...] Ein scharfer Stich in die Flanken würde sie schon zähmen'] (59–60): an image that, once again, foreshadows Freud's horseman analogy. In a crossover between mind and matter, even Fischer's tattered psyche repeatedly takes on a subversive somatic life of its own. The 'wayward, wilful thoughts' ['eigenwillige[] Gedanken'] (58) must be brought to heel, but to no avail as they rip into the narrative fabric, vocalized in Fischer's violent declarations of authority, concretized in the slapstick of flailing body parts, and internalized in shards of hallucination and free indirect discourse. 'Eigenwillig', revealingly, refers both to renegade thoughts and renegade limbs.

In the light of this tangle of body and mind, we should in turn read these figurations of *Willenskultur* against Döblin's specific clinical backdrop. Fischer 'presents', as both Reiner Marx and Christine Emig have argued, as an obsessive-compulsive neurotic tipped over into a symptomatology of paranoid schizophrenia;[82] and the affinities between the fragmentary aesthetics of modernism and the sensory and psychical 'hyperreflexivity' of schizophrenia, which had first emerged as a diagnostic category in the 1890s, have been comprehensively mapped out by Louis Sass in his groundbreaking study *Madness and Modernism*.[83] Döblin's observations of the confabulations of a Korsakoff sufferer, which made up the case study of his psychiatric dissertation, certainly helped to shape Fischer's particular psychopathology: 'Die Tänzerin' and 'Die Ermordung' were written in 1904 and 1905 respectively, a gestation which closely associates them with the doctoral work.[84]

Acutely susceptible to symptoms of depersonalization and dissociation, Korsakoff sufferers experience the complete collapse of a meaningful narrative, as their disturbances of association lead to the irrevocable confusion of the real with the fictional, and of particular memories with the wrong contexts.[85] Even dream-like tales of 'cock-and-bull stories' and 'encounters with wild animals' ['Räubergeschichten' and 'Begegnungen mit wilden Tieren'] are translated into imagined personal experience (*Gedächtnisstörungen* 44–45). The story foregrounds that ambiguous space between the fantastical products of the poet and the patient's synaptic disturbances. In the dissertation the combined products of dreams, third-person accounts and free imagination come to be mixed up and re-placed in radically different contexts (*Gedächtnisstörungen* 48). In his account of the personal impact of the syndrome, in 'A Matter of Identity', in *The Man who Mistook his Wife for a Hat*, the neurologist Oliver Sacks argued that the fictionalized 'pseudo-narratives' of his

Korsakoff patients might be read as unwitting over-compensations for their lack of those self-narratives through which past experiences shape 'normal' identities and hermeneutics in the present.[86] In a similar vein, Döblin shows confabulation to be internally coherent, if false: a mixture of disorientation on the one hand, and the residual capacity for weaving perceptions and ideas into elaborately false memories on the other (*Gedächtnisstörungen* 46).[87] Fischer does not 'confabulate' in Döblin's clinical sense, but aspects of precisely this symptomatology are nonetheless woven into the story's bodily and mental confusion, speaking not just to the confusion itself, but also to his desperate attempt narratively to overcome it.

Fischer's confabulations take on a mythic logic, which forms the third thread to the narrative fabric. In her seminal study, Emig convincingly showed how this motif directly draws upon the theme of primal guilt and revenge central to Aeschylus' trilogy of tragedies, the *Oresteia*.[88] What so fascinated Döblin about the trilogy, Emig argues, was its portrayal of mythic revenge, at the hands of the female furies, for Orestes' injury to nature's chthonic, figuratively female forces. This nourishes Clytemnestra's posthumous claim for mythic justice through the Furies, which must ultimately give way to Athena's establishment of the Law of the Father underpinning civilization.[89] This is a principle of ancient tragic necessity, described by Adorno as lying at the origins of mythology, through which vengeance is meted out on the individual as punishment for insufficiencies embodied and injuries inflicted by virtue of being human, and so marginally split over against nature. In Fischer's frantic flight through the forest (62–63), we might even hear the echo of Orestes' steps in the final play of the *Oresteia*, the *Eumenides*, as he is pursued by the vengeful Furies 'throughout all the long mainland as your steps take you constantly wandering the earth beyond the ocean and the cities round which it flows'.[90]

For all its persuasiveness, I suggest that Emig's reading narrows the story's suggestiveness to a particular set of mythic contours, whereas its peculiar irritant quality in fact lies in its stubborn refusal to allow its symptoms to be subsumed to its symbols, or vice versa. Intimations of vengeance and justice make for an unsettling oscillation between the symbolic and the psychiatric. Trees 'assemble in judgment' ['treten zum Gericht zusammen'] as Fischer runs through the forest; but this mythic statement of guilt has already been reduced to mental chaos as one particularly resinous tree suddenly transmogrifies into a weeping one (62). We hear the 'singing' and 'howling' of the electric tram as he narrowly escapes from a forest and a mountain which 'hisses threats behind him, shaking its fists' ['drohsam rauscht, die Fäuste schüttelt'] (63) — an uncanny meeting point of perception and hallucination, the aesthetics of Expressionism and technological modernity. His suicidal thoughts vacillate between his anger at a life now beholden to atonement and his regret that the buttercup is no longer alive to enjoy the sunshine and the cuckoo's call.

On the anniversary of her death he pretends to be oblivious, only to devote half the day to her memory when she seems to insist on commemoration, in an anticipation of Josef K.'s submission to the absent-yet-present Court in Kafka's *Der Proceß* (1925) (65). And yet, the metaphysics is made irresistibly comic as we view it in clinical and figurative counterpoint to a Korsakoff patient's deepening paranoia (*Gedächtnisstörungen* 46). A growing fear of his crime's ramifications is reflected in the despairing question about what 'they' will do with him. His sense of disorientation is visualized as he gropes his way from tree to tree to avoid slipping on a newly smooth ground, and as the forest presses in around him, we are confronted with a sudden dip into free indirect discourse in the panicked realization that '[h]e has to get out' ['[e]r muß hinaus']. A pine tree then 'knocks him down with raised hands' ['schlägt mit aufgehobenen Händen auf ihn nieder'], before he careers down the last slope of the forest into the village street lights, his clothes in tatters (62–63). Döblin's grammatical shift from the preterite to the present tense combines with a shift of focalization between psychiatric observation, hallucination, and free indirect discourse. Through a narrative doubling that mirrors the *Doppelgänger* vision, these slippages, in the space between madness and myth, mimic Fischer's mental and bodily dislocation.

As with the collection's other protagonists, both his primal crime and desperate attempts at atonement metastasize into a drive to flatten out his own fleshliness; but this intertwines with a mimetic impulse towards those corporeal and libidinal aspects of who he 'is'. For Thomas Anz, the grotesquely exaggerated decapitation of the buttercup embodies Fischer's repression of the libidinal dimensions of his inner existence. Viewed from this perspective, his madness is an expressionistic figure: an ever-failing bid to control or even eliminate the flesh, which Döblin's stories push to its extremes in order to critique the repressed narratives of bourgeois existence, not to mention Wilhelmine ideologies of self-controlled masculinity.[91] Nonetheless, this figural reading, ironized in Fischer's obsessive fondling of his effeminately clean-shaven chin (57), should be filtered through the lens of the story's angular materiality and directness *as* an experimental text grounded in the psychiatric case study. His consciousness of guilt ['schuldbewußt'] is evoked in connection to his decision to push his walking stick up into his sleeve in order to stabilize himself (60);[92] and it is palpably tied up, not least in his neurotic self-observations, with a pained sense of 'this' being within 'this' body, always insufficient and inchoately in breach of something.[93] 'Guilt' is figured here not as the marker of a particular act of perpetration, but rather as what Stegemann calls a crime against the 'ethos of life's [vitalistic] pathos' ['das Ethos des Lebenspathos']: the tragic existential wages of being marginally split over against an ultimately all-consuming nature.[94]

In the light of this painful splitting, the story stakes a truth claim in its invitation to think humanness in terms of the point of clash between being a body, and so entangled with an external and internal nature, and being irreducible to both.[95] But Fischer's *Doppelgänger* vision brings that contradiction down into the fundamentally asymbolic and anti-hermeneutic spaces of psychopathology. The retrospective hallucination of the decapitation links Fischer's repressed sexuality to a compulsion to negate the fleshly being that he is:

> Plötzlich sah Herr Michael Fischer, während sein Blick über den Wegrand strich, wie eine untersetzte Gestalt, er selbst, von dem Rasen zurücktritt, auf die Blumen stürzte und einer Butterblume den Kopf glatt abschlug. [...] Diese Blume dort glich den anderen auf ein Haar. Diese eine lockte seinen Blick, seine Hand, seinen Stock. Sein Arm hob sich, das Stöckchen sauste, wupp, flog der Kopf ab. Der Kopf überstürzte sich in der Luft, verschwand im Gras. Wild

schlug das Herz des Kaufmanns. Plump sank jetzt der gelöste Pflanzenkopf und wühlte sich in das Gras. Tiefer, immer tiefer, durch die Grasdecke hindurch, in den Boden hinein. Jetzt fing er an zu sausen, in das Erdinnere, daß keine Hände ihn mehr halten konnten. Und von oben, aus dem Körperstumpf, tropfte es, quoll aus dem Halse weißes Blut, nach in das Loch, erst wenig, wie einem Gelähmten, dem der Speichel aus dem Mundwinkel läuft, dann in dickem Strom, rann schleimig, mit gelbem Schaum auf Herrn Michael zu, der vergeblich zu entfliehen suchte, nach rechts hüpfte, nach links hüpfte, der drüber wegspringen wollte, gegen dessen Füße es schon anbrandete. (SE 57–58)

[As his gaze ranged at a loose end over the edge of the path, Herr Michael Fischer suddenly saw a stocky figure, himself, step back from the grass, lunge at the flowers and cleanly chop the head of a buttercup off. [...] All the flowers looked exactly identical. This one in particular attracted his gaze, his hand, his stick. His arm went up, his little stick whipped down, whoosh, the head flew straight off. The head somersaulted into the air, disappeared into the grass. The businessman's heart pounded. The chopped-off planthead sank awkwardly and burrowed its way into the grass. Deeper, ever deeper it went, through the grass, into the earth. Now it really hurtled downwards in the earth's core, where no hand could pluck it. And from the top of it, from the stump of its body something was dripping, a spurt of white blood from the neck into the hole, at first a trickle, like spittle dribbling from the corner of an invalid's mouth, then in a wide stream. It ran slimy, flowing towards Herr Michael, who tried in vain to jump out of the way, jumped to the left, jumped to the right, tried to jump over this stream, which was now surging and beating at his feet.]

As Torsten Hoffmann suggests, the anthropomorphism of the buttercup mirrors Fischer's desire to do away with the body and destroy the traces of nature within himself.[96] It is an act of violence born *in* the body and symbolically unleashed on the 'Kopf', here enmeshed with 'Pflanzen'. Rather like *Berlin Alexanderplatz*'s 'Franz Beaverhead' ['Biberkopf'], the hybrid 'Pflanzenkopf' intertwines mind and matter. Throughout Fischer's ensuing mental torment, the repressed returns as revenant: a motif of the uncanniness through which things unnervingly close to us that should have remained hidden unexpectedly resurface, and the familiar takes on unfamiliar complexions.[97] This is not to add another psychoanalytic interpretation to a tottering pile, but rather to suggest that in the joints of its discourses — mythic and psychiatric — the text oscillates between virulent, fearful disgust and clandestine excitement. Fischer's desperation to avoid the 'schleimig' stream of resinous blood is offset by the sexually violent fantasy of an ejaculation and a literal deflowering, here refigured as an uncontrollable flood. The excitement with which he stares at the mutilation finds expression as he 'shivered wildly at his own audacity, he would never have imagined himself so depraved' ['erschauerte wüst über seine eigene Tollkühnheit, er hätte sich nie für so verworfen gehalten'] (58). Not only that, but deep down, 'he lusted for the flower and the murder scene' ['lüsterte ihn nach der Blume und der Mordstelle'] (60). However, these frissons overlap with disgust and terror as he imagines the orgasm's disgusting residue, a yellow stinking sludge, which, in strikingly medical vocabulary, is 'mucoid like vomit' ['schleimartig wie Erbrochenes'] (59). The stink — the smudged trace of a *fin-de-siècle* culture of decadence, and most notorious in the form of the pervasive 'yellow smell' of

Charlotte Perkins Gilman's 'The Yellow Wallpaper' (1892) — hints at the abject residue of female genital discharge, the excretion of nature's ultimate metonym.[98] The crossovers between sexuality and nature myth are mirrored in the chthonic image of the buttercup head boring its way into the depths of the earth.

Fischer's desire to eliminate the body and the bodily is tied up with his inseparability from both. We recall Johannes's polymorphously perverse fascination with his sweet peas in *Der schwarze Vorhang*, which serves as an uncanny gateway to his sadomasochistic relationship with Irene: 'He often caressed and stroked their baby hairs and tendrils, their twines, which feel their way forward like the steps of a blind man. He let them play tenderly against his cheek' ['Über ihre weichen, hellen Kinderhärchen und Ranken, Windungen, welche spürsam wie die Schritte eines Blinden sind, streichelte er oft liebkosend hin, ließ sie zart gegen seine Wangen spielen'] (SV 114). The symbiosis of terror and desire is made even clearer here, as Fischer 'fearfully feasted' ['labte sich ängstlich'] on the auditory hallucinations of her furious screams (SE 65). In *Dialektik der Aufklärung*, Adorno and Horkheimer identify the tragic flip-side of fascism's theatrical violence as a repressed mimetic desire for reconciliation with precisely those traces of nature it has attempted to expunge. The violence itself is the perverted mimesis of its victim's flailing gestures of pain.[99] The shadow side of Döblin's unsettling case study, in turn, lies in the recognition that Fischer's flailing attempts to restore a sense of order entwines him ever more intimately with what he wants to subjugate — and discloses his paradoxical yearning to be reconciled with it. The sight of him breaking down in tears for the first time since childhood over his inability to be rid of his crime, 'almost until his heart broke' ['daß ihm fast das Herz brach'], manages to be both comic and disconcertingly moving (64).

'Die Ermordung' ends as mind succumbs to matter, just as matter succumbs to mind. After contractually deceiving the forest, Fischer declares open season on all buttercups, and — as the narrative itself snaps coldly shut — vanishes into the literal and mental darkness of the forest (67). By tricking nature, he is tricked by it in turn. Psychopathology and myth finally reunite, but that reunion is ironically what forecloses any narrative resolution. The story's formidable achievement lies in the way in which it allows medical discourses and mythic motifs to enter the same narrative and hermeneutic space, without ever quite cancelling one another out. Like the tangled bank in which his walking stick becomes fatefully caught, the story's tangle of discourses both tempts us into an interpretation and, in the same motion, resists any attempt at one. Fischer's loosening hold on body and mind, as he searches in vain for the originary buttercup corpse, is mirrored in our own search for the elusive key to a pathological text. Legible simultaneously as a twisted case study, a psychosocial critique of the repressions underpinning Wilhelmine masculinity, and a reworking of nature myth, it is irreducible to any one line of interpretation and securely rooted in none.

If Fischer's body asserts itself through a disintegrating mind, then the mind triumphs just as ambivalently in 'Die Tänzerin'. Ella's body asserts its own ineluctability as a semi-autonomous being, as the voice that she used to order it about itself falls silent. The harbinger archetype of the *Doppelgänger* is embodied in the 'fear of death' that creepily stands behind her bed as she sleeps (SE 19). Although she subjects it to stringent control ('she locked the body up, put it in chains [...] she suppressed her pain') ['[s]ie sperrte den Leib, legte ihn in Ketten [...] ihren Schmerz verheimlichte sie'] (19–20), it nonetheless becomes — as for the nun — a limit point of discourse, and an outer border of description and discipline. In another subtle focalizing shift between objective observation and free indirect discourse, the body is 'othered' as it slips through epithets that intimate the dancer's crumbling sovereignty: 'her mouth swallowed the medicine [...] she thought about what he would be making of it, he the body, this childish one, oh this domineering one, this sinister one' ['[i]hr Mund schluckte Medizin [...] [sie] sann darüber nach, was er daraus machte, er der Leib, der kindische, o der herrische, der finstere'] (19).

Ella's story is shot through with her repression of her bad flesh, this repulsive 'piece of carrion' ['Stück Aas'] (18–19, 20); but this, in turn, is an overcompensating disguise for the deeper sense of shame at her entanglement with it. In order quite literally to defend her own integrity from the physiological therapies of the perplexed doctors — the hammers, the needles, the medicines — she must retreat further into her 'fox's den' ['Fuchsbau'], thus exposing her dependency on it; and yet she also tries to make some kind of truce with the body by making it her spokesman when they do their rounds, a kind of physiological deputizing that only enhances its power (20). Ella's emotionless rationality repeatedly betrays its beholdenness to the body, not least in the unwittingly libidinal freighting of the observation that she 'desired' ['begehrte'] silk and canvas to stitch the image of her own suicide. Her embroidered pre-performance of suicide is a final performance of agency over both the body and its doctors: she stitches in symbolic red thread a highly stylized image of herself thumbing her nose at a doctor with her left hand and stabbing herself to death with the right. As Cowan argues, we encounter here a dark parody of the therapeutic use of embroidery as a means of instilling a sense of order over a chaotic mental environment in the psychiatric clinics of the early twentieth century.[100] This grotesque moment of mimesis is a parody of control that betrays the subject's beholdenness to the very nature it seems to have tamed.

Ella's endgame brings this paradox all the way down into the quirks of the body. She despises her own suffering and that of her fellow patients, and her final fantasy of a deathly waltz with her body is shot through with a contemptuous lust for violence. In a startling inversion of a gendered hierarchy of mind and matter, we learn that

> [s]ie wollte einen Walzer, einen wundersüßen, mit ihm tanzen, der ihr Herr geworden war, mit dem Leib. Mit einer Bewegung ihres Willens konnte sie ihn noch einmal bei den Händen fassen, den Leib, das träge Tier, ihn hinwerfen, herumwerfen, und er war nicht mehr der Herr über sie.
>
> [...] [Sie] stieß sich, die Decke abwerfend, die Nähschere in die linke Brust. Ein geller Schrei stand irgendwo in der Ecke des Saales. Noch im Tode hatte die Tänzerin den kalten verächtlichen Zug um den Mund. (SE 21)
>
> [[s]he wanted to dance a waltz, a wonderful sweet waltz, with him, he who had become her master, with the body. With a movement of the will she could

take him by the hands once more, this body, this indolent animal, and throw it down, throw it around, and it was no longer her master.

[...] And throwing off the blanket, she plunged the sewing scissors into her left breast. A piercing cry stood somewhere in the corner of the room. And still in death the dancer had that cold, contemptuous look on her lips.]

It is through the physicalized 'will' that the dancer can hurl the body around; and her performative reconciliation is of course anything but. The story ends in the insuperable division of the two: an uncannily disembodied cry finds its counterpart in a smirking corpse, as the body plays its final trick on its dead occupant. The dancer's terminal bid for mastery through disembodiment is inescapably embodied.

## Redeeming 'ein Stück Aas'?

Both protagonists try to exert sovereign control over their inner narratives, Michael Fischer by trying to expiate his crime, and Ella by embroidering her imminent suicide. But these simultaneously forceful and fragile attempts to sustain personal narrative sense are continually subverted by the bodies that underwrite them. It is by taking a discourse of wilful self-narrativization to its pathological extremes that Döblin speaks directly to questions of embodiment and embodied identity that still preoccupy us today. While they are manifestly critiques of the patriarchal repressions of Wilhelmine culture, his miniatures also have an indisputable contemporary resonance, critiquing ideologies of therapy that still today remain keyed to the ideal of an autonomous and self-determined subjectivity. As Cowan argues with reference to Michael Foucault's 'techniques of the self', the culture (and therapies) of the will find one of their twenty-first century descendants in the 'motivational paradigm' central to contemporary forms of life coaching.[101] In an analogous manner to Ella's self-discipline, the subject's narrative sovereignty over its body imprisons and conscripts that body's resources.

Perhaps more subtly, Fischer and Ella also challenge the dualisms that still latently underpin much of the humanistic thinking behind contemporary clinical and medical encounters. Pioneers of the medical-humanist innovation of 'narrative medicine', such as Rita Charon, have done profoundly valuable work to distinguish a patient's intimately personal experience and 'narrative' of embodiment from the practitioner's clinical gaze.[102] Sure enough, we read that with every one of their clinical questions, the doctors take away 'another piece' of Ella (SE 20). But for all its suggestion of empowerment, the promise of meaningful self-narrative itself entrenches dualisms of mind and matter, language and body, and meaning and materiality. In short, we may risk reducing patients to biochemical machines with personal narratives — and subjectivities — simply 'bolted on'.[103] Herr Fischer and Ella the dancer may seem overly schematic, or else inaccessibly pathological, but their stylized strangeness is precisely what invites us critically to rethink these dualisms, and to rethink ourselves as caught between mind and body, normality and pathology, rationalism and irrationality.

Taken as a whole, Döblin's eclectic early stories provide us with negative aesthetic spaces, refusing to suggest any resolution to their own strange contradictions. However, their ethical power lies in their ways of both rethinking and revalorizing human embodiment beyond its traditional dualisms. More than that, the twists and contortions of the strange protagonists testify to the oblique promise of a human life lived in reconciliation with its body and its surrounding nature: in short, the stories leave behind a hermeneutic remnant. As I will show in my discussions of *Unser Dasein* and *Berlin Alexanderplatz*, the paradoxes exposed in Döblin's early writing lay the foundations for a creaturely reconception of selfhood that might challenge the humanistic models upon which we have come tacitly to rely.

With the emergence of ethical possibilities within negativity in mind, I want to close by moving forward slightly to 1920 and casting a glance at Döblin's reimagining of the Gospel story, 'Die Flucht aus dem Himmel' ['The Flight from Heaven']. The narrative finds its playful premise in Jesus's giving God the slip and escaping from heaven, something which, as we are archly told, was completely unheard of (SE 321). After an extensive search, Mary finds him in Palestine. What follows is the start of both an Oedipal and a social-revolutionary rebellion against God the Father, as we observe the Son's bizarrely incestuous relationship with his mother, his repudiation of his own divinity, and his desire to create a new society among the beggars and the slaves (323). But there opens up an unbridgeable divide between the Law of the Father and the messy realities of life on Earth, from which various Lazaruses had been quite happy to be free. This is a parodistic inversion of Jesus' bitter sense of forsakenness in the Garden of Gethsemane. This awareness of divine isolation would nourish a literary trope of godlessness in the Garden of Gethsemane: one which had come to the fore in Rilke's 'Der Ölbaum-Garten' ['The Garden of Gethsemane'] in his *Neue Gedichte* (1907), but which also reflects the broader Expressionist motif of an intensely human, suffering Christ.[104]

In Döblin's reworking, Gethsemane is the site of Jesus's recognition that he doesn't have the makings of a rebel after all, and that there is no place for the transformative love he has come to preach, let alone the appetite for another deity in a world that is already teeming with them. When Mary begs him to throw off his guise of humanness, his cryptic question — 'If I could do it, would I still be your son?' ['Könnte ich es, wäre ich dann dein Sohn?'] (323–24) — resonates with Rilke's sense of abandonment, but also with the ambivalence of Döblin's personal mytho-theology in the 1910s and 1920s, combining as it did an interest in the motifs of Mariology with an emphatic rejection of Christian dogmas.[105] The strangeness of the *dénouement*, as it moves straight from the Passion to the Ascension, lies in its mediation of the rejection of salvation through the residual suggestion of hope. Despite exhibiting his humanness on the cross, Jesus's wretched death only exposes the gap between heaven and the Son's battered and ravaged body: having completely failed to anticipate the depth of pain on earth, he heads straight back up, where his Father shouts in his ear that He has never forsaken him, and the story concludes with the sardonic observation that 'he knew that mankind could be redeemed' ['[e]r [Jesus] wußte, die Menschheit konnte gerettet werden'] (325).

We can certainly hear pessimistic resonances with Kafka,[106] but the affinities testify to something more ambivalent than a universe simply deprived of reconciliation. The bitter irony of 'I have not forsaken you' ['Ich habe dich nicht verlassen'] (324), in response to Jesus's famous question, points forward to the gatekeeper's booming words as he shuts the gate on the dying traveller in Kafka's parable 'Vor dem Gesetz' ['Before the Law'] near the close of *Der Proceß* [*The Trial*] (1925). Josef K.'s subjection to the Law — the wages of insufficient righteousness — combines implacably with his exclusion from it; and yet the notion that 'this entrance was meant only for you' ['dieser Eingang [...] nur für dich bestimmt [war]'],[107] before it is closed forever, refracts a similar hint of 'mineness', and with that, the possibility of an otherwise unthinkable moment of redemption. Despite Kafka's marked differences from Döblin, the latter clearly found much inspiration for his own developing sense of the modern epic work. As he recognized in an article in 1927 for *Die literarische Welt* [*The Literary World*], there is an epiphanic appearance to Kafka's novels and short stories: their dream-like realities are obliquely meaningful in ways that are neither symbolic nor allegorical (AzL 285–86), and their strange surface traces hint at truths that are deeper, stranger and even less decipherable.

In this retrospective light, there is one final ambiguity to Döblin's parable, a twist in the tale that seems to keep a utopian possibility faintly alive. The crucified Christ is reduced to one of the abject forms already so familiar to us. His mouth is parched, his eyeballs 'covered in a fish-white film' ['fischweiß überhautet'], before his ascended body — to the shock of those who crucified him — slumps at God's feet. The second 'I have not forsaken you' comes from Mary, the ultimate Christian symbol of reconciliation of body and spirit, as Jesus sighs and calls out for her. However, the first one is unaccounted for in the text, one of Döblin's countless moments of indeterminacy of gaze and address, as the chasm between the heavenly and the earthly is made irresolvably ambiguous.

'Die Flucht' closes with the rejection of transcendent Christian redemption, just as it dispenses with the irreverent Expressionist fantasy of a worldly Jesus establishing a proto-socialist utopia on earth. But as we encounter the convulsed, creaturely body of a failed Saviour, we cannot quite shake the faint hope for a reconciled mode of humanness, even within the vicissitudes of embodied life. I now turn to another failed rebellion; and I want to ask whether that reconciliation — between self and body, and self and nature — can even be positively imagined in literature, let alone realized in life.

## Notes to Chapter 1

My translations from the stories owe much to the excellent model provided by Damion Searls in his translated selection of Döblin's short prose, *Bright Magic: Stories* (New York: NYRB Classics, 2016).

1. Max Jungnickel, *Bühnen-Roland Nr. 47*, 21 November 1912, reproduced in *Alfred Döblin im Spiegel der zeitgenössischen Kritik*, ed. by Ingrid Schuster and Ingrid Bode (Bern and Munich: Francke, 1973), p. 7.
2. See also Otto Pick, *Pester Lloyd*, 1 May 1913, reproduced ibid., pp. 12–13.
3. See Wilfried F. Schoeller, *Alfred Döblin: Eine Biographie* (Munich: Hanser, 2011), p. 69.
4. See ibid., pp. 68–69.

5. See ibid., p. 71.
6. See ibid., pp. 101–05; cf. Sabine Kyora, 'Der Novellenzyklus *Die Ermordung einer Butterblume und andere Erzählungen* (1912)', in *Döblin-Handbuch*, ed. by Becker pp. 29–41 (p. 29). On Döblin's relationship with literary Expressionism, see Sabina Becker, 'Döblin und die literarische Moderne 1910–1933', in *Döblin-Handbuch*, ed. by Becker, pp. 330–40 (pp. 333–35).
7. See Christina Althen, 'Alfred Döblins medizinische Ausbildung dargestellt anhand von Quellen', in *Internationales Alfred Döblin Kolloquium Zürich 2015: Exil als Schicksalsreise. Alfred Döblin und das literarische Exil 1933–1950*, ed. by Sabina Becker and Sabine Schneider (Bern: Lang, 2017), pp. 27–45.
8. Schoeller, p. 90. This antagonism would find expression in a newspaper article published in the *Berliner Volkszeitung* in 1928, which was titled, after Goethe's *Faust*, 'Zwei Seelen in einer Brust' ['Two souls in one breast'] (SLW 103–06). In this ironic diptych of self-accounts, the public service doctor in working-class Lichtenberg and the prominent member of Berlin's literary scene share how little they apparently have in common with one another.
9. See Becker, 'Döblin und die literarische Moderne 1910–1933', p. 334.
10. Thomas Anz casts madness itself as a powerful metaphor for the social outsider in Expressionism: see his study, *Literatur der Existenz: Literarische Psychopathographie und ihre soziale Bedeutung im Frühexpressionismus* (Stuttgart: Metzler, 1977), especially pp. 39–44.
11. 'G. Kl.', in Schuster and Bode, pp. 11–12 (p. 11) (first publ. in *Hamburgischer Correspondent*, 22 June 1913).
12. 'Fr. Gr.', ibid., pp. 10–11 (p. 11) (first publ. in *Zentralblatt für Kinderheilkunde*, 18 (1913)).
13. Cf., in particular, Müller-Salget, *Alfred Döblin*, pp. 60–61.
14. See Schäffner, especially pp. 383–88. In relation to the interplay of discourses and forms of *Wissen* in the short stories, see Sabina Becker and Robert Krause, '"Tatsachenphantasie": Alfred Döblins Poetik des Wissens im Kontext der Moderne', in *'Tatsachenphantasie'*, ed. by Becker and Krause, pp. 9–26; cf. Genz, especially pp. 80–82.
15. David Midgley, 'The Early Fiction of Alfred Döblin: The Short Story between Case Study and Parable', in *Kafka und die kleine Prosa der Moderne: Kafka and Short Modernist Prose*, ed. by Manfred Engel and Ritchie Robertson (Würzburg: Königshausen & Neumann, 2011), pp. 209–23 (p. 210).
16. Helga Stegemann's path-breaking study of 1978 identified the *Ermordung* collection's symbolism as part and parcel of the vitalistic nature that surrounds and envelops its set-pieces and *personae*: see her *Studien zu Alfred Döblins Bildlichkeit: Die Ermordung einer Butterblume und andere Erzählungen* (Bern: Lang, 1978), especially pp. 11–28. She finds a hermeneutic in Döblin's apparent aesthetic affirmation of dissolution into nature, and in her identification of a metaphysics of immanence, she anticipates Monika Fick's later investigation of the monistic psychophysical underpinnings — the fusion of sensuality and spirituality — in the literary and intellectual culture of the German *fin de siècle*: see Monika Fick, *Sinnenwelt und Weltseele: Der psychophysische Monismus in der Literatur der Jahrhundertwende* (Tübingen: Niemeyer, 1993), pp. 1–20, especially p. 7.
17. Anz draws a metonymic and metaphorical connection between an aesthetics of ugliness, and the fragmented reality of inner and outer existence portrayed in Expressionism: see *Literatur der Existenz*, especially pp. 167–75.
18. See Cowan, pp. 1–20. This implicitly dualistic hierarchy underpinned such work as that of the German experimental psychologist Narziß Ach, who conducted experiments designed to strengthen the will's capacity to overcome an associative tendency towards repetition, by having patients repeat meaningless series of syllables. These experiments built on the work of such figures as the French psychophysiologist Théodule Ribot, whose work of 1884, *Les maladies de la volonté*, cast the healthily functioning will as a faculty of self-control: a 'braking mechanism' over unruly bodily reactions (see Cowan, pp. 2 and 8–9).
19. See Cowan, especially pp. 31–39 and 180–88.
20. For the most recent account of Max Döblin's shattering abandonment of his family and brief flight to America with a female employee in July 1888, an experience which unquestionably resonates in this story, see Schoeller, especially pp. 32–34.
21. In the last part of his medical doctoral dissertation of 1905, *Gedächtnisstörungen bei der Korsakoffschen Psychose* [*Memory Disturbances through Korsakoff Syndrome*], he had offered an

extended observation of his patient, the 54-year-old Korsakoff sufferer, a farmer and family man identified in the study only as 'E.F.G.'. This case-study report is marked by a cataloguing of physiological states, yielding little promise of any interpretative key — in the light of the contemporary idea of the psychiatrist *qua* storyteller — to decipher their randomness: 'Conjunctiva a light yellow, body a little distended. [...] The brute force of the arms diminished; insecure gait. [...] Slight tremor in tongue and hands' ['Conjunction leicht gelblich verfärbt, Leib wenig aufgetrieben. [...] Grobe Kraft der Arme gering; Gang unsicher. [...] Geringer Tremor der Zunge und der Hände'] (*Gedächtnisstörungen*, 51). Throughout the early stories, we can find the imprint of Emil Kraepelin's influential attempts to construct a systematic diagnostics, and so to read his patient's symptoms as a *text*, on the basis of the observation of disturbances in 'normal' patterns of volition and agency. On the psychiatric and hermeneutic significance of the patient's prehistory, see Emil Kraepelin, *Psychiatrie: Ein Lehrbuch für Studirende* [sic] *und Aerzte*, 7th edn, 2 vols (Leipzig: Barth, 1903), I, especially pp. 340–43.
22. See Mirjana Stancic, 'Döblins frühe Erzählungen *Die Segelfahrt* und *Die falsche Tür*: Ein interkultureller Annäherungsversuch', in *Internationales Alfred Döblin Kolloquium Warschau 2013. Interkulturelle Aspekte im Schaffen Alfred Döblins*, ed. by Marion Brandt and Grazyna Kwiecinska (Bern: Lang, 2015), pp. 159–72.
23. Stegemann (p. 47) highlights the senses in which the early Nietzsche's metaphysics provided a means of affirming the transience of life 'in the here and now' [*im Diesseits*], in spite of Döblin's early mistrust of the ethical implications of Nietzsche's thought.
24. 'Unter dem unaufhörlichen Wechsel der Erscheinungen die ewig schöpferische, ewig zum Dasein zwingende [...] Urmutter!': Nietzsche, *KG*, III.1, 103–04 (here p. 104); Nietzsche, *The Birth of Tragedy*, p. 80.
25. '[D]as Nichts im Rücken, vor sich das Nichts': Kobel, p. 82.
26. "Das Allerbeste ist für dich gänzlich unerreichbar: nicht geboren zu sein, nicht zu sein, nichts zu sein. Das Zweitbeste aber ist für dich — bald zu sterben." Nietzsche, *KG*, III.1, 31; Nietzsche, *The Birth of Tragedy*, p. 23.
27. See Andrew J. Webber, *The Doppelgänger: Double Visions in German Literature* (Oxford: Clarendon Press, 1996), p. 317; cf. pp. 41–48, especially p. 47. On repetition as a source of uncanny feeling, see Freud, 'Das Unheimliche', in *GW*, XII, 227–68 (pp. 249–51).
28. Freud, *GW*, XIII: *Jenseits des Lustprinzips*, pp. 61–62; see also *GW*, XII: 'Das Unheimliche', p. 257. Here, Freud finds the pinnacle of the uncanny in the fearful phantasy of being buried alive. Psychoanalysis, he claims, has taught us that this 'terrible phantasy' of a return to the ground embodies merely the mutated and transmogrified form of 'another one, [...] which originally had nothing frightening or spooky to it, but was rather characterized by a certain lasciviousness: namely, the phantasy of life in the maternal body' ['einer anderen [...], die ursprünglich nichts Schreckhaftes war, sondern von einer gewissen Lüsternheit getragen wurde, nämlich der Phantasie vom Leben im Mutterleib']. Cf. Webber, *The Doppelgänger*, p. 47.
29. Stegemann, p. 18.
30. The fact that the figure of the *Doppelgänger* would be incorporated into psychoanalysis nine years later, in the form of Freud's essay on 'the uncanny', highlights the fruitfulness of reading the stories against the backdrop of his later, metapsychological theories, as I will argue in the next part of the chapter: see Freud, *GW*, XII, 253–57.
31. Nietzsche, *KG*, III.1, 43 (the emphasis is in the original); cf. Stegemann, p. 58.
32. Sascha Michel reads this richly intertextual novella as tied up with the young Döblin's broader antipathy to the ethics of the triumphantly self-willing *Ich* that he considered to be inherent in Nietzsche's metaphysics, especially in *Also sprach Zarathustra*: see Sascha Michel, 'Der schwarze Vorhang: Roman von den Worten und Zufällen (1919)', in *Döblin-Handbuch*, ed. by Becker, pp. 24–28 (pp. 27–28); cf. my discussion of Döblin's earliest engagements with Nietzsche in my Introduction.
33. Freud describes this as the 'love–hate ambivalence of the death drive' ['Liebe–Haß Ambivalenz des Todestriebes'], wavering as it does between destruction and erotic dissolution (Freud, *GW*, XIII, 58). Of the co-dependent and conterminous relationship of sexuality and violence, and the complementarity of sadism and masochism, he writes that 'from time immemorial we have

acknowledged a sadistic component to the sexual drive. [...] As the complementary partial drive of sadism, masochism [is] to be understood as a reverse-action of sadism against the individual ego' ['[w]ir haben von jeher eine sadistische Komponente des Sexualtriebs anerkannt. [...] [D]er dem Sadismus komplementäre Partialtrieb des Masochismus [ist] als eine Rückwendung des Sadismus gegen das eigene Ich zu verstehen'] (*GW*, XIII, 58–59).

34. Cf. Nicholas Saul, 'Love, Death and *Liebestod* in German Romanticism', in *The Cambridge Companion to German Romanticism*, ed. by Nicholas Saul (Cambridge: Cambridge University Press, 2009), pp. 163–74 (especially pp. 164–65 and 171–72).
35. Adorno, *GS*, VII: *Ästhetische Theorie*, p. 172.
36. See Christina Althen, 'Nachwort', in Alfred Döblin, *Die Ermordung einer Butterblume und andere Erzählungen*, ed. by Althen, 5th edn (Munich: DTV, 2012), pp. 131–47 (p. 140).
37. See Sander, *Alfred Döblin*, p. 23.
38. Rather than offer us a sense of psychological causality and continuity, Döblin's focus on decentred movement and body language touches on a mythic desire for a discharge of inner and outer stimuli, and a proverbial and literal return to nature in the ultimate discharge in death. This modernist trope would find theoretical expression, among other places, in Freud's *Nirwanaprinzip*, a term that he borrowed from the British analyst Barbara Low: see here George Makari, *Revolution in Mind: The Creation of Psychoanalysis*, 2nd edn (London: Duckworth, 2010), p. 317. In *Jenseits des Lustprinzips*, Freud betrays the speculative quality of his own theory, and its positioning at the outer edges of empirical science:

> Daß wir als die herrschende Tendenz des Seelenlebens, vielleicht des Nervenlebens überhaupt, das Streben nach Herabsetzung, Konstanterhaltung, Aufhebung der inneren Reizspannung erkannten (das *Nirwanaprinzip* nach einem Ausdruck von Barbara *Low*), wie es im Lustprinzip zum Ausdruck kommt, das ist ja eines unserer stärksten Motive, an die Existenz von Todestrieben zu glauben. (Freud, *GW*, XIII, 60, emphasis in the original.)

> [The fact that we have recognized the governing tendency of the life of the psyche, perhaps of nervous existence in general, to be a striving for the decrease, for a keeping constant, for a removal of inner tension as a result of stimuli (the 'Nirvana principle', to quote Barbara *Low*'s phrase), as it comes to expression in the pleasure principle: this, of course, is one of our strongest reasons to believe in the existence of death drives.]

39. See Ingrid Maaß, *Regression und Individuation: Alfred Döblins Naturphilosophie und späte Romane vor dem Hintergrund einer Affinität zu Freuds Metapsychologie* (Frankfurt a.M.: Lang, 1997), p. 9.
40. See Thomas Anz, 'Alfred Döblin und die Psychoanalyse: Ein kritischer Bericht zur Forschung', in *Internationales Alfred-Döblin-Kolloquium Leiden 1995*, ed. by Gabriele Sander (Berlin: Lang, 1997), pp. 9–30 (p. 19). See also Schoeller, pp. 79–80. Hoche's later significance to the development of the National Socialists' T4 euthanasia programme is one of the darker coincidences of this chapter in Döblin's story.
41. See Maaß, p. 29. This reductively materialistic procedure underpinned both Döblin's and Freud's medical training.
42. See ibid., pp. 30–31.
43. See Veronika Fuechtner, '"Arzt und Dichter": Döblin's Medical, Psychiatric, and Psychoanalytical Work', in *A Companion to the Works of Alfred Döblin*, ed. by Roland Dollinger and others (Rochester, NY: Camden House, 2004), pp. 111–40 (especially pp. 114–16); and Sander, *Alfred Döblin*, pp. 21–22.
44. See Fuechtner, pp. 115–20.
45. Anz, 'Alfred Döblin und die Psychoanalyse', p. 18; Fuechtner, p. 119.
46. See Maaß, pp. 24–25; and Fuechtner, pp. 119–20. When Freud was awarded the 1930 Goethe Prize, Döblin (who had enthusiastically lobbied for the award) conceded that he had moved from an initial scepticism towards his recognition of the qualified effectiveness of psychoanalysis.
47. Cf. Freud, *GW*, XIII, 239–45; cf. pp. 251–55.
48. Fuechtner, p. 117.
49. While she does not analyse Döblin's literary anticipations of Freud's metapsychology in the

short stories, Maaß discusses the affinities between the metapsychological theories and Döblin's developing nature philosophy in *Regression und Individuation* (see pp. 29–77).
50. On the syncretism at play here, see Ruth Neubauer-Petzoldt, 'Döblins *Der Ritter Blaubart* und seine synkretische Montagetechnik', in *Alfred Döblin: Paradigms of Modernism*, ed. by Davies and Schonfield, pp. 74–101 (pp. 93–99).
51. This is a connection briefly pointed out by Midgley in 'The Early Fiction of Alfred Döblin', pp. 220–21.
52. Mererid Puw Davies, *The Tale of Bluebeard in German Literature: From the Eighteenth Century to the Present* (Oxford: Clarendon Press, 2001), pp. 41 and 47; cf. p. 201.
53. Midgley, 'The Early Fiction of Alfred Döblin', pp. 219 and 223.
54. See Stegemann, pp. 137–39.
55. Freud, *GW*, XIII, 253; cf. Döblin, KS II, 264.
56. Freud, *GW*, XIII, 58.
57. For his discussion of the evolutionary connections that link the earliest and smallest protozoa to the humans of the present, see Wilhelm Bölsche, *Das Liebesleben in der Natur: Eine Entwickelungsgeschichte der Liebe*, 3 vols (Florence and Leipzig: Diederichs, 1898–1903), I, especially p. 6. On the echoes of Bölsche in Döblin's stories, see Midgley, 'The Early Fiction of Alfred Döblin', p. 220.
58. Bölsche, I, 9.
59. Ibid., pp. 100–06.
60. Nicholas Saul, 'Darwin in German Literary Culture 1890–1913', in *The Literary and Cultural Reception of Charles Darwin*, ed. by Thomas F. Glick and Elinor Shaffer, 3 vols (London: Bloomsbury, 2014), III, 46–77 (p. 53).
61. In her discussion of the story, Neubauer-Petzoldt (pp. 76–77) foregrounds the significance of the mythical — on Cassirer's account — as offering alternative means of thinking our relationship with the instrumentalized 'rationalities' of the modern world. See Ernst Cassirer, *Philosophie der symbolischen Formen: Zweiter Teil — Das mythische Denken* (Berlin: Bruno Cassirer, 1925), pp. 66 and 75–77. I shall return to Cassirer's suggestion of the mythic re-enchantment of the world in the context of *Berge Meere und Giganten*.
62. See Theodor Storm, *Der Schimmelreiter*, in Storm, *Werke: Gesamtausgabe in drei Bänden* (Stuttgart: J. G. Cotta'sche Buchhandlung, 1958), III: *Novellen — Schriften — Briefe*, pp. 405–06.
63. In this vein, Stegemann (p. 141) points to the repeated *Jugendstil* motif of the birch trees: a mythic 'tapering off' which forms a pattern of circularity with the birch trees at the story's opening.
64. See Stephanie Catani, 'Die Geburt des Döblinismus aus dem Geist des Fin de Siècle: Döblins frühe Erzählungen im Spannungsfeld von Ästhetik, Poetik und Medizin', in *Alfred Döblin: Paradigms of Modernism*, ed. by Davies and Schonfield, pp. 28–45 (p. 45).
65. Freud, *GW*, XIII, 13.
66. Of this attempt to exert a measure of control over one's own narrative towards death, Freud writes:

> Die theoretische Bedeutung der Selbsterhaltungs-, Macht- und Geltungstriebe schrumpft, in diesem Licht gesehen, ein; es sind Partialtriebe, dazu bestimmt, den eigenen Todesweg des Organismus zu sichern und andere Möglichkeiten der Rückkehr zum Anorganischen als die immanenten fernzuhalten[.] [...] Es ist wie ein Zauderrhythmus im Leben der Organismen; die eine Triebgruppe stürmt nach vorwärts, um das Endziel des Lebens möglichst bald zu erreichen, die andere schnellt an einer gewissen Stelle dieses Weges zurück, um ihn von einem bestimmten Punkt an nochmals zu machen und so die Dauer des Weges zu verlängern. (Freud, *GW*, XIII, 41, 43)
>
> [The theoretical significance of the drives of self-preservation, power and survival shrivels into insignificance in this light; these are partial drives, conditioned to ensure the organism's own path towards death and to prevent any possibilities of a return to the inorganic other than the immanent ones[.] [...] It is like an oscillating rhythm in the life of the organism; one set of drives rushes forwards to reach the end-goal of life as soon as possible, the other springs back at a certain point on the way there, only to

make the journey again along that same stretch from a certain point and therefore to extend and prolong the route.]

For a discussion of the proto-linguistic (i.e. meaning-making) qualities of the *fort-da*, see Paul Ricoeur's reading of it in his study, *Freud and Philosophy: An Essay on Interpretation*, trans. by Denis Savage (New Haven, CT: Yale University Press, 1970), pp. 285–94 and 378–92.

67. Cf. n. 33, above.
68. See here Kyora, p. 34; cf. Stegemann, p. 97.
69. In his ethical and political critique in *Republic*, Plato regarded mimesis as a form of distorting imitation, whereas Aristotle's *Poetics* developed a more positive theory of mimesis as doing aesthetic justice to the particularity of its 'natural' objects: see here Matthew Potolsky, *Mimesis* (New York: Routledge, 2006), pp. 15 and 32–36.
70. Ibid., pp. 140–41; cf. Benjamin, GS, II.1: *Frühe Arbeiten zur Bildungs- und Kulturkritik*, pp. 206–07.
71. Horkheimer and Adorno, *Dialektik der Aufklärung*, p. 26.
72. Ibid., pp. 29–30.
73. Ibid., pp. 32–49.
74. Adorno, GS, VII, *Ästhetische Theorie*, p. 166.
75. Ibid., p. 199; cf. p. 203.
76. Josef Früchtl underscores the aporia between 'Destruktion' and 'Versöhnung' at the heart of the mimetic, linking it to the Freudian *Todestriebe* in his study, *Mimesis: Konstellationen eines Zentralbegriffs bei Adorno* (Würzburg: Königshausen & Neumann, 1986), pp. 39–41 and 260.
77. For Adorno's theorization of this dialectical struggle within the artwork itself, see GS, VII, *Ästhetische Theorie*, p. 18. See also my brief discussion of Adorno in the Introduction.
78. See Cowan, pp. 180–81.
79. For a discussion of this parody, see Catani, pp. 41–42.
80. See Cowan, pp. 3–20.
81. See ibid., especially pp. 11–16.
82. See Reiner Marx, 'Literatur und Zwangsneurose: Eine Gegenübertragungsimprovisation zu Alfred Döblins früher Erzählung "Die Ermordung einer Butterblume"', in *Internationales Alfred-Döblin-Kolloquium Leiden 1995*, ed. by Sander, pp. 49–60 (p. 56); and Christine Emig, 'Butterblume — Mutterblume: Psychiatrischer und "naturphilosophischer" Diskurs in Alfred Döblins Die Ermordung einer Butterblume', *Scientia Poetica*, 9 (2005), 195–215 (p. 196).
83. See Louis Sass, *Madness and Modernism: Insanity in the Light of Modern Art, Literature, and Thought*, rev. edn (Oxford: Oxford University Press, 2017), especially pp. 1 and 12–21.
84. See Susanne Mahler, 'Poetik des Vergessens', in Alfred Döblin, *Gedächtnisstörungen bei der Korsakoffschen Psychose* (Leipzig: Tropen, 2006), pp. 91–106 (pp. 95–96).
85. Ibid., p. 102.
86. See Oliver Sacks, *The Man Who Mistook His Wife for a Hat*, 2nd edn (London: Picador, 2011), pp. 116–17.
87. In his dissertation, Döblin revealingly describes a healthily functioning memory as the faculty that 'liberates' the individual from her or his beholdenness to stimulations (*Gedächtnisstörungen* 14).
88. Emig (pp. 202–06) argues that Döblin's detailed knowledge of the *Oresteia* is provable from at least 1903 onwards; and as I shall analyse it in my final chapter, Aeschylus' drama is subjected to a parodistic reworking in *Berlin Alexanderplatz*, which is at once light-hearted and disturbing.
89. Aeschylus, *Eumenides*, in *Oresteia*, ed. and trans. by Christopher Collard (Oxford: Oxford University Press, 2008), *Eum.*, ll. 733–1051 (pp. 105–13); see here Emig, pp. 203–05.
90. Aeschylus, *Eum.*, ll. 75–77 (p. 87).
91. See Anz, *Literatur der Existenz*, pp. 122–25.
92. This anatomical doubling of a walking stick as a prosthetic, used to shore up an unruly or fractured 'Will', is also encountered in Rainer Maria Rilke's *Die Aufzeichnungen des Malte Laurids Brigge* (1910), in the vignette of a man afflicted by St. Vitus' Dance who is trying, in vain, to bring his limbs under control by holding his stick against his back and pushing it up into his collar: see Rilke, *Werke: Kommentierte Ausgabe in vier Bänden*, ed. by Manfred Engel, Ulrich Fülleborn, Horst Nalewski and August Stahl, 4 vols (Frankfurt a.M. and Leipzig: Insel, 1996), III: *Prosa und Dramen*, ed. by August Stahl, p. 502.

93. Horkheimer and Adorno, *Dialektik der Aufklärung*, p. 28.
94. Stegemann, p. 123.
95. As we shall see in Chapter 4, this imbalance is developed at far greater length in *Unser Dasein* (1933).
96. Torsten Hoffmann, '"Inzwischen ginger seine Füße weiter": Autonome Körperteile in den frühen Erzählungen und medizinischen Essays von Alfred Döblin und Gottfried Benn', in *Alfred Döblin: Paradigms of Modernism*, ed. by Davies and Schonfield, pp. 46–73 (pp. 55–57).
97. See Freud, 'Das Unheimliche', in *GW*, XII, 230–37 and 259–62.
98. Charlotte Perkins Gilman, 'The Yellow Wallpaper', in *The Oxford Book of Gothic Tales*, ed. by Chris Baldick (Oxford: Oxford University Press, 1993), pp. 249–63 (p. 259). On Freud's more or less explicit linking of the prominence of smell to female sexuality, see Mary Jacobus, 'An Unnecessary Maze of Sign-Reading', in Jacobus, *Reading Women: Essays in Feminist Criticism* (London: Methuen, 1986), pp. 229–48 (p. 243).
99. Horkheimer and Adorno, *Dialektik der Aufklärung*, p. 208.
100. See Cowan, p. 217.
101. Ibid., pp. 1–2 and 260–64.
102. See Rita Charon, *Narrative Medicine: Honoring the Stories of Illness* (Oxford: Oxford University Press, 2006), especially p. 22.
103. For a cogent critique of recent humanistic developments in the medical humanities, see Jeffrey P. Bishop, 'Rejecting Medical Humanism', *Journal of Medical Humanities*, 29 (2008), 13–25 (especially pp. 19–22).
104. 'Those who have lost themselves all things forsake. | They are cast out by their fathers | Banished from their mothers' wombs.' ['Die Sich-Verlierenden läßt alles los, | und sie sind preisgegeben von den Vätern | und ausgeschlossen aus der Mütter Schooß.'] See Rilke, *Werke*, I: *Gedichte 1895 bis 1910*, pp. 459–60.
105. See Marcel Reich-Ranicki, *Sieben Wegbereiter: Schriftsteller des zwanzigsten Jahrhunderts* (Stuttgart: DVA, 2002), p. 130. Cf. Döblin's essay 'Jenseits von Gott' of 1919 (KS I, especially pp. 246–50).
106. Cf. Midgley, 'The Early Fiction of Alfred Döblin', pp. 222–23.
107. Franz Kafka, *Schriften, Tagebücher, Briefe: Kritische Ausgabe*, ed. by Jürgen Born, Gerhard Neumann, Malcolm Pasley and Jost Schillemeit (Frankfurt a.M.: Fischer, 1990): *Der Proceß*, ed. by Malcolm Pasley, pp. 294–95.

CHAPTER 2

❖

# Another Time, Another Place: *Die drei Sprünge des Wang-lun*

In a recent study of science fiction, the Marxist critic Fredric Jameson argued that the paradox of Utopia lies in the fact that, almost by definition, it cannot be thought: as a *no-place*, it offers us neither a narrative nor a conceptual bridge. An intractable dilemma of utopian science fiction, in particular, is its inability to account for the 'break that simultaneously secures the radical difference of the new Utopian society'.[1] From our vantage point in the damaged reality of the present, narrative fiction can never quite make the imaginative leap to a redeemed space and time that always remains palpably out of reach. In turn, the writing of the past constantly suppresses historical alternatives: new openings and different directions are continually sealed off in a narrative that seeks to justify the world of the present by drawing it into a royal road of progress into the future. To put it simply, meaningful utopia remains positively unimaginable.

This problem finds one of its most famous articulations in Walter Benjamin's 'Über den Begriff der Geschichte' ['On the Concept of History', also known as the 'Theses on the Philosophy of History']. Benjamin wrote this allusive series of meditations in the winter of 1939–40, mere months before his suicide on the Franco-Spanish border while fleeing the advance of the German armies across continental Europe, and shortly after the Molotov–Ribbentrop Pact of August 1939. They were an expression of his profound disappointment at what he saw as the utter failure of Communism in allying with Fascism;[2] but central to the 'Theses', too, was a deeper critique of the violence done to past and present in the thinking and writing of history. Benjamin offers a trenchant critique of nineteenth-century historicism, particularly its explicit project of writing an objective account of history 'the way it really was' ['wie es denn eigentlich gewesen ist'], in a near-exact quotation of Leopold von Ranke.[3] Tied up with this claim to scientific objectivity was a form of ideological violence to parallel the relentlessly recurring cycles of physical violence. Benjamin argues in his sixth thesis that this sanctioned form of objective History instilled a deep, monolithic 'Konformismus'. It is, of course, the victors who get to write it; and he warns that both the artefacts of historical record and those who receive them from earlier generations will become little more than the tools of the ruling classes. Neither the living nor the dead will ever truly be 'safe' from their repeated, and repeatedly successful, attempts to silence unsanctioned and incommensurable voices.⁴ If Benjamin targets his attack most insistently and urgently at the terrifying logics of totalitarianism, he also criticizes aspects of the tradition of German Social Democracy: its commitment to a form of political gradualism in the late nineteenth century had subjected German workers to the alienating impact of technological progress in the name of political progress and social change.

Although the 'angel of history' from Thesis IX, modelled on Paul Klee's *Angelus Novus* of 1920, is now a well-worn cliché, he still embodies Benjamin's central argument. He is blown violently backwards into the future, his wings caught in a storm, and can only look on helplessly as the rubble heap of historical disasters piles up and the dead lie unredeemed. This storm represents 'progress'.⁵ The gradualist myth of infinite social and political perfectibility is tied up with its own supposed unfolding through 'homogeneous, empty time' ['die homogene und leere Zeit']:⁶ it is a myth that disguises a reality of discontinuities, catastrophes, and an abject lack of progress. By contrast, it is in the discontinuities that hope might be found. For all the recurrence of this ever-same cycle of chaos, Benjamin sees the possibility of redemption as emerging in a fleeting constellation between the 'now' and a similar historical memory that 'flashes up in the moment of danger' ['im Augenblick einer Gefahr aufblitzt'].⁷ In a shard of what he calls 'messianic time', the seemingly past historical event enters into an illuminating and subversive communion with the catastrophes of the 'now', a transient meeting which will be forever lost if the affinity is not recognized.⁸ The 'now-time' ['Jetztzeit'], this ever-charged moment of possibility, is what fills history. It is the ever-vanishing moment of historical possibility, or 'the small gateway in time through which the Messiah might enter' ['die kleine Pforte, durch die der Messias treten konnte'];⁹ and in the figure of the Messiah, Benjamin highlights the unforeseeability of the revolutionary change, and the radical difference of what *might* be to come.

This might seem an odd opening for a chapter about a novel set in eighteenth-century China. On first encounters, indeed, Benjamin's final philosophical work apparently has little in common with Döblin's breakthrough fiction. The Marxist thinker wrote his 'Theses' more than a quarter of a century after Döblin completed the manuscript of *Die drei Sprünge des Wang-lun*, and in very different historical and intellectual circumstances. This Expressionist author, still something of an 'insider tip' on the Berlin literary scene by 1915,¹⁰ was occupied with a syncretism between a Daoist philosophy of *wu wei* (non-action), an idiosyncratic strain of philosophical vitalism, and a growing personal sense of the injustices of forms of imperialist politics. However, even after a little over eighteen months of medical service at Saargmünd on the Western Front, in 1916, Döblin still understood his vocation as a writer in a relatively apolitical sense (cf. *Briefe*, I, 87). At the same time, he was the (not untypical) product of a culture of belligerent nationalism, as several essays in praise of the elemental unifying force of German aggression during the First World War would show.¹¹ As the victim of that nationalism in its eventual form, the Benjamin of the 1930s was trying to reimagine the possibility of political hope by establishing a speculative link between historical materialism and a form of Jewish messianism.¹² In spite of their differences in time, place and orientation,

Benjamin's pessimism over the linearity of historical progress nonetheless bears illuminating resemblances to Döblin's portrayals of pasts both real and imagined. The description of history as a single catastrophe, heaping rubble upon rubble, is in keeping with the experimental prose of an author sceptical of linear narrative and historical meaning.[13] His novels are strewn with unredeemed bodies and rubble, and their many discontinuities resist easy comprehension, let alone interpretation, at almost every turn; and yet, I suggest that Benjamin can help us to detect the fleeting promises of ethical and political change in the warp and weft of Döblin's epic writing.

My focus here is not on the more recognizably historical novels, which have enjoyed cogent recent treatments elsewhere.[14] Instead, I want to consider Döblin's first experiment in telling a reimagined past in a novel which remains his most successful, in commercial terms, after *Berlin Alexanderplatz*. Released in 1916 but backdated to the previous year, *Die drei Sprünge des Wang-lun* plays out under the Emperorship of the Manchu (Qing) Dynasty. Its primary source of historical inspiration was an uprising against the dynasty by one Wang-lun, who made a claim to be the incarnation of the Buddha Maitreya and the next Emperor, and led several thousand adherents of the so-called White Lotus Sect during the 1770s. The rebellion, which flared up in the north-eastern province of Shantung (commonly romanized as Shandong), was triggered by a combination of political, economic and religious grievances. Not only was the local population trapped in a state of unending economic precariousness, but the sect, whose origins in northern China dated back some two centuries, was increasingly coming into conflict with the rigid Confucianism of the Manchus.[15] The uprising ended abjectly in defeat at the hands of Imperial troops towards the end of 1774, with Wang-lun burning himself alive in the final battle in the city of Linqing, in order to evade capture.

Rather than an 'historical novel' *per se*, or even a fictional reconstruction, Döblin's epic provides us with a vivid reconfiguration. It earned Döblin his literary breakthrough, winning the prestigious Fontane Prize in 1916, and reaching its twelfth edition by 1923. As one critic remarked, the fragmented and acausal prose style was strongly reminiscent of the visual techniques of cubism, which was burgeoning through the work of Picasso and others at that exact moment in European cultural life.[16] In turn, readers lavished praise on a portrayal which, even in the context of a contemporary appetite for all things Chinese, at the very least seemed unprecedented in its ethnographic authenticity. Some even went so far as to suggest that the novel might be a translation, or at least an adaptation, from a Chinese source text, and that Döblin seemed to have learned Chinese (which he had not).[17] Brecht devoured *Wang-lun* in September 1920, and it prompted his own aesthetic and political interest in the Daoist principle of non-resistance, which would come to offer a valuable dialectical counterpart to his Leninist conceptions of active political interventionism.[18] On his later admission, it also strongly shaped his own developing ideas about epic theatre. The novel is pivotal to Döblin's own developing conception of an epic poetics; and Brecht would even suggest, in an essay titled 'Über Alfred Döblin' in 1943–44, that the novelist had taught him more than anyone else about the nature of the epic, singling out *Wang-lun* in particular.[19] While the fascination it held for Germany's greatest twentieth-century political playwright alone arguably justifies its discussion, I am primarily interested here in the aesthetic and philosophical modes through which it discloses its ethical and political insights.

Ritchie Robertson argues that Döblin unfurls for us a 'China of the imagination', with a sense of political and religious engagement but a relatively tenuous connection to a Chinese present; and he sets it against Georg Lukács's famous definition of the historical novel as an inherently political genre with a recognizable connection to the present.[20] Döblin's recent biographer, Wilfried Schoeller, has gone further still in suggesting that despite its historical and socio-political content, the novel is primarily an imaginative 'work of enchantment' with a mass of exotic yet essentially exchangeable cultural and historical details (SLW 29).[21] But even though this is a manifestly fictional China, how do we account for its insistent relevance and attraction for its modern European audience? What is it about the novel that was, and remains, so timely?

In this chapter, I will first introduce *Wang-lun*, before setting it in the context of its political and cultural milieu of a fascination with Chinese history and culture. This will lead into a detailed reading of the text, structured around the paradox of 'non-resistance' in the shape of *wu wei*. An exploration of its apparent impossibility in the face of violence and real political power will be followed by a closing discussion of the novel's unremitting hope for it. By bringing two later concepts into dialogue with one another — Brecht's *Verfremdungseffekt* and Benjamin's 'Jetztzeit' — I suggest that Döblin's writing evokes a dynamic sense of temporality that both withholds and, at the same time, holds out that social and political hope. In stark contrast to Lukács's sense of the bourgeois historical novel of the nineteenth century as aiming to grasp epochs in their totality, and so portray a sense of continuity across reforms and revolutions,[22] Döblin is intensely concerned with the myriad ruptures, the now-times, that fracture both past and present. His radicalism here is just as political as it is aesthetic, and his achievement is to show how the modern epic novel might become a form of political critique in its own right.

## Radicalism with Chinese Characteristics?

*Wang-lun* is both liberal with its historical facts and distractingly non-linear, a pattern that was to become a hallmark of the epic works. The first of four 'books' opens by introducing us to the sect of the 'Truly Powerless' ['die Wahrhaft Schwachen'], before looping into the backstory of its protagonist. Wang-lun is introduced to us as a rough-and-ready nobody, the son of a peasant fisherman from Shantung. The murder of an innocent Muslim by a member of the Imperial police provokes in him an instinctive moment of identification and a burning desire for revenge. After killing an officer, Wang-lun flees to Chihli Province, and specifically into the mountains. Both an agonized preoccupation with the memory of his crime and his encounter with the wretchedness of other social outcasts prompt him into a form of resistance to the authorities. In one of Döblin's many poetic licences, this takes the form of the Daoist doctrine of *wu wei*, literally 'no action', as a way of living that entails a conscious renunciation of both violence and sexual activity. The Truly Powerless attract growing numbers of adherents throughout the plains and mountains of Chihli. The story then forks. Wang-lun travels to solicit material and military protection from the 'White Waterlily' ['Weiße Wasserlilie'], a secret society of prosperous merchants committed to the restoration of the Ming Dynasty. Buoyed by the sect's growth, the renegade Buddhist monk Ma-noh, Wang's friend and erstwhile influence, makes himself its *de facto* leader, abandons the policy of celibacy, and distorts *wu wei* into a very different kind of non-resistance: orgiastic gratification. This culminates in the mass rape of women and girls, Ma-noh's repulsively dubbed 'Broken Melons' ['Gebrochene Melonen']. In desperate defence of this non-resistance, the priest-king Ma and a significantly reduced band of devotees face siege and near-certain death in the city of Yang-chou-fu at the hands of the Emperor's troops, bent as they are on spiritual martyrdom and a redemptive entrance into the so-called Western Paradise. After failing to persuade Ma of the need for a peaceful end to the siege, Wang takes the decision to poison the city's water supply in order to prevent his former comrades' massacre.

A grisly and protracted scene of mass poisoning rounds off the second book, and the disturbing news of it prompts Wang's retirement into obscurity as a cormorant fisherman. A narrative shift to the Manchu Court in the third book, 'Der Herr der gelben Erde' [Lord of the Yellow Earth], whisks us off to a cloistered world where the appeasement of angered ancestors jostles alongside the bloody compromises of *Realpolitik*. Emperor Khien-lung's ultimate decision to crush the Truly Powerless brings Wang back into battle. His own quest for the throne as the restored Ming Emperor falters with his failure to take Beijing. The final barricading of the rebel soldiers in Linqing in the fourth book prompts Wang's return to the principle of *wu wei*, albeit this time with sword in hand. Wang departs his story almost as unheroically as he enters it, burned alive in a conflagration in the midst of battle.

We are certainly dealing here with 'both an aesthetic construction and a political exploration of the pros and cons of non-resistance'.[23] However, even this fairly uncontroversial assessment begs the critical question of the aesthetic function of the novel's exotic setting: why China? In the wake of an increasing number of post-colonialist approaches, Oliver Jahraus has recently drawn upon the concept of 'Chinoiserie' to identify two tendencies in the artistic appropriation of China in early twentieth-century German culture.[24] Its first definition is simply as a Western cultural artefact that imitates Chinese cultural production; and that aspect is borne out in Döblin's own immersion in travel accounts, philological and historical studies of culture, religion and philosophy, as well as a letter to Martin Buber of October 1912, in which he expressed a wish for 'all kinds of Chinese miscellanea' to make his world as credible as possible (*Briefe* I, 58).[25] The second sense of 'Chinoiserie', however, relates to the use of the religious and political sectarianism of 1770s China as a projection screen for European intellectual and political dilemmas.

Both tendencies are at work in the novel, and their interplay shapes its peculiar combination of the historical and the timeless, the transient and the symbolic. The German cultural fascination with China was, of course, deeply political, and Döblin's work was no exception to that trend. The brutal suppression of the Boxer Rebellion in 1901 by an alliance of colonial powers, including Germany and the British Empire, opened the way for a period of intensified diplomatic and cultural exchange. In 1906, a Chinese government delegation travelled to Germany, among other countries, to study the Prussian monarchy as a possible model for a Chinese constitutional state; and the subsequent decade witnessed a burgeoning (if distinctly paternalistic) German interest in Chinese culture, history and philosophy. A slew of publications on Chinese literature and philosophy during this period included the *Reden und Gleichnisse* of Zhuangzi, edited by Martin Buber in 1910. The theologian and Protestant missionary Richard Wilhelm's translations of Confucius's *Gespräche*, Laozi's *Tao-te Ching*, and *Das wahre Buch vom quellenden Urgrund* [*The True Book of the Gushing Source*], ascribed to Liezi, appeared in 1911. The latter two works in particular became important sources for the novel.[26] In a kind of colonial-political reverse, both Döblin and other democratically minded authors saw some inspiration for opposition to the corrupt and oppressive Wilhelmine monarchy in the rise of political resistance movements in China, which culminated in the establishment of a Chinese Republic under Sun Yat-sen and the abdication of the last emperor of the Qing Dynasty, Puyi, in February 1912.[27] Döblin's growing aversion to oppressive forms of colonial power found a focal point in the figures of Wang-lun and Emperor Khien-lun. In an early indication of his own sympathy for forms of political radicalism, the central trigger of inspiration for the novel is thought to have been a newspaper article in the *Vossische Zeitung* about a revolt by Korean gold-panners in Siberia in the spring of 1912, which had been violently crushed by Tsarist troops at the cost of 150 lives.[28] Intertwining with this consciousness of real-world events was Döblin's growing personal interest in Daoism, which was to leave a deep and lasting imprint. Nor was he by any means alone in his enthusiasm at a time when Expressionist writers and thinkers were preoccupied with making connections between ancient Chinese philosophy and contemporary social and political movements.

Daoist thought itself originated in part in the *Tao-te Ching*, traditionally accredited in its earliest form to Laozi in approximately the sixth century BCE. Through the mediation of scholars such as Richard Wilhelm, writers such as Klabund, Hermann Hesse, Döblin and Brecht found fertile creative soil in the *Dao*. As the primal ground and source of everything that comes into being, it is both a union of creative and destructive energies and a formless and infinite chaos. It gives rise to a universe of endless flux, the movement of which is understood in classical Chinese philosophy in the broad terms of the dialectic of *yang* and *yin*. This picture of endless change, and incessant forming and dissolving, was a particularly compelling one for early modernist writers influenced by the philosophical trends of vitalism and *Lebensphilosophie*. Among German philosophers, it was Schopenhauer whose pessimistic vitalism did the most to encourage an active philosophical interest in Buddhism within European intellectual culture; and a trickle of translations of

Daoist texts throughout the nineteenth century introduced Daoism to European thinkers and authors, albeit more gradually and at a later stage than either Buddhism or Hinduism.[29]

What was especially attractive to the Expressionists was the doctrine of *wu wei* at the heart of Daoism. *Wu wei* describes a principle of behaviour whose enactment attunes the human being to the *Dao*. Far from setting up a dualistic distinction between action and non-action, agency and acquiescent passivity, it expresses the ideal of the human being's reconciliation and harmony with the primal shape and nature of every phenomenon. Inextricable from this is an ethos of non-coercion towards both human beings and things. 'Nicht-Handeln', or 'No Action', is characterized by a dialectical interdependence of strength and weakness, which is expressed in both the *Tao-te Ching* and *Wang-lun* through the metaphorics of water: simultaneously weak and irresistibly powerful, and in tune with nature's course.[30] *Wu wei*'s ecological orientation is reflected in a refusal to subjugate nature to human ends; and its political dimension lies in its resistance to instrumentalist norms and practices.[31] But the concept's reception in European intellectual culture, from the 1820s onwards, was also shaped by the central tenets of the Christian Gospels, with their own ethical inversions of 'strength' and 'weakness'. Through Wilhelm's translations, in the light of his more proselytizing predecessors, Judaeo-Christian concepts entered into a simultaneously distorting and creative relationship with the *Tao-te Ching*.[32]

Daoism's potential for political radicalism would receive its most explicit European treatment a few years after *Wang-lun*, in Max Weber's magisterial *Die Wirtschaftsethik der Weltreligionen: Konfuzianismus und Taoismus* [*The Economic Ethics of World Religions: Confucianism and Daoism*] (1920). This study drew a contrast between a Confucian concentration on the stability of family and state order with Daoism's orientation towards an 'emptying one's self completely of worldly interests and passions, to the point of complete non-activity' ['absolute Entleerung des eigenen Ich von Weltinteressen und Leidenschaften bis zu völliger Nichttätigkeit'].[33] To put it differently, Weber was distinguishing between a humanist social and political orthodoxy supported by Confucianism as the official religious and philosophical foundation of the Chinese state bureaucracy, and the philosophy of decentralization and dissolution advanced in Daoism.[34] That millennia-old distinction, in turn, makes up part of the intellectual and institutional context of the ebbing and flowing war between the Imperial authorities and the Truly Powerless. Wang-lun's Daoism in Döblin's novel is a bold stroke of poetic licence, but it is set against a very real historical resentment at Confucian state power.

In view of this web of political and philosophical affinities, Döblin's retrospective remarks about his engagement with China may seem somewhat facetious, if not wilfully misleading. In a retrospective essay of 1921, he rather blithely claimed that the mass of 'factual' and 'historical' materials absorbed in his copious research for a novel ended up being substantially forgotten within a matter of hours. He deployed his historical, ethnographic and geographical materials not as 'facts', but rather as the accessories and stimulants of what, in a post-authorial and even posthumanist vein, he describes as 'a whole surging psychical process'. In an admission of the arbitrariness of this novel's setting, he even denies any particular interest in 'travelling' to China. After all, what did this place have to do with an author who barely even knew Europe (SLW 29)? Nor was he particularly averse to having it both ways in his claims on the exotic, making the rather telling admission in 1927 that he felt more secure in writing about India and China than about his own stamping ground of Berlin (SLW 79). These self-appraisals veer towards an all-too-familiar form of cultural colonialism, through which the Other is reduced to little more than a cabinet of retooled curiosities. A novelist may well have a point in claiming that the strange is easier to write about than the familiar, but we are entitled to ask exactly why that is the case.

Even in that critical light, though, I want to suggest that the novel's timeliness is the product *not* of straightforward cultural appropriation, but rather of a hybridity of the familiar and the strange. This sense of fusion is not only evident in the use of Daoist thought to explore the urgent question of non-resistance as a political possibility, but also comes to the fore in Döblin's Expressionist diction. The energetic flow of the prose, swollen with the materials of a history never quite under the author's control, was aesthetically of a piece with a novel that aimed to challenge and subvert hegemonies of all kinds.

## The Contradictions of *wu wei*

Still, subversion on its own rarely translates into a realistic alternative, even with a palette of exotic ideas to hand. Instead of pretending that it does, Döblin shows just how hard it is to move from resistance into something meaningfully new, whether in eighteenth-century China or in pre-war Europe. The very paradox of *wu wei*, in fact, lies in its practical impossibility, speaking as it does to the ideal of acting (and reacting) by not acting, and resisting by not resisting. A doctrine of non-coercion towards nature is paralleled in the refusal to be a part of any system grounded in force or violence of any kind. It is, after all, the arbitrary and extrajudicial murder of the Muslim Su-koh that first drives Wang-lun into the mountains. But the Truly Powerless are introduced to us, at the very start of Book 1, as an amorphous and adamantly insubstantial movement. Under the sign of *wu wei*, they have no fixed abode, living in vegetarian harmony with the nature that sustains them, and they refuse to gather converts. Their constitution itself is rooted in violence, and we read that they plunder and occupy the village of Pat'a-ling; but this gregarious band of criminals is a ragbag agglomeration of discharged soldiers, cripples without independent means of support, men who have lost families in floods, and those subjected to the near-annual hardship of the failed harvest. In one of the novel's uncanny crossovers between this motley band and the nature they are striving to emulate, 'many of these human waves surged across the face of this enormous Empire' ['derartige Menschenwellen wogten in dem ungeheuren Reiche viel'] (61).

As their charismatic leader, Wang-lun asserts that trying to conquer the world through 'action' fails (49). This ethos of non-coercion and non-conquest certainly anticipates Franz Biberkopf's resignation to the need to give up his masculinist dreams of 'conquering' Berlin, and this was to become one of Döblin's abiding ethical fascinations. But if Biberkopf's tribulations are inflected with Old Testament myths, resonances with the New Testament vibrate throughout *Wang-lun*. We read that 'whoever acts, loses the world; and whoever holds on to it, loses it' ['[w]er handelt, verliert sie; wer festhält, verliert sie'] (49). This near-direct transposition from Richard Wilhelm's translation of *Tao-te Ching* replaces 'corrupts' ['verdirbt'] in the first clause with a repetition of 'loses' ['verliert']:[35] a possible (not untypical) copying error on Döblin's part which only highlights the proximity to Matthew 16. 25: 'For whosoever will save his life shall lose it: and whosoever will lose his life for my sake shall find it' (King James Version). A later expression of non-action draws upon the metaphorics of water in *Das wahre Buch vom quellenden Urgrund*. 'Not acting' means being 'weak and obedient' to the laws of nature like 'water', and slipping from every leaf 'like light'. We can only counteract the inherent destructiveness of fate by not resisting and acquiescing in the course of nature: a way of living which, in another transposition from Liezi's attributed work, recasts weakness as strength (82–83).[36]

Döblin offers us a programmatic formulation of *wu wei*, then, albeit one which — through the lens of Wilhelm's translations — echoes aspects of Christian teaching: the counter-cultural interplay of strength and weakness, and life and death, suggest parallels with such passages as the Beatitudes in Matthew 5.[37] More interesting than the syncretism itself, however, is the aesthetic effect of putting these schematic statements in Wang-lun's mouth. Far from laying out a spiritual ideal that might help nurture a realistic political ethos, these syncretic maxims highlight their own artifice and, with this, their own impracticability.

*Wu wei* is caught up in its own ethical contradictions right from the outset. One of the most striking examples is Wang's own slightly sinister ideal of non-coercive leadership, through which he claims that he will not lead them, but 'if you have my will, I will lead you. You must agree with me in this very moment' ['[w]enn ihr meinen Willen habt, will ich euch auch führen. Ihr müßt mir zustimmen, gleich und in diesem Augenblick'] (82). The echoes of Jesus of Nazareth's demands for uncompromising obedience are striking, and they become even more so in the promise not to forsake his followers, and the assertion that whoever strikes them will feel their own weakness. For all these noble ideals, Wang's actions amount to a series of calculations made recognizably from within the world of *Realpolitik*. Time and again, the plot reveals the ease with which ideals of a new way of living collapse into new forms of violence. Wang's approach to the White Waterlily at the end of Book 1 is characterized by a hard-nosed sense of the need for military and political protection from this secret society. Understandably suspicious, the Waterlily's representative, the merchant Chen-yao-fen, wants to know what it is that Wang-lun's inchoate band really wants. In return for the offer of shelter and pressure on the Imperial authorities, Wang can offer this secret society a steadily growing army in return. Far from remaining amorphous and turning its evasive cheek, the Truly Powerless must stick together so as to avoid returning to petty criminality, a reality that Wang illustrates by pointing to the caustic lye which Chen cannot simply pour away if he wants it to grow crystals and take shape. Both the promise and the danger are borne out in a moment of impulsive violence: having been invited for supper with the society's unconvinced representatives, Wang assaults one of the guests in a flash of violent class politics, a threat that is as wordlessly heeded as it is made, as Chen finally indicates his support (89–102).

The White Waterlily is Döblin's astute picture of a shadowy elite, pulling the strings of change behind the scenes, and all too ready to fold in the face of real violence — but grubby compromise is, of course, the game that Wang also has to play. If he flouts both the spirit and letter of *wu wei* in order to guarantee its survival, then the story's subsequent course suggests he has no real alternative. Döblin's own politics would develop during the 1920s into an idiosyncratic socialism with an anarchist inflection: he was deeply sceptical of state powers and borders, a worldview born of his sense of power's inherent corruptibility.[38] Certainly, the Confucian ideology of the Qing Dynasty tacitly relies upon age-old tools of oppression; but even more strikingly, Ma-noh's attempts to build an island kingdom of the Truly Powerless descend into the millenarian politics of the religious cult. These apparent opposites dominate the third and second books respectively, but their extreme differences also conceal surprising dynamic similarities. Khien-lung is tormented by the thought of his own crumbling legacy, not least in relation to Confucian ancestor worship. After all, his is a rule, and a state, grounded in the mythic places of the past, while Ma-noh's kingdom is founded in the empty redemptive promises of the immediate future. The two are mirror images of one another, both of them beholden to a sense of time, memory and hope that is rooted in phantasm, and all the more dangerous for it.[39]

Under Ma-noh's *de facto* leadership, a diffuse agglomeration seems to evolve into a coherent movement. The Truly Powerless rapidly recruit adherents from all sections of society, and soon begin to attract an influx of women and girls. In a portrayal of a mass movement of discontent which represents the land itself in the anatomical terms of an ailing and twitching body, we read that '[a] twinge permeated western and southern Chihli, a rheumatic ache pulsed through the arm, the shoulder, over the feet, a stabbing pain in the teeth, pins and needles just above the left eye' ['[d]urch das westliche und südliche Tschi-li ging ein Ziehen, ein rheumatisches Unbehagen, im Arm, in der Schulter, über den Fußrücken, schmerzhaftes Zucken in einem Zahn, Nervenstechen über dem linken Auge'] (105).

This translation of inchoate discontent into a catalogue of medical symptoms is unnervingly appropriate to a movement that is beginning to understand its telos as the transcendence to a collective Nirvana. In the intellectual discourse of Expressionism, under the influence of Schopenhauer and Nietzsche, this Buddhist concept was refigured in terms of the physiological discharge of all individual desires, impulses and tensions. Ma-noh's elite 'ring of the pious' emerges with the paradoxical belief that through the sheer force of contemplation, they would be able to attain the ultimate stage of spiritual purification known, among other names, as the Western Paradise (122). In another moment of syncretism, Döblin draws upon the Buddhist doctrine of the Western Paradise, the realm of the buddha Amitābha and the ultimate goal of rebirth.[40] At the so-called Day of Consummation of the Glorious Shakyamuni (the Buddha himself), a barque is built to celebrate the 'Blessed Traverse' of the goddess Kuan-yin to the Western Paradise, to which (on some Buddhist mythologies) she sends her adherents on a lotus flower. Kuan-yin's barque is ceremonially burned in the midst of a gala of jugglers, acrobats and a wildly dancing eunuch (129–34). Ma-noh himself expresses a yearning for transcendence which is closely linked to a discourse of discharge, claiming that he is tied to 'the wheel of existence' ['das Rad des Daseins'], which is dragging him through an endless chain of abject reincarnations (141). It is hardly surprising that the admission into the sect of large numbers of women and girls triggers the redefinition of transcendence in terms of sexual discharge. The inauguration of a 'women's hill' allows *wu wei* to be conveniently recast as purification through gratification. Men, it seems, shouldn't have to resist their impulses, as Ma tells the returning Wang in a grim sleight of hand and reminder that some things change very slowly, if they change at all (160–65).

A cocktail of apocalyptic millenarianism, narcissism and promiscuity is bitterly familiar from recent decades, most notoriously in the abuse that Jim Jones (like Ma, an apostate) perpetrated among the inhabitants of Jonestown, Guyana in the late 1970s.[41] But Döblin's figurations have a strong contemporary inflection to them. In *Jenseits des Lustprinzips*, as we saw in the previous chapter, Freud would take up the psychoanalyst Barbara Low's concept of the 'Nirvana Principle' to link the 'pleasure principle' and the 'death drives'. Here he identifies the governing tendency of psychical life as a striving for the reduction and the removal of instinctual tension, culminating in the ultimate self-evacuation of death itself. In turn, he characterizes this discharge in terms of Schopenhauer's Buddhist-inflected renunciation of will, thus linking self-preservative sexual impulses to a repressed and deferred desire for dissolution and death.[42]

Ma instigates mass rape. In a Dionysiac communion of the Truly Powerless and the lush surrounding nature, we read that the terrified women and girls, many of whom come from respectable families, 'pressed their bodies against the ground' as the ground 'crepitated back against them' ['knisterte [...] gegen sie her']. In a grotesque travesty of the water imagery of *wu wei*, the men's orgasms are figured in terms of pulsating waves which break against their bodies. Bushes shake and tussocks jostle together as backs and heads re-emerge from coitus (148–50). Ma somehow justifies all this under the cloak of a Daoist ideal of reconciliation with nature: a yearned-for peace between the positive and masculine *yang* and the negative, feminine force of *yin* (151). What is so disturbing is that his promise of transcendence in the here and now is realized in an unholy alliance of sexuality and violence, and dissolution and destruction. As so often in Döblin's works, an ideal of perfect presence can be consummated only in the violence of disappearance.

Outraged at Ma's refusal to abandon his dogma of non-resistance in the face of the Island of the Broken Melon's inevitable defeat at the hands of the Imperial forces, it is Wang, in a disturbing twist, who brings this religious fiefdom to its delirious point of consummation (and destruction) by poisoning the water supply of the city in which it lies besieged (274–79). Ma, however, provides the novel's most damning picture of the narcissistic spiritual leader characterized both by the absoluteness of the power bestowed by the cult, and by that power's utter emptiness of any real content, any sense of meaning. When he anoints himself as a priest-king, we learn, in a deceptively simple aside, that Ma compulsively 'draws' an ever more absolute power to himself because he feels that he would otherwise succumb to power's responsibility ['weil er fühlte, sonst der Verantwortung zu erliegen']. Utopia is not an ethical ideal inspiring a process of imperfect approximation, but rather something immediately imaginable and realizable: something 'nearby [...], already purchased, overpaid-for tenfold' ['Nahes [...] Gekauftes und zehnfach Überbezahltes'] (224). This is a clear indictment of a political utopianism conceived in terms of imminent possibility, as what seems to be an expression of reclaimed sovereignty switches over into its opposite. The contradictory but painstaking ideal of *wu wei* gives way to a sense of powerless inevitability, as we learn that 'against fate, there was no salvation other than not resisting' ['[g]egen das Schicksal gab es keine Rettung als Nichtwiderstreben'] (225). What Döblin offers us, I suggest, is a shrewd statement on the fatalistic dynamics of uncritical utopian thinking. A community blindly committed to a moment of complete transformation can only achieve its purpose by destroying itself. Utopia and dystopia, as we shall see in the next chapter, are two sides of exactly the same coin.

While the redemptive hopes of the Broken Melon are grounded in a sense of apocalyptic futurity, Khien-lung's rule is rooted in a Confucian veneration of the dead and the preservation of their legacy in the present. He is tormented by the unappeasable anger of his ancestors for allowing the people of the illegitimate Island of the Broken Melon to be killed, if presumably by Wang-lun. The third book presents the Emperor's political dilemma as to whether he should use force to eradicate all traces of the *wu wei* sect, or spare them. Invited for counsel, the ageing Tashi-Lama, Lobsang Paldan Jische, makes the perilous journey from Tibet to Beijing. He scorns the Emperor's suggestion that he can atone for a hundred 'restless' ghosts with a series of neatly curated sacrifices, telling him instead to show mercy (320–21). But if Ma-noh's priesthood marks out the contradictions of millenarianism and the dangers of bad messianism, to invert Benjamin, Khien-lung's preoccupation with Imperial order illustrates the impossibility of non-resistance from a very different angle.

Despite considering Paldan Jische's exhortation of clemency, the Emperor is persuaded by his son Kia-king, following a failed coup by marginalized court reactionaries and his own suicide attempt, that the anger of the ancestors stems from his own negligence towards the rebels and their undermining of civic and political order in China's eighteen provinces. In one of Chinese history's repeated refrains, he warns of incipient sedition from Tibet, as the Dynasty exposes itself to threats from both the North and the West (370–71). The third book's final, programmatic reaffirmation of sovereignty situates the question of Imperial order firmly within the ideological ken of Confucianism: the Dragon Throne, we are assured, will defend the teachings of Confucius and of Heaven (373).

Once again, an apparently esoteric series of exchanges is a vehicle for an incisive piece of political critique. The Dynasty's Confucian ideology marks out a parallel with questions of political sovereignty and resistance in pre- and post-First World War Europe. In such texts as the *Doctrine of the Mean* [*Zhongyong*], one of the foundational Four Books of Confucianism, we find laid out an ideal of harmony between heaven, earth and humanity: a balance that relies on a government's commitment to its people's self-cultivation, while enforcing the people's duty to uphold order through collaboration and cooperation.[43] However, even a peaceful polity is shown to rest on a monopoly of violence. Khien-lung explains to the Lama that the kingdom of the Truly Powerless poses a danger to the Empire's integrity not through any particular act of resistance, but rather in its passive refusal to be part of the machineries of state and economy. He insists that fields have to be ploughed and sown, and taxes levied and collected, and he follows this up with the patriarchal threat of corporal punishment for runaway sons and wives, and death by cuts and drowning for the 'women of easy virtue' and concubines who have joined them (319).

## *Wu wei* and Non-violence

In short, if *wu wei* is a refusal to take part in an instrumentalist economy, then that refusal amounts to a kind of negative insurgency: a General Strike of sorts, which draws out and exposes the structural violence of state power. Between 1920 and 1921, Walter Benjamin would write his enigmatic 'Critique of Violence' ['Zur Kritik der Gewalt'], which can shed some retrospective light on the concepts of legitimate violence at play in the novel. Benjamin's enthusiasm for the revolutionary potential of the masses in the immediate wake of the revolutions in Russia and Germany intersected with the urgent contemporary question of exactly what forms of violence ['Gewalt'] revolutionary movements could lay claim to outside state apparatuses. Under the inspiration of Ernst Bloch, as well as the broadly political and metaphysical thinkers Charles Péguy, Georges Sorel and Erich Unger, the Critique also aimed to break with the means–end utilitarianism of both authoritarian and democratic politics, thus sketching out the utopian space for a new moral and social order. In an inversion of the orthodox understanding of a 'state under the rule of law' [*Rechtsstaat*], which deploys violence only at its limit points and as a just means, Benjamin situated the foundation of the state itself in an originating and self-justifying 'Gewalt'.[44] The extrajudicial slaughter of Su-koh is the originating moment of violence that propels Wang into spiritual and political awareness, and it also embodies the arbitrary violence at the heart of a corrupt regime that prefers to eschew direct force and to let the people be, 'so long as they allowed themselves to be ruled' ['wenn es sich nur beherrschen ließ'] (91). Drawing a distinction between 'natural' and 'positive' law, Benjamin argues that the former, rooted in evolutionary history, concerns itself primarily with the justice of ends, whereas the latter is preoccupied with the justice of means.[45] If violence as a means is directed towards *natural* ends, as for example in the waging of war for self-preservation, then it amounts to unsanctioned, 'law-making' and so power-making violence ['rechtsetzende Gewalt']; whereas the structural violence of the state, latent yet physically manifest when required, is figured as 'law-preserving' ['rechtserhaltend'].[46] In the Broken Melon's apocalyptic preoccupation with a future redemption, as well as Khien-lung's obsession with his legacy, Döblin exposes an illegitimate act of violence as the originating and grounding moment of political sovereignty. In the face of that brute fact, *wu wei*'s original ideal under Wang-lun — its refusal to bend to coercion — can offer no realistic answer. As we will see again in *Berge Meere und Giganten*, in the planned deportation of the peaceful 'settlers' and the ecological catastrophe that follows from that decision, a refusal of the system's violence simply provokes the system's violent response.

After his return to lead the remnants of the Truly Powerless in Book 4, Wang-lun certainly acknowledges the impossibility of *wu wei* as a practicable dogma; but he also questions the scope and meaning of the Emperor's power in the face of the truly irresistible forces of nature. In a question that again anticipates Benjamin's originating moment of *Gewalt*, he asks if Khien-lung's right to eradicate the Truly Powerless, supposedly equal to the 'rights' of nature itself, derives simply from his distant ancestor's defeat of the Ming Dynasty (413–14). The only realistic response is not to persist in 'powerlessness', a stance he now describes as suicidal ['[e]in Wahrhaft Schwacher kann nur Selbstmörder sein'] (416), but rather, with the White Waterlily as would-be kingmakers, to take up arms as the restorer of the Ming and march on Beijing (419–20). If this seems simply to mark a capitulation to the originally *mythic* means-and-ends cycle of violence, power and law, Wang's encounter with a robber brings about his final epiphanic turn, which in turn provokes the symbolic 'three leaps' of the title. The leaps themselves take place shortly before the final clash between rebel and Imperial troops, and they represent Wang-lun's attempt to illustrate his engagement with *wu wei* to his trusted lieutenant Yellow Bell ['Gelbe Glocke']. The first leap, over a shallow stream in a quiet corner of the besieged city of Linqing, symbolizes the embrace of non-resistance, a philosophy that ends in catastrophe with the founding and grisly end of the Island of the Broken Melon. It is Wang's *coup de grâce*, in poisoning its denizens, which is reflected in the second leap, back over the stream, into the use of force. After his retirement into life as a provincial fisherman, the march on Beijing is the culmination of this acceptance of military and political realities. Finally, the third leap returns him to the original side of the stream, and the principle of non-action through *wu wei*. The exhortation to Yellow Bell to 'bring me my sword' in preparation for battle seems to represent a moment of synthesis of agency and passivity; but the conclusion to this strangely static tableau is an ambiguous one. Not only does his resort to the sword, his so-called 'Yellow Leaper', leave the dialectic of action and non-action unresolved, but the scene's staginess foregrounds its own irresolution (480–81).

The staginess and artifice represent, I suggest, a deliberate aesthetic choice. As Anke Detken rightly argues, the retrospective enactment of the three leaps mark the consummation of a novel which was to help shape Brecht's concept of epic theatre, and specifically his later development of the *Verfremdungseffekt*.[47] His enthusiastic initial response to *Wang-lun* came in a journal entry of September 1920, just days after the iconic assertion on 9 September that 'a man with one theory is lost' ['[e]in Mann mit einer Theorie ist verloren'], and that he needs to stuff a host of different ones into his pockets like newspapers hot off the press.[48] The seminal essay of 1935, 'Vergnügungstheater oder Lehrtheater?' ['Theatre for Pleasure or Theatre for Instruction?'], outlined the principles of a theory for epic drama. Here, he praised Döblin for a conception of the epic in which, in contrast to an orientation towards a central character or plot, the world would be presented in all its living and moving parts, and capable of being dissected as such: as Döblin had argued in 1917, the epic should be able to be cut up into ten pieces like an earthworm, with every piece still moving of its own accord (SÄPL 125–26).[49] Quoting this observation, Brecht points out that 'pleasure' and 'instruction' are by no means antithetical in a theatre that aims not simply to reflect capitalism's internal contradictions, but also to effect meaningful change. A so-called 'process of alienation' ['Entfremdungsprozeß'] should make any instinctive identification with the play's characters impossible, thus opening up space for reflection on how their constitutive economic, social and psychological circumstances might be different.[50] This Hegelian term would give way to the neologism 'Verfremdung', which found its first substantial definition in the essay 'Verfremdungseffekte in der chinesischen Schauspielkunst' ['Alienation Effects in Chinese Acting'] of 1936. Going beyond a description of the audience's cognitive processes, 'Verfremdung' was meant to encapsulate the radical defamiliarization, the 'making strange', of the people and events enacted on stage.[51]

In counterpoint to readings which have tended to foreground the exoticism of the novel, Detken has suggested that Döblin's use of masks and maskings — not least the stag mask which he wears to avenge Su-koh's murder (41–43) — serves this purpose of defamiliarization. The scene of the three leaps is a significant point of culmination because it represents a moment of retroactive 'showing' and 'enacting' rather than a diegetic 'telling', which reconstitutes Wang-lun not as a unitary protagonist but a rather as a moveable nodal point of irresolvable contradictions. Its point is to encourage the reader critically to read *back* and also to read *across* the text.[52]

In 'Der Bau des epischen Werks', Döblin would argue that the purpose of the epic work was not to portray psychologically 'relatable' characters, but rather to sound out the elemental truths of human existence. As such, Wang-lun may be read as a figurative thread around which a swelling cast of events and individuals coagulate (SÄPL 218–19, 238–39). In a pointed reminder of our ambiguous hero's essential insignificance, the novel's close leaves wide open the question that Wang-lun poses in his three leaps. The wife of the Emperor's field commander, mourning her dead children and vowing revenge on Wang, asks herself, 'Be still, do not resist, can I do it?' ['Stille sein, nicht widerstreben, kann ich es denn?'], in a melancholy meditation on *wu wei*'s residual possibilities (WL 495). Her question mediates passivity through agency and negation through affirmation; and the open question, with its implicit turn towards the reader, anticipates the appeal to the audience at the end of Brecht's *Der gute Mensch von Sezuan* [*The Good Person of*

*Sezuan*], which was first performed in Zurich in 1943.⁵³ The oscillation between the unconditionally generous and compliant Shen Te — the gods' last hope in their increasingly desperate search for one good person — and her invented cousin, the hard-nosed representative of an exploitative capitalism, Shui Ta, has a recognizably Daoist undertone, just as Brecht's own interest in his Chinese milieu was more strongly shaped by its historical brutality and poverty.⁵⁴ After repeatedly switching personae throughout the play in order to maintain an imperilled picture of integrity while Shui Ta's tobacco factory grows apace, Shen Te reveals herself to be Shui Ta at his trial for her suspected murder. 'Your former order | to be good and yet to live | tore me in two like lightning' ['[e]uer einstiger Befehl | Gut zu sein und doch zu leben | Zerriß mich wie ein Blitz in zwei Hälften'], she claims in an arrestingly programmatic moment of despair.⁵⁵ After the gods depart in a reverse-*deus ex machina* with the amusingly apposite valediction of '[l]eb wohl, mach's gut!', and the suggestion that she will probably only need her cousin once a month, an actor appears in front of the curtain, in a final distancing effect, with the request that the audience provide their own ending. In the insistence that 'there must be a good person, must, must, must!' ['Es muß ein guter da sein, muß, muß, muß!'],⁵⁶ there is an infusion of desperate hope and utter uncertainty similar to the one hovering over the end of *Wang-lun*. The despair is even more pronounced here, of course, in a play completed in exile from National Socialist Germany, and Döblin's and Brecht's cognate techniques of *Verfremdung* highlight different senses of what exactly is irreconcilable here. The impossibility of continuing to survive and simply be human, while submitting peacefully to nature's course, is encapsulated in Wang's recurring dream about being swallowed up by a tree:

> Es ist beschlossen, vollendet, jauchzte Wang. Glücklich schlief er ein. Im Traum stand er unter einer Sykomore, an deren Stamm er sich hielt. Über seinen Kopf wuchs der Wipfel des Baumes in die grüne Breite und Höhe, so daß er, als die schweren Äste sich senkten, ganz eingehüllt und versunken im kühlen Blattwerk war und niemand ihn mehr sehen konnte von den vielen Menschen, die vorüberspazierten und sich an dem unerschöpflichen Wachstum ergötzten. (WL 482)

> Er plätscherte von dem Traum, der ihm Nacht um Nacht erschiene: er stünde an dem Stamm, erst sei es wie eine Sykomore. Allmählich finge der Baum an, so schlank und gleichzeitig so zottig um ihn zu wuchern, ihn wie eine Trauerweide schwelgerisch zu überhängen, wie ein grüner Sarg umzuschließen. Manchmal beim Aufwachen nehme sein Kopf den Traum mit, und dann käme ihm vor, daß sich der dünne Baumstamm nach Art eines saftigen Schmarotzers um seine Beine, seinen Leib und Arme gestengelt habe, so daß er sie nicht herausziehen konnte aus dem wässerigen Mark und ganz aufgesogen wurde von der reichen Pflanze, an deren Anblick sich alle beglückten. (487)

> [It is decided, it is finished, Wang rejoiced. Contented, he fell asleep. In a dream he stood under a sycamore, grasping its trunk. Above his head the tip of the tree sprawled outwards in its green height and breadth, and as the heavy branches drooped, he was utterly engulfed by the cool foliage, invisible to the many passers-by who delighted in this inexhaustible growth.]

> [He babbled about the dream that appeared to him night after night: he stood next to the trunk, which seemed at first to be a sycamore. Gradually the tree began to grow around him, so delicately but also with such exuberance, it hung over him voluptuously, began to enclose him like a green coffin. Sometimes when waking, his head would take the dream with it, and then it was as if the slender tree trunk had enveloped his legs, torso and arms like a parasitic vine, so tight that he was trapped in the watery pith, completely swallowed up by the succulent plant, a sight which delighted everyone who walked by.]

This surreal fantasy strikes an alienating note, combining a desire for disappearance into nature with an almost autoerotic yearning both to watch and tell it at the same time.[57] The subject is split over against himself, as the weirdly messianic 'es ist [...] vollendet', in the wake of his final qualified turn back into *wu wei*, yields to an even stranger sacrifice to a sycamore tree. Wang-lun yearns for the same kind of self-discharge that fuelled Ma-noh's distortion of mass sexuality into a quasi-religious principle, while distancing himself through dreamwork. We can recognize the near-identity of perfect self-presence and utter absence that so fascinated Döblin, and which finds such suggestive (because exotic) vehicles throughout the novel in the tropes of Daoism and Buddhism. That uncanny sense of nature as something at once strangely familiar — a home from home — and yet alien comes to the fore in the parasitical 'Schmarotzer', as well as the creepy agency of 'stengeln', a neologism from 'Stängel' ['stalks']. In short, we have a miniature fantasy of utopia: a picture of *wu wei* which, if realized, would destroy the Truly Powerless both individually and collectively. Sure enough, these passages are prefaced by the disciplining threat of a savage beating for some undesirable new arrivals in this doomed and dwindling community, and they are followed several pages later by the almost incidental mention of Wang's unceremonious incineration (491).

Ambiguity prevails, then, even as Wang finally leaps back into an embrace of 'not resisting'. Both the three leaps and Wang's dream are the symbolic culminations of a novel that persistently warns against utopianism by showing how difficult, even deadly, it is to try to fashion pacifism into a new kind of society and polity. Indeed, Wang is killed with sword in hand, and the corpses of his followers are left to rot ignominiously in the streets. The euphemistic language of state-bureaucratic violence rounds off the failed rebellion, as we learn that 'concluding government measures in this affair' lasted a whole month. An eventual arrangement to have the rebels buried under mounds of rubble in shallow graves where evil spirits congregate is signed off in the narrative with the bathetic observation that the humped mounds of rubble looked like the backs of two giant moles scrabbling their way out of the earth (491–92). *Verfremdung* is a complex and evolving idea, but one of its central impetuses for Brecht is its sense of practical hope in and in spite of despair at the present. In that connection it is highly significant that Döblin's novel as a whole ends not with a denial but a question, and the hint of an opening onto something hitherto unseen. And in a similar vein to many other moments of vicarious pleasure throughout his prose, Wang's dream image is one of paradox and contradiction, but it also leaves behind its hope for reconciliation, its own hermeneutic remnant.

I now want to show that Döblin's writing unfurls a different way of thinking about utopia in precisely this light. In contrast to a politics grounded either in a dead (and non-existent) past or a utopian future, the failures of which we have countenanced with Ma-noh and Khien-lung, his novel illustrates the possibilities of change latent in the energies of the now-time. As will become clear, this dynamic would broaden out considerably during the evolution of his poetics and anthropology, but it is in *Wang-lun* that it found its most immediate expression.

## Life in the Now-Time

Döblin completed the manuscript of *Wang-lun* in the spring of 1913, and May saw the publication of perhaps his single most famous statement of aesthetics, the so-called 'Berliner Programm', addressed to 'novelists and their critics' (SÄPL 119). This manifesto should be read not just against the backdrop of the novel's gestation, but also as an attempt to articulate his freshly minted concept of 'Döblinismus': an aesthetic programme that initially developed between 1911 and 1913.[58] Döblin's literary practice and theory were two sides of a symbiosis, and both the novel and the manifesto crystallized a radical new literary approach to reproducing the immediacy of the moment in time, the 'now'. This poetics was to develop into the aesthetic correlate of the ethics of non-resistance and non-coercion that so fascinated him, and it would lay the groundwork for his full-blown theory of the modern epic work.

Döblin had coined his neologism in direct response to Futurism, a predominantly Italian aesthetic and social movement whose main principles were outlined by the poet Filippo Tommaso Marinetti in his first 'Futurist Manifesto' ['Manifesto del Futurismo'] in 1909. Futurism would come to span the whole range of art forms, from poetry, through music, fine art and sculpture, to urban design, and it was characterized by an intense preoccupation with the acceleration and violence of modern technology and urban life, along with a vociferous rejection of 'the old' and 'the traditional'. Marinetti's poetics was marked by a break with Realism's focus on psychologies and unitary personalities, a rupture with conventions of syntax, and an obsession with the sounds and textures of words often ripped violently out of their semantic fields. The aesthetics of Futurism had exerted a formative influence on Döblin's markedly non-psychological and anti-subjective aesthetics, which first came to fruition in his short stories. Marinetti's novel *Mafarka il futurista* (1910), however, provoked his critical reassessment.[59] In an 'Open Letter to F. T. Marinetti', in March 1913, he praised the latter's principle of 'getting even closer to life itself' ['[d]ichter heran müssen wir an das Leben'] in a supercharged form of 'naturalism' (SÄPL 113–14, 115). A modern poetics worthy of the name should avoid needless embellishment, sticking instead to an unvarnished representation of 'hardness, coldness and fire, softness, the transcendent, the shocking' ['Härte, Kälte und Feuer, Weichheit, Transcendentales und Erschütterndes'] (113). But in an allusion to Futurism's notorious veneration of violence, Döblin also takes Marinetti severely to task over his indiscriminate shattering of sense and meaning 'for the sake of the sheer plasticity of battle' ['der Schlachtenplastik zu Liebe'] (116). Döblinism can be understood in this light as a distinctive aesthetics that in part adopted, refined, yet decisively moved beyond Futurist innovations.

In the 'Berliner Programm', Döblin heavily criticizes what he calls the artificial 'rationalism' of the nineteenth-century novel's penchant for psychological realism (SÄPL 120–21). As he had argued in an essay written during the gestation period of his early short stories, 'Das Recht auf Rhetorik' ['The Right to Rhetoric'] (1909), psychology 'is more about logic than it is about actual psyche' ['kennt mehr Logik als Psyche'], and amounts to little more than a crutch to shore up a lack of poetic intuition (KS I, 62–63). Rather than letting himself become caught up in linear narrative's claims to accurate psychological representation, the author must 'press backwards from "anger" and "love" to what is real, what is concrete' ['von "Zorn" und "Liebe" auf das Konkrete zurück[zu]dringen'] (SÄPL 121). What he means by this is that words of thought and affect sit at a faded remove from the sensory immediacy of observed phenomena, that is, the visible, audible and even calculable 'stuff' that happens; the ever-changing relations of cause and effect (121). In the wake of the reworked case studies of his short stories, as well as his doctoral dissertation, his fascination with the interplay of psychiatry and aesthetics is made explicit here.

Modern scientific psychiatry had emerged in the 1870s as a discrete discipline and approach to mental disorders. Under Emil Kraepelin's formative influence, it increasingly turned away from neurology's classificatory process of 'mapping the brain', and towards an observational act of describing patients' behaviour as the manifestation of a corporeal whole.[60] For Kraepelin, the psyche was a hypothetical, non-substantial construct emerging in the course of self-observation and clinical description: the relationship between mind and body was non-dualistic, but also resistant to direct causal analysis.[61] In one of his most famous prescriptions, Dr Döblin issues an invitation to 'learn from psychiatry, the only science that concerns itself with the human being in its psychical entirety' ['[m]an lerne von der Psychiatrie, der einzigen Wissenschaft, die sich mit dem seelischen ganzen Menschen befaßt'] (SÄPL 120). This branch of medicine, he tells us, occupies itself with the recording of visible symptoms and manifestations; and analogously, the prose writer should eschew the classic literary questions of 'why' and 'how' even in the face of supposed psychological normality (SÄPL 121). This resistance to any sense of causal motivation reflects precisely the scepticism towards locating the origins of mental disorders in psychological causes that I discussed in the previous chapter.

What emerges through these clinical figurations is a questioning not just of the literary conventions of Romanticism and Realism, but also the unity and sovereignty of the human subject itself. In a reassignment of the hermeneutics of a text from author to reader, Döblin asserts that the 'Hegemonie' of the author should be broken. This call has a subversive edge to it: we have to reckon here not just with the author's 'self-denial' ['Selbstverleugnung'], but also with a root-and-branch undermining of a centralizing authority. Reinforcing a sense of emptying and renouncing, and with echoes of the 'self-evacuation' that Weber would so astutely identify in Daoism,[62] he pushes a fantasy of 'kenosis' ['Entäußerung'] to its extremes with the suggestion that 'I' am no longer myself, but rather the street, the lanterns, this or that event, nothing more (122). This strikingly religious language culminates in nothing less than a demand for the end of the self as we know it in prose: an evacuation which is mirrored in the suggestion that 'the earth must steam again' ['[d]ie Erde muß wieder dampfen'], free of the controlling gaze of both the author and the human subject (123).

Andreas Solbach has highlighted deep parallels between the tenets of Daoism and this anti-subjective poetics, suggesting of the novel that Döblin 'lets himself be carried along by the nature of his material; he does not interfere high-handedly in its flow but rather allows [or gives the impression of allowing] his material to unfold entirely of its own accord'.[63] His writing style, in short, was to embody an ideal of non-resistance. However, the innovation of Döblin's prose relates not simply to its subversion of sovereignty, but also to a new way of figuring the relationship between time and space in prose. If he was seeking a way of capturing different spatial angles and perspectives of an object or a sequence of events *in* time,[64] then this in turn involved a form of representation that was quite new to the tradition of the German novel. What is significant here is not an attempt to convey time and space as objective dimensions, but rather the evocation of a particular kind of materiality and temporality within literary language itself, through its own creative energies. Language must renounce its own claims to substantive reference, whether in relation to things, concepts or affects, an argument that reflects the profound influence of Fritz Mauthner's philosophy of language scepticism.[65] The author, in turn, should wrest as much 'plasticity and liveliness' ['Plastik und Lebendigkeit'] as possible from his or her words, an emphasis on poetic texture which shifts our focus from the expression of phenomena to the phenomena of their expressions (SÄPL 121–22).

The point is that we are presented not with a kind of writing that simply submits itself to the flux of things and sensations, but which assembles something new, with its own kind of texture and tactility, from those raw materials. 'We don't narrate, we build' ['man erzählt nicht, sondern baut'], as Döblin has it. What this so-called 'cinema style' ['Kinostil'] suggests is a forerunner to the montage technique that Benjamin would identify as central to *Berlin Alexanderplatz*. In a non-linear melding of time and space within the frame of prose, Döblin moots a portrayal not just of 'successive flow' ['Hintereinander'] but also of 'juxtaposition' ['Nebeneinander']. Rather than Marinetti's arbitrary pell-mell of words, this juxtaposition is a spatio-temporal nodal point out of which new perspectives and meanings might emerge. The comparison with music is revealing, drawing as it does a parallel with an art form that elicits its effects in the in-between spaces of materials, their sounds and their notes (121–22); and we find precisely that interplay of successiveness and simultaneity expressed in Döblin's Socratic Dialogue on the philosophy of music, *Gespräche mit Kalypso* (SÄPL 64).

The Programme's final call to arms of 'Tatsachenphantasie!' is perhaps his most suggestive, conveying in its oxymoron a tension between the subjective and the objective, authorial presence and absence, and the factual and the fantastical (123). Critical to it too, as I outlined in my Introduction, is a dialectical relationship between the heterogeneity of the discourses, motifs and 'facts' making up a novel, and the almost auto-generative flow of an authorial and readerly imagination that endlessly reorders them. But if 'Tatsachenphantasie' can be understood as a watchword of Döblin's epic poetics, then this has to do not with a sense of abdicated sovereignty, but with the creation of new constellations. That sense of forging something new is what underpins the final announcement that the novel must be reborn as a 'modern epic' (123).

The reduction of a unitary self to a bundle of actions, sensations and impulses is made clear in Wang's first encounter with Ma. The first description of the monk is a testament to Döblin's filmic switches of focus — between the very large and the minutely small — and it also encapsulates his proverbially psychiatric prose. As we saw in Chapter 1, in the aesthetic parallels between his characters' wordless gestures and the close physiological observations of his Korsakoff patient, any sense of psychological causality, let alone a reconstructible hermeneutic, yields instead to a sequence of observations marked, in a pattern characteristic of the novel's overall structure, by an aesthetic of jumps and jump-cuts. There is a distinct physicality-in-motion to the description of the two protagonists' early moments of acquaintance. In an almost literal manifestation of Döblin's calls for 'concreteness' and 'plasticity', and through the focalization of an early twentieth-century narrator, we read that Ma-noh's movements and gestures give the impression of an eccentric old man, his uncertain eyes 'flinch[ing] from every object like bouncing rubber balls' ['die vor jedem Gegenstand zurückwichen wie aufschlagende Gummibälle'] (WL 50). Various crossovers between internal and external physiological responses combine with an interplay of human and non-human, the sentient and the inanimate, the tersely observational and the poetic. The quartz statue of the goddess Kuan-yin, for example, is depicted in faintly hallucinatory motion, complete with her 'countless' arms and a mouth which curls up slightly, 'as when a gentle wind brushes over pasture plants' ['wie wenn ein leichter Wind über eine Weidenpflanzung fegt'] (51). Ma's later descent into outright psychopathology is prefigured here in flashes of egomania, notably his screaming into his buddhas' ears, and throwing himself at their feet in despair, when they refuse to heed his demands.

This, then, is a poetics devoid of psychological reconstruction — even at his zenith, on the throne of his Island of the Broken Melon, Ma-noh is described as 'inscrutable' (224). In the early interactions between the two men, we see more than a hint of the anxious homoeroticism characteristic of many of Döblin's male partnerships. As Wang kneels on a mat in Ma's hut and repeats the latter's sutras back to him, the small man 'sat down breathless next to him, anxiously fingered him, sniffed at him. Twice, in an outburst of rage, he showed him the door' ['fühlte sich ängstlich an ihn *heran*, beschnüffelte ihn. Zweimal wies er Wang in einer Aufwallung die Tür'] (55, my emphasis). What is both bizarre and fascinating here is the interdependence at play between physical and affective intimacy on the one hand, and stony unknowability on the other; and Armin Schäfer has cogently drawn attention to Döblin's intuitive grasp of the minute physiological signs that pass, below the level of language, between individuals who have no hope of 'knowing' one another but are at least subconsciously striving 'to understanding *how* [the other] can be experienced'.[66] That sense of mutual experiencing in the moment finds its way almost directly into the Programme, where he argues that we must 'feel our way towards' ['*heranspüren*'] the uniqueness of every occurrence and grasp both the physiognomy and the particular development of each event (SÄPL 122, my emphasis). Döblin himself is feeling his way towards a prose that might reproduce the materiality of a moment in time and space — however incommensurable with linear prose that may be.

Set in the author's present, the opening Dedication reminds us that this temporality is never straightforwardly of the here and now, but rather echoes and resonates repeatedly with the sounds of other times and other places. 'Lest I forget — ' is, revealingly, the twice-repeated opening line. We are treated to the description of a busy Berlin street, in which the phenomenological immediacy of the sounds leaves a strangely abstract impression when translated into language. 'Electric flute sounds all along the rail' ['[e]in elektrisches Flöten schienenentlang'] is the surreal description of a tram's intermittent screech. The milk-white arc lamps bombard the window panes and heap 'cartloads' of light into the room: a description marked by a characteristic criss-crossing of sensory boundaries, but also a defamiliarization in the unexpected tenor–vehicle combination. All the narrator wants to do is shut the window, admitting that he is unable to orient himself with the city's myriad vibrations ringing in his ears:

> Ich weiß nicht, wessen Stimmen das sind, wessen Seele solch tausendtönniges Gewölbe von Resonanz braucht.
> Dieser himmlische Taubenflug der Aeroplane.
> Diese schlüpfenden Kamine unter dem Boden.
> Dieses Blitzen von Worten über hundert Meilen:
> Wem dient es?
> Die Menschen auf dem Trottoir kenne ich doch. Ihre Telefunken sind neu. Die Grimassen der Habgier, die feindliche Sattheit des bläulich rasierten Kinns, die dünne Schnüffelnase der Geilheit, die Roheit, an deren Geleeblut das Herz sich klein puppert, der wässerige Hundeblick der Ehrsucht, ihre Kehlen haben die Jahrhunderte durchkläfft und sie angefüllt mit — Fortschritt.
> O, ich kenne das. Ich, vom Wind gestriegelt.
> Daß ich nicht vergesse —
> Im Leben dieser Erde sind zweitausend Jahre ein Jahr. (WL 7–8)

> [I don't know whose voices these all are, whose soul needs to echo and resonate throughout such a vast vault.
> This heavenly doveflight of aeroplanes.
> These flue pipes coiling and sliding underground.
> This flashing of words over a hundred miles:
> Who is this all for?
> Yes, I know the people out there on the pavement. Their telegraphs are new. The greedy grimaces, the hostile satiety of a blue-shaven chin, the thin, snuffling nose of lechery, the coarseness, its heart, like a doll, trapped in jellied blood, the watery dog-eye of envy, their throats have yapped down the centuries and filled them up with — progress.
> Oh, I've seen all this — I, combed by the wind.
> Lest I forget —
> In the life of this earth two thousand years are one year.]

At the end of the dedication, 'this powerless book' ['diese[s] ohnmächtige[] Buch'] is dedicated to Liezi and the work traditionally ascribed to (but not authored by) him, *Das wahre Buch vom quellenden Urgrund*, from which the narrator directly quotes (WL 8).[67] We can see here the imprint of a Futurist yen for modern technology and, at the same time, the recognition of vast expanses of time and funds of countercultural wisdom, both of which precede and will outlast the present's particular version of human greed.[68] This surreal prose poem of sorts, with its twisted images of dog-eat-dog greed and mindless advance, resonates with the myth of linear progress through homogeneous empty time:[69] there is a weary nod to the eternal recurrence of the same in the sound of empty yapping down the centuries. And yet, the unreflective historylessness of the lived present is modulated through the call to 'remember' the wisdom of Daoism, itself a testament to its relevance to the Europe of the 1910s. The figure of 'resonance' carries with it a semantic field of vibrations and echoes, a suggestion of megaphones and telephones, and disembodied voices. The juxtaposition of aeroplanes, flue pipes and telegraphs, the first two uncannily crossing over with the nature that they penetrate, represents a first attempt at literary montage, bringing together the spatially and temporally disparate in the immediacy of the here and now. Benjamin argued of the 'present' that it should be figured not as the culmination of a linear history but rather as a moment shot through 'with splinters of messianic time' ['in welcher Splitter der messianischen [Zeit] eingesprengt sind'].[70] The present always contains within it a fleeting *possible* connection with moments in the past that would otherwise be irredeemably lost. The past flits by, and can only be seized and momentarily understood 'as an image that flashes up at the moment of its recognizability, and is never seen again'.[71] I now want to suggest, in an extended coda, that such a sense of connection is central to *Wang-lun*'s hope for a space in which a non-coercive human existence might be imaginable, and its own Dedication partially redeemable.

\* \* \* \* \*

In his review of 1930, Benjamin would praise *Berlin Alexanderplatz* for a use of literary montage, which, in its displacements and rearrangements, opened up daring new vistas for the modern novel as a genre. I will consider the effects of montage in the city novel in more detail in my final chapter. However, Walter Muschg traces the origins of this genre subversion back to *Wang-lun*, which, far being (merely) a powerless book, amounted to nothing less than what he calls a 'declaration of war on the bourgeois art of the start of the twentieth century'.[72] It is this bold project which sketches out the space for imagining ethical and political change. I suggest that Döblin's aesthetic reflects a budding political sensibility that he had yet to make explicit, and that this is tied up with an underexplored rethinking of the dynamics of memory within the present moment.

As we can see in the narrative's opening call 'not to forget', the present is irrevocably infused with the past — and all the more intensely so for modernity's attempts to deny or even repress it. The trope of the past's precarious recognizability in the present recurs throughout Benjamin's later work, finding revolutionary expression in the 'Theses'. In his posthumously published masterpiece *Das Passagen-Werk* [*The Arcades Project*], we read that every now is 'the now of a particular recognizability'. In precisely this moment, 'truth is charged to the bursting point with time'. Benjamin goes on to suggest that 'what has been comes together in a flash with the now to form a constellation' in what Benjamin calls 'dialectics at a standstill': a fleeting relationship of association that can never be reduced to the past shining light on the conditions of the present, or vice versa.[73] By momentarily identifying with the past, the present suddenly recognizes itself in reflection, identifying with the suffering endured by previous generations and responding to their persistent yet unredeemed claims to utopia.[74]

The image of flashing affinities and similarities can also be found in Benjamin's language philosophy of the 1930s. In the essay 'Lehre vom Ähnlichen' ['Doctrine of the Similar'] (1933), he argues of our mimetic faculties that the very *perception* of similarity of objects across gaps of space or time is in every case bound to a phenomenon of 'flashing up' ['Aufblitzen']. Just as a constellation of stars offers itself fleetingly to the eye, so this perception of similarity 'flits past, can possibly be won again, but cannot really be held fast as can other perceptions'.[75] In a conception that would influence Adorno, Benjamin argues that mankind's original relationship with nature was grounded in our bodily and sensory connections to it; and as he points out at the start of 'Über das mimetische Vermögen' ['On the Mimetic Faculty'], a revised version of the 'Doctrine' essay which was also published in 1933, man's 'gift for seeing similarity is nothing but a rudiment of the once powerful compulsion to become similar and to behave mimetically'.[76] Long before the emergence of a rational conception of nature, primitive man strove to control and shape it through an imitation of its changes and its movements. The dynamics of mimetic expression fed into a sensuous and corporeal form of language. But while traces of this sensuous correspondence and affinity persist in metaphor, language's development as a primarily semiotic and communicative medium marks a movement out of 'sensuous' and into 'non-sensuous' forms of correspondence and, with this, a progressive abstraction and disenchantment.[77] Six years later, in 'Über einige Motive bei Baudelaire' ['On some motifs in Baudelaire'] (1939), Benjamin would further develop this theory of correspondence with his concept of 'aura'. An object's 'aura' is manifest in its uncanny and ungraspable ability to 'look at us'. It is never exhausted by our gaze, and our experience of it is marked by what he identifies as our 'transposition of a response common in human relationships to the relationship between the inanimate or natural objects and man'.[78] In short, it harks back to a less technologized and less alienated mimetic relationship, a sense of non-coercion that would in turn shape Adorno's articulation of mimesis.

What is at stake for Benjamin in particular is the very possibility of aura in an instrumentalized modern world. As a phenomenon, it corresponds to the data of what Marcel Proust, in *À la recherche du temps perdu* [*In Search of Lost Time*], portrayed as 'mémoire involontaire': a form of memory produced by events which leave their mark below the threshold of consciousness, and which emerges fragmentarily at moments of unexpected stimulus.[79] As Aleida Assmann suggests, 'the auratic' may persist in the unexpected, epiphanic moments of connections within a poetics (like Döblin's) that aims to reproduce the sensory and psychical 'shock experiences' of modern life.[80] But what is especially significant here is that a figure of transient similarities across time and space, beyond our conscious control, is what holds Benjamin's constellation of ideas together.[81] I want to illustrate this sense of epiphany, and explain its profound significance for *Wang-lun*, with the help of several rather different examples.

The first is drawn from the battle between the Imperial armies and Wang-lun's rebel force on the threshold of the Forbidden City, shortly before his final defeat. The depth of material desperation feeding into this final upsurge against the Manchu Dynasty reaches its gruesome culmination in a welter of jumping, writhing and bursting bodies. An extreme drought spreads, and in another hybridization of the land and its hungry inhabitants, we learn that 'canals snaked along like empty intestines, carving their dry, greasy-putrid cavities through the landscape' ['Kanäle schlängelten sich wie leere Därme, mit trockener, schmierigfauler Höhlung durch die Landschaft'] (WL 430). This is an uncanny animation of the inanimate. The sticky near-onomatopoeia of 'schmierigfaul' is just one instance of a mode of description bent on reproducing the immediacy of sights, sounds, textures and smells; and in the hybridization we glimpse a marked similarity to the 'open, rust-flecked' plumbing channel which snakes its way along the outer wall of the half-demolished house in Rilke's *Aufzeichnungen des Malte Laurids Brigge* [*Notebooks of Malte Laurids Brigge*] of 1910, in what Malte describes as 'unspeakably disgusting, squashily wormlike, almost digesting motions' ['in unsäglich widerlichen, wurmweichen, gleichsam verdauenden Bewegungen'].[82] As Yuan Tan has argued, Döblin is not averse to violently reducing his human beings to disposable objects, just as he conversely endows objects with 'living' characteristics;[83] and the latter, if in a different tenor, is also a feature of Rilke's prose. Just as interesting, though, is the way in which fragmentary physiological details, the subject of a neurotic close-up focus in Döblin's early short stories, are blown up here into convulsing, fleshy masses. The unitary subject is dissolved, and with it, the bare worth of the existence it is supposed to underwrite.

Benjamin's angel sees history not as a chain of events, but rather 'one single catastrophe, which keeps piling wreckage upon wreckage',[84] an image which brings Döblin's chaotic battle scenes insistently to mind. In his description of the decisive battle for Beijing, he shows us human life's sheer destructibility. Döblin's mass of gerunds is just one example of a semantic network of twitching, jumping and leaping throughout the text. We read of a 'grotesque thrashing around, a wrenching, the wild swinging of arms, silhouettes leaping, ghostly dashing through shadowed barrack yards and backstreets' ['[g]roteskes Zappeln, Verrenken, Armschwingen, Hüpfen von Silhouetten, gespensterhaftes Rennen über verschattete Kasernenhöfe und Gassen'] (WL 436). A fondness for asyndeton makes itself felt at moments of chaos and violence in the novels, and there is a notable parallel with the grim description of the mass rape among the Broken Melons (145). A particular marker of this anatomical — proverbially psychiatric — prose is its keen sense of the meaninglessness of events when reproduced in an imitation of 'real time'. As Döblin dissolves individuals and individual bodies, so their parts, movements and sounds are substantivized. But we are repeatedly reminded of a narrator's shadowy presence, as the battle for Beijing is shot through with moments of mediation and montage. The use of water throughout the text, not least in Wang's own idealized description of the Truly Powerless as water which is always flowing and taking the form of its vessel (175), comes to a head in an imagery of bursting vessels and stomachs. We are told, with a disgusted alliteration, how the rebels, having burst the Forbidden City's North Gate, 'disgorged their misshapen forms, the stink of graves and backstreets, into the imposing Imperial City' ['ergossen ihre verzerrten Gebärden, den Gestank der Gräben und Gassen in die strenge Kaiserstadt'] (436). The bulging masses of bodies 'bubbled' and finally 'burst' upon contact with the spear of a fresh Imperial regiment (437). Finally, the city 'vomited out' the rebels, and one final inhalation culminates, in another arrangement of snapshots on the page, in the 'explosion of a boiler' ['[d]as Platzen eines Kessels'] (438).

These descriptions seem to promise quite the opposite of redemption, parodying the fluid metaphorics of *wu wei* in a grotesque hydraulics. But as so often in the novel, Döblin's images here never point purely to a loss of control or meaning. At their most indiscriminate, in a lurid Expressionist diction that quite often confuses and irritates more than it enlightens, they mimic the narrative chaos of history, the piles of corpses and rubble littering the battlefields. But at their best, they have a properly arresting effect on the reader in their uncanny hints of other times and places:

> Das blendende Weißrot des Feuermeers im Osten der Tartarenstadt trug in das Bild die Durchschneidung der Helligkeiten und schwerer Schatten ein. Das nördliche neue Kornmagazin loderte. Von dem Funkenregen wurde das südlicher gelegene unermeßliche Reislager befruchtet und gedieh in Minuten zu einer im Wind tosenden flammenden Riesenmohnblüte. Unter diesen feierlichen Lichtern wühlten die zuckenden Massen ineinander. [...] Schwirren, Platzen, Prasseln in überhitzter Luft von allen Seiten, überschüttend die herkömmlichen Geräusche des Frage- und Antwortspiels zwischen dem Tod und dem menschlichen Leben. (WL 435–36)

> [The blinding white-red of the sea of fire in the eastern quarters of the Tartar City brought into the picture a criss-crossing of bright lights and dark shadows. The new granary to the north blazed. The vast rice storehouse further to the south was fertilized by the shower of sparks and bloomed in minutes into an enormous poppy, flaming in the wind. Under these ceremonial lights the flashing masses dug ferociously into one another. [...] A buzzing, a bursting, a crepitating in the scorching air rushing in from all sides, overwhelming the usual noises of that game of question-and-answer between death and human life.]

With its senses of flashing, as well as twitching and thrashing, the verb 'zucken' is a perennial favourite of Döblin's, and this passage sets those meanings in play. David Dollenmayer has identified a pattern of 'spiritual ruptures and alternation' as both central to the novel's thrust, and ultimately embodied in the three leaps.[85] This dialectic of leaps and shifts finds explicit expression in the morbid game of question and answer that rounds off the passage, a rare reminder of the human complexion of the life that is imperilled here. Döblin's 'Kinostil', manifest as it is in the jump cut-like parataxis of his prose, is crystallized here in a cinematic vignette. In a vivid moment of mediation embedded in the description, the rice storehouse is fertilized and blooms into a poppy. Despite presenting a picture of destruction, there is in these unusual metaphors not just the sense of a gruesome ending but rather an aesthetic opening into something inchoately new.[86] It is through their constitutive uncanniness — that metaphorical combination of the familiar and the strange — that they faintly prefigure a possible reconciliation with nature, even an aesthetic redemption of the present's suffering.

This, I suggest, is an instance of Döblin's hermeneutic remnant. In *Wang-lun*, it takes the form of a *Verfremdung* that reaches from the novel's structuring principle and backbone, in the shape of his three leaps, right down into the fine-grained details of metaphor and simile. And it is here, in a modulation on Detken's Brechtian argument,[87] that the novel's exotic strain of 'Tatsachenphantasie', its reworking of myriad chinoiseries, becomes integral to its hints of possible change. Once again, the copula of metaphor disappears, and the narrator himself is made strange in an orientalized, painterly description of a thunderstorm raging above the warring forces: 'up in the black air a huge gong hung from an invisible cord over the armies, its beats baiting them. Two white panthers leapt over one another' ['[a]us schwarzer Luft hing an unsichtbarer Leine ein Riesengong über den Armeen, dessen Schläge hetzten. Zwei weiße Panther übersprangen sich'] (439). The narrative's quality of defamiliarization foregrounds the contradictions inherent in an ethics and politics of non-action. Conversely, though, it also expresses the hope for a form of reconciliation with nature beyond the cycles of mythic violence in which the text's ebb and flow between Khien-lung and the Truly Powerless becomes caught.

I will outline this reconciliation in greater detail in my discussion of global war and environmental catastrophe in the next chapter. Its peculiar quality for Döblin first flourishes here, though, and has certain important aspects in common with Benjamin's 'aura'. Central to aura, as I have suggested, is an ungraspable sense of subjectivity, and with it an otherness, in the objects of history, art and nature. *Wang-lun* is littered not only with images that hybridize man and nature, but also descriptions of nature which sprout up in the plot like unkempt, marginally utopian, patches of wilderness. A passage dwelling on the 'immense lushness' ['unermeßliches Wachsen'] around Chinan-fu adds virtually nothing substantive to the plot's forward thrust, but its pointlessness is part of the point. We see thrushes and ravens chasing each other from their perches on locust trees whose leaves start 'buzzing', as if the trees themselves were suppressing convulsive laughter (WL 24). An incommensurable thing called nature repeatedly juts into the picture, reminding us of its own animistic agency in the margins beyond human violence and coercion. For all its epic scope, Döblin's novel makes a point of remembering the contingent, the ignored and the unimportant; and that sense of remembering, paradoxically enough, is central to a poetics rooted in the temporality of the moment. By casting its sideways glance at otherwise forgotten and abject things, events and individuals, the novel opens up the space for their representation and, with this, their marginal redemption in prose.

In that light, my final example of this chapter is one that symbolically frames both Wang-lun's story and the novel as a whole. This is the memory of an act of violence which turns out to be pivotal to Wang's leaps, but whose real significance cuts right across the dialectic of violence and non-violence, action and non-action. The impact on Wang of the murder of the Muslim Su-koh by an Imperial policeman in the city of Tsi-nan-fu is characterized by multiple 'flashbacks'. The witnessed killing, in itself a contingent moment in the text, splits into a series of simultaneous moments of consciousness, a splitting which maps with remarkable complexity the mental processes through which we reconstitute memories of events after the fact:

> Wang schrie hell mit den andern auf, die von den Ecken der Straßen dies angesehen hatten. Er wollte zuspringen, aber er zitterte, konnte nicht von der Stelle, seine Glieder waren plötzlich von einer Schwäche und Lähmung befallen. Er trieb mit der Menschenflut im Zickzack über die Plätze, seiner nicht ganz bewußt. Seine Blicke liefen hilflos über die Gesichter, die Gänsekiele und die Ladenschilder, die goldbemalten. Er erkannte keine Farben. Eine immer wachsende Ängstlichkeit trieb ihn vorwärts. Fünf Säbel fuhren dicht nacheinander durch die Luft, zehn Schritte vor ihm, wohin er sah. Und dann ein graues Durcheinander, Übereinander.
>
> Su-koh, sein ernster Bruder, lag ungerettet auf der Straße.
> Su-koh war sein Bruder.
> Su-koh war ungerettet geblieben.
> Su-koh lag auf der Straße.
> An der Mauer.
> 'Wo ist denn die Mauer?' (WL 39)
>
> [Wang let out a sharp cry, as did the other onlookers from their street corners. He wanted to jump into the fray, but he was trembling, he couldn't move, his limbs were overcome by a sudden paralysis. In the midst of the flood of human bodies, he ran in a zigzag across the city squares, not quite conscious of himself. He glanced helplessly around at the faces, quills, gold-painted shop signs. He couldn't discern colours. The fear grew and grew and drove him on. Five sabres sliced through the air, one after the other, a mere ten feet in front of him, right there, in front of his eyes. And then a blurred chaos, one thing on top of another.
>
> Su-koh, that sincere brother of his, lay unrescued in the street.
> Su-koh was his brother.
> Su-koh remained unrescued.
> Su-koh lay in the street.
> By the wall.
> 'But where is the wall?']

Wang's response is certainly an impulsive one. In a snapshot of ham-fisted authoritarianism, this innocent wick manufacturer had been arrested and tortured on account of his nephew's involvement in an uprising in the region of Kansu, before being summarily stabbed under conditions of open season on the local Muslim community. Wang's decision to avenge his friend is not a rational response to injustice but the product, as Schäfer argues, of a series of extreme physiological reactions.[88] Not only does his own murderous act of revenge against the soldier in question, replayed over several pages, draw its heightened energy and sense of dissociated confusion from an adrenaline-fuelled body and mind; but those reactions culminate in retrospect in an 'all-encompassing rapture, an unconditional investment in Su's fate' ['die Hingerissenheit und unbedingte Teilnahme an Sus Schicksal'] (75). In a flashback to the moment of the murder, Wang 'felt the overwhelming pressure of suffering, in the back of his head, on his tongue, in the hollow of his breast' ['fühlte er den überwältigenden Druck des Leidens, im Hinterkopf, auf der Zunge, in der Höhlung der Brust'] (44).[89]

Without wanting to deny the physiological and psychological impulse of revenge, I suggest that we might also fruitfully read it as a trace of Benjamin's now-time. His argument, as I have shown above, is that articulating the past historically does not entail recognizing it as it really was, but rather seizing and appropriating a memory as it flashes up in a moment of historical danger.[90] It is telling that the picture of Su-koh lying 'unrescued' recurrently flashes across the screen of Wang's consciousness. To avoid immediate reprisal, we recall, he flees northwards into the mountains. His aimless wandering is punctuated by moments of intense physiological and psychological focus, as his mind flashes back to a picture of flashing sabres against the wall in Tsi-nan-fu, and the image of Su-koh languishing in a roadside shrine for homeless spirits (WL 48). The simultaneity of perspectives on his friend in the flashback immediately after the murder ('sein Bruder', 'ungerettet', 'auf der Straße') charges the moment with an intensified sense of spatiality, and its closing question opens up this cascade of thoughts and feelings to an indeterminate response.

Wang's revenge killing takes on a weirdly ceremonial complexion as he dons his stag mask to carry it out, but it also happens in something of a textual blur. Yet another flashback reconstitutes this moment of killing in a series of staggered, fragmented stills that arrest and poetize the flow of the prose (44–45).[91] There are suggestive nods here not to the execution of justice, but rather to the rescuing of the 'ungerettet' Su-koh, such that he would 'stand up again and walk about again' ['[w]o bekam man ein Mittel her, daß Su-koh, sein Bruder, wieder aufstand und herumging?'] (40). Significantly, it is Wang's encounter in the final book with a robber, on whom he is to pass judgment, which marks the final moment of connection and partial redemption. Wang sees his own alternative fate mirrored in this starving criminal: a story that might have played out for him, without 'this or that coincidence', starting with Su-koh. He even retrospectively blames Su-koh for leading him away from this path of existential solidarity. But the plainly epiphanic recognition of this stranger as '[s]ein Bruder, sein Bruder!', rather than simply another member of the Truly Powerless, resonates with Su's fate, just as it marks Wang's coming face to face with a picture of his past self (473–74). It is this arresting moment of self-recognition, crystallized in the detail of Wang's comparing his hands with those of the robber, which triggers his final turn back into *wu wei*. His third leap cannot sidestep its own contradictions, but it may still enact a hope of sorts for a place and time in which the dead and forgotten are remembered and recognized.

If with a sense of the tragedies that revolution can bring about, Benjamin, too, describes it (in a Marxian vein) as a dialectical 'leap' between present and past.[92] In its resistance to forms of political power bent on forgetting for the sake of their own survival, the final leap marks the first enactment of a revolutionary promise; and given that hegemonic power both originates in and perpetuates cycles of violence, Wang-lun's stylized gestures embody a rearticulated hope for *wu wei*. Döblin's aesthetic commitment to the temporal moment points to a world, however remote, that might one day belong to the Truly Powerless.

In an essay of 1921, Döblin argued that his underlying purpose as a novelist was to do justice to the 'now'. His was a constant fight against the clarified and fixed sequence of what is dead and gone, for the sake of the 'dark, the unformed, the unfurling, what can never quite come to light — for the sake of the momentary' ['zu Gunsten des Dunklen, Weichen, sich erst Enthüllenden, dauernd an der Enthüllung Verhinderten, — zu Gunsten des Momentanen'] (SLW 33). This epiphanic commitment is rooted in the ongoing struggle to 'do justice to the minute' ['[m]an kämpft um das Recht der Minute'] (SLW 33): a typically robust formulation which carries a chiefly aesthetic meaning in the light of the 'Berliner Programm', but which also connotes an ethical act of restoring and redeeming. The narrator's opening call not to forget might in conclusion, then, be read in several intersecting ways. As we have seen, the Daoist teachings to which the work is dedicated represent a rich and eminently usable fund of thinking that reached far beneath and behind Europe's frenetic present. The retold story of Wang-lun, insignificant as it might be in the flow of world (and even Chinese) history, was meant to equip its readers with ways of thinking differently about aspects of a contemporary reality. Perhaps more importantly still, the very act of remembering, whether conscious or *involontaire*, orients itself not primarily towards the past, but rather to the unfilled spaces of the present and the future.

It is by seizing that past, as it flits across our present, that we might redeem its catastrophes and find a way, hoping beyond hope, of shaping what futures we still have in the light of them. In one of German modernism's most starkly innovative novels, Döblin began to articulate that fragile hope. As the work's closing question suggests, we should keep on leaping, even as we remain persistently critical of where we land, and ready to ask (and leap) again. Turning now to the science fiction, I want to elaborate on this critical sense of utopia in the context of yet another, very different, time and place.

## Notes to Chapter 2

1. Fredric Jameson, *Archaeologies of the Future: The Desire Called Utopia and Other Science Fictions* (London: Verso, 2007), pp. 85–86 and 90.
2. See Marc de Wilde, 'Benjamin's Politics of Remembrance', in *A Companion to the Works of Walter Benjamin*, ed. by Rolf J. Goebel (Rochester, NY: Camden House, 2009), pp. 177–94 (pp. 177–79).
3. Walter Benjamin, 'Über den Begriff der Geschichte', in GS, 1.2, 693–704 (p. 695): Thesis VI; *Selected Writings: 1938–40*, ed. by Howard Eiland and Michael W. Jennings, Gary Smith and others, 4 vols (Cambridge, MA: Belknap Press, 2003), IV, 391.

4. Ibid., Thesis VI.
5. Ibid., pp. 697–98, Thesis IX.
6. Ibid., p. 701, Thesis XIII.
7. Ibid., p. 695, Thesis VI; *Selected Writings*, IV, 391.
8. Ibid., p. 695, Thesis V; ibid., pp. 390–91.
9. Ibid., p. 704, Anhang B; ibid., p. 397.
10. See Gabriele Sander, '"Chinesischer Roman": *Die drei Sprünge des Wang-lun* (1915)', in *Döblin-Handbuch*, ed. by Becker, pp. 41–50 (p. 43).
11. For a nuanced engagement with this uncomfortable contradiction, see Ritchie Robertson, 'Alfred Döblin as Pacifist and Chauvinist: *Die drei Sprünge des Wang-lun* and Wartime Propaganda', in *Pacifist and Anti-Militarist Writing in German, 1889–1928*, ed. by Andreas Kramer and Ritchie Robertson (Munich: Iudicium, 2018), pp. 199–210.
12. On this idiosyncratic and much-contested alliance, see de Wilde, especially pp. 180–81. In contrast, Döblin's distinctly non-messianic engagement with Judaism in its religious, cultural and political dimensions would only really develop through his encounters with Polish Jewish communities in the autumn of 1924, as portrayed in *Reise in Polen* (1925): see here Klaus Müller-Salget, 'Döblin and Judaism', in *A Companion to the Works of Alfred Döblin*, ed. by Dollinger and others, pp. 233–46 (especially pp. 235–36).
13. Cf. Benjamin, GS, I.2, 697, Thesis IX.
14. In his reading of *Wallenstein* (1920), Steffan Davies has shown how Döblin challenged the nineteenth-century tradition of the historical novel. In a decisive move away from the 'sense-giving' aspects of the genre — reflecting the precepts of historicism — his retelling of the Thirty Years War was an innovative portrayal of history's chaos and contingency. See Steffan Davies, 'Writing History', especially pp. 129, 137. Cf. Helmuth Kiesel, 'Döblin's *November 1918*', in *A Companion to the Works of Alfred Döblin*, ed. by Dollinger and others, pp. 215–32.
15. See Robertson, 'Alfred Döblin as Pacifist and Chauvinist', p. 201; cf. Susan Naquin, *Shantung Rebellion: The Wang-lun Uprising of 1774* (New Haven, CT: Yale University Press, 1981), p. 12.
16. See Schuster and Bode, p. 29.
17. See Sander, '"Chinesischer Roman"', pp. 43–44; and Anke Detken, 'Zwischen China und Brecht: Masken und Formen der Verfremdung in Döblins *Die drei Sprünge des Wang-lun*', in *Alfred Döblin: Paradigms of Modernism*, ed. by Davies and Schonfield, pp. 102–20 (pp. 103–04).
18. See Heinrich Detering, *Bertolt Brecht und Laotse* (Göttingen: Wallstein, 2008), p. 46. On the enduring political importance of Daoist philosophy for Brecht, see also Stephen Parker, *Bertolt Brecht: A Literary Life* (London: Methuen, 2014), especially p. 155.
19. Brecht, 'Über Alfred Döblin', in *Werke*, XXIII, 23.
20. Robertson, 'Alfred Döblin as Pacifist and Chauvinist', pp. 203–04.
21. Cf. Schoeller, p. 121.
22. Cf. Georg Lukács, *The Historical Novel*, trans. by Hannah Mitchell and Stanley Mitchell (London: Merlin Press, 1962), p. 23.
23. Robertson, 'Alfred Döblin as Pacifist and Chauvinist', p. 202.
24. See Jahraus, pp. 67–71.
25. See Sander, '"Chinesischer Roman"', p. 42.
26. The semi-legendary figure of Laozi, who lived and worked in the sixth century BCE, is generally considered to be the first philosopher of Daoism, and the traditionally accredited author of the *Tao-te Ching*, one of Daoism's foundational texts. Even less is known about Liezi's life; but along with Laozi, he is reckoned to have been one of three foundational Daoist thinkers. It is thought that he lived in the fourth century BCE, and he is the presumed author of the eponymous work *Liezi*. See Max Kaltenmark and Roger T. Ames, 'Laozi', *Encyclopaedia Britannica* <https://www.britannica.com/biography/Laozi>; and Roger T. Ames, 'Liezi', *Encyclopaedia Britannica* <https://www.britannica.com/biography/Liezi-Daoist-philosopher> [accessed 2 October 2019].
27. On this anti-imperialist connection see Joch, p. 416.
28. See Sander, '"Chinesischer Roman"', pp. 41–42.
29. See Weijian Liu, *Die daoistische Philosophie im Werk von Hesse, Döblin und Brecht* (Bochum: Brockmeyer, 1991), pp. 30–32; cf. Sheppard, pp. 40 and 283–86. On the growing reception of Daoist thought see Detering, pp. 22–24.

30. See Wilhelm, pp. 32–33; cf. Liu, pp. 12–14.
31. See here Karyn L. Lai, *An Introduction to Chinese Philosophy* (Cambridge: Cambridge University Press, 2008), especially p. 98. As Lai argues, Daoism's embrace of 'multiplicity and plurality' and 'hesitancy about social order and uniformity' conditioned its inherent resistance to human attempts to 'classify, control and manipulate' nature (p. 9).
32. See Detering, pp. 23–28.
33. Max Weber, *Gesamtausgabe*, ed. by Horst Baier and others (Tübingen: Mohr, 1984–), I.19: *Schriften und Reden*, ed. by Helwig Schmidt-Glintzer in coordination with Petra Kolonko (1991), p. 383; see Detering, pp. 43–45.
34. See Detering, pp. 43–45. On the long-standing link between the doctrine of moral self-cultivation in Confucian thought and the maintenance of Chinese state order, see Lai, especially pp. 35–51. The Confucian ideology that education instils moral wisdom underpinned the Chinese Civil Servant Examination system. This was in existence from the period of the Han Dynasty (206 BCE–220 CE) until its abolition in 1905, and it was grounded in the conviction that 'scholars of the classical texts would also be ethically adept practitioners of good government' (Lai, p. 35).
35. See Sander, 'Anmerkungen', in Alfred Döblin, *Die drei Sprünge des Wang-lun*, ed. by Sander and Solbach, p. 582.
36. See ibid., p. 590.
37. Yuan Tan has detailed Döblin's misunderstandings of *wu wei* along Western philosophical and theological lines. As he suggests, Döblin's *wu wei* was distorted by a continued attachment to the dualisms of European thought, as evidenced in the novel's insistent return to the individualizing ethical paradox of its final question, 'Be still, do not resist, have I the strength?' ['Stille sein, nicht widerstreben, kann ich es denn?'] (WL 495): see here Yuan Tan, *Der Chinese in der deutschen Literatur* (Göttingen: Cuvillier, 2007), especially pp. 98–102 and 107–12. Both the *Dao* and *wu wei* also fed into his later works of nature philosophy, not least in such figurations as the 'primal meaning' ['Ursinn'] in *Das Ich über der Natur* and the dialectic and interdependence of 'acting and suffering' ['Handeln' and 'Leiden'] in *Unser Dasein*. See Döblin, IN, especially 194–200, 205–06 and 211–20; and UD, especially 183–87. For a detailed discussion of these concepts in Döblin's nature philosophy and anthropology, see Chapter 4.
38. For an overview of Döblin's political development in the 1920s, see Wulf Koepke, 'Döblin's Political Writings during the Weimar Republic', in *A Companion to the Works of Alfred Döblin*, ed. by Dollinger and others, pp. 183–92 (especially pp. 188–91).
39. Andreas Solbach briefly draws attention to these contrasting temporalities in his 'Nachwort', in Döblin, *Die drei Sprünge des Wang-lun*, ed. by Sander and Solbach, pp. 638–70 (p. 669).
40. Sander has comprehensively outlined the sources of Döblin's knowledge of the Buddhist doctrine of Nirvana, most notably the recent philological and anthropological studies of Chinese religious practices by Wilhelm Grube (1901, 1902 and 1910), Jan Jakob Maria de Groot (1901–10), and Carl Friedrich Koeppen (1859 and 1906): see Sander, 'Anmerkungen', in *Die drei Sprünge des Wang-lun*, especially pp. 584 and 596.
41. For this brief comparison, see Robertson 'Alfred Döblin as Pacifist and Chauvinist', p. 207.
42. See Freud, GW, XIII, 53 and 60–62.
43. See Lai, pp. 45–47 and 49.
44. For an excellent exposition of the essay's political and intellectual contexts, see Axel Honneth, '"Zur Kritik der Gewalt"', in *Benjamin-Handbuch: Leben — Werk — Wirkung*, ed. by Burkhardt Lindner (Stuttgart: Metzler, 2006), pp. 193–210 (especially pp. 193–94).
45. See Benjamin, GS, II.1, 180.
46. Ibid., especially pp. 186–87 and 198. For Benjamin, the proletarian General Strike ideally embodied a moment of immediate, non-instrumental 'Gewalt' which would overthrow the means–end justifications of state violence (p. 194). As David Dollenmayer has astutely noted, Döblin's politicized choice of terms (not least in references to 'farmers and workers', and even the anachronistic description of beleaguered salt makers as 'trade unionists' ['Gewerkschaftler']), draws a clear connection with the social and economic struggles of the Kaiserreich, which were also a prominent part of Benjamin's political hinterland in writing his essay. See Dollenmayer,

'The Advent of Döblinism', in *A Companion to the Works of Alfred Döblin*, ed. by Dollinger and others, pp. 55–74 (p. 63).
47. See Detken, pp. 108–10.
48. Brecht, *Werke*, XXVI: *Journale I: 1913–1941*, ed. by Marianne Conrad and Werner Hecht, p. 160.
49. Brecht, *Werke*, XXII: *Schriften II: 1933–1942*, ed. by Inge Gellert and Werner Hecht, pp. 107–08.
50. Ibid., pp. 108–09.
51. See Parker, especially pp. 352–53.
52. See Detken, especially pp. 107–10 and 112–16.
53. For a critical comparison of the open questions at the ends of Döblin's novel and Brecht's play, see ibid., pp. 119–20.
54. For the first comprehensive discussion of the split between the alter egos, and the play's links to Döblin's novel, see Osman Durrani, 'Shen Te, Shui Ta, and *Die drei Sprünge des Wang-lun*', *Oxford German Studies*, 12 (1981), 111–21 (pp. 116–17).
55. Brecht, *Werke*, VI: *Stücke VI*, ed. by Klaus-Detlef Müller, p. 275.
56. Ibid., pp. 277 and 279.
57. Nicholas Royle outlines the parallels between the *Verfremdungseffekt* and Freud's conception of the uncanny in 'Das Unheimliche' (1919). 'The uncanny' emerges from the interplay of the familiar and the unfamiliar, coming to light when that which should have stayed hidden is exposed. In a similar dynamic, the purpose of *Verfremdung*, on Brecht's understanding, is in part to make what seems familiar, 'peculiar, striking and unexpected'. See Nicholas Royle, *The uncanny* [sic] (Manchester: Manchester University Press, 2003), p. 5.
58. See Becker, 'Döblin und die literarische Moderne 1910–1933', pp. 330–31.
59. Ibid., p. 331.
60. Mathias Kiefer has highlighted the influence of both Gustav Fechner (1801–87) and Wilhelm Wundt (1832–1920) on the grounding physiological presuppositions of this observational psychiatry. See Kiefer, *Die Entwicklung des Seelenbegriffs in der deutschen Psychiatrie ab der zweiten Hälfte des 19. Jahrhunderts unter dem Einfluss zeitgenössischer Philosophie* (Essen: Die Blaue Eule, 1996), pp. 67–74.
61. See Fuechtner, pp. 112–13.
62. Cf. n. 33 above.
63. 'Er läßt sich von der Natur seines Materials tragen, er greift nicht eigenmächtig in den Gang des Ganzen ein und er erlaubt dem Material, sich ungestört zu entfalten' (Solbach, p. 670).
64. Cf. ibid., p. 669.
65. From his earliest forays into literary writing onwards, Döblin was an avowed admirer of Mauthner, and addressed him as none other than his 'intellectual comrade' in a letter of July 1922, celebrating their common sense of the 'continuum of clarity *and* scepticism' (*Briefe*, I, 121). Mauthner — his gaze turned inwards — had argued in his three-part *Beiträge zu einer Kritik der Sprache* [*Contributions to a Critique of Language*] (1901 and 1902) that we are incapable of developing a language to describe our inner (internal) experiences, as the language we do use always carries physical implications. Because language is a tool that is practically adapted for understanding the outside world, it is incapable of making and stating accurate models and judgments of our subjective lives. See Mauthner, *Beiträge zu einer Kritik der Sprache*, 3rd edn, 3 vols (Leipzig: Meiner, 1923), I, 235 and 416–17.
66. Armin Schäfer, 'The Physiology of Charisma: Alfred Döblin's Novel *The Three Leaps of Wang-lun*', *New German Critique*, 114 (2011), 79–93 (p. 85). The emphasis is mine.
67. In a commentary on the essential purposelessness of human life, quoted from Richard Wilhelm's translation, we read that 'we go and don't know where. We stay and we don't know where. We eat and we don't know why. All this is the mighty life-force of heaven and earth' ['[w]ir gehen und wissen nicht wohin. Wir bleiben und wissen nicht wo. Wir essen und wissen nicht warum. Das alles ist die starke Lebenskraft von Himmel und Erde'] (WL 8): see Sander, 'Anmerkungen', in *Die drei Sprünge des Wang-lun*, p. 568. In a nod to the futile rapaciousness of contemporary capitalism, Döblin slightly modifies the original's question of possession to: "who then can speak of profiting, possessing?" [' "wer kann da sprechen von Gewinnen, Besitzen?" '].
68. See Solbach, pp. 666–67.

69. Cf. Benjamin, *GS*, I.2, 697: Thesis XIV; *Selected Writings*, IV, 395.
70. Benjamin, *GS*, I.2, 704, Anhang A; *Selected Writings*, IV, 397.
71. 'Nur als Bild, das auf Nimmerwiedersehen im Augenblick seiner Erkennbarkeit eben aufblitzt, ist die Vergangenheit festzuhalten' (ibid., p. 695, Thesis V; *Selected Writings*, IV, 390).
72. Walter Muschg, 'Nachwort des Herausgebers', in Döblin, *Die drei Sprünge des Wang-lun*, ed. by Muschg (Olten and Freiburg i.Br.: Walter, 1960), pp. 481–502 (p. 491).
73. '[J]edes Jetzt ist das Jetzt einer bestimmten Erkennbarkeit. In ihm ist die Wahrheit mit Zeit bis zum Zerspringen geladen. [...] Nicht so ist es, daß das Vergangene sein Licht auf das Gegenwärtige oder das Gegenwärtige sein Licht auf das Vergangene wirft, sondern Bild ist dasjenige, worin das Gewesene mit dem Jetzt blitzhaft zu einer Konstellation zusammentritt. Mit andern Worten: Bild ist die Dialektik im Stillstand.' (Benjamin, *GS*, V.1: *Das Passagen-Werk*, p. 578) [[E]ach 'now' is the now of a particular recognizability. In it, truth is charged to the bursting point with time. [...] It is not that what is past casts its light on what is present, or what is present its light on what is past; rather, image is that wherein what has been comes together in a flash with the now to form a constellation. In other words: image is dialectics at a standstill.] (Benjamin, *The Arcades Project*, trans. by Howard Eiland and Kevin McLaughlin (Cambridge, MA: Belknap Press, 1999), p. 463)
74. See de Wilde, p. 187.
75. '[Die Wahrnehmung von Ähnlichkeiten] ist in jedem Fall an ein Aufblitzen gebunden. Sie huscht vorbei, ist vielleicht wiederzugewinnen, aber kann nicht eigentlich wie andere Wahrnehmungen festgehalten werden. Sie bietet sich dem Auge ebenso flüchtig, vorübergehend wie eine Gestirnkonstellation.' (Benjamin, *GS*, II.1, 206–07) [The perception of similarity is in any case bound to a flashing up. It flits past, can possibly be won again, but cannot really be held fast as can other perceptions. It offers itself to the eye as fleetingly and transitorily as a constellation of stars.] (*Selected Writings: 1931–1934*, ed. by Michael W. Jennings, Howard Eiland and Gary Smith (Cambridge, MA: Belknap Press, 1999), II.2, 695–96)
76. 'Die Gabe, Ähnlichkeit zu sehen, die er besitzt, ist nichts als ein Rudiment des ehemals gewaltigen Zwanges, ähnlich zu werden und sich zu verhalten. Vielleicht besitzt er keine höhere Funktion, die nicht entscheidend durch mimetisches Vermögen mitbedingt ist.' (Benjamin, *GS*, II.1, 210) [His gift for seeing similarity is nothing but a rudiment of the once powerful compulsion to become similar and to behave mimetically. There is perhaps not a single one of his higher functions in which his mimetic faculty does not play a decisive role.] (*Selected Writings*, II.2, 720)
77. See ibid., p. 213.
78. 'Die Erfahrung der Aura beruht [...] auf der Übertragung einer in der menschlichen Gesellschaft geläufigen Reaktionsform auf das Verhältnis des Unbelebten oder der Natur zum Menschen.' Benjamin, *GS*, I.2, 646; Benjamin, *Charles Baudelaire: A Lyric Poet in the Era of High Capitalism*, trans. by Harry Zohn (London: New Left Books, 1973), p. 148.
79. Benjamin, *GS*, I.2, 612–13.
80. Aleida Assmann, 'How Long Does the Present Last? Seven Approaches to a Fleeting Phenomenon', in *Time in German Literature and Culture, 1900–2015: Between Acceleration and Slowness*, ed. by Anne Fuchs and J. J. Long (Houndmills and Basingstoke: Palgrave Macmillan, 2016), pp. 39–53 (p. 46).
81. Richard Wolin highlights the recurrence of the metaphor of 'flitting resemblances' and 'flashing lights' across Benjamin's later works: see Wolin, *Walter Benjamin: An Aesthetic of Redemption* (New York: Columbia University Press, 1982), p. 245.
82. Rilke, *Werke*, III, 485; Rilke, *The Notebooks of Malte Laurids Brigge*, trans. by Robert Vilain (Oxford: Oxford University Press, 2016), p. 27.
83. See Tan, especially pp. 145–46.
84. '[E]ine einzige Katastrophe, die unablässig Trümmer auf Trümmer häuft': Benjamin, *GS*, I.2, 697, Thesis IX; 'On the Concept of History', p. 392.
85. Dollenmayer, 'The Advent of Döblinism', p. 62.
86. In a flashing of correspondences between moments in cultural tradition, this garish constellation of images brings to mind the hallucinatory nightmare of the Viet Cong's ever-same attack

on the Do Lung Bridge, shortly before the climax of Francis Ford Coppola's *Apocalypse Now* (1979). It is revealing that Coppola himself consciously drew upon the fragmentary aesthetics of modernism, not least its penchant for montage, in order to recapture the horror and absurdity of his source text, Conrad's *Heart of Darkness*. For a cogent account of the return to 'modernist' techniques among filmmakers of the 1970s, particularly in representations of the Second World War and Vietnam, see Margot Norris, 'Modernism and Vietnam: Francis Ford Coppola's *Apocalypse Now*', *Modern Fiction Studies*, 44.3 (1998), 730–66 (especially p. 731).

87. Cf. Detken, especially pp. 119–20.
88. Schäfer, p. 83.
89. See ibid., p. 84. In this connection, see also Dollenmayer, 'The Advent of Döblinism', p. 63.
90. Benjamin, GS, 1.2, 695, Thesis VI.
91. 'Mask gripped, thrust over the head of the T'ouszu, throttled, cast aside. [...] Thrust it over his head, the mask over the T'ouszu, then away. Thrusted over the head of the T'ouszu, then away, away' ['[D]ie Maske gefaßt und über den Kopf des Tou-ssee gestülpt, erdrosselt, weggeworfen. [...] Über den Kopf stülpen die Maske dem Tou-ssee, und dann weg. Über den Kopf des Toussee gestülpt, dann weg, weg'] (WL 44–45).
92. Benjamin, GS, 1.2, 701, Thesis XIV; 'On the Concept of History', p. 395.

CHAPTER 3

# Of Cyborgs and Other Monsters: *Berge Meere und Giganten*

In his book of 2008, *In Defence of Lost Causes*, Slavoj Žižek suggested that Nature does not really exist. Being the Romantics in denial that we are, we sustain the illusion of an essentially harmonious natural world thrown off-balance by our incursions. 'Our' environment is something with which we might be somehow reconciled if finally we learned to live sustainably. However, when boiled down to its mechanisms, Nature, this over-determined mass of things that are 'other' than us, is little more than a series of countless catastrophes. Žižek's example of oil production is startling for its sheer terseness. The product of a 'past [organic] cataclysm of unimaginable dimensions', our primary energy source here becomes a metonymy for a natural world which is unfolding before our eyes as an immense imbalance sheet of huge losses and ever more marginal gains. The planet itself will go on and on, of course, but we are simply one desperately contingent — if increasingly destructive — part of what is in effect a great big system of broken equilibria.[1]

The Romantic ideal of human reconciliation with Nature finds one of its most influential modern articulations in Heidegger's concept of *Earth*, in 'Der Ursprung des Kunstwerkes', which was written between 1935 and 1936. This is the ineluctable seedbed out of which we create our *World*, our spaces of social, cultural and political meaning. Earth is entirely irreducible to World but also lies at its root.[2] It is through a dialectical relationship with Earth that we define and continually reconfigure who we are as human beings;[3] but Žižek's argument is that there is no longer any such thing as Earth, no 'Big Other' reassuringly 'there' to root our plans and projects. As we master the rules of nature's construction, it slowly loses its impenetrability and becomes endlessly manipulable; but as we can see from the impact of our accelerating climate crisis, as well as advances in biogenetics, the more powerfully we manipulate, the more powerless we become. As the Anthropocene hurtles towards a further temperature rise of significantly more than 2°C by the end of the twenty-first century, we are creating self-sustaining feedback loops that we neither fully understand nor control.[4] But even as Earth crumbles away into the terrifyingly abstract numbers of hard science, we continually fall back, if only subconsciously, on our Romantic dreams of reconciliation. We must instead come to terms with a brutally contingent yet implicated relationship. The appropriate response, if we can call it that, is certainly not a resigned fatalism, but rather the radical ownership of our individual and collective role in all this brokenness; and the increasingly prominent discourse around a 'Green New Deal' in both the United States and Europe (at the time of writing) suggests that we are at least starting to build the right kinds of coalition.[5] Žižek's call elicits a clear echo in the eco-critic Timothy Morton's advocacy of a so-called 'dark ecology' grounded in our entwined affinity with, yet at a marginal distance from, our damaged environment: the 'sticky mess that we're in and that we are'.[6]

Döblin's *Berge Meere und Giganten* is overshadowed in the cultural imagination by more famous siblings like *Berlin Alexanderplatz*, not to mention Thomas Mann's *Der Zauberberg*, which was published in the same year. But as Günter Grass recognized in an article of 1978 in *Die Zeit*, here was a novel that spoke with frightening relevance to a globalizing world scarred by revolutionary political violence and unforeseeable environmental and demographic change.[7] In its prescient engagement with these themes, I suggest that it yields fresh insights into those debates over our environment that 'dark ecology' has thrown bracingly open: debates which reach far beyond the traditional ken of ecocriticism, and which both enlarge and in the same motion subvert our understanding of 'the environment'. One of his guiding impetuses, as he was to claim in 1948, was a question regarding technology that is of almost unparalleled relevance today: 'What will become of human beings if they carry on living with it in this way?' ['was wird aus dem Menschen, wenn er es mit ihr so weitertreibt?'] (SLW 293).

First, though, we should bear in mind some contextual caveats. Like all fictions of the future, this one is a refraction of its time and place. It was coloured by the catastrophes of the recent past, and most personally by Döblin's encounters with the human fallout of industrialized warfare. His employment during the war as a military doctor in Saargemünd, and from 1917 in Hagenau, Alsace, shaped a deeply critical attitude towards war and violence that overtook the chauvinism briefly outlined in the previous chapter. His sense of patriotism found particularly virulent expression in his article 'Reims' (1914), a pugnacious justification of the German army's attack on the city's cathedral which doubled as yet another manifesto of Futurist aesthetics (SPG 17–25); and even by 1918, a strain of aggressive nationalism was still evident in such essays as 'Drei Demokratien' ['Three Democracies'] (SPG 33–44). However, as Schoeller argues, his initial enthusiasm for the war was rather more tempered than that of some of his literary contemporaries.[8] His treatment of serious injuries, along with his encounters with the Spanish flu, fed into his grisly portrait of warfare as both a military and civilian catastrophe in *Wallenstein* (1920). On top of that, his personal sense of relative powerlessness behind the lines brought him to wonder how a post-war politics might actually function, while acknowledging his and other intellectuals' urgent need to take on more political responsibility (*Briefe*, 1, 87).[9] *Berge Meere und Giganten* was one literary product of that sense of engagement: as Alexander Honold argues, it alloyed technologized destruction with a sense of the industrialization of the earth, and the unprecedented mobilization of its masses.[10]

As usual, there was an idiosyncratic personal motivation at play as well, and one that brought humankind's destructiveness into proximity with the measureless power of nature. His accompanying remarks to the novel (of the same year) trace its origins back to the entirely unremarkable sight of sand and pebbles on a Baltic shoreline in the summer and early autumn of 1921. From this angle, it is a celebration of the endless, mysterious change and transformation of nature (SLW 51–52). As Döblin's organic response to a resonance between his *Ich* and the grandeur of Nature, the novel's purpose was to eulogize this 'world being' (351). The Goethean invocations of the novel's opening Dedication greet this awesome Other as the 'thousand-named, nameless one' ['Tausendnamigen Namenlosen'] (BMG 7), recasting the writing process as a pseudo-religious worship of and self-protection from a sublime monstrosity. The Daoist dedication of *Wang-lun* had clearly laid the foundations for what was now a much more explicit engagement with Nature itself.

The narrative proper of *Berge Meere und Giganten* opens in the late twentieth century with the picture of a world severed from the warnings of its past, and so prone to embark on fresh cycles of destruction: we are told that there was no one still alive who had lived through the war that they called the World War (13). The grim cyclicality of what follows never drowns out the sense of a book dedicated to something far greater than a chronically forgetful and self-destructive human race. Nonetheless, that recent destruction was ringing in Europe's ears. The unprecedented experience of modern warfare provided a more general focal point for varied literary and philosophical, utopian and dystopian, responses within the Weimar Republic. A febrile and fractured political and intellectual culture nurtured what Jeffrey Herf has called a 'reactionary modernism': a strain of nationalism characterized by an anti-Enlightenment and explicitly anti-democratic yearning for boundless technological advance.[11] The *Kultur–Zivilisation* dichotomy elaborated by Oswald Spengler in the two-part *Der Untergang des Abendlandes* [*Decline of the West*] (1918 and 1922) and *Der Mensch und die Technik* [*Man and Technology*] (1931), for example, developed this commonplace of German intellectual history, particularly salient since the mid-nineteenth century, into a full-scale morphology of culture. Under the influence of such intellectuals as Georg Simmel and Thomas Mann, Spengler articulated a distinction between a supposedly organic and autotelic 'culture', and a 'civilization' characterized by mechanization, individualism and a growing sense of spiritual and moral rootlessness.[12] A flinty cultural pessimism was the only thinkable stance in the face of imperialist 'world cities' beholden to the abstract and lifeless idea of money.[13] And yet, in his Faustian devotion to 'the machine', man has become the slave of technology in the figures of the entrepreneur, the engineer and the factory owner. A new 'Caesarism', through which the 'master will' is ultimately to triumph over a capitalistic 'will for plunder', must be pursued to its destined end, even in the face of destruction.[14] In *Der Arbeiter* [*The Worker*] (1932), in turn, Ernst Jünger called on 'soldier-workers' to forge a resolutely obedient yet paradoxically emancipated breed committed to a technocratic state, undergirded by the conterminous rule of 'freedom' and 'order'.[15]

In a less mandarin vein, the new democracy's climate of animosity and unrest had created a febrile context for futuristic literary fantasies among writers of both the radical Right and Left. The persistence of the notorious 'stab in the back' myth [*Dolchstoßlegende*], after 1918, marked one focal point for fantasies of the redemption of a Germany undermined by an eclectic group of internal enemies, from seditious 'red' workers to Jewish financiers, and the trappings of a decadent Western civilization more generally.[16] But the years following the First World War also saw the emergence of a market for fantastical projections of technological modernity, the most prominent of which was Thea von Harbou's *Metropolis* (1926). Fritz Lang's film version of 1927 crystallized an insidious transition from Expressionism to the illusory reconciliations of National Socialism. Socialist visions from the period, particularly in the works of authors such as Johannes R. Becher, were also shot through with hostility to the political status quo, whether expressed in terms of utopia or dystopia.[17] If the Republic's lesser science fictions were functions of social and political fears and antipathies, and predominantly the products of political extremes, then *Berge Meere und Giganten* is altogether more ambiguous. Its marginal suggestions of a less destructive way of living are the fruits of dystopian catastrophe and collapse. Nonetheless, it derived much of its contemporary allure — or its powers of repulsion — from an intensely contemporary appeal to Spenglerian cultural pessimism, as well as a broader hostility both to civilization and to its hallmark, modern technology.[18]

In the first part of *Der Untergang des Abendlandes* (1918), Spengler had developed the sublime, post-Nietzschean conceit of a technological Will to Power that is bent on conquering and overcoming an abstract and utterly unbounded nature. Western civilization's reverence of the dogma of power and energy has become symptomatic of a movement of 'eternal becoming' that is pushing Western physics 'close to the limits of its inner possibilities'.[19] This sense of transcending the limits of the thinkable is powerfully echoed, as I shall discuss below, in the catastrophic decision in the novel's twenty-seventh century to embark on the so-called Uralic War with the aim of enlivening emasculated Europeans: '[T]hey should go to the limits of the real and the possible, beyond the imaginable' ['An die Wirklichen und Möglichen sollten sie, über das Erdenkbare hinaus mußten sie fahren'] (BMG 98). The hint of the novel itself as an unbounded experiment reflects technological modernity's own Faustian experiments with the earth and its peoples.

Döblin's textual experiment expands *Tatsachenphantasie* to an unprecedented scale and extent, projecting the materials and discourses of real history into wildly imaginative fictional spaces. In his own remarks on the novel, he spoke of a lively, even properly living, writing process that became a self-sustaining movement from biological to astronomical and geological materials (SLW 50). Many of the narrative characteristics of *Wang-lun*, notably its multifaceted challenge to pretences of sovereignty, can be found here in even more vivid form. There was much enthusiasm for Döblin's new offering in some critical quarters, but his growing proclivity for experimentation was too much for others. A number of reviewers declared themselves bemused by this monster, not least the fact that it 'batters and overruns the reader with utterly outsized happenings and forms'.[20] Some took exception to the novel's sheer technocratic hermeticism. The impression that it had been written by a machine rather than a human being added, in turn, to a sense of alienation.[21] With the hindsight of almost a century, I want to suggest that this anti-humanist quality in fact works in both directions. It draws 'Döblinismus' into frightening proximity with the dehumanizing violence of Europe's early twentieth century; but conversely, it also opens up new spaces for us to think about our species' posthuman futures in the twenty-first. *Berge Meere und Giganten* speaks more urgently and relevantly than ever to our own age, disfigured as it is by the spectre of populism, a notably apocalyptic political discourse, and the existential threats of military, ecological or biological catastrophe.

I begin my chapter by revisiting Döblin's essay of 1924 on the aesthetics of modern technology, 'Der Geist des naturalistischen Zeitalters' ['The Spirit of the Naturalistic Age'], which provides us with something of a compass to help negotiate the novel's more intractable conflicts between nature and humanity. As will become evident, the new sense of modern 'spirituality' anticipated in the essay remains just as distant and badly needed as ever. Following this, I turn to the novel itself, showing how it sets in motion a 'dystopian utopia' of humankind's attempts to manipulate nature to *his* own ends. But these biopolitical attempts at conquest end up eviscerating precisely those modes of human existence that they strive to regulate and preserve. The novel traces out modern society's dialectic of progress and regression, enlightenment and mythology;[22] and it does so by showing that technocratic attempts to subdue the earth derive their power from nature itself, only to collapse back into it. As in *Wang-lun*, we once again encounter the folly of thoroughgoing attempts to build heaven on earth. The chapter then turns to suggest how Döblin's inter-discursive and porous poetics open up marginal spaces for radically reshaping our ways of thinking about nature and our relationship to it. From that perspective, I close by arguing more hopefully that the novel fruitfully recasts humanness not in terms of an essence or an identity, but in terms of its 'cyborgness'.

My understanding of the cyborg is inevitably shaped in part by the ironizing and ironized chimeras of Donna Haraway's visions: those 'theorized and fabricated hybrids of machine and organism' which, she argues, we had all inescapably become by the late twentieth century.[23] However, this postmodern cyborg, a creature straddling the borders between fiction and social reality, should be read primarily in the context of the gender politics of the late 1980s. In other words, as a consumerist yet subversive composite of 'information systems, texts, and ergonomically controlled laboring and reproducing systems',[24] it is a far cry from Döblin's more elemental imaginings. My reading here is rooted in modernist conceptions of the cyborg, and it takes a contemporary cue from N. Katherine Hayles's *How We Became Posthuman* (1999). Rather than fixating on the fashionably disembodied 'cybernetic construction' of the posthuman, Hayles redraws this slippery figure as a radically decentred, post-Nietzschean hybrid of mind and matter, the cognitive and the embodied, the human and the animal.[25] Döblin's figurations reflect and refract those entanglements. His cyborgs stray onto the contaminated terrain of dark ecology; and this constellation might help to enrich our sense of post-humanism and the posthuman. If we are to eke out better ways of existing, then we could do worse than travel with Döblin for a while.

## 'Sie sind der Korallenstock'

As I showed in Chapter 2, the starting point of Döblin's radical aesthetics was its break with the presuppositions of bourgeois humanism; and this went hand in hand with a radical challenge to any residual sense of a unitary subject. In a kind of *apologia* for his novel's effects of depersonalization and alienation, in his 'Bemerkungen zu "Berge Meere und Giganten"', Döblin claimed that the anonymous, post-industrial masses should emerge as the true protagonists of the modern epic (SLW 56). The novel is a vast intertwining of natural and human history, and in this respect it finds fruitful affinities in 'Der Geist des naturalistischen Zeitalters'. The essay's description of the machine age as 'naturalistic' is itself revealing because it motions towards an aesthetic response to its phenomena. Dismissing the distinction between culture and civilization as bespeaking a sentimental nostalgia for past ages and aesthetic forms (SÄPL 168), Döblin confronts a society and a nature transformed beyond recognition by technology, and he considers the cultural, aesthetic and ethical implications of those changes.

At the heart of Döblin's essay lies the conscious ambivalence of his own attitude towards technological progress. On one level, technology is marked by an obsessive impulse towards identification, subjugation and control. We are shown a *Zeitgeist* in which the old social function of war, as a periodic outlet for excess energy, has been replaced by technology as a form of eternal warfare (SÄPL 173). Metonymized here as the waterfalls of hydroelectric dams, nature is no longer permitted to exist 'for itself', but is invariably given over to objectification and manipulation (176): an image which brings to mind Heidegger's use of hydroelectric works on the Rhine as an illustration of 'standing reserve' ['Bestand'] in his famous essay of 1954, 'The Question Concerning Technology' ['Die Frage nach der Technik'].[26] Means and ends become interchangeable, as the rapacious accumulation of capital fuels an insatiable drive for expansion. The capitalists and industrialists of the age are obsessed above all with the exploitation of the natural world, followed by its defeat and subjugation ['Bezwingung und Unterwerfung'] (181). In a later essay of 1938, titled 'Prometheus und das Primitive' ['Prometheus and the Primitive'], he would expand on this argument to suggest that Western civilization has been overcome by a Promethean thirst for endless reinvention and progress (SPG 351). Our desire to conquer and dominate nature, however, conceals a perverse desire to restore a mythical, prelapsarian union with it (358).[27]

This desire is part of the paradox that Döblin is negotiating here. Certainly, he seems to present us with the idea, as Horkheimer and Adorno were to have it, that enlightenment amounted to a full-scale 'disenchantment' of the world.[28] The nuance to his account, though, lies in its hints of new existential possibilities for humankind in its relationship to modern technology, in short, in the suggestion of a movement beyond what he dubs the 'technical' and 'naturalistic' impulse (173). Far from simply disenchanting nature, the remorseless advance of science and technology also uncovers a new kind of mysticism: one that is grounded neither in old dreams of transcendence, nor in a kind of reactionary essentialism, but rather in an immanent sense of what is always in excess of the measurable and manipulable. In the light of the conscious affinities between Döblin's aesthetics and Fritz Mauthner's philosophy of language, he invokes the latter's 'godless mysticism' as the epitome of a new kind of natural religiosity that respects the limits of what is observable and quantifiable, but also moves beyond them. Mysticism becomes science's limit point, the mystery of non-identity and the obscurity of the unknown (SÄPL 188). If nature itself is a secret, then its physics — its measurable and quantifiable physical manifestations — are in need not just of explanation but also qualitative *interpretation* (SLW 51). This suggestion is in part a throwback to the interdependence of observation and intuition at the heart of Goethe's science,[29] but it also points forward to a phenomenological rethinking of the irreducible 'thingliness' of materiality.[30] As I will show in my discussion of his nature-philosophy, Döblin persistently censures the natural sciences for reducing their objects to quantifiable laws, relationships and compounds (cf. IN 72).

If science and natural theology are once again becoming entwined, then so too are natural and human history. Man's evolution into a 'Kollektivwesen Mensch', a 'collective human being' that represents a macrocosm of the individual, highlights the inextricability of species-being and human community from its organic and inorganic environments (SÄPL 177–79). If cities are a proverbially organic expression of man's tendency towards forms of collectivity, the spirit of the age has made the city its organ and its instrument, the site for the ever-more intertwined 'social being' ['Gesellschaftswesen'] of the urban collective. The machine age has seen the configurations of metropolitan life decisively shift, in a kind of evolutionary development akin to the path that our own lungs have taken from their hydrostatic origins in fish (178). The evolutionary adaptation of an animal's hide or antlers finds a powerful analogue in man's instincts to weave clothes and to fashion tools and weapons. Just as human physiology and anatomy reveal themselves in their innately technological structures, their *techne*, so human technology is merely the product of a functional, yet at the same time metaphorical, advance on its natural forebears (UD 103, 171). In a form of distributed cognition *avant la lettre*, he describes how human habitations themselves remain separate from their inhabitants' bodies, but integral to their species-being. The hides, antlers and behavioural habits of animals enrich their coexistence with their environments; and yet so too do huts, weapons and clothes enrich our coexistence with ours. No longer mere appendages, these are prostheses, 'the extended man' ['der erweiterte Mensch'] (SÄPL 180). Döblin is drawing here upon a modernist fascination with prosthetic forms and figures, not least in respect of the deep structural analogues and resonances between the biological and the technological:[31] we are always already natural cyborgs, and that cyborgness is becoming ever more salient and pronounced in our naturalistic age. Our task is to work out its anthropological and ethical ramifications.

But what exactly are they? Döblin suggests that modern Europe remains incapable of realizing them, caught as it is in a spiritual and cultural time lag. He argues that the 'technological' is simply an incipient symptom of something hidden, and a cultural and spiritual potential that has yet to be revealed. After a century of paradigm-shifting advances in the physical sciences, 'nature' is paradoxically revealing itself as a mystery which this age must learn to grasp in new vocabularies (SÄPL 183, 190). However, the naturalistic age is marked by a deep incongruity between its cutting-edge technological practices and a sense of 'spirituality' ['Geistigkeit'] that remains rooted in earlier eras: we have yet to discover, or develop, a form of spirituality that might make sense of, let alone do justice to, the massively accelerated drives of modern technology (187). On the one hand, this drive is inherently imperialistic, erasing as it does natural, cultural and national boundaries (in another play with the essay's recurrent trope of 'Grenzen'); but on the other, a modern technical imperialism intensifies under the malignancy of ethnic nationalism, a slightly ironic observation as we consider that the example Döblin reaches for — in the mid-1920s — is not a European one, but the Ku Klux Klan (SÄPL 182, 188).

In short, we live in a 'confusion' of different eras, world-views and paradigms, with significant segments (in a strikingly organic metaphor) 'not fully cooked through, poorly baked' ['undurchgoren, schlecht gebacken'] (187); and it is striking that in his famous essay of 1935, 'Das Kunstwerk im Zeitalter seiner technischen Reproduzierbarkeit' ['The Work of Art in the Age of Mechanical Reproducibility'], Benjamin would associate the bellicosity of imperialism in the modern era with the fact that 'society had not sufficiently matured to make technology its organ' ['die Gesellschaft [war] nicht reif genug [...], sich die Technik zu ihrem Organ zu machen'].[32] As both thinkers argue in organic terms, technological modernity must first grow into its own prostheses. Döblin rounds off and simultaneously opens up 'Der Geist' with a nod to the Renaissance-era astronomer Nicolaus Copernicus, whose work initiated the paradigm shift of the so-called Copernican Revolution. We are still grappling with the spiritual ramifications of heliocentrism in the place (it is implied) of monotheism, and our troubled relationship with technology is simply one symptom of that struggle.

While it of course has yet to materialize, a distinctly utopian vision of human coexistence is beginning to emerge in 'Der Geist'. An inherently collective form of urban modernity combines with a sense of its near-identity with the patterns and forms of nature: we have to reckon with a new sense of our own species-being, to borrow a term from Marx. Döblin's description of techno-metropolises as the 'coral colony for man's collective being' ['Korallenstock für das Kollektivwesen Mensch'] is the most arresting visualization of this ideal (SÄPL 180), and alongside images of termite mounds and honeycombs (178), it is an image that will spring into life in *Berlin Alexanderplatz*, where the life of the city is refracted through that of the individual, and vice versa. Coral, in particular, evokes an intermixing of different, even conflicting, ages, cultures and customs in modernity (187). These metaphors of natural collectivity both reveal, and are themselves the product of, deep structural and systemic affinities between the natural world, human technology and metropolitan modernity; and with this, they suggest the incipient emergence of a posthuman vision. 'Humanismus' in Döblin's specific context primarily refers to the persistence of Renaissance humanism, with its ideology of universalism (172). However, it is also associated here with art forms which, preoccupied as they are with their Romantic and Biedermeier subject matters, are manifestly failing to do justice to modernity (185). Döblin acknowledges the non-representational anti-naturalism, even the 'non-naturalism' ['Anaturalismus'], of both Futurism and constructivism (187). Closing out a lyrical tour, early on in the essay, of the products of mass manufacture, he makes the provocative suggestion that the electric dynamo ['Dynamomaschine'] can compete with Cologne Cathedral, and that pioneering processes of glucose synthesis — to take two examples from an exuberant list — can hold their own with any of the great humanistic achievements of art and culture (174–76).

Quite apart from being a characteristic bit of coat trailing on Döblin's part, this also suggests a way of reframing aesthetics that might bring *poiesis* into proximity with *techne* and *physis*, in a new entwining of art, technology and the natural world.[33] Nonetheless, what is central to Döblin's attempt to deconstruct the culture–civilization antithesis is the recognition of 'Kultur' itself not simply as a figuratively organic phenomenon, but rather as a self-cognizing and evolving entity with its own particular cerebral networks and organ systems, both metaphoric and uncannily literal (172). As I shall discuss in more detail in the next chapter, Döblin would further flesh out the deep structural similarities and identities between the organic and the inorganic, and the social and the cultural, with the help of the electro-magnetic and musical metaphor of 'Resonanz' in *Unser Dasein* (UD 168–71); but his projection here is of a form of technology — and by metonymic extension civilization — that might be harmonized with a nature both external and internal, without and within.

Perhaps unsurprisingly, this yields some rather striking political idealism: the suggestion that the world is constructing a 'huge collective entity' ['ein Gesellschaftswesen'] as nation-states are hollowed out (SÄPL 190) evokes a naïve vision of something akin to globalization. Likewise, the prediction that patriarchy will atrophy in the face of an increased female presence in the industrial workforce after the First World War overlaps with the premature gender-political suggestion that the difference between men and women is steadily disappearing (184). However, Döblin's essay does not shy away from the ethical engagement of an incipient attempt to sketch out a new meaning, even a new kind of spirituality, for a world that is dramatically losing its political, social and ethical contours. *Berge Meere und Giganten* is the projection, by contrast, of a world that loses them with nothing to take their place.

## *Menschenmassen*

The breathless narrative takes no prisoners, often quite literally. We are plunged into the thick of things from the outset with an account of a neo-colonialist export of technology from Europe and America to Asia and Africa. The Great War has passed into oblivion, while generations of humans and animals have come and gone (BMG 13). What the novel confronts its readers with from the outset, then, is their severance as historical contemporaries and descendants from a radically different kind of narrative context. Against that backdrop, Döblin's mediation of sober historical report through mythology has the effect of blurring genre boundaries between history and myth, linearity and cyclicality, and metonymy and allegory.

Indeed, the blurring of boundaries reflects a world of ever more outlandish projects of conquest, both of the natural world and of other human beings. The novel as a whole, stretching over 630 pages, is divided into nine books, and tracks the fates of an immense turnover of characters from an indeterminate point in the twentieth century through to the twenty-seventh. The first four books, which will be the focus in this section, focus on the perennial conflict between sprawling European and American city-states ['Stadtschaften']. The urban centres of Berlin, Paris, Brussels, London and New York have seen national and cultural differences dissolve within them; but this has been accompanied by the consolidation of oligarchical and technocratic power in the hands of a small number of ruling families. Books 1 and 2 chronicle in detail the city states' technological attempts to meet the challenges of large-scale social and demographic change, including overpopulation, followed by declining birth dates and mass immigration from Africa. The lethargy of urban populations, induced by mass consumerism, inspires a radically destructive response in the form of all-out warfare between the European and Asian continents.

At the start of the third book, Marke, Consul of Berlin, presides over a period of de-urbanization in the wake of this devastation, forcing his citizens onto the land. His reign is followed by the rise to power of the ambitious scientist Marduk, who brutally exploits his own biotechnical expertise to consolidate his consulship, before being usurped by an equally brutal Congolese rival, Zimbo. Meanwhile, a trickle of anti-technological and anti-civilizational sentiment has swelled into an urban exodus that now threatens the functioning and order of the city-states, particularly in the form of the radically egalitarian 'settlers' ['Siedler'] in Book 5. In London, it is decided that Greenland must be colonized in part to channel this subversive overspill; and the extraordinary account of the engineered rupture of Iceland's volcanoes, and the use of the energy to melt the Greenland icecap, provides the violent forward thrusts of 6 and 7.

Döblin himself conceived this as the recapitulation of the Uralic War, this time on a planetary scale, as he remarked in his own commentary (SLW 57). The reconstitution of dinosaur- and dragon-like monsters, antediluvian remnants resuscitated in the deluge, embodies nature's mythic revenge for this grand plan. The monsters make for Europe, where the response of the city senates is to bio-engineer the eponymous defensive 'giants', while relocating their citizens underground. These giants are huge, tower-like composites of human, animal and vegetable matter; but power-hungry technocrats are themselves prompted to apply these growth technologies to themselves in a bid to transform themselves into huge human–animal hybrids. Havoc is again wreaked; but the final book sees a precarious alliance begin to develop between the traumatized survivors of the Greenland exhibition, under their leader Kylin, and a reinvigorated group of settlers led by the mysterious (albeit slightly sinister) Venaska. If not quite as literally as in *Wang-lun*, Döblin's epic ends with a question mark over its own utopian possibilities.

Underlying this epic plot is the drumbeat of history's repetition, or at least its loud echoing across generations; and this feature of Döblin's imagined twentieth century strikes us almost immediately from the outset of Book 1. As the Western peoples unthinkingly bequeath their futuristic, beguilingly under-described and underdetermined technologies to their descendants (13–14), we can trace a pattern of unreflective inevitability: a mythic circularity centred upon each emerging generation's calculation and subjugation of natural forces. We hear echoes of the hopeless circularity of the Book of Ecclesiastes as the narrator recounts that 'generation upon generation' ['Geschlecht um Geschlecht'] had followed one another into the grave (13).[34] There is a dialectical dynamic at work here: while Döblin celebrates an immanent and non-theistic mysticism as continuous with a modern and technological mode of being, the flip-side of this is what Horkheimer and Adorno in *Dialektik der Aufklärung* call a principle of technocratic 'immanence'.[35] This concept embodies the fusion of myth and enlightenment, and the tendency of both to want to identify everything that comes under their sway. Central to this argument is a sense of 'enlightenment' not as an historical epoch, but rather what Simon Jarvis calls a series of 'intellectual and practical operations' that disenchant, categorize and control the world.[36] But the dialectical aspect of the argument is that the cyclical processes of myth always become enlightenment, just as enlightenment in its turn reverts to the ever-same cycles of mythology. The mythical identification and explanation of everything as a repetition feeds directly into a categorization and control of nature.[37]

Without divulging the details, the narrator tells us that machines of terrible capabilities have been developed, and the people are compulsively beholden to them. Ominously enough, these are black boxes, characterized in one of Döblin's trademark strange concretizations as 'effervescent with power' ['sprühend an Vermögen']: we are confronted with magical entities that escape the control of their inventors to become the very 'will that flew before them' ['Wille, der vor ihnen flog'] (14). What Döblin wants to portray, in critical affinity with Spengler,[38] is the utter collapse of dualities, as instrumental rationality and mythology enter the same spaces, means metastasize into ends, and technology alloys itself with a form of animistic magic.

For all its sense of alienation, though, the narrative repeatedly evokes the grotesque distortion of natural human impulses through technology, not least in the eroticized description of industrial colonialization in the West's export of machines to Africa, China and Japan. The machine lovers from the Western city-states are compelled to parade, then sell off, their steel 'beloveds' ['Geliebte'] (14). We catch a whiff of the interplay of violence and sexuality that is latent in Adorno's sense of man's compulsive investment in cycles of technologization. His recasting of the world as nothing more than one 'gigantic analytic judgment' ['gigantisches analytisches Urteil'] represents enlightenment's thoroughgoing (mythical) subjugation of both nature and humanity to a rigid schema of category and function. It suggests not a fundamental abstraction from nature, but rather our ever deeper entwining in the 'mechanism of coercion' ['Zwangsmechanismus'], of our formulae, our machines and our technologies.[39] Human labour leads us away from myth in a bid to escape the dominion of nature, only to fall repeatedly under myth's spell.[40] This dialectical reverse marks out the inextricability of nature and human history, and it illuminates the decisive collapse of humanistic conceptions of individual and society: the mythical, dehumanizing quality of Döblin's prose speaks to a reshaping of the human collectivity as so much raw material.

If technocracy fails to give a definitive answer to anything, so too does populist democracy. Attempts to restrict public access to science and technology simply give rise to riots in the late twenty-fourth century, calling for the abolition of all advanced technology. But this in turn gives way to a movement of quasi-religious worship of machines led by a self-appointed prophetess who declares that we human beings must 'break open the stars! Break open the sun!' ['[d]ie Sterne aufbrechen! Die Sonne aufbrechen!'] (67–70). There is an interchange here between man and machine, as the anthropomorphism of technology is accompanied by man's reduction to mechanism; and the crossover is complete in the suggestion that the droning and the rattling of the machines itself became sexually arousing. In a violent inversion, man's dream of subjugating nature is inverted in a series of propitiatory sacrifices to the machines (69–70). This machine–human hybridization draws upon a radical cyborgness, an aesthetic interplay of nature and artifice, which speaks to the blurred distinction between metonymy and metaphor at the heart of Döblin's stripped-down prose. It rests on the marginal gap between prosaic identification and the uncannily unidentified, and (here) between biology and technology. A woman hurls herself into one of the machines, to the horror of onlookers:

> Keinen Augenblick änderte die Maschine ihren Lauf, herrisch dröhnte sie in ihrer steinenern Umfassung. Sie wühlte in ihrem Bett, schlang den Frauenleib, salbte sich mit seinem gießenden hellroten Blut. Riesig überschmetterte sie Kreischen und Schreckensstille der Menschen. Ein Mann auf der Umfassung, klein geduckt, Gesicht, das nicht zeigte ob es lächelte oder weinte. "Hin ist hin. Was ist ein Leib für eine Maschine. Wieviel muß eine Maschine fressen, um ein Mensch zu sein." (BMG 70–71)
>
> [The machine didn't grind to a halt for even a moment, it droned on imperiously in its stone casing. It scrabbled around in its bed, swallowed the female body whole, anointed itself with the spurting, bright red blood. It thunderously drowned out both the shrieks and the stunned silence of the humans. A man up on the side of the casing, crouched low, his face not showing whether it [sic] was smiling or crying. 'What's gone is gone. What's a body to a machine. How much must a machine eat to be a man.']

The splatter of this scene, with its characterization of 'the machine' as a ravenous monster, shows a three-way collapse of man, technology and nature, culminating in the chiasmus of one of Döblin's characteristically strange non sequiturs: a questioning of identities and essences in the vanishing spaces between metal and flesh. 'Anointed' hints at the machines' virtually consecrated status, which acquires a further irony as it spits out its swallowed bodies, before gobbling them up as they roll back in (71). It 'purred, as if it was rubbing itself, and seemed to hesitate for a moment' ['schnurrte [...], als wenn sie sich innerlich riebe und zögerte']; and in the near-chiastic description of how it then 'thunderblared and ironraged on' ['*donner*schmetterte eisen*toste* weiter' (my emphasis)], the hybridization of nature, machine and man is brought down into the neologistic fabric of a language that itself becomes a kind of cyborg. The anti-psychological thrust of the 'Berliner Programm' here intensifies into an assault upon human essentialisms, and humanism itself.

I am dwelling upon the novel's early sections because of their attempts to describe and circumscribe what we humans actually *are*, attempts that repeatedly meet with violence, followed by the deafening absence of an answer. A new sense of what it might now mean to be human only begins to emerge, as we shall see, in the novel's final pages. But in the cyclical centuries before then, countless bodies both individual and politic act out an intimate link between identification, objectification and dehumanization; and they also foreground what Michel Foucault would recognize as the pathetic transience of modern 'man' in the final part of *The Order of Things* (1966). He dates 'man's' coming-into-being to the end of the eighteenth century, and identifies the Kantian emergence of an 'empirico-transcendental doublet' as delineating a being 'such that knowledge will be attained in him of what renders all knowledge possible'.[41] But in the face of the ever-growing salience of what he calls the 'unthought', that alien and irrational remainder, after Schopenhauer's Will, which can never quite be symbolized, Foucault warns of man's discursive disappearance from history like 'a face drawn in the sand at the edge of the sea'.[42] And it is in that light that Döblin's narrative enacts the sheer vulnerability of the human being as a transcendental, reflexive entity, and its susceptibility to manipulation and biotechnical change.

As if on cue, the sinister 'doctrine of water and storm' ['Wasser- und Sturmlehre'] emerges in the middle of the twenty-fifth century. The aim is to eliminate individuality, to stop history, and to flatten out humanity's painful splitting over against nature in a bid to restabilize society (BMG 77). By the following century, this has fed into the logic of artificial foodstuff-manufacture in the *Mekifabriken*, a generation of food synthesis factories so called after their inventor. Despite their separation in scores of years, these innovations are eerily similar: in an echo of history that we hear throughout the novel, one is the symptom of a rejection of technological mastery for the sake of rejoining nature, while the other amounts to a technocratic mastery of human physiologies. In both cases, our species-being is reduced to something that is rigidly identified and controlled.

In *Das Leben des Menschen* [*The Life of Man*], a book that shaped Döblin's figuration of the deep affinities between biological forms and human technology, the doctor and popular science writer Fritz Kahn pointed to a 'natural order of things' [*Naturgeschehen*] which 'follows mathematical laws and takes mechanical forms' ['sich nach Gesetzen, die wir mathematisch, und in Formen, die wir mechanisch nennen, vollzieht'].[43] The doctrine of water and storm embodies the Meki scientists' reduction of nature to a schema of calculation, and therefore manipulation. But it also reflects the text's more general dissolution of the difference and distance between humankind, animal and machine, an equation that also found highly influential expression in Franz Reuleaux's kinematic definitions of human physiology in terms of machine technology in his *Lehrbuch der Kinematik* [*Textbook of Kinematics*] of 1875.[44] In a dystopian extension of the 'homogeneity' of the human collective discussed in 'Der Geist des naturalistischen Zeitalters' (SÄPL 190), the engineers Surrer from Edinburgh and Sörrensen from Norway aim to bio-engineer their cities to imitate both the purposiveness and the machine-like patterns of cooperation to be found in animal communities (BMG 76–77). This is the markedly biopolitical idea that it is in the masses' interests to give up an individual form of life that has never been fully realized, and so is implicitly unworthy of life: what is left behind is a vegetative 'steady state', a 'gleichmäßigen Dauerzustand', with strong echoes, as Wolfgang Schäffner has suggested, of Ludwig Boltzmann's thermodynamics (77).[45] In short, the fabric of Döblin's poetology of knowledge vibrates with the merging, if also distinct, sounds of very different scientific disciplines and discourses. The use of such adverbs as 'vegetativ' feeds into a broader continuity in Döblin's thinking between plant, animal and human life: a set of associations which, as we shall see in his figurative use of 'resonance', collapses, or at the very least blurs, the distinction between man and nature, as well as between metonymy and metaphor.

Human existence is marked by both continuity and discontinuity with a nature whose animal, vegetable and mineral elements continue to resonate within us (UD 168). The paradox of stopping history itself in order to safeguard the future of the species speaks to a disdain for the individual life as an incommensurable waste product. This 'levelling out to the point of a human mass' ['Einebnung zur Menschenmasse'] amounts chillingly to an extirpation of all aspects of incommensurability, suffering and shame, which we have come to associate with the murderous development of eugenic discourse in the 1930s and 1940s. We are told that 'a remorseless winnowing, a weeding out, came to be seen as an absolute necessity' ['[e]rbarmungsloses Sichten und Ausscheiden wurde als selbstverständlich angesehen']. The weakest members of society are systematically neglected, and all remaining inherited 'human feeling' ['Humanitätsgefühl'] begins to fade away (BMG 78).

For all these attempts to make humankind history-less, there are strong historical resonances here with contemporary eugenic movements within Weimar culture. The emergence of aggressively eugenicist 'women's associations', for example, aims at doing away with the family itself, turning childbirth into a weapon against the patriarchy and, with Spartan harshness, exterminating children of unknown provenance.[46] The portrayal of synthetic food manufacture echoes the distribution of food substitutes during the Great War, and there are here — in the face of Döblin's own critiques in 1914 of an insufficient understanding of the biochemistry even of natural nutrition (KS 1, 170) — further echoes of Kahn's own celebrations of the inevitable future manufacture of artificial foodstuffs.[47] In a near-mirror image of *Wang-lun*, novels set in the future 'tend to be really about the present', as is evident here in the traces of the Western Front in the ravages of the Uralic War.[48] Döblin's portrait of a dehumanized future in the terms of a biopolitical present is part of a broader contemporary science-fiction discourse around the relationship between eugenics and political control. Aldous Huxley's *Brave New World* (1932) shows a population subjected to a regime that dehumanizes more humanely. The novel opens with a briskly satirical tour through the Central London Hatchery and Conditioning Centre, where the messy inefficiency of viviparity has been replaced with the Fordist mass-insemination and bottling of embryos. While the elite Alphas and Betas are the direct products of this process, the fertilized eggs of the lower classes are subject to irradiation and multiplication through 'Bokanovsky's Process'. The 'Social Predestination' room, with its ironically neo-Calvinistic suggestion of a new theology, links collectivity, happiness and historylessness, as the members of each social class are indoctrinated to identify with their own kind. 'History is bunk', one of 'Our Ford's' sayings, is the slogan under which the Centre Controller 'whisks' away the remnants of a shared cultural past.[49] The question of security remains a common denominator in both Döblin's and Huxley's works. In view of the dangers of both independent thought and an independent communion with nature, we read that a gaggle of Delta babies are being conditioned to be 'safe from books and botany all their lives',[50] just as a soldier within the 'Menschenmasse' should be fully satisfied in his service, and socially useless (and therefore dangerous) as soon as he leaves his rank and file (BMG 77).[51] Khien-lung's fear of the Truly Powerless, on account of their resistance to instrumentation, finds its futuristic echo here.

The *Mekifabriken* are a product of a particularly fierce ardour for technological progress and, with this, a separation from nature itself. Just as epidemics used to devastate human populations, so now a surge of new inventions precipitates the relentless establishment, then abandonment, of new factories, facilities and cities, followed by mass unemployment (BMG 80). And this Cockaigne of material plenty finds its political correlate in ever finer-grained forms of population control (81–83). Biopower seeps into the smallest recesses, as the synthesis of artificial nutrition exploits what Döblin would later explicitly recognize as the existence of infinitely small 'building blocks' in nature far beneath the threshold of the visible (UD 125; IN 73, 79). The fractal-like limitlessness of nature's building blocks finds its counterpart in a limitless technological push 'right down into the material [...], right down into the elements' ['auf die Mutterstoffe [...], ins Elementare'], as the later drive to bio-engineer the eponymous giants is described. A peculiarly philosophical word for *materia*, 'Mutterstoff' aligns with a traditionally gendered characterization of nature as female, and it also exemplifies the markedly Germanic nature of Döblin's word choice throughout the novel (BMG 537). In contrast to Latin (and ancient Greek) derivations of scientific terms, Döblin's choice of their Germanic equivalents arguably maintains a tension between the classificatory drive of the natural sciences on the one hand, and the recalcitrant materiality of its objects on the other. Nonetheless, their reduction to yet another self-sustaining analytic judgment finds another twisted allegory in the scientists' ironic celebration at having ended man's dependence on the elements. Harvested organs and brains are doused in nutritional fluids, alongside the biopsied bodies of the laboratory's purple-clad experimental subjects who every now and then issue hymn-like moans from their glass coffins. The imitation of these biological processes leads to ever less of a reliance on the animal and plant matter growing in the neighbouring rooms, themselves entwined in a chaos of wires and pipes (84–88).

Döblin's antiseptic aesthetic of glass and rubber, the silence, the protective face-masks, and the rubber soles of the green-clad laboratory workers, resonate with the 'pale, corpse-coloured rubber' and the wintriness responding 'to wintriness' in the tropical heat of Huxley's incubation room:[52] a German case of 'techno-primitivism', as David Trotter has recently termed British modernism's fetishistic fascination with new materials that were straddling a rapidly developing divide between the natural and the synthetic from the 1920s onwards.[53] Forms of surveillance and control compound each other. The panoptical qualities of light are reflected in 'the dazzlingly lit, white-tiled observation halls' ['die blendend erleuchteten weißgekachelten Beobachtungshallen'] (87), a synonymity of illumination and control which speaks to George Orwell's description of the Ministry of Love in *Nineteen Eighty-Four* as a windowless and timeless place of white porcelain bricks where, as Orwell has it in an inversion of divine truth, 'the lights would never be turned out'.[54] The city-states move underground in the twenty-seventh century in a bid to protect their peoples against Greenland's ante- and postdiluvian monsters. The darkness of the excavated tunnels is overcome by a plasma-like material that clings viscously to bodies and clothes as it illuminates lion and bullfights, the bread and circuses designed to keep the people grotesquely entertained and in order (526–27). These tropes of literal enlightenment and penetration, with their dissected brains and entrails, and metastasizing wires and pipes, embody the narrative's own experimental reshaping of its human masses; but the shadow-side of this, of course, is humanity's evisceration as a form of existence distinguished by any of the old markers of human dignity (86).[55] In short, 'the human' is articulated not in terms of a definable and universal essence, but rather a raw material continuously modelled and remodelled to fit ever-changing moulds. As Döblin perspicuously comments of the technological age in 'Der Geist', man is being more intensively 'worked on' than ever before (SÄPL 189).

The biopolitical resonances here could hardly be stronger. In *Society Must Be Defended*, one of his fullest statements on biopolitics, Foucault would suggest that the late nineteenth century was marked by the ever-tighter intertwining of politics and biology. He describes biopolitical sovereignty as 'the acquisition of power over man insofar as man is a living being', its final frontier becoming a total control over a population that has been comprehensively rethought as a biological problem. Central to this idea is the state-sanctioned effacement of incommensurability through 'regulatory' strategies, focused on the collective body reconceived as a circulation of 'general biological processes'.[56] Döblin's pulsating theme is a desire to eliminate all traces of an incommensurable natural world. Squeezing out nature's residue amounts to the elimination of time, history and collective memory.

On this reading, the Uralic War is the *ne plus ultra* of biopolitics, waged in a bid to galvanize fattened and lethargic populations after a glut of consumerism. The scenes of annihilation — with the use of weaponized walls of flame on both sides — represent the final frontier of sovereignty:[57]

> Feuer Rauch, den Horizont abschließend, keine Lücke lassend, die rollende Mauer. [...]
> Hochgeschleudert unter Donnerschlag rauchte blutflammte die Erde, verzehrte sich geifernd in die Luft, aufgehoben in einem wirbelnden puffenden Qualm [...] Flamme neben Flamme wie die Blockzähne der großen Egge, über Wiesen Ackerboden, zwischen Dörfern Landstraßen, vom Toten Meer zum Ladogasee Cherson Poltawa Mohilew Pskow Waldai. Den gleichen wolkenbezogenen Himmel angrellend Tag und Nacht, ihn rüttelnd erschütternd mit Stößen zu Donner und Widerdonner. Menschen Häuser Steine Hügel Tiere Wälder restlos zerklafternd aufhebend hochwerfend verschüttend, Flußtäler zerreißend ausfüllend. (BMG 108–09)

> [Fire, smoke, closing off the horizon, leaving no gap, the rolling wall. [...] Hurled up with a thunderclap, the earth smoked, blood-flamed, salivated and consumed itself in the air, shooting up in a burst of swirling puffing smoke. [...] Flame upon flame like the teeth of a huge harrow, sweeping across meadows, crops, between villages, country roads, from the Dead Sea to Lake Ladoga, to Kherson, Poltava, Mahilyow, Pskov, Valday. Screaming at the same clouded sky day and night, shaking and jolting it with thunderclap after thunderclap. Remorselessly pulling apart, hurling up, filling in the gaps between humans, houses, stones, hills, animals, forests, tearing apart and filling up river valleys.]

Through a trademark lack of punctuation and piling up of nouns, passages like this bring the human, the biological and the technological into a destructive relationship of near-identity with each other. Elemental weapons shoot forth explosives, gases, and minerals with the aim of leaving nothing unincorporated, undestroyed, unburied, unfilled. The upshot of these pages, an echo of the horrors of the Western Front, is a frighteningly prescient scorched-earth campaign conducted by both the Westerners and the 'Asians', which launches on waves of widespread popular support. We glimpse flashes of anthropomorphic agency, a hint of nature's retaliation in the midst of these attempts to weaponize it. That element-mixing hybridization of 'rauchte blutflammte die Erde' speaks to Döblin's ontology of endless change and movement (IN 22–27), but in another discursive mishmash, it also suggests Presocratic traces of the fundamental elements of air, water, earth and fire. Such images as that of 'volatalizing earth' ['vergasende Erde'] testify to a natural world both coming spectacularly undone and returning to its elemental constellations (BMG 109–10).[58] For all this flattening and annihilation, though, it is in the glimpses of non-human agency that we might find the hints of something different.

What this description illustrates, I suggest, is the way in which Döblin's prose critiques the violence it portrays by enacting it. The dynamics of mimesis are pushed to their extremes in a spirit of violent imitation. Because it cannot credibly take up a position of resistance in a gap-less totality of ideological and physical violence, art is forced to critique that violence by mimicking it, thus in some sense defusing it. Sure enough, there is an aggressive poetic relish to these descriptions. Döblin's narrative textures modulate between hermeticism and porousness, closedness and openness: between all-flattening violence, and an excess (and excessive) materiality that refuses to be flattened. The sheer semantic disjointedness, and visceral panic, in Döblin's account of the Uralic War also points to the collapse of meaningful narrative itself in the face of events and experiences so far beyond, or beneath, the bounds of meaningful 'telling'. To return, too, to Benjamin's sense of history as the growing rubble of the ever-same, the prospect of developing narrative meaning has disappeared under the — literally shocking — psychical conditions of modernity.[59] But amidst this dehumanization, I suggest, we can find remainders of humanness; and it is here that we might at least begin to find our way out of the narrative's closed circuits of biopolitics. A much later torture scene involves a group of captured rebels who had been arrayed against the tyrannical Consul Marduk, years after the war, in a messy series of conflicts and skirmishes bent on deposing him; and it is marked by a voyeuristic narrative desire to penetrate the bodies of its portrayed victims, while obliquely remembering their suffering.

The narrator seems to revel in the shock experiences he (or it) is mimicking, while reminding us of the bloodied bodies just beneath. We read, for example, how the chains 'didn't end at the hands, feet, knees, bodies of the prisoners, but split into horsehairs, which were pulled through the tongue the arm muscles, the chest muscles' ['endeten nicht an den Händen Füßen Knien Leibern der Gefangenen, sondern gingen in Roßhaare aus, die durch die Zunge Armmuskeln Brustmuskeln gezogen waren']. It is with a perverse mix of admiration and disdain that their captors watch these bloodied, contorted bodies try desperately to worm themselves free (255). Both disgustingly intimate and strikingly clinical, this almost Sadean sequence brings the violence of Döblin's vast canvases right into the flesh and sinews of its victims. As human testaments to this disfiguring control over the natural and the human, the aesthetic of 'shock' comes most viscerally to the fore at flesh-level, in the various sparrings and strange acts of violence between the novel's individual figures. Robertson has justly suggested that the text's sporadic and scattered human relationships lack a certain human interest.[60] However, in view of the collapse of meaningful human life that Döblin wants to portray, this criticism partly misses the point. In their *Verfremdungseffekte*, these vignettes externalize mythic forces of dehumanization, and so open up new ways of thinking about the modern human being. To put it differently, it is only by taking humanity to its violent vanishing points that Döblin might disclose the marginal trace of its redemption.

We need only recall the sadistic autocrat Melise von Bordeaux, who in the twenty-third century establishes a realm that reaches from her namesake to beyond Toulouse. Her murderous masquerades as Persephone, and then Hades, 'the underworld itself', bring the text's biopolitical dynamic right down into the fabric of the *Eros–Thanatos* dialectic. Following her summary executions, in the form of an erotic, smothering embrace of her victims and a bizarre semi-absorption of their bodies, she swells up with their very 'beings' (56). Facing her victim's naked body, which mechanically and uncannily 'undulated to and fro, as if in search of a movement' ['wogte hin und her, wie auf der Suche nach einer Bewegung'], Melise's *raison d'être* — in a mythic extrapolation of Ella the dancer — is the expulsion of human flesh itself from the fields and the earth (55–56).

But what lingers here, with its echoes of Ma-noh's ill-fated reign over the Truly Powerless, is the meaninglessness of absolute sovereignty: a radical emptiness mirrored in the blackness of the window, centuries later, through which Marion Divoise jumps to her death after the shame of an orgasm in a sexual wager with the brutal Marduk, one of Melise's spiritual successors (185–86). Following an almost direct reversal of Ilsebill's cry for life in 'Der Ritter Blaubart', her very insides scream a desire to die, and she hurls herself out, her suicide speaking to a despair at being an uncontrollable human body, indeed at simply existing in the first place.

In a jarringly negative hermeneutic remnant, this scene both withholds and at the same time leaves marginally open the possibility of some kind of resolution. What remains most insistently after the collapse of Marion's wager is the terrifying sense of a human being with nowhere left to go in the vistas of what it commonly means to 'be human'. From the largest to the most intimate scales, Döblin imitates in prose a species-being that is mechanized, violated and driven repeatedly to its points of disappearance.

**The Mythic and the Primitive**

In the extraordinary decision of the Western city-states to melt the Greenland icecap, at the close of the fifth book, biopolitics finally leaps beyond even the bounds of the real and the possible. The aim of this technological project is to reclaim vast new swathes of land to which to deport the increasingly uncontrollable masses of settlers, while (once again) exciting and reinvigorating city populations which have once again grown decadent and lethargic (353–58). But in a kind of explosion of the mythic revenge we encountered above in 'Die Ermordung einer Butterblume', technology's 'Other' — the residue of nature — returns to reassert itself. In inaugurating cycles of destruction (through the Uralic War) and hypertrophic growth (in Marduk's experiments, in the super-accelerated evolution of the Greenland monsters, and the growth of the eponymous giants), biopower's sovereignty over body and population tips over into biological proliferation and destruction.

As the preface to this fateful decision, the fifth book, 'Das Auslaufen der Städte' ['The Discharge of the Cities'], with its strikingly hydraulic title, had taken as its focus a primitivist revival in the wake of the protracted guerrilla war between Marduk and his eventual usurper Zimbo. After his own biotechnical experiments, Marduk had succumbed to one of the latest elemental bio-weapons, and the narrator recounts in detail how his body gradually fails through an assailment of every nook and cranny, before literally freezing shut (279). In a counter-movement to this chaotic *quid pro quo* of skirmishes, torture scenes and murders, as well as the emasculating effects of synthetic nourishment, there is a mass movement of de-urbanization, and a new embrace of ancient superstitions under the sway of wandering shamans. An oral tradition re-emerges, and so-called 'settlers' establish communities of sexual liberation and equality.

Tellingly right at the novel's heart, the dramatized tales of the Fulbe tribe open up a subversive and contrapuntal space of cultural primitivism (309–39).[61] The story of the lion Liongo's doomed attempt to win the hand of the chieftain Mutiyamba's daughter is a thinly veiled allegory for the senates' oppression of their peoples; but the machinations of the devious stray dog, Kri, which culminate in Liongo's being tied up and eventually sacrificed, remind us of the contract of social control inherent in the mimetic forms of deception familiar to us from the tricks that Odysseus plays on the nature within both himself and his crew, in protection against the sirens.[62] This African variant on a European troubadour culture suggests yet another hybrid, but it is also totemic of the novel's movement into the mythical and the primitive, and its embrace of the in-between spaces of myth: the gaps and points of overlap between self and nature, and between the problematic discourses that Döblin uses to mark them out.

It is grimly telling, for example, that the melting of Greenland's glaciers, with the help of supercharged, pyroelectric tourmaline sheets, is characterized in terms of the gargantuan rape of (feminized) nature. We read of a 'high-pitched singing and flaming ardour of the tourmaline net' ['[h]ohes Singen des flammenbrünstigen [Turmalin]netzes'], which adds a strongly sexual flavour to this all-out assault on the icy landmass, exposing the bare rock beneath, and making everything its own and its own kind (481, 480). In this light, Nevzat Kaya has suggested that the narrative bears the misogynistic mark of a millennia-old feminization of nature, pointing in particular to broader cultural parallels between Johann Jakob Bachofen's influential exploration of the dialectics of the patriarchal and the matriarchal in *Das Mutterrecht* [*Mother-Right*] (1861), and the interplay of Apollo and Dionysus in *Die Geburt der Tragödie*.[63] Nietzsche associates the chaotic excesses of the Dionysiac with a breaking of 'the spell of individuation' and a passage 'to the Mothers of being, to the innermost core of things' ['zu den Müttern des Sein's [sic], zu dem innersten Kern der Dinge'].[64] In shaping this idiom,[65] Bachofen had identified the wild, sensual Dionysus as the ultimate women's god, bursting apart the shackles of matriarchy, destroying ordered distinctions, and dissolving life itself back into the elemental laws of matter.[66] Sure enough, in counterpoint to the rape of Greenland, the toppling of Iceland's volcanoes suggests an enormous act of castration, as jagged mountaintops are simply snapped off (384). And as if in a Dionysian soundtrack to all this, the notion of music as the 'copy' ['Abbild'] of the roiling, seething Will itself resounds in the humans' ecstatic yet terrified responses to the electrically charged tourmaline sheets as they are borne away from the remains of Iceland in their ships:[67]

> Die schrecklichen Turmaline strahlten sangen. [...] Wie viele verkamen, stürzten ab. Als jetzt die Sirenen schrien, standen sie auf den Decks über dem rollenden Meer. Es bebte trommelwirbelte schleuderte sich hinter ihren Hälsen herum, daß sie ächzten und ihre Füße weich wurden. [...] [Die Menschen] [w]inselten vor Schreck haltlos, als die Lohe am Horizont unbändig höher höher höher höher schritt. Zugleich zuckte in ihnen die Sehnsucht: Dahin!

Sehnsucht nach dem Feuer! Das Feuer Islands! Das furchtbare geliebte Land! (458–59)

[The terrible tourmalines radiated, sang. [...] How very many of them died, plummeted to their ends. When now the sirens sang, they stood on the decks above the roiling sea. From behind them came a trembling, a drumwhirling, a colossal tossing and turning, which made them groan and made their feet soft. [...] Entirely disoriented, [the humans] whimpered with fear as the glow on the horizon rose inexorably higher, higher, higher, higher. And there flickered a yearning: Onwards! Yearning for fire! Iceland's fire! The terrible beloved land!]

Very much of their time, these mythic figurations are marked far less by technological mastery than by an unbounded resistance to it, in other words by nature's life-giving and destroying *mythos*. As Döblin would put it in *Das Ich über der Natur*, this is a natural world of constant, noisy displacement, reconstitution and relocation (IN 99), sublimely indifferent to its human subjugators yet vital to their contingent existences. In a bid to encourage a progressive revaluation of the mythical in early twentieth-century German culture, David Pan has identified the marked traces of 'primitive' art and culture in Expressionism.[68] Central to this nexus of ethnology, psychology and philosophy was a fascination with supposedly pre-logical cultural forms and configurations of thinking. Wolfgang Riedel has in turn highlighted an intimate associative relationship between a mythic past, a distant utopian future, and a disenchanted present. In the face of the alienations of modernity, the lost Arcadia contained within it the suggestion of a new Elysium.[69] Integral to early twentieth-century cultural discourses of primitivism, though, was not simply a crisis of disenchantment, and the sense of a need to rethink aesthetics in the face of cultic art forms and modes of thinking,[70] but also a proliferation of ideologies surrounding questions of nature and naturalness themselves.

Obliquely in keeping with Döblin's own argument that artistic and intellectual movements in the machine age contained within them the traces of very different times and epochs (SÄPL 185), we should note that his novel, too, is stained with the racialism of artistic and literary primitivism. Long before Claude Lévi-Strauss's anthropological designations of 'la pensée sauvage' in his work of the same title in 1962, in reference to belief systems beyond the reach of Western rationality, ethnologists in the early years of the century were conceiving a phylogenetic and ontogenetic movement of evolutionary progress from the 'wild', the 'early' and the 'undeveloped', to the civilized and the developed.[71] As Nicola Gess shows, intertwined developments in ethnology, developmental psychology, and psychopathology at the *fin de siècle* fed into the paradigm of 'the primitive' as an idea with which they could explain modes of thinking and behaviour in modernity's supposedly related Others: primitive peoples, children and the mentally ill. Such pre-logical belief systems and patterns, which allowed a supposedly more immediate access to nature, were described by turns as magical, mythical or mystical. But in the decades following Edward Burnett Tylor's reintroduction of the term 'animism' into European cultural currency in his seminal work of anthropology, *Primitive Culture* (1871), they also became a site for ways of thinking about marginal forms of artistic and poetic consciousness.[72] In short, what emerged within particular streams of literary and artistic modernism was the conscious reappropriation of these ideas against the backdrop of a highly ambivalent relationship between concepts of cultural progress and regression.[73]

We certainly find this imprint in Döblin's narrative, not least in the artistic utopia of the troubadours.[74] The Fulbe put on their plays in the forests outside Western European cities, and — in an unsettling parallel with Spengler's critiques of urban deracination[75] — the decadent denizens of the Meki factories are revitalized by the 'untameable naïvety' ['unbezwingliche Naivität'] of these red and brown people (307–08). Their lustre and liveliness come uncomfortably close to cultural associations between the primitive man and the child, but an even darker shadow side becomes all too evident at several moments in the text. In the complicated build-up to Marduk's deposition and death, for example, we have read that the flow of African blood into Europe through interbreeding has brought about regression to cannibalism (233). These openly racist tropes, which Sander suggests had most likely been absorbed uncritically from the ethnographic materials,[76] leave an ugly stain, reminding us of Adorno's argument that works of art are invariably compromised and polluted by their constitutive materials and discourses. Nonetheless, there is at the same time an arguable sense in which Döblin shows figurative elements of the 'mythic' to pull against prevailing ideologies of unquestioning progress, thereby opening up spaces for thinking differently. We can recognize that undialectical appropriations of mythic thought threaten dialectically to switch over into irrational forms of instrumental rationality, and culminate in the orchestrated primitivism, the mimesis of mimesis, inherent in the violence of fascism.[77] Still, we might also salvage the residual value of myth as a dialectical site of resistance.

The aesthetic and the existential certainly enter into proximity with each other in Döblin's primitivist intimation that his narrative itself represented a kind of self-defence against an indefinable but overwhelming 'natural' Other. 'Me against my nothingness' ['Ich gegen mein Nichts'], is Döblin's encapsulation of writing itself as a form of self-preservation in the face of sublime insignificance: a desperate bid to shore some text against the ruinous recognition that 'I — am — not' ['Ich — bin — nicht'] (SLW 51). The author's elemental purpose is to write the world, but also in a sense to write against it, and the writing process itself is entwined with his or her embodied existence. The novel's opening eulogy to nature as the thing with both a thousand names and none at all (BMG 7), with its pointed sense of Romantic irony, reminds us of Faust's advocacy, in Goethe's famous garden scene, of a poetic engagement with God as the nameless all-embracer and all-sustainer ['Allumfasser' and 'Allerhalter'], who 'moves in an eternal secret | invisible, visible next to you' ['webt in ewigem Geheimnis | Unsichtbar sichtbar neben dir'].[78]

The obverse of this is that nature writing is by definition a dangerous kind of tangling up in what is alien and destructive. We hear clear echoes of the Daoist doctrine of *wu wei*, not least in the tension between the individual and nature. But Döblin infuses these influences, in turn, with a sense of mythic consciousness. In his work on myth, the second part of the seminal *Philosophie der symbolischen Formen* [*Philosophy of Symbolic Forms*], which was published a year after Döblin's novel in 1925, Ernst Cassirer explores a kind of mythic thinking that paradoxically depends on a sense of non-identity. Myth here is concerned not with objectification and identity, but rather with a sense of metaphorical affinity. In straddling the identical and the non-identical, metaphor grows out of the shape-shifting economies of myth and the mythic — but its symbolic value lies in its material continuity with the nature that it describes or, rather, discloses through the logic of *pars pro toto*.[79] Invoking the work of the philologist and orientalist Max Müller, Cassirer points to the constitutive ambiguities of metaphor as a kind of copula between human language and myth.[80] In a related vein, Döblin would argue in 'Prometheus und das Primitive' that our technological relationship with nature should be reconceived in terms of this human continuity with a nature that is full of its own kinds of meaning. Supposedly 'mystical' peoples are characterized, fancifully, by a deep-lying sense of affinity: a primal 'flame' ['Flamme'] that embodies a deep sense of kinship with the myriad named and anthropomorphized forces of nature (SPG 346, 349). As we saw in the flashing moments of affinity and recognition in *Wang-lun*, in relation to Benjamin's concept of mimesis, elements of mythic thought, far from simply being regressive, can powerfully challenge a way of thinking that rests on classification and control.

In spite of Döblin's suggestions of mythical communion, though, this speculative anthropology is not a simplistic paean to lost naturalness. Rather, it recognizes technology as both a cultural and a natural extension of who and what we are in nature. Technology is its own testament to its origins in the earth, and to its inventors' intricate bodily connections to both (SPG 348); and we might recall the primal structures of mimesis as the remembrance of the otherness of 'things', and the hope for a less coercive form of life among them.[81] In my extended closing discussion, I suggest that Döblin sees a post-catastrophic rethinking of humanity, such as it is, as lying in the uncanny and in-between spaces of affinity, rather than the essentialist spaces of identity.

## Towards Cyborg Redemption?

What distinguishes Döblin's novel from later, English-language dystopias, is its aesthetic resistance to any humanistic 'way back' from catastrophe. As *Brave New World* approaches its *dénouement*, the Savage — Huxley's ironic primitivist inversion of Shakespeare's Caliban — makes an impassioned defence to Mustapha Mond of humanness as meaningful precisely in its sense of tragedy and imbalance. The so-called World Controller's doublethink allows him to accept both this and, at the same time, the need for biopolitical 'stability'.[82] In subtle contrast, Döblin's achievement is to show how the old tenets of humanism itself might need to give way to something quite different.

By examining the text's constitutive porousness, I want to trace a path out of his closed circuits of violence into that 'different' space. The pointlessly hubristic melting of Greenland's glaciers by covering them with electrically charged sheets of tourmaline unleashes ecological catastrophe. In a modulation on the myth of Prometheus, vast tourmaline sheets transform Iceland's fire into electricity, which, in melting Greenland's ice, generates heat and light sufficient to resuscitate the remains of prehistoric creatures. In the emergence of the *Untiere* from beneath the rapidly melting icecap, we encounter a characteristic fusion of the chaotic and the mechanistic, as biology spins out of control. We are told that these monsters are creatures without biological parallel or precedent (BMG 487–88), as we can see in wild new combinations of animal, vegetable and mineral — as well as the turbo-charged evolutionary repurposing of ancient body parts. A utopian dream of human mastery has switched over into the nightmare of nature's self-sustaining reproduction.[83]

The entirely rational metastasizes into the entirely irrational, and vice versa, in an enactment of the monstrous effects of environmental abuse: the natural world's collapse into pure mechanism, beyond the bounds of human control and understanding, is allegorized in a massively accelerated process of anthropogenic evolution. Permeating these descriptions is a Dionysiac interplay of form and formlessness, growth and disintegration, but also the suggestion of a nature that has assumed a wild new agency across the exposed plains beneath the melted ice. 'In these flooded grasslands, these lively forests, there grew and died countless animals' ['In diesen wasserdurchzogenen Wiesen, lustigen Wäldern wuchsen verkamen zahllose Tiere']. A few chaotic lines later, 'forests and grasslands grew into one another, forming a single breathing entity' ['[z]u einem einzigen hauchenden Wesen wuchsen Wälder und Wiesen des Meeres ineinander'] (485): a chiasmus of terrifying configurations and wild new rhythms of growth, echoed in breathless alliteration.

The novel's accounts of melting, disintegration and recombination are characterized not by a sense of mechanistic closure, but rather by gaps and openings: those points of fracture that 'let other discourses in'.[84] The melding of the living with the dead, such that animals become the body parts of plants and vice versa, is a playful allegory of the ways in which *Tatsachenphantasie* gathers and fantastically reappropriates materials from radically different times and places. We read that 'remnants of animals, seeds, plants, splinters from a time millions of years gone, were again exposed to the light, this time a new light' ['[d]ie Tiertrümmer Samen Pflanzen, Splitter einer jahrmillionenfernen Zeit waren wieder dem Licht preisgegeben, jetzt einem anderen Licht'] (486–87). The products are

> keine Wesen, wie sie die Erde früher getragen hatte. Um bloßliegende Glieder, Köpfe Knochen Zähne Schwanzstücke Wirbel, um Farnblätter Stempelteile Wurzelstümpfe sammelten sich die Wasser die Salze Erden; oft wuchs es sich zu Geschöpfen aus, die den alten dieser Erdzeit ähnelten, oft drehten sich sonderbare Wesen, sogen an der Erde, tanzten. Das waren Köpfe Schädel, deren Kiefer Beine geworden waren, der Rachen ein Darm, die Augenlöcher Münder. Rippen rollten sich als Würmer.
> [...]
> Oft rissen sich Bäume und Tiere nicht ganz aus dem Boden, blieben drin stecken, waren ein Mittelding zwischen wuchernden Erdstoffen und lebendigen Wesen.
> Oft schleppten sie wie einen Eidotter Erdmasse mit sich fort, Beutel, ganze Säcke, an Strängen wie Nabelschnüre und fielen hin, andern zum Opfer, wenn der Dottersack leer war.

Oft fuhren Gebüsche drohend wie Arme gegeneinander, schienen sich ersticken zu wollen. Dann brachen ihre Äste bei der Berührung; sie schmolzen zusammen; gemeinsam flutete ihre Nahrung in alle; ein großes Wesen erhob sich. (BMG 487–89)

[beings of a kind the earth had never seen before. The waters, the salts, the soils coagulated around the exposed limbs, heads, bones, teeth, silversides, spines, around fern leaves, pistils, root stumps; these pieces often grew into creatures which looked like their ancestors from prehistoric ages, there gyrated many strange beings which sucked on the earth, danced. Here were heads, skulls, whose jawbones had become legs, pharynxes an intestine, the eye sockets mouths. Ribs rolled as worms.
[...]
Often trees and animals failed to tear themselves completely loose of the earth, they stayed stuck there, became a hybrid of proliferating soil matter and living organisms.
Often they dragged huge clods of earth along with them like an egg yolk, bags, whole sacs, hoisted along on ropes like umbilical cords, before falling victim to other creatures when the yolk sac was empty.
Often bushes threateningly set about each other like arms, looked like they were bent on suffocating each other. Then their branches broke off in contact with each other; they melded together, their sustenance came flooding together; a huge new being arose.]

This is a dramatic collapse of purpose and function. These incommensurate component parts are thrown together from incommensurate semantic fields: pistils and silversides jostle alongside one another. Such unprecedentedly monstrous forms are the aesthetic correlates to the absolute intertwining of the mechanisms of nature and technology. Seeming opposites collapse into one another. The attempted subjugation of what is always proximally 'other', that is, the trace of nature, switches violently into a subjection to it. Nature's proverbial fight-back reflects what Foucault identifies as a 'biopower in excess of sovereign right': an uncontrolled extension of control over nature which makes life itself metastasize and proliferate in boundless forms that cannot be reharnessed.[85] If Döblin's visions seem the product of an overcharged imagination, there is nonetheless a self-generative energy to his nature that comes disturbingly close to our contemporary reality. The effects of positive feedback triggered by global-scale ice melt depend on so many complex variables, indeed, that the exact shape of oceanic and atmospheric change remains extremely difficult to predict.[86] In that light, what is perhaps most striking about the fate of Döblin's Greenland is the way in which it embodies nature's refusal to bend to our expectations and models.

The idea of climate change reviving humankind's phylogenetic evolutionary-biological and mythic connection to its ancient reptilian ancestors is a science fiction trope that would later be developed by J. G. Ballard in his dystopia *The Drowned World* (1962).[87] Ballard's novel portrays a future London reduced to a postdiluvian primeval swamp by drastic (if natural) environmental heating as a result of solar storms. Amidst the ever more searing tropical heat, the remnants of civilization have long since relocated to its remaining outpost at Camp Byrd in the

Arctic Circle, where the climate remains tolerable. A military detail, tasked with combing a newly Triassic Europe for survivors to take north, crosses paths with the appealingly ambivalent figure of Dr Robert Kerans, who finds it increasingly difficult to resist the oneiric pull of regression into the womb of nature. Döblin's environmental collapse is of course anthropogenic. But what is notable about his deluge, in contrast to Ballard's, is the way in which it uses elements of myth to delineate an essentially alien nature, rather than drawing upon nature's alienness to flesh out uncannily familiar myths of primordial return.

The montage in this chaotic passage epitomizes a radical immeasurability and uncontrollability; but it also points to the ways in which mythic modes of description may be reappropriated to illustrate dynamics that may otherwise seem too far removed from our present reality for intuitive digestion. In a related vein to its reception of Eastern philosophies and religions (which I discussed above), Richard Sheppard has shown how readily German modernism also drew upon the philosophy of the Presocratics, particularly Heraclitus's notion of the universe as perpetual flux, which is crystallized in the flow of ever 'different waters' in the same rivers.[88] Despite the characteristic lack of biographical proof,[89] there are affinities with numerous Presocratic tropes in these two passages, including the Heraclitean idea of 'strife' as creation through antagonism and the motif of fire as vacillating between creation and destruction. These bizarre monsters remind us of Empedocles' individual body parts that come, through the elemental clash of Love and Strife, to form outlandish new beings in an ancient articulation of the process of natural selection.[90] Only the best-equipped organisms survive, as we read in an Empedoclean fragment from Claudius Aelianus's *De Natura Animalium*:

> [Der Erde] entsproßten viele Kinnbacken ohne Hälse, nackte Arme irrten hin und her sonder Schultern, und Augen allein schweiften umher der Stirnen bar. [...] [Es] wuchsen viele Geschöpfe hervor mit doppeltem Gesicht und doppelter Brust, Kuhsprößlinge mit Menschenvorderteil, andere wieder tauchten umgekehrt auf als Menschengeschöpfe mit Ochsenköpfen.[91]

> [From the earth there sprang many jaws without throats, bare arms wandered here and there without shoulders, and eyes roamed around alone without foreheads. [...] There grew forth many creatures with double faces and double chests, cow offspring with human fronts, others emerged in reverse as human-likes creatures with the heads of oxen.]

Provable connections here are less significant than the recognition that Döblin, whether consciously or not, was drawing upon and joining up a range of discourses and motifs, from doctrines of evolutionary biology through to the mythical suggestiveness of modernism. Indeed, this Presocratic sense of purposelessness anticipates features of Darwin's nineteenth-century theories of natural selection, which, as Schäffner suggests, were part and parcel of a contemporary — paradigmatic — recognition of the utterly mechanistic nature of life itself.[92] In short, destruction and creation are mythically and scientifically conterminous.

When people come into contact with the monsters' blood and mucus after their migration to Europe, they are swallowed up by their own metastasizing organs.

The cognate energy within the electrified tourmaline sheets is in turn harnessed by the technocrats of the city states in a bid to bio-engineer the colossal hybrids of humans, plants, animals and minerals, the 'tower people' [*Turmmenschen*], as Europe's first lines of defence against the monsters. Subsequently, the technocrats use these energies on their own bodies in a frenzy of futuristic alchemy and accelerated synthetic growth (BMG 536–37). Any sense of difference and distance entirely breaks down, accompanied by another telling failure to learn from history: in their destructive shape-shifting, such power-hungry city-state senators as Delvil are repeating Marduk's own experiments of artificial growth. This time, though, Greenland has yielded the quintessence of the growth-inducing power in the form of its fire (139, 515). At yet another vanishing point, human abstraction from nature now returns full-circle into undialectical identification with it. Biopower ends up eating itself.

Döblin's mishmash of the scientific and the mythic, then, reminds us that far from being an object to be located and mastered, nature is always intricately entwined with who we are. It is both the fluid and the sticky residue in the joints of our constructs and constructions, be they cultural, technological, or both. Along with our creations, we too are the products of in-between spaces. Even the appearance in the final book of the alluring demiurge Venaska, whom some call the moon goddess in a synthesis of the Goddess Diana and the Virgin Mary,[93] does not spell anything like a realizable utopia. Her influence among the newly emerging group of settlers, the so-called 'snakes', testifies to their desire to re-establish a utopia of egalitarian and heterodox sexual and social relations, along with a reconciled *modus vivendi* with nature. We are told that the snakes first 'bloomed' in the Valley of the Charente. In an ambiguous wavering between 'gentleness' and 'ardour', we learn that as these peoples cross the land, 'the wine and the herbs grew into them' ['der Wein und die Bodenwürze in sie stiegen']; and in a reconciliatory vein, their erotic impulses towards each other were deep and strong 'after their long alienation' ['nach der langen Entfremdung'] (563).

However, Venaska herself embodies a oneness with nature that marks out her alienness from her human followers. Her distinctly homoerotic sensual power reveals an utter lack of any of the corporeal shame that afflicts Döblin's humans. Like Calypso in Döblin's *Gespräche mit Kalypso*, she is a mythic site at which the distinction between death and life vanishes, and with that the meaningfulness of mortality itself. Her intoxicating effects on her lovers, the hysterical mix of 'effervescing, moaning, jangling, pleading, threatening, raging' ['Sprudeln Stöhnen Keifen Flehen Drohen Wüten'] and 'shaking, smiling, soft whispering, begging' ['Abzittern Lächeln sanftes Flüstern Betteln'], bringing this semi-divine being into the dangerous realm of the ecstatic yet destructive *mythos* of Dionysus (575). Following an epidemic of violent promiscuity centred on the wildly bisexual Tika On (577–79), as well as the recognition by Kylin, the leader of the Greenland expedition, of her disquieting non-humanness, Venaska eventually sinks back into the Earth along with the giants, her own kind (616–21). As the embodiment of Iceland's fire, she reflects the novel's problematic feminization of nature; and yet it is through that ancient discourse that she speaks to the inherent instability of any positive image of reconciliation with it.

★ ★ ★ ★ ★

Timothy Morton writes that nature is never something that unambiguously exists in essence or in substance, whether out there or in here, but rather an infinitely complex constellation of historical and discursive mechanisms. Refiguring the primitivist terms often misappropriated to invoke an ahistorical utopia of naturalness and harmony, he contends that this 'nature' might even be figured in radically historical terms as a 'shape-shifting trickster' through which '[l]ife-forms are constantly coming and going, mutating and becoming extinct'.[94] This unsettling of definitions is certainly not a recipe for apathy in the face of insignificance. By recognizing the Earth's persistent refusal to orient itself towards us, and the alarming possibility of our extinction, we might instead develop a more urgent sense of our entwinement with it.

Döblin's science fiction presciently responds to these concerns in part, I suggest, by having us think of ourselves as modern cyborgs. We are hybrids of the organic and the inorganic, the human and the non-human, and the mythic and the real, shorn of fixed borders and of any real linguistic and technological mastery over whatever, or whoever, is other than us. Returning to that strange zoogony in the passages above, we are struck by the description of trees and animals coming to constitute an indefinable 'middle thing' between the organic and the inorganic (487). The uncanny growth recalls Freud's sense of 'uncanniness' as finding its roots in ancient animist beliefs. Freud tellingly invokes *mana*[95] — that polymorphous primal energy which can be the power 'possessed by a spirit', but can also be the force of a 'non-spiritual object';[96] and with this, in turn, we recall what Cassirer describes as an animistic non-distinction of self and other, and the living and the dead (484).[97] Döblin's description of organic-inorganic forms, with its hint of Freud's uncanny 'severed limbs and feet that dance by themselves' ['[a]bgetrennte Glieder' and 'Füße, die für sich allein tanzen'],[98] slips between metaphor, simile and metonymy. The description of huge clods of earth as yolk sacs links into a grotesque mention of umbilical cords. Bushes throttle each other like flailing arms. Elsewhere, technology itself is vested with its own uncanny agency as attempts are made to create sunken islands by evaporating demarcated sections of sea off the coast of Greenland. The machines metamorphose, in their descriptions, into the herons and cranes that they resemble (463).

I suggested above that the narrative's neologisms lend its very fabric a cyborg-like quality, as if in an aesthetic correlate to the numerous techno-organic people and things that populate it. I want to argue in conclusion that it is in these individual figurations that we might unexpectedly find the hope for an escape from Benjamin's rubble of catastrophe both natural and historical. To draw things into a stretto with one final example from the novel, Iceland's volcanoes are broken open through the intense electrical heating of sandwiched quartets of gigantic metal plates:

Die Platten, aufeinander gepreßte Blätter, glühten. Das oberste geladene Blatt strahlte schmolz. Und wie sich seine Masse mit der des zweiten Blattes mischte, stieg ihre Hitze. Die brünstig ineinander brennenden ersten und zweiten rissen das starre dritte in den Brand. Knisternd spaltete sich das, tropfte seitlich und an der Bruchstelle, um plötzlich erweichend mit einem Schrei sich in das Feuer zu geben, das weiß niedrig immer bläulich durchsichtiger wurde. Und wie die pfeifenden keuchenden streng und starr sengenden saugenden sich rund rollten, bog sich das letzte Blatt, streckte sich wie in einem Krampf, schlug sich um, gezogen gespannt zu einem haarfeinen Glas, einer schillernden Haut um die singenden drei. Die Kugel wuchs hoch, weiß, blauweiß, hellblau, dehnte sich, dehnte sich. Schmelzend zersprang sie und im Augenblick war jede Farbe aus dem armhohen Brand verschwunden. War nichts da als ein strenger starrer befehlender Hauch, ein Röcheln. (BMG 380)

[The plates, sheets pressed together, glowed. When it was charged, the uppermost sheet radiated, melted. And as its liquid mass mixed with that of the second, it became hotter. The first and second sheets seared each other with a hot passion, and now dragged the rigid third sheet into the fire. The whole thing crackled and split down the middle, dripped at the sides and at the point of fracture, only to surrender suddenly to the fire with a scream, fire that turned white at its bottom, then became more blueish and ever more transparent. And as the whistling, panting, searing, sucking plants rolled each other into a sphere, the final sheet curled round, stretched out as if in a spasm, folded back on itself, pulled and stretched out to a hair-fine glass, a glittering skin around its three singing companions. The sphere swelled, rose, grew white, blue-white, dark blue, it stretched, it stretched. Melting, it exploded, and in that very moment every single colour had vanished from the fire, which was of no more than an arm's height. Everything had gone, there was nothing left apart from a stern, imperious breath, a death rattle.]

Adverbs like 'brünstig', together with such participles as 'keuchend', again suggest the rape and forced orgasm of nature: a jarring motif in the book's ongoing war between man and his world. And yet, the narrative's function here is altogether more complex than that. The narrator's role is to chronicle impossibly alien and distant events from a non-focalized 'nowhere'. But here, he (or it) intones sibilantly about the curling and writhing plates, recounting how the fourth one cloaks its companions in a gleaming skin, in a cyborg-like anthropomorphism. The sphere finally gives up the ghost with a creaturely death rattle, as does the rock that it is supposed to break open. In the repeated '[U]nd wie', and the repetition of 'dehnte sich, dehnte sich', there is an uncanny hint of subjective focalization in the midst of what seems a posthuman 'poetry of fact' devoid of 'any human perspective'.[99] A persistent narrative trace subtly recalls us to our place — however precarious — in the mesh.

In concert, these details make for a highly distinctive poetics of technology, which, as in the uncanny glittering skin that forms around the singing metal sheets, blurs and, in precisely the same motion, preserves the borders between the technological and the natural: between human prostheses and an Other that never fails to bite back. There is an exuberant linguistic hybridity in a near-onomatopoeic coming together and parting of machines and natural forms, and of language and its matter. Döblin's language itself again becomes a cyborg. What these rich textual effects suggest, I argue, is that if the idea and reality of 'the human' is to have any future at all in ever-stranger and more dangerous landscapes, it is by embracing a cyborgness rooted in interconnections, crossovers and uncanny in-betweens. In *How We Became Posthuman*, Hayles identifies post-humanism, not in terms of the virtual disembodiments and re-embodiments of cybernetics, but with the recognition that, as humans, our humanness lies caught in the unmasterable spaces between our bodies and our myriad different prostheses.[100] *Berge Meere und Giganten* is motioning towards a version of this insight, which Döblin would articulate in *Unser Dasein*. Human technology here is only one small step further on from what we already are: prosthetic extensions of natural embodiment, which in their turn 'jut back into nature itself' ['in die Natur hineinragt']. And this intertwining, Döblin argues, shows how profoundly dangerous it is simply to oppose the two (UD 103).

In Hayles's words, the human body itself emerges as a 'congealed metaphor', made up of both a 'sedimented' evolutionary history and myriad incarnate 'constraints and possibilities'.[101] What we encounter in this constellation, I argue, is a play of proximity *and* difference. Our environment is no longer to be understood as an aestheticized object, sublimely 'over there', but rather as a space teeming with things — strangers and neighbours — both unsettlingly familiar and irresistibly weird.[102] By calling for a deep recognition of this 'non-identity',[103] dark ecology resituates the idea of the posthuman at the uncanny heart of the environmental question.

Döblin's novel draws to a close with its own sense of that non-identity. The traumatized survivors from the Greenland expedition look to re-establish forms of civilization within the spaces 'in between', scattering across the Earth with the post-apocalyptic masses in a manner reminiscent of the Apostles touched by the Pentecostal flames. As Kylin admits, we either use the Promethean flame of technology with a sense of responsibility, vanishingly close to us as it is, or else we burn in it: 'I look the fire in the face. [...] I confront it head-on. [...] I either burn out or go on.' ['Ich sehe [dem Feuer] ins Gesicht. [...] Ich stelle mich ihm gegenüber. [...] Entweder ich brenne aus oder ich bleibe.'] (BMG 552–53). If the concealed spiritual kernel of technology, as Döblin argued in 'Prometheus und das Primitive', was 'to come closer to nature again' (SPG 348), the suggestion of this ever-failing reconciliation is already lurking silently in the joints of this novel. The hermeneutic remnant, that negative but hopeful trace of a literary knowledge of something different, comes insistently to the fore. In Kylin's programmatic new credo, we can even hear the echo of *Wang-lun*'s opening call not to forget. 'The fire' is obsessively interchanged with 'Greenland', and it is clear that any future society will need to be grounded in a newly responsible sense of individual and collective memory.

The novel's close duly hints at some kind of *rapprochement*, if not quite reconciliation: 'Black the ether above them, studded with little balls of sun, sparkling, bursting star clusters. Breast by breast lay the blackness with the humans. Light gleamed from them' ['Schwarz der Äther über ihnen, mit kleinen Sonnenbällen, funkelnden verschlackenden Sternhaufen. Brust an Brust lag die Schwärze mit den Menschen, Licht glomm aus ihnen'] (BMG 631). Utopia this emphatically is not. Nature, or what passes for it, remains an endless cycle of destruction and regeneration, and there is a strong chance that human history will resume its old forgetful habits and the sorry circles will redraw themselves in a slightly different orbit. Still, there is something obliquely hopeful in that mirror image of stars and man-made lights, with that strangely concretized blackness lying breast by breast with the communities that it shrouds. *Berge Meere und Giganten* pushes the dynamics of biopolitics to their extremes, as nature is reduced to the repetitive drives of technology, and technology is subsumed under an undifferentiated function of nature. For all his scepticism of linear progress and fascination with outlandish forms, though, Döblin seems finally to keep open the possibility of breaking the text's violent cycles and moving into something sustainably different. Little bodes well and the odds are almost impossibly long, but a rethought humanity might, at the very least, be quite a good idea.[104]

## Notes to Chapter 3

1. Slavoj Žižek, *In Defence of Lost Causes* (London: Verso, 2008), p. 441.
2. See Martin Heidegger, *Holzwege*, 8th edn (Frankfurt a.M.: Vittorio Klostermann, 2003), especially pp. 37–38.
3. Ibid., p. 51.
4. See Adrian E. Raftery and others, 'Less than 2 °C warming by 2100 unlikely', *Nature Climate Change*, 7 (2017), 637–41; cf. Žižek, *In Defence of Lost Causes*, pp. 435–36.
5. On the changing political discourse around climate change, see John Vidal, 'Has the politics of climate change finally reached a tipping point?', *The Guardian*, 15 May 2019, <https://www.theguardian.com/commentisfree/2019/may/15/climate-change-politics-environmental-crisis-government> [accessed 9 June 2019].
6. See Morton, *Ecology without Nature*, p. 188; cf. p. 205.
7. See Günter Grass, 'Im Wettlauf mit den Utopien', *Die Zeit*, 16 June 1978, reproduced in Grass, *Werkausgabe*, XI, 715–36.
8. See Oliver Bernhardt, *Alfred Döblin* (Munich: DTV, 2007), p. 47. For a nuanced account of Döblin's response to the outbreak of the war — in contrast to the more overtly bellicose poetry and rhetoric of the likes of Brecht and Thomas Mann — see Schoeller, pp. 137–42.
9. On the personal impact of Döblin's wartime postings, see Davies, 'Writing History', pp. 134–37.
10. Alexander Honold, 'Exotisch entgrenzte Kriegslandschaften: Alfred Döblins Weg zum "Geonarrativ": Berge Meere und Giganten', in *Literarischer Primitivismus*, ed. by Nicola Gess (Berlin: De Gruyter, 2013), pp. 211–34 (pp. 214–15).
11. See Jeffrey Herf, *Reactionary Modernism: Technology, Culture, and Politics in Weimar and the Third Reich* (Cambridge: Cambridge University Press, 1984), pp. 12–17 and 24–30.
12. See Aram Yengoyan, 'Betrachtungen über Vorstellungen von Kultur, Zivilisation, Politik und Ästhetik: Franz Boas, Georg Simmel und Thomas Mann mit besonderem Nachdruck auf ihre Verwirklichung als Geist, Weltanschauung und Völkergedanken', *Social Analysis*, 41.3 (1997), 24–41 (especially pp. 26–32).
13. Oswald Spengler, *Der Untergang des Abendlandes: Umrisse einer Morphologie der Weltgeschichte* (Munich: Beck, 1969), pp. 668–73.
14. Ibid., pp. 1190–93; see also Spengler, *Der Mensch und die Technik* (Munich: Beck, 1931), pp. 88–89.
15. Ernst Jünger, *Der Arbeiter: Herrschaft und Gesellschaft* (Stuttgart: Klett-Cotta, 1982), pp. 15–16.
16. See here Peter S. Fisher, *Fantasy and Politics: Visions of the Future in the Weimar Republic* (Madison: University of Wisconsin Press, 1991), p. 22; cf. pp. 3–16.
17. Ibid., pp. 103–07, 126–28 and 157–220.
18. See Gabriele Sander, *'An die Grenzen des Wirklichen und Möglichen': Studien zu Alfred Döblins*

*Roman* Berge Meere und Giganten (Bern: Lang, 1988), p. 11. Döblin launches an attack on the distinction between culture and civilization at the beginning of *Der Geist des naturalistischen Zeitalters* (1924) (SÄPL 168–69). He was also a fierce critic (in *Der deutsche Maskenball* [*The German Masked Ball*] of 1921, and *Wissen und Verändern!* [*To Know and to Change!*] of 1931) of the totalization of Spengler's cultural morphology, as well as the arch-conservative thinker's profound distaste for the German proletariat (WuV, especially pp. 79 and 250).

19. 'nahe an die Grenzen ihrer inneren Möglichkeiten': Spengler, *Der Untergang des Abendlandes*, especially pp. 533 and 538.
20. Volker Klotz, 'Nachwort', in Alfred Döblin, *Berge Meere und Giganten*, ed. by Klotz (Freiburg i.Br.: Walter, 1977), pp. 515–39 (p. 515).
21. See Erich Ebermayer, 'Berge, Meere und Giganten', quoted in Sander, *'An die Grenzen'*, especially pp. 11–12 (first publ. in *Leipziger Tageblatt*, 9 March 1924, p. 14); Fred Hildenbrandt, 'Döblins "Berge, Meere und Giganten"', in Schuster and Bode, pp. 138–40 (p. 138) (first publ. in *Berliner Tageblatt*, 31 May 1924).
22. Roland Dollinger sketches out, but does not develop in depth, a conceptual link with *Dialektik der Aufklärung* in 'Technology and Nature: From Döblin's *Berge Meere und Giganten* to a Philosophy of Nature', in *A Companion to the Works of Alfred Döblin*, ed. by Dollinger and others (Rochester, NY: Camden House, 2004), pp. 93–109 (pp. 99–100).
23. Donna J. Haraway, 'A Cyborg Manifesto: Science, Technology, and Socialist Feminism in the Late Twentieth Century', in Haraway, *Simians, Cyborgs and Women: The Reinvention of Nature* (London: Free Association Books, 1991), pp. 149–81 (p. 150).
24. Haraway, 'Introduction', in Haraway, *Simians, Cyborgs and Women*, pp. 1–7 (p. 1).
25. N. Katherine Hayles, *How We Became Posthuman: Virtual Bodies in Cybernetics, Literature, and Informatics* (Chicago: University of Chicago Press, 1999), p. 4.
26. Heidegger, *Gesamtausgabe*, ed. by Friedrich-Wilhelm von Herrmann, 102 vols (Frankfurt a.M.: Vittorio Klostermann, 1975–) [henceforth *GA*], VII: *Vorträge und Aufsätze*, ed. by von Herrmann, pp. 16 and 18.
27. On the pervasive (Western) cultural desire to return to this prelapsarian 'place', see Carolyn Merchant, *Reinventing Eden: The Fate of Nature in Western Culture*, 2nd edn (New York: Routledge, 2013), pp. 10–11.
28. Horkheimer and Adorno, p. 19.
29. On the centrality of observation (of 'seeing') to Goethe's science, see Nicholas Boyle, *Goethe: The Poet and the Age*, II: *Revolution and Renunciation (1790–1803)* (Oxford: Clarendon Press, 2000), pp. 599 and 677.
30. 'Interpreting' becomes central to Heidegger's distinction between ever-incomplete understanding, and objective *explaining*, as the crucial difference between hermeneutics and the natural sciences: see Martin Heidegger, *Sein und Zeit*, 19th edn (Tübingen: Niemeyer, 2006), pp. 152–53.
31. This fascination with the interplay between biology and technology came to the fore in the writing of such diverse figures as Spengler and the biologist and proto-systems theorist Jakob von Uexküll: see Spengler, *Der Mensch und die Technik*, pp. 6–13; cf. Jakob von Uexküll, *Theoretische Biologie*, 2nd edn (Berlin: Springer, 1928), especially pp. 145–76. Franz Reuleaux' pioneering two-part *Lehrbuch der Kinematik* (1875, 1900) shone light on the innate mechanicity of the human body (see Schäffner, pp. 224–28). For a cogent discussion of the intensive interplay of organic and technological forms in modernist literature, thought and popular science more generally, see also Tim Armstrong, *Modernism, Technology and the Body: A Cultural Study* (Cambridge: Cambridge University Press, 1998), especially pp. 77–105.
32. Benjamin, *GS*, 1.2, 468.
33. For the most famous analysis of the deep originary interdependence of the craft of art, technology's drive to 'make' and 'fashion', and the organic processes mirrored in both, see Heidegger, 'Die Frage nach der Technik', in Heidegger, *GA*, VII, especially pp. 25 and 29.
34. Cf. Ecclesiastes 1. 1–4.
35. Horkheimer and Adorno, *Dialektik der Aufklärung*, p. 28.
36. Jarvis, p. 24.
37. Horkheimer and Adorno, *Dialektik der Aufklärung*, especially pp. 20, 26 and 28.

38. Spengler, *Der Mensch und die Technik*, p. 75. Spengler laments here that modern technology of its nature forced its inventors and operators, as slaves of the 'machine', to follow 'in the direction of its trajectory' ['in die Richtung ihrer Bahn'].
39. Horkheimer and Adorno, *Dialektik der Aufklärung*, pp. 44 and 56.
40. Ibid., p. 49.
41. Michel Foucault, *The Order of Things: An Archaeology of the Human Sciences* (London: Routledge, 2002), p. 347.
42. Ibid., p. 422; cf. pp. 371–73 and 418–22.
43. Fritz Kahn, *Das Leben des Menschen: Eine volkstümliche Anatomie, Biologie, Physiologie und Entwicklungsgeschichte des Menschen*, 5 vols (Stuttgart: Franckh'sche Verlagshandlung, 1922–29), I, 125. At the end of his essay 'Metapsychologie und Biologie' ['Metapsychology and Biology'], in December 1922, Döblin enthused that the first volume of Kahn's bestseller, packed as it was with 'extraordinarily vivid blow-up images' ['ungewöhnlich plastische Vergrößerungen'] in its metaphors for human technicity and the natural world at large, was not simply a work of popular science, but also 'an entirely original feeling for and portrayal of this science' ['eine ganz originelle Durchfühlung und Darstellung dieses Wissens'] (KS II, 193). On Kahn's likely influence on Döblin, see Annette Ripper's strongly Foucauldian reading in her 'Überlegungen zur Aneignung des Körpers und zum Aspekt der Bio-Macht in Alfred Döblins *Berge Meere und Giganten*', *Musil-Forum*, 30 (2007), 194–220 (especially pp. 202 and 210–11).
44. See Schäffner, pp. 219 and 226–27.
45. There are recognizable discursive overlaps here with James Clerk Maxwell's statistical theories of Social Physics in the 1860s and 1870s, as well as Boltzmann's development of the field of 'statistical mechanics' from 1877 onwards: see Schäffner, pp. 308–09.
46. This draws upon a number of prominent scientific and public discourses around eugenics in Weimar culture, which included neo-Malthusian debates about population control and regulation, as well as more drastic suggestions, after the theories of Francis Galton and Alfred Ploetz, of the need to control racial hygiene right down to the level of individual cells: see Ripper, pp. 204–09.
47. See ibid., pp. 202 and 210–11; cf. Kahn, p. 110.
48. Ritchie Robertson, 'Alfred Döblin's Feeling for Snow: The Poetry of Fact in *Berge Meere und Giganten*', in *Alfred Döblin: Paradigms of Modernism*, ed. by Davies and Schonfield, pp. 215–28 (pp. 218–19).
49. Aldous Huxley, *Brave New World and Brave New World Revisited* (New York: Harper Perennial, 2005), pp. 40–41.
50. Ibid., p. 30.
51. In the British and American context, Tim Armstrong has shown how the Eugenics movement — which spearheaded the idea of state intervention into human populations in the 1920s and 1930s — enjoyed considerable acceptance from scientists and writers across the political spectrum, from George Bernard Shaw to W. B. Yeats: see Armstrong, 'Modernism, Technology, and the Life Sciences', in *The Cambridge Companion to Literature and Science*, ed. by Steven Meyer (Cambridge: Cambridge University Press, 2018), pp. 223–41 (pp. 228–35).
52. Huxley, p. 15.
53. David Trotter, *Literature in the First Media Age: Britain between the Wars* (Cambridge, MA: Harvard University Press, 2013), pp. 32–34.
54. George Orwell, *Nineteen Eighty-Four* (London: Penguin, 2000), p. 241; cf. John 1. 5–10. On Döblin's extensive metaphorics of light, see Oliver Jungen, *Döblin, die Stadt und das Licht* (Munich: Iudicium, 2001).
55. Carl Gelderloos cogently argues that Döblin's paratactic prose radically fragments the human body in these laboratory descriptions, and that the interpenetration of technology and nature 'serves as a model for the way that nature and technology are increasingly interwoven in the instrumental body throughout the novel': see Gelderloos, '"Jetzt kommt das Leben": The Technological Body in Alfred Döblin's *Berge Meere und Giganten*', *The German Quarterly*, 88.3 (2015), 291–316 (p. 297).
56. Michel Foucault, *Society Must Be Defended: Lectures at the Collège de France, 1975–76*, trans. by David Macey (London: Allen Lane, 2003), especially pp. 239 and 249.

57. We can read this particular dynamic in parallel with the perpetual wars of political control in Orwell's novel. For Foucault, the culmination of biopolitics in the twentieth century is the state's ultimate power to take life. Its conclusion is the destruction of life itself in the form of atomic warfare, as biopolitics exceeds the bounds of human sovereignty itself and tips over into self-sustaining systems of destruction: cf. *Society Must Be Defended*, pp. 253 and 257. Foucault shines a retrospective light on Döblin's vision of destruction in his analysis of Nazism as predicated on *Vernichtungskrieg*, that is, on the limitless extension of the sovereign 'right to take life' (see pp. 259–63).
58. On these 'fundamental elements', see James Warren, *Presocratics* (Stocksfield: Acumen, 2007), pp. 29–30.
59. See Benjamin, *GS*, I.2, 697. On Benjamin's distinction between *Erlebnis* and *Erfahrung* in modernity, see his essay *Über einige Motive bei Baudelaire* [*On Some Motifs in Baudelaire*], *GS*, I.2, 605–54 (especially pp. 612–18). This differentiation draws upon Freud's speculations, in *Jenseits des Lustprinzips*, on the experiential indigestibility of the shock experiences of trench warfare (see Freud, *GW*, XIII, 26–27). Embattled consciousness is unable hermeneutically to register the unprecedented shock of these stimuli as they break through the ego's figurative 'protective shield' ['Reizschutz'], and is thus unable to reorder them into personally meaningful experience.
60. Robertson, 'Alfred Döblin's Feeling for Snow', pp. 222–23.
61. Sander has shown that Döblin most likely drew his raw material from a variety of recent ethnographic sources, including the sixth edition of *Meyers Konversations-Lexikon* (1902–08), and Georg Schweinfurth's ethnographic accounts of his travels in East Central Africa, in *Im Herzen von Afrika* (4th edn, 1922). See here Sander, '"Der uralte noch immer traumverlorene Erdteil": Die Afrika-Thematik in Alfred Döblins Roman *Berge Meere und Giganten*', in *Alfred Döblin: Paradigms of Modernism*, ed. by Davies and Schonfield, pp. 229–44 (pp. 237–44).
62. For analyses of this mythic-sacrificial contract as representing the repressive origins of the 'enlightened' subject in separation from nature, see Horkheimer and Adorno, *Dialektik der Aufklärung*, pp. 76–78; see Larson Powell's reading of this part of the novel in *The Technological Unconscious in German Modernist Literature: Nature in Rilke, Benn, Brecht, and Döblin* (Rochester, NY: Camden House, 2008), p. 164. In this primitivist connection, see also René Girard's discussion, where he links this contract to the logic of sacrifice, in *Violence and the Sacred*, trans. by Patrick Gregory (London: Bloomsbury, 2013), pp. 6–7.
63. Nevzat Kaya, '"Tellurische Rationalitätskritik": Zur Weiblichkeitskonzeption in *Berge Meere und Giganten*', in *Internationales Alfred Döblin Kolloquium 1999*, ed. by Torsten Hahn (Berlin: Lang, 2002), pp. 131–40 (especially pp. 133–36).
64. Nietzsche, *KG*, III.1, 99; Nietzsche, *The Birth of Tragedy*, p. 76.
65. Nietzsche knew Bachofen well in person and his early work is littered with the traces of the anthropologist's ideas: see here Frances Nesbitt Oppel, *Nietzsche on Gender: Beyond Man and Woman* (Charlottesville: University of Virginia Press, 2005), pp. 38–39.
66. See Johann Jakob Bachofen, *Das Mutterrecht: Eine Untersuchung über die Gynaikokratie der alten Welt nach ihrer religiösen und rechtlichen Natur*, ed. by Hans-Jürgen Heinrichs (Frankfurt a.M.: Suhrkamp, 1975), pp. 39 and 40. Döblin very briefly and negatively invokes Bachofen's contribution to *völkisch* thought in an essay of 1946, titled 'Die Deutsche Utopie von 1933 und die Literatur' ['Literature and the German Utopia of 1933'] (SÄPL 380).
67. Nietzsche is celebrating Schopenhauer's eulogy of music as the art form that comes closest to capturing Will: namely, the essence of the 'thing in itself' of the world. See Nietzsche, *KG*, III.1, 100.
68. See David Pan, *Primitive Renaissance: Rethinking German Expressionism* (Lincoln, NA: University of Nebraska Press, 2001), pp. 5–6.
69. Wolfgang Riedel, *Nach der Achsendrehung: Literarische Anthropologie im 20. Jahrhundert* (Würzburg: Königshausen & Neumann, 2014), pp. 7–11.
70. Cf. Doris Kaufmann, '"Primitivismus": Zur Geschichte eines semantischen Feldes 1900–1930', in *Literarischer Primitivismus*, ed. by Gess, pp. 93–124 (pp. 94–97).
71. Riedel, *Nach der Achsendrehung*, p. 10.
72. Nicola Gess, 'Literarischer Primitivismus: Chancen und Grenzen eines Begriffs', in *Literarischer Primitivismus*, ed. by Gess, pp. 1–10 (pp. 3 and 5).

73. See Erhard Schüttpelz, 'Zur Definition des literarischen Primitivismus', in *Literarischer Primitivismus*, ed. by Gess, pp. 13–28 (especially pp. 14–15 and 24–25).
74. Sander points to the ethnographical work of Leo Frobenius, who studied the tradition of bardic singing among the Fulbe (see 'Die Afrika-Thematik', pp. 241–42).
75. See Spengler, *Der Untergang des Abendlandes*, pp. 668–73.
76. See Sander, 'Die Afrika-Thematik', especially pp. 239–40.
77. See Horkheimer and Adorno, *Dialektik der Aufklärung*, p. 209; cf. p. 25.
78. Goethe, *Werke*, III: *Faust*, 3450 (p. 110).
79. Cassirer, *Philosophie der symbolischen Formen: Zweiter Teil — Das mythische Denken*, p. 66.
80. Ibid., pp. 28–29.
81. See Horkheimer and Adorno, *Dialektik der Aufklärung*, p. 21; cf. J. M. Bernstein, *Adorno: Disenchantment and Ethics* (Cambridge: Cambridge University Press, 2001), pp. 194–95.
82. See Huxley, pp. 206–15.
83. See Foucault, *Society Must Be Defended*, p. 254. Cf. Žižek's concept of 'second nature' in the Anthropocene, through which our hubristic dream of a scientific mastery of the natural world metastasizes into a technological 'progress that would exponentially reproduce itself and go on and on autonomously': Žižek, *In Defence of Lost Causes*, p. 435.
84. Davies and Schonfield, 'Introduction', p. 6.
85. Horkheimer and Adorno, p. 210; cf. Foucault, *Society Must be Defended*, p. 254.
86. See Nicholas R. Gollidge and others, 'Global Environmental Consequences of Twenty-First-Century Ice-Sheet Melt', *Nature*, 566 (2019) 65–72 (pp. 70–71), <https://doi.org/10.1038/s41586-019-0889-9>.
87. See J. G. Ballard, *The Drowned World* (London: Fourth Estate, 2014), especially pp. 74 and 112–13.
88. 'Fragment 214', reproduced in G. S. Kirk, J. E. Raven and Malcolm Schofield, *The Presocratic Philosophers: A Critical History with a Selection of Texts*, 2nd edn (Cambridge: Cambridge University Press, 1983), pp. 194–95. On Heraclitus's aesthetic significance for literary and philosophical modernisms, see Sheppard, pp. 28, 38 and 275.
89. In the wake of numerous early references to Aeschylus and Euripides (e.g. KS I, 30, 62), Döblin's later 'Kleines Notizbuch' of 1948 associates the mythical value of ancient Greek drama with the fires of Etna into which Empedocles had legendarily thrown himself (KS IV, 370).
90. As Christina Althen has shown, Döblin's medical training in Berlin between 1900 and 1904 included lectures on Greek literature and philosophy from the resolutely anti-Nietzschean Ulrich von Wilamowitz-Moellendorff: see 'Alfred Döblins medizinische Ausbildung', pp. 27–45. If he had encountered early Greek philosophy — for example in the lecture series 'Perikles und seine Zeit', delivered by Wilamowitz-Moellendorff in the Winter Semester of 1901–02 — he would probably have been made aware of Ritter and Preller's influential collection of Pre-Socratic fragments, from 1857; and given that Hermann Diels was Professor of Classics at Berlin while Döblin was studying there, he may well have come into contact with Diels's influential three-volume collection, *Die Fragmente der Vorsokratiker*, first published in 1903. On Empedocles' articulation of an ancient form of natural selection, see Warren, p. 144.
91. See *Die Fragmente der Vorsokratiker: Griechisch und Deutsch*, ed. by Hermann Diels (Berlin: Weidmann, 1903), pp. 199–200.
92. See Warren, p. 144; cf. Schäffner, pp. 314–15; see also Kahn, p. 125. This mechanistic conception of evolution in German culture owed much to Ernst Haeckel's early championing of Darwinism in his *Generelle Morphologie der Organismen* [*General Morphology of Organisms*] (Berlin: Reimer, 1866). Despite the intriguing Presocratic affinities, Sander tellingly finds the immediate roots of these strange passages in Döblin's notes from his reading of Matthias Jakob Schleiden's *Das Meer* [*The Sea*] (1869, 3rd edn: 1888): Schleiden, too, was an early German champion of Darwin. See Sander, 'Anmerkungen', in *Berge Meere und Giganten*, ed. by Sander, pp. 687–764 (p. 752).
93. See Sander, 'Anmerkungen', p. 759.
94. Morton, *Ecology without Nature*, p. 21.
95. Freud, *GW*, XII, 253.
96. Marcel Mauss, *A General Theory of Magic*, trans. by Robert Brain (London: Routledge, 2001), p. 136.

97. Cassirer, p. 48.
98. Freud, GW, XII, 257.
99. Cf. Robertson, 'Alfred Döblin's Feeling for Snow', pp. 221, 215.
100. Hayles, pp. 2–4.
101. Ibid., p. 284.
102. See Morton, *Ecology without Nature*, pp. 119 and 187–93.
103. Ibid., pp. 185–96.
104. This is a longer and substantially revised version of my previously published article 'Monsters and Other Cyborgs: The "Posthuman" in *Berge Meere und Giganten*', in *Internationales Alfred-Döblin-Kolloquium Cambridge 2017: Natur, Technik und das (Post-)Humane in den Schriften Alfred Döblins*, ed. by Steffan Davies and David Midgley, *Jahrbuch für Internationale Germanistik*, Series A, 133 (Bern: Lang, 2019), pp. 243–59.

# CHAPTER 4

# After the Deluge: The Anthropology and Nature-Philosophy

For all our temporary contracts with nature, Döblin's science fiction leaves us with the suspicion of our own sublime insignificance. Both our sense-making and our making sense as human beings remain inextricable from nature's fundamentally alien materiality; and while our collective existences might now mean something, our meaning as individuals seems to crumble away. Kylin seems able to restore a sense of communal meaning and responsibility, and we are just about able to sustain the hope that things might be different 'next time'. However, this reaffirmation of human worth remains an oddly abstract and impersonal promise, threatening never quite to become flesh-and-blood reality.

The motif of the individual's disappearance into nature is one to which Döblin repeatedly returned throughout his career; and as we have seen, it is invariably tied up with the reality of our deep connection to that nature. There is a particularly memorable disappearance at the close of 'Die Segelfahrt', of course, but the motif also rounds off Döblin's early mock-dramatic duologue of music philosophy, *Gespräche mit Kalypso* [*Conversations with Calypso*], which was published in 1910 in *Der Sturm*, towards the end of the gestation period of the early stories. 'I can't find myself, I don't know who I am, who I should still become' ['"[M]ich" finde ich nicht, ich weiß nicht, wer ich bin, wer ich noch sein soll'] (SÄPL 109), as the musician, Döblin's male protagonist, cries shortly before the island of his imprisonment finally sinks into the sea. At the close of a winding discussion that has criss-crossed borders between musicology, psychology and metaphysics, he returns one final time to the intractable problem of selfhood in a universe that continually undermines our conceptions of it. Who or what am I? What is left of my significance and my meanings in the face of the impersonal forces of nature? And as the sea threatens to roll in, where, if anywhere, could or should I go from here? In the end, the surrounding sea swallows up everything, staking its claim to a stage only temporarily hired out for a discussion about music (111–12).

As a meditation on aesthetics and human existence, the *Gespräche* are set up as a loose reimagining of the Calypso episode at the start of the fifth book of Homer's *Odyssey*. Odysseus is imprisoned on the island home of the divine nymph, who has fallen desperately in love with him. Homer's epic poem sees him renounce the prospect of immortal life with Calypso for the sake of a return to Penelope and his *oikos* in Ithaca.[1] But instead of having the musician escape Calypso's island with Zeus' help, Döblin's Odysseus, like Copetta and his would-be lover, disappears into the sea (111). He never does make it back, and the subject's allegorical homecoming in Homer's original is abruptly curtailed. In the many endeavours of Odysseus and his crew to escape the destructive clutches of nature, the *Odyssey* has often been read as an epic account of the pre-modern self, and — in a more speculative vein — as one of the original poetic foundations of the unitary subject in 'enlightened' modernity.[2] Given his familiarity with the epic, we should read one subtext of Döblin's duologue as a root-and-branch challenge to this sense of selfhood. Following on the heels of his musician, we may yet disappear, discursively and eventually literally, like the human face drawn in the sand at the edge of the sea at the end of Foucault's *The Order of Things*.[3]

The *Gespräche* are an illuminating but relatively unrefined attempt at an aesthetic and metaphysical system, and I will bring aspects of that early sketch into play at several points in this chapter. The work provides a fruitful symbolic starting point for discussing Döblin's more developed anthropology and nature-philosophy, though, because it quite literally removes the ground from beneath the feet of the unitary and transcendental subject, thus leaving open the space for the emergence of something radically different. *Wang-lun* and *Berge Meere und Giganten* unfolded natural and human worlds that crush the individual human subject like an enormous iron tank, as Döblin would bluntly put it in retrospect in 1948 (SLW 308). For all their intimations of social and political hope, though, many of their visions are depersonalizing and even dehumanizing in character, and the landscapes they leave behind are ravaged and damaged ones. Döblin saw his Indian epic poem *Manas* (1927) as representing an aesthetic movement away from impersonal masses, and towards the 'individual human being' ['Einzelmenschen'] (SLW 310–11). However, the seeds for this revalidation of the individual can be found in the travelogue *Reise in Polen* (1925). Döblin's labyrinthine account of his two-month tour of Poland during the autumn of 1924 served as a point of crystallization of a number of linked, if variegated, interests. The contemporary questions of Polish and Jewish self-determination, the former a particularly salient and fraught one in the wake of the Peace of Riga of 1921, formed a political backdrop for his growing fascination with two different spiritual traditions. Specifically, he was attracted to Hasidic Judaism's conception of its tzaddik, its righteous man, or 'more-than-a-man' ['Mehr-als-Menschen'], for whom 'pure thought and feeling was everything' ['[d]er reine Gedanke, das Gefühl war ihm alles'] (RP 134–35); and in the sculpture of the crucified Christ in the Basilica in Kraków, he encountered Roman Catholicism's mediation of divinity through human corporeality and wretchedness (239–40).[4] Döblin observed unexpected parallels between the two traditions in their investment of spirituality in human corporeality, in close reflection of nature, which itself 'also thinks in pictures, in forms, in plastic configurations' ['denkt auch in Bildern, in Formen, Gestaltungen'] (166).

These thematic threads are interwoven with a wealth of heterogeneous and primarily external observations of (an often miserably poor) urban life. However, the text's closing scene, on the Danzig shoreline, is marked by a qualified optimism over the agency and dignity of the individual. Observing the ebbing and flowing of the Baltic Sea, Döblin implicitly compares political self-determination with the dialectical struggle of the individual with nature. In short, the human being is no longer merely a dispensable piece of flotsam and jetsam, but a newly enfranchised natural, social and political agent. Over against the seemingly insuperable power of nature, 'the spirit and the will are legitimate, fruitful and strong' ['[d]er Geist und der Wille sind legitim, fruchtbar und stark'] (344).

In the light of this turn towards the individual in Döblin's writing and thinking during the latter half of the 1920s,[5] my primary purpose in this chapter is to home in on his rethinking of human subjectivity and human meaning in his compendious essay of nature-philosophy and anthropology, *Unser Dasein* (1933). He published it shortly before his flight into exile in March of that year, shortly after the peak of his literary fame in the wake of *Berlin Alexanderplatz*. It was one of the books burned by the National Socialists and, as such, enjoyed no contemporary reception or discussion. In recent years, however, this overlooked 'step-child' of Döblin research, as Thomas Keil has put it, has enjoyed a deserved critical revival, not least on account of its eclecticism of form and genre and its creative negotiations at the interface of philosophy, science and literature.[6] At the point of exile, the essay was only the latest in a series of heterogeneous writings on philosophy that reached back to his early critical essays on Nietzsche in 1902 and 1903. Döblin's guiding philosophical interest, as first manifest here, was in finding a metaphysical mode of thought that might compensate for the 'disintegrative effects of empirical enquiry'.[7] He was certainly not alone in this quest, but rather one of a large number of thinkers and writers developing cognate ideas.

In the wake of a century dominated by the increasing prominence and authority of the natural sciences, along with the continued erosion of old religious certainties, there was an urgently felt need throughout European intellectual and literary cultures to find new kinds of unifying metaphysical vision.[8] Döblin's ongoing response to this dilemma was rooted in his own precocious reading of philosophy while he was still at school, admitting as he did in 'Epilog' that he read 'Spinoza, Schopenhauer and Nietzsche, and most intensively, Spinoza' ['Spinoza, Schopenhauer und Nietzsche, am intensivsten Spinoza'] (SLW 289); and this diet came to be complemented by an early sympathy for Hegelian Idealism. This range of canonical influences — enriched, as we have seen, by materials from radically different times and places — fed into a form of philosophizing which in turn fed off its own inherent contradictions. Döblin's thinking and writing were almost obsessively preoccupied with the recalcitrant materiality of the 'things of the world' (SLW 239–40, 289), but he was equally concerned with finding ways of reconciling the antitheses that populate Western philosophy, such as subject and object, mind and body, and unity and diversity.[9]

*Das Ich über der Natur* (1927), Döblin's first substantial philosophical treatise, was in large part an amalgam of earlier, smaller pieces. It was published in the same year as the epic poem *Manas*, and while the critical reception of both books was varied in tone, both sold badly. As Benjamin Bühler has justifiably argued, *Das Ich* ends up resolving its contradictions with its distinctly monistic and even pantheistic appeal to an ineluctable 'primal meaning' ['Ursinn'].[10] While in itself an interesting reflection of its author's yen for immanent metaphysical meaning, Döblin's final call for a 'new theology' arguably sells the book's protagonists, 'Ich' and 'Natur', rather short (IN 242). In that light, my primary focus here is the later and more comprehensive *Unser Dasein*, which, in its fierce defence of the quiddity, or the 'thisness', of the human subject, aims to elaborate on the contradictions inherent in the earlier essay's central relationship.

Over the course of almost 500 pages, *Unser Dasein* guides its reader through a dazzling array of themes and literary and philosophical styles and strategies, often employing an arrestingly informal and playful idiom in order to engage us as participants in its exploration of the dimensions of our existence. As the preface quirkily puts it, ours is a human (and natural) world replete with 'small, bigger, and great truths' ['geringe, größere und große Wahrheiten'], ranging from the phenomenon of, for example, the lamp standing on my desk, through the fact that *I* am 'there' as a living and breathing human being, to the weightiest questions of all: who I am; what 'life' actually is; and how that life relates to the earth and everything in it (UD 5). Eight 'books' are intercalated with three more recognizably literary diversions. The first three books explore at length the tensions between the subjective existence of the 'Ich' and the supposedly objective world of 'things'; and Book 3, in particular, turns its attention to the interplay of organic and inorganic forms in nature, in their complex relationship with that 'Ich'. A compelling negotiation with the temporality and finitude of human existence in Book 4 is followed by a new theory of art, and its connection to nature, in the fifth book. Following this, a disparate collection of illustrative case studies and sketches precedes a history of the Jews and Judaism in Book 7, and a somewhat scattergun engagement with Western peoples and nation states rounds the work off. Because the sheer range rather brings to mind Douglas Adams's title *Life, the Universe and Everything* (complete with a not dissimilar sense of humour), my treatment here will necessarily be selective and focus on what I consider the most interesting and original contributions to our overarching theme of humankind's relationship with nature.

The chapter will begin by engaging closely with Döblin's thinking about subjectivity in *Unser Dasein*, in dialogue with his forebears and contemporaries. Recent scholarship has already excavated the sources and affinities of the essay's ideas, and this kind of philological work, which I build on here, is vital to mapping out the orientations of those ideas at particular points.[11] Proof of direct influence can often be difficult to establish beyond points of analogy and affinity; and as is ever the case with Döblin, a delineation of his creative reworkings is far more fruitful than an attempt to trace the exact origins of their ingredients. Nonetheless, my exploration of the parallels will lay the foundations for the chapter's final two sections, where I unfold Döblin's hermeneutics of human existence in its relations both to nature and to its own mortality. Drawing on the figure of metaphor, I argue that Döblin successfully finds a way of thinking through our embeddedness in nature: in other words, our contradictory existence as both an insignificant 'part' of nature, and its reflective and co-creative 'counterpart'. My contention is that metaphor's hybrid epistemic status — mediating between identity and non-identity — mirrors that ontological state of being, and so it helps us to develop a concept of human 'truth' that might circumvent the pitfalls of both anthropocentrism and radical relativism. In conclusion, I consider how the reality of human finitude itself unlocks a valuable perspective on this sense of truth. If Döblin cannot answer his musician's agonized questions, then he might at least be able radically to reframe them.

**Finding the Fugitive Self**

In view of the text's distinct non-linearity, it is perhaps a good idea to start at the very end of *Unser Dasein*, where Döblin pulls together his multifarious strands, before working our way through the detail of the text. In a fragment close to the end of the essay, he adumbrates the lacuna in which his *Ich* finds itself caught: that indeterminate space between mind, body and nature that is a persistent topos in his pre-exile work. The mode of existence that emerges at the close of the essay is marked neither by freedom of will nor by an exhaustive scientific determinism, but is a third entity that subsists in the space between 'duality' and 'unity': a form of being both inextricable from nature and yet irreducibly 'more' than it (UD 475). To put it differently, Döblin articulates, or rather idealizes, what I have identified as the hermeneutic remnant at the heart of his fiction. He is striving towards a positive image of reconciliation between humankind and nature, rather than the domination of one by the other (which tends, as we have seen, to switch over into its opposite). The mutually constitutive antagonism of *Welt* and *Ich* is captured in the chiastic assertion that 'what happens in the world concerns me, and my concerns concern the world' ['[w]as in der Welt vorgeht, erkenne ich als meine Sache, und meine Sache ist etwas, das die Welt angeht'] (UD 475). This is followed by the qualifying gloss that as both part and counterpart of nature, I belong to it, just as I also jut into it and 'reshape it' (475). *Unser Dasein* is addressed to the enduring human paradox of being passive and active, powerless and powerful, at one and the same time.

The first book opens with a reflection on the profound difficulty of locating and identifying this self (15–17), a difficulty reflected in the fact that Döblin circles around this question, if in slightly different orbits, throughout the work as a whole. As a hybrid text, it acts out the quiddity of the *Ich*; or to put it differently, it actively dramatizes its own anthropology. Bühler argues that Döblin elevates 'literary strategies to an authentic principle of knowledge':[12] in other words, the literary assumes an epistemological role in the constitution of knowledge about the subject and its relationship with *Welt*. But in order to do justice to the specificity of *Unser Dasein* as a text, we should move from an epistemological assessment of a symbiosis of 'literary' and 'biological' knowledge to an ontological investigation of its implications for the very entity of an embodied self.

The individual's existence between the material and the intellectual, and subject and object, precludes an all-unifying metaphysical vision — and this refusal finds affinities in contemporary philosophical attempts to move beyond preoccupations with questions of monism and dualism in an attempt to account for the nature of humanness. Heidegger was resituating the supposedly forgotten question of 'being' at the heart of philosophy through his phenomenology of Dasein in *Sein und Zeit* (1927), while Helmuth Plessner's 'philosophical anthropology', as developed in *Die Stufen des Organischen und der Mensch* [*Levels of Organic Life and the Human*] (1928), recast the human being in terms of its 'eccentric positionality' ['exzentrische Positionalität']: that is, our sense of simultaneously 'having' a body as an object and 'being' it as a subject.[13] The hybridity in Döblin's text is formally enacted in its cross-genre interplay of the rhetorical, the dialogical and the discursive. At an early stage in the first book, 'Das Ich und die Dingwelt' ['The I and the World of things'], the narrator marvels at the marginal difference and distance between the 'I' and the sheer materiality, the thingness, of its body. He wonders aloud at his *Doppelgänger*, commenting that 'such a fantastical animal is there — and — sits with me here on this chair. We sit and walk together. Siamese twins are nothing compared to us' ['Ja, solch phantastisches Tier ist da — und — sitzt mit mir hier auf dem Stuhl. Wir sitzen und gehen immer zusammen. Die siamesischen Zwillinge sind nichts gegen uns'] (21). One of the text's multiple thought experiments brings this sense of non-locatability right down to the question of death and its relationship with the self. If I shoot you in the stomach, you might die: your *Ich* is no longer 'there', but it is your body — not your *Ich* — that I have attacked. By addressing his readers as his interlocutors, Döblin draws us into his text and highlights a form of self-knowledge that is realizable only in dialogue: discursive and theoretical modes of knowledge hit their epistemic limits when confronted with the black box of selfhood.

This suture between experiencing in a body, and actually being that body, is captured in Döblin's hybrid conception of the human as both a natural 'part of the world' ['Stück der Welt'] and the world's reshaping 'counterpart' ['Gegenstück']. This finds its experiential counterpoint in the recognition that the 'body' and the phenomenon of 'living' ['Leib' and 'Leben'], and its subjective correlates in 'er*leiben*' and 'er*leben*' [being manifest as a body and experiencing in and through it], intimately belong together (29). The near-homonymy of 'erleben' and the neologism 'erleiben' mirrors both their difference and their uncanny proximity. Döblin's sense of the intertwining of our body and our experience of it as ours clearly recalls the early stories, most graphically the *danse macabre* between Ella and her body. However, the distinctly negative dynamics of the early narratives give way here to a more energetic set of reflections on the paradoxes of embodiment. A reeling-off of medical-anatomical details, in a miniature *Tatsachenphantasie*, is both an admission of the strangeness of this organic montage of such apparently heterogeneous components and, at the same time, a moment of wonder at the fact (21). Oscillating between the objective and the subjective, Döblin observes 'this hand, these fingers, these eyes', before marvelling that 'it is my, my, my hand' (30). There is a clear affinity here with Schopenhauer's sense of the paradox of selfhood as the irresolvable 'knot of the world' ['Weltknoten'],[14] caught between *knowing* and *willing*.[15] This sense of subjectivity is reflected in a powerful sense of 'mineness', but it finds its most powerful expression *ex negativo* in a radical recognition of alterity, that is, in the strange otherness of the material to which the self is attached. Döblin marvels at how the body, as a finely tuned set of mechanisms, can be described as 'a factory, a company' ['eine Fabrik, einen Konzern'], while at the same time, uncannily, 'this is — You!' ['dies bist — Du!'] (27).

Still, what is so striking in this direct appeal to the reader *qua* interlocutor is the sheer insufficiency of performance and the performative. The dialogue subtitled 'So which of the two of us has the I?' (63–65) riffs playfully on this sense of unexchangeability; and the replies to such questions of self-definition reveal the unbridgeable gap between self and other, and, with that, the difficulty of any truly intersubjective recognition. I cannot give an answer, I only ever experience one 'self', I am what I am, laments one interlocutor, effectively emptying her *Ich* of definability (65). That this rhetorical quest for a definition continues throughout *Unser Dasein* testifies to the inexhaustibility of self-performance; but it also speaks to the more interesting idea of an identity that persistently and irreducibly exceeds its own self-performances.

That insufficiency, even lack, is worth exploring in some depth, as Döblin may be able to help us nuance our current postmodernist ideologies around self-identity as a performative construct. Certainly, the narrator seems on first encounters to face no limits in performance, inasmuch as he acts out a remainder-less convergence of mind and matter, and soul and body. The assertion that '"I" — see, hear, taste, smell, touch, I feel, want, think. Therefore I am, that's it' ['"[i]ch" — sehe, höre, schmecke, rieche, taste, ich fühle, will, denke. So bin Ich, das ist alles'] (22), seems to find a chiastic complement in the reversal of subject and predicate through the statement that 'I exist [am there — in sensing, in feeling, in thinking, in wanting' ['[i]ch bin da — im Empfinden, Fühlen, Denken, Wollen'] (23). Perhaps unexpectedly for a writer so obviously opposed to Descartes's dualisms of mind and matter, this is a strikingly physicalized homage to him. Following on from the famous *cogito ergo sum* in *Discours de la méthode* [*Discourse on Method*] (1637), we read in Descartes's *Méditations* of 1647 that 'this thing which thinks' is 'a thing which doubts, which conceives, which affirms, which denies, wants, does not want, which also imagines, and which feels'.[16] His listing of increasingly embodied predicates (of imagining and feeling) seems to suggest the emergence of the subject through a cognizance of its own performance; and, indeed, such prominent philosophers as Jaakko Hintikka have pointed to the logical difficulty of inferring from predicates of existence to a thinking essence without the performative (rather than strictly logical) statement of a 'thinking thing'.[17] If Döblin himself circles around the chicken-and-egg conundrum of essence and existence, he remains painfully conscious of the inadequacy of performance either to identify subjectivity, or else to account for it in the first place.

His 'search for the I' (16–17) is a burlesque attempt quite literally to chase subjectivity to ground. A thinly disguised parody of the absurd lengths that philosophers go to in order to secure a grounding for subjectivity, it is a hectic tour through the centre of town, appealing to neighbours, a policeman and a cobbler for information of the 'I's' whereabouts. The 'we' of the passage finally sinks in despair into the 'grave' of its bed after its futile search. Finally, we rise after a night of dreaming in which this mystery has been disclosed, only to feel the tears on our face ['die Tränen im Gesicht'] and immediately know that 'in our dreaming, our crying, was "I"' ['in Träumen, im Weinen war Ich'] (17). But the illusion of consummation, in the assonance of 'Gesicht' and 'Ich', is itself ironized through a tongue-in-cheek doggerel that strongly resembles the fairground *Moritate* in *Berlin Alexanderplatz*.[18] As is characteristic of its looping structure, the text later returns to this performance in a supposed 're-establishment' of the I, in the words of a section title towards the end of one of Döblin's literary digressions. But far from being re-established, 'I' am simply dissipated in my own gibberish:

> Da redet man so hin und her und ist Geschwätz und gar nichts mehr. Man redet lang und redet schräg, man redet über jeden Weg, man redet tief, man redet hoch, man redet in die Erd ein Loch. Man redet um die Ecke rum, man redet alle Leute krumm, sie biegen krumm sich wie ein Schlauch, sie halten sich entsetzt den Bauch. (UD 276)
>
> [You talk yourself near and far and you're nothing but talk, that's all you are. You talk at length, you talk across, you talk yourself down road after road, you talk yourself deep, you talk yourself tall, you talk straight into the earth a hole. You talk round a corner, you talk them all sick, they double up like a hose, they hold their stomach, they hold their nose.]

This — in very liberal translation — is a *reductio ad absurdum* to pure textual performance: an empty spinning of gears, a mill with no grist, and an unmistakable parody of the doggerel of Wilhelm Busch's famous and highly influential children's tale, *Max und Moritz* (1865). Language collapses into materiality, and the problem of linguistic ordering without any content to order finds its flipside in the dilemma of there being nothing apart from unordered content. Some twenty years after Döblin's call for authors to learn from psychiatry and embrace *Tatsachenphantasie*, he suggests here that 'seeing' be distilled into colours, shapes and their mutations, and 'tasting' give way to the sweet, the sour and the salty (UD 278). Even the objectification of 'seeing' a room has to give way to the phenomenological reality of the room *as* a room *for me*. 'I experience myself in the room', or even 'I experience myself as the room' (to take the phenomenology to its extreme) is now distilled simply into 'room'.

If the predicate of 'seeing' itself is dismissed as a superannuated form of metaphysics, Döblin's next move is to deconstruct the personalized 'I' itself. We can hear the echoes of Ernst Mach's and Fritz Mauthner's dissolution of the relationship of representation between subject and language, not least in the suggestion that world and self in effect collapse into one another, and 'thus fill and concretize each other' ['füllen, konkretisieren sich so'] (278).[19] In *Die Analyse der Empfindungen und das Verhältnis des Physischen zum Psychischen* [*The Analysis of Sensations*], originally published in 1886, Mach declared the self 'irredeemable' ['unrettbar'] in the face of the primacy of the sensations, and salvageable only as a convenient practical fiction.

His reduction of subjectivity to a contingent nexus of thoughts, sensations, moods and memories had a significant influence on Mauthner and therefore, indirectly, on Döblin;[20] and we certainly recall here the atomizing declaration in the 'Berliner Programm' that 'I am not I', but rather the streets and the lanterns, this or that event, and nothing more (SÄPL 122). Still, Döblin draws this tangle of aesthetics, epistemology and ontology into a more positive figuration in *Unser Dasein*. If I cannot be restored to what I was, then maybe I can at least reformulate who or what I am.

This thing called 'I' may be without substance and heft. But it is both in and through the phenomena of the world that I exist and constitute myself. If 'world' is there, then I am there as its co-constituent (277–79, 285). In short, world and subject converge in the same space. The 'Ich' is now a superfluous form of description of human life — an arbitrary designation of a boundary, a social performance and a relic deserving of little more than an honorary place in the 'museum of languages' (286). It is telling that Döblin now explicitly substitutes the word 'Dasein' as the only viable designation for a mode of living that is shaped by, and which actively shapes, its world, as performance gives way to a form of co-constitution and co-construction. After an extended wrestling with subjectivity, Döblin emerges with a language that comes close to Heidegger's phenomenology, which had first been comprehensively developed a few years earlier in *Sein und Zeit*. There is no smoking-gun evidence of Heidegger's direct influence on Döblin;[21] but what is significant is that both thinkers, from within overlapping intellectual contexts, were working to find a path beyond the dualisms of subject and object, immanence and transcendence, and consciousness and unconsciousness.[22] If for Heidegger this took the form of a revolutionary new approach to the question of being itself, Döblin's cognate orientation was towards a hermeneutics of humankind both in and as nature. In the next section, I want to turn to examine some of the philosophical foundations and affinities of that hermeneutics.

## Beyond Idealism?

Although *Ich* seems to be rebranded here as *Dasein*, the rebrand hardly solves the product's problems, nor does it manage to do away with its old nomenclature. Döblin's core difficulty throughout his essay lies in finding ways of affirming both the concept and the reality of subjectivity without papering over its paradoxes. As we have seen, the attempt to locate the *Ich* simply in its facticity — its 'thisness' — ultimately reveals itself to be tautological. As 'part and counterpart of nature', my Dasein rests on the dual pillars of 'experience and physical form' ['Erleben und Gestalt'] (UD 31), the psychological and biological aspects of my personhood. It constitutes, shapes and reshapes itself in what is described as an open-ended to-and-fro between person and world (30). Döblin spells out the relationship here:

> Ein Spannungsablauf erfolgt dauernd, und so geht Erlebtes, als Ich über das Medium und aus der Apparatur der Person in Welt, Natur, Geschichte über, und es schwingt Welt, Natur, Geschichte in die Person und das Ich zurück.

> Das ist die ununterbrochene kämpferische, ringende Erschließung der 'Welt' durch die 'Person', den Fühl- und Aktionskörper, und die ständige Durchtränkung der 'Person' mit 'Welt'.
> Immer wieder wird der Mensch von Erde zu Erde, immer wieder wird die Erde von Mensch zu Mensch. (UD 30)
>
> [There is a continual tension in which what is experienced, in the form of the 'I', passes over into world, nature and history via the medium and in the physiology of the 'person', and world, nature and history vibrates back into the person and the 'I'.
> This is the uninterrupted, combative, pugnacious opening up of the 'world' through the 'person', the feeling and acting body, and it is the constant imbuement of 'person' with 'world'.
> Time and again, man passes from dust to dust, and time and again the earth passes from man to man.]

There are two chiastic crossovers in motion here. Playing with a recurrent vocabulary of swinging, vibrating and oscillating ['schwingt'], which will come into focus in relation to my discussion of *Resonanz* below, the first rhetorically highlights the intertwining of 'Ich' as the seat of subjectivity, and 'Person' as its embodied instantiation. The second chiasmus (dust to dust, man to man) encapsulates a material reality of co-constitution, which plays out through an emollient vocabulary of softening and imbuing on the one hand, and the metaphorics of fighting and forceful opening on the other. But it also leaves many questions unanswered. In one of the text's many semi-literary quirks, and a small example of the parodistic homilies peppering *Berlin Alexanderplatz*, a mocking voice, a 'Spottvogel', issues a miniature jeremiad on the dangers of too much philosophizing (17).[23] And even if the mocker's song 'dies away' at the close of the book, its very mention textualizes, and therefore ironizes, the ensuing investigation.

Döblin is well aware of the limits of traditional philosophical and scientific paradigms and vocabularies, an awareness that does not exactly make matters any less tortuous for him (or us) in his renegotiations of the self. Since 'reality', such as it is, now emerges in the mutual interaction of person and world, he roundly rejects the dissecting scientific methods that are exhaustively brought to bear by a band of thinkers described in broad-brush and pejorative terms as 'realists, determinists and materialists'. The 'x des Ich', its incalculable qualitative difference from the rest of the material world, cannot be explained away through laws of physical or mechanical causality (184). We will encounter a parodistic example in *Berlin Alexanderplatz*, in the flashback to Biberkopf's manslaughter of his girlfriend Ida: another instance of the toing and froing between novel and essay. Beyond this jarring parody, though, the essay persists in asking a question about the epistemological limitations of the natural sciences: a question that had preoccupied Romantic *Naturphilosophie*, and reoccupied a prominent place in German philosophy following the demise of positivism, and in the wake of a burgeoning interest in Nietzsche around 1900. Edmund Husserl's concept of a pre-scientific 'life-world' ['Lebenswelt'] is perhaps the most obvious point of comparison;[24] but the life philosophy of Dilthey, Bergson and Simmel also portrayed a world irreducible to theoretical abstractions and scientific explanations. Life philosophy aimed to reconceive life itself 'as a creative process, with the continuity of mental experiences associated with that process, and with "inner perception" or intuition as a privileged mode of understanding that process'.[25] It was in 1910 that Dilthey drew his highly influential distinction between 'describing' and 'explaining' as being integral to the human and natural sciences respectively.[26] Working through and beyond Dilthey's influence in his posthumously published work *Lebensanschauung* [*View of Life*] (1918), Simmel argued that scientific 'explanations', while provable in relation to one other, ultimately lacked an ineluctable philosophical grounding.[27] In a similar vein, Döblin contends that while the world is determinable within certain borders and parameters, it remains indeterminate and ungroundable in scientific terms (184–85). Under the influence of Simmel,[28] Heidegger in turn argued in *Sein und Zeit* that both scientific models and the metaphysical schemata underlying them are preceded by a Dasein characterized first and foremost by its temporality, its ineluctable 'Da' in space and time.[29]

Very much part of this kind of discourse, Döblin makes a distinction between the empirically measurable and analysable 'seen world' of the natural sciences, and its 'lived' counterpart.[30] Optics and acoustics, to take his two specific examples, form what he calls an 'incomplete world-view', representing as they do mere abstractions from a real, concrete world. This emerges in dialogue with human beings, who bring to bear their irreducibly human concerns and orientations: their feeling, willing and thinking, their joys and pains, aspirations and aversions, and values and norms (85). Even if he concedes the seemingly self-indulgent lyricism of all this, he sees the multifariousness of human experience as just as valid a part of nature as chemistry and physics, and as making their laws 'shiver' and 'shimmer' (87): a suggestion which is almost certainly reworked from one of *Berlin Alexanderplatz*'s vignettes (cf. BA 39–40). Crucially, these truths can no longer be considered merely in the terms of a science, but rather from the perspective of 'Praxis', under the sign of 'action' ['Handlung'] (UD 85). There are striking parallels here with Simmel's argument that our lives *are* praxes, that we unfurl different truths in relation to different life experiences, and that our processes of adaptation to different praxes are themselves 'part of this behaviour, and of the world' ['ein Stück dieses Verhaltens und dieser Welt'].[31] Heidegger's phenomenology further radicalized this practical orientation into a conception of Dasein as always 'projecting' or 'pushing forward' into a space of existential possibilities: a 'Worumwillen', or a 'for-the-sake-of-which', which refers to Dasein's network of everyday purposes and practices.[32]

These cognate ideas about subjectively determined truth found their origins not only in Schopenhauer and Nietzsche, but also in the German Idealist tradition of the late eighteenth and early nineteenth centuries. Hegel's concept of 'objective spirit' exerted a formative influence upon Dilthey's and Simmel's work; and F. W. J. Schelling provided a conceptual vocabulary for rethinking an intuitively grasped natural and human world of endless creative change in the wake of both positivism and the alienation brought about by industrialization.[33] Thomas Keil has, in turn, underscored the proximity of Döblin's negotiations with the 'Ich' to the philosophies of both Schelling and J. G. Fichte.[34] Fichte's famous definition of

'Intelligenz' — the intellective self — as 'a deed and absolutely nothing else' ['ein Tun und absolut nichts weiter'] recasts the 'I' in terms of action rather than as a substance or an essence;[35] and this figuration of subjectivity in terms of agency is echoed in Döblin's suggestion that 'Ich' brings its objective reality into existence through an act of positing. '"I" exists, "I" acts and experiences world' ['Ich ist, Ich handelt und erlebt Welt']. The subject is redefined here as a 'centre' which 'creates form' from within itself — a process described as 'acting' ['Handeln'] (UD 73, 85). At the close of Book 2, the meaning-giving and stabilizing function of the 'I' crystallizes in the rather extravagant suggestion that it is what 'holds together' and gives meaning to an otherwise chaotic and meaningless world (92). Crucially, this notion of nature's radical otherness is a powerful corrective to any residually Idealist sense of self. It draws into question the scope of its self-creating performance and exposes a growing fracture in the text between an individualized and an all-embracing, even pantheistic, conception of the 'Ich'.

Döblin had first comprehensively developed the concept of an *Ur-Ich* in *Das Ich über der Natur*, and it is a concept that suggests close parallels with Schelling's notion of a cosmic *Ich* as the all-uniting and unconditional substance of everything that is, that exists.[36] In his early essay on the dialectics of subject and object, Schelling had defined this 'Ich' as the absolutely self-identical ground of all existence, the grounding of Being and of the reality of all entities:[37] an 'I' that could not be identified as an object because this would itself require a further regress to a prior ontological and epistemological principle. In *Das Ich über der Natur*, Döblin is thinking along similar lines. 'The world embodies, in its whole, the multi-dimensional expression of a primal I, a primal meaning' ['[d]ie Welt stellt im ganzen die vieldimensionale Äußerung eines Ur-Ichs, eines Ur-Sinns dar']; and to this, he adds that the 'Ur-Ich' in effect subsists as a meaning-giving creative force throughout material reality (IN 243). This *Ur-Ich*, however, underpins an individual 'Ich' which is itself a panoply of individual components: a so-called 'Nature-I' ['Natur-Ich'] encapsulates our biological and environmental make-ups; our 'Passion-I' and 'Societal-I' ['Passions-Ich' and 'Gesellschafts-Ich'] stand for our incorporation into the masses; and on those foundations, our so-called 'Private-I' and 'Action-I' ['Privat-Ich' and 'Aktions-Ich'] embody my *self*, the person that I unexchangeably am (IN 117–20, 166–71).

In a mythologized form, the *Ur-Ich* forms the metaphysical ground bass of the epic poem *Manas*. Manas, the son of the King of Udaipur, has returned home from victory in battle, only to fall into a deep depression, in which he yearns for his own end at the hands of Schiwa, the deity of destruction. 'He seeks pain. | He wants to shudder and suffer' ['Er sucht den Schmerz. | Er will schauern und leiden'], in a rebellious bid to declare himself an *Ich* (*Manas*, 20). But this antagonism finds poetic resolution as the god is confronted with the fact of being himself nothing more than the progeny, the derivative, of an all-pervasive and ineluctable creative power (*Manas* 359).[38] There is a vein of this immanent and all-grounding meaning running through *Unser Dasein*. Along similar transcendent-yet-immanent lines to Schelling's concept of the *Ich*, Döblin argued that the 'I' is present in its indivisibility wherever 'the world' is directly experienced (UD 58). In a conceptualization reminiscent of

Baruch Spinoza's distinction between the divine *natura naturans* and a determinate *natura naturata* in his *Ethics*,[39] we learn that this 'I', as an ultimately indivisible phenomenon, is omnipresent throughout the vegetable, animal and mineral worlds, and that it is what holds everything together (88, 280).

Schelling's monism had developed in critical response to the determinism implicit in Spinoza.[40] And despite the clearly monistic inflection of *Das Ich über der Natur*, what is intriguing about *Unser Dasein* is its unmistakable turn away from monism, not into dualism, but rather into a dialectical relationship that is qualitatively different from both. The remnants of this pantheistic and universalist conception of the *Ur-Ich* are now giving way to a sense of the 'I' individually grounded in and shaped and carried by a material and corporeal reality that remains irreducibly other.[41] In short, monism is giving way to a sense of hybridity, and the polyvalent principle of the *Ich* is being rethought in agonistic yet creative symbiosis with something of which it is also an integral part. Our Dasein is 'this little bit of nothing' ['[d]ieses bißchen Nichts'] (234); and this, in turn, exposes a profound contradiction within the text between an *Ich* that continually invests meaning in an otherwise meaningless reality and a human life — dissipated among individual subjects — that exists in an insignificant metonymic continuity with nature. In turn, there is a marked lacuna between the fluctuating, forming yet dissolving energies of the natural world, and the sense that this nature carries its own non-anthropomorphic meaning within it. In spite of Idealism's formidable intellectual resources, Döblin has to concede that the 'form, shape, number, and order' pervasive throughout nature cannot be straightforwardly understood in terms of an *Ur-Ich*, and that they therefore remain irreducible to our human meaning-making capacities (179).

At the close of the third book, Döblin describes 'form' as mere 'stabilizing posts on a vast avenue' ['Pfähle auf einer ungeheuren Chaussee']: points of 'rest and respite in a constant flight' which have no fixity or permanence to them, but like crests of waves, simply sink back into the flux (177). And once again, we can hear the rumbling of Schopenhauer's Will beneath the surface: that formless, essentially non-rational urge that pervades both us and the universe. In *Die Welt als Wille und Vorstellung*, the human subject is relegated to a fundamentally illusionary and entirely contingent status against the amorphous backdrop of the will.[42] For Schopenhauer, music provides us with the most direct and unmediated access to the will. As the 'direct likeness' ['unmittelbar[] Abbild'] of the will itself, it expresses emotions in their essence, and its harmonies and rhythms are an auditory echo of the patterns and numbers to be found in nature.[43] While Döblin explicitly challenges Schopenhauer's claim that music gives us near-unmediated and disinterested access to a metaphysical will (UD 244–45), his celebration of music's expressive capacities nonetheless recognizes the ways in which it meaningfully connects us, and our thoughts and feelings, to a non-human world caught between presence and absence, and form and formlessness (257–60).[44]

This critical distinction from Schopenhauer, with an infusion of Idealism, is a repeated theme throughout Döblin's work, and it proves to be an important facet of his developing nature-philosophy. The complex affinity between the two is particularly significant here because it provides an aesthetic parallel to Döblin's sense of a world and universe whose meaning is irrefutable yet radically different from 'meaning' as we humans understand it. This basic contradiction is encapsulated in the section title that rounds off the third book, titled 'Progress of the world — but where exactly to?' ['Fortgang der Welt, aber wohin?'] (UD 177). The problem is that part and counterpart of nature seem to collapse into one another as soon as we recognize ourselves to be just one more exchangeable piece of the tapestry. We contain within us 'traces of the animal, the vegetable, the mineral, and the inorganic' (168). This residue of 'a real connection' with these 'non-moral' natural forms is echoed in musical tones and rhythms (169, 242–43), but it also points to our participation in a cycle of destruction, regeneration and natural meaning that remains irreducible to human projections. Perhaps Döblin's most memorable illustration of this is the cycle of organic and inorganic rebirth at the end of *Berge Meere und Giganten*:

> Und wenn die Herzen stillstanden, die Zellen sich trennten und auflösten, waren sie neue Seelen, zerfallendes Eiweiß Ammoniak Aminosäuren, Kohlensäure und Wasser, Wasser das sich in Dampf verwandelte. Leid- und lustbegierig, wanderungssüchtig, Seelenvereine in Schneelandschaften, in dem pendelnden weiten Meer, in den blasenden Stürmen, den Steinvölkern, die der Boden zu Bergen hochtrieb. (BMG 631)

> [And when their hearts stopped and their cells divided and dissolved, they became new souls, disintegrating protein, ammonia, amino acids, carbonic acid and water, water that transformed itself into steam. Eager to suffer, eager for desire, itching to move and travel, communities of souls in vast snowy landscapes, in the wide swelling sea, in the raging storms, in the stone peoples which the earth's floor pushed and moulded into mountains.]

What follows this penultimate paragraph is the novel's final ceasefire between humanity and nature. Döblin places an aesthetic complexion here on a supposedly scientific observation of the continued interaction and element-exchange between the organic and the inorganic, and between the human and the non-human. The strange images ('stone peoples') anthropomorphize those natural forms that we will eventually rejoin. As so often with Döblin's use of metaphor, the uncanniness foregrounds the oscillation of this thing called 'nature' between familiarity and otherness. While that Other underpins and structures our figurative capacities, it also remains marginally outside our epistemic and technological mastery. Döblin's 'Fortgang' encapsulates his contradictory perspective on man's relationship with nature, and his refusal to restrict himself to any particular scientific or philosophical model. In other words, the unsystematic and sometimes contradictory nature of his meditations mirrors the insoluble contradictions of our own existences. We are an insignificant component of its endless flow, merely one composite form amidst infinite others (UD 177–79). At the same time, the 'Ich' remains the 'motor' behind the world's temporality and materiality, at least as understood from a human perspective (207). As he concedes at an early point in the essay, both our 'experiencing', and the 'world of things and forms' that we experience, are mutually irreducible yet inseparable. Contradiction is where our life happens (27–28), and so contradiction must be the starting point of any attempt to make sense of it.

## Metaphor and Hybridity

Although we are embedded in natural patterns and cycles, we are forever working to reshape them to our own purposes. Our contradictory combination of connection and transcendence as 'Stück' and 'Gegenstück' (part and counterpart) determines both the possibilities and the limitations of our existences. I suggest that this links both our constitution of our world, and our knowledge of it, to the dialectics of metaphor. Although it is never explicitly mentioned in *Unser Dasein*, the figure of metaphor provides us with a conceptual tool for grasping what Döblin sees as our place and worth in the world: it serves as a robust means of thinking through the contradictions from which human existence lives, but on whose edges it repeatedly snags.

Because we are a finite part of an indeterminate picture, both our knowing and the conditions of that knowing are possible and articulable only from within that picture.[45] As we saw in the previous section, any 'scientific' world-view is ultimately ungroundable, and therefore, in Döblin's similar formulation, 'incomplete' (UD 84–85). To develop this idea further, our capacity to explain and understand things and beings, both scientifically and in terms of their relationship to us, rests on our ability to identify each of them in terms of something else. Our ways of coping with and knowing our world, as the embodied beings that we are, depend on a web of interconnections, contiguities and overlaps; and so, what 'objective' knowledge we have originates in a metaphorical interplay of identity and non-identity, presence and absence.[46] Andrew Bowie has argued that this dialectic, which is integral to the question of 'being' in Heidegger's phenomenology, can be traced back to Early Romantic irony, as well as to Schelling's struggle to reconcile his anthropomorphic metaphors with his metaphysics.[47] I now want to situate Döblin's anthropology and nature-philosophy in relation to this tradition's twentieth-century legacy. Metaphor becomes the central, if tacit, component not only of his epistemology, but also of the very phenomenon of being human, being finite and being hybrid. It offers an answer to the musician's call for meaning, suggesting as it does a way of making new sense of our contingent material existences.

Perhaps the most prominent statement on metaphor in relation to literary modernism can be found in Nietzsche's 'Über Wahrheit und Lüge im außermoralischen Sinne' ['On Truth and Lying in the Extra-Moral Sense'], written in 1873 but only published in 1896. In an essay that has been repeatedly read as a precursor of Deconstruction, Nietzsche underscored the fundamental arbitrariness and contingency of our edifice of truths: systems of interlocking concepts that are little more than metaphors denuded of their original sensory and cognitive immediacy.[48] However, Döblin's implicit understanding of metaphor as constituting our networks of knowledge — whether practical, philosophical, scientific or technological — requires a far richer conceptual vocabulary than one grounded in the straightforward rejection of objective truth.[49] In fact, it requires a way of thinking that might help to reconfigure the idea of objective truth itself.

His discussion of the changing functionality of a table is a powerful case in point, illustrating how metaphor undergirds both our practical interactions with the world and our hybrid relationship with it. The table is presented to us, in markedly animistic terms, as an entity with its own natural history and agency, even its own 'Ich' (UD 88–89). This seems little more than a fanciful extension of the figure of the 'Ich' far beyond the realm of the human. We might think of the stonepeoples at the very end of *Berge Meere und Giganten*; and in *Unser Dasein*, Döblin explicitly attributes a purposive 'Ich' to both animals and plants (96–99). This suggestion of innate organic purpose brings to light parallels with the biologist Hans Driesch's philosophical vitalism.[50] What is of primary interest here, though, is not the mark of philosophical or scientific influence, but rather the relationship between the 'human being' and the 'table' that Döblin imaginatively works out. The wood is no longer living, but in a transformation that is as real as it is figurative, it assumes a new kind of life 'through me' ['an mir'] and 'tailored to me' ['zugeschnitten [...] auf mich']. Once again, we glimpse the natural cyborg — even a form of distributed cognition — in the suggestion that the table commutes from one configuration to another in the form of one of my organs: a prosthetic extension of my biological existence in space and time. As the table continues its lifecycle, cracks and starts to rot away, it 'liberates' itself from its oppressive human masters, and finds a new purpose in dialogue with the elements (89–90). The comparison with a slaughtered animal, the components of which pass into new configurations, evokes the celebrated abattoir scene in *Berlin Alexanderplatz* (89; BA 136–43). Integral to the phenomenon of the table is neither its geometrical dimensions, nor the entelechy of its parent tree or even its biochemical makeup, but rather its practical existence *for* us *as* something: as a 'tool', a prosthetic organ and technological supplement to our existences. Its functionality is concrete and literal, but its purpose is malleable and metaphorical: we understand and use it as a particular thing that is at once meaningful for us and yet never quite exhausts its, or indeed our, ontological possibilities. This is an account of practical meanings that refuses to reduce them to the status of congealed metaphors, but rather sees them as living, shifting and fluid. In short, transience, contingency and truth-value come to occupy exactly the same space.

This phenomenological 'as-structure' of understanding is perhaps most familiar to us from Heidegger's *Sein und Zeit*. On the basis of its finite being-in-the-world, Dasein understands the world and itself primordially not in theoretical or scientific terms, but rather in terms of the 'the ready at hand', that is, through the practical objects, purposes and connections that populate and structure its worlds.[51] Using his famous example of the practical use of a hammer in a similar vein to the example of the table, Heidegger shows how human existence is definable fundamentally not as a dualism of mind and matter, but as the moving centre of a finite network of purposes and projects.[52]

However, despite Döblin's striking use of a similar nomenclature, his new *Ich* is certainly not simply conterminous with Heidegger's Dasein. Döblin's movement beyond the old debates between monism and dualism also takes place, as I have suggested, in relation to life philosophy, with its sense of the coexistence of form and the continuity, and determinacy and indeterminacy.[53] But perhaps most significantly, it reveals profound affinities with an emergent form of biology that was striving to understand the material reality of nature from the embodied positions of individual beings.

Döblin figures the human body through a metaphorics of technology and industry. It is the corporation, its factory, and, rather less grandiosely, the tool carrier of the *Ich* (28–29). There is a hint of the prosthetic, and of the idea of distributed cognition and function, in the suggestion that our own 'world surroundings' ['Weltumkreis'] and the attuning of human physiologies and their environments together ensure that the 'Umkreis' and its centre, the embodied individual, cannot be thought in any sense in isolation or separation from one another. The 'blood-warm, blood-pulsating, unknowable reality of this "environment"' ['blutwarme, blutgetränkte, unkenntliche Realität dieser "Umwelt"'] (29), in turn, suggests striking figurative similarities with the biologist Jakob von Uexküll's doctrine of *Umweltlehre*, which he had first elaborated in *Umwelt und Innenwelt der Tiere* [*Outer World and Inner World of Animals*] (1909).

'Umwelt' denoted a phenomenal world that was inextricable from the embodied experiences and worlds of different animals; and rather than analysing animals as interacting sets of mechanisms, Uexküll aimed to investigate the embodied means by which they perceive and constitute their surroundings, and at the same time act constructively upon them.[54] In a concise statement of his developing ideas in his *Biologische Briefe an eine Dame* [*Biological Letters to a Woman*], published in 1919 in the *Deutsche Rundschau*, Uexküll outlines the animal's physiological 'situation plan' ['Situationsplan'], through which its so-called 'inner environment' ['Innenwelt'], with its chain of organs of reception and action, exists in an intimate symbiosis with its 'outer environment' ['Außenwelt'] of individually relevant characteristics and objects ['Merkmale']: a relationship that is characterized by an interplay of stimulation and reception, and reaction and reshaping.[55] Each animal 'subject' forms the 'centre' of its 'perception environment' ['Merkwelt'], the stimulations of which prompt its interventions into its 'effect environment' ['Wirkwelt'] as an agent.[56]

What particularly captured the attention and imagination of his contemporaries was Uexküll's attempt to subjectivize the meaning and purpose of specific environments for specific animals. In his *Streifzüge durch die Umwelten von Tieren und Menschen* [*A Foray into the Worlds of Animals and Humans*], which was published a year after *Unser Dasein*, he develops the thesis that each (human or animal) subject lives in a specific world, and that environments themselves constitute radically subjective realities. This articulation is followed by the concluding description of an oak tree as an object understood in radically different terms from the perspectives of different perceptual environments. The different beings perceive and interact with the same 'object' in radically different ways, for different purposes;[57] and yet, as Uexküll goes on to argue in his *Bedeutungslehre* [*Theory of Meaning*], published in 1940, it is through these relations of symbiosis and co-adaptation that a process of physiological and environmental harmonization ['Harmonie'] and counterpoint ['Kontrapunkt'] occurs. That is, objects and organisms come to fulfil specific functions and assume specific 'meanings' *only in relation* to one another.[58] While

Döblin makes no mention of a personal engagement, Keil has outlined the points of connection between the two.[59] The biologist's theories of non-anthropocentric worlds combined universally valid truths with a valorization of individual expression and behaviour, thus making them a compelling point of reference not only for Heidegger, but also for such poets and writers as Gottfried Benn, Rilke and Thomas Mann.[60]

Central to our purposes is the emergence of an understanding of nature not through the mechanistic causalities of physics and chemistry, but rather through an intuitive — and by extension metaphorical — connection to the living world: an intellectual tradition which found some of its complex roots in Schelling's *Naturphilosophie* and Goethe's morphological observations of nature.[61] While metaphor remains a human faculty dependent on language for its realization, we can see many qualitatively different structures of 'intuiting-as' and 'understanding-as' in operation both across species boundaries and throughout interlinked ecosystems. Through his seemingly poetic use of metaphor in a bid to delineate the *Umkreise* of different forms of 'Ich', Döblin is not simply reducing the world to an anthropomorphic construct, or else indiscriminately re-enchanting it. Nor is it his aim, like Plessner, to offer a functionalistic account of our eccentric positionality. Rather, through his use of metaphor as a heuristic tool of description and explanation, he aims to make approximate sense of ultimately unknowable beings and their environments. This non-coercive epistemic purpose in turn shines ontological light on a human life lived through metaphor: irrespective of the uniqueness of our species, we are defined by our hybrid state of 'being' our own biological networks, being entangled in wider environmental and social networks, and yet able reflexively to describe and reshape those networks at the same time.

I suggest that *Unser Dasein*'s sense of *Ich* as a 'centre' paradoxically opens up a decentred anthropology that is rooted in different forms of sense-making from within myriad different environments. Drawing attention to a network of functions and interdependencies, Döblin contends that there is no such thing as a purposeless 'Natur' which is 'merely for itself and in itself' ['für sich und in sich']. In *Bedeutungslehre*, Uexküll finely observes that the microscopic grooves on the surface of a flower's stem not only 'provide the tactile perception mark of the ant's feelers', but also 'serve the ant as a carrier of the effect mark of its feet':[62] in other words, he argues that these aspects of the ant's and the stem's physiologies become attuned to one another. Döblin makes a strikingly similar observation that the nectar serves the bees, and that the antelope, as prey, interlocks with the specifically evolved locomotive and masticatory apparatus of the lion (96). In short, while an organism's overall physiological constitution and operation seem to form an organic 'whole and a closed system' ['Ganzheit, geschlossenes System'], its mutually constitutive interactions with its ecosystem — its birth, its search for food, its metabolic processes, its death — mark out its organic openness and incompleteness. The organism's system is not a microcosm of a much larger nature, but rather the decentred and disposable component of ever-larger systems, destined ultimately for its own dissolution into them (96–97). As if through a series of speculative and metaphorical shifts between biological and existential categories, Döblin elaborates a chain of evolutionary development here. With its borderless systems, flora remains literally rooted in and symbiotic with its immediate environment, whereas animals and humans have to move, to transcend their physical borders, in order simply to survive (99–102). Animals, in turn, remain 'tied to their place and environment' ['ortsgebunden'] in ways that we, in our capacities for reflexivity and goal-directed movement, do not (108). I have already considered the decentredness that is integral to our experience of embodiment; and as Ursula Elm and Keil have recognized, there are certain important parallels with Plessner's concept of eccentric positionality.[63] Nonetheless, there are also instructive differences. While Plessner aims to provide a functionalistic theory of eccentric positionality — combining empirical and theoretical biology with philosophy — Döblin's approach to our transcendence of borders (as well as that of other species) is far more speculative in its application of different disciplinary categories.[64]

However, far from simply reducing other *Umkreise* to anthropomorphic modes of figuration, I suggest that both the openness and the mutability of nature's systems in fact lend themselves the fluid epistemic logic of metaphor. The reason for this is that in its combination of identity and non-identity, metaphor serves as a means of delineating and describing other centres of existence — other forms of *Ich* — which are at once knowable and yet ontologically impenetrable. As the correlate of our reflexive and hybrid positionality as 'Gegenstück' as well as 'Stück', our capacity for metaphor lends real meaning and worth to that positionality: we are part of a world we can meaningfully know and shape, but which also eludes our mastery and control. Perhaps the most striking example is Döblin's radical break with Cartesianism in his description of human consciousness not as the seat and essence of our *Ich*, but rather as an evolutionary prosthesis evolved to cope with a specific *Umkreis*. In one of his many techno-natural metaphors, he even compares it to a car lamp, a snail's feelers. Is the lamp the car, and are the feelers the snail? (105). A plant, we are told, 'thinks and feels' even without a brain (106); and a crystal, an entity figuratively caught between the living and non-living, develops functional corners and surfaces which elude any sense of organic purpose, but which might also be figured as organs 'from the perspective of the crystal', an impossible point from which we are nevertheless invited to try to think (116–17).[65] As we know from contemporary discussions about the respective ontological statuses of biological and computer viruses, for example, both scientific and philosophical advances happen through the 'understanding-as' operations of metaphor: operations which allow new analogies, models and hypotheses to emerge.[66] In a neat extension of the thought experiment of the table, we learn that technological prostheses emerge from our understanding and conscious adaptation of the energies, forms and processes of nature (103). Building on the cyborg configurations that we encountered in *Berge Meere und Giganten* and 'Der Geist des naturalistischen Zeitalters', the implication here is that our humanness is most fully understood and realized in our natural cyborgness: a mode of existence which operates in continuity with its own appendages and extensions.

Integral to Döblin's discussion, then, is an ontology of cooperative agency which extends across borders between species, and between organic and inorganic forms; and central to this is a relationship of de-hierarchized interplay between nature, humanity, its technologies and societies. In a sideways glance at evolutionary theory — with shades of Haeckel's biogenetic law that ontogeny recapitulates phylogeny[67] — Döblin argues that we carry the traces of the animal, the vegetable and the mineral 'baked' within us, and that something of these traces 'sounds through and resonates' even in our state of advanced evolution ['klingt [...] durch und mit'] (168). This metaphor of sounding and resounding is significant because it draws upon the figure of 'Resonanz': the phenomenon that shows itself when a system is subjected to an oscillating force with a near-identical frequency to its own natural one. Döblin's discussion of resonance draws syncretically on examples from mechanics, electricity and music technology (169–72). Harking back to his discussions of harmony and counterpoint in *Gespräche mit Kalypso*, and with echoes in Uexküll's *Bedeutungslehre*, its figurative potential undoubtedly emerged in part from his own encounters with Hans Kayser's theories of harmonics, which investigated the links between waves in sound and matter within the newly emergent science of quantum physics.[68]

*Resonanz* speaks to a deep interplay and co-relation of the organic and inorganic structures of nature on the one hand, and those of human physiology, anatomy and homeostasis on the other. In turn, it exhibits its own figurative and conceptual adaptability. Not only does it refer to the similarities of structures, dynamics and processes throughout the natural and human worlds; it also evokes our ability to understand, adapt and reuse them as the models, structures and processes that make sense for us and fulfil our purposes. In an implicit statement on metaphor's epistemological significance, Döblin argues that cognition itself objectively rests on the 'the hints of similarities and identities between the knowing and the knower' ['Anklingen von Ähnlichkeiten und Gleichheiten zwischen dem Erkennen und dem Erkennenden'] (171). Systemic and dynamic affinities and resonances are not simply biological, physical and material, but also psychological, social and political.

This comes to the fore in a brief example of the Muslim conquest of Roman Egypt in the seventh century, where Döblin poses the question of the relative strengths of human and natural forces. Who is the mightier: Muhammad or the Nile? He suggests that the physiological and cultural traits of the Egyptian people reveal a striking continuity that has been substantially shaped by the surrounding landscape. Döblin's materialistic reading is that ideas and ideologies can only take root in a resonant earth and environment; and while peoples and communities invariably undergo evolutionary and societal adaptations over immensely long periods, our dialectical existence as both 'part' and 'counterpart' allows us to shape and reshape our environment just as it shapes us (175–76). It is beyond the scope of this study to discuss the idiosyncratic and rather jejune expositions of Western political systems in Book 8; but it is certainly worth noting *Unser Dasein*'s astute and (in the early 1930s) timely opposition to the idea of the nation-state as an ossified and impoverished construct that must be thrown off for the sake of flexible forms of collectivity grounded in *Resonanz* (351–53, 424–26). Fixed borders of most kinds are profoundly suspect to Döblin.

For all the utopianism of this ontology, I argue that it lays the foundations for a posthuman vision of diversity in interconnection. This sense of interconnection is grounded in the processes and structures of metaphor, and it offers a powerful challenge to our ideologies of autonomy and inherent superiority over the rest of nature. If nature has 'no corners' ['keine Winkel'] (168), then it certainly has nothing that looks like a centre, either.[69]

## Incompletely Complete?

Our capacity for metaphor is a testament to our unique place in this network. It is our restlessly human appetite for supplementation, for the endless creation of new extensions and new prostheses, and it is what perhaps most clearly sets our species-being apart from those that interact with us and share our worlds. Human reality is co-constituted through a process of mutual action and counter-action between human beings and their worlds. The redefinition of my 'Ich' as a 'centre' is in this sense not an anthropocentric flight of fancy, but rather a reconfiguration of human existence in the dynamic and ever-shifting terms of 'action' ['Handeln']. This Döblin describes as the capacity to shape our environments, combined with an openness to be shaped in turn (UD 85, 187, 207). In this definition of human agency as a mediating dynamic between activity and passivity, and 'acting' and 'suffering', we can see a clear development of the Daoist ideas articulated by Wang-lun; but we can also see a parallel with the ethics of responsible political action and interaction sketched out at the end of *Berlin Alexanderplatz* (BA 453–54).[70] Döblin's concept of 'Handeln' offers us a perspective on humankind that does not erase the agency of the human, but rather recalls us to our irreplaceably human capacities for recognition, agency and responsibility within webs that traverse the old borders of nature and culture.[71]

There are profound and far-reaching implications here for how we think of ourselves as communitarian and ecological beings; but more generally, there are also important contemporary insights into the ways in which we shape and mould an external reality that shapes and moulds us. As the psychiatrist Iain McGilchrist argues on the basis of recent research in neurobiology and neuropsychology, we need to rethink human 'experience' of the world in terms of a creative and participatory dynamic rather than a predetermined essence. There is undoubtedly something real that exists independently of us, but we nonetheless 'play a vital role in bringing it into being', thus in effect becoming 'partners in creation'.[72] This, I suggest, is the sense of co-creation that Döblin is articulating in his anthropology. While eschewing anything that looks like an objective reality 'out there' to be known and mastered, this concept also transcends the proto-postmodernist self-performances that he exposes as empty and, for all their ideological temptations, meaningless.

However, our status as co-creators is bought at the cost of our own finitude and our eventual subsumption under nature's cycles. This reckoning brings our discussion full circle, and as we think back to the musician's questions at the close of the *Gespräche*, we might now ask how our finitude underwrites our sense of human worth and purpose, rather than simply undermining it. We also arrive at what is perhaps the most tragic contradiction of all: the fact that our need for completeness and fulfilment is inextricable from finitude. This finds its biological expression in our species existence as radically 'open systems', but as I indicated above, that organic and systemic openness also encapsulates a painful existential paradox. This is the idea with which I now want to close my discussion; and having ranged across the whole of the natural world in Book 3, Döblin devotes much of the following book to examining the minutiae of individual human existence, particularly in relation to the experience of time and temporality.

Our existence in the here and now is never as present as we think it is, but is rather shot through with its own disintegration, disappearance and eventual absence. As Döblin weightily puts it, 'wrapped up in the moment of the "now", along with life and existence, is disappearance and complete and utter death' ['Im Jetzt ist momentan mit dem Leben und dem Dasein auch das Verschwinden und der völlige Tod gegeben']. In fact, the moment of the 'now' repeatedly 'flashes' with life and death at one and the same time (UD 217). The incompleteness of our lived present is what induces in us our inexhaustible metaphorical tendency to make and draw comparisons, and to interpret the people and things that populate our worlds as things and people that make sense *for* us.

The 'now' is constituted by the before-and-after logic of causality, but it also brings simultaneous moments, things and events into play with one another, thus prompting us 'to make comparisons, to meld together, to amalgamate' ['zu Vergleichen, zum Aneinanderschmelzen, Amalgamieren'] (216–17, 219). The temporality of the 'now' is recast, then, not as a moment of fullness and presence in time and space, but rather a point of radical incompleteness in an unceasing search for completion and consumption. It is a 'trial, a court, a decision' ['eine Probe, ein Gericht, eine Entscheidung'] (219). The sense that we can never fully occupy this moment combines, in the language of judging and deciding, with the suggestion of a radical ethical claim. This idea recalls the Benjaminian flashes of 'now time' in *Wang-lun*: those fleeting moments of affinity that demand our attention as agents with the capacity for change, before disappearing, unredeemed. And as repeatedly happens with his favourite tropes, Döblin now draws his literary figurations of temporality into a full-blooded account of what makes us inherently human, and our disposable lives inherently worthwhile:

> Die Unvollendbarkeit gehört zum Dasein eines jeden von uns. Die Unvollendbarkeit des Menschenwesens aber, die Trauer und Tragik, die aus dem simpelsten Dasein fließt, zeigt etwas Hoheitsvolles an. Was da klagt, was schließlich resigniert, ist nicht die einfache warme tierische Natur, die sich erkalten fühlt. Es ist deutlich mehr. In dem Beengen, Versagen, Erkalten fühlt etwas in uns Grenzen, die es unter keinen Umständen anerkennen will. In dem Schmerz um die Unvollendung, um die Krankheit und den Tod ist mehr als die banale Klage: ich möchte doch glücklich und gesund und unsterblich sein. Ich möchte — Vollendung. Wer da klagt, was da Schmerz empfindet, weiß — um Vollendung. (238)

[Uncompletability is part and parcel of the existence of every last one of us. But this human uncompletability, the sorrow and tragedy that flows from the simplest human existence, has something high and noble to it. What cries out here, what finally gives up hope, is not simply, warm, animal nature, which feels itself growing cold. It's significantly more. In the narrowing, the failing, the fading, the growing cold, we feel that something within us pushes up against boundaries, boundaries it doesn't want to acknowledge under any circumstances. In our pain at our own incompleteness, sickness and death, we can hear more than just the banal cry: but I want to be happy and healthy and immortal. I would like — completion. If you cry, if something within you feels that pain, then you know about — completion.]

The repeated dash, followed by the gnomic 'completion', shows Döblin to be struggling against the limits of description as he tries to account for our irrational grounding in meaning, our continual striving for it even in the face of its apparent absence. What sustains this hope is a reinvestment in everyday purposes and projects even as life narrows towards its point of disappearance. As Döblin had argued a few pages earlier of this hint of completeness, the nature which reincorporates and recycles us also runs 'straight through us'; and as an implicated part-counterpart to this natural world, it is my role and purpose in life 'to co-order and consummate this world' ['diese Welt mit zu ordnen und zu vollziehen'] (224, 227). Döblin's refiguration of death as inherent in life is certainly part of a broader philosophical fascination with finitude in the intellectual cultures of modernism, suggesting as it does powerful echoes of Freud, Simmel and Heidegger.[73] But by viewing Döblin's book-length search for 'our existence' through this prism of incomplete completeness, we can appreciate the predication of human meaning on contingency and finitude. In this mediation between that meaning and its negation, our myriad forms and their dissolution, and the representable and the unrepresentable, we begin to understand the possibility of meaningful human life both in and through its own contingency. Our finiteness is precisely what makes us 'make sense' as the beings we both are and might become. To put it in more existential terms, the very fact that we suffer, desire and love, invests our worlds with truth. This mundane but very real sense of our significance both 'casts us to the ground' ['zu Boden wirft'] and in the same motion 'elevates us' ['erhebt'] (69): Döblin is, in short, circling around (while never quite pinning down) the sublime fact of meaning, despite everything, in a post-Copernican and post-Darwinian world.

His attachment to this contradiction would come to shape his own intellectual and spiritual development during the years of exile. Christoph Bartscherer suggests that the dialectical interplay of 'greatness' ['grandeur'] and 'misery' ['misère'] in Blaise Pascal's *Pensées sur la religion* [*Thoughts on Religion*] (1670) may well have appealed to him.[74] Pascal argued that 'despite the view of all the miseries that touch us, which grab us by the throat, we have an instinct that we can't repress, which lifts us up' ['malgré la vue de toutes nos misères qui nous touchent, qui nous tiennent à la gorge, nous avons un instinct que nous ne pouvons réprimer qui nous élève'].[75] It is this paradox of an existence caught between 'infinity' and 'the void', between nothing and everything,[76] which for Pascal was to find its resolution in the figure of Christ. Christ's figural reconciliation of these contradictions, which had struck Döblin so strongly in Kraków, would become a significant intellectual impetus in his conversion to Catholicism.[77] However, in *Unser Dasein*, he had not yet found a metaphysical resolution for the contradictions, and he takes issue with systems of thought and belief that try. He rejects the abnegation of sensory reality in the ultimate pursuit of a nirvana of nothing: that Buddhist ideology was, of course, also found desperately wanting in Ma-noh's bad utopia (UD 228–30, 298–99). Although it is shot through with imperfection and disintegration, life should be lived to its fullest sensory, emotional and intellectual measure (475–77). And it is telling that Döblin mounts an impassioned defence of embodied human consciousness against its alleged devaluation — in the face of the impulses of the body and the unconscious — at the hands of Nietzsche, Freud and Marx (191–92).

While there is nothing about our existences that bespeaks it, still we 'should and must aim for completion' ['auf Vollendung soll und muß es aber gehen'] (238). This residual promise of something ineffably 'more', just as the scientific, philosophical and anthropological evidence piles up against it, remains the ground bass and underlying theme of Döblin's anthropology and nature-philosophy. It lies at the root of its inexhaustible sense of hope; and I will discuss art's particular role in redeeming that paradox in relation to *Berlin Alexanderplatz*. Nonetheless, for all the temptation to reduce *Unser Dasein* to a philosophical 'guidebook' for Döblin's literature and life, I hope to have shown that its multifaceted palette of approaches and styles makes it a unique and exciting work in its own right, which succeeds in capturing the messy but inherently dignified realities of existences lived out as both parts and counterparts of nature. By refusing to resolve its own contradictions, it presents us with a hermeneutic of the subject as both shaping agent and shaped participant. And *Unser Dasein*'s final sentence and parting shot — 'end and no end' ['*Ende und kein Ende*'] (478) — is perhaps that subject's most fitting epitaph.

## Notes to Chapter 4

1. 'She is a mortal, while you are immortal and ageless. But even so, I wish and long day in and day out to reach my home, and to see the day of my return': Homer, *Odyssey*, ed. and trans. by A. T. Murray, 2 vols, The Loeb Classical Library, 104–05 (Cambridge, MA: Harvard University Press, 1995), I: v. 218–20. Erich Kleinschmidt suggests that Döblin's immediate inspiration for the setting may have come from his encounter with Arnold Böcklin's painting of Calypso with a harp in the Kunstmuseum in Basel in July 1905 (*Odysseus und Kalypso*, 1882). But Döblin's acquaintance with the epic probably drew upon J. H. Voß's well-established German rendering of the description of Calypso, later in the epic, as 'the one gifted with language' ['die mit Sprache Begabte'] (*Odyssee*, XII. 449): see Erich Kleinschmidt, 'Editorische Nachweise und Kommentar', in Döblin, *Schriften zu Ästhetik, Poetik und Literatur*, ed. by Kleinschmidt (Olten: Walter, 1989), pp. 603–739 (p. 616). Moreover, Döblin's populating the island with hybrid 'bird people' ['Vogelmenschen'] represents a musically resonant reappropriation of the Sirens from the *Odyssey*'s twelfth book (see SÄPL II, 111).
2. See, most recently, Michal Rozynek, *A Philosophy of Nationhood and the Modern Self* (London: Palgrave Macmillan, 2017), pp. 60–61. For one of the classic analyses of the *Odyssey*'s figurative significance for the emergence of the Western concept of selfhood, see the chapter 'Odysseus oder Mythos und Aufklärung' ['Odysseus or Myth and Enlightenment'], in Horkheimer and Adorno, *Dialektik der Aufklärung*, pp. 61–99.

3. Cf. Foucault, *The Order of Things*, p. 422.
4. On Döblin's formative spiritual encounters during his journey, see Friedrich Emde, *Alfred Döblin: Sein Weg zum Christentum* (Tübingen: Narr, 1999), pp. 124–37; see also Sander, *Alfred Döblin*, p. 135.
5. For a compact but nuanced consideration of Döblin's aesthetic and philosophical development during this period, see Marion Brandt, '*Reise in Polen* (1925)', in *Döblin-Handbuch*, ed. by Becker, pp. 288–94 (p. 291).
6. On the text's gestation and (lack of) contemporary reception, see Thomas Keil, *Alfred Döblins 'Unser Dasein': Quellenphilologische Untersuchungen* (Würzburg: Königshausen & Neumann, 2005), pp. 23–28, and Christine Maillard, '*Unser Dasein* (1933)', in *Döblin-Handbuch*, pp. 280–85 (pp. 280–82). Detailed explorations of the text's hybridity of genres and perspectives include Keil's and Maillard's readings, as well as Benjamin Bühler's monograph, *Lebende Körper: Biologisches und anthropologisches Wissen bei Rilke, Döblin und Jünger* (Würzburg: Königshausen & Neumann, 2004), especially pp. 218–43. In her recent study of the history and the figurative potentiality of liquid crystals for a radical politics, Esther Leslie investigates Döblin's explorations of the crossovers between nature's organic and inorganic forms in *Unser Dasein*. She draws his discussion of crystalline forms in particular into proximity with his conception of human beings as capable of endless formations and re-formations. See Esther Leslie, *Liquid Crystals: The Science and Art of a Fluid Form* (London: Reaktion, 2016), especially pp. 146–52.
7. Midgley, 'Metaphysical Speculation and the Fascination of the Real', p. 13.
8. See Riedel, '*Homo Natura*', pp. 47, 52–53; cf. Hoock, pp. 33–51.
9. See here Midgley, 'Metaphysical Speculation and the Fascination of the Real', pp. 13–14; and Carl Gelderloos, '*Das Ich über der Natur* (1927)', in *Döblin-Handbuch*, ed. by Becker, pp. 276–80 (especially p. 277).
10. Bühler, pp. 215–17.
11. In relation to Döblin's proximity to *Lebensphilosophie*, see Elm, pp. 22–96; on the text's proximity to Freud's metapsychological thinking, see Maaß, pp. 37–64; and for a detailed study of his (admittedly not entirely documentable) intellectual and scientific sources, see Keil, pp. 59–129.
12. See Bühler, pp. 234–35.
13. As Jos de Mul argues, the near-parallel development of these paradigms reflected radically different approaches to the 'nature' of the human being. From his perspective as a trained biologist, Plessner formulated our uniquely decentred position in nature in terms of our particular sense of *space*, whereas Heidegger conceived his de-biologized concept of Dasein in terms of its sense of *time*: see Jos de Mul, 'Artificial by Nature: An Introduction to Plessner's Philosophical Anthropology', in *Plessner's Philosophical Anthropology: Perspectives and Prospects*, ed. by Jos de Mul (Amsterdam: Amsterdam University Press, 2014), pp. 11–40 (especially pp. 14–15).
14. See Arthur Schopenhauer, *Sämtliche Werke*, ed. by Wolfgang Frhr. von Löhneysen, 5 vols (Stuttgart and Frankfurt a.M.: Cotta/Insel, 1960–65), III: *Über die vierfache Wurzel des Satzes vom zureichenden Grunde*, p. 171.
15. Schopenhauer's emblematic distinction between 'will' and 'representation' ['Wille' and 'Vorstellung'], as it relates to the *Ich*, suggests one (possibly direct) influence on Döblin here. This concept, as it develops over Schopenhauer's career, incorporates two mutually dependent aspects. Each of us is an embodied subject of willing on the one hand, and a subject of knowledge on the other, capable of arriving at objective knowledge about both the world and our own biological beings through representations. Even before he had fully developed his philosophy of Will, the early work *Über die vierfache Wurzel des Satzes vom zureichenden Grunde* [*On the Fourfold Root of the Principle of Sufficient Reason*] (1813) articulated the antinomy at play here. In the second part of *Die Welt als Wille und Vorstellung* [*The World as Will and Representation*] (1844), the correlate of this dual existence is the experience of our physical body as an analysable set of mechanisms on the one hand, and a manifestation of the depersonalizing *Wille* on the other (as ineffably subjective, indexical existence). Christopher Janaway points to the 'enduring perplexity' of Schopenhauer's hybrid conception of existence, which goes beyond the bounds of objective knowledge in order to account for 'one's awareness of being oneself, indeed of being "inside" one's experience': see Christopher Janaway, *Schopenhauer* (Oxford: Oxford University

Press, 1994), p. 44. On the nuances of Döblin's engagement with Schopenhauer, see Hannelore Qual, *Natur und Utopie: Weltanschauung und Gesellschaftsbild in Alfred Döblins Roman 'Berge Meere und Giganten'* (Munich: Iudicium, 1992), especially pp. 40–41; see also Keil, p. 64.
16. 'Mais qu'est-ce donc que je suis? Une chose qui pense. Qu'est-ce qu'une chose qui pense? C'est-à-dire une chose qui doute, qui conçoit, qui affirme, qui nie, qui veut, qui ne veut pas, qui imagine aussi, et qui sent.' René Descartes, *Méditations métaphysiques*, ed. by Jean-Marie Beyssade and Michelle Beyssade (Paris: Flammarion, 1979), *Méditation* II, 137.
17. See, for example, Jaakko Hintikka, '*Cogito, Ergo Sum*: Inference or Performance?', *Philosophical Review*, 71 (1962), 3–32 (p. 25). Bühler (pp. 230–31) points to Döblin's debt to Descartes's search for self-knowledge, but he does not fully sound out the echoes between the thinkers.
18. 'Moritate', or didactic murder ballads, were common in the oral cultures of German towns and cities from the seventeenth century onwards. Klaus Müller-Salget explains this particular stylistic resemblance with reference to the common gestation period of the two texts, in his study, *Alfred Döblin*, p. 290.
19. See Ernst Mach, *Die Analyse der Empfindungen und das Verhältnis des Physischen zum Psychischen*, 3rd edn (Jena: Fischer, 1902), p. 17.
20. Ibid., pp. 17 and 20–22. On the influence of Mach's metaphysics, or rather his anti-metaphysics, on Mauthner, see Gershon Weiler, *Mauthner's Critique of Language* (Cambridge: Cambridge University Press, 1970), especially pp. 141 and 150.
21. Döblin's only explicit reference to Heidegger did not come until 1957, in a letter from the Sanatorium Wiesneck to his fellow writer Ludwig Marcuse, in which he speculated that the by-then deeply controversial philosopher was probably wandering the forests around Freiburg like one of his beloved peasants (*Briefe*, I, 484).
22. For a cogent discussion of Heidegger's profoundly influential move beyond these dualisms, see Hubert L. Dreyfus, *Being-in-the-World: A Commentary on Heidegger's 'Being and Time'*, Division I (Cambridge, MA: MIT Press, 1991), especially pp. 3–9.
23. 'A fellow who speculates is like an animal on a barren heath, chased around by an evil spirit, and all around the grass is green and lush' ['Ein Kerl, der spekuliert, ist wie ein Tier auf dürrer Heide, von einem bösen Geist herumgeführt, und ringsumher liegt schöne grüne Weide'] (UD 17).
24. See Edmund Husserl, *Die Krisis der europäischen Wissenschaften und die transzendentale Phänomenologie: Eine Einleitung in die phänomenologische Philosophie*, ed. by Walter Biemel (The Hague: Nijhoff, 1954), p. 20.
25. Midgley, 'After Materialism', p. 161.
26. See Wilhelm Dilthey, *Gesammelte Schriften*, ed. by Bernhard Groethuysen and others, 26 vols (Leipzig and Berlin: Teubner, 1914–2006), VII: *Der Aufbau der Geschichtlichen Welt in den Geisteswissenschaften*, ed. by Groethuysen (1926), pp. 85–86 and 148.
27. See Georg Simmel, *Lebensanschauung: Vier metaphysische Kapitel*, 2nd edn (Munich and Leipzig: Duncker & Humblot, 1922), p. 57; cf. pp. 60–61.
28. On these conceptual and biographical links, see Donald N. Levine and Daniel Silver, 'Introduction', in Georg Simmel, *The View of Life: Four Metaphysical Essays with Journal Aphorisms*, ed. by Levine and Silver (Chicago, IL: University of Chicago Press, 2010), pp. ix–xxix (especially pp. x and xxvii).
29. Heidegger, *Sein und Zeit*, p. 148. Heidegger argues that scientific knowledge is grounded in a de-temporalizing equation of *Sein* with what he calls a 'constant presence-at-hand' ['ständige[] Vorhandenheit'], in other words, analysable and measurable objectivity: see *Sein und Zeit*, p. 96.
30. Elm (pp. 10–13) shows that we can discern substantial philosophical affinities between his thinking and that of Simmel, Dilthey and Bergson.
31. Simmel, *Lebensanschauung*, pp. 52–53.
32. Heidegger, *Sein und Zeit*, p. 143; see here Dreyfus, p. 35.
33. See Midgley, 'After Materialism', pp. 161–62.
34. See Keil, pp. 132–33.
35. Johann Gottlieb Fichte, *Schriften zur Wissenschaftslehre: Werke I*, ed. by Wilhelm G. Jacobs (Frankfurt a.M.: Deutscher Klassiker Verlag, 1997), p. 122.

36. Cf. Keil, pp. 134–35; see also David Midgley, '"Was heißt eigentlich ganz tot?" Zur thematischen und poetologischen Bedeutung der Seelenwanderung bei Alfred Döblin', in *Poetik der Seelenwanderung*, ed. by Martin Hense and Jutta Müller-Tamm (Freiburg i.Br.: Rombach, 2014), pp. 169–84 (p. 174). As Midgley shows, it is likely that Döblin came into contact with aspects of Schelling's philosophy through the so-called 'objective Idealism' ['objektive[r] Idealismus'] of the philosopher Friedrich Paulsen, whom he first encountered during his student years in Berlin. Paulsen's *Einleitung in die Philosophie* (1892; 7th edn, 1900) was devoted in large part to investigating the dimensions and intellectual ramifications of an 'all-pervasive ensoulment' ['Allbeseelung'] within nature, over against the monistic materialisms expounded by such figures as Ernst Haeckel and Ludwig Büchner.
37. F. W. J. Schelling, 'Of the I as Principle of Philosophy, or On the Unconditional in Human Knowledge', in *The Unconditional in Human Knowledge: Four Early Essays (1794–1796)*, trans. and ed. by Fritz Marti (Lewisburg, PA: Bucknell University Press, 1980), pp. 63–128 (Section 13, p. 95); Schelling, *Vom Ich als Princip der Philosophie, oder Über das Unbedingte im menschlichen Wissen* (Tübingen: Herbrandt, 1795), Section 13, pp. 84–85.
38. For a discussion of the text's driving paradox, see David Midgley, 'Epische Dichtung: *Manas* (1927)', in *Döblin-Handbuch*, ed. by Becker, pp. 97–101 (pp. 99–100).
39. Cf. Baruch Spinoza, *Die Ethik*, trans. by Jakob Stern (Stuttgart: Reclam, 1977), pp. 5 and 595.
40. See Andrew Bowie, *Schelling and Modern European Philosophy: An Introduction* (Cambridge: Cambridge University Press, 1993), pp. 9–10.
41. Elm, p. 168.
42. Schopenhauer, *SW*, II, 360.
43. Ibid., I, 364, 366 and 372.
44. This interpretation of music as an art form that traces out the suture between man and nature reaches back to the dialogues between Calypso and the musician in *Gespräche mit Kalypso* (cf. SÄPL 45, 47, 62–65, 95).
45. As Simmel puts it in *Lebensanschauung* (p. 102), humans find themselves caught in a space between 'knowing and not-knowing', reliant on their epistemic capacities but unable to ground or explain them.
46. Paul Ricoeur argues that metaphor, and with it linguistic meaning itself, emerges through the constitutive tension 'between identity and difference in the interplay of resemblance': see Ricoeur, *The Rule of Metaphor: The Creation of Meaning in Language*, trans. by Robert Czerny, 3rd edn (London: Routledge, 2003), p. 292.
47. See Andrew Bowie, *From Romanticism to Critical Theory: The Philosophy of German Literary Theory* (London: Routledge, 1997), especially pp. 69–75; cf. Bowie, *Schelling*, pp. 5–12.
48. See Nietzsche, *KG*, III.2 ('Über Wahrheit und Lüge im außermoralischen Sinne'), pp. 373 and 376; Nietzsche, *The Birth of Tragedy and Other Writings*, ed. by Geuss and Speirs: 'On Truth and Lying in a Non-Moral Sense' (pp. 141–53), p. 144. Cf. here Georg Braungart, *Leibhafter Sinn: Der andere Diskurs der Moderne* (Tübingen Niemeyer, 1995), p. 1.
49. Georg Simmel underlines the paradox that we can neither affirm nor deny the concept of truth without already presupposing the existence of 'truth' itself: see Simmel, *Lebensanschauung*, p. 57. In turn, Charles Taylor has argued along similar lines in his dialogue with Deconstruction, arguing that Derrida's *différance* always silently posits the 'presence' that it sets out to disaffirm: see Charles Taylor, *Philosophical Arguments* (Cambridge, MA: Harvard University Press, 1995), p. viii.
50. On the likely imprint of Hans Driesch's vitalism on Döblin, see Bühler, p. 216, and Keil, pp. 74–79. This suggestion of innate organic purpose comes particularly close to Driesch's concept of entelechy, which aimed to go beyond philosophical distinctions between teleology and mechanism. In his work *Philosophie des Organischen* [*A Philosophy of the Organic*], based on in his Gifford Lectures in Aberdeen in 1907–08, Driesch defined entelechy as an organism's 'essence': entelechy was its regulating and directing 'centre', one which had no physical or spatial existence, and which was reducible neither to a substance nor to a form of energy. As the incarnation of every single actual and potential feature within the organism, it caused its material system to develop according to the model that it imposed: see Hans Driesch, *Philosophie des Organischen*, 4th edn (Leipzig: Quelle & Meyer, 1928), p. 379.

51. Heidegger, *Sein und Zeit*, p. 149.
52. Ibid., pp. 69 and 143–45.
53. See Simmel, *Lebensanschauung*, p. 16; cf. Thomas Isermann's discussion in *Der Text und das Unsagbare: Studien zu Religionssuche und Werkpoetik bei Alfred Döblin* (Idstein: Schulz-Kirchner, 1989), p. 13.
54. For a summary of Uexküll's theories of animals in interaction with their environments, see David Wachter, 'Amoeba, Dragonfly, Gazelle: Animal Poetics around 1908', in *Biological Discourses: The Language of Science and Literature around 1900*, ed. by Robert Craig and Ina Linge (Oxford: Lang, 2017), pp. 371–96 (especially pp. 377–82).
55. See Jakob von Uexküll, 'Biologische Briefe an eine Dame', *Deutsche Rundschau*, 178 (1919), 132–48, 179, 277–93, 309–23, 451–68 (pp. 144–45), quoted in Malte Herwig, 'The Unwitting Muse: Jakob von Uexküll's Theory of Umwelt and Twentieth-Century Literature', *Semiotica*, 134.1 (2001), 553–92 (pp. 565–66).
56. See Thure von Uexküll's summary, 'Die Umweltforschung als subjekt- und objektumgreifende Naturforschung' ['Environment research as a subject- and object-encompassing form of nature research'], in Jakob von Uexküll and Georg Kriszat, *Streifzüge durch die Umwelten von Tieren und Menschen: Ein Bilderbuch unsichtbarer Welten/Bedeutungslehre* (Frankfurt a.M.: Fischer, 1970), pp. xxiii–xlviii (especially pp. xxxiv–xlviii).
57. See Jakob von Uexküll and Georg Kriszat, *Streifzüge*, pp. 93–100.
58. Jakob von Uexküll, *Bedeutungslehre*, pp. 107–79 (especially pp. 107–13 and 154–63).
59. See Keil, pp. 82–83 and 87–91.
60. For an overview of Uexküll's direct literary reception, see Herwig, especially p. 554. In his *Grundbegriffe der Metaphysik* [*The Fundamental Concept of Metaphysics*], published in 1930, Heidegger praises Uexküll's emphasis on the organism's inextricability from Umwelt, despite his reservations about the biologist's yoking of the purportedly closed biological existence of animals to the understanding-as 'openness' of human existence: See Heidegger, *GA*, XXIX–XXX: *Grundbegriffe der Metaphysik*, pp. 380, 383.
61. See Herwig, pp. 570–71. As Uexküll argues in the 'Briefe' (p. 144), the intuitive poet is able to speculate on aspects of an animal's disposition and orientation which, because they are empirically unobservable and so unanalysable, remain closed off to the natural scientist.
62. 'Die Riefelung der Stengeloberfläche dient der Ameise neben der Erzeugung des Tastmerkmals ihrer Fühler auch als Wirkmalträger ihrer Füße' (Uexküll, *Bedeutungslehre*, p. 112).
63. In *Die Stufen des organischen und der Mensch* [*Levels of the Organic and the Human Being*] (1928), Plessner invoked the concept of 'eccentric positionality' to capture both the *a priori* and empirical reality that, unlike animals which remain centred 'in' their bodies, we are decentred: we 'are' our bodies and 'have' them at the same time, capable as we are both of experiencing and 'experiencing experience'. In other words, we can take up a reflective position 'behind' ourselves as embodied beings. See Helmuth Plessner, *Gesammelte Schriften*, IV: *Die Stufen des Organischen und der Mensch. Einleitung in die philosophische Anthropologie*, ed. by Günter Dux, Odo Marquard, Elisabeth Ströker and others (Frankfurt a.M.: Suhrkamp, 1981), especially pp. 360–65; cf. Elm, pp. 67–71. Keil (pp. 139–41) has qualified such philosophical similarities, tracing them back to common influences in the seminal (and arguably discipline-founding) anthropological work of Johann Gottfried Herder, which also highlighted man's constitutive incompleteness.
64. See Bühler, pp. 220–21.
65. Keil draws a close parallel between Döblin's fascination with this ambiguous scientific status and Ernst Haeckel's monistic projection of 'life' onto crystalline forms in his study *Kristallseelen: Studien über das anorganische Leben* [*Crystal Souls: Studies of Inorganic Life*] (1917). Keil suggests that this work influenced Döblin primarily through the theorist of harmony, Hans Kayser, who viewed the crystal as the harmonic basis of life itself (see Keil, pp. 112–23).
66. With close reference to Schelling's awareness of the heuristic status of metaphor, Bowie points to a growing recognition of metaphor's centrality both to the elaboration and to the fine-tuning of scientific theories, not least on the basis of the philosophies and histories of science in the work of such thinkers as Thomas Kuhn, Mary Hesse, Donald Davidson and Michel Foucault: see Bowie, *Schelling*, p. 5.

67. See Ernst Haeckel, *Generelle Morphologie der Organismen* (Berlin: Reimer, 1866), p. 8. Haeckel's influence on the intellectual culture of early twentieth-century Germany was profound, not least through his popularization and adaptation of Darwin's evolutionary theory. Nonetheless, Döblin's polemical opposition to Haeckel's monistic materialism is evident in a number of strongly disparaging remarks, notably in 1927 and 1938 (KS III, 106; SPG 367): see Keil, p. 150. As Bühler (p. 223) argues, the persistence of inorganic and organic patterns across generations and epochs also bears traces of Jean-Baptiste Lamarck's model of 'epigenetic memory'.
68. Like Keil, Leslie (p. 150) has also outlined this connection, pointing out that Döblin had in his possession a copy of Kayser's *Orpheus: Vom Klang der Welt* [*Orpheus: On the Sound of the World*], and that he mentioned the book in an article for the *Vossische Zeitung* at the end of 1927.
69. In this ramifying and self-reproducing vision, we can find a definite foretaste of what Timothy Morton calls 'the mesh': a tangled bank of interconnections between the organic, the inorganic and the human, in which '[n]othing exists all by itself, and so nothing is fully "itself"'. Morton's sense of an interplay between nature, technology and the human carries significant ethical implications for their malleable coexistence: see Timothy Morton, *The Ecological Thought* (Cambridge, MA: Harvard University Press, 2010), p. 15.
70. Bühler (pp. 242–43) has justly highlighted the biopolitical dimensions — the simultaneous open-endedness, malleability *and* violent manipulability — of Döblin's figuration of the *Ich* in *Unser Dasein*.
71. This is a way of thinking about humanity and humanness that also closely resembles contemporary movements in so-called 'ecological posthumanism', which aims to rethink the human being in close co-dependence with nature. The hybrid 'nature–culture' portmanteau of ecological posthumanism represents a significant critical development because it aims to transcend many of the old dualisms of essentialism and constructivism. For a cogent summary discussion, see Heather I. Sullivan and Bernhard L. Malkmus, 'The Challenge of Ecology to the Humanities: An Introduction', *New German Critique*, 43.2 (2016), 1–20 (especially pp. 11–14).
72. See Iain McGilchrist, *The Master and his Emissary: The Divided Brain and the Making of the Western World*, 2nd edn (New Haven, CT: Yale University Press, 2012), pp. 5 and 28–30.
73. Simmel's conception of death as an immanent presence in life in *Lebensanschauung* (1918) is reflected in the extraordinary suggestion that the life that 'we consume' in the approach to death is, at the same time, the life that 'we use' in order to flee from it: '[d]as Leben, das wir dazu verbrauchen, uns dem Tode zu nähern, verbrauchen wir dazu, ihn zu fliehen' (Simmel, *Lebensanschauung*, p. 107). There is a striking similarity here with Freud's description of an oscillation between 'death drives' and 'life drives' as marking out the individual's circuitous route towards death: a dynamic that Döblin probably had in the back of his mind while writing these passages (see Freud, GW, XIII, 41). But in a different philosophical vein, we can also detect parallels with Heidegger's profoundly influential sense of death of Dasein's '*ownmost* possibility' ['*eigenste* Möglichkeit'], that is, the final reduction of all our structures and relations of meaning to a point of complete aloneness in the face of death. In the footnotes of *Sein und Zeit*, Heidegger recognizes Simmel's place in a much older (Christian) intellectual tradition of situating death at the heart of life. However, in a distinction between his hermeneutic phenomenology and life philosophy, he argues that Simmel has not yet succeeded in separating the ontological and existential implications of death from death as a biological fact (*Sein und Zeit*, p. 249; cf. p. 263).
74. See here Christoph Bartscherer, 'Robinson the Castaway: Döblin's Christian Faith as Reflected in his Autobiography *Schicksalsreise* and his Religious Dialogues *Der unsterbliche Mensch* and *Der Kampf mit dem Engel*', in *A Companion to the Works of Alfred Döblin*, ed. by Dollinger and others, pp. 247–70 (pp. 261–63).
75. Blaise Pascal, *Pensées*, in Pascal, *Oeuvres complètes*, ed. by Louis Lafuma (Paris: Seuil, 1963), fragment 633.
76. Ibid., fragment 199.
77. See Bartscherer, 'Robinson the Castaway', pp. 263–65.

CHAPTER 5

❖

# A Creaturely Carnival: *Berlin Alexanderplatz*

*Berlin Alexanderplatz* is now such a recognizable landmark that, rather like one of Nietzsche's hackneyed metaphors, it has become part of the furniture, to be dusted down and presented when a venerable example of experimental modernism is needed. It is a subversive masterpiece at once familiar and awkwardly under-read. The regular comparisons with *Ulysses* (1922), perhaps the most obvious hook for English-speaking readers, have long since been nuanced into a finer appreciation of Döblin's unique achievement.[1] However, it is telling that even recent readings have continued to take the classic — indisputable — line that this is, first and foremost, German literature's greatest example of a city noisily narrating itself. In its denial of a protagonist-centred perspective and its polyphonic mimesis of the city, it remains a uniquely successful confluence of 'the political, the avant-garde, and the urban'.[2] To put it simply, it is *the* literary monument to the febrile Berlin of the late Weimar Republic.

The Alexanderplatz, or just the 'Alex', as it is still colloquially known, was central to Berlin's twentieth-century life. It was, and remains, one of the city's major transport hubs. In the wake of a boom period that had begun in the late nineteenth century, it had by 1928 come to epitomize the city's aspirations to be a site of change, exchange and capital. At the same time, it embodied that capital's seedier sides in the form of barely hidden poverty and rampant crime.[3] Its pile drivers, tramlines, product lines, jagged edges and dark corners are central to Döblin's novel. But if the Alex is one of the book's two protagonists, Franz Biberkopf is decidedly the other; and here I would like to refocus attention slightly on an antihero who, for almost a century of critical reception, has provoked a mixture of fascination, sympathy and repulsion. *Berlin Alexanderplatz* holds out the promise of Biberkopf's spiritual awakening, and it sets up a decidedly physical meditation on intractable questions of life and death. As Döblin discussed in 'Der Bau des epischen Werks', it even suggests the penetration of Berlin's asphalt and concrete, its blood, and its pungent and sometimes repellent smells, in search of the existential strata beneath (SÄPL 219, 245). The novel, in short, fleshes out an epiphanic theory of the epic concerned with existential questions as they are refracted through surface realities.

Döblin famously claimed that the second part of the title, '[d]ie Geschichte vom Franz Biberkopf', was appended to the book's main title at the insistence of his publisher (SLW 312). Quite irrespective of its verifiability, the anecdote has long spoken to the sense of two very different books joined at the hip. It is the narrated and the narrating city, but also a kind of *Bildungsroman* of a former Berlin cement and transport worker released from a stint in prison for the manslaughter of his girlfriend. Biberkopf's story sees him move in chaotic succession from selling neckties to hawking Nazi papers, through an involvement with a gang of petty criminals, to losing his arm after being pushed from a getaway car, and finally becoming a pimp, only to have his new girlfriend, Mieze, murdered by his sinister fellow criminal, Reinhold. What follows is a nervous and existential breakdown; his admittance to the mental hospital out at Berlin-Buch; and the life-changing revelation — dispensed by an ironized Grim Reaper — that he has been engaged in a hubristic and self-destructive process of self-preservation. In this chapter, I want to show that the intertwining of these two aspects (Biberkopf and Berlin) calls for a fresh interpretation: one that refuses to reduce it to the didactic tale of a violent Everyman, or else to read it in essence as an epistemological and aesthetic playground of urban texts and discourses.[4] My argument is that a 'creaturely' reading best captures this deep symbiosis, and by briefly revisiting the novel's background, I want to unearth its significance for Döblin's radical question of the self and its place in nature.

From 1919 onwards, Döblin had run a clinic as a public service doctor in working-class Lichtenberg, a proximity to the Alexanderplatz that underwrote his own identity as both implicated local and detached observer — even something of an outsider.[5] Nonetheless, after a journey that had already taken in eighteenth-century China, seventeenth-century Europe and a mythical India, not to mention the giants and monsters of the distant future, this was a surprisingly belated literary homecoming to a city which, as he had repeatedly pointed out, was his fuel and his lifeblood.[6] His portrayal of Biberkopf as a manifestly traumatized Front veteran unquestionably drew upon his professional treatment of the psychological and social effects of industrialized warfare — compounded by the sensory onslaught of urban modernity — among his working-class patients.[7] But alongside his day job and his literary writing, as I have shown, Döblin continued to cultivate his keen interest in the interface between medicine, biology and philosophy.[8] *Berlin Alexanderplatz* both grew out of this intellectual hinterland and fed idiosyncratically back into it. Under increasing pressure from his publisher, Samuel Fischer, in the wake of the lack of commercial success of *Manas*, he had begun work on the novel in October of that year. He started compiling material for *Unser Dasein* in 1928, and the chronological proximity betokens the strong conceptual and figural relationship between the works.[9]

In his own retrospective overview of *Berlin Alexanderplatz* in 1932, Döblin revealed how strongly its energies were shaped by the ceaseless interplay of form and formlessness, and creation and dissolution: a dialectic that characterizes the strains of *Lebensphilosophie* which were to leave their mark on *Unser Dasein*.[10] As Döblin suggests, Biberkopf's urban environment is marked by a vitalistic dynamic of 'simultaneous construction and disintegration' ['Aufbau und Zerfall zugleich'], through which figurations of forming and ordering draw relentlessly upon energies of destruction and disintegration (SLW 216).

As I shall discuss in the first part of this chapter, this damaged war veteran proves repeatedly, and violently, unable to subsume his experiences under a socially acceptable role in the city. But amidst the rubble left in the wake of Biberkopf's aggressive sense of his own masculinity, and the anodyne nature of his social reintegration at the novel's close, I turn in the chapter's second section to the idea of creatureliness. Eric Santner's influential concept of the 'creature' in literary modernism captures man's hybrid existence at the ambiguous 'jointure of nature and culture, the inscription of biological life into historical forms of life'.[11] In dialogue with this particular sense of the creature as a hybrid of biology and society, I briefly bring Mikhail Bakhtin's idea of the carnival to bear on the coexistence of form and formlessness in the novel. Bakhtin's theory of the polyphonic potential of the modern novel, as articulated in his theories of heteroglossia in the essay 'Discourse in the Novel' (written in 1934–35), has already been convincingly applied to Döblin's distinctly polyphonic practice in *Berlin Alexanderplatz*.[12] But the topos of the Renaissance carnival is also profoundly relevant to the heteroglossia of modernism, particularly as it relates to the notion — refracted through the figure of the messily incomplete human form — that there is a vital meaningfulness tied up with the negations that are integral to the life-giving energies of ribald humour, subversion and irony.[13]

The novel's celebrated montage sequences put into play the messy plasticity of a modern urban existence caught between inexorable creation and forces of ironization and carnivalization. But these montages also enact their own — figurative and literal — proximity to organic processes. This organic dimension to the epic novel is crucial to Döblin's literary practice, not least because it marks the point at which his aesthetics and poetics overlap with his anthropology. In *Unser Dasein*, as we recall, the idiosyncrasy of 'being human' lies in the fact that we are at once part of nature and its counterpart (UD 49, 291). As an organism, I am a structured *form* ['Gestalt'] open to and symbiotic with the natural world through a constant to-and-fro of nourishment and metabolic process ['Nahrungssuche, Stoffwechsel'] via the visible 'umbilical cord' of the organs; but I am also a cognizing and experiencing 'I', forever split over against it (95, 29). Döblin draws an intriguing, if implicit, metaphorical link between these two — respectively biological and existential — aspects. The open system of the human individual evokes an impression of wholeness, but it also remains incomplete and impermanent, tethered as it is to its environment. The individual's 'self-formation' and 'system character' ['Eigenformung' and 'Systemcharakter'] is offset by the fact that it is embedded in far larger systems (96).

In straddling this creaturely divide, the work of art is the figurative imprint of the human self as both a subject straining towards an ever-elusive sense of autonomy (and completeness), and the human being as a physiological and social *Gestalt*: just one more disposable part of organic, environmental, and — by metonymic and metaphoric extension — social webs (UD 241–42). As I briefly showed in my Introduction, Ernst Haeckel had brought a 'spiritualized and progressivist interpretation' to bear on Darwin's theories of natural selection in such influential works as his *Natürliche Schöpfungsgeschichte* [*The Natural History of Creation*], published in 1868;[14] and this monistic reworking fed in turn into the recognizably Romantic idea of a deep affinity between the laws that form inorganic matter into organic beings and those employed to create art.[15] As Haeckel had argued in the supplementary commentary to the lavishly illustrated *Kunstformen der Natur* [*Art Forms in Nature*] (1904) the distinctive characteristic of all organic entities — from unicellular protozoa all the way up — was an innate purposiveness ['Zweckmäßigkeit'] that fed into an ever-greater degree of completeness. Indeed, Haeckel rounds off his commentary with the observation that the adaptive and creative processes of evolution have culminated in 'the most complete art form of the primates, man' ['vollkommensten Kunstform der Primaten, im Menschen'].[16]

In a related discursive field, Döblin had argued in 1928 that works of art are dynamically akin to works of nature. Human beings are both 'created and creating nature' ['geschaffene und schaffende Natur'], a hybridity reflected in Döblin's understanding of his literary works as never entirely 'his' product, but rather 'emerging from a gamete in me like the young sprout from the growth-point of a plant' ['aus [...] einer Keimzelle in mir entstanden wie der junge Sproß aus dem "Auge" der Pflanze'] (SLW 107). This mediation between creativity and createdness highlights the anthropological truth-value of the work of art; and this quotation evokes the uncanny figurative proximity of botanical and human reproduction that has been persuasively discussed elsewhere in the specific context of the early works.[17] But in *Unser Dasein*, Döblin suggests that our perennial incompleteness is offset by the paradox that we nonetheless embody an 'approach to completeness' ['Anlauf zur Ganzheit'], or the intimation of fully realized selfhood (UD 73). The work accordingly figures, in strikingly Kantian terms, as 'a whole without any particular purpose in the world' ['Ganzes ohne zwecklichen Bezug der Welt gegenüber'] (UD 249). It is the mirror image of our peculiar kind of existence between being part and counterpart, both an embedded part of nature's cycles and yet painfully separate from them. Art is inherently meaningful, and it draws its forms and its energies from the myriad organic processes of disintegration, decay and regeneration to which its creators are subject. But if these are the theoretical underpinnings of artistic creation, what is their relevance to a novel set in the restive working-class neighbourhoods of eastern Berlin in 1928? Can this urban masterpiece, the product of a uniquely energetic yet dangerous juncture in the city's history, be credibly described as creaturely? And if so, what are the ethical implications for the stridently masculine creature at its heart?

## Sovereign Masculinity?

The modern metropolis had certainly dealt a body blow to the unitary subject, any stable sense of linear narrative and a cumulative personal history. As the sociologist Georg Simmel had argued in his seminal essay on urban consciousness of 1903, 'Die Großstädte und das Geistesleben' ['The Metropolis and Mental Life'], the city dweller must reckon with an unprecedented *'intensification of nervous stimulation'* ['*Steigerung des Nervenlebens*'], resulting from a rapid and uninterrupted exchange, a two-way switch, between outer and inner stimuli.[18] Simmel's theories of urban consciousness speak to the barrage of incommensurable sensory information afflicting urban life, but when mixed in with the trauma of Döblin's front veteran and figure of the *lumpenproletariat*, the implications of this theory are thrown into ever-messier literary relief as the novel progresses.

The urban narrative proper opens with this sense of depersonalization. However, it also reflects a radical and traumatic sense of decentring within the urban subject, which anticipates Döblin's meditations in *Unser Dasein* on what he calls '[das] Anonyme', that is, the amorphous, anonymous yet vital presence of nature, of which the individual *Ich* is an embedded yet vanishingly insignificant part (UD 230). From the very outset, the city is cast as an organic entity with a supra-individual life of its own: 'it had happy faces, it laughed, waited on the traffic island opposite Aschinger in pairs or in threes, smoked cigarettes, leafed through newspapers' ['[e]s hatte fröhliche Gesichter, es lachte, wartete auf der Schutzinsel gegenüber Aschinger zu zweit oder zu dritt, rauchte Zigaretten, blätterte in Zeitungen']. But for all the vital signs, this life barely disguises a constitutive void below the bustle. '[O]utside, everything was in motion but — just beneath the surface — nothing! It — was — not — alive!' ['[d]raußen bewegte sich alles, aber — dahinter — war nichts! Es — lebte — nicht!'] (BA 16).

The suggestion of an abyss is accompanied by the intimation of the city's own fleshliness, an organic twist to which I shall return below. We catch a sideways glance of a man and woman downing beer and forking meat into their mouths. The hallucinatory consolation that 'they weren't bleeding' ['sie bluteten nicht'] is redolent of a very different kind of encounter with urban modernity, namely, that of the impoverished Danish aristocrat and poet Malte Laurids Brigge in Rilke's Paris of 1910. The resonances may help us to grasp what is at stake here. As we briefly saw in the example of the plumbing channel in Chapter 2, Malte's fragmentary descriptions of exposure reveal those traumatic points at which the fabric, or the flesh, of the city momentarily comes away to expose the contingent materiality beneath. Mere pages into his notebooks, he notices a woman who has started and fallen forward, so that 'her face remained stuck in her hands' ['das Gesicht in den zwei Händen blieb'].[19] His horror at the open head, denuded of its covering, is echoed in other moments of ill fit between the fabric of the city and its mediating human and social faces.[20] This sense of collapse is reflected, from a different angle, in *Berlin Alexanderplatz*'s interplay between the semiotic systems of the city and the constant threat of their disintegration: as soon as the surface is pulled away, 'it — was — not — alive'. Unlike Malte, Biberkopf is unable to rework the onslaught into literary writing; and an admixture of fear and barely contained violence bubbles to the surface in the narrative's miniature montages of *erlebte Rede*, disembodied voices, raw sensory data, and sporadic moments of clarity:

> Lebhafte Straßen tauchten auf, die Seestraße, Leute stiegen ein und aus. In ihm schrie *es* entsetzt: *Achtung, Achtung*, es geht los. Seine Nasenspitze vereiste, über seine Backe schwirrte *es*. 'Zwölf Uhr Mittagszeitung', 'B. Z.', 'Die neuste

Illustrirte', 'Die Funkstunde neu', 'Noch jemand zugestiegen?' Die Schupos haben jetzt blaue Uniformen. Er stieg *unbeachtet* wieder aus dem Wagen, war unter Menschen. Was war denn? Nichts. Haltung, ausgehungertes Schwein, reiß dich zusammen, kriegst meine Faust zu riechen. Gewimmel, welch Gewimmel. Wie sich das bewegte. (BA 15, my emphasis)

[Busy streets appeared, Seestraße, people got on and off. Something inside him screamed, terrified: look out, look out, it's kicking off. The tip of his nose froze, a twanging and buzzing across his cheek. 'Zwölf Uhr Mittagszeitung!', 'B. Z.!', 'Berliner Illustrierte!', 'Funkstunde!'. 'Any more fares please?' The coppers wear blue now. He got off the tram, unnoticed, and was back among people. What now? Nothing. Head up you scrawny little shit, get it together mate, I'll thump you. Swarms, all these swarms. Look at them move.]

We are repeatedly disoriented by the narrative's sidesteps into snippets and fragments of thought, speech and discourse. The insignificance of Biberkopf's own historical depth in this chaotic patchwork comes to the fore in his 'unbeachtet' exit from the tram, in pointed contrast to the call for 'Achtung, Achtung'. The text parrots his internalized prison orders, echoing an institutionalized emasculation. And to cap it all, an hallucination of sliding roofs puts paid to any stable sense of centred agency in an image of mental chaos and imbalance which recurs throughout the text (16–17). Even as Franz manages superficially to stabilize himself and walk through Berlin without the attendant hallucinations at the start of Book 4, the chaos of his first re-entry is never far from the surface: 'those roofs can start swaying, swinging, shaking, sliding like sand they are. Just like that, they're gone, like a hat from a head' ['[z]u schwanken können sie anfangen, zu schaukeln, zu schütteln. Rutschen können die Dächer, wie Sand schräg herunter, wie ein Hut vom Kopf'] (131).[21] As in the uncanny twists of Döblin's short stories, this sibilant fusion of displaced hats and sliding roofs, and city and psyche, welds psyche into cityscape, melding symptom with symbol as it does so.

Beleaguered metropolitan man is unable to master the sensory and psychical shocks of urban existence.[22] The panic at a loss of mental control is only narrowly averted in the reminder that the roofs are nailed on, an illusion of stability which shades over into a yearning for the lost contours of wartime manhood in the sloganeering of 'firm and true stands the Watch, the Watch on the Rhine!' ['[f]est steht und treu die Wacht, die Wacht am Rhein'] (131). The narrative, then, shimmies in and out of adjoining psychical and discursive spaces — and these flashes of machismo hint at both the gathering clouds of the late 1920s and the persistent residue of trench warfare beyond the fluid bounds of individual consciousness, as Döblin the urban general practitioner had acknowledged in a number of essays in the early years of the decade. The border between inner and outer breaks down as the symptoms of the individual spill over into the texts of the collective.[23]

Against these overlaps of city and psyche, *Berlin Alexanderplatz*'s queasily sliding roofs are mirrored in a textual tendency towards instability; and they enter into an allegorical association with countless other fusions of psyche and city, most prominently the Alex's resident pile driver, which hammers away at the 'heads' of steel piles in a markedly physical symbol of the city's psychical barrage (165). I shall return to the pile driver's uncanny embodiment of psychical instability at the end of the chapter. What is particularly significant here, though, is that in mediating the violence of the city and its protagonist through a play of motifs and discourses, the novel exposes the precariousness of the idea of a sovereign subject. This illusion of sovereignty is a stridently masculine one, and its portrayal in *Berlin Alexanderplatz* is both complex and controversial. It is worth examining in some detail here because it provides an important foil to Döblin's creaturely vision.

The text is certainly rife with images of would-be masculine dominance. The chapter title of the notorious rape of Minna at the end of Book 1 — 'Victory all down the line! Franz Biberkopf buys a veal cutlet!' ['Sieg auf der ganzen Linie! Franz Biberkopf kauft ein Kalbsfilet'] (37) — on one level reinforces a link between militarism and sexual conquest. On another, it encapsulates both the narrative's bathos and its critique of sexual violence through a juxtaposition of physical conquest and violation with a paltry compensation — Biberkopf's token of restored manliness — in the form of a veal cutlet. Franz's orgasmic rediscovery of virility in the assault is accompanied by the comically overblown collapse of the laws of nature, where the victim simply 'melts away like water' ['zerfließt wie Wasser'] in a nod to the continua of organic and inorganic compounds central to *Das Ich über der Natur* (BA 39–40; cf. IN 105). The dissolution of gravitational and centrifugal forces in the face of this violent orgasm plays ironically off against the fanciful suggestion, in *Unser Dasein*, that the qualia of human experience make the laws of physics and chemistry shiver, tremble and totter (UD 87).

A mock-sublime shift into the natural sciences finds its counterpoint in its companion set piece, namely the flashback to the manslaughter of Ida, which sets up the finale to the second book. There is a disjuncture between the sufferings of Agamemnon and Orestes at the hands of Clytemnestra and the Furies in Aeschylus' *Oresteia*, one of Döblin's mythopoeic ports of call in figuring the relationship between man and nature,[24] and the disconcertingly detached and objective reporting of the female death in terms of the Newtonian laws of motion (BA 99). By suggesting that the formulae of Newtonian kinetics do exhaustively explain everything about this crime without the need to factor in the Furies, the narrator shines light on those points of mismatch between discourses and languages (BA 100; cf. UD 184). This modernist heteroglossia finds a particularly famous example right at the start of Robert Musil's *Der Mann ohne Eigenschaften* [*The Man without Qualities*], as a meteorologically exact account of weather conditions gives way to the conventions of nineteenth-century literary Realism.[25]

Here, the Furies that plague Orestes in the final play of the *Oresteia* give way to the phlegmatic concession that these are very different times, and that Biberkopf is troubled by no such qualms. The relay system of lit beacons used to announce the fall of Troy in *Agamemnon* has been replaced by the telegraph and electronic recording systems; but even as this diversion makes light of the subsequent recounting of Clytemnestra's passionate murder of her husband, the invocation of this ancient 'beast' still makes its unsightly mark on the text. As Maria Tatar has persuasively shown in her analysis of the misogyny latent in the fabric of the narrative, the 'vanishing corpse' of the repeatedly female victim contrasts with the narrator's repeated tendency to 'gender the incarnation of murderous evil as feminine'.[26] However, Tatar fails fully to acknowledge the extent to which Döblin's own portrayals conceal a persistent undercurrent of irony. In both a prefiguration and an echo of her sister's and Mieze's eventual fate, Ida simply 'melts away into slurry' ['zerfließt in Jauche'] (BA 102). In keeping with the dialectical dynamics of Döblin's prose, the repetition of 'zerfließen' is significant, I suggest, precisely because its dehumanizing function undercuts the narrator by restoring a negative trace — a remainder or reminder — of humanness.

We are told in no uncertain terms that the application of Newtonian laws of motion to the manslaughter of Ida leaves nothing unaccounted-for in its equations (100); but this is a direct (and deliberate) inversion of the observation of experimental science, in *Unser Dasein*, that it is the human element that represents the unknown and invisible quantity in any equation at all (UD 184). The curiously slapstick description of Ida's succumbing wordlessly to Franz's blows, simply opening her mouth in 'strange, pout-like fashion' ['schnutenartig merkwürdig den Mund aufsperrte'], gives way to the concession that she is simply no longer *there*, in terse contrast to the apparently sovereign 'da' (BA 99, 102). By presenting us with a manifestly inadequate kinetic account of Ida's manslaughter and reducing the text's female victims to water and slurry, the narrator brings to the fore both his own descriptive inadequacy and the machismo that his descriptions seem to make light of.

Franz's desire for 'da(sein)', his yearning for an elusive sense of sovereignty and security, certainly comes ironically to the fore at various points throughout the text (19, 43, 449), rooted as it is in his masculine sense of selfhood. The ever-more self-confident voice of fascism in late Weimar political discourse, with its false Edenic promises of law and order (82), is linked to Biberkopf's need to regain a modicum of control over a chaotic external world: a yearning for simple solutions that is just as unsettlingly familiar to our own historical moment. He has nothing against the Jews, apparently, but still, '[l]aw and order, law must reign in paradise, which everyone must recognize' ['Ordnung. Denn Ordnung muß im Paradiese sein, das sieht ja wohl ein jeder ein'] (82).[27] A political argument wih some Communists in Henschke's bar provokes a desire to restore the tranquillity of a proverbial Eden by lashing out,[28] only for him suddenly to realize in horror, as he brandishes a chair, that the city is an irredeemably meaningless place (95). These intimations of paradise, and elusive traces of mastery over body and city, find their dialectical opposite in Franz's desire to disappear and become nothing at all. As he stews self-indulgently over one of his personal misfortunes, we can hear an echo of Michael Fischer's own desire for self-control as the extermination of everything that is 'other' and incommensurable in 'Die Ermordung einer Butterblume': 'everything must be made clean, washed away. [...] From earth thou camest, to earth thou returnest' ['[m]uß alles sauber werden, muß alles weg [...] [v]on Erde bist du gekommen, zu Erde sollst du wieder werden'] (119). We have moved from the idyll of Eden to a melancholy recognition of man's transience in Genesis 3. 19; and in this interplay of disappearance and redemption, we once again recall Ma-noh's bad messianism in *Wang-lun*. Utopia is never that easily bought.

The novel's self-conscious intertextuality, indeed, repeatedly reminds us of that heavy price, exposing its roots in the embodied memories of the characters, as well as in the physical fabric of the city itself. Franz's repeated desire for a peaceful release from the sensory tensions of the city, for example, finds a recurrent counterpart in the repetitions that surround yet mentally decentre him ['da gehen wir hin, rummer di bummer di kieker di nell, rummer di bummer di kieker di nell, rummer di bummer'] (37); and as so often in the text's many echoes, we can actually hear the traumatic hybridization of the city into Franz's consciousness, and vice versa. The 'bum bum' of the Tegel prison bell — that echo of internalized discipline — mixes with the 'rumm rumm' of the pile driver (19, 165).

This shifting field of echoes and inversions constitutes a precarious foundation for Franz's trumpeted resocialization as an autonomous Berliner at the close of the novel. After his breakdown in the wake of Mieze's death, he undergoes a hallucinatory 'drastic cure' in the asylum at Buch, where Death castigates Franz for his destructive desire for sovereignty over his own life, before amusingly making mincemeat of him with mock-cathartic violence (431–32). He now sees the light, having accepted his role in Mieze's death, and can properly 'read' the city. There's always something kicking off on the Alex, but the main thing is that he's all 'there' again ['Hauptsache: er ist da'] (449). At the close of a novel-length school of hard knocks, figured in terms of an allegorical hammer which repeatedly swings against him, we are granted an *anagnorisis* of sorts, as Franz, his head well and truly pummelled, has his eyes opened and can read the street sign above him, illuminated by a lantern (453): the city is re-set as a newly legible text. In his new incarnation as a factory doorman, the rechristened Franz Karl Biberkopf takes down numbers and keeps a watchful eye on who comes in and out, freed of those urges to master an environment that he now accepts he never can fully control. The Alex is metonymically and symbolically 'there' to sustain him, and the roofs are mercifully no longer sliding off the houses (454, 447).

At first blush, Döblin seems to provide an answer to the chaos with which the novel has bombarded Biberkopf and his readers. However, numerous commentators have rightly questioned the answer; and it is in these questions, in turn, that we can find the seeds of a creaturely alternative. In his review of 1930, Walter Benjamin argued that the close of the novel sacrificed the courage of its fragmentary aesthetic by offering us an otherworldly picture of this hoodlum's redemption: the false consciousness and consolation of the old bourgeois *Bildungsroman*.[29] The re-emergent Franz certainly seems to embody the sense of watchful bourgeois detachment that Simmel in his essay of 1903 thought central to personal freedom at the heart of the modern city. Things are not as they seem, though, as the preservation of metropolitan individuality depends on suppressed antagonism, a defensiveness that threatens to break out into violence at any moment of closer contact.[30] Psychical stability finds itself underwritten by the threat of physical violence, and social control is upheld by a barely internalized communal and ideological force. An entreaty to stay awake, keep your eyes open and look out, tips over into a reprise of one of the text's cacophonous marching orders. 'Keep in step and make no fuss:

march in time with the rest of us' ['Halt das Maul und fasse Schritt, marschiere mit uns andern mit'] (454).

This disjointed end mediates its celebration of collectivity through the threats of collective violence. We may well take at face value the banal homily that a ship will always come unmoored without a big anchor, and a human being needs his fellows to stay afloat (454). But there is a jarring question mark over the mentally and socially stable 'new man'. The strange jumble of the finale, I suggest, undermines any positive picture of sovereign masculinity. Tatar suggests that Franz's redemption arrives in the form of a complete shedding of his bestial side, in other words, the disturbing 'desexualization' of a rapist.[31] After the twists and turns of the preceding narrative, it seems as if Franz has been rehabilitated, and we are duly presented with the anodyne picture of him eating cake with Eva and calmly reflecting on the past and the future (451). In a more explicitly political vein, Adorno and Horkheimer argued in 1947 that Döblin's novel embodied the ideological submission of the individual to the mechanistic will of the collective: this was fascism's falsely humanitarian side, the 'miracle of integration' ['Wunder der Integration'] reserved for those little people, like Biberkopf, who swallow their rebelliousness and finally learn to conform.[32] However, I suggest that it is the aesthetic failure of Biberkopf's reintegration that opens up the space for alternative readings. The narrative's warnings against the coercions and blandishments of the masses are undermined by the hints of collective violence in the shape of an army marching left and right and left and right. The drums of war echo those rhythmic figurations of '[n]atural history and urban technology' that Webber has cogently identified throughout the novel,[33] not least as the deathly reverberations of '*krumm* [...] *fällt um* [...] *stumm, widebum, widebum*' resonate with the 'rumm rumm' rumbling of the Alex's pile driver (455). In short, a sense of aesthetic closure and social resolution finds itself undercut, along with the protagonist it is supposed to underwrite. The onomatopoeic overlap in the text between the linguistic and the material — between the psychical and the physical, the city's brutality and the emergent forces of nature — highlights the illusion of the sovereign or unitary subject; but more immediately, it demolishes the myth of sovereignty and unity that Biberkopf has been trying desperately to hold on to throughout his story.

We are left, then, with a strangely unknowable and docile protagonist who is neither a convincing hero nor a fully fleshed-out penitent. Just as we are manifestly encouraged to dismiss his delusions of grandeur, so we are rightly reluctant to accept his final redemption. However, the rumbling and echoing of the book's close add a final layer of ambiguity in reminding us of the natural and urban forces that Biberkopf proves unable to control. This underlines his creatureliness; and by following his creaturely traces, I argue that the novel in fact offers us a far more nuanced sense of self, and of humanness, than its surface bravado might suggest.

## Of Men and Other Creatures

As a description of the human being caught in the overlapping spaces of self, nature and city, my urban creature mirrors aspects of Eric Santner's creaturely life. One of his focal points is the embodied facticity, the sheer thisness, of being human.[34] To develop the dialectic of body and mind that I have discussed at length above, humanness is a hybrid of body and language, the somatic and the representational. Being human means being non-conterminous with that biological being, and painfully aware of the contingency of the sub-significational 'abyss' in our bodily existence,[35] a gap and point of absence which gives rise to meaning and language, but which we only ever fragmentarily paper over with language and meaning. Against this unstable backdrop, creaturely life arises in the individual's 'conscious and self-conscious relation to things, crossed with borders and articulated within a matrix of representations that position him [sic], qua *subject* over against the world, qua *object* of mastery'.[36] 'Flesh' here is not primarily the meaty or rubbery mass to which we normally attach the word, but rather it invokes 'the semiotic and somatic stresses' of creaturely life. It speaks to the 'missing piece of the world' at the heart of self-conscious human existence, the uncanny and uncomfortable sense of ill fit that is what we are.[37]

On Santner's account, Rilke is one of the writers most explicitly committed to an articulation of creaturely life in literary modernism. In the eighth of his *Duineser Elegien* (1923), the poet laments that we are always fatefully 'opposite [...] | and nothing but that, forever opposite' ['[g]egenüber [...] | und nichts als das und immer gegenüber']. Our hybrid existence as nature's part and counterpart situates us in an embedded yet detached dialectic with our world. We hear by contrast that 'with all its eyes, the natural world sees | the Open' ['[m]it allen Augen sieht die Kreatur | das Offene'], as Rilke strives to poetize his animals' dwelling in what Santner, tracing out a 'biological metaphysics' after Schopenhauer and Nietzsche, calls the 'unimaginable enjoyment of self-being in otherness'.[38] This blissful self-being cannot be imagined because any sense of self and self-consciousness is predicated on a point of detachment and absence: it is baldly incompatible with the animal's biological attunement to nature's rhythms and its — supposed, imagined — acceptance of them.

As it develops beyond Rilke, Santner's creature is marked less by its (imagined) transcendence of a human–animal divide, than by its embodiment of the specific claims, transfers and new investitures of sovereignty in modern political life.[39] However, the entwinements and distinctions that *Berlin Alexanderplatz* draws out between natural and urban worlds can help illuminate the problems and potentialities of the urban self as a kind of creature. Recent scholarship has brought the pain of human detachment from the animal world into dialogue with the so-called 'crisis of language' ['Sprachkrise'] in European intellectual culture around 1900, showing how far the very fact of human language spoke to an insurmountable sense of alienation from nature. A peculiarly 'animalized' conception of the human had emerged through the writings of Darwin, Nietzsche and Freud, but this sense of species proximity only further highlighted the differences and distances.[40] Human beings are riveted to their animal condition, and that connection resonates strongly with the hybridity that we encountered above in *Unser Dasein*; but it also takes on a specific symbolic form in Biberkopf's proximity to animality. After hearing the picaresque tale of the conman Stefan Zannowich, as told by the marginal Galician Jews Nachum and Eliser, whom he encounters after leaving Tegel prison at the start of the novel, he laments that he is little more than a 'damn bloody animal' ['verfluchtes Mistvieh'], to be driven out of his corner of the shed for disposal by the 'filthy swine with his dog wagon' ['Schweinekerl mit dem Hundewagen'], despite not even being completely dead (BA 30): in short, an abject creature released back into society, but excluded from civic participation. In further development of the paradox, the intercalation of Abraham's near-sacrifice of Isaac in Genesis, complete with a preposterously jubilant Yahweh, is followed by the narrator's rueful comment that man (Franz) has his eyes, that 'there's lots of stuff in him, and it's all topsy-turvy' ['in dem steckt viel drin und alles durcheinander'], and that he is burdened with a dreadful brain: an altogether sorry state of affairs in contrast to the humble sow, who is happy to consist of flesh and fat (286). And as Franz later lies in a state of deep unconsciousness in the asylum at Buch, he laments that it is better to cower under the earth than to live in a human body. In contrast to that unreachable but idealized state of otherness — akin to Rilke's 'Open' — Franz emerges, in the hallucinated goading by the field mice around the asylum, as 'the most repugnant creature' ['das widrigste Geschöpf'], conscious of being set apart from nature yet desperate to rejoin nature's cycles (428–29). Man's status as 'the most repugnant creature' is reminiscent of Nietzsche's description of man, in *Der Antichrist*, as 'the most wayward and the sickest of all animals' ['das mißrathenste Thier, das krankhafteste'], if also the most interesting of all.[41] But it also painfully recalls Rilke's lament in the Fourth Elegy that we are never quite biologically 'in tune' like the migratory birds, even though '[b]lühn und verdorrn ist uns zugleich bewußt' [we are conscious of blooming and withering at one and the same time].[42]

These suggestions of a misshapen in-between space show us a Franz Biberkopf who is irreducible both to sovereign agency on the one hand, and to the cycles of nature on the other. He is, painfully, neither one thing nor the other. It is through the topos of Berlin's central slaughterhouse, with its premonitions of sacrifice, that this sense of contingency and violence might nonetheless lay an unexpected foundation for a new set of perspectives on humanness. The chapter title 'For the same fate awaits both man and cattle; as one dies, so dies the other' ['Denn es geht dem Menschen wie dem Vieh; wie dies stirbt, so stirbt er auch'] (136), is a reworking of Ecclesiastes 3. 19, and reflects the individual's subjection to the same biological facticity of death as the abattoir's pigs and bullocks. The narrator reels off the slaughterhouse's exact floor area, livestock turnover and administrative apparatus, finally presenting us, when the first round of slaughter is done, with the tastefully appointed butcher's shop on the other side, and reassuring the swine that it's nothing personal (136–43). We are confronted here with the sanitizing logic of modern food production as simultaneously central to properly 'civilized' urban life and emblematic of its underwriting violence. The image of condemned swine clambering over one another in fright now seems a chilling omen,[43] and myriad anthropomorphisms call to mind Giorgio Agamben's 'state of exception': that blurring of the internal threshold between the *polis* and the 'state of nature', *physis*; and between the sacrifice-worthy and abjectly unworthy, in the figure of 'homo sacer'.[44] After being assured of the legitimacy of the abattoir workers' duties as food providers, we are treated to graphic accounts of the slaughter, firstly of swine, and secondly of a bullock:

> (i) [D]as Beil ist heruntergesaust, getaucht in das Gedränge mit der stumpfen Seite auf einen Kopf, noch einen Kopf. Das war ein Augenblick. Das zappelt unten. Das strampelt. Das schleudert sich auf die Seite. Das weiß nichts mehr. Und liegt da. Was machen die Beine, der Kopf. Aber das macht das Schwein nicht, das machen die Beine als Privatperson. [...] Ritsch, ritsch, die Adern rechts, die Adern links. Rasch rühren. So. Jetzt läßt das Zucken nach. Jetzt liegst du still. Wir sind am Ende von Physiologie und Theologie, die Physik beginnt. (139–40)

> [The axe came hurtling down, plunging into the melee, with the blunt side crashing down on one head, now another head. All in a flash. There's a thrashing around right at the bottom of pile. They are floundering. The pigs throw themselves on their side. They lose consciousness. They lie there. What are the legs doing, what's the head doing? But it's not the pig doing that, it's the legs which are behaving like private citizens. [...] Rip, rip, veins to the left, veins to the right. Quick, stand at ease. So. Now the twitching begins to subside. Now you lie still. We're at the end of physiology and theology, and so the physics begins.]

> (ii) Da steht der aber hinter ihm, der Schlächter, mit dem aufgehobenen Hammer. Blick dich nicht um. Der Hammer, von dem starken Mann mit beiden Fäusten aufgehoben, ist hinter ihm, über ihm und dann: wumm herunter. Die Muskelkraft eines starken Mannes wie ein Keil eisern in das Genick. Und im Moment, der Hammer ist noch nicht abgehoben, schnellen die vier Beine des Tieres hoch, der ganze schwere Körper scheint anzufliegen. [...] Jetzt wird das Messer angesetzt werden, und das Blut wird herausstürzen, ich kann es mir schon denken, armdick im Strahl, schwarzes, schönes, jubelndes Blut. Dann wird der ganze lustige Festjubel das Haus verlassen, die Gäste tanzen hinaus, ein Tumult, und weg die fröhlichen Weiden, der warme Stall, das duftende Futter, alles weg, fortgeblasen, ein leeres Loch, Finsternis, jetzt kommt ein neues Weltbild. [...] Das Leben röchelt sich nun aus, der Atem läßt nach. Schwer dreht sich der Hinterleib, kippt. Das ist die Erde, die Schwerkraft. (141–42)

> [But there he stands behind him, the butcher, with the raised hammer. Don't look round! The hammer, which the strong man lifts with both his fists, is behind him, above him, and then: boom, down it comes. The muscles of a strapping chap like an iron wedge to the neck. And this very instant, the hammer has not yet been raised, the animal's four legs jolt, the whole heavy body seems to come flying upwards. [...] Now the knife will be prepared, and the blood will gush out — I can see it now — the jet as thick as an arm, lovely black rejoicing blood. Then the deafening cheers of the party leave the building, the guests dance out, a big tumult, and gone are those happy meadows, the warm stall, that fragrant feed, everything gone, blown away, an

empty hole, darkness; look, here comes a new world picture. [...] Life wheezes itself away, breathing subsides. The abdomen turns, heavily, then keels over. This is the earth, and here comes gravity.]

What strikes us here and in the surrounding passages, besides the bloody corporeal detail, is the narrator's carnivalesque relish: the imagined, 'jubilant' gushing of the bullock's blood is described in terms of a ritual celebration, and it immediately segues into an hallucination of revellers spilling out of their party, as life drains from the corpse (142). The first quotation sets in motion Döblin's dynamics of *Tatsachenphantasie*. There are echoes of the discursive play in Franz's earlier rape of Minna — with its suggestion of self-annulling laws of physics — in the description of the pig's moving through physiology and theology to the final jurisdiction of physics (BA 140; cf. 39). The borders between man and animal break down in the near-anthropomorphisms of jerking legs and limbs, the comic suggestion — in preparation for the slaughter — that the pigs are taking a 'Russian-Roman bath' ['russisch-römisches Bad'], and the reproduction of noises associated elsewhere in the text with Franz himself. For example, the disjointed 'das Leben röchelt sich nun aus' (ii) falls among other instances of the visceral but ironically medical death-rattle of 'röcheln', which in turn jostle alongside sounds that characteristically blur and invert the divide between animal and man, nature and city (138; cf. 142, 178). In modernist affinity with Bakhtin's conception of the medieval and Renaissance carnival, thought as a literal and figurative site of endlessly 'degrading and simultaneously regenerating functions', or rather disintegrating and redeveloping meanings,[45] the messiness of the abattoir continually feeds into myriad resonances with myths of slaughter, death and renewal throughout the narrative fabric.

In fact, reverberations of animal-killing can be heard time and again as the novel progresses, but these are not predicated simply on a semantic field of death. Mieze's brutal murder at the hands of Reinhold at the close of Book 7 is intercut with flashbacks to the knives and the arteries of the abattoir (139–40) — a filmic technique which makes Döblin's invocation of the 'Kinostil' in the 'Berliner Programm' (SÄPL 121) all the more suggestive; and the crime is also overshadowed by a burlesque travesty of the Grim Reaper (BA 352; cf. 185). The swinging hatchet, crashing down on the heads of slaughterhouse swine and Franz alike, sees the site of food production, right at the seam between man and nature, perversely mirror the site of his ritual sacrifice at the hands of the hatchet-wielding Death in the mental hospital out at Buch (139, 431). Ritchie Robertson has argued that as Gretchen redeems Faust, 'so the pure-hearted prostitute Mieze seems to redeem Biberkopf by her violent death';[46] but when read in the shadow of the abattoir, the novel's troubling sacrificial economy — through which he is supposedly resocialized and so redeemed — is far more prone to slippage and irony than Robertson's reading might suggest.[47] Franz's recognition of the need to accept responsibility for Mieze's violent death through his own hubristic bluff and bluster is of a piece with the collapse of sense of sovereignty in the face of his own mortality and the radical uncontrollability of his environment. However, this new openness to otherness, embodied in the refrain of 'letting things come' ['herankommen lassen'] (435–36), is itself carnivalized and subverted by being made bluntly explicit. Death casts himself as a bizarre hybrid of messianism, baroque figuration and low-cultural *Volkslied*, complete with a bemusing Berlin accent, and such self-ironizing claims as the parody of John 14. 6 in the claim that 'I am life and the truest power' ['[i]ch bin das Leben und die wahrste Kraft'] (431). And when Franz finally emerges from the asylum after much hacking, chopping, screaming, and clinical disagreement over whether he needs a physiological or psychotherapeutic cure, metaphoric catharsis gives way to a strikingly humdrum reincorporation into Berlin society. He is now Franz Karl Biberkopf, after his maternal grandfather, but he has the same papers and the same appearance.

Against that shifting backdrop, I suggest that instead of presenting us principally with the tale of a rapist's moral epiphany, the novel shows us how symbolic meanings are chopped up like so much organic matter and messily reassembled in new forms. It is by bringing the creature and the carnival together that we can see how these energies of regeneration and re-formation might link into the narrative of Berlin as a whole. We read that on a different kind of metaphysics, and beyond the centimetres into which he is being chopped up, Franz's body is certainly not dead, but rather 'all of it lives on' ['[es] lebt alles weiter'] (432). This process of renewal finds an amusing biological parallel in the image of Franz's broken soul containing many plant germs and drifting, in a dream state, out of the asylum on a daily basis to scatter more over the wintry ground (429). These organic metaphors nourish a vitalistic aesthetic that redeems fragmentation through fragmentation. In other words, the novel's symbols of violence, sacrifice and degeneration continually shade into their opposites of regrowth. Combinations and constellations of very different notes or themes set in motion a dynamic of interaction and interpenetration (SÄPL 41). To recall Charles Taylor's argument, the peculiar epiphanies of modernist literature are refracted through their fragmentary materials and forms; but the poetics of modernism are particularly characterized by an orientation of aesthetic disclosure away from the writing or speaking subject towards something altogether more disparate and fragmented. The 'epiphanic centre of gravity', as Taylor writes, 'begins to be displaced from the self to the flow of experience, to new forms of unity, to language conceived in a variety of ways'.[48] In view of this sense of shifting epiphany, my suggestion is that the various languages of the narrative evoke transient new perspectives in the in-between spaces of their echoes.

To that end, biblical allegory is repeatedly reworked through natural history, evincing new perspectives in its new constellations. The uncanny vignette of singing trees (345), which prefaces Mieze's murder at Reinhold's hands, recalls the image in Jeremiah 17 of a God-fearing man as a tree planted in living waters, which flashes up at the fateful moment of Franz's commitment to the Pums criminal gang in the novel's fifth book. What unfurls here is a portmanteau of myth and biological process which plays on different senses of 'verlassen' ['relying' or 'abandoning'] in its almost organic shift from Franz's assurances to his criminal associates that 'you can count on me' ['auf mir kannste dich verlassen', 'auf mir ist Verlaß'] (178, 206), to a repeated condemnation of 'the man abandoned in the wilderness' ['Verlassenen in der Steppe'] who relies on his own fleshly strength (198, 212). And even this condemnation is twisted through figurations of decay and renewal in waters that are apostrophized as living in a very different sense, with rotting plants and indolently stirring fish and snails (198).[49] This melancholic textual carnival embodies Döblin's mediations of allegory and symbol through fleshly reality. The contingencies of mental confabulation, as we saw them enacted in the psychiatric poetics of the early prose, are strewn throughout the text and invested with new significance in combination and constellation with each other.

But the implications here are by no means simply hermeneutic. I want to suggest that we find enacted through this figurative dynamic the ethical suggestion of a creaturely openness in the face of an uncontrollable, transient and chaotic world: a two-way movement of softening, opening and penetration between subject and world. We recall that in *Unser Dasein*, Döblin resorts to a gendered discourse in order to articulate the human being's position in relation to nature, connoting the opposite poles of 'person' and 'world' as 'masculine' and 'feminine' (187). Nonetheless, his concept of 'acting' ['Handeln'], with its unmistakable inflections of the Daoist *wu wei*, dissolves this polarity of subject and object into a dialectical relationship between nature and self. A mutual and open-ended 'enrichment' unfolds within a relationship marked by porousness and temporality. Döblin's objection to the self's ossification and secession from nature is marked by a rejection of the very idea of a unitary subject conceived as sovereign over nature (UD 168–71, 187). What we see here, I argue, is not simply the implicit rejection of a masculinist model of subjectivity, but also an aesthetic of openness to what is strange, unmasterable, and simply 'other'. Precisely this openness, though, refuses to let us sand down the text's jagged edges and dissolve its unsightly residues. What it offers instead is a literary reflection on a creaturely life that of its nature can never quite be rounded out and reduced to its animal underpinnings. We read, for example, of a gap or point of emptiness that repeatedly opens up in the fabric of the text beneath the shifting forms of material, urban and discursive reality at moments of particular crisis (BA 95, 142, 336). And as we saw in quotation (ii) above, this 'empty hole' ['leeres Loch'], and nothing less than a new metaphysics, comes suddenly into focus as the bullock is slaughtered in the abattoir.

The unflinching description of Mieze's violent death at the hands of Reinhold sheds light on this moment of contingency and point of fracture. We read that 'her body contracts contract is what her body, Mieze's body, does' ['[i]hr Körper zusammen zusammen zieht sich ihr Körper, Miezes Körper']. As she is strangled, her body itself seems to shrink from symbolic significance and disappear into its own hole; and in a distinctly filmic movement, the text immediately cuts to the image of an animal being bludgeoned senseless as the blood flows into the metal basins of the abattoir (352). Mieze is situated both inside and outside the novel's sacrificial and symbolic economy: a redemptive force, but also a bodily presence that is simultaneously both less and more than its own symbolic role. Just as interesting, though, is the way in which the narrative highlights its own textuality, and in so doing reminds us that as the novel's voyeurs, we are always looking at marginally more than an abject animal. The inversions of 'zusammen' and 'zieht' disrupt and poetize the metonymic flow, thereby foregrounding the strangeness of this mechanistic description of human death. Once again, the text refuses comfortable answers, as our minds are cast back to the description of her screams while she is beaten up by Franz in front of his sexual rival: 'screaming, screaming, endlessly from her mouth, torturous screaming [...] a wall of screams, scream-lances against all this, higher, shriller still, scream-stones' ['Schreien, Schreien unaufhörlich aus ihrem Mund, qualvolles Schreien [...] eine Schreimauer, Schreilanzen gegen das da, höher hin, Schreisteine'] (336). As language is pushed to its extremes, it fragments and assumes strange forms; but this fragmentation itself, as a form of mimesis in Adorno's sense, puts up aesthetic resistance to the modes of violence it enacts. These irreverent moments of play, of excess meaning on the cusp of violence, nonsense or nothingness, speak to a creaturely life in language that barely (but nonetheless) transcends the cycles of biological and urban violence in which it is caught. With this creatureliness firmly in mind, I now return in my closing section to the Alex and its environs; and my contention is that in channelling and echoing Berlin's vibrant textuality, this epic gives us at least a first glimpse of what it might mean to be a modern urban creature.

## Carnivals and Cityscapes

Reflecting on the modern author's dispersion among different languages and texts, Döblin argued in 'Der Bau des epischen Werks' that while the writer thinks that he [sic] is the one doing the writing, he is in fact being both written and spoken at the same time (SÄPL 243). Far from being an instrument at our sovereign disposal, language is a proverbially living being with both expressive and coercive power over its concepts and speakers. In affinity with music, it speaks immanently from within itself, shaping and reshaping the concepts that grow in it (242). Despite his reservations about the novel's end, Benjamin admired the way in which the narrative's dissipation among Bible verses, snippets from popular songs, and statistics — its 'montage'-like quality — violently 'breaks open' the structure and style of the novel as a genre ['sprengt ihn im Aufbau wie auch stilistisch'] and so opens up new, 'epic' possibilities.[50]

In the 'Berliner Programm', we recall, Döblin had overthrown the author's sovereignty by suggesting that reality should be portrayed as it exists in front of us, rather than the way it is mediated through language (SÄPL 122); and his aim for epic writing, as Benjamin recognized in relation to montage techniques familiar from Dada, was to get as close as possible to the materiality of the things themselves. But there is the sense in which 'showing' rather than 'telling' the city always involves a refractive speaking from a particular perspective, from somewhere: the montage at the start of Book 2 claims that the Rosenthaler Platz is chattering away at itself (BA 51), and a supposed sensory immediacy is always mediated through a seductive logic of texts and advertising blandishments (123–24). Sure enough, Berlin itself is Döblin's megaphone, his novel a noisy 'monument to Berlinese' ['ein

Monument des Berlinischen'].⁵¹ His celebrated montage sequences certainly serve to set in motion the radical temporality, and with this the moments of absence, at the heart of the sensory and textual presence of the city. Even when Döblin gets as close as he can to reproducing this temporal and spatial 'thisness' — in the resort to pictograms, pasted into the narrative at the opening of Book 2 from Berlin's latest telephone book — he simply highlights the unnerving absence that led him to supplement his text with yet more text in the first place.

The city's spatio-temporal movement from one moment to the next, and one place to the next, is portrayed metonymically in the imitation of tram travel, as Döblin follows the route of tram no. 68 through the city (52). The spatial displacement reflected in the enumerated stops suggests a constant temporal and textual displacement and absenting: in short, an echo of the idea, further developed in *Unser Dasein*, that 'now follows upon now' ['auf Jetzt folgt Jetzt'] with no end-point or consummation (UD 219). This effect of absence-in-presence is only further intensified in the uncannily animistic descriptions of streets radiating from or converging on the Rosenthaler Platz (BA 53). We are thrown head first into the ever-becomingness of the city as advertising jingles jostle alongside enumerations of company departments and snippets of such contingent and incomplete personal narratives as that of young Max Rüst who, as a kind of forebear of Tom Tykwer's flash-forwards in one of the iconic films of post-Reunification Berlin, *Lola rennt* (1998), will die 'at the still incomplete age of 55 years' ['im noch nicht vollendeten Alter von 55 Jahren'] (54).

Arguing that Döblin recasts the city itself as an emptily functional narrator, Klaus Scherpe suggests that the novel hollows out its own discourses and motifs, leaving behind 'isolated functional effects of meaning, incidental signs of an already prestructured world of images and signifiers'.⁵² There is certainly an excitable exchangeability to the surfaces and languages of Weimar capitalism and, with this, the sense of a linguistic and textual authority that has been dissipated among the population at large. In his analysis of the contours and contradictions of creaturely life in modernity, Santner has pointed to a figuratively fleshly transfer of sovereignty from the king, the royal, to the people at large.⁵³ One correlate of this dissipation of sovereignty is a disturbing equivalence of the languages of advertising on the one hand and reactionary populism on the other. The start of Book 4 sees a regurgitation of the notorious *Dolchstoßlegende* — Philipp Scheidemann had promised us peace, freedom and bread! — alongside the flogging of caramel malt beer to expectant mothers (123).⁵⁴ In the conjoining of the discourses of capitalism and a budding fascism, the consumerist language of expectation melds with the menace of broken political promises. The particular ways in which individuals are coercively spoken to, even in a sense spoken, by the city comes to the fore in a prostitute's regurgitation of the jingle for Mampe brandy in a bid to offer Franz something that will help him get it up: 'Come on big man, one more Mampe. If it's your eyes, go to Mampe, let that open them' ['Sinds die Augen, geh zu Mampe, gieß dir ein auf die Lampe'] (BA 36). In short, Franz's yearning for sovereignty is inscribed and recirculated in the city's exchangeable texts. Even this jingle turns back on itself, however, by playfully anticipating the 'lantern' and the 'open eyes' of Franz's *anagnorisis* (BA 453). And it is in this light that I want to argue for a complex relationship between Berlin's polyphonic texts and the emergence within them of creaturely selfhood.

The doctrine implicit in 'letting things come' is characterized, in the adapted terms of yet another text (John 1. 1), as the recognizably modernist 'word of death', stonily present in Franz's mouth as he lies in his asylum bed at Buch (BA 435).[55] In another ironic inversion of Franz's aggressive taunts to 'let them come' (BA 73, 265), the idea is presented in schematic terms as an embrace of the transience, unmasterability and impenetrability of the city and its circulating texts. But as the idea would develop explicitly in *Unser Dasein*, letting things come also embodies the undeterminable sense of our connections with, and dependencies on, other people and things in the subjectively lived moment in time, each and every 'now' (UD 212–19). In a particularly revealing crossover between the novel and the essay, this speaks to the need for Franz to sacrifice his obduracy in the face of the constantly changing surface of the city. More than that, it suggests that his decentred presence as an urban self can meaningfully vibrate, and find an intimation of completeness, only within a web of mutating processes, interactions and texts (UD 213). Simmel's sense of mistrustful urban coexistence gives way to a praxis of urban collectivity, which depends upon the recognition of interdependence and a shared sense of creaturely finiteness and fragility. The urban gesture of 'letting things come' affirms this nowtime precisely not as a discrete 'Jetzt', but rather as a plenitude of converging and diverging connections and possibilities. As I suggested in my previous chapter, this is a nodal point of metaphorical meanings, which is meaningful yet radically open and resistant to fixed and definite judgments and decisions (215, 219). By homing in on two specific examples from the fabric of Berlin itself, my final suggestion is that this creaturely anthropology unfurls not primarily within the protagonist's personal journey to epiphany, but rather out on the street itself. In short, the two halves of the novel — Biberkopf and the Alexanderplatz — reveal their noisy interdependence.

★ ★ ★ ★ ★

By 1928, the Alex had become synonymous with urban reconstruction, and Döblin's montage sequences bring to lively presence a cityscape that is in the midst of *Umbau*.[56] It is in this space between form and formlessness that the idea of 'letting things come' finds purchase as both an openness to contingency and a renewed and reinvigorated locus of creaturely meaning in the city. The laying of the new U-Bahn line, which would be opened in December 1930, finds its way into the narrative at the start of the urban panoramas of Books 4 and 5 (BA 123, 165). The mentions seem properly coincidental, and simply another example of Döblin's desire to give a vivid account of a real contemporary time and space. What strikes us, however, is the way in which this street-level description of the city points beyond itself, and shades over into something of symbolic significance. The riffing invocation of security and protection companies near the start of the fourth book, for example, playfully invokes the panoptical quality of the novel's own textual strategies (106). In a dynamic of seemingly free association, mimicking a dynamic of urban transit, the narrative shifts from the 'Watch and Safeguard Service for Greater Berlin' ['*Wach*-und Schutzdienst für Groß-Berlin und außerhalb'], through the tellingly named 'Germania Protective Agency' ['*Wach*bereitschaft Deutschland'], to a nonsensical play on '*Wach*smann als Erzieher' and 'Flachsmann als Erzieher', before ending up ridiculously in the contiguous and entirely random Adler's Laundrette ['*Wäsch*erei Adler'] with its speciality in 'fine gents' and ladies' underwear' ['feine Herren- und Damen*wäsch*e'] (124, my emphases).

In an extensive discussion of James Joyce in *The Modes of Modern Writing*, David Lodge points to a high-modernist proclivity for scattering words from seemingly incommensurable realms of signification through the fabric of a mundane, metonymic narrative reality.[57] Döblin's use of montage is interesting in this connection because of the way in which the contingent details of the city's furniture and infrastructure interact with the narrative's central thrust. Against repeated rumbles of the *Dolchstoßlegende* (123), the verbiage brings echoes of the motifs of '*Wacht* am Rhein' and '*wach* sein' into dialogue with the hardware of the city (cf. BA 131, 454, my emphases), before ironizing both in a moment of textual play. Biberkopf's story is fused into Berlin's spatiality and temporality, and his persistent desire for a militaristic sense of his own power and control is repeatedly carnivalized. As if in delight at the plasticity of its own language, the narrative acts out its own proximity to disintegration and nonsense. This contingency, of course, threatens to tip over into the pre-texts and the preparatory violence of fascism. However, the narrative's playfulness also points beyond itself as a mimesis of a mode of urban life that is open to radical difference and otherness in the city's frenetic here and now, as Döblin describes modernity itself in *Unser Dasein* (213). The cityscape's proximity to disintegration, its tendency to come apart at the seams, is what opens up new perspectives and reinvestments.

Once again, then, at the heart of the breaking down, we discover an inexhaustible drive to build back up, as the carnivalization of meanings feeds into transient reconfigurations, and fragmentation lays the ground for re-creation. Appropriately enough, this brings us back to the Alex's pile driver, whose pounding has echoed throughout our discussions. Book 5's negotiations with building work open with an onomatopoeic description of how the pile driver slams away at the Alex (165). This biologically inflected portrayal of collective animal activity — people swarming all over the ground 'like bees' — contrasts markedly with Biberkopf's own bluster at his ability to rise above the city, to be a masculine conqueror of all.[58] We are told to shed no tears over the condemned Hahn department store, as it is simply part of a natural cycle of rejuvenation, to be cannibalized into something new, just as the former statue of the Berolina might be recast into medals. As Döblin had argued with a Darwinian flourish in 'Der Geist des naturalistischen Zeitalters', cities were themselves natural histories, the products of the evolutionary tendency of our species towards collaborative forms of existence. If that essay of 1924 had invited its readers to reconsider the dynamics of human collectivity for the technological age,

*Berlin Alexanderplatz* presents us with Döblin's literary response, the modern city itself incarnate as a collective creature.

However, the personification of the piles for the U-Bahn exceeds even these natural cycles, motioning to a creaturely meaning that is always marginally in excess of the biological reality of simply 'being human'. There is a miniature process of subjective association on the part of passers-by who have time outside the city's frenetic circulation of texts briefly to watch the pile driver hammering piles into the ground, the three 'bangs' an echo of the novel's three 'hammer blows' of fate. In their witnessing of the battered 'heads', we glimpse a playful allegory of the modern epic itself. And in the observation of how slickly it all passes off, there is a hint at the readers' shared experience in following Biberkopf's trials and tribulations, not to mention a nod to the ideal of a shared public space and a collective encounter with the work of art:

> Rumm rumm haut die Dampframme auf dem Alexanderplatz.
> Viele Menschen haben Zeit und gucken sich an, wie die Ramme haut. Ein Mann oben zieht immer eine Kette, dann pafft es oben, und ratz hat die Stange eins auf den Kopf. Da stehen die Männer und Frauen und besonders die Jungens und freuen sich, wie das geschmiert geht: ratz kriegt die Stange eins auf den Kopf. Nachher ist sie klein wie eine Fingerspitze, dann kriegt sie aber noch immer eins, da kann sie machen, was sie will. Zuletzt ist sie weg, Donnerwetter, die haben sie fein eingepökelt, man zieht befriedigt ab. (165)
>
> [Boom boom, the steam pounds away on the Alex. Many people have time spare, and watch the pile driver pounding away. Up top there's a man pulling at a chain, then a puff of steam, and bang! The pile gets it right on the head. There are men and women standing around and lots of youngsters as well and they love how slick it all is: bang! The pile gets it right on the head. It gets smaller, smaller, as small as a fingertip, then it gets it again, there, they can do what they like with that one. Bloody hell, they've given that a good old whack, and people head off, satisfied.]

Throughout this study, I have argued that Döblin's aesthetic leaves behind a so-called hermeneutic remnant, even in the wake of senseless moments of coercion, violence and collapse. My introduction to this chapter went further still, suggesting that art itself comes to elicit the oblique suggestion of purposiveness — a meaningful form of life — in the face of contingency and incompleteness. Crystallized in these shared moments on the Alex is a filmic and uncanny suggestion of completeness in the midst of urban violence and disintegration, as the cyborg-like pole is gratifyingly driven into the ground like a shrinking fingertip; and the imagined pleasure of spectatorship recalls Wang-lun's autoerotic dream of being consumed by a sycamore as passers-by rejoice in its growth. Our Berlin scene shows a disappearance into a different kind of hole and, in the hammer blows, a cathartic glimpse of Biberkopf's ravaged body and mind. Echoes of the pile driver, in the form of inculcated verb declensions,[59] intertwine with advertisements for Loeser und Wolff cigars and cigarillos, in another hint at Weimar Berlin's seductive mix of consumerist freedom and biopolitical control. But as one of the city's contingent carnival pleasures, this is a moment that refracts the aesthetic promise of completion and consumption into the novel's many random and nondescript Berlin vignettes (126–27). And out on the Alex, that's more than enough to let the nameless fellow Berliners move off and get on with their intersecting days, satisfied, with the sense that something, however small, has been finished: something is done. 'Bloody hell, they've given that a good old whack.'

The novel's enduring achievement is certainly not to redeem its deeply troubled and troubling protagonist in an economy of resolution and resocialization, to the ominous drumbeat of '*onwards, onwards to freedom*' ['*in die Freiheit, die Freiheit hinein*'] (454). Rather, it brings to expression many fleeting promises of creaturely life and creaturely meaning from within its unredeemed fabric, leaving Franz's own future as one of the little people wide open, albeit with his head now screwed on (we hope), as the novel's cacophony of noises fades to silence. The would-be redemptive logic of the narrative's close gives way to something more ramifying and uncertain: the suggestion of meaningful human life, decentred and reconstituted in language, and denuded of its ideologies of sovereignty.

The events of the following decade illustrated the lethal historical contingencies that this disorientation was to help prise open; and although National Socialism had not found fertile political ground in Berlin during the 1920s, we can see that many of the ingredients for what was to come were already in place by 1928. Indeed, the image of the pile driver speaks not just to completion, but also to the violence of re-forming and re-moulding, as we recall the narrator's rather sinister opening promise that this ne'er-do-well would be 'bent into shape' ['zurechtgebogen'] by the end (11). But at the same time, the text's openness and polyvalence confound and subvert our interpretations and judgments; and it is to that subversiveness that we owe its enduring aesthetic and ethical power. If the urban self is to be rethought, it is neither in punishment and redemption, nor in orders to stay on your guard and keep your eyes open, but rather in those moments of *Resonanz* at the limits of language, beyond sovereign control, and teetering on the edge of absurdity. Franz is by no means the only creature in town.[60]

## Notes to Chapter 5

1. Döblin published an enthusiastic review of James Joyce's masterpiece in 1928, lauding its 'radicality' ['Radikalität'] and its 'uncommon sense of reality and truth to life' ['ungewöhnliche Echtheit und Naturtreue'] (AzL 287, 290). In a retrospective essay on *Berlin Alexanderplatz*, he acknowledged that *Ulysses* — whose first German translation had appeared in 1927 — had proved to be a 'good wind' in his sails during the latter parts of work on his own novel (SLW 217). His enduring frustration at the constant comparisons obscures the changes in Döblin's style that occurred after the encounter, as Robert Weninger argues in his monograph *The German Joyce* (Gainesville, FL: University Press of Florida, 2012), pp. 42–46. Nonetheless, the objection also reflects Döblin's own — entirely justified — sense that he was striking out on an original path, especially in respect of the work's mythic and symbolic textures (SLW 217). Perhaps pre-emptively, he had argued in his review that Joyce's particular response to the crisis of identity and the problem of the modern novel merely represented *one* possible answer (AzL 288).
2. Andreas Huyssen, *Miniature Metropolis: Literature in an Age of Photography and Film* (Cambridge, MA: Harvard University Press, 2015), p. 156; see also David Dollenmayer, 'Narration and the City', in *A New History of German Literature*, ed. by David E. Wellbery (Cambridge, MA: Harvard University Press, 2004), pp. 764–69 (p. 767).

3. Webber, *Berlin in the Twentieth Century*, p. 189.
4. See Keller, pp. 155–56; cf., for example, Horn, pp. 719–39.
5. Webber traces a sense of outsiderness all the way back to the family's move from Stettin to Berlin in October 1888 when Döblin was ten years old: see *Berlin in the Twentieth Century*, pp. 189–90; cf. SLW 110–11. Döblin's sense of his own Jewish identity and heritage had been sharpened by his tour of Poland, as recounted in *Reise in Polen* (1925): see Müller-Salget, 'Döblin and Judaism', p. 235. Jewish modes of storytelling can be found in *Berlin Alexanderplatz*, not least in the playful 'delight in fiction' exhibited by the Jew Nachum in his recounting of the tale of the conman Stefan Zannowich. As Stephanie Bird has shown, the three interludes of Biberkopf's encounters with the Galician Jewish immigrants — outsiders even in Berlin — form something of a subversive counterpoint to the epic's central didactic narrative thrust (BA 21–31, 43–45, 130–35): see Stephanie Bird, 'Nachum der Weise: On Storytelling, Eyes, and Misunderstanding in *Berlin Alexanderplatz*', in *Alfred Döblin: Paradigms of Modernism*, ed. by Davies and Schonfield, pp. 245–60 (especially pp. 246–51).
6. See Sabina Becker, 'Großstadtroman: *Berlin Alexanderplatz. Die Geschichte vom Franz Biberkopf* (1929)', in *Döblin Handbuch*, ed. by Becker, pp. 102–23 (p. 102).
7. See Fuechtner, pp. 118 and 123. A brief conversation between Biberkopf and the polisher Georg Dreske in Book 2, concerning his recent involvement with the Nazis, reveals that he is a veteran of the trenches at Arras (BA 84).
8. See Midgley, 'Metaphysical Speculation and the Fascination of the Real', p. 13.
9. For concise accounts of the genesis of both texts, see Becker, 'Großstadtroman: *Berlin Alexanderplatz*', pp. 102–03; and Maillard, '*Unser Dasein* (1933)', pp. 280–81.
10. See Elm, pp. 10–23.
11. Eric L. Santner, *The Royal Remains: The People's Two Bodies and the Endgames of Sovereignty* (Chicago, IL: University of Chicago Press, 2011), p. 13.
12. See Anne Nesbet, 'Schizoglossia and *Berlin Alexanderplatz*', *Qui Parle*, 2.1 (1988), 125–41.
13. See Mikhail Bakhtin, *Rabelais and his World*, trans. by Helene Iswolsky (Bloomington: Indiana University Press, 1984), especially pp. 10 and 15–21.
14. Saul, 'Darwin in German Literary Culture 1890–1913', p. 48.
15. See ibid., p. 51.
16. See Ernst Haeckel, *Kunstformen der Natur: Supplement-Heft; Allgemeine Erläuterung und systematische Übersicht* (Leipzig and Vienna: Verlag des Bibliographischen Instituts, 1904), pp. 8 and 47.
17. See Linda Leskau, 'Botanical Perversions: On the Depathologization of Perversions in Texts by Alfred Döblin and Hanns Heinz Ewers', in *Biological Discourses*, ed. by Craig and Linge, pp. 211–34.
18. Georg Simmel, 'Die Großstädte und das Geistesleben', in *Das Individuum und die Freiheit: Essais* (Berlin: Wagenbach, 1984), pp. 192–204 (p. 192); Simmel, 'The Metropolis and Mental Life', trans. by H. H. Gerth, in *Classic Essays on the Culture of Cities*, ed. by Richard Sennett (Englewood Cliffs, NJ: Prentice Hall, 1969), pp. 47–60 (p. 48). The emphasis is in the original.
19. Rilke, *Werke*, III, 457; Rilke, *The Notebooks*, p. 5.
20. Santner uses the term 'flesh' to describe this phenomenon of ill fit between our biological vitality and our meaning-making networks: see *The Royal Remains*, pp. 4–5.
21. In reflection of this instability, David Lodge identifies a characteristically modernist slippage of metaphor's 'word-selection' onto metonymy's axis of 'combination'. See Lodge, *The Modes of Modern Writing: Metaphor, Metonymy, and the Typology of Modern Literature* (London: Arnold, 1977), pp. 73–77, 139–44.
22. See my discussion of Benjamin's theorization of shock experiences above, in the context of *Berge Meere und Giganten*: cf. Benjamin, GS, 1.2, 615.
23. See Fuechtner, pp. 118 and 123.
24. See also my discussion of 'Die Ermordung einer Butterblume' in relation to the *Oresteia*, in Chapter 1.
25. The novel's deliberate epistemological false start of 'over the Atlantic there prevailed a barometric minimum' ['[ü]ber dem Atlantik befand sich ein barometrisches Minimum'] feeds ironically into the straightforward 'it was a fine August day in 1913' ['[e]s war ein schöner Augusttag des

Jahres 1913']. From the outset, Musil playfully paves the way for a highly complex intertwining of seemingly incommensurate modes of knowledge, be they functionalistic or humanistic: see Musil, *Der Mann ohne Eigenschaften* (Hamburg: Rowohlt, 1952), p. 9.
26. Cf. Maria Tatar, *Lustmord: Sexual Murder in Weimar Germany* (Princeton, NJ: Princeton University Press, 1995), p. 148. As Roger Kingerlee has remarked in qualification of these portrayals of masculinity, there is an unmistakable irony to Biberkopf's self-projections. Kingerlee thus problematizes lines of interpretation which straightforwardly attack Döblin's elision between Franz as violent perpetrator, and Franz as a victim of a figuratively female 'Other' of formlessness, chaos and — in the Whore of Babylon, 'drunk on the blood of the saints' ['trunken vom Blut der Heiligen'] — mythic violence (BA 237, 380). See Kingerlee, *Psychological Models of Masculinity in Döblin, Musil, and Jahnn: Männliches, Allzumännliches* (Lewiston, NY: Mellen, 2001), pp. 78–80; cf. Tatar, pp. 145 and 151–52.
27. There are echoes here of the febrile political climate on and around the Alexanderplatz by 1928. As Peter Jelavich reminds us, it had already seen violence in the crushing of the Spartacist Uprising in 1919, as well as a series of 'notorious, pogrom-like assaults' in 1923 on the Jewish Community living in the nearby Scheunenviertel. See Jelavich, *Berlin Alexanderplatz: Radio, Film, and the Death of Weimar Culture* (Berkeley: University of California Press, 2006), pp. 3 and 7.
28. See here Genesis 1. 26. For an incisive critique of the patriarchal dimensions to Edenic fantasies of a restored sovereignty over nature, see Merchant, p. 65.
29. Benjamin, GS, III, 236.
30. Dollenmayer reads in *Berlin Alexanderplatz* a 'textbook example' of this type of freedom: see Dollenmayer, 'Narration and the City', p. 767. Cf. Simmel, 'Die Großstädte und das Geistesleben', pp. 192–94 and 198–99 ;'The Metropolis and Mental Life', pp. 48–49 and 53–54.
31. Tatar, pp. 141–42.
32. Horkheimer and Adorno, *Dialektik der Aufklärung*, p. 177; *Dialectic of Enlightenment*, p. 154.
33. Webber, *Berlin in the Twentieth Century*, p. 215.
34. See Eric L. Santner, *On Creaturely Life: Rilke, Benjamin, Sebald* (Chicago, IL: University of Chicago Press, 2006), pp. 22–24. Cf. Webber, who invokes, but does not develop at length, the concepts of 'the creature' and 'bare life' in his discussion of the novel in *Berlin in the Twentieth Century*, pp. 205–06 and 212.
35. Slavoj Žižek, *For They Know Not what They Do: Enjoyment as a Political Factor* (London: Verso, 1991), p. 201; see also Santner, *The Royal Remains*, pp. 69–76.
36. Santner, *On Creaturely Life*, p. xix.
37. Santner, *The Royal Remains*, p. 5.
38. Rilke, *Werke*, II: *Gedichte 1910 bis 1926*, pp. 224–25; Santner, *On Creaturely Life*, p. 2 (cf. p. 6).
39. Cf. Santner, *On Creaturely Life*, pp. xix, 38–39.
40. See Kári Driscoll, 'Toward a Poetics of Animality: Hofmannsthal, Rilke, Pirandello, Kafka' (unpublished PhD dissertation, Columbia University, 2014), especially pp. 3–4 and 5–6; cf. Riedel, *Nach der Achsendrehung*, pp. ix–x. As Riedel shows, this sense of man's deep rootedness in his natural environment fed into the growth of 'philosophical anthropology' in the 1920s (pp. x, 149).
41. For Nietzsche, man is 'das missrathenste Thier, das krankhafteste': Nietzsche, KG, VI 3: *Der Antichrist*, section 14, p. 178; cf. UD 101.
42. Rilke, *Werke*, II, 211.
43. On the hint of the death camps here, see Dollenmayer, 'Narration and the City', p. 768.
44. See Giorgio Agamben, *Homo Sacer: Sovereign Power and Bare Life*, trans. by Daniel Heller-Roazen (Stanford, CA: Stanford University Press, 1998), pp. 90 and 107–10. As Agamben argues, the Hobbesian state of nature is 'not a real epoch chronologically prior to the foundation of the City but a principle internal to the City' (p. 105). This sense of a crossover is central to Santner's sense of 'creaturely life': see *The Royal Remains*, pp. 56–57.
45. See Bakhtin, p. 23.
46. Ritchie Robertson, 'From Naturalism to National Socialism (1890–1945)', in *The Cambridge History of German Literature*, ed. by Helen Watanabe-O'Kelly (Cambridge: Cambridge University Press, 1997), pp. 327–92 (p. 363).

47. Cf. also Tatar, pp. 141 and 145.
48. Taylor, *Sources of the Self*, p. 465.
49. See Keller, pp. 160–62.
50. Benjamin, GS, III, 232. For the most sophisticated and extensive recent discussion of Döblin's use of montage as achieving 'perceptual disruption' with the help of 'ready-made' media, and therefore doing away with a 'controlling fictional narrator', see Mario Slugan, *Montage as Perceptual Experience: 'Berlin Alexanderplatz' from Döblin to Fassbinder* (Rochester, NY: Camden House, 2017), pp. 65–107 (especially pp. 65–67).
51. Ibid., p. 233.
52. Klaus R. Scherpe, 'The City as Narrator', in *Modernity and the Text: Revisions of German Modernism*, ed. by David Bathrick und Andreas Huyssen (New York: Columbia University Press, 1989), pp. 162–79 (p. 170); cf. Simmel, 'Die Großstädte und das Geistesleben', pp. 194–95. In a similar vein, Adorno argues in his essay of 1954, 'Standort des Erzählers im zeitgenössischen Roman' ['The Position of the Narrator in the Contemporary Novel'], that narrated experience itself has lost its significance in modernity because the world has become an entirely quantifiable totality, its myriad parts and personal narratives essentially interchangeable. See Adorno, GS, XI: *Noten zur Literatur I*, p. 42.
53. See Santner, *The Royal Remains*, pp. 34–38.
54. Philip Scheidemann served as the second Minister President ['Ministerpräsident'] of the Weimar Republic, between February and June 1919. Döblin's narrative makes a number of direct references to the persistent 'stab in the back myth', which blamed Germany's defeat in the First World War on an eclectic group of internal enemies, from seditious 'red' workers to Jewish financiers (see BA 84–85). See Eberhard Kolb, *The Weimar Republic*, trans. by P. S. Falda and R. J. Park (London: Routledge, 2004), p. 140.
55. In an affinity which speaks to a modernist discourse in thinking about death as immanent *in* life, the figure of death as a fruit in the mouth of the living comes to expression in a striking image in Rilke's Fourth Elegy. In celebration of the silent and indescribable immanence of death in the proverbially complete life of the child, the elegist asks: 'Who will carve a child's death | out of grey bread which becomes hard, — or leave | it in its round mouth like the core | of a fine apple?' ['Wer macht den Kindertod | aus grauem Brot, das hart wird, — oder läßt | ihn drin im runden Mund, so wie den Gröps | von einem schönen Apfel?'] (Rilke, *Werke*, II, 213)
56. See Jelavich, pp. 3–8.
57. See Lodge, pp. 134–35. In his review of *Ulysses*, Döblin praised Joyce's consummately 'plastic' and 'three-dimensional' portrayal of his Dubliners. Revealingly, he also marvelled at how Joyce incorporated into his epic 'a huge mass of knowledge, book wisdom, atmospheres, fantasies novel' ['eine Unsumme von Wissen, Bibliotheksweisheit, Stimmungen und Phantasien'] (AzL 290). The development of Döblin's style in the course of his work on the novel testifies, despite his own qualifications, to Joyce's imprint: see Weninger, p. 42, and n. 1 at the start of this chapter.
58. See David Midgley, '"Wie die Bienen sind sie über den Boden her." Zu den biologischen Bezügen der Massendarstellungen in Döblins Romanen', in *Internationales Alfred-Döblin-Kolloquium Berlin 2011: Massen und Medien bei Alfred Döblin*, ed. by Stefan Keppler-Tasaki (Bern: Lang, 2014), pp. 51–65 (p. 64).
59. 'I smash up everything, you smash up everything, he smashes up everything' ['Ich zerschlage alles, du zerschlägst alles, er zerschlägt alles'] (BA 166).
60. This is a longer and substantially revised version of my previously published book chapter, 'The City as Creature: Reconfiguring the Creaturely Self in Alfred Döblin's *Berlin Alexanderplatz*', in *Biological Discourses*, ed. by Craig and Linge, pp. 397–422.

# CONCLUSION: REDEMPTION AFTER ALL?

Alfred Döblin's development as a writer and thinker between 1900 and 1933 was a characteristically restless and convoluted process. Each of his works experimented with a particular set of ideas, materials and their contradictions, before suggesting a series of intractable new questions (or reconfigured old ones). Döblin's metaphor of a ball thrown from work to work suggests an unfurling dialogue, the passing-on of a creative baton (SLW 311). Read as a form of self-reconstruction, the image is a tendentious one; but as I hope to have shown in this book, there is nonetheless a recognizable sense of developing purpose to his fictional and theoretical work before the years of exile. In an idiosyncratically positive vein for a radical modernist, Döblin became ever more concerned during this period with rethinking and remoulding 'the human being', rather than simply leaving it in interesting-looking pieces by the roadside, crying to be put back together by someone else. Whether he managed that, or simply pulled off an even more compelling failure in the shape of his greatest novel, must surely remain open to debate. At any rate, his proverbial ball hit something of a wall at the end of *Berlin Alexanderplatz*.

In a subsequent letter to the Berlin Germanist Julius Petersen on 18 September 1931, Döblin argued that the novel's ambiguous close was tied up with a thorny new dualism at the heart of human existence. Rather than a binary of body and soul, the relationship between which remained unresolved in his literary practice, this was a mediation between a sense of the human being as little more than a disintegrating and replaceable part of nature and society, and a reinvestment in humanity and humanness itself as a creating, completing and redeeming force. And yet, crucially, Döblin leaves open the possibility of a sequel in his suggestion that Franz Biberkopf, as a knot of contradictions, remained unredeemed in the face of his own supposed redemption. In keeping with that broken logic, even the book itself is without redemption (*Briefe*, 1, 165). He contends that it offers a kind of bridge to a riverbank which is still conspicuous for its absence, a place of redemption he calls 'heaven'. Continuing the story there, he adds, would obviously have been impossible (165–66). For all of Döblin's ambiguous hopes for a new and better kind of society, then, his epic novel had to default on a definitive moment of catharsis or resolution. As we saw in different veins in both *Die drei Sprünge des Wang-lun* and *Berge Meere und Giganten*, the story of Franz Biberkopf comes up short: certainly not without hints of social and political hope, but never quite able to offer a positive image of something substantially different.

The implicit question is similar to one that I posed at the start of Chapter 4, when contemplating the musician's fate at the close of *Gespräche mit Kalypso*: where could, or should, Biberkopf go from here? For all the caveats of authorial intentionality that we have considered, work has been done elsewhere on Döblin's personal response to the question, not least in suggesting that this inchoate metaphysical need found a personal answer in Christianity while in exile.[1] In contrast to Brecht's derogatory attribution of this unexpected turn to the 'particularly hard blows' ['besonders harte schläge [sic]'] of Döblin's exile and traumatic journey through France in 1940, a lack of commercial or literary success in California, and the scattering of his immediate family,[2] the decision revealed a deep continuity with the thinking that had preceded it. The shattering recognition, in the cathedral at Mende in France in June 1940, that Christ was one and the same with the 'Urgrund', the eternal ground of existence (SR 169), should not be read as a wild aberration, but rather as a profoundly personal crystallization of a career-long reinvestment of metaphysical (and now properly theological) meaning in mortal and corporeal reality. As Christoph Bartscherer has argued, Döblin's personal Catholicism was infused with the dialectic of self and nature that had emerged in his nature-philosophy: it was humanity's hybridity, its implication in yet marginal separation from its own biological existence, which marked out both its intense misery and ineluctable dignity.[3]

But what is most interesting about Döblin's works up to 1933 is certainly not their existence as way posts on a journey towards redemption; in other words, that point at which Günter Grass admitted that he and his teacher had to disagree and part ways.[4] Far more compelling are the thorny paradoxes that refuse to submit to the explanations of metaphysical schemata, or else the false consolations and redemptions of political or spiritual ideologies. The early short stories offer hauntingly negative fables of madness and death. On far larger canvases, *Wang-lun* and *Berge Meere und Giganten* illustrate the devastating consequences of simplistic utopianism when extended to groups and societies. While *Unser Dasein* works to paint a more positive picture, it circles around the central contradiction in human life between 'completion' ['Vollendung'] and 'uncompletability' ['Unvollendbarkeit'] (UD 238). In short, the self is caught in a state of indeterminacy between the suggestion of wholeness — redeemed existence — in the here and now, and a dynamic reality of transience, dissolution and disintegration. One of Döblin's persistent concerns is to show that the hope for a reconciled and meaningful form of modern life is shot through with negativity and irony: 'building up' ['Aufbau'] is predicated on relentless 'disintegration' ['Zerfall'] and 'dissolution' ['Auflösung'] (SLW 216; cf. UD 241–42); and the success of his city masterpiece depends on its intimations, but ultimate refusal, of completeness in both content and form. One of the famous final lines, 'We know what we know, the price we paid was not low' ['Wir wissen, was wir wissen, wir habens [sic] teuer bezahlen müssen'] (BA 454), is either tantalizingly or frustratingly ambiguous.

I want to propose two related conclusions to my arguments in this book, each of which takes a slightly different orbit around the dialectics of nature and self. Firstly, instead of a clear-cut teleological (and ideological) movement towards the rethought and refigured individual, Döblin's works represent multifaceted meditations on the corporeal, mental and discursive imbalance, fragmentation and even destruction of the self in modernity — as well as illuminating the ways in which this disparate self might somehow be rethought or reconfigured. In the face of meaning's fragmentation — its dispersal among discourses and even its reduction to distinctions between normality and psychopathology — the argument in my first chapter homed in on what I called the 'hermeneutic remnant' in the early short stories. The stories present us with discursive spaces in which the fraught relationship between self and nature, self and body, and even self and self, is repeatedly fractured and refigured. However, in the midst of the violence and madness, the narratives come close to what Adorno calls the 'semblance of non-semblance' ['Schein des Scheinlosen']: in other words, the oblique and ever-broken yet persistent promise of a reconciled and dignified existence in the here and the now.[5]

*Wang-lun* wrestles expansively with the idea of human insignificance in the face of the realities of nature and history. However, as we saw in Chapter 2, the novel presents an ambiguous picture. The 'three leaps' seem to arrive at an idealized commitment to subjective agency and resistance beyond the passivity of *wu wei*, but Wang's weirdly erotic dreams of being swallowed up in the ramifying roots of a sycamore tree testifies to a fetishistic fascination of destruction, of *Nichtsein*, of nothingness (WL 482, 487). A gesture of non-resistance to the violence of politics, society and nature unavoidably entails the destruction of the self. But my contention was that Döblin's innovative prose style — as theorized in the 'Berliner Programm' — unlocks the transhistorical memories and energies of what Benjamin called the 'now-time' ['Jetztzeit']. This, in turn, provides a moment of hope against hope for an otherwise unforeseeable social and political change, with regard to both our environments and our fellow human beings. With the kind of provocation that was strongly to shape Brecht's theatrical practice, *Wang-lun* denies us a resolution to its dialectical puzzle, inviting us instead to keep asking and keep leaping.

While the profound complexity of genre debates over historical fiction has precluded my discussion of it in this study, the end of *Wallenstein* once again brings the question of 'history' into dialogue with the violent realities of nature. Just as Wang-lun meets his end by being ignominiously burned alive, so the interlinked trajectories of Wallenstein and Ferdinand deny the retelling of history any redemptive force. As Steffan Davies has cogently argued, *Wallenstein* made a path-breaking contribution to the tradition of the historical novel by moving beyond the historicist assumptions of reconstructibility and comprehensibility in narrative. Nineteenth-century historicism had instilled a belief that the past 'imparts meaning' and, with this, a residual sense of teleology in relation to the present. This teleological myth had been shattered in the collective social and cultural imagination by the senseless material destruction of the First World War;[6] and *Wallenstein* reads out the last rites.

The Holy Roman Emperor Ferdinand II's death is an absurd departure from the 'facts' of historical reality, in keeping with his personal and figurative contrast to the brutal realism of his imperial military leader. His final retreat into the forest is a wholesale retreat from worldly office, and it speaks to a barely repressed desire for a lost communion with nature. But the barely disguised homoeroticism of his closing interactions with a forest goblin ('Kobold') is in no sense the consummation of that, embodying instead a brutal negation. The Kobold fatally stabs Ferdinand in a typically strange twist, and our last close-up is of this strange embodiment of the forest uncomprehendingly rocking the Emperor's suspended body on tree branches (W 732–33). The twist brings human history itself right down into the meaningless twists and abrupt violations of natural life. Might Döblin's strange turns of fantasy bring us closer to this chaotic reality than either literary Realism or its relations and descendants?

That question took on barely imaginable dimensions and implications as Döblin put the real history books down and turned to his vast history of the future, *Berge Meere und Giganten*. The narrative's biopolitical manipulations and violent dialectical inversions seem to reduce humanity to identifiable, malleable and violable masses; but the text's myriad lacunae — between man and nature, and nature and technology — come to represent those spaces in which humanness might be rethought in terms of hybridity. *Unser Dasein* in its turn develops this hybridity into an anthropology that bears remarkable discursive similarities with the philosophical innovations of Simmel, Heidegger and Uexküll. Döblin shows how our dialectical existences both in and apart from nature provide the seedbed for our meaningfulness as human beings. *Berlin Alexanderplatz* sees this hybrid reveal itself as a creature. The urban creature emerges as the uncanny shadow-side to the violent Franz, while helping us to rethink our urban forms of life as shared spaces of human meaning in the midst of precariousness, transience and provisionality.

Throughout our discussions, then, we have seen humanness re-emerge not in the terms of a timeless essence or even a fixed identity, but rather in marginal spaces both within and outside the powers and discourses that threaten to objectify, reduce or simply annihilate it. Döblin's works are characterized by a central hermeneutic tension: one that cannot simply be subsumed to the cyclical rhythms of *Aufbau* and *Zerfall*. As I have shown, they variously hint at disclosures of literary or anthropological meaning, but that meaning, such as it is, is repeatedly fragmented, negated, or simply reabsorbed into the vagaries of text and discourse. Michael Fischer's case study evokes tragic hints of the *Oresteia*, but it collapses into outright madness in his confabulated narrative of mythic justice; and as he lies in the mental hospital, argued over by different diagnosticians, Franz Biberkopf is purified and rectified by a Death who channels the rhetoric of the Messiah through the Berlin street dialect of the Grim Reaper. If these works are exemplars of epiphanic modernism, in Taylor's sense of the inextricability of content and form,[7] then their oblique hints of reconciliation are compelling only on account of the disruptive presence of the materials and discourses that they try to point beyond: those recalcitrant 'things' which, in Adorno's words, 'stand in resistance to art' ['das ihr Widerstrebende'].[8] The work of art, as a figment of wholeness and autonomy (UD 241), makes its negative promise of human freedom and dignity only through its inextricability from materials and realities that are palpably, even violently, 'other' than it.

In close relation to this idea, my second conclusion is that Döblin succeeds in positively reaffirming the modern self as a dynamic hybrid. As the aesthetic correlate to hybridity, it is in the figure of metaphor and metaphoricity that he illuminates the crossovers between literature and philosophy, and aesthetics and anthropology. In his recent work of literary anthropology, *Nach der Achsendrehung*, Wolfgang Riedel points out, with Simmel, that philosophy in the wake of Schopenhauer marked a radical turn towards man's 'animal' or 'instinctual' nature. The legacy of this reorientation was not simply a reduction of 'the human being' to another cog in Darwin's evolutionary machine: rather, the developments of both psychoanalysis and, later, philosophical anthropology were beating new disciplinary paths between the biological study of man, and the hermeneutic-anthropological study of the human. Riedel suggests that it is only through literature that we might do justice to an ambivalent liminal space between nature and culture, and between our biological and social beings. In spite of its inseparability from them, modernist literature is not merely a cultural epiphenomenon in respect of philosophy or the natural sciences, but rather stakes its truth claims in its transformative interactions with both.[9]

Döblin's work in the spaces between literature and philosophy reveals the intricate relationship of the two. As we saw in *Unser Dasein*, the lively interaction of self and world is something that is reducible to neither metaphysical nor scientific schemata; and metaphor accordingly emerges as the focal point of a performative and dynamic relationship between self and world, and between the conceptual and the literary (UD 29–30). To put it differently, Döblin was not so much absorbing and appropriating the influences of his milieu, as doing much original shaping himself. In 1932, as I briefly mentioned in my discussion of the novel, he insisted that *Berlin Alexanderplatz*'s similarities to *Ulysses* showed how 'the same time can produce similar phenomena, indeed the same thing, in various different places' ['[d]ieselbe Zeit kann unabhängig voneinander Ähnliches, ja Gleiches an verschiedenen Stellen erzeugen'] (SLW 217). Rather than a retrospective anxiety of influence, this speaks to the notion of affinities as 'instances of resonance' ['Resonanzerscheinungen'] (UD 174): circulating theories and ideas that resonated across boundaries and were worked into new forms. Heidegger's considerable fame in the years after *Sein und Zeit* was justifiably predicated on his radically new questions about being;[10] but Simmel's and Döblin's cognate reconceptions of subjective meaning remind us that even the path-breaking philosopher was himself part of a richly variegated intellectual horizon. Döblin's works, then, should perhaps not be understood primarily in epistemological-aesthetic terms as 'paradigms and repositories of modernism',[11] but rather as important contributions in their own right towards the rethinking of embodiment and human identity in modernity.

## Humanness Regained?

It is by bringing my two conclusions together that we can best understand Döblin's enduring importance to us as a writer and thinker. At the close of my first chapter, I argued that the contorted, shameful, terrifying or terrified bodies of the short stories invite us to rethink embodiment in terms that go beyond the old separations and dualisms of subject and object, and mind and matter. My subsequent discussions traced out various catastrophic attempts to demarcate the one from the other, with the aim of achieving illusionary sovereignty over oneself, other individuals, or something called Nature. In a similar vein, as Rowan Williams has argued in relation to both medical and environmental ethics, we need to be wary of a philosophical 'habit of opposing purely active subject to passive object'. The notion that 'the material universe appears as an essentially *symbolic* complex' has us reimagine a participatory, if often fractious, dialogue that implicates (but never precisely situates) both us *and* it.[12] I suggest that Döblin presents us with a version of the challenge that Williams poses here. This is neither a revival of animism nor a disguised version of secular humanism, but rather a reinvestment in materiality that might help us better to appreciate the claims to dignity of the strangers, the neighbours, and even the *things* that share or disrupt our worlds. It is here, in turn, that a new kind of materialism — if we can call it that — stakes its powerful ethical claim. Only through a recovered sense of mystery and alterity can we be certain to avoid judging 'the acceptability or normalcy of another bodily presence' in terms of its comprehensibility and recognisability to us, as Williams puts it.[13] Our bemused or even disgusted inability to identify and categorize in terms that are familiar to us should be no barrier to a serious and committed ethical engagement with our myriad Others, be they human or non-human. Aesthetics and ethics join in configurations that are as unsettling as they are unexpected, and the strange bodies populating Döblin's works — the monsters, cyborgs and Berliners — add sharp edges to this ethical demand precisely because they defy easy understanding. In some cases, most notably in *Berge Meere und Giganten*, their constructions are so bizarre that they confound any understanding at all.

Nevertheless, Döblin leaves us with the unaccountable and paradoxical sense that even the bare fact of being an uncanny human presence in the world remains meaningful and worthwhile, however chaotic or violent our surroundings. From this angle, there is something distinctly modernist about the hints of reconciliation and redemption that momentarily flicker in his prose; and once again, revealing parallels suggest themselves. Kafka's *Der Proceß* draws to a famously bleak end, as Josef K. is executed 'like a dog', both inside and outside the Law at the same time. But the preceding paragraphs suggest, if not a way out, then at the least the vanishing image of a life that might just about be worth living after all — even if the revelation, of course, comes far too late. In anticipation of the final moment, K. suddenly notices a figure gesturing out of a top-floor window, and with it, a sense of human connection shot through with uncertainty. Who was this person? A friend? An enemy? A participant in the ritual? Someone who perhaps wanted to help? An individual? Everyone? While the Law itself might be unshakeable, 'it cannot resist one who wants to live' ['einem Menschen, der leben will, widersteht sie nicht'].[14] That deceptively simple paradox also rises repeatedly to the surface of Döblin's works, if in rather different forms. In one of its scattered cosmic diversions, *Berlin Alexanderplatz* briefly switches into a meditation on the miracle of sunlight as the thing that sustains human life even in the face of our arbitrariness and disposability. Moving through the walls and rooms of the surrounding tenements, Book 4 took us on a panoramic tour of myriad small and insignificant, yet mundanely meaningful,

Berlin lives and narratives (BA 125–27). We now learn just how dispensable we are in the far grander scheme of things. The Sun, after all, is over 300,000 times as massive as Earth, and what are we in relation to it, after all? Still, we are here, we are alive, and we do make a strange kind of sense in spite of it all. This is a world that we can see, touch and experience, and which carries on meaning something to us in spite of its ultimate meaninglessness and our contingency. There must have been some kind of mix-up, the narrator adds: a mistake somewhere along the line in those huge numbers with the countless zeros (212–13).

In short, and on a dialectical logic, the laws and forces that would dehumanize and crush us never entirely manage it — despite triumphing time and again. Döblin is still more than capable of giving us bad dreams, as Grass warned. He shatters our humanist delusions and exposes our cheap destructibility. On those shaky foundations, he reveals the all too real dangers of biopolitical manipulation and control, while furnishing us with new if risky ways of refashioning ourselves as beings entwined with our natural worlds. But his greatest achievement is also his subtlest. In an age caught like our own between pessimism, cynicism and despair, Alfred Döblin quite simply keeps faith with what it is that makes us so absurdly, vanishingly human.

## Notes to the Conclusion

1. See, for example, Emde, pp. 237–312; and Christoph Bartscherer, *Das Ich und die Natur: Alfred Döblins literarischer Weg im Licht seiner Religionsphilosophie* (Paderborn: Igel, 1997), especially pp. 6–14.
2. Brecht, *Werke*, XXVII, 165.
3. See Bartscherer, *Das Ich und die Natur*, pp. 177–80 and 236–37.
4. Grass, *Werkausgabe*, IX, 238.
5. Adorno, GS, VII, *Ästhetische Theorie*, pp. 199 and 203.
6. Davies, 'Writing History', pp. 121–43 (especially p. 121).
7. Taylor, *Sources of the Self*, p. 429.
8. Adorno, VII, *Ästhetische Theorie*, p. 18.
9. See Riedel, *Nach der Achsendrehung*, pp. ix–xix.
10. On the internationally covered debate between Martin Heidegger and Ernst Cassirer in Davos in the spring of 1929, see Rüdiger Safranski, *Martin Heidegger: Between Good and Evil*, trans. by Ewald Osers (Cambridge, MA: Harvard University Press, 1998), pp. 183–88.
11. Davies and Schonfield (p. 6) have convincingly identified this as one way of interpreting and assessing Döblin's significance as a modernist writer.
12. Rowan Williams, *The Edge of Words: God and the Habits of Language* (London: Bloomsbury, 2014), pp. 101–02.
13. Ibid., pp. 115–17.
14. Kafka, *Der Proceß*, p. 312. For a cogent discussion of K.'s final ethical awakening, see Ritchie Robertson, *Kafka: Judaism, Politics, and Literature* (Oxford: Oxford University Press, 1985), pp. 127–29.

# BIBLIOGRAPHY

## Works by Alfred Döblin

*Aufsätze zur Literatur*, ed. by Walter Muschg (Olten: Walter, 1963)
*Ausgewählte Werke in Einzelbänden*, ed. by Walter Muschg, Anthony W. Riley, and Christina Alten (Olten, Solothurn, Düsseldorf and Zurich: Walter, 1960–2007)
*Berge Meere und Giganten*, ed. by Gabriele Sander (Düsseldorf: Walter, 2006)
*Berlin Alexanderplatz: Die Geschichte vom Franz Biberkopf*, ed. by Werner Stauffacher (Zurich: Walter, 1996)
*Briefe*, 1, ed. by Heinz Graber (Olten: Walter, 1970)
*Das Ich über der Natur* (Berlin: Fischer, 1927)
*Der deutsche Maskenball. Von Linke Poot / Wissen und Verändern!*, ed. by Walter Muschg (Olten: Walter, 1972)
*Die drei Sprünge des Wang-lun: Chinesischer Roman*, ed. by Gabriele Sander and Andreas Solbach (Düsseldorf and Zurich: Walter, 2007)
*Die Ermordung einer Butterblume: Sämtliche Erzählungen*, ed. by Christina Althen (Düsseldorf: Walter, 2001)
*Gedächtnisstörungen bei der Korsakoffschen Psychose* (Munich: Tropen, 2006)
*Jagende Rosse: Der schwarze Vorhang und andere frühe Erzählwerke*, ed. by Anthony W. Riley (Olten: Walter, 1981)
*Kleine Schriften I: 1902–1921*, ed. by Anthony W. Riley (Olten: Walter, 1985)
*Kleine Schriften II: 1922–1924*, ed. by Anthony W. Riley (Olten: Walter, 1990)
*Kleine Schriften III: 1925–1933*, ed. by Anthony W. Riley (Zurich: Walter, 1999)
*Kleine Schriften IV: 1933–1953*, ed. by Anthony W. Riley and Christina Althen (Düsseldorf: Walter, 2005)
*Manas: Epische Dichtung*, ed. by Walter Muschg (Olten: Walter, 1961)
*Reise in Polen*, ed. by Walter Muschg (Olten: Walter, 1968)
*Schicksalsreise: Bericht und Bekenntnis*, ed. by Anthony W. Riley (Solothurn: Walter, 1993)
*Schriften zu Ästhetik, Poetik und Literatur*, ed. by Erich Kleinschmidt (Olten: Walter, 1989)
*Schriften zu Leben und Werk*, ed. by Erich Kleinschmidt (Olten: Walter, 1986)
*Schriften zur Politik und Gesellschaft*, ed. by Heinz Graber (Olten: Walter, 1972)
*Unser Dasein*, ed. by Walter Muschg (Olten: Walter, 1964)
*Wallenstein*, ed. by Erwin Kobel (Düsseldorf and Zurich: Walter, 2001)

## Main Philosophical Works

ADORNO, THEODOR W., *Gesammelte Schriften*, ed. by Rolf Tiedemann and others, 20 vols (Frankfurt a.M.: Suhrkamp, 1970–2003)
BENJAMIN, WALTER, *The Arcades Project*, trans. by Howard Eiland and Kevin McLaughlin (Cambridge, MA: Belknap Press, 1999)
—— *Charles Baudelaire: A Lyric Poet in the Era of High Capitalism*, trans. by Harry Zohn (London: New Left Books, 1973)

——— *Gesammelte Schriften*, ed. by Rolf Tiedemann and Hermann Schweppenhäuser, 7 vols (Frankfurt a.M.: Suhrkamp, 1972)
——— *Selected Writings*, ed. by Howard Eiland, Michael W. Jennings, Gary Smith and others, 4 vols (Cambridge, MA: Belknap Press, 1999 and 2003)
BERGSON, HENRI, *Essai sur les données immédiates de la conscience*, 8th edn (Paris: Alcan, 1911)
CASSIRER, ERNST, *Philosophie der symbolischen Formen: Zweiter Teil — Das mythische Denken* (Berlin: Bruno Cassirer, 1925)
DESCARTES, RENÉ, *Méditations métaphysiques*, ed. by Jean-Marie Beyssade and Michelle Beyssade (Paris: Flammarion, 1979)
DILTHEY, WILHELM, *Gesammelte Schriften*, ed. by Bernhard Groethuysen and others, 26 vols (Leipzig and Berlin: Teubner, 1914–2006)
DRIESCH, HANS, *Philosophie des Organischen*, 4th edn (Leipzig: Quelle & Meyer, 1928)
FICHTE, JOHANN GOTTLIEB, *Schriften zur Wissenschaftslehre: Werke I*, ed. by Wilhelm G. Jacobs (Frankfurt a.M.: Deutscher Klassiker Verlag, 1997)
FREUD, SIGMUND, *Gesammelte Werke*, ed. by Anna Freud and others, 18 vols (London: Imago, 1991)
HEIDEGGER, MARTIN, *Gesamtausgabe*, ed. by Friedrich-Wilhelm von Herrmann and others, 102 vols (Frankfurt a.M.: Klostermann, 1975–)
——— *Holzwege*, 8th edn (Frankfurt a.M.: Klostermann, 2003)
——— *Sein und Zeit*, 19th edn (Tübingen: Niemeyer, 2006)
HORKHEIMER, MAX and THEODOR W. ADORNO, *Dialektik der Aufklärung: Philosophische Fragmente*, in Theodor W. Adorno, *Gesammelte Schriften*, ed. by Rolf Tiedemann and others, 20 vols (Frankfurt a.M.: Suhrkamp, 1970–2003), III (1984)
——— *Dialectic of Enlightenment*, trans. by John Cumming (London: Verso, 1997)
HUSSERL, EDMUND, *Die Krisis der europäischen Wissenschaften und die transzendentale Phänomenologie: Eine Einleitung in die phänomenologische Philosophie*, ed. by Walter Biemel (The Hague: Nijhoff, 1954)
MACH, ERNST, *Die Analyse der Empfindungen und das Verhältnis des Physischen zum Psychischen*, 3rd edn (Jena: Fischer, 1902)
MAUTHNER, FRITZ, *Beiträge zu einer Kritik der Sprache*, 3rd edn, 3 vols (Leipzig: Meiner, 1923)
NIETZSCHE, FRIEDRICH, *Sämtliche Werke: Kritische Gesamtausgabe*, ed. by Giorgio Colli and Mazzino Montinari (Berlin: De Gruyter, 1967–)
——— *The Birth of Tragedy and Other Writings*, ed. by Raymond Geuss and Ronald Speirs (Cambridge: Cambridge University Press, 1999)
PASCAL, BLAISE, *Oeuvres complètes*, ed. by Louis Lafuma (Paris: Seuil, 1963)
PLESSNER, HELMUTH, *Gesammelte Schriften, IV: Die Stufen des Organischen und der Mensch. Einleitung in die philosophische Anthropologie*, ed. by Günter Dux, Odo Marquard, Elisabeth Ströker and others (Frankfurt a.M.: Suhrkamp, 1981)
SCHELLING, F. W. J., 'Of the I as Principle of Philosophy, or On the Unconditional in Human Knowledge', in *The Unconditional in Human Knowledge: Four Early Essays (1794–1796)*, trans. and ed. by Fritz Marti (Lewisburg, PA: Bucknell University Press, 1980), pp. 63-128
——— *Vom Ich als Princip der Philosophie, oder Über das Unbedingte im menschlichen Wissen* (Tübingen: Herbrandt, 1795)
SCHOPENHAUER, ARTHUR, *Sämtliche Werke*, ed. by Wolfgang Frhr. von Löhneysen, 5 vols (Stuttgart and Frankfurt a.M.: Cotta/Insel, 1960–65)
SIMMEL, GEORG, 'Die Großstädte und das Geistesleben', in *Das Individuum und die Freiheit: Essais* (Berlin: Wagenbach, 1984), pp. 192–204
——— *Lebensanschauung: Vier metaphysische Kapitel*, 2nd edn (Munich and Leipzig: Duncker & Humblot, 1922)

―― 'The Metropolis and Mental Life', trans. by H. H. Gerth, in *Classic Essays on the Culture of Cities*, ed. by Richard Sennett (Englewood Cliffs, NJ: Prentice Hall, 1969), pp. 47–60

SPENGLER, OSWALD, *Der Mensch und die Technik: Beitrag zu einer Philosophie des Lebens* (Munich: Beck, 1931)

―― *Der Untergang des Abendlandes: Umrisse einer Morphologie der Weltgeschichte* (Munich: Beck, 1969)

SPINOZA, BARUCH, *Die Ethik*, trans. by Jakob Stern (Stuttgart: Reclam 1977)

WEBER, MAX, *Gesamtausgabe*, ed. by Horst Baier and others (Tübingen: Mohr, 1984– )

## Other Primary Texts

AESCHYLUS, *Oresteia*, ed. and trans. by Christopher Collard (Oxford: Oxford University Press, 2008)

BACHOFEN, JOHANN JAKOB, *Das Mutterrecht: Eine Untersuchung über die Gynaikokratie der alten Welt nach ihrer religiösen und rechtlichen Natur*, ed. by Hans-Jürgen Heinrichs (Frankfurt a.M.: Suhrkamp, 1975)

BALLARD, J. G., *The Drowned World* (London: Fourth Estate, 2014)

BÖLSCHE, WILHELM, *Das Liebesleben in der Natur*, 3 vols (Florence and Leipzig: Diederichs, 1898–1902)

BRECHT, BERTOLT, *Werke: Große kommentierte Berliner und Frankfurter Ausgabe*, 30 vols, ed. by Werner Hecht, Jan Knopf, Werner Mittenzwei and Klaus-Detlef Müller (Berlin and Weimar: Aufbau-Verlag, 1993)

DIELS, HERMANN, ed., *Die Fragmente der Vorsokratiker: Griechisch und Deutsch* (Berlin: Weidmann, 1903)

GILMAN, CHARLOTTE PERKINS, 'The Yellow Wallpaper', in *The Oxford Book of Gothic Tales*, ed. by Chris Baldick (Oxford: Oxford University Press, 1993), pp. 249–63

GOETHE, JOHANN WOLFGANG VON, *Werke: Hamburger Ausgabe in 14 Bänden*, ed. by Erich Trunz, 10th edn (Munich: Beck, 1973–76)

GRASS, GÜNTER, *Werkausgabe in zehn Bänden*, ed. by Volker Neuhaus (Darmstadt and Neuwied: Luchterhand, 1987)

HAECKEL, ERNST, *Generelle Morphologie der Organismen* (Berlin: Reimer, 1866)

―― *Kunstformen der Natur: Supplement-Heft; Allgemeine Erläuterung und systematische Übersicht* (Leipzig and Vienna: Verlag des Bibliographischen Instituts, 1904)

HOMER, *Odyssey*, ed. and trans. by A. T. Murray, 2 vols, *The Loeb Classical Library*, 104–05 (Cambridge, MA: Harvard University Press, 1995)

HUXLEY, ALDOUS, *Brave New World and Brave New World Revisited* (New York: Harper Perennial, 2005)

JÜNGER, ERNST, *Der Arbeiter: Herrschaft und Gesellschaft* (Stuttgart: Klett-Cotta, 1982)

KAHN, FRITZ, *Das Leben des Menschen: Eine volkstümliche Anatomie, Biologie, Physiologie und Entwicklungsgeschichte des Menschen*, 5 vols (Stuttgart: Franckh'sche Verlagshandlung, 1922–29)

KAFKA, FRANZ, *Schriften, Tagebücher, Briefe: Kritische Ausgabe*, ed. by Jürgen Born, Gerhard Neumann, Malcolm Pasley and Jost Schillemeit (Frankfurt a.M.: Fischer, 1990): *Der Proceß*, ed. by Malcolm Pasley

KRAEPELIN, EMIL, *Psychiatrie: Ein Lehrbuch für Studirende [sic] und Aerzte*, 7th edn, 2 vols (Leipzig: Barth, 1903)

MAUSS, MARCEL, *A General Theory of Magic*, trans. by Robert Brain (London: Routledge, 2001)

MUSIL, ROBERT, *Der Mann ohne Eigenschaften* (Hamburg: Rowohlt, 1952)

ORWELL, GEORGE, *Nineteen Eighty-Four* (London: Penguin, 2000)

Rilke, Rainer Maria, *Werke: Kommentierte Ausgabe in vier Bänden*, ed. by Manfred Engel, Ulrich Fülleborn, Horst Nalewski and August Stahl, 4 vols (Frankfurt a.M. and Leipzig: Insel, 1996)
—— *The Notebooks of Malte Laurids Brigge*, trans. by Robert Vilain (Oxford: Oxford University Press, 2016)
Storm, Theodor, *Werke: Gesamtausgabe in drei Bänden*, III: *Novellen — Schriften — Briefe* (Stuttgart: J. G. Cotta'sche Buchhandlung, 1958)
Uexküll, Jakob von, *Bedeutungslehre*, in Jakob von Uexküll and Georg Kriszat, *Streifzüge durch die Umwelten von Tieren und Menschen: Ein Bilderbuch unsichtbarer Welten / Bedeutungslehre* (Frankfurt a.M.: Fischer 1970), pp. 107–79
—— 'Biologische Briefe an eine Dame', *Deutsche Rundschau*, 178 (1919), 132–48, 179, 277–93, 309–23, 451–68
—— *Theoretische Biologie*, 2nd edn (Berlin: Springer, 1928)
Uexküll, Thure von, 'Die Umweltforschung als subjekt- und objektumgreifende Naturforschung', in Jakob von Uexküll and Georg Kriszat, *Streifzüge durch die Umwelten von Tieren und Menschen: Ein Bilderbuch unsichtbarer Welten/Bedeutungslehre* (Frankfurt a.M.: Fischer, 1970), pp. xxiii–xlviii

## Secondary Literature

Agamben, Giorgio, *Homo Sacer: Sovereign Power and Bare Life*, trans. by Daniel Heller-Roazen (Stanford, CA: Stanford University Press, 1998)
Althen, Christina, 'Alfred Döblins medizinische Ausbildung dargestellt anhand von Quellen', in *Internationales Alfred Döblin Kolloquium Zürich 2015: Exil als Schicksalsreise. Alfred Döblin und das literarische Exil 1933–1950*, ed. by Sabina Becker and Sabine Schneider (Bern: Lang, 2017), pp. 27–45
—— 'Nachwort', in Alfred Döblin, *Die Ermordung einer Butterblume und andere Erzählungen*, ed. by Christina Althen, 5th edn (Munich: DTV, 2012), pp. 131–47
Ames, Roger T., 'Liezi', *Encyclopaedia Britannica*, <https://www.britannica.com/biography/Liezi-Daoist-philosopher>
Anz, Thomas, 'Alfred Döblin und die Psychoanalyse: Ein kritischer Bericht zur Forschung', in *Internationales Alfred-Döblin-Kolloquium Leiden 1995*, ed. by Gabriele Sander (Bern: Lang, 1997), pp. 9–30
—— *Literatur der Existenz: Literarische Psychopathographie und ihre soziale Bedeutung im Frühexpressionismus* (Stuttgart: Metzler, 1977)
Armstrong, Tim, *Modernism, Technology and the Body: A Cultural Study* (Cambridge: Cambridge University Press, 1998)
—— 'Modernism, Technology, and the Life Sciences', in *The Cambridge Companion to Literature and Science*, ed. by Steven Meyer (Cambridge: Cambridge University Press, 2018), pp. 223–41
Assmann, Aleida, 'How Long Does the Present Last? Seven Approaches to a Fleeting Phenomenon', in *Time in German Literature and Culture, 1900–2015: Between Acceleration and Slowness*, ed. by Anne Fuchs and J. J. Long (Houndmills and Basingstoke: Palgrave Macmillan, 2016), pp. 39–53
Bakhtin, Mikhail, *Rabelais and his World*, trans. by Helene Iswolsky (Bloomington: Indiana University Press, 1984)
Barthes, Roland, *The Death of the Author*, reproduced in Barthes, *Image — Music — Text*, ed. and trans. by Stephen Heath (London: Fontana, 1977), pp. 142–48
Bartscherer, Christoph, *Das Ich und die Natur: Alfred Döblins literarischer Weg im Licht seiner Religionsphilosophie* (Paderborn: Igel, 1997)
—— 'Robinson the Castaway: Döblin's Christian Faith as Reflected in his Autobiography

*Schicksalsreise* and his Religious Dialogues *Der unsterbliche Mensch* and *Der Kampf mit dem Engel*', in *A Companion to the Works of Alfred Döblin*, ed. by Roland Dollinger and others (Rochester, NY: Camden House, 2004), pp. 247–70

BECKER, SABINA, 'Döblin und die literarische Moderne 1910–1933', in *Döblin-Handbuch: Leben — Werk — Wirkung*, ed. by Sabina Becker (Stuttgart: Metzler, 2016), pp. 330–40.

——— 'Großstadtroman: Berlin Alexanderplatz. Die Geschichte vom Franz Biberkopf (1929)', in *Döblin-Handbuch: Leben — Werk — Wirkung*, ed. by Becker (Stuttgart: Metzler, 2016), pp. 102–23

——— ed., *Döblin-Handbuch: Leben — Werk — Wirkung* (Stuttgart: Metzler, 2016)

BECKER, SABINA, and ROBERT KRAUSE, '"Tatsachenphantasie": Alfred Döblins Poetik des Wissens im Kontext der Moderne', in *Internationales Alfred Döblin Kolloquium Emmendingen 2007: 'Tatsachenphantasie'. Alfred Döblins Poetik des Wissens im Kontext der Moderne*, ed. by Becker and Krause (Bern: Lang, 2008), pp. 9–26

BERNHARDT, OLIVER, *Alfred Döblin* (Munich: DTV, 2007)

BERNSTEIN, J. M., *Adorno: Disenchantment and Ethics* (Cambridge: Cambridge University Press, 2001)

BIRD, STEPHANIE, 'Nachum der Weise: On Storytelling, Eyes, and Misunderstanding in *Berlin Alexanderplatz*', in *Alfred Döblin: Paradigms of Modernism*, ed. by Steffan Davies and Ernest Schonfield (Berlin: De Gruyter, 2009), pp. 245–60

BISHOP, JEFFREY P., 'Rejecting Medical Humanism', *Journal of Medical Humanities*, 29 (2008), 13–25

BOWIE, ANDREW, *From Romanticism to Critical Theory: The Philosophy of German Literary Theory* (London: Routledge, 1997)

——— *Schelling and Modern European Philosophy: An Introduction* (Cambridge: Cambridge University Press, 1993)

BOYLE, NICHOLAS, *Goethe: The Poet and the Age*, II: *Revolution and Renunciation (1790–1803)* (Oxford: Clarendon Press, 2000)

BRANDT, MARION, 'Interkulturalität', in *Döblin-Handbuch: Leben — Werk — Wirkung*, ed. by Sabina Becker (Stuttgart: Metzler, 2016), pp. 343–46

——— 'Reise in Polen (1925)', in *Döblin-Handbuch: Leben — Werk — Wirkung*, ed. by Sabina Becker (Stuttgart: Metzler, 2016), pp. 288–94

BRAUNGART, GEORG, *Leibhafter Sinn: Der andere Diskurs der Moderne* (Tübingen: Niemeyer, 1995)

BÜHLER, BENJAMIN, *Lebende Körper: Biologisches und anthropologisches Wissen bei Rilke, Döblin und Jünger* (Würzburg: Königshausen & Neumann, 2004)

CATANI, STEPHANIE, 'Die Geburt des Döblinismus aus dem Geist des Fin de Siècle: Döblins frühe Erzählungen im Spannungsfeld von Ästhetik, Poetik und Medizin', in *Alfred Döblin: Paradigms of Modernism*, ed. by Steffan Davies and Ernest Schonfield (Berlin: De Gruyter, 2009), pp. 28–45

CHARON, RITA, *Narrative Medicine: Honoring the Stories of Illness* (Oxford: Oxford University Press, 2006)

COWAN, MICHAEL J., *Cult of the Will: Nervousness and German Modernity* (University Park: Pennsylvania State University Press, 2008)

CRAIG, ROBERT, 'The City as Creature: Reconfiguring the Creaturely Self in Alfred Döblin's *Berlin Alexanderplatz*', in *Biological Discourses: The Language of Science and Literature around 1900*, ed. by Robert Craig and Ina Linge (Oxford: Lang, 2017), pp. 397–422

——— 'Monsters and Other Cyborgs: The "Posthuman" in *Berge Meere und Giganten*', in *Internationales Alfred-Döblin-Kolloquium Cambridge 2017: Natur, Technik und das (Post-) Humane in den Schriften Alfred Döblins*, ed. by Steffan Davies and David Midgley, *Jahrbuch für Internationale Germanistik*, Series A, 133 (Bern: Lang, 2019), pp. 243–59

DAVIES, MERERID PUW, *The Tale of Bluebeard in German Literature: From the Eighteenth Century to the Present* (Oxford: Clarendon Press, 2001)

DAVIES, STEFFAN, 'Writing History: Why *Ferdinand der Andere* is called *Wallenstein*', in *Alfred Döblin: Paradigms of Modernism*, ed. by Davies and Schonfield (Berlin: De Gruyter, 2009), pp. 121–43

DAVIES, STEFFAN, and ERNEST SCHONFIELD, eds, *Alfred Döblin: Paradigms of Modernism* (Berlin: De Gruyter, 2009)

——'Introduction', in *Alfred Döblin: Paradigms of Modernism*, ed. by Steffan Davies and Ernest Schonfield (Berlin: De Gruyter, 2009), pp. 1–6

DE MUL, JOS, 'Artificial by Nature: An Introduction to Plessner's Philosophical Anthropology', in *Plessner's Philosophical Anthropology: Perspectives and Prospects*, ed. by Jos de Mul (Amsterdam: Amsterdam University Press, 2014), pp. 11–40

DETERING, HEINRICH, *Bertolt Brecht und Laotse* (Göttingen: Wallstein, 2008)

DETKEN, ANKE, 'Zwischen China und Brecht: Masken und Formen der Verfremdung in Döblins *Die drei Sprünge des Wang-lun*', in *Alfred Döblin: Paradigms of Modernism*, ed. by Steffan Davies and Ernest Schonfield (Berlin: De Gruyter, 2009), pp. 102–20

DE WILDE, MARC, 'Benjamin's Politics of Remembrance', in *A Companion to the Works of Walter Benjamin*, ed. by Rolf J. Goebel (Rochester, NY: Camden House, 2009), pp. 177–94

DOLLENMAYER, DAVID, 'The Advent of Döblinism: *Die drei Sprünge des Wang-lun* and *Wadzeks Kampf mit der Dampfturbine*', in *A Companion to the Works of Alfred Döblin*, ed. by Roland Dollinger and others (Rochester, NY: Camden House, 2004), pp. 55–74

——'Narration and the City', in *A New History of German Literature*, ed. by David E. Wellbery (Cambridge, MA: Harvard University Press, 2004), pp. 764–69

DOLLINGER, ROLAND, 'Technology and Nature: From Döblin's *Berge Meere und Giganten* to a Philosophy of Nature', in *A Companion to the Works of Alfred Döblin*, ed. by Roland Dollinger and others (Rochester, NY: Camden House, 2004), pp. 93–110

DOLLINGER, ROLAND, WULF KOEPKE, and HEIDI THOMANN TEWARSON, eds, *A Companion to the Works of Alfred Döblin* (Rochester, NY: Camden House, 2004)

DREYFUS, HUBERT L., *Being-in-the-World: A Commentary on Heidegger's 'Being and Time', Division I* (Cambridge, MA: MIT Press, 1991)

DRISCOLL, KÁRI, 'Toward a Poetics of Animality: Hofmannsthal, Rilke, Pirandello, Kafka', unpublished PhD dissertation, Columbia University, 2014

DURRANI, OSMAN, 'Shen Te, Shui Ta, and *Die drei Sprünge des Wang-lun*', *Oxford German Studies*, 12 (1981), 111–21

EAGLETON, TERRY, *The Ideology of the Aesthetic* (Oxford: Blackwell, 1990)

ELM, URSULA, *Literatur als 'Lebensanschauung': Zum ideengeschichtlichen Hintergrund von Alfred Döblins 'Berlin Alexanderplatz'* (Bielefeld: Aisthesis, 1991)

EMDE, FRIEDRICH, *Alfred Döblin: Sein Weg zum Christentum* (Tübingen: Narr, 1999)

EMIG, CHRISTINE, 'Butterblume — Mutterblume: Psychiatrischer und "naturphilosophischer" Diskurs in Alfred Döblins *Die Ermordung einer Butterblume*', *Scientia Poetica*, 9 (2005), 195–215

FICK, MONIKA, *Sinnenwelt und Weltseele: Der psychophysische Monismus in der Literatur der Jahrhundertwende* (Tübingen: Niemeyer, 1993)

FISHER, PETER S., *Fantasy and Politics: Visions of the Future in the Weimar Republic* (Madison: University of Wisconsin Press, 1991)

FOUCAULT, MICHEL, *The Order of Things: An Archaeology of the Human Sciences* (London: Routledge, 2002)

——*Society Must Be Defended: Lectures at the Collège de France, 1975–76*, trans. by David Macey (London: Allen Lane, 2003)

FRÜCHTL, JOSEF, *Mimesis: Konstellation eines Zentralbegriffs bei Adorno* (Würzburg: Königshausen & Neumann, 1986)

FUECHTNER, VERONIKA, '"Arzt und Dichter": Döblin's Medical, Psychiatric, and Psychoanalytical Work', in *A Companion to the Works of Alfred Döblin*, ed. by Roland Dollinger and others (Rochester, NY: Camden House, 2004), pp. 111–40

GELDERLOOS, CARL, 'Das Ich über der Natur (1927)', in *Döblin-Handbuch: Leben — Werk — Wirkung*, ed. by Sabina Becker (Stuttgart: Metzler, 2016), pp. 276–80

—— '"Jetzt kommt das Leben": The Technological Body in Alfred Döblin's *Berge Meere und Giganten*', *The German Quarterly*, 88.3 (2015), 291–316

GENZ, JULIA, 'Döblins Schreibweise der Evokation und Aussparung: Psychoanalytische und psychiatrische Diskurse in *Die Tänzerin und der Leib*', in *Internationales Alfred Döblin Kolloquium Emmendingen 2007: 'Tatsachenphantasie'. Alfred Döblins Poetik des Wissens im Kontext der Moderne*, ed. by Sabina Becker and Robert Krause (Bern: Lang, 2008), pp. 69–82

GESS, NICOLA, ed., *Literarischer Primitivismus* (Berlin: De Gruyter, 2013)

—— 'Literarischer Primitivismus: Chancen und Grenzen eines Begriffs', in *Literarischer Primitivismus*, ed. by Nicola Gess (Berlin: De Gruyter, 2013), pp. 1–10

GIRARD, RENÉ, *Violence and the Sacred*, trans. by Patrick Gregory (London: Bloomsbury, 2013)

GOLLIDGE, NICHOLAS R., and OTHERS, 'Global Environmental Consequences of Twenty-First-Century Ice-Sheet Melt', *Nature*, 566 (2019) 65–72 (pp. 70–71), <https://doi.org/10.1038/s41586-019-0889-9>

HARAWAY, DONNA J., 'A Cyborg Manifesto: Science, Technology, and Socialist-Feminism in the Late Twentieth Century', in Haraway, *Simians, Cyborgs and Women: The Reinvention of Nature* (London: Free Association Books, 1991), pp. 149–81

HAYLES, N. KATHERINE, *How We Became Posthuman: Virtual Bodies in Cybernetics, Literature, and Informatics* (Chicago: University of Chicago Press, 1999)

HERF, JEFFREY, *Reactionary Modernism: Technology, Culture, and Politics in Weimar and the Third Reich* (Cambridge: Cambridge University Press, 1984)

HERWIG, MALTE, 'The Unwitting Muse: Jakob von Uexküll's Theory of Umwelt and Twentieth-Century Literature', *Semiotica*, 134.1 (2001), 553–92

HINTIKKA, JAAKKO, '*Cogito, Ergo Sum*: Inference or Performance?', *Philosophical Review*, 71 (1962), 3–32

HOFFMANN, TORSTEN, '"Inzwischen gingen seine Füße weiter": Autonome Körperteile in den frühen Erzählungen und medizinischen Essays von Alfred Döblin und Gottfried Benn', in *Alfred Döblin: Paradigms of Modernism*, ed. by Steffan Davies and Ernest Schonfield (Berlin: De Gruyter, 2009), pp. 46–73

HONNETH, AXEL, '"Zur Kritik der Gewalt"', in *Benjamin-Handbuch: Leben — Werk — Wirkung*, ed. by Burkhardt Lindner (Stuttgart: Metzler, 2006), pp. 193–210

HONOLD, ALEXANDER, 'Exotisch entgrenzte Kriegslandschaften: Alfred Döblins Weg zum "Geonarrativ": *Berge Meere und Giganten*', in *Literarischer Primitivismus*, ed. by Nicola Gess (Berlin: De Gruyter, 2013), pp. 211–34

HOOCK, BIRGIT, *Modernität als Paradox: Der Begriff der 'Moderne' und seine Anwendung auf das Werk Alfred Döblins (bis 1933)* (Tübingen: Niemeyer, 1997)

HORN, EVA, 'Literary Research: Narration and the Epistemology of the Human Sciences in Alfred Döblin', *Modern Language Notes*, 118 (2003), 719–39 <http://dx.doi.org/10.1353/mln.2003.0057>

HUYSSEN, ANDREAS, *Miniature Metropolis: Literature in an Age of Photography and Film* (Cambridge, MA: Harvard University Press, 2015)

ISERMANN, THOMAS, *Der Text und das Unsagbare: Studien zu Religionssuche und Werkpoetik bei Alfred Döblin* (Idstein: Schulz-Kirchner, 1989)

JACOBUS, MARY, 'An Unnecessary Maze of Sign-Reading', in Mary Jacobus, *Reading Women: Essays in Feminist Criticism* (London: Methuen, 1986), pp. 229–48

JAHRAUS, OLIVER, 'Chinoiserien, Chinawaren, chinesischer Roman: Döblins "Die drei Sprünge des Wang-lun" mit einem Seitenblick auf Bertoluccis "Der letzte Kaiser"', in *Alfred Döblin: Neufassung*, ed. by Sabina Kyora, Text + Kritik: Zeitschrift für Literatur, 13/14 (2018), 66–77

JAMESON, FREDRIC, *Archaeologies of the Future: The Desire Called Utopia and Other Science Fictions* (London: Verso, 2007)

JANAWAY, CHRISTOPHER, *Schopenhauer* (Oxford: Oxford University Press, 1994)

JARVIS, SIMON, *Adorno: A Critical Introduction* (Cambridge: Polity, 1998)

JELAVICH, PETER, *Berlin Alexanderplatz: Radio, Film, and the Death of Weimar Culture* (Berkeley: University of California Press, 2006)

JOCH, MARKUS, 'Der Platz des irdischen Friedens. Sommer 1912 [sic]: Alfred Döblin beginnt die Arbeit am *Wang-lun*', in *Mit Deutschland um die Welt: Eine Kulturgeschichte des Fremden in der Kolonialzeit*, ed. by Alexander Honold and Klaus R. Scherpe (Stuttgart: Metzler, 2004), pp. 415–21

JUNGEN, OLIVER, *Döblin, die Stadt und das Licht* (Munich: Iudicium, 2001)

KALTENMARK, MARK, and ROGER T. AMES, 'Laozi', *Encyclopaedia Britannica* <https://www.britannica.com/biography/Laozi>

KAUFMANN, DORIS, '"Primitivismus": Zur Geschichte eines semantischen Feldes, 1900–1930', in *Literarischer Primitivismus*, ed. by Nicola Gess (Berlin: De Gruyter, 2013), pp. 93–124

KAYA, NEVZAT, '"Tellurische Rationalitätskritik": Zur Weiblichkeitskonzeption in *Berge Meere und Giganten*', in *Internationales Alfred Döblin Kolloquium 1999*, ed. by Torsten Hahn (Berlin: Lang, 2002), pp. 131–40

KEIL, THOMAS, *Alfred Döblins 'Unser Dasein': Quellenphilologische Untersuchungen* (Würzburg: Königshausen & Neumann, 2005)

KELLER, OTTO, *Döblins Montageroman als Epos der Moderne* (Munich: Fink, 1980)

KIEFER, MATHIAS, *Die Entwicklung des Seelenbegriffs in der deutschen Psychiatrie ab der zweiten Hälfte des 19. Jahrhunderts unter dem Einfluss zeitgenössischer Philosophie* (Essen: Die Blaue Eule, 1996)

KIESEL, HELMUTH, 'Döblin's *November 1918*', in *A Companion to the Works of Alfred Döblin* ed. by Roland Dollinger and others (Rochester, NY: Camden House, 2004), pp. 215–32

KINGERLEE, ROGER, *Psychological Models of Masculinity in Döblin, Musil, and Jahnn: Männliches, Allzumännliches* (Lewiston, NY: Mellen, 2001)

KIRK, G. S., J. E. RAVEN and MALCOLM SCHOFIELD, *The Presocratic Philosophers: A Critical History with a Selection of Texts*, 2nd edn (Cambridge: Cambridge University Press, 1983)

KLEINSCHMIDT, ERICH, 'Editorische Nachweise und Kommentar', in Alfred Döblin, *Schriften zu Ästhetik, Poetik und Literatur*, ed. by Kleinschmidt (Olten: Walter, 1989), pp. 603–739

KLOTZ, VOLKER, 'Nachwort', in Alfred Döblin, *Berge Meere und Giganten*, ed. by Klotz (Freiburg i.Br.: Walter, 1977), pp. 515–39

KOBEL, ERWIN, *Alfred Döblin: Erzählkunst im Umbruch* (New York: De Gruyter, 1985)

KOEPKE, WULF, 'Döblin's Political Writings during the Weimar Republic', in *A Companion to the Works of Alfred Döblin*, ed. by Roland Dollinger and others (Rochester, NY: Camden House, 2004), pp. 183–92

KOLB, EBERHARD, *The Weimar Republic*, trans. by P. S. Falda and R. J. Park (London: Routledge, 2004)

KYORA, SABINE, 'Der Novellenzyklus *Die Ermordung einer Butterblume und andere Erzählungen* (1912)', in *Döblin-Handbuch: Leben — Werk — Wirkung*, ed. by Sabina Becker (Stuttgart: Metzler, 2016), pp. 29–41

LAI, KARYN L., *An Introduction to Chinese Philosophy* (Cambridge: Cambridge University Press, 2008)

LESKAU, LINDA, 'Botanical Perversions: On the Depathologization of Perversions in Texts by Alfred Döblin and Hanns Heinz Ewers', in *Biological Discourses: The Language of Science and Literature around 1900*, ed. by Robert Craig and Ina Linge (Oxford: Lang, 2017), pp. 211–34

LESLIE, ESTHER, *Liquid Crystals: The Science and Art of a Fluid Form* (London: Reaktion, 2016)

LEVINE, DONALD N., and DANIEL SILVER, 'Introduction', in Georg Simmel, *The View of Life: Four Metaphysical Essays with Journal Aphorisms*, ed. by Levine and Silver (Chicago, IL: University of Chicago Press, 2010), pp. ix–xxix

LION, FERDINAND, 'Das Werk Alfred Döblins: Zum fünfzigsten Geburtstag des Dichters am 10. August 1928', *Neue Rundschau*, 39.2 (1928), 161–73

LIU, WEIJIAN, *Die daoistische Philosophie im Werk von Hesse, Döblin und Brecht* (Bochum: Brockmeyer, 1991)

LODGE, DAVID, *The Modes of Modern Writing: Metaphor, Metonymy, and the Typology of Modern Literature* (London: Arnold, 1977)

LUKÁCS, GEORG, *The Historical Novel*, trans. by Hannah Mitchell and Stanley Mitchell (London: Merlin Press, 1962)

MAASS, INGRID, *Regression und Individuation: Alfred Döblins Naturphilosophie und späte Romane vor dem Hintergrund einer Affinität zu Freuds Metapsychologie* (Frankfurt a.M.: Lang, 1997)

MAHLER, SUSANNE, 'Poetik des Vergessens', in Alfred Döblin, *Gedächtnisstörungen bei der Korsakoffschen Psychose*, ed. by Susanne Mahler (Leipzig: Tropen, 2006), pp. 91–106

MAILLARD, CHRISTINE, '*Unser Dasein* (1933)', in *Döblin-Handbuch: Leben — Werk — Wirkung*, ed. by Sabina Becker (Stuttgart: Metzler, 2016), pp. 280–85

MAKARI, GEORGE, *Revolution in Mind: The Creation of Psychoanalysis*, 2nd edn (London: Duckworth, 2010)

MARX, REINER, 'Literatur und Zwangsneurose: Eine Gegenübertragungsimprovisation zu Alfred Döblins früher Erzählung "Die Ermordung einer Butterblume"', in *Internationales Alfred-Döblin-Kolloquium Leiden 1995*, ed. by Gabriele Sander (Bern: Lang, 1997), pp. 49–60

McGILCHRIST, IAIN, *The Master and his Emissary: The Divided Brain and the Making of the Western World*, 2nd edn (New Haven, CT: Yale University Press, 2012)

McGOWAN, MORAY, 'German Writing in the West (1945–1990)', in *The Cambridge History of German Literature*, ed. by Helen Watanabe O'Kelly (Cambridge: Cambridge University Press, 1997), pp. 440–506

MERCHANT, CAROLYN, *Reinventing Eden: The Fate of Nature in Western Culture*, 2nd edn (New York: Routledge, 2013)

MICHEL, SASCHA, '*Der schwarze Vorhang. Roman von den Worten und Zufällen* (1919)', in *Döblin-Handbuch: Leben — Werk — Wirkung*, ed. by Sabina Becker (Stuttgart: Metzler, 2016), pp. 24–28

MIDGLEY, DAVID, 'After Materialism: Reflections of Idealism in *Lebensphilosophie*: Dilthey, Bergson and Simmel', in *The Impact of Idealism*, ed. by Nicholas Boyle, Liz Disley and John Walker, 4 vols (Cambridge: Cambridge University Press, 2013), II: *Historical, Social, and Political Thought: The Legacy of Post-Kantian Thought*, 161–85

—— '"Creative Evolution": Bergson's Critique of Science and its Reception in the German-Speaking World', in *The Evolution of Literature: Legacies of Darwin in European Cultures*, ed. by Nicholas Saul and Simon J. James (Amsterdam: Rodopi, 2011), pp. 283–99

—— 'The Early Fiction of Alfred Döblin: The Short Story between Case Study and Parable', in *Kafka und die kleine Prosa der Moderne: Kafka and Short Modernist Prose*, ed. by Manfred Engel and Ritchie Robertson (Würzburg: Königshausen & Neumann, 2011), pp. 209–23

—— 'Epische Dichtung: *Manas* (1927)', in *Döblin-Handbuch: Leben — Werk — Wirkung*, ed. by Sabina Becker (Stuttgart: Metzler, 2016), pp. 97–101

—— 'Metaphysical Speculation and the Fascination of the Real: On the Connections between Döblin's Philosophical Writing and his Major Fiction before *Berlin Alexanderplatz*', in *Alfred Döblin: Paradigms of Modernism*, ed. by Steffan Davies and Ernest Schonfield (Berlin: De Gruyter, 2009), pp. 7–27

—— '"Was heißt eigentlich ganz tot?" Zur thematischen und poetologischen Bedeutung der Seelenwanderung bei Alfred Döblin', in *Poetik der Seelenwanderung*, ed. by Martin Hense and Jutta Müller-Tamm, (Freiburg i.Br.: Rombach, 2014), pp. 169–84

—— '"Wie die Bienen sind sie über den Boden her." Zu den biologischen Bezügen der Massendarstellungen in Döblins Romanen', in *Internationales Alfred-Döblin-Kolloquium Berlin 2011: Massen und Medien bei Alfred Döblin*, ed. by Stefan Keppler-Tasaki (Bern: Lang, 2014), pp. 51–66

MORTON, TIMOTHY, *Ecology without Nature: Rethinking Environmental Aesthetics* (Cambridge, MA: Harvard University Press, 2007)

—— *The Ecological Thought* (Cambridge, MA: Harvard University Press, 2010)

MÜLLER-SALGET, KLAUS, *Alfred Döblin: Werk und Entwicklung* (Bonn: Bouvier, 1972)

—— 'Döblin and Judaism', in *A Companion to the Works of Alfred Döblin*, ed. by Roland Dollinger, Wulf Koepke and Heidi Thomann Tewarson (Rochester, NY: Camden House, 2004), pp. 233–46

MUSCHG, WALTER, 'Nachwort des Herausgebers', in Döblin, *Die drei Sprünge des Wang-lun*, ed. by Walter Muschg (Olten and Freiburg i.Br.: Walter, 1960), pp. 481–502

NAQUIN, SUSAN, *Shantung Rebellion: The Wang Lun Uprising of 1774* (New Haven, CT: Yale University Press, 1981)

NESBET, ANNE, 'Schizoglossia and *Berlin Alexanderplatz*', *Qui Parle*, 2.1 (1988), 125–41

NEUBAUER-PETZOLDT, RUTH, 'Döblins *Der Ritter Blaubart* und seine synkretische Montagetechnik', in *Alfred Döblin: Paradigms of Modernism*, ed. by Steffan Davies and Ernest Schonfield (Berlin: De Gruyter, 2009), pp. 74–101

NORRIS, MARGOT, 'Modernism and Vietnam: Francis Ford Coppola's *Apocalypse Now*', *Modern Fiction Studies*, 44.3 (1998), 730–66

OPPEL, FRANCES NESBITT, *Nietzsche on Gender: Beyond Man and Woman* (Charlottesville: University of Virginia Press, 2005)

PAN, DAVID, *Primitive Renaissance: Rethinking German Expressionism* (Lincoln, NA: University of Nebraska Press, 2001)

PARKER, STEPHEN, *Bertolt Brecht: A Literary Life* (London: Methuen, 2014)

POTOLSKY, MATTHEW, *Mimesis* (New York: Routledge, 2006)

POWELL, LARSON, *The Technological Unconscious in German Modernist Literature: Nature in Rilke, Benn, Brecht, and Döblin* (Rochester, NY: Camden House, 2008).

QUAL, HANNELORE, *Natur und Utopie: Weltanschauung und Gesellschaftsbild in Alfred Döblins Roman 'Berge Meere und Giganten'* (Munich: Iudicium, 1992)

RAFTERY, ADRIAN E., and OTHERS, 'Less than 2 °C warming by 2100 unlikely', *Nature Climate Change*, 7 (2017) 637–41

REICH-RANICKI, MARCEL, *Sieben Wegbereiter: Schriftsteller des zwanzigsten Jahrhunderts* (Stuttgart: DVA, 2002)

RICHARDS, ROBERT J., *The Tragic Sense of Life: Ernst Haeckel and the Struggle over Evolutionary Thought* (Chicago, IL: University of Chicago Press, 2008)

RICOEUR, PAUL, *Freud and Philosophy: An Essay on Interpretation*, trans. by Denis Savage (New Haven, CT: Yale University Press, 1970)

—— *The Rule of Metaphor: The Creation of Meaning in Language*, trans. by Robert Czerny, 3rd edn (London: Routledge, 2003)

RIEDEL, WOLFGANG, *'Homo Natura': Literarische Anthropologie um 1900* (Berlin: De Gruyter, 1996)

―― *Nach der Achsendrehung: Literarische Anthropologie im 20. Jahrhundert* (Würzburg: Königshausen & Neumann, 2014)
RIPPER, ANNETTE, 'Überlegungen zur Aneignung des Körpers und zum Aspekt der Bio-Macht in Alfred Döblins *Berge Meere und Giganten*', *Musil-Forum*, 30 (2007), 194–220
ROBERTSON, RITCHIE, 'Alfred Döblin as Pacifist and Chauvinist: *Die drei Sprünge des Wang-lun* and Wartime Propaganda', in *Pacifist and Anti-Militarist Writing in German, 1889–1928*, ed. by Andreas Kramer and Ritchie Robertson (Munich: Iudicium, 2018), pp. 199–210
―― 'Alfred Döblin's Feeling for Snow: The Poetry of Fact in *Berge Meere und Giganten*', in *Alfred Döblin: Paradigms of Modernism*, ed. by Steffan Davies and Ernest Schonfield (Berlin: De Gruyter, 2009), pp. 215–28
―― 'From Naturalism to National Socialism (1890–1945)', in *The Cambridge History of German Literature*, ed. by Helen Watanabe-O'Kelly (Cambridge: Cambridge University Press, 1997), pp. 327–92
―― *Kafka: Judaism, Politics, and Literature* (Oxford: Oxford University Press, 1985)
―― 'Modernism and the Self: 1890–1924', in *Philosophy and German Literature, 1700–1990*, ed. by Nicholas Saul (Cambridge: Cambridge University Press, 2002), pp. 150–96
ROYLE, NICHOLAS, *The uncanny* [sic] (Manchester: Manchester University Press, 2003)
ROZYNEK, MICHAL, *A Philosophy of Nationhood and the Modern Self* (London: Palgrave Macmillan, 2017)
SACKS, OLIVER, *The Man Who Mistook His Wife for a Hat*, 2nd edn (London: Picador, 2011)
SAFRANSKI, RÜDIGER, *Martin Heidegger: Between Good and Evil*, trans. by Ewald Osers (Cambridge, MA: Harvard University Press, 1998)
SANDER, GABRIELE, *Alfred Döblin* (Stuttgart: Reclam, 2001)
―― *'An die Grenzen des Wirklichen und Möglichen': Studien zu Alfred Döblins Roman* Berge Meere und Giganten (Bern: Lang, 1988)
―― 'Anmerkungen', in Alfred Döblin, *Berge Meere und Giganten*, ed. by Gabriele Sander (Zurich: Walter, 2006), pp. 687–764
―― 'Anmerkungen', in Alfred Döblin, *Die drei Sprünge des Wang-lun: Chinesischer Roman*, ed. by Gabriele Sander and Andreas Solbach (Düsseldorf and Zurich: Walter, 2007), pp. 568–637
―― '"Chinesischer Roman": *Die drei Sprünge des Wang-lun* (1915)', in *Döblin-Handbuch: Leben — Werk — Wirkung*, ed. by Sabina Becker (Stuttgart: Metzler, 2016), pp. 41–50
―― '"Der uralte noch immer traumverlorene Erdteil": Die Afrika-Thematik in Alfred Döblins Roman *Berge Meere und Giganten*', in *Alfred Döblin: Paradigms of Modernism*, ed. by Steffan Davies and Ernest Schonfield (Berlin: De Gruyter, 2009), pp. 229–44
―― 'Literarische Wirkungsgeschichte', in *Döblin-Handbuch: Leben — Werk — Wirkung*, ed. by Sabina Becker (Stuttgart: Metzler, 2016), pp. 9–11
―― 'Rezeption zu Lebzeiten', in *Döblin-Handbuch: Leben — Werk — Wirkung*, ed. by Sabina Becker (Stuttgart: Metzler, 2016), pp. 2–4
SANTNER, ERIC L., *On Creaturely Life: Rilke, Benjamin, Sebald* (Chicago, IL: University of Chicago Press, 2006)
―― *The Royal Remains: The People's Two Bodies and the Endgames of Sovereignty* (Chicago, IL: University of Chicago Press, 2011)
SASS, LOUIS, *Madness and Modernism: Insanity in the Light of Modern Art, Literature, and Thought*, rev. edn (Oxford: Oxford University Press, 2017)
SAUL, NICHOLAS, 'Darwin in German Literary Culture 1890–1913', in *The Literary and Cultural Reception of Charles Darwin*, ed. by Thomas F. Glick and Elinor Shaffer, 3 vols (London: Bloomsbury, 2014), III, 46–77
―― 'Love, Death and *Liebestod* in German Romanticism', in *The Cambridge Companion to German Romanticism*, ed. by Nicholas Saul (Cambridge: Cambridge University Press, 2009), pp. 163–74

SCHÄFER, ARMIN, 'The Physiology of Charisma: Alfred Döblin's Novel *The Three Leaps of Wang-lun*', *New German Critique*, 114 (2011), 79–93

SCHÄFFNER, WOLFGANG, *Die Ordnung des Wahns: Zur Poetologie psychiatrischen Wissens bei Alfred Döblin* (Munich: Fink, 1995)

SCHERPE, KLAUS R., 'The City as Narrator', in *Modernity and the Text: Revisions of German Modernism*, ed. by David Bathrick und Andreas Huyssen (New York: Columbia University Press, 1989), pp. 162–79

SCHOELLER, WILFRIED F., *Alfred Döblin: Eine Biographie* (Munich: Hanser, 2011)

SCHULTZ, KARLA L., *Mimesis on the Move: Theodor Adorno's Concept of Imitation* (Bern: Lang, 1990)

SCHUSTER, INGRID, and INGRID BODE, eds, *Alfred Döblin im Spiegel der zeitgenössischen Kritik* (Bern and Munich: Francke, 1973)

SCHÜTTPELZ, ERHARD, 'Zur Definition des literarischen Primitivismus', in *Literarischer Primitivismus*, ed. by Nicola Gess (Berlin: De Gruyter, 2013), pp. 13–28

SHEPPARD, RICHARD, *Modernism — Dada — Postmodernism* (Evanston, IL: Northwestern University Press, 2000)

SIEBENPFEIFFER, HANIA, 'Dokumentarische Erzählung: *Die beiden Freundinnen und ihr Giftmord* (1924)', in *Döblin-Handbuch: Leben — Werk — Wirkung*, ed. by Sabina Becker (Stuttgart: Metzler, 2016), pp. 93–97

SLUGAN, MARIO, *Montage as Perceptual Experience: 'Berlin Alexanderplatz' from Döblin to Fassbinder* (Rochester, NY: Camden House, 2017)

SOLBACH, ANDREAS, 'Nachwort', in Alfred Döblin, *Die drei Sprünge des Wang-lun: Chinesischer Roman*, ed. by Gabriele Sander and Andreas Solbach (Düsseldorf and Zurich: Walter, 2007), pp. 638–70.

SOPER, KATE, *What is Nature? Culture, Politics and the Non-Human* (Oxford: Blackwell, 1995)

STANCIC, MIRJANA, 'Auseinandersetzung mit Friedrich Nietzsche', in *Döblin-Handbuch: Leben — Werk — Wirkung*, ed. by Sabina Becker (Stuttgart: Metzler, 2016), pp. 273–75

—— 'Döblins frühe Erzählungen *Die Segelfahrt* und *Die falsche Tür*: Ein interkultureller Annäherungsversuch', in *Internationales Alfred Döblin Kolloquium Warschau 2013: Interkulturelle Aspekte im Schaffen Alfred Döblins*, ed. by Marion Brandt and Grazyna Kwiecinska (Bern: Lang, 2015), pp. 159–72

STEGEMANN, HELGA, *Studien zu Alfred Döblins Bildlichkeit: Die Ermordung einer Butterblume und andere Erzählungen* (Bern: Lang, 1978)

SULLIVAN, HEATHER I. and BERNHARD L. MALKMUS, 'The Challenge of Ecology to the Humanities: An Introduction', *New German Critique*, 43.2 (2016), 1–20

TAN, YUAN, *Der Chinese in der deutschen Literatur* (Göttingen: Cuvillier, 2007)

TATAR, MARIA, *Lustmord: Sexual Murder in Weimar Germany* (Princeton, NJ: Princeton University Press, 1995)

TAYLOR, CHARLES, *Philosophical Arguments* (Cambridge, MA: Harvard University Press, 1995)

—— *Sources of the Self: The Making of the Modern Identity* (Cambridge: Cambridge University Press, 1989)

THIRLWELL, ADAM, 'An Explosion of Pure Fact', *The New York Review of Books*, 25 October 2018 <https://www.nybooks.com/articles/2018/10/25/berlin-alexanderplatz-explosion-pure-fact/> [accessed 21 November 2019]

TROTTER, DAVID, *Literature in the First Media Age: Britain between the Wars* (Cambridge, MA: Harvard University Press, 2013)

VIDAL, JOHN, 'Has the politics of climate change finally reached a tipping point?', *The Guardian*, 15 May 2019, <https://www.theguardian.com/commentisfree/2019/may/15/climate-change-politics-environmental-crisis-government>

WACHTER, DAVID, 'Amoeba, Dragonfly, Gazelle: Animal Poetics around 1908', in *Biological Discourses: The Language of Science and Literature around 1900*, ed. by Robert Craig and Ina Linge (Oxford: Lang, 2017), pp. 371–96
WARREN, JAMES, *Presocratics* (Stocksfield: Acumen, 2007)
WEBBER, ANDREW J., *Berlin in the Twentieth Century: A Cultural Topography* (Cambridge: Cambridge University Press, 2008)
—— *The Doppelgänger: Double Visions in German Literature* (Oxford: Clarendon Press, 1996)
WEILER, GERSHON, *Mauthner's Critique of Language* (Cambridge: Cambridge University Press, 1970)
WENINGER, ROBERT K., *The German Joyce* (Gainesville, FL: University Press of Florida, 2012)
WILLIAMS, ROWAN, *The Edge of Words: God and the Habits of Language* (London: Bloomsbury, 2014)
WOLIN, RICHARD, *Walter Benjamin: An Aesthetic of Redemption* (New York: Columbia University Press, 1982)
WÜBBEN, YVONNE, 'Tatsachenphantasien: Alfred Döblins Die Ermordung einer Butterblume im Kontext von Experimentalpsychologie und psychiatrischer Krankheitslehre', in *Internationales Alfred Döblin Kolloquium Emmendingen 2007: 'Tatsachenphantasie'. Alfred Döblins Poetik des Wissens im Kontext der Moderne*, ed. by Sabina Becker and Robert Krause (Bern: Lang, 2008), pp. 84–100
YENGOYAN, ARAM, 'Betrachtungen über Vorstellungen von Kultur, Zivilisation, Politik und Ästhetik: Franz Boas, Georg Simmel und Thomas Mann mit besonderem Nachdruck auf ihre Verwirklichung als Geist, Weltanschuung und Völkergedanken', *Social Analysis*, 41.3 (1997), 24–41
ŽIŽEK, SLAVOJ, *For They Know Not What They Do: Enjoyment as a Political Factor* (London: Verso, 1991).
—— *In Defence of Lost Causes* (London: Verso, 2008)

# INDEX

Adorno, Theodor W. 13, 42, 112,
   *Ästhetische Theorie* 10, 27, 38, 183, 184
   *Dialektik der Aufklärung* 7, 10, 38, 45, 57, 96, 101–02, 112, 124 n. 62
   on Döblin 165
   mimesis 38, 79, 107–08, 172
   'Standort des Erzählers im zeitgenössischen Roman' 180 n. 52
Aelianus, Claudius 116
Aeschylus 125 n. 89
   *Oresteia* 42, 162, 184
Agamben, Giorgio 168
Althen, Christina 20, 125 n. 90
animals and animality 143–45, 166–69
animism 28, 111, 118, 186
Anz, Thomas 43
*Apocalypse Now* 89–90 n. 86
Aristotle 38
Armstrong, Tim 122 n. 31, 123 n. 51
Assmann, Aleida 79–80

Bachofen, Johann Jakob 110
Bakhtin, Mikhail, *see* carnivalesque, the
Ballard, J. G., *The Drowned World* 14, 115–16
Barthes, Roland 2, 28
Bartscherer, Christoph 149, 182
Becher, Johannes R. 94
Becker, Sabina 50 nn. 9 & 14, 88 n. 58, 178 n. 6
Benjamin, Walter 12, 13, 56–58, 67, 80, 85
   'aura' 79, 82
   'Das Kunstwerk im Zeitalter seiner technischen Reproduzierbarkeit' 98
   *Das Passagen-Werk* 79
   on Döblin 12, 16 n. 34, 78, 164, 172–73
   'Jetztzeit' 57, 59, 84 148, 183
   'Lehre vom Ähnlichen' 38, 79
   Messianism 57
   mimesis 38, 79, 113
   'Über das mimetische Vermögen' 38, 79
   'Über den Begriff der Geschichte' 56–58, 78, 80, 108
   'Über einige Motive bei Baudelaire' 79, 124 n. 59
   'Zur Kritik der Gewalt' 68–69
Benn, Gottfried 20, 144
Bergson, Henri 6, 136–37
Biblical allusions:
   New Testament 38, 48–49, 62, 64, 170, 174
   Old Testament 36, 101, 163, 167, 170
   Virgin Mary 32, 35, 48–49, 117
*Bildungsroman* 157, 164
biopolitics and biopower 103–07, 109, 117, 121
Bloch, Ernst 68
Bluebeard 19, 32
Bölsche, Wilhelm 34
Boltzmann, Ludwig 104
Bowie, Andrew 141
Brecht, Bertolt 2, 12, 13, 182, 183
   and Daoism 61
   *Der gute Mensch von Sezuan* 70–71
   epic theatre 58
   influence of Döblin 58–59, 70
   *Verfremdungseffekt* 59, 69–72, 82, 108
Buber, Martin 60, 61
Buddhism 6, 61–62, 65–66, 72
   Nirvana 34, 65–66, 150
Bühler, Benjamin 130, 131
Busch, Wilhelm 134

carnivalesque, the 158, 169–71
Carossa, Hans 20
Cassirer, Ernst 53 n. 61, 112–13, 118
Catani, Stephanie 37
Charon, Rita:
   and narrative medicine 47
China, Expressionist interest in 60–61
   *see also* Daoism
Christianity, *see* Biblical allusions
Confucianism 58, 62, 65, 67–68
Copernicus, Nicolaus 98, 149
Cowan, Michael 13, 22, 40, 46, 47
creatureliness 14, 38, 48, 158, 166–72
cyborgs 12–13, 14, 95–97, 102–03, 118–20, 142–43, 145, 176

Dada 172
Daoism 6, 9–10, 13, 57, 60–63, 74–75, 93, 147
   Laozi 61
   Liezi 61, 64, 78
   *wu wei* 9–10, 60, 63–73, 84–85, 112, 171
Darwin, Charles 3–4, 34, 116, 149, 159, 166
Davies, Mererid Puw 32
Davies, Steffan 9, 12, 86 n. 14, 183
death, personifications of 36–38, 169–70
*Der Sturm* [literary magazine] 6, 20, 127

Descartes, René 133
determinism 131, 136, 139
Detken, Anke 69, 70, 82
*deus sive natura* 4
Dilthey, Wilhelm 6, 136–37
Döblin, Alfred:
  career and life:
    and Berlin 14, 157, 178 n. 5
    and Catholicism 1, 11–12, 128, 149–50, 182
    interest in China 60–63
    interest in Daoism, *see* Daoism
    'Döblinismus' 73, 95
    epic writing 11, 12, 21–22, 58–59, 70, 75–76, 96, 156, 158, 172
    in exile 11–12, 182
    and Expressionism 13, 19–21, 22, 26, 42, 48–49, 65
    and the Fontane Prize 58
    and the Great War 57, 92
      *see also* the Great War, memory of
    historical fiction 3, 12, 58–59, 86 n. 14, 183
    and Judaism 86 n. 12, 128, 178 n. 5
    'Kinostil' 75, 82, 169
    marriage to Erna Reiss 28
    medical training and work 20–21, 30–32, 57, 92, 157
    and nationalism, *see* nationalisms
    and psychoanalysis 30–32
    racism 112
    relationship with father, Max Döblin 23, 50 n. 20
    relationship with Frieda Kunke 28
    return to Germany after World War II 1
    and socialism 65
    'Tatsachenphantasie' 8, 20–21, 75–76, 82, 94, 114, 132, 134, 169
    theory of art 158–59, 184
  works:
    autobiography and travel writing:
      *Reise in Polen* 128–29
      *Schicksalsreise* 1
    essays and manifestos:
      'Arzt und Dichter' 31
      'Bemerkungen zu "Berge Meere und Giganten"' 96
      'Berliner Programm' 2, 8, 21, 24, **73–76**, 85, 103, 135, 169, 172, 183
      'Das Recht auf Rhetorik' 74
      'Der Bau des epischen Werks' 11, 21–22, 70, 156, 172
      'Der Geist des naturalistischen Zeitalters' 95, **96–99**, 106, 145, 175–76
      'Drei Demokratien' 92
      'Epilog' 8, 26, 129, 156–57
      'Futuristische Worttechnik: Offener Brief an F. T. Marinetti' 73–74
      'Leib und Seele' 30
      'Mein Buch "Berlin Alexanderplatz"' 157–58
      'Persönliches und Unpersönliches' 5
      'Prometheus und das Primitive' 96, 113, 120
      'Reims' 92
    medical writings:
      'Aufmerksamkeitsstörungen bei Hysterie' 30
      *Gedächtnisstörungen bei der Korsakoffschen Psychose* 41–43, 50–51 n. 21
      'Praxis der Psychoanalyse' 31
      'Psychoanalyse von heute' 31
    novels and epic poems:
      *Berge Meere und Giganten* 1, 3, 9, 13–14, 35, 69, **91–126**, 128, 140, 142, 145, 184
      *Berlin Alexanderplatz* 1–3, 8, 14, 27, 30, 34, 36, 44, 78, 98, 134, 136–37, 142, 147, **156–81**, 184, 186–87
      *Der schwarze Vorhang* 13, 20, 23, 27, 28, 45
      *Die drei Sprünge des Wang-lun* 3, 9, 11, 13, **56–90**, 113, 120, 128, 148, 163, 183
      *Hamlet oder Die lange Nacht nimmt ein Ende* 1
      *Jagende Rosse* 19
      *Manas: Epische Dichtung* 128, 138, 157
      *Wadzeks Kampf mit der Dampfturbine* 12
      *Wallenstein* 12, 86 n. 14, 92, 183–84
    novellas and short stories:
      'Das Stiftsfräulein und der Tod' **36–38**
      'Der Ritter Blaubart' **32–36**, 109
      *Die beiden Freundinnen und ihr Giftmord* 12
      'Die Ermordung einer Butterblume' 8–9, 13, **39–45**, 109, 163
      'Die Flucht aus dem Himmel' **48–49**
      'Die Segelfahrt' **23–28**, 127
      'Die Tänzerin und der Leib' 8–9, 39–40, **45–47**, 109
      'Die Verwandlung' **28–29**
    philosophical and anthropological works:
      *Das Ich über der Natur* 87 n. 37, 107, 111, **129–30**, 138–39, 162
      'Der Wille zur Macht als Erkenntnis bei Friedrich Nietzsche' 4–5
      *Gespräche mit Kalypso: Über die Musik* 6, 27, 40, 75, 117, 127, 146, 147–48, 182
      *Unser Dasein* 11, 14, 31, 48, 87 n. 37, 99, 120, **129–55**, 157, 158–59, 160, 162–63, 171, 173–74, 175, 182, 184
      'Zu Nietzsches Morallehre' 4–5
*Dolchstoßlegende* 94, 173, 175
Dollenmayer, David 81–82
*Doppelgänger* motif 25–26, 43, 45–46
Driesch, Hans 142
dualisms 13, 47–48, 132, 133, 139, 142, 185

ecology and ecocriticism 7, 91, 118
Elm, Ursula 145
Emig, Christine 41, 42
Empedocles 116, 125 n. 89
  *see also* Presocratics

epiphany in modernism 10–11, 79–80, 170
eugenics 104–05

Fassbinder, Rainer Werner 2
*femme fragile* 40
Fichte, Johann Gottlieb 137–38
S. Fischer Verlag 20, 157
Foucault, Michel 8, 47, 115
   *Madness and Civilization* 8
   *The Order of Things* 103, 128
   *Society Must Be Defended* 106–07, 115
   see also biopolitics and biopower
Freud, Sigmund 4, 30–32, 149–50, 166
   *Das Ich und das Es* 31, 34
   'Das Unheimliche' 25, 88 n. 57, 118
   death drive 25, 27, 34, 39
   'Eine Schwierigkeit in der Psychoanalyse' 4
   *fort-da* 36–37
   *Jenseits des Lustprinzips* 26, 31, 34, 36, 66, 124 n. 59
   *Zur Psychopathologie des Alltagslebens* 30
Fuechtner, Veronika 30
Futurism 73, 75, 99

Gelderloos, Carl 123 n. 55
general strike 68
Genz, Julia 8–9
Gess, Nicola 111
Gilman, Charlotte Perkins 44–45
Goethe, Johann Wolfgang von 5, 26, 50 n. 8, 93, 97, 112, 144, 169
Grass, Günter 1, 2, 92, 182, 187
Great War, memory of 106–08, 161, 183
Grimm, Jacob and Wilhelm 32
guilt 28–29, 42, 43

Haeckel, Ernst 3, 31, 146
   *Die Welträthsel* 3–4
   *Generelle Morphologie der Organismen* 125 n. 92, 155 n. 67
   *Kristallseelen: Studien über das anorganische Leben* 154 n. 65
   *Kunstformen der Natur* 159
   *Natürliche Schöpfungsgeschichte* 3–4, 158–59
Haraway, Donna J. 95
Harbou, Thea von 94
Hartmann, Eduard von 4
Hayles, N. Katherine 95, 120
Hegel, Georg Wilhelm Friedrich 129, 137
Heidegger, Martin 141, 144, 149, 185
   'Der Ursprung des Kunstwerkes' 10, 91
   'Die Frage nach der Technik' 96, 122 n. 33
   *Sein und Zeit* 14, 122 n. 31, 132, 135, 137, 142, 155 n. 73
Heraclitus 116
Herf, Jeffrey 93

hermeneutic remnant 10, 22, 48, 82, 109, 120, 131, 176, 183
Hesse, Hermann 61
Heym, Georg 21
Hinduism 61–62
Hintikka, Jaakko 133
Hirschfeld, Magnus 20
Hoche, Alfred Erich 20, 30
Hoffmann, Torsten 44
Homer, *Odyssey* 7, 110, 127–28
homoeroticism 76, 117, 183–84
Honold, Alexander 92
Hoock, Birgit 8
Horkheimer, Max, see Adorno, Theodor W, *Dialektik der Aufklärung*
Horn, Eva 9
Husserl, Edmund 136
Huxley, Aldous, *Brave New World* 14, 105–06, 113

Idealism, German 6, 137–40

Jahnn, Hans Henny 2
Jahraus Oliver 60
Jameson, Fredric 56
Jaques-Dalcroze, Émile 40
Jarvis, Simon 101
Jones, Jim 66
Joyce, James, *Ulysses* 156, 175, 185
*Jugendstil* 35
Juncker, Axel 20
Jünger, Ernst 93

Kafka, Franz 28, 29, 42, 49, 186
   influence on Döblin 49
Kahn, Fritz 103–04
Kant, Immanuel 159
Kästner, Erich 2
Kaya, Nevzat 110
Keil, Thomas 129, 137, 144, 145
Keller, Otto 8
Keun, Irmgard 2
Kirchner, Ernst Ludwig 37
Klabund 61
Klee, Paul 57
Kobel, Erwin 25
Kraepelin, Emil 30, 50–51 n. 21, 74

Lang, Fritz 94
*Lebensphilosophie* 5–6, 14, 61, 136–37, 142–43, 157
Leslie, Esther 151 n. 6
Lévi-Strauss, Claude 111
*Liebestod* 13, 23, 27
Lion, Ferdinand 6
Lodge, David 175
Lukács, Georg 59
*Lustmord* 20, 37

Maaß, Ingrid 30
McGilchrist, Iain 147
Mach, Ernst 4, 134–35
Mann, Klaus 2
Mann, Thomas 26, 92, 93, 144
Marinetti, Filippo Tommaso, *see* Futurism
Marx, Karl 98, 150
Marx, Reiner 41
Mauthner, Fritz 75, 97, 134–35
medical humanities 13
mental illness 20–21
   aboulia 41
   of Franz Biberkopf 157, 161
   Korsakoff syndrome 20, 41–42
   nervousness 41
   neurasthenia 41
   paranoid schizophrenia 41
   war neuroses 37, 157, 161
metaphor and metaphoricity 14, 112–13, 141–47
Midgley, David 5–6, 22, 34, 153 n. 36
monism 130, 132, 139
monsters 12–13, 114–18
montage 75, 78, 116, 158, 172–73, 175
Morton, Timothy 7, 118
   dark ecology 92, 96, 120
   'the mesh' 155 n. 69
Müller, Max 113
Müller-Salget, Klaus 8
Muschg, Walter 78
Musil, Robert 162

National Socialism 1, 56–57, 71, 94, 129, 177
nationalisms 57–58, 92, 98, 128–29, 146
natural sciences 136–37
nature 7–9, 35, 82, 91–126
   and anthropomorphism 138–47
   and climate catastrophe 91–92, 113–17
   and the self 23–47, 112, 135–47, *see also* self and subjectivity
   and the sublime 27, 93, 112
   and technology, *see* technology
   *see also* violence against nature
Newton, Isaac 162
Nietzsche, Friedrich 2–3, 4–6, 10, 25, 31, 65, 129, 136, 150, 156, 166
   and Deconstruction 141
   *Der Antichrist* 167
   *Die Geburt der Tragödie* 6, 25, 26, 110
   eternal recurrence 5
   'Über Wahrheit und Lüge im außermoralischen Sinne' 141
   Übermensch 5, 27

oral tradition 109–10, 112
Orwell, George, *Nineteen Eighty-Four* 106

Pan, David 111
Perrault, Charles 32, 33
Pascal, Blaise 149–50
Petersen, Julius 181
Plato 34, 38
Plessner, Helmuth 132, 144–45, 151 n. 13
posthuman, the 2, 3, 14, 95–96, 119–20, 146–47, 155 n. 71
Powell, Larson 124 n. 62
Presocratics, the 107, 116
primitivism 109–12
   techno-primitivism 106
Proust, Marcel 79
psychiatry 8–9, 20–21, 30, 74

Ranke, Leopold von 56
Realism, literary 73–74, 184
*Resonanz* 99, 136, 146, 177, 185
Reuleaux, Franz 104
Ricoeur, Paul 53–54 n. 66, 153 n. 46
Riedel, Wolfgang 111, 185
Rilke, Rainer Maria 20, 144
   *Die Aufzeichnungen des Malte Laurids Brigge* 54 n. 92, 80, 160
   *Duineser Elegien* 166, 167, 180 n. 55
   *Neue Gedichte* 48
Ripper, Annette 123 n. 43
Robertson, Ritchie 4, 59, 108, 169
Romantic irony 112, 141
Romanticism 10, 27, 31–32, 74, 91–92, 159
   and *Naturphilosophie* 136

Sacks, Oliver 41–42
Sander, Gabriele 9, 112
Santner, Eric L. 158, 166, 173
Sass, Louis 41
Saul, Nicholas 34
Schäfer, Armin 76, 83–84
Schäffner Wolfgang 8, 104, 116
Scheidemann, Philipp 173
Schelling, F. W. J. 137–39, 141, 144
Scherpe, Klaus 173
Schoeller, Wilfried F. 20, 92
Schonfield, Ernest 9
Schopenhauer, Arthur 2–3, 4, 6, 10, 31, 61–62, 65, 66, 103, 129, 139, 151 n. 14–15, 166, 185
   *Die Welt als Wille und Vorstellung* 139
   and music 139
   *Über die vierfache Wurzel des Satzes vom zureichenden Grunde* 132–33
science fiction 91–126
self and hybridity 139, 141–47, 184–85
self and subjectivity 131–35
Sheppard, Richard 3, 116
Simmel, Ernst 30
Simmel, Georg 6, 93, 136–37, 149, 184, 185

'Die Großstädte und das Geistesleben' 159–60, 164, 174
*Lebensanschauung* 137, 155 n. 73
Solbach, Andreas 75
Spengler, Oswald 93, 94, 101, 112
Spinoza, Baruch 3, 4, 6, 129, 138–39
*Sprachkrise* 166
Stancic, Mirjana 4, 24
Stegemann, Helga 26, 43
Storm, Theodor 32, 35
synthetic foodstuffs 104–05

Tan, Yuan 80
Tatar, Maria 162–63, 165
Taylor, Charles 10, 28, 153 n. 49, 170
technology 96–111, 113, 118–21, 143, 145
  *see also* nature
Trotter, David 106
Tykwer, Tom 173
Tylor, Edward Burnett 111

Uexküll, Jakob von 122 n. 31, 143–44, 146, 184
utopia and utopianism 48–49, 56, 66–67, 72–73, 82, 95, 163

violence:
  against nature 43–45, 106–08, 110–11, 113–17, 166–69
  non-violence 63–73, *see also* Daoism
  sadomasochism and sexual violence 20, 27, 37, 65–66, 162–63, 169
  *see also* Lustmord
  state violence 67–69, 72, 103–07
  in war 80–82, 106–08
vitalism, philosophical 57, 61, 142
*Vossische Zeitung* 61

Walden, Herwarth 20
Webber, Andrew J. 25, 165
Weber, Max 62
Wilhelm, Richard 61–62, 64
*Willenskultur* 22, 40–41
Williams, Rowan 186
women, Döblin's portrayals of 32, 45–47, 65–67, 99, 108–09, 110–11, 117–18, 162–63, 171–72
Wübben, Yvonne 8–9

yin and yang 61, 66

Žižek, Slavoj 91–92

www.ingramcontent.com/pod-product-compliance
Lightning Source LLC
Chambersburg PA
CBHW050453110426
42743CB00017B/3348

"'*La vida contigo es un tango.* Life with you is a tango, / sometimes tricky, sometimes sweaty, always bold, / daring, grace, guts, and comedy!' In 'El Tango,' one of many tributes to the woman he adores, poet and storyteller Armando García-Dávila sums up his artful dance. With love up his sleeve—charming, savvy—he moves across life's floor, hugging his Mexican roots, embracing spirituality. Betrayed by the Catholic Church of his youth, the poet steps back from institutions, trusting instead the tell-tale intimacy of family and community. In 'American God,' a prose-poem, he revisits his questioning childhood. 'Other kids went to church in newer cars, with newer clothes, with newer parents. . . . But if we praised the same God in the same way, then why did He bless *them* so much more than us?' To the beat of one heart, Armando García-Dávila's *Profile* shines a lyric light into America's ballrooms, backyards, and closets."

—AL YOUNG, California's poet laureate emeritus

"This lovely, well-written book of verse and stories touched my heart. These poems and stories travel back and forth in time evoking childhood memories of the Catholic Church paired with a writer's close analysis of the betrayal of innocence and the senselessness of war. However, interwoven throughout these painful moments is a poet's eye for finding those moments in life which also heal. Lines such as 'And the only sounds interrupting this immense meditation would be the wisps of butterfly wings, and a prayerful chant quietly echoing in each canyon.

'Love.' 'Love.' 'Love.'

Those words help to remind us, that despite the perplexity of life, there is tremendous power in the transformative act of remembering and being present to the beauty of living."

—IANTHE BRAUTIGAN SWENSEN, author of *You Can't Catch Death* (2001)

"'La vida contigo es un tango. ¡Algunas veces difícil, otras húmeda, siempre atrevida, desafiante, elegante, sin miedo y cómica!' En 'El tango,' uno de los muchos tributos a la mujer que adora, el poeta y cuentista, Armando García-Dávila nos entrega su baile artístico. Con el amor como vanguardia—es encantador, inteligente—se mueve a través del piso de la vida, abrazando sus raíces mexicanas, abrazando su espiritualidad. Traicionado por la Iglesia católica durante su niñez, el poeta se retira de las instituciones, confiando en su lugar en las tradiciones íntimas de su familia y su comunidad. En 'El dios norteamericano', un poema en prosa, Armando visita su niñez, una vez más cuestionándola.

'Otros niños iban a la iglesia en carros nuevos, con ropa más nueva, con padres más nuevos. . . . Pero si todos alabábamos al mismo dios de la misma manera, ¿entonces por qué Él bendecía mucho más a ellos que a nosotros?' Al latido del corazón, 'Perfil' de Armando García-Dávila alumbra su lírica con una brillantez hacia los salones de baile, los patios traseros y los roperos de los Estados Unidos".

—AL YOUNG, poeta Emérito Laureado de California

"Este adorable y bien escrito libro en verso y prosa me llegó al corazón. Estos poemas y cuentos viajan por el tiempo de ida y regreso evocando memorias de la Iglesia católica de su niñez, a la misma vez que como escritor analiza la guerra sin sentido y la traición a la inocencia. No obstante, los momentos dolorosos del poeta se hallan entretejidos en la vista por hallar aquellos momentos en la vida que también sanan el alma. Líneas como 'Y que el único sonido que interrumpa esta inmensa meditación sea el movimiento de las alas de la mariposa y que el canto resuene como un eco en cada cañón.

'Amor'. 'Amor'. 'Amor'.

Estas palabras nos ayudan a recordar que a pesar de lo perplejo de la vida, hay mucho poder en el acto transformativo de recordar y el estar presente en la belleza de vivir".

—IANTHE BRAUTIGAN SWENSEN, autor de *"No puedes agarrar la muerte"* (2001)

"A writer's heart displayed is a beautiful thing, especially when the view includes honesty, courage, and wisdom. In his new book, *Profile*, Armando García-Dávila shows us the passionate, loving, laughing, angry, proud, and wise heart that beats in his chest. At first flush these forty-seven poems and seven stories feel safe and warm, like Armando's studio on a hilltop in Santa Rosa, until you realize the risks he takes—and asks us to take—in many of his pieces.

'Want to be free?' Armando asks. 'Lay your ego by the side of the road and in your sternest voice give the command, "Stay!" Then run like hell until you can't hear its protests anymore.'

In 'The Muse,' Armando writes: 'Poetry barged through my door one day. . . . When in good humor, she gave herself without pause or shame, and the verses flowed freely. . . . Other times she ripped a tooth from my jawbone in barter for a single line.'

Armando's love poems do what the finest of that genre always have: make us feel what we're called upon to give and receive to call ourselves human. Armando is a Sonoma County treasure, and in the world I want to live in he'd be a treasure in all of California and beyond, wherever the young, the sensitive, the passionate, the hungry, the hurt, the abandoned, and the brave demand respect and truth."

—DAVID BECKMAN, author of *Language Factory of the Mind* (2012)

"Armando is full of passion and questions as are his dancing words."

—SUSAN SWARTZ, author of *The Juicy Tomatoes Guide to Ripe Living after 50* (2006)

"El corazón de un escritor es una cosa hermosa, especialmente cuando la vista incluye honestidad, coraje y sabiduría. En su nuevo libro Perfil, Armando García-Dávila revela sus pasiones, amores, carcajadas, enojos, orgullos y la sabiduría del corazón que late en su pecho. A primera vista estos cuarenta y siete poemas y siete cuentos se sienten seguros y calurosos, como el estudio de Armando localizado en una cima de Santa Rosa, hasta que te das cuenta de los riesgos que está tomando—y nos pide que también nosotros los tomemos en muchos de sus escritos.

'¿Quieres ser libre?' Pregunta Armando. 'Deja tu ego en la orilla del camino y con voz firme ordénale que ¡Se quede! Después corre rápido hasta que ya no escuches las protestas'.

En 'La musa' Armando escribe: 'La poesía entró por la puerta un día...Cuando está de buen humor, se entrega sin pausa y vergüenza, y los versos emanan libremente...en otras ocasiones, me arranca un diente de la encía y negocia por un simple verso'.

Los poemas de amor de Armando presentan lo más fino que ese género siempre ha tenido: nos hacen sentir que hemos sido llamados para dar y recibir, para llamarnos humanos. Armando es un tesoro del condado de Sonoma, y del mundo que quiero vivir, en el que él será un tesoro en todo California y más allá, donde esté el joven, el sensible, el apasionado, el hambriento, el lastimado, el abandonado y el valiente demandando el respeto y la verdad".

—David Beckman, autor de *"Fábrica del idioma de la mente"* (2012)

"Armando está lleno de pasión y sus preguntas son como sus palabras que danzan".

—Susan Swartz, autor de *"La guía de tomates jugosos viviendo después de los 50"* (2006)

"How wonderful to have in hand this hot book. Call it 'An Armando García-Dávila Reader.' A collection of new and old work, poems, prose poems, and stories, it explores love, death, sex, and labor. The author's voice cries out from the wilderness, laments the loss of faith and celebrates the renewal of faith in poems that shock, arouse, and evoke the beauty of earthly and heavenly bodies and extoll the earth itself. In *Profile: Poems and Stories*, García-Dávila reveals himself as a dreamer waking to the agony and the ecstasy of life, rousing and arousing readers from sleep, from forgetfulness and from their own addictions."

—JONAH RASKIN, author of *Rock 'n' Roll Women* (2012) and *A Few French Scenes* (2013)

"¡Qué maravilloso es tener este cardente libro a la mano! Llámalo 'Lecturas de Armando García-Dávila'. Una colección de escritos nuevos y viejos, poemas en verso, poemas en prosa y cuentos, ellos exploran el amor, la muerte, el sexo y el trabajo. El autor con voces a gritos viene desde la profundidad selvática, con lamentos de una fe perdida y la celebración de una fe renovada en poemas que sorprenden, emocionan y evocan la belleza de los cuerpos terrenales y celestiales alabando la tierra misma. En Perfil: Poemas y Cuentos, García-Dávila se revela como un soñador caminando en la agonía y el éxtasis de la vida, inspirando y despertando a los lectores de un sueño de olvido y de sus propias adicciones".
—JONAH RASKIN, autor de *"Mujeres rock 'n' roll"* (2012) y *"Unas pocas escenas francesas"* (2013)

# PERFIL
## POEMAS Y CUENTOS

# PROFILE
## POEMS AND STORIES

## Also by Armando García-Dávila

*Out Of My Heart/De Mi Corazon.* Poetry published in English and Spanish by Thumbprint Press. (1999)

*At the Edge of the River/Al Lado Del Rio.* Prose and poetry published in English and Spanish by Running Wolf Press. (2007)

## Works in Other Publications

Poetry and short stories were a regular feature in *La Voz*, a bilingual newspaper.

*Bless Me Father for I Have Sinned* and *The Pendulum.* Humorous short stories featured in *Bust Out Stories,* a Thumbprint Press magazine.

*Healdsburg Alive! Eight Sonoma County Writers Pay Homage to a Great Northern California Town.* (2012)

## Awards

*Bless Me Father for I Have Sinned* and *If I Could* were awarded first place blue ribbons at the Marin County Fair. (1998)

Healdsburg, California, Literary Laureate—2002/2003.

# PERFIL
## POEMAS Y CUENTOS

# PROFILE
## POEMS AND STORIES

### Armando García-Dávila

McCaa Books • Santa Rosa

McCaa Books
1604 Deer Run
Santa Rosa, CA 95405-7535

Copyright © 2015 by Armando García-Dávila
All Rights Reserved

Without limiting the rights under copyright reserved above, no part of this publication may be reproduced, distributed, or transmitted in any form or by any means, or stored in a database or retrieval system, without the prior written permission of both the copyright owner and the publisher of this book except in the case of brief quotations embodied in critical articles or reviews.

ISBN 978-0-9960695-4-0
First published in 2015 by McCaa Books,
an imprint of McCaa Publications.
Second printing, October 2016.

Printed in the United States of America
Set in Minion Pro

www.mccaabooks.com

*To Kathy who has always been there for me. "I love you more than I could ever express, sweetheart."*

*To Doris whose financial and emotional support has made this possible. "I love and miss you."*

*A Kathy que siempre me ha brindado su apoyo. "Mi amor, te amo más de lo que pueda expresar".*

*A Doris, la cual su apoyo financiero y emocional han hecho esto posible. "Te amo y te extraño".*

# CONTENTS

| | |
|---|---|
| Preface | 20 |

## *Poems*

| | |
|---|---|
| The Day Will Come | 24 |
| Dead List | 26 |
| Distracted | 30 |
| A Free Man | 34 |
| If I Could | 36 |
| J.C. | 40 |
| Lonely | 42 |
| Mother Sea | 44 |
| October Corn | 50 |
| Roadside Flowers | 56 |
| Two Springs | 58 |
| The Herd | 62 |
| The Muse | 64 |
| The Pit | 68 |
| Where Are You? | 72 |
| 120/80 | 76 |
| Carry Me | 80 |
| The Greatest Poem | 84 |
| You've Got Mail | 88 |
| A Respite | 94 |
| Could You Love Me? | 96 |
| Embers | 98 |

# CONTENIDO

| | |
|---|---:|
| Prefacio | 21 |

## Poemas

| | |
|---|---:|
| El día vendrá | 25 |
| Lista de muertos | 27 |
| Distraido | 31 |
| Un hombre libre | 35 |
| Si Yo Pudiera | 37 |
| J.C. | 41 |
| Solitario | 43 |
| Madre Mar | 45 |
| El maíz de octubre | 51 |
| Las flores del camino | 57 |
| Dos primaveras | 59 |
| La manada | 63 |
| La musa | 65 |
| El hoyo | 69 |
| ¿En donde estas? | 73 |
| 120/80 | 77 |
| Cárgame | 81 |
| El poema grandioso | 85 |
| Haz recibido correo | 89 |
| Un descanso | 95 |
| ¿Me podrias amar? | 97 |
| Cenizas | 99 |

| | |
|---|---|
| An Exquisite Eve | 100 |
| Her Song | 102 |
| If I Loved You Yesterday | 104 |
| Listen | 106 |
| Of Little Boys and Kisses | 108 |
| Of Love and Uncertainty | 110 |
| Loving Her | 112 |
| *Mi Leona* | 114 |
| Regular Love | 116 |
| Silence | 118 |
| *El Tango* | 120 |
| A Winter's Alcove | 122 |
| Wishing | 124 |
| Your Light | 126 |
| "Yes!" | 128 |
| American God | 132 |
| The *Campesinos' Maestra* | 134 |
| *El Jardinero* | 138 |
| *El Paletero* | 142 |
| *El Gran Viento* | 144 |
| Monks of the Field | 148 |
| *El Otro Lado* | 152 |
| *Fresas* | 156 |
| Which Foot? | 160 |
| Wild Flowers | 164 |

| | |
|---|---|
| Una eva exquisita | 101 |
| Su eanción | 103 |
| Si yo te amé ayer | 105 |
| Escucha | 107 |
| De iños pequeños y besos | 109 |
| De amor e incertidumbre | 111 |
| Amándola | 113 |
| Mi leona | 115 |
| Amor regular | 117 |
| Silencio | 119 |
| El tango | 121 |
| La alcoba de invierno | 123 |
| Deseando | 125 |
| Tu luz | 127 |
| "¡Sí!" | 129 |
| El dios norteamericano | 133 |
| La maestra de los campes nos | 135 |
| El jardinero | 139 |
| El paletero | 143 |
| El gran viento | 145 |
| Los monjes del campo | 149 |
| El otro lado | 153 |
| Fresas | 157 |
| ¿Cual pie? | 161 |
| Flores silvestres | 165 |

## Stories

| | |
|---|---|
| Bless Me Father for I Have Sinned | 170 |
| Don't Fall Asleep | 190 |
| *Chato's* Steal | 196 |
| Voice Behind the Wall | 210 |
| Portrait of a Rose | 228 |
| Lord, Snow, and Dawn | 242 |
| Love at First Sight | 276 |
| | |
| Acknowledgments | 284 |
| About the Author | 288 |

## Cuentos

| | |
|---|---|
| Bendiceme padre por pecador | 171 |
| No te quedes dormido | 191 |
| El robo del chato | 197 |
| La voz detrás de la pared | 211 |
| Retrato de una rosa | 229 |
| "El Señor", Nieves, y Aurora | 243 |
| Amor a primera vista | 277 |
| | |
| Reconocimientos | 285 |
| Acerca del autor | 289 |

# PREFACE

WHAT FOLLOWS IN THIS BOOK are some revelations of my life and soul through a few poems and short stories. I have no pretensions to seek your understanding or forgiveness. I only hope you enjoy the pathos, sense of seeking, and humor in my work.

The Catholic Church and our family's Mexican roots and modest means provided the foundation of my young years. I remain indebted to my parents, older brother, twin brother, and four sisters for the core of my being. Without them, I would be but a shadow.

However, the church confused me early in life as I came to realize the fallibility of the institution. My intention in writing about it is not to offend but to simply offer its effects on me as an innocent and malleable child.

> Armando García-Dávila
> October 2016

# PREFACIO

Lo que sigue en este libro son algunas revelaciones de mi vida y de mi alma a través de unos pocos poemas y cuentos breves. No tengo pretensiones de obtener su comprensión o perdón. Sólo espero que disfrute de los sentimientos y el sentido de la búsqueda y el humor en mi trabajo.

La Iglesia católica, las raíces mexicanas de nuestra familia y modestos medios fueron los que ofrecieron las bases para mi juventud. Agradezco a mis padres, mi hermano mayor, mi gemelo y a mis cuatro hermanas desde el centro de mi ser. Sin ellos, yo sería nada más que una sombra.

Sin embargo, la Iglesia me traicionó desde muy temprano en la vida, a medida que llegué a comprender el engaño de esta institución. Mi intención al escribir de ella no es para ofender sino simplemente ofrecer sus efectos sobre mí como un niño inocente y obediente.

Armando García-Dávila
octubre 2016

*Poems*

*Poemas*

*PROFILE / PERFIL*

# The Day Will Come

And the day will come when you hit the switch,
but the room will remain dark.

Computers will not hum, monitors will not glow,
and boys will have no flashing games
to play.

Gas pumps will remain silent, and we will
be forced to walk.

Those who don't know how to start a fire will
be cold.

The comfortably wealthy will be greatly
inconvenienced.

And those who live under bridges will not notice
the difference.

## El día vendrá

Y el día vendrá cuando prendas el apagador,
pero el cuarto se quedará a obscuras.

Las computadoras no zumbarán, el monitor no
brillará y los niños no tendrán juegos luminosos
con que jugar.

Las estaciones de gasolina estarán calladas y
estaremos forzados a caminar.

Aquellos que no saben cómo prender el fuego
tendrán frío.

La comodidad de los ricos será profundamente
inconveniente.

Y aquellos que viven bajo los puentes no notarán
la diferencia.

*PROFILE / PERFIL*

# Dead List

Black, cold, still outdoors, storm clouds shroud the sunrise. A dove perches in the apple tree outside my kitchen window. A solitary "coo" escapes her beak. I look up and bid her my usual "good morning," wondering if she will sing today with the sky so dark.

Steam rises from my coffee cup; first sip tastes best. I'm always intrigued reading obituaries in the morning paper; entire lives reduced to a handful of words.

"I check da dead list," Tony, my neighbor used to say. He was a World War I veteran, fought for Italy. "Name not on list. Good day today!" I was saddened when his name finally appeared. I miss him. He made me laugh, his irreverence toward the pope, his telling me that my back spasms were because I wasn't "getting enough." The man in me laughed, the altar boy embarrassed.

Sad when the old die, tragic when they're young. Saw an infant's coffin carried by a single pallbearer at a funeral once. And Philip, my best friend in the sixth grade, died one rainy afternoon. The cave he had been digging collapsed in on him. Ma showed me his obituary. Strange seeing his desk empty in our classroom the next day. Grief-stricken, his mother collapsed at the memorial service.

# Lista de muertos

Negras, frías, aún afuera, las nubes de la tormenta envuelven el amanecer. Una paloma se posa en el árbol de manzanas, afuera de la ventana de mi cocina. De su pico se escapa un solitario "cu". Miro hacia afuera y la saludo con mi diario "buenos días", preguntándome si va a cantar hoy a pesar del cielo negro.

El vapor de mi café se eleva; el primer sorbo siempre es el mejor. Es intrigante leer los anuncios de defunción en el periódico de la mañana; vidas enteras reducidas a un puñado de palabras.

Mi vecino Toño solía decir, "reviso la lista de los muertos". Era un veterano de la Primera Guerra Mundial, peleó por Italia. "¡Buen día hoy, no está mi nombre en la lista!" Me puse triste cuando su nombre por fin apareció en la lista. Lo extraño. Cómo me hacía reír con sus irreverencias hacia el Papa y me decía que el dolor de la cintura era porque no tenía suficiente sexo. El hombre en mí reía, el monaguillo se apenaba.

Es triste cuando los ancianos mueren, es trágico cuando son jóvenes. Una vez vi al sepulturero cargar el sólo el ataúd de un bebé. Y Philip, mi mejor amigo de sexto año en la escuela, murió una tarde lluviosa. La cueva que estaba escarbando se desplomó sobre él. Mi amá me enseñó el anuncio de su defunción. Al día siguiente fue extraño ver su escritorio vacío en mi clase. Su madre se desmayó de tanta tristeza en su funeral.

*PROFILE / PERFIL*

And last year a young woman's husband made the dead list. He was a soldier killed in the war, she pregnant with their first, named the boy after his father.

Endless this checking of dead lists. The lists from Thermopylae, from Waterloo, Bull Run, Normandy, Da Nang, Baghdad, too many to name.

And we will not be seeing the coffins bearing America's colors return home. No day of mourning for them. Each blood sacrifice reduced to an item in the obits.

I consider making another cup of coffee, but lightning explodes overhead. My kitchen turns dark. Glasses in the cupboards rattle. Thunder roars through the valley, shattering the predawn peace. Hail mercilessly pounds the apple tree. Countless blossoms fall to the ground, fruit never to be realized.

And I hear nothing more from the dove.

Y el año pasado, el esposo de una mujer joven se incorporó a la lista de los muertos. Era un soldado que murió en la guerra. Éste era su primer embarazo. Le puso al niño el nombre de su padre ya muerto.

La lista de muertos es interminable. Las listas de Thermopylae, Waterloo, Bull Run, Normandía, Da Nang, Bagdad, tantas por mencionar.

Y no vamos a ver los ataúdes con los colores de los Estados Unidos regresar a casa. No va haber un día de luto para ellos. Cada sangre sacrificada es reducida a un obituario.

Quiero hacer más café, pero los relámpagos truenan en el cielo. Mi cocina se obscurece y los vasos en la vitrina tiemblan. Los relámpagos rugen por el valle, quebrando el calmado amanecer. El granizo no tiene misericordia del árbol de manzanas. Incontables flores caen al suelo, de las cuales nunca habrá un fruto.

Y no escucho más a la paloma.

*PROFILE / PERFIL*

# **Distracted**

The rising sun bears witness to the commotion of our hectic lives each day. Thunderous machines tear down and rebuild cities, repair streets, as we race to work amid racing engines and honking horns. Helicopters hover high overhead advising us of road conditions that could make us late; we need to hurry. Our car radios fill our ears with happy announcers, happy music, happy advertisers that make us laugh, make us want.

Employers, important appointments, churches, and families compete for our precious time.

And we don't dare miss our television programs. I'm pulling for the pretty young lady vying to be the next singing idol.

We roar at the stadium as the ball soars across the field like a bird on the wing. Oh, what a play!

You understand that it's hard for us to hear much else, don't you?

We do have feelings about the issue though. You know the one about *our* war in *your* country. We see it on the news, your homes turned to rubble, you weeping for your children who have been consumed by fire and hate. And our young warriors who have lost their legs, their arms, their sanity, as one politician screams into his opponent's deaf ear.

## Distraido

El sol de la mañana es testigo de la conmoción, de la vida agitada que vivimos cada día. Máquinas ruidosas destruyen y construyen ciudades, apresurados vamos al trabajo, las calles son reparadas en medio de motores en carrera tocando el claxon. Los helicópteros vuelan en el aire dándonos las noticias del tráfico y el estado de las carreteras. Hay que darse prisa. El radio transmite anuncios felices, música feliz, los locutores bromistas nos hacen reír, nos hacen querer algo.

Jefes de trabajo, citas importantes, las iglesias y la familia compiten por nuestro precioso tiempo.

Y no nos atrevemos a pedernos nuestros programas de televisión. Voy a votar por la joven bonita para que sea la ganadora del programa *"idol"*.

Rugimos en los estadios cuando la pelota gira por la cancha, como si fuera un pájaro en vuelo ¡Qué jugada!

¿Entiendes que es difícil para nosotros escuchar otra cosa? ¿O no?

El tema no despierta emociones. ¿Sabes? El tema de nuestra guerra en tu país. Lo vemos en las noticias, tu casa destruida, lloras por tus hijos, los cuales han sido consumidos por el fuego y el odio. Y nuestros guerreros jóvenes han perdido las piernas, los brazos, su cordura, y al mismo tiempo un político le grita a su oponente con oídos sordos.

*PROFILE / PERFIL*

This incessant ranting and uproar frightens and confuses us. We close our eyes and ears to it lest it drives us mad. We turn to sedatives and wine for a blissful moment of serenity in our harried and lonely lives.

But after the sun has set on our frenzied world, and the moon has made its way high into the dark night, and it is so still that even the crickets have quieted, and at long last there is a moment of solitude, this is when the dreaded question begins haunting our troubled sleep.

"What, in the name of God, are we doing?"

Then mercifully the alarm clock shrieks and the din begins anew.

*POEMS / POEMAS*

El incesante tumulto del escándalo nos da miedo y nos confunde. Cerramos los ojos, tapamos los oídos para no volvernos locos. A cambio, consumimos calmantes y vino para tener un momento de paz y serenidad en nuestra rápida y solitaria vida.

Pero cuando el sol está en el ocaso de nuestra rápida vida y la luna está en lo alto de la negra noche, cuando todo está en silencio, hasta los grillos están callados, al fin, hay un momento de soledad, éste es el momento cuando la temida pregunta empieza a espantar nuestro sueño ya acosado.

"¿En el nombre de Dios, qué es lo que estamos haciendo?".

Entonces, milagrosamente la alarma del reloj suena y el ruido comienza otra vez.

*PROFILE / PERFIL*

# A Free Man

Want to be a free man? It's simple. Start by shedding your clothes. They say too much about who you wish to be.

Next, to eliminate the compulsion to dominate, remove your testicles and set them on a shelf out of reach.

Lay your ego by the side of the road and in your sternest voice give the command, "Stay!" Then run like hell until you can't hear its protests.

Erase your history so that you are not a man anymore, nor Catholic, Protestant, Jew, or Muslim. You aren't Mexican, German, or Chinese.

Don't consider the future; in fact, so you won't think at all, put your brain in the freezer (thinking is overrated).

Find a clock and smash it between two stones, then feel your way through days and nights.

Forgive yourself and your children for not being enough. Forgive your ex, forgive God for not giving you the answers you think He owes you.

Now find a place in the shade, and listen to everyone, particularly children and birds. Sit quietly until you recognize the miracle of breath.

*POEMS / POEMAS*

# Un hombre libre

¿Quieres ser un hombre libre? Es muy simple. Empieza por quitarte la ropa. Tu ropa denuncia tus anhelos de quién quieres ser.

Después, elimina el deseo de dominar, quítate los testículos y ponlos en una repisa difícil de alcanzar.

Deja tu ego en la orilla del camino y con una voz de comando ordénale que "¡Se quede!" Después échate a correr rápido hasta que ya no escuches las protestas.

Borra tu historia para que ya no seas ese hombre, católico, protestante, judío, o musulmán. Para que no seas mexicano, alemán o chino.

No consideres el futuro. En realidad no pienses nada, mete tu cerebro en el congelador. El pensamiento exagera.

Busca un reloj y rómpelo en medio de dos piedras, después siente tu camino por los días y las noches.

Perdónate y perdona a tus hijos por no ser lo esperado. Perdona a tu ex, perdona a Dios por no darte las respuestas que tú crees él te debe.

Ahora sí, busca un lugar en la sombra y escucha a todos, especialmente a los niños y los pájaros. Siéntate callado hasta que reconozcas el milagro del respiro.

*PROFILE / PERFIL*

# If I Could

If only for a moment, I would silence the world's motors, and the roar of the airplane would not be so much as a hum, and the thunder of the locomotive would become less than a moan.

No blaring horns, no screeching brakes, no screaming police sirens would come from the avenue. The din of Industry would cease, and the factory would fall into a coma. Its smoke would lift, allowing the forest to inhale deeply, and once again we would drink from the river.

The miracles of the dawn and the dusk would reclaim their sacred stillness.

The parrot would stop his incessant squawking, and children would play a game of statues. The wino, realizing the gift of his existence, would leave his bottle corked.

The right would swing to the left, and the left would not know where to turn. Politicians would be left without plots to hatch, and the devil, he would run out of tricks.

## Si yo pudiera

Si tan sólo por un momento apagara los motores del mundo, que los rugidos del avión se conviertan en un suspiro y que el trueno de la locomotora se convierta en tan sólo un lamento.

Que no hubiera cláxones escandalosos, frenos arrastrándose, que las sirenas de la policía no se escuchen desde la avenida. Que el ruido de las fábricas se apague y que las fábricas estén en coma. Que el humo se vaya para que el bosque respire profundo, para que una vez más podamos beber del río.

Para que los milagros del amanecer y anochecer reclamen su sagrada quietud.

Que el cotorro pare su constante parloteo y que los niños jueguen a las estatuas. Que el borracho reconozca el regalo de su existencia y deje la botella sellada.

Que la derecha se mueva a la izquierda y que la izquierda no sepa hacia dónde ir. Que los políticos estén sin la mordida y que al diablo se le acaben los trucos.

*PROFILE / PERFIL*

Shouts would turn to whispers, whispers to thoughts, and thoughts to prayer. Chicks, in their nests, would sleep. And in every canton and hamlet, in every town and city, one would hear only the rhythmic breathing of deep slumber and the throbbing of his own heart. And the only sounds interrupting this immense meditation would be the wisps of butterfly wings, and a prayerful chant quietly echoing in each canyon.

"Love."   "Love."   "Love."

Que los gritos se conviertan en susurros, los susurros en pensamientos y los pensamientos en oración. Para que los pollitos en sus nidos duerman. Que en cada casa y choza, que en cada ciudad y pueblo, uno pueda escuchar nada más que el ritmo del sueño profundo y el latido de su corazón. Y que el único sonido que interrumpa esta inmensa meditación sea el movimiento de las alas de la mariposa y que el canto resuene como un eco en cada cañón.

"Amor". "Amor". "Amor".

*PROFILE / PERFIL*

# J.C.

I didn't ask You to die for me. Maybe You should've been a carpenter instead of a preacher. Would the world be any different if You had? Would the Crusaders have killed in the name of someone else instead?

Your mother would have been spared the anguish of seeing her son tortured to death. Wouldn't that have been better? You could have given her grandchildren who would have delighted her in her old age, and I would have been spared the guilt of causing Your agony.

I didn't ask You to die for me.

## J.C.

No te pedí que murieras por mí. Quizás deberías haber sido carpintero en lugar de predicador. ¿Habría sido el mundo diferente si tú lo hubieras sido? ¿Habrían matado los cruzados en el nombre de otro?

Tu madre se habría ahorrado la angustia de ver a su hijo torturado hasta la muerte. ¿No sido hubiera eso mejor? Le habrías dado nietos para deleitarla en su vejez y yo me habría ahorrado la culpa de haberte causado tu agonía.

No te pedí que murieras por mí.

*PROFILE / PERFIL*

# Lonely

No one knocks on my door. No one calls me on the phone. There were no notes left on my porch today, nor a letter in the mail.

A nutshell lies on the ground, its meat stolen by an uncaring squirrel.

I heated my dinner and ate. It was quietly good. I will retire, my bed will be warmed solely by my body.

Tomorrow I will eat breakfast, make a lunch, and go to labor. When I return, I will listen to *Moonlight Sonata*,

and no one

will knock

on my door.

*POEMS / POEMAS*

## Solitario

Nadie toca mi puerta. Nadie me llama por teléfono. No hay notas en mi portal el día de hoy, ni una carta en el correo.

La cáscara de una nuez está en el piso, el fruto fue robado por una ardilla descarada.

Calenté mi cena y comí. Estaba calladamente buena. Me acostaré. Mi cama estará calentada sólo con mi cuerpo.

Mañana desayunaré, prepararé mi almuerzo e iré a trabajar. Cuando regrese, escucharé la *Sonata de la luz de la luna*

y nadie

tocará

a mi puerta.

*PROFILE / PERFIL*

# Mother Sea

Swell, break, crash — swell, break, crash.

Cells morph into plankton in Mother Sea, plankton to fish, fish to amphibians to reptiles, mammals, into you, into me. We owned gills once, or did they own us? And what of this dream of being able to breathe underwater. A dream? Or a primal memory?

Swell, break, crash — swell, break, crash.

Mother Sea taps the universe's rhythm at her shores.

Phoenicians, Egyptians, Greeks, and Persians explored and conquered by learning to navigate her waters. South China Sea to The Sea of Galilee, Chinese on their junks, Palestinians and Jews in their modest boats, Altus in the frigid Arctic, Brazilians at a sweltering equator, all go about their daily trade of drawing sustenance from her rich stores, by hand, with basket, spear, hook, and net. Oh Mother Sea from whom all good things come, give us this day our daily fish.

Children run screaming from a rushing shore-break, then gleefully chase it back, not noticing the globe's grand arcing horizon, unaware that the entire world lies there at their feet. Lovers on a white sandy beach lie on a blanket basking in the sun, "by the sea, by the sea, by the beautiful sea."

*POEMS / POEMAS*

# Madre Mar

Crece, se rompe, choca — crece, se rompe, choca.

En la Madre Mar, las células se transforman en plancton, el plancton en peces, los peces en anfibios, en reptiles, en mamíferos, en ti. En mí. ¿En un tiempo teníamos branquias, o ellas nos tenían a nosotros? Y qué pasa con el sueño de poder respirar bajo el agua. ¿Un sueño? ¿O una memoria primitiva?

Crece, se rompe, choca — crece, se rompe, choca.

La Madre Mar toca los ritmos del universo en sus costas.

Los fenicios, egipcios, griegos y persas exploraron y conquistaron cuando aprendieron a navegar sus mares. Del Mar del Sur de China, al Mar de Galilea, los chinos en sus chatarras, los palestinos y judíos en sus barcas humildes, los esquimales en el frío Ártico, los brasileños en el caluroso Ecuador. Todos tienen su sustento basado en la venta cotidiana, desde las ricas tiendas, hechas a mano, con canastas, flechas, ganchos y redes. ¡Oh Madre Mar! De dónde vienen todos esos productos, danos nuestro pescado de cada día.

Los niños huyen de la playa gritando, donde las olas se rompen, después contentos siguen corriendo a las olas, ni siquiera perciben el gran arco horizontal del mundo. Sin darse cuenta que el mundo entero está a sus pies. Los amantes recostados en la playa sobre una cobija se broncean bajo el sol, "en el mar, en el mar, en el hermoso mar".

*PROFILE / PERFIL*

And in the sea it shall be finished. Minute krill by the million are filtered out in the jowls of colossal baleen whales. A horseshoe crab emerges from a tide pool; its life quickly ends in a sandpiper's beak. A woman paces a widow's walk, looks out to the sea praying for the sight of her man's returning trawler. A wife lays her husband's ashes into the surf.

Roman, Spanish, British mariners, admirals and seamen, captains and oarsmen, whalers and their crews, have all tasted the sea's salt, and lost to "the deep" in storm and war. Once mighty armadas, royal galleons of timber, sail, and flaming cannon, countless slave ships, and fleets of cargo ships, ships of hardened iron, and deafening engines, their holds laden rich with silk, oil, grain, and ore, are now scores upon scores of rusting skeletons, linking continents like highways of death, across the ocean's cold silent bed.

## POEMS / POEMAS

Y en el mar todo terminará. Millones de pequeños crustáceos se filtran como balas por minuto en las colosales bocas de las ballenas. Un cangrejo sale de la marea; su vida termina abruptamente cuando cae el pico de un andarríos. Una mujer anda con el paso de una viuda, divisando al mar con la esperanza de que su hombre regrese. Una esposa deposita las cenizas de su esposo en el oleaje.

Marineros romanos, españoles, ingleses, almirantes, capitanes, remeros, balleneros y sus trabajadores, todos han probado el mar salado y se han perdido en "la profundidad" de la tormenta y la guerra. En ese entonces de poderosos ejércitos, los galeones reales llevando la madera, ondeando sus velas con sus poderosos cañones. Innumerables barcos de esclavos y barcos de carga, barcos de hierro endurecido, los ensordecedores motores, con su carga de ricas y suaves sedas, aceite, granos y metales; ahora convertidos en montones sobre montones de esqueletos oxidados, uniendo continentes como caminos de la muerte, a través de la callada y fría cama del océano.

*PROFILE / PERFIL*

Swell, break, crash — swell, break, crash.

Patiently, relentlessly, wave by wave, minute-by-minute, by day and night, and into the millennia, Mother Sea pounds rock coasts to sand. When agitated she spins sky above, assails the land with gale wind and torrential rain, claiming city and village, claiming forest and earth, man and beast alike, drawing all to her watery bosom.

Remember man that thou art of the sea, and unto the sea thou shalt return. The sea gives, and the sea takes.

Swell, break, crash — swell, break, crash.

Blessed be the name of Mother Sea.

Crece, se rompe, choca — crece, se rompe, choca.

Pacientemente, implacablemente, ola tras ola, minuto a minuto, de día y noche, durante milenios, la Madre Mar arremete contra las rocas convirtiéndolas en arena. Cuando se agita, gira hacia el cielo, acomete contra la tierra cargada de viento y fuertes tormentas reclamando los pueblos y ciudades, reclamando el bosque y la tierra, el hombre y la bestia por igual, llevándose todo a su pecho lleno de agua.

Recuerda hombre que tú eres del mar y que al mar regresas. El mar da y el mar quita.

Crece, se rompe, choca — crece, se rompe, choca.

Bendito sea el nombre de la Madre Mar.

*PROFILE / PERFIL*

# October Corn

The corn stalks in my vegetable garden, a deep green not long ago, have yellowed with age. Once straight, tall, and virile, they are now bent and twisted like decrepit old men. Tomato plants are stressed by fall's chilly night air, and those tomatoes left on the vine will not ripen. It pains me seeing summer's sweetness slowly fading away, but it's all a part of the plan, you know; one's strength giving way to aching bones.

My twin, Fernando, and I went trick or treating as little ones. Tony, our big brother, dressed us as pirates. I got an eye-patch, Fernando a handkerchief tied around his head. Tony made us wooden swords and had me go shirtless into the night. He said real pirates braved the cold, and so I did and didn't allow myself to shiver. Our older sisters took us house-to-house, neighborhood to neighborhood, in a frenzied drive for as much candy as we could gather; pirates pilfering booty. Only Christmas surpassed Halloween in fun, and getting something good for simply being young. These days I'm preoccupied with the business of supporting my family and home.

*POEMS / POEMAS*

# El maíz de octubre

En mi siembra, los tallos de maíz. No hace mucho estaban verde obscuro, ahora han madurado con un color amarillo. Antes estaban derechos, altos y viriles, ahora están doblados y torcidos, como hombres viejos y decrépitos. Mis plantas de jitomates están estresadas por el viento frío de otoño y los jitomates que quedan en la vaina no van a madurar. Me duele ver la dulzura del verano irse lentamente, pero todo es parte del plan, ¿no? la fuerza se va para dar paso a los huesos adoloridos.

Cuando éramos niños, mi gemelo, Fernando, y yo íbamos a pedir nuestra calaverita. Toño nuestro hermano mayor, nos vistió de piratas. A mí me puso un parche en el ojo, a Fernando le puso un paliacate amarrado en la cabeza. Toño nos hizo espadas de madera y me hizo ir sin camisa por la noche. Me dijo que los piratas verdaderos eran valientes con el frío, entonces no me permití temblar. Nuestras hermanas mayores nos llevaban de casa en casa por todo el barrio, en una carrera loca para ver cuántos dulces nos daban; dentro de una bota de pirata. Solamente la Navidad superaba al Halloween en lo divertido y en ver los relajos que nos daban simplemente por ser niños. Ahora, me preocupo por mi negocio y cómo voy a mantener a mi familia y mi casa.

*PROFILE / PERFIL*

Newspapers tell me the last of the apples and grapes are being harvested as our country's latest war reaps our young soldiers, squandering funds that could be used to feed the hungry, clothe the naked, and cure the sick. It saddened me to read that Paul Newman died. They say he was old and sick, though I only knew him to be young, handsome, and generous. Someone wrote a poem about his life the next day. I'm glad to see that a poet wrote about something that mattered.

My *Tia* Sara, a grandaunt who lived in Mexico, died when I was a boy. She was old, and wrinkled as a prune. She wore dark ankle-length dresses and flesh-colored stockings that covered what little skin that might be exposed. Her long hair was always braided into a pair of long, gray snakes that were wrapped tight against her scalp. She went to bed one night never to rise again. Ma's cousin, my *Tia* Concha, washed Sara's lifeless body and hair, combed and braided her hair, powdered her face, applied rouge and stuffed wads of newspaper in her mouth to fill her cheeks sunken by death's cold hand. The family had a traditional *"velorio"* for Sara. They laid her out surrounded by candles in her living room. Everyone knelt and prayed for her soul. My uncles dug her grave, and buried her the next day.

*POEMS / POEMAS*

Los periódicos dan las noticias que la siembra de manzanas y uvas están en las últimas etapas de las cosecha y que nuestro país en la última guerra está cosechando nuestros soldados jóvenes, derrochando los fondos del gobierno que podrían ser usados para darle de comer al hambriento, darle ropa al desnudo y curar al enfermo. Me pone triste al leer que Paul Newman ha muerto. Dicen que estaba viejo y enfermo. Sólo lo conocí como joven, guapo y generoso. Alguien escribió un poema de su vida al día siguiente. Me dio gusto ver que un poeta escribió acerca de algo importante.

Mi tía abuela, Sara, que vivía en México, murió cuando yo era un niño. Estaba vieja y arrugada como una ciruela. Usaba ropa obscura que le llegaba hasta el tobillo y sus medias eran de color piel para cubrir cualquier parte del cuerpo que estuviera descubierta. Su cabello largo siempre estaba en dos largas trenzas grises en forma de serpientes que se moldeaban alrededor de su cabeza. Una noche se fue a dormir y nunca despertó. La tía Concha, la prima de mi mamá, lavó su pelo y el cuerpo inerte de mi tía Sara. La peinó y le hizo trenzas, le puso maquillaje, le puso chapetas y bolas de papel periódico en la boca para que se viera más llena, sus mejillas estaban hundidas por la mano fría de la muerte. La familia le hizo un velorio tradicional a Sara. La acostaron en la sala rodeada de velas. Todos los asistentes se arrodillaron y rezaron por su alma. Mis tíos cavaron su tumba y la enterraron al día siguiente.

*PROFILE / PERFIL*

She receiver a proper memorial service, even if she was a gossip who doled out advice that hadn't been asked for. My Ma and Pa, and most of my uncles and aunts, have passed on, irreplaceable losses. It saddens me that they are not with me anymore. At least they come to visit with me in dreams once in a while. I take comfort knowing that we will be together again one day.

I love the Day of the Dead, a custom rooted in ancient Mexico. A good way to honor those who have passed to the other world, a way to accept and even poke fun at death, instead of fearing him; a good way to prepare for our own inevitable appointment with him. We can fear or laugh and accept him, for in the end there's no choice in the matter. It's all a part of the deal. Aren't we like stalks of corn? Small tender sprouts in spring, strong and sturdy in summer, frail in autumn, dried and lifeless in winter.

Let us be like the Mexican *Calaveras*, the skeletons who play music, dance and sing, replacing fear with a fiesta. Let us celebrate then, for today we are on this side of the great divide, honoring those on the other, and hoping that one day, we will be remembered in a respectful manner, even if we are imperfect. Raise your cups of *atole*, of *chocolate caliente*, raise your *pan dulce*. Here's to life *mis hermanos y hermanas*, here's to death.

Sara tuvo un buen velorio, a pesar de que era una chismosa, quien siempre se entrometía para dar consejos sin ser pedidos. Mi papá y mi mamá, casi todos mis tíos y tías se han muerto, pérdidas irreparables. Me pongo triste porque ya no están conmigo. Al menos me visitan en mis sueños de vez en cuando. Me relajo porque sé que algún día vamos a estar juntos otra vez.

Adoro el Día de los Muertos, una tradición arraigada del México ancestral. Es una bonita manera de honrar a aquellos que se han ido al otro mundo, una manera de aceptar, hasta de burlarse de la muerte, en vez de temerla, es una manera de prepararnos para la inevitable cita con ella. Le podemos temer, o reír y aceptarla, para mí al final no hay otra cosa que escoger. Todo es parte del acuerdo ¿No es cierto acaso que somos como las plantas de maíz? Pequeñas plantas en la primavera, fuertes y maduras en el verano, frágiles en otoño, secas y ya sin vida en el invierno.

Seamos como las calaveras mexicanas, como los esqueletos que tocan música, que bailan y cantan, reemplacemos el miedo con la fiesta. Celebremos entonces, porque ahora estamos en este lado de gran división, honrando a aquellos que se fueron al otro lado, esperando que un día, también nosotros seamos honrados, aunque aquí seamos imperfectos. Levantemos nuestras tasas de atole, de chocolate caliente, levantemos nuestro pan dulce. Salud a la vida hermanos y hermanas, salud a la muerte.

*PROFILE / PERFIL*

# Roadside Flowers

See how they brighten the sterile ground of the byway.

Are they not a testament to beauty in this rushed world of asphalt and automobiles?

Can one not help but see them, and think if only for a moment, that there is so much more than one's quick life of appointments and destinations, which after all, will only be forgotten the very next day?

See how these delicate blossoms adorn the small white cross reminding you that a profound event took place on this spot that you pass each day on your way to seemingly important business.

"Someone made an unforeseen and final stop here," they whisper into each driver's ear.

And all that is left to a man are his humble roadside flowers, and his anguished warnings to a hurried planet, that his little girl, and her mommy, saw their last day on this ground made hallowed by the passing of their souls.

See how the shining purple ribbons wave in the wake of each passing car.

*POEMS / POEMAS*

# Las flores del camino

Mira como ellas alumbran la tierra esteríl del camino.

¿No son ellas un testimonio de belleza en este mundo acelerado lleno de asfalto y automóviles?

Uno no puede dejar de verlas y pensar ¿Si tan sólo fuera por un momento, que hay mucho más que una vida rápida de horarios y destinos, los cuales, después de todo, serán olvidados el próximo día?

Mira cómo estas delicadas flores adornan la pequeña cruz blanca, recordándote que un evento profundo ocurrió en este lugar por donde tú pasas cada día haciendo negocios que parecen ser importantes.

"Alguien hizo una parada imprevista y final aquí", ellos susurran al oído de cada chofer.

Y todo lo que le queda a un hombre, son sus humildes flores del camino y su angustiosa preocupación de un planeta acelerado, que su pequeña niña y su mamá vieron el último día en esta tierra santificada al paso de las almas.

Mira cómo los brillantes listones morados se mueven con el paso de cada automóvil.

*PROFILE / PERFIL*

# Two Springs

he wonders
will the telephone ever ring again
it has been a long quiet winter
with not enough work

bank accounts dwindle
wife needs grocery money
daughter a new sweater
mortgage electricity equipment loans payroll taxes
insurances all must be paid

his workers need to earn income
to support their own families
is the economy improving enough
will the telephone ring with clients this year

generations earlier a man sees his tribe's stored berries,
nuts, dried meats and fish reduced then rationed
he stands on a knoll looking to the horizon hoping
for signs that buffalo will return
will there be meat to nourish his people
or will the great spirit send the herds to other grazing
grounds this year
will there be a desperate hunt fueled by hunger
he paces nervously
As the season of cold wanes

*POEMS / POEMAS*

## Dos primaveras

él se pregunta
volvera el teléfono a sonar otra vez
ha sido un largo y callado invierno
sin suficiente trabajo

Las cuentas del banco se esfuman
la esposa necesita dinero para la comida
la hija necesita un suéter nuevo
el pago de la casa la luz,los préstamos los impuestos del sueldo
los seguros, todos deben ser pagados

sus trabajadores necesecitan recibir salarios
para mantener a sus famílias
estará la economía mejorando lo suficiente
sonará el telfonó con clientes este año

hace muchas generaciones atras un hombre ve que las
provisiones de su tribu: bayas, nueces, las carnes y los
pescados secos disminuyen después son racionadas
parado en loma mira hacia el horizonte esperando las
señales de que el búfalo regresará
habra carne para alimentar a su gente  este año o el gran
espíritu mandará las manadas a otras tierras con pasto
habra una caza desesperada alimentada por el hambre
se pasean nervioso
mientras que la estación del frío desaparece

*PROFILE / PERFIL*

the days get noticeably longer
rain and warming soil awaken hibernating seeds
grass turns gray hills green
multiple days of sun and blue skies stir the earth
from its long cold sleep

one man hears the telephone ring
the other thundering hooves in the distance

los dias comienzan a alargarse
la lluvia y la tierra tibia despiertan las semillas
después de haber hibernado
el pasto convierte a las colinas grises en verde
múltiples días de sol y cielos azules despiertan a la tierra
de su largo sueño frío

un hombre escucha el teléfono sonar
el otro escucha la tierra retumbar en la distancia

*PROFILE / PERFIL*

# The Herd

A great herd of clouds, the color of enraged buffalo, thundered onto the Mendocino coast. They stampeded out light, turning all to black fear.

They mounted earth over and over, making hard love to her. Their potent semen impregnated her, bringing forth the birth of a million, million, million white seeds, coloring her otherwise gray skin a hope-filled, green.

Realizing that she was able to reproduce yet again, and ending her barrenness, earth took to the joy of motherhood, as if for the first time.

*POEMS / POEMAS*

# La manada

Una gran manada de nubes de color búfalo enfurecido tronó en la Costa de Mendocino. Vinieron en estampida apagando la luz y convirtiendo todo en un negro temeroso.

Ellos montaron la tierra una vez y otra vez haciendo el amor con fuerza. Su potente semen la impregnó, trayendo así el nacimiento de millones y millones de semillas blancas, coloreando su piel gris al color verde de esperanza.

Dándose cuenta que podía reproducir otra vez, poniendo fin a su infecundidad, la madre tierra se dejó llevar por la maternidad como si fuera la primera vez.

*PROFILE / PERFIL*

# The Muse

Poetry barged through my door one day. There was no stealth in her movements, no cloak to hide her red hair, red lips and red attitude. She caressed, cuddled and had her way with me.

She came from the ocean during the red tide. I didn't beckon or invite her, she simply swept me away.

She came in Spanish and English and took my long words and whittled them to their core.

When in good humor, she gave herself without pause, or shame, and the verses flowed freely in meter and cadence as from a spigot. Other times she ripped a tooth from my jawbone in barter for a single line.

She had little patience with cowardice or hesitation and was a grand, jealous, and mischievous lover, often calling on me when I was long asleep, or slicing hot roast.

I began thinking that I understood her and could have my way with her. She jeered, and threw her head back and laughed when I wrote the false words she gave me as a tease.

*POEMS / POEMAS*

# La musa

La poesía se metió por mi puerta un día. No había disimulo en sus movimientos, no tenía una capa para esconder su cabello rojo, sus labios rojos y su actitud roja. Ella me acarició, me abrazó e hizo lo que quiso conmigo.

Vino del océano, cuando la marea era verde en el horizonte y rojo en la costa. No le hice señales ni la invité a entrar, simplemente barrió conmigo.

Entró en español e inglés, tomando mis largas palabras y diseñó su esencia.
Cuando está de buen humor, se da sin vergüenza o pausa y los versos fluyen libremente sin medida y con la cadencia de un grifo. Otras veces ella arranca un diente de mi mandíbula a intercambio de una sola línea.

Ella tiene poca paciencia con la cobardía o las dudas. Y es una gran amante, celosa y traviesa que seguido me llama cuando estoy dormido profundamente, o cuando rebano el lomo asado caliente.

Empecé a pensar que la entendía y que podría hacer con ella lo que quisiera. Pero se burló, echó la cabeza hacia atrás y se rió cuando escribí las falsas palabras que me había dado para vacilarme.

*PROFILE / PERFIL*

So much do I want to understand her. I craved her friendship and devotion. She paused and looked at me for a moment, then spoke without color. "If you come to understand me, the magic will disappear," she warned. "I can only have spontaneous and lustful lovers. I have loved you as I have loved so many like you."

She smiled, lifted her blouse, and demanded that I tickle her pink nipple, then reached into her bag and put a peanut-sized phrase in my hand because she was in a generous mood.

¡Cómo quiero entenderla! ¡Cómo deseo su amistad y devoción! Ella se detuvo y me miró por un momento, después habló sin color alguno. "Si vienes a entenderme, la magia desaparecerá", me advirtió. "Sólo puedo tener amantes espontáneos y libidinosos. Te he amado como he amado a tantos como tú". ·

Ella sonrió, se levantó la blusa y demandó que acariciara su pezón rosa, después buscó en su bolsa una frase del tamaño de un cacahuate y lo puso en mi mano porque estaba de humor generoso.

*PROFILE / PERFIL*

# The Pit

I know the fear of God, Satan, the world, and what it is to lose a childhood to the haunting fear of eternal damnation in the fiery pit of hell.

I know what it is to be ridiculed for having a different name, and feeling shame for being of my people.

I know what it is to be told, "You're not one of us, your skin is too light, you talk and dress like them, you're one of them."

I know what it is to lose even in victory.

I know how pent up fear and rage, express themselves through the tearing of one's own skin.

I know what it is to not trust the self, and the helpless feeling of being hired, realizing that a termination will soon come.

I know what it is to be the lesser of the males, and the pain of a broken back.

I know the dead eyes of life-term prisoners, the black whirlpool of drug addiction and its demonic dreams.

*POEMS / POEMAS*

# El hoyo

Conozco el miedo a Dios, a Satanás, al mundo y a lo que significa perder la niñez, al miedo persistente de condena eterna en el hoyo furioso del infierno.

Sé lo que es ser ridiculizado por tener un nombre diferente y sentir vergüenza por ser parte de mi gente.

Sé lo que es cuando te dicen "Tú no eres uno de nosotros, tu piel es demasiado clara, tú hablas y te vistes como ellos, tú eres uno de ellos".

Sé lo que es perder aun siendo victorioso.

Sé cómo reprimir el coraje y el miedo que se expresan rasgándose su propia piel.

Sé lo que es en no tener confianza en sí mismo y el sentimiento desvalido de ser contratado sabiendo que una terminación vendrá pronto.

Sé lo que es ser el más bajo de los hombres y el dolor de una espalda rota.

Conozco los ojos muertos de los prisioneros de por vida, el remolino negro del enviciamiento a las drogas y sus sueños demoníacos.

*PROFILE / PERFIL*

I know the jealousy and disdain of those who are joyous, and hate for those whom you are supposed to care for, and what it is to be deceived by someone you trust, and lie to someone you love.

I know what it is to slowly lose strength and the melting away of youth.

I know the dream of the drowned buck, with its magnificent antlers and its blank stare, as the final air bubbles emit from its splendid black nostrils.

I know what it is to desperately want to please, and to desperately love someone who will never love you.

I know the past and future of failure, what it is to hate the self, what it is to want to hide where no one can ever find you, and the temptation of wanting to sleep forever.

*POEMS / POEMAS*

Conozco los celos y el desdén por aquellos que están contentos y el odio a esos que se supone debes de cuidar y lo que es ser engañado por alguien de tu confianza, así como el mentir a alguien a quien amas.

Sé lo que es perder la fuerza lentamente y ver tu juventud desvanecerse.

Sé del sueño del ciervo ahogado. Sus cuernos magníficos, su mirada fija y sus burbujas finales emitidas de su nariz negra.

Sé lo que es querer agradar desesperadamente y desesperadamente amar a alguien que nunca te amará.

Sé lo que es el pasado y el futuro del fracaso, lo que es odiarse a uno mismo, lo que es querer esconderse en un lugar en donde nadie te encuentre y la tentación de querer dormir por siempre.

*PROFILE / PERFIL*

# Where Are You?

Where are You when the torturer singes, rips, and breaks?

When the infant was pulled from the well, and breathed her last, did You care?

Are You saddened when a child starves, or when a cat toys with a mouse before tearing it to pieces? Or is it also sport for You?

Were You there when they told old man Contreras that his son hung himself in the jail cell? He tithed every week to Your house, even as his family was in need.

Were You there when the widower leaped from the bridge? Could You have not whispered *something* into his ear?

And where were You when she cast her children into the lake?

Can't You stop the little innocents from being fondled?

## ¿En dónde estás?

¿En dónde estás cuando el torturador quema, desgarra y destroza?

Cuando el infante fue sacado del pozo y tuvo su último respiro, ¿Te importó?

¿Te pones triste cuando un niño se muere de hambre, o cuando el gato juega con el ratón antes de destrozarlo y comérselo? ¿O todo es simplemente un juego para ti?

¿Estabas presente cuando le dijeron al viejo Contreras que su hijo se ahorcó en su celda? Contreras dio limosnas cada semana en tu casa, a pesar de que su familia lo necesitaba.

¿Estabas presente cuando el viudo saltó del puente? ¿No pudiste acaso susurrarle algo en el oído?

¿Y dónde estuviste cuando ella arrojó a sus hijos al lago?

¿No podrías detener el que los pequeños inocentes sean molestados sexualmente?

*PROFILE / PERFIL*

Come now, You could curl a finger and stop the burning tree from toppling onto the fawn.

Weren't You there when they found out Anne and her family and took them away?

Are You there when the emaciated, in the stench of their own urine, take a final drink?

Were You there when Lily wasted away? She died in agony as the disease spread. She was one of Your faithful servants, to the end. Was it necessary for her to suffer so much, or does it matter to You?

Where were You when He cried, "Why hast Thou forsaken Me?"

When our voices rise through the stained glassed windows of Your houses and land at Your feet, where are You?

No me digas que no puedes mover un dedo para detener
que el árbol en llamas cayera sobre el cervatillo.

¿No estabas ahí cuando arrastraron a Ana y a su familia
y se los llevaron?

¿Estabas ahí cuando el escuálido apestoso tomó el último
trago? Envuelto en la inmundicia de sus orines.

¿Estabas presente cuando Lily se murió? Su muerte fue
una terrible agonía cuando la enfermedad se expandió
por todo el cuerpo. Ella era una de tus fieles ciervos,
hasta el final. Dime si fue necesario que sufriera tanto
hasta la muerte ¿O de veras te importa?

"¿Dónde estabas cuando él lloró?" "¿Por qué me
mantienes lejos, por qué me haz desamparado?"

Cuando nuestras voces se levantan y cruzan las ventanas
de tu casa, abnegados a tus pies, ¿Dónde estás?

*PROFILE /PERFIL*

## **120/80**

Her machine buzzes a warning. Its red digital numbers blink on and off, 208/110, 208/110. My wife gasps and removes the Velcro band wrapped around my arm. "Maybe it's not so bad!" I say. "It's the silent killer," she tells me, and makes an appointment with my doctor. "Hmm," he says, "she's right, you know, pressure's much too high. A perfect reading for you is 120/80. Take this blue pill daily, but be advised, it may have a side effect. Come back in two weeks." I don't miss a single day taking the little blue pill that will make me perfect.

Two weeks later her machine's buzzer shrieks, red numbers blink on and off 195/96, 195/96. "Still way too high!" she says removing the band and dialing my doc. "The pill's causing me to drool, doctor!" I say wiping my chin. "Hmm," he says "don't worry, we'll get you to 120/80. You want to be perfect don't you? Add another blue pill to bring it down a little and take this green one to stop the flow. Come back in two weeks." "No-flow," reads the bottle's label. "Might have a side effect." I don't miss a day taking two blue and one green pill that will surely get me there.

I close my eyes and cross my fingers for good luck when she straps on the machine. "180/96," she says then reaches for the phone. I sit, grateful that at least the damn buzzer's been silenced.

*POEMS / POEMAS*

## 120/80

El aparato dispara en señal de advertencia. Es rojo y los números digitales se prenden y apagan, 208/110, 208/110. Mi esposa respira profundo y remueve la banda del velcro de mi brazo. "¡Quizás no está tan mal!", le digo". Ella me responde "es la muerte silenciosa", y hace una cita con mi doctor. "Mmm", murmulla el doctor "ella está en lo correcto, la presión está muy alta. La medida perfecta sería 120/80. Tómate esta pastilla azul una vez al día, pero te advierto, quizás tenga efectos secundarios. Regresa en dos semanas". No dejo de tomar cada día la pastilla azul que me hará perfecto.

Dos semanas después los disparos de su aparato gritan los números rojos 195/96, 195/96. "¡Sigue muy alta!" Me dice mientras remueve la banda y llama al doctor. "¡La pastilla me hace babear mucho doctor!" Le digo mientras me limpio la baba. "Mmm", dice, "no te preocupes te bajaremos a 120/80. ¿Quieres estar perfecto, no es así? Incrementa la dosis a dos pastillas al día y tómate esta verde para detener la baba. Regresa en dos semanas". "Para no babear," dice el sello de la botella. "Quizás tenga efectos secundarios". No fallo un sólo día de tomar las dos pastillas azules y la verde que de seguro me van a ayudar a estar mejor.

Cierro los ojos y cruzo los dedos para la buena suerte cuando me envuelve el brazo en la banda del aparato. "180/96," me dice al mismo tiempo que toma el teléfono. Yo sigo sentado agradecido de al menos el ruido ha sido silenciado.

*PROFILE / PERFIL*

"The No-flow is causing me to hallucinate, doc. I've been hearing politicians in my head giving speeches and they're telling the truth!" "Oh my!" says the doctor. "Oh my!" says the wife. "A pink one to supplement the blues and a yellow for the politicians, you're so close. It'd be a shame not to make it. See you in two weeks." Everyday it's two blue, a green, a pink, and a yellow that will make me perfect.

She straps on the machine and it reads, 143/84. She goes for the phone; I break down in tears. "The yellows have got me preaching from the Bible downtown on Sunday mornings, doc, and I'm getting a following!" "Here you are dear boy, a purple with red stripes for the preaching and this pretty turquoise with orange spots that'll finally get you to perfection, could have a slight side effect."

Doctor and wife stand quietly on the hillside overlooking the valley. Birds chirp in a tree, a breeze flutters the ribbon around the bouquet of flowers. The headstone reads: "Armando García-Dávila - A perfect 120/80: Cholesterol 400!"

"Doctor, las pastillas para no babear me están dando alucinaciones. He estado escuchando a políticos dentro de mi cabeza ¡Sus ponencias dicen la verdad!" ¿De veras?", pregunta el doctor "¿De veras?", pregunta mi esposa. "Una rosa para suplementar las tristezas y una amarilla para los políticos, ya estás muy cerca. Sería una pena no llegar al número deseado. Te veo en dos semanas". Todos los días tomo dos azules, una verde, una rosa y una amarilla para que me hagan perfecto.

Ella me toma la presión y lee, 143/84. Va por el teléfono. Yo me pongo a llorar. "¡Doctor, las amarillas me han puesto a predicar la Biblia los domingos por la mañana en el centro de la ciudad! ¡Y ya tengo a varios seguidores!" "Aquí tienes mi querido niño, la morada con las rayas rojas para el predicamento y esta bonita de color turquesa con puntos anaranjados, esa es la que finalmente te va a llevar a la perfección. Podría tener un efecto secundario".

El doctor y mi esposa están parados en silencio en la colina mirando hacia el valle. Los pájaros cantan en el árbol, la brisa mueve el moño en el ramo de flores. La lápida dice: "Armando García-Dávila – ¡Perfecto 120/80!: ¡Colesterol 400!"

*PROFILE /PERFIL*

# Carry Me

The truth is I am tired of it. You know how it goes. One tires of the pace and of carrying this load of muscle and blood and bone. My toes bicker constantly with one another. My ankles and calves complain and whine. "This road of sixty-plus years is so much harder than it was. Where did the soft grasses and mud puddles you frequented go? And where are your mother's arms?"

My hands tire of tying shoelaces, shaving the same face, and brushing ever-thinning hair.

My eyes tire of reading angry newspapers and seeing the reflection of a progressively wrinkled face in the mirror each morning and of viewing inane television programs. Each eye has taken to a separate interest of late. While one adores gazing at flowers, the other leers at women. On Sunday last, one eye admired the red and white flowers in a planter box as the other gawked in the opposite direction at a pair of nicely filled nylons. Damn, it hurt and was terribly embarrassing walking into that telephone pole.

## Cárgame

La verdad es que estoy cansado de todo. Tú sabes cómo es esto. Uno se cansa del ritmo de llevar esta carga de músculos, sangre y huesos. Los dedos de mis pies se quejan constantemente uno con el otro. Mis tobillos y pantorrillas se quejan y gimen. "Este camino de sesenta y tantos años y más es mucho más difícil de lo que era antes. ¿A dónde se fueron los pastos suaves y los charcos a los que antes ibas? ¿En dónde están los brazos de tu madre?"

Mis manos se cansan de amarrarme los zapatos, de rasurarme la cara y de cepillarme el poco pelo.

Mis ojos están cansados de leer periódicos enojados y de ver cada mañana la imagen de una cara en el espejo que progresivamente está arrugándose y de ver programación estúpida en la televisión. Últimamente cada ojo ha tomado intereses separados. Mientras uno adora contemplar las flores el otro mira de reojo a las mujeres. El domingo pasado, un ojo admiraba las flores blancas y rojas en la caja donde las plantamos mientras que el otro se quedaba abstraído en dirección opuesta, mirando a un par de piernas con medias. Demonios, fue totalmente vergonzoso chocar contra el poste del teléfono

.

*PROFILE /PERFIL*

My soul is tired, tired of carrying so many loads of fear; the devil's sly craft at getting me to sin incurring God's eternal wrath, and the dread of phallic missiles that would incinerate the world in the batting of an eye. The thought of the earth sick with fever, her continents of ice fracturing and melting. It's a worrisome business!

I tire of doling out my earnings to men in suits: insurers, tax collectors, mortgage brokers. The mere sight of my checkbook brings me to uncontrolled weeping.

I tire of politicians and their organ-grinder masters, manipulating with promises of honey, while delivering bile.

I'm fed up with Christians who declare the remission of a disease of one of their own "a miracle from God," and children of other lands torn to bloody flesh by our bombs of war as nothing more than "collateral damage."

I've had it with "holy" men telling *me* whom I should hate. It would be delicious to stand in the middle of a packed fundamentalist service and scream out, "He died. He's not coming back. Get over it!"

Mi alma está cansada, cansada de llevar muchas cargas
de miedo; la magia astuta del diablo para que yo peque
incurriendo a la eterna furia de Dios y el terror de los
misiles fálicos que incinerarían el mundo en un abrir y
cerrar de ojos. El pensamiento de un mundo enfermo
con fiebre y sus continentes de hielo fracturados y
derritiéndose ¡Es un negocio preocupante!

Estoy cansado de dar mi sueldo a hombres con trajes;
aseguradores, cobradores de impuestos y de préstamos
hipotecarios. Ver mi chequera a simple vista me hace
llorar incontrolablemente.

Estoy cansado de los políticos y su órgano triturador,
manipulando con las promesas de miel, mientras
derraman ira.

Estoy harto de los cristianos que declaran como suya la
remisión de una enfermedad, "es un milagro de Dios"
dicen, mientras los niños en otras tierras vuelan en
sangrientos pedazos de carne por nuestras bombas de la
guerra, como si fuera nada más un "daño colateral".

Ya me cansé de escuchar a los hombres "sagrados"
decirme a quién odiar. Sería delicioso parame en una
junta llena de fundamentalistas y gritar abiertamente
"Él murió. No regresará. ¡Olvídense!"

*PROFILE /PERFIL*

# The Greatest Poem

Soon I shall write the greatest poem ever written. I will be met at city gates and carried on the shoulders of cheering citizens to the town's square where mayors and councilmen will gather to hear me recite it.

The envy of every poet will run in green torrents down streets and into gutters. No anthology will be complete without *my* poem. Neruda, Whitman, Lorca, Borges, Homer, ha! Their names will all be listed after mine.

It won't be easy. I will reveal deep vulnerabilities causing men to cry and women to throw their fists in the air and shout, "You go, man!"

I will write of my convictions and philosophies, sparking new religions. Lamas and popes will give me their cell phone numbers.

I will never have to write a single verse again, living large off the royalties. Publishing houses will beg me to write more, anything! They will send me fat advances on works yet to be started.

*POEMS / POEMAS*

# El poema grandioso

Muy pronto voy a escribir el poema más grandioso jamás escrito. Los ciudadanos de la ciudad me van a buscar en el portón de la ciudad y contentos me van a llevar en sus hombros a la plaza central donde los alcaldes y los hombres del concilio se juntarán para escuchar cuando lo recite.

La envidia verde de todos los poetas correrá como torrentes por las calles hasta llegar a las alcantarillas. No habrá una antología completa sin *mi* poema. Neruda, Whitman, Lorca, Borges, Homero ¡Ja! Sus nombres estarán en las listas después del mío.

No será fácil. Al revelar las vulnerabilidades más profundas haré llorar a los hombres y las mujeres de gusto levantarán sus puños al aire gritando "¡Así se hace señor!".

Mi escritura estará basada en mi filosofía y mis convicciones, creando nuevas religiones. Lamas y papas me darán el número de sus celulares.

No voy a tener que escribir un simple verso otra vez, voy a vivir de mis regalías. Las compañías publicitarias me rogarán que escriba más ¡lo que sea! Me mandarán grandes pagos por adelantado por un trabajo no empezado

.

*PROFILE /PERFIL*

I shall write the greatest poem ever written, right after dinner, or a refreshing nap. The muse will kneel at my feet massaging them as she nibbles on my ear whispering honey verses into it.

Brace yourselves because very soon, I shall write the greatest poem ever written.

Voy a escribir el poema más grandioso que jamás haya sido escrito, después de la cena, o de una buena siesta. La musa arrodillada me dará masaje en los pies mientras que besuquea mi oído y susurra versos enmelados.

Prepárense porque muy pronto voy a escribir el poema más grandioso que jamás se haya escrito.

*PROFILE /PERFIL*

# You've Got Mail

It took a while before I finally gave in to buying the machine. "It will bring you the world," my grandchildren said. "But the world is too damn big to fit into this thing," I argued. "Haven't you heard of libraries where there are atlases? It's all the world you need!" "Whatever, grandpa," they said.

First it was learning how to turn it on. "Hold the button down," they said. "Don't let it go too quickly, hold it down a sec."

Then it was single clicking and double clicking using a rat. Like a fly caught in a spider web, I became more and more entangled in the web, in the electronic web, the World Wide Web.

A man's voice tells me, "You've got mail!" It's nice to hear people are sending me mail. I've never gotten all that much. But it turns out to be tasteless mail, there're no stamps or envelopes to lick, no taste at all! And I'm getting mail that I haven't asked for, but it isn't junk mail. Oh no, it's "spam," they tell me, but spam without eggs? Then it's not spam! "You've got mail," the man says every time I turn on the machine. He's starting to get annoying.

*POEMS / POEMAS*

# Haz recibido correo

Me tomó un buen tiempo el decidir comprar el aparato. "Te va a traer el mundo", mis nietos me decían. "Pero el maldito mundo es muy grande para caber en esta cosa", les dije. "¿Nunca has oído de las bibliotecas donde están los libros de mapas? ¡Tienen todo el mundo que tú necesitas!"
"Como quieras, abuelo," me dijeron.

Primero tuve que aprender a prender el aparato. "Mantén apretado el botón", me dijeron. "No lo sueltes tan rápido, apriétalo por un segundo".

Después era dando un clic y dos clics usando un ratón. Como una mosca atrapada en la telaraña. Estuve más y más atrapado en la telaraña, en la telaraña electrónica, la telaraña mundial.

La voz de un hombre me dice "¡Haz recibido correo!", es agradable saber que la gente me está mandando correo. Nunca había recibido tanto correo. Pero resulta ser un correo sin sentido, no hay timbres o sobres sellados con la lengua ¡no hay ningún sabor! Y estoy recibiendo correo que no he pedido, pero no es correo de basura ¡Oh no! es "spam", me dicen, ¿pero *spam* sin huevos? ¡Entonces no es *spam*! "Haz recibido correo", el hombre me dice cada vez que prendo el aparato. Me empieza a molestar.

*PROFILE /PERFIL*

The machine gets sick now and then. It's always a virus and it takes a "geek doctor" who is summoned with the cure. He isn't half my age. Tap, tap, tap "that'll be $80," he says. "At least, my regular doctor takes my blood pressure and weighs me and gives me a bottle of sample pills," I tell the shaggy-haired geek doctor as I hand over my money. He doesn't even wear a smock to cover his tattered Levis.

"Whatever," he says rolling his eyes. "Whatever? Whatever? What's with this *whatever* crap?"

And now I've been set up with friends on the "Facebook," friends I didn't ask for or even remember having in the first place, and there are legions of them! I wish I could sit and have a beer with just one of my newfound friends. I complained about it to one of them. He "unfriended" me. Jerk.

There are cookies in the machine, but cookies without oatmeal or raisins? Then they're not cookies!

Now they're telling me that I should have a blackberry. I'd really like to have a blackberry, but just one? I'm told that these don't have juice to stain my fingers. "Then they're not goddamned blackberries!" "Whateverrr, Grandpa."

El aparato se enferma de vez en cuando, es siempre un virus y se necesita un "doctor cerebro" el cual ha sido llamado para la cura. No tiene ni siquiera la mitad de mi edad. Tap, tap, tap "van a ser $80", me dice. "Al menos mi doctor regular me toma la presión arterial, me pesa y me da una botella de pastillas de muestra", le comento al doctor melenudo mientras le doy mi dinero. Ni siquiera usa una bata blanca para cubrir sus *levis* desgastados.

"¡Como quiera!", me dice con la mirada exasperada. "¿Cómo quiera? ¿Cómo quiera? ¿Qué pasa con esta mierda de *¡cómo quiera!*?"

Y ahora me han inscrito en el "Facebook", para tener amigos. Amigos que en primer lugar ni pedí, o que ni siquiera recuerdo. ¡De veras que hay legiones de ellos! ¡Cómo me gustaría sentarme y tomar una cerveza con alguno de mis nuevos amigos! Me quejé de eso con uno de ellos. Dejó de "ser mi amigo". Sangrón.

¿Hay galletas en el aparato, pero galletas sin avena o pasitas? ¡Entonces esas no son galletas!

Ahora me dicen que debería tener un *blackberry*. ¿Qué de veras me gustaría tener un *blackberry*, pero nada más uno? Me dicen que éstas no tienen el jugo que me mancha los dedos. "¡Entonces no son las fregadas zarzamoras!" "¡Cómo quierasss, abuelo!".

*PROFILE /PERFIL*

And there are people with a "My-Space," well what about the lady who would like to have *her* space or the poor bastard that would like *his* space or a group that might want their spaces? This my space guy sounds a little self-absorbed to me. He must be the same twit who tweets his twitter.

I'm not sold on this brand new world, not sold at all.

I turn on the machine. "You've got mail," the man says.

Go fuck yourself.

Y hay gente con *"My-Space"*. Bueno ¿y qué tal la dama que quiere tener su espacio, o el pobre bastardo que le gustaría tener su espacio, o el grupo que quizás quiera su espacio? Esto de mi espacio me parece un poco egoísta. Debe de ser el mismo que twit, quien *tweets* a su *twitter*.

Deveras que no acabo de entender esta marca del nuevo mundo, no lo entiendo del todo.

Prendo el aparato. "Has recibido correo," el hombre me dice.

Vete a la chingada.

*PROFILE / PERFIL*

# A Respite

There was tiredness in my love's eyes tonight.
But that I could have gently massaged her toes and feet,
her ankles and calves, her forehead, and flawless skin.

But that I could have disrobed her, covered her with a
quilt of down, kissed her weary hand, and let her drift
into a slumber to dream the romantic dreams of an
untroubled world.

## Un descanso

Se veía cansancio en los ojos de mi amada esta noche.
Pero que yo podía darle suavemente un masaje a sus
dedos y pies, sus tobillos y pantorrillas, su frente y
hermosa piel.

Pero que yo podía desvestirla, cubrirla con una cobija de
plumas, besar su cansada mano, y dejarla flotar hacia un
sueño de sueños románticos de un mundo sin problemas.

*PROFILE / PERFIL*

# Could You Love Me?

If I loved you? If, I, loved, you.

Could you love me?

Would you be here when the morning light greets the songs of the sparrows, or would I be left with a hundred cries, and your seed swimming in my belly?

If I would lay with you in the soft, supple grasses of spring, and satisfy your carnal desires, would you be here after our nap? And would you be able to love me without touching my hair, my breasts, or so much as my hand?

If I perfumed the straw of my bed for you, and painted my lips in scarlet, and rubbed your back, and danced naked for you, would you be willing to stroll next to me at the shore on a Sunday afternoon?

If I tickled you with my tongue when God sleeps, would you dance a lazy dance with me? Would you write verses and stanzas to my name?

If I anointed myself with oil and slithered with you under satin blankets, and made you feel like the red-plumed rooster, would you be here when the morning light greets the songs of the sparrows? Or would I be left with a hundred cries and your seed swimming in my belly?

## ¿Me podrias amar?

¿Si yo te amara? Si, yo, te, amara.

¿Me podrias amar?

¿Estarías aquí cuando la luz de la mañana salude las canciones de los gorriones o me quedaré con cien llantos y tu semilla nadando en mi vientre?

¿Si me acostara contigo en el pasto blando y suave de la primavera y satisficiera tus deseos carnales, estarás aquí después de nuestra siesta? ¿Serías capaz de amarme sin tocar mi cabello, mis pechos, o tanto así como mi mano?

Si perfumara la paja de mi cama para ti y pintara mis labios color carmesí y te sobara la espalda y bailara desnuda para ti ¿Serías capaz de caminar junto a mí por la costa un domingo por la tarde?

Si te hiciera cosquillas con mi lengua, cuando duerme Dios ¿Bailarías conmigo una canción lenta? ¿Escribirías versos y estrofas a mi nombre?

Si me cubriera con aceite y me deslizara bajo tus cobijas de satín y hacerte sentir como el gallo rojo emplumado ¿Estarías aquí cuando la luz de la mañana salude las canciones de los gorriones o me quedaré con cien llantos y tu semilla nadando en mi vientre?

*PROFILE / PERFIL*

# Embers

The flames have subsided, and the heat has been absorbed in the walls. Glowing embers warm the house on this winter's eve.

It's no longer the passion of a new love, but her rubbing my sore back and neck after my day of labor. It's the soup she prepares for me and the glass of water she brings to take the dryness from my mouth in the middle of the night.

"Please be safe," she says when I leave each morning.

Walking through the park is our joy, and laughter the aphrodisiac.

The blaze of our love has subsided, the heartwood of oak, now embers, glow in the hearth warming our home from winter's chill.

*POEMS / POEMAS*

# Cenizas

Las flamas se han calmado y el calor ha sido absorbido por las paredes. Las cenizas brillantes calientan la casa esta noche de inverno.

No es ya más la pasión de un nuevo amor, pero la forma en que me da masaje en el cuello y la espalda después de un día de trabajo. Es la sopa que me hace y el vaso de agua que me da para saciar la sed a media noche.

"Por favor ten cuidado", me dice cuando me voy cada mañana.

Nuestro gusto es el paseo por el parque y la risa es un afrodisíaco.

La llama de nuestro amor ha amainado, la leña de roble, ahora cenizas brillantes, mantiene el corazón de la casa caliente en este invierno helado.

*PROFILE / PERFIL*

# An Exquisite Eve

Gently, I will knock on your door, when the heavens are clothed in sheer black silk. You will lie exquisitely naked by the flame of a candle.

Whispering, I will quietly love you in air sweetened by the flower of a jasmine, and we will sing the psalms of Eros.

*POEMS / POEMAS*

## Una Eva exquisita

Suavemente, yo tocaré en tu puerta cuando los cielos sean vestidos de seda negra y pura. Tú te acostarás exquisitamente desnuda por la llama de una vela.

Susurrando, te amaré silenciosamente en aire endulzado por la flor de un jazmín y cantaremos los salmos de Eros.

*PROFILE / PERFIL*

# Her Song

My melancholy, like a cold Irish fog, is centuries old, and saps life from my body and spirit. It turns children and puppies into nuisances and draws cynical amusement from the misfortunes of others.

Her song, whispered into my ear, is a beacon in this abysmal night of blue solitude. I hear its melody over the wail of the black wind. The power of her hymn is subtle yet steady, veering neither to the right or left, and warms from the stomach.

She gazes at the reflection of my fractured life in the shard of a broken mirror, seeing it whole.
Seeing, it whole.

She kisses my cold fingers and takes the green knives of self-deprecation and doubt from them, and puts them to sleep in their sheaves, then speaks the wondrous words of understanding. She lifts the cartload of guilt from my back, and dumps it into a deep ravine, where it is swept away by the white foam of tumultuous azure waters to the sea, for krill to devour.

"There is light," she assures. "Take my candlestick," she says. "But I can't see the handle," I reply. She laughs, then embraces me.

## Su canción

Mi melancolía, como una niebla fría irlandesa, tiene centenares de edad, le quita vida a mi cuerpo y espíritu. Molesta a niños y cachorros y dibuja cínicamente la mala suerte de los otros.

Su canción, susurra en mi oído, es un faro en esta noche abismal de soledad azul. Oigo su melodía sobre el lamento del viento negro. Escucho su melodía por encima del lamento del viento negro. La fuerza de su himno es sutil pero estable, no vira ni a la derecha ni a la izquierda, y calienta desde el estómago.

Ella contempla las reflexiones de mi vida fracturada en los fragmentos del espejo roto, viéndolo completo. Viéndolo, completo.

Ella besa mis dedos fríos y toma los cuchillos verdes de deprecación propia, duda de ellos y los regresa a dormir en su funda, entonces pronuncia las palabras maravillosas de entendimiento. Ella toma el bulto lleno de culpas de mi espalda y lo tira en un barranco profundo, en donde es arrastrado por la espuma blanca de aguas tumultuosas azul celeste hacia el mar, para que los crustáceos lo devoren.

"Hay luz", asegura ella. "Toma mi candelabro", me dice. "Pero no puedo ver el asa", contesto. Ella se ríe, entonces me abraza.

*PROFILE / PERFIL*

# If I Loved You Yesterday

If I loved you yesterday, I love you more today.

If I loved you at dawn, then I love you all the more as the sun bids a good evening to the blue and green earth.

If I loved you when the hourglass was turned and one grain followed another, I loved you more with each falling particle, until the last nestled atop the mound.

If I loved you with this breath, then I loved you all the more with the next, and with each batting of an eye, and with each flutter of the hummingbird's wing, I loved you again and more.

I will heap my love for you after my day of labor, and sleep to dream of you, and then awake to love you more than the night before, because, my love, if I loved you yesterday, I love you more today.

## Si yo te amé ayer

Si yo te amé ayer, te amo mas hoy.

Si yo te amé al amanecer, entonces yo te amo aún más, como cuando el sol intenta dar las buenas noches para la tierra azul y verde.

Si yo te amé cuando el reloj de arena estaba volteado y un grano sigue al otro, te amo más con cada partícula que cae hasta que la última caiga en la cima del montón.

Si yo te amé con este respiro, entonces te amaré aún más con el siguiente, y después con cada pestañeo del ojo, y con cada aleteo del colibrí, te amo otra vez y más.

Amontonaré mi amor por ti después de un día de trabajo, y dormiré para soñar contigo, y entonces despertaré para amarte más que la noche anterior. Porque mi amor, si te amé ayer, te amo más ahora.

*PROFILE / PERFIL*

# Listen

Is it too much to ask?
Open a door for me.
Walk next to me.
Hug me once a day.

I will color my hair. I will paint my face to hide who I am, if it pleases you, just tell me that you love me once in a while. I'll hang those words on my wall, remembering that they passed through your lips.

And when the hour is late, before the lamp's flame has been snuffed, sit with me to tell me of your day.

And when the madness of the world spins like a black tornado, throwing me one side to another, hold your tongue, take my hand, then simply and quietly listen to me.

## Escucha

¿Es mucho pedirte?
Me abras la puerta.
Camines junto a mí.
Me des un abrazo al día.

Me teñiré el pelo. Me voy a poner maquillaje para
esconder quien soy yo, si eso te satisface, nada más dime
que me amas de vez en cuando. Colgaré esas palabras en
mi pared, para acordarme que salieron de tus labios.

Y cuando la hora marque la noche, antes de que la luz de
la lámpara muera, siéntate conmigo y dime cómo fue tu
día.

Y cuando la locura del mundo gire como un tornado
negro y loco, aventándome de un lado al otro, detén
la lengua, toma mi mano, entonces simplemente
escúchame.

*PROFILE / PERFIL*

# Of Little Boys and Kisses

Today my thoughts are the joyous thoughts of a little boy on a swing, for I know that she will be there to greet me on my return. I anticipate her smile wrapped around my tired eyes.

Hurry night, hurry day, break into a trot, pass quickly that the hour may soon arrive, that the smile and pocketful of kisses she has saved for me will not be in the distance, but here before my longing soul, that the minute may come that we shall embrace, that the second may come that our lips may lose their arid hours apart to be moistened by the kiss that says,

"Hello my love, how I have missed you."

*POEMS / POEMAS*

## De niños pequeños y besos

Hoy mis pensamientos son de pensamientos jubilosos de un niño pequeño en un columpio, porque yo sé que ella estará ahí para saludarme a mi regreso. Anticipo su sonrisa envuelta alrededor de mis ojos cansados.

Noche apresúrate, día apresúrate, que se quiebra en un paso rápido, pasa rápidamente para que la hora pueda llegar, para que la sonrisa y un paquete lleno de besos que ella ha guardado para mí no estará en la distancia, pero aquí ante mi alma añorada, que el minuto pueda venir en que estemos abrazados, que el segundo pueda venir en que nuestros labios separados puedan perder sus horas áridas para que sean humedecidos por el beso que dice,

"Hola mi amor, cómo te he extrañado".

*PROFILE / PERFIL*

# Of Love and Uncertainty

Uncertainty is all there is, my love.

Planets collide and explode in this chaotic universe. Gophers and beavers drown in their dens in this imperfect world. And one day there will be no day, for the earth shall cease its spinning.

We will take each other's hand, and walk this lonely trail together, each stone, each bend in the path a threat to our journey.

There are those who see us stumble. "Ha!" they say. "Did I not warn you of having faith in another?"

Fools we will be then, one to another, walking in light, wandering in shadows, for in the end my love, all that there is, is uncertainty and each other.

*POEMS / POEMAS*

# De amor e incertidumbre

Todo lo que hay es incertidumbre, mi amor.

Los planetas chocan y explotan en este caótico universo. En este mundo imperfecto las tuzas y los castores se ahogan en sus madrigueras. Y un día no va a haber un día, porque el mundo va a dejar de girar.

Nos vamos a tomar de las manos y vamos a caminar juntos este camino solitario, cada piedra, cada curva en el camino será una amenaza en nuestro viaje.
Hay aquellos que nos ven tropezarnos. "¡Ah!" dicen "¿No te advertí que hay que tener fe el uno en el otro?".

Seremos entonces unos tontos, uno al otro, caminando en la luz, confusos en las sombras, porque al final mi amor, todo lo que hay, es incertidumbre y nosotros.

*PROFILE / PERFIL*

# Loving Her

How I love her clean, soft flesh that smells of fresh cream on a Sunday morning.

How I love her tender breasts of jasmine that call to my mischievous fingers and tongue.

How I love her soft, moist crevasse playing a game of tag with my braggart rooster.

How I love her lying on me, lips to lips, navel to navel, toes to toes.

How I love the sweet breeze of her breath.

How I love her hair against the snowy pillow, like a mermaid's tiara around her radiant face that could surely launch a thousand ships.

## **Amándola**

Cómo amo su piel suave, limpia que huele a la loción fresca de la mañana del domingo.

Cómo amo su tierno pecho de jazmines que llaman a mis traviesos dedos y lengua.

Cómo amo su pelvis jugando al toque de mi crecido gallo.

Cómo la amo recostada sobre mí, boca con boca, ombligo con ombligo, dedos con dedos.

Cómo amo su cálido aliento.

Cómo amo su pelo sobre mi almohada blanca, como la corona de una sirena alrededor de su cara radiante que seguramente lanzaría mil barcos

.

*PROFILE / PERFIL*

# *Mi Leona*

My love is a lioness, ripping her passions into my neck and shoulder. She is a thousand, thousand kisses, falling on me like hot rain. She is a hundred red explosions.

My love is an agitated ocean, pounding wave after wave, covering my jagged crags in her white foam, again and again, and then again, pitching her steam high into the air.

Her sensual fingers explore, and pinch, and rub, making love to my arms and chest and hair.

My love is Cupid's mischievous arrow, pricking me here, and there, and here again.

Naked, she is beauty and all things desirable, like the silver moons of August. Her shoulders are the whitest powdered snow, inviting *me*, to be the first to pass over them.

Our loving is angry and joyful and laughter and tears and delicious perspiration.

# Mi leona

Mi amor es una leona rasgando sus pasiones en mi cuello y hombro. Ella es miles y miles de besos que caen a mí como lluvia caliente. Ella es cien explosiones rojas.

Mi amor es un océano agitado golpeando ola tras ola, cubriendo mis dentados peñascos con su espuma blanca una vez y otra vez y después otra vez, lanzando su vapor alto en el aire.

Sus dedos sensuales exploran, pellizcan y frotan, haciéndole el amor a mis brazos y pecho y cabello.

Mi amor es la flecha traviesa de Cupido, picándome aquí y allá y aquí de nuevo.

Desnuda ella es belleza y todas las cosas deseadas, como las lunas plateadas de agosto. Sus hombros son las nieves empolvadas más blancas, invitándome que sea el primero a pasar por ellas.

Hacernos el amor es enojado, y jubiloso, y risa, y sudor delicioso.

*PROFILE / PERFIL*

# Regular Love

Hello my sweetheart. How was your day at work? I thought of you. I wondered and hoped that you were having a good day.

I love the days of the week with you: Tuesday, Wednesday, Thursday when you come home. I love the humdrum of the everyday, me writing at my desk, you taking a well-earned break laughing or crying with Oprah.

I love sitting with you having dinner and talking of nothing important. I love lying in bed with you, you with the remote in your hand catching the last of the news, me finishing a crossword puzzle. I love turning out the light, kissing you and saying, "Good night babe," then rolling over to feel your warmth under the covers and drifting off to sleep.

I love the regular.

## Amor regular

Hola mi amor. ¿Cómo estuvo tu día en el trabajo? Pensé en ti. Espero que hayas tenido un buen día.

Adoro los días de la semana contigo: martes, miércoles, jueves, cuando vienes a casa. Amo la rutina de todos los días, yo escribiendo en mi escritorio, tú hablando, riendo, llorando mientras tomas un bien merecido descanso en la compañía de Oprah.

Amo sentarme contigo mientras cenamos, mientras hablamos de cosas sin importancia. Amo estar en la cama contigo, tú con el control remoto en la mano viendo las noticias y yo resolviendo un rompecabezas. Amo cuando apagamos las luces y te beso "Buenas noches bebita", después me doy la vuelta para sentir tu calor debajo de las cobijas y quedarme dormido.

Amo lo regular

.

*PROFILE / PERFIL*

# Silence

It frightens me when you are silent.
It is as if you can see through me, as if I am made of glass, and my words stand naked before you with no place to hide.

It is disquieting when you don't speak.
It is as if the world has disappeared, as if time, light, shadows, the moon are no more, and the only things that I can be sure of are the darkness, and the cold, and loneliness.

Ah, *loneliness* who carried me in his back pocket for so long before I met you.

But just the same, I am frightened by your silence. And your eyes, black as obsidian, are perfect mysteries revealing nothing to me, perfect mirrors, reflecting only what is before them:

a truth, a lie, a frightened child.

*POEMS / POEMAS*

# Silencio

Me atemorizo cuando estás callada.
Es como si pudieras ver a través de mí, como si yo fuera hecho de cristal y mis palabras se presentan desnudas ante ti sin un lugar para esconderse.

Me preocupa cuando no hablas. Es como si el mundo desapareciera, como si el tiempo, la luz, la sombra, y la luna no estuvieran, y la única cosa de la que pudiera estar seguro es la obscuridad, el frío y la soledad.

¡Ah! La soledad, quien me lleva en el bolsillo trasero, mucho antes de conocerte.

Pero es simplemente lo mismo, estoy temeroso de tu silencio. Y tus negros ojos como la obsidiana, son unos misterios perfectos que no me revelan nada, espejos perfectos, que sólo reflejan lo que está enfrente de ti:

una verdad, una mentira, una niño atemorizada.

*PROFILE / PERFIL*

# *El Tango*

*La vida contigo es un tango.* Life with you is a tango, sometimes tricky, sometimes sweaty, always bold, daring, grace, guts, and comedy!

You press your forehead to mine looking into my eyes, and stare into my soul, keeping me in time, in step, in tune.

My dance is slapstick, yours pure art. I, the clown, you, the ballerina. You take my hand in yours, put your arm on my shoulder and gently nudge, gently guide my clumsy self side to side to life's rhythms.

You whisper the cadences into my ear, "One, two, three, one, two, and one. Turn this way, now dip, hold me tight, tighter, like you mean it! Now turn."

They look on with envy, "They dance so well together." Ha! But that they only knew which is the dancer

Life with you is a tango, *la vida contigo es un tango, un tango fantastico!*

## El tango

La vida contigo es un tango. ¡Algunas veces difícil, otras húmeda, siempre atrevida, desafiante, elegante, sin miedo y cómica!

Pones tu frente en la mía, mirándome a los ojos, viendo dentro de mi alma, manteniéndome al tiempo, al paso, al ritmo.

Mi ritmo es payaso, el tuyo es arte puro, yo soy el payaso, tú eres la bailarina. Tomas mi mano en la tuya, pones tu brazo en mi hombro y gentilmente me empujas, gentilmente guías mi lado torpe de lado a lado en los ritmos de la vida.

Murmuras las cadencias del ritmo en mi oído. "Uno, dos, tres, uno, dos y uno. ¡Date la vuelta así, ahora baja, detenme apretada, más apretada, como si de veras lo sintieras! Ahora vuelta".

Nos miran con envidia "Bailan muy bien juntos" ¡Ja! Si sólo supieran quién es el bailador.

¡La vida contigo es un tango, un tango fantástico!

*PROFILE / PERFIL*

# A Winter's Alcove

There are sorrowful, chilled fogs these days that remind one of his mortality. We are in that season when the sun loses the eternal tug-of-war with the icy moon, as exhausted leaves fall like wounded soldiers from desperate trees.

It is the time when the earth falls into her hibernation, to conceive the unhappy dreams of lost loves, a time when we are reminded of whom we have offended, and forgotten, and left behind. It is the time of cold rains and hungry animals.

Let me kiss you, turn your collar up to the gray cold, take your hand, and strut the joyous walk of love, defying the face of the storm. I will create a warm alcove for you in this river of iced waters, put my arms around your sadness and for one brief and exotic moment take you to where we will lie naked on warm blessed sands, bask in the sun, and laugh at our melancholy.

Let us heap our fears in the cold night where they will feel at home, polish our joys, and wear them around our necks.

# La alcoba de invierno

Hay nieblas tristes y frías estos días que nos recuerdan su mortalidad. Estamos en la estación del tiempo cuando el sol pierde la guerra eterna del estira y afloja con la helada luna, mientras que las hojas del otoño caen como soldados heridos de los árboles desesperados.

Es un tiempo cuando la tierra llega a su invernada, para concebir los sueños infelices de los amores perdidos, es un tiempo que nos hace recordar a quienes hemos ofendido y olvidado o dejado. Es el tiempo de lluvias frías y animales hambrientos.

Permíteme besarte, vuelve tu cuello arriba, hacia al frío gris, toma tu mano y pavonea el ardado alegre del amor desafiando la cara de la tormenta. Crearé una alcoba seca para ti en este río de aguas heladas, pongo mis brazos alrededor de tu tristeza y por un momento breve y exótico te llevaré a donde nos acostaremos desnudos sobre las arenas benditas y calurosas, gozaremos bajo el sol y nos reiremos de nuestra melancolía.

Vamos a amontonar nuestros miedos en la noche fría, en donde se sentirán como en su casa, pulamos nuestras alegrías y colguémoslas en nuestros cuellos.

*PROFILE / PERFIL*

# Wishing

How I wish that we didn't know each other's name, but only knew about one another through our eyes and lips and the yellow fruit that we like to eat.

How I wish that your hand was on my cheek, and that your aroma filled my room, and your smile was my nightlight.

How I wish that our pasts were erased, and that our hands had chalk to playfully script our futures in pinks and reds and crimsons.

How I wish I could put you on my bicycle and take you to the swings in the park.

How I wish you understood just how happy you make me, like a Sunday at the beach.

And how I like it when our souls chat like children anxiously waiting in line for ice cream.

## **Deseando**

Cómo deseo que no supiéramos nuestros nombres, sino sólo conocernos por medio de nuestros ojos y labios y la fruta amarilla que nos gusta comer.

Cómo deseo que tu mano esté en mi mejilla, y que tu aroma llene mi cuarto, y que tu sonrisa sea mi luz de noche.

Cómo deseo que nuestros pasados fueran borrados y que nuestras manos tuvieran gis para crear historias juguetonas de nuestro futuro en colores rosas, rojos y carmesís.

Cómo deseo poder llevarte en mi bicicleta a los columpios del parque.

Cómo deseo que tú entendieras lo feliz que me haces, como un domingo en la playa.

Y cómo me gusta cuando nuestras almas platican como ansiosos niños formados para comer un helado.

*PROFILE / PERFIL*

# Your Light

Who are you? From where does your light come?

Did you come on the wind from an Eastern winter, or did you emerge from a river of rose petals and chocolate?

Do you like the feel of sun-warmed soil under your toes, and soft cotton against your skin, or do you get your full-moon energy from blue silk at midnight?

It's been a happy dream chatting with your spirit. But I need to hear your laugh, touch your cheek, and hold your hand.

We must eat strawberries together while cooling our feet in a stream.

I want to wink and blush, steal a kiss, and contain shy laughter.

If I could hear the waves pound on the shore with you, and smell your hair. Perhaps then, I could understand from where your light comes.

*POEMS / POEMAS*

# Tu luz

¿Quién eres? ¿De dónde viene tu luz?

¿Viniste del viento de un invierno oriental, o emergiste de un río de chocolate y pétalos de rosa?

¿Te gusta sentir la tierra caliente tocando los dedos de tus pies y el algodón suave sobre tu piel, u obtienes tu energía de la luna sedosa azul de la media noche?

Ha sido un sueño feliz platicar con tu espíritu. Pero necesito oír tu risa, tocar tu mejilla y tomar tu mano.

Debemos de comer fresas mientras que refrescamos nuestros pies en un arroyo.

Quiero pestañear y ruborizarme, robarte un beso y contener una risa tímida.

Si pudiera oír el rugir de las olas contigo y oler tu cabello. Quizás entonces, podría entender de dónde viene tu luz.

*PROFILE / PERFIL*

# "Yes!"

"Yes!"

Good God Almighty. She said, "Yes!"

I got on my knee and asked her, and she said, "Yes!"

My legs trembled, my voice quavered for the damned uncertainty, but she said, "Yes," with tears in her opened eyes she said, "Yes!"

I have so little to offer, but it seems to be enough for her that I am, simply who I am! "Quick, I better give her the ring so that she can't change her mind."

Will she continue to pat my cheek and laugh at my countless follies? Will she continue to smile every single day when she sees me?

"Oh crazy woman do you understand whom you are getting involved with?"

*POEMS / POEMAS*

## "¡Sí!"

"¡Sí!"

¡Ay! bendito sea Dios. Ella dijo, "¡Sí!".

Me pusé de rodillas y le pregunté, y ella dijo, "¡Sí!".

Mis piernas temblaron, mi voz se quebrantó por la incertidumbre maldita, pero ella dijo "Sí" con lágrimas en sus ojos abiertos. Ella dijo "¡Sí!".

¡Tengo tan poco que ofrecerle, pero parece que es suficiente para ella que yo sea, simplemente quien soy! "Rápido, es mejor que le dé el anillo, así ella no podrá cambiar de idea".

¿Continuará ella acariciando mi mejilla y riendo de mis locuras incontables? ¿Continuará ella sonriendo cada día que me vea?

"¡Oh, mujer loca! ¿Entiendes tú con quién te estás involucrando?"

*PROFILE / PERFIL*

"Three immense Titans of ancient Greece could not hold the love that I have for you. Cupid has emptied his quiver into my hindquarters!"

Winter, summer, and autumn will be a springtime of joy each day. Daytime will provide the sun's light to see her face, and the night means sharing a bed, and sleep will bring the dreams of love and a world void of sadness.

I will give coins to beggars, candy to children, and smile at each stranger, because she said, "Yes, I will take this journey with you, yes, I will be your partner, yes, I will walk arm in arm, shoulder to shoulder with you."

Good God almighty. She said, "Yes!"

"¡Tres titanes inmensos de la Grecia antigua no pueden sostener el amor que yo tengo para ti! ¡El cupido ha vaciado su caja de flechas en mi trasero!".

Invierno, verano y otoño serán una primavera de regocijo cada día. El día proporcionará la luz solar para ver su rostro, la noche significa el compartir una cama y el dormir traerá los sueños de amor y un mundo vacío de tristeza.

La daré monedas a los mendigos, dulces a los niños y sonreiré a cada extraño, porqué ella dijo "Sí, yo tomaré este viaje contigo, sí, yo seré tu compañera, sí, yo caminaré brazo con brazo y hombro con hombro contigo".

¡Ay bendito sea Dios! Ella dijo "¡Sí!".

*PROFILE / PERFIL*

# American God

I was embarrassed being seen by beautiful Patricia with my family in our rattling station wagon on Sunday mornings. A Mexican Noah, my father. His ark of dents and worn tires filled with his creatures who had no choice in the matter.

Ma kept our clothes washed and pressed, but detergent and an iron could not mask faded shirts and pants worn through at the knees.

Other kids went to church in newer cars, with newer clothes, with newer parents.

We shared pews with Patricia and her family and the rest of the *Norte Americanos*. We all prayed in English, prayed in Latin, said the same orations, sang the same hymns.

But if we praised the same God in the same way, then why did He bless *them* so much more than us?

*POEMS / POEMAS*

# El dios norteamericano

Me apenaba que la hermosa Patricia me viera con mi familia en la chatarra de camioneta los domingos por la mañana. Mi papá, un Noé mexicano. Su arca de abolladuras y llantas gastadas llena de criaturas, que no tenían decisión alguna en el asunto.

Mi mamá mantenía nuestra ropa limpia y planchada, pero ni el jabón de ropa ni la plancha escondían las camisas descoloridas y los pantalones gastados de las rodillas.

Otros niños iban a la iglesia en carros más nuevos, con ropa más nueva, con padres más nuevos.

Compartíamos la banca con Patricia y su familia, así como con el resto de los norteamericanos. Todos rezábamos en inglés, en latín, decíamos las mismas oraciones, cantábamos los mismos himnos.

¿Pero si todos rezábamos al mismo dios, de la misma manera? Entonces ¿Por qué Él bendecía mucho más a ellos que a nosotros?

*PROFILE / PERFIL*

# The *Campesinos' Maestra*

And it was in that season when the countryside is a painter's pallet of yellows and reds and crimsons that I met her.

She walked in a deliberate step even as *campesinos* in stained and soiled pants ran row to row slicing stems, stretched from the weight of bunches, sagging with the liquid sugar of the vines. Instinctively they found only the ripe.

Cut go.    Cut go.    Cut go.

But it was her wont to smile and speak with the certitude of a warm breeze, soft, gentile, quiet, but unquestioned resolve.

She had countless children under her charge loving each as her own, encouraging all to reach for the brass ring of life's carousel.

And the *campesinos*, who never knew such a teacher, continued their jog up and down row after row, parcel after parcel, acre after endless acre, making their wage kicking dust into the air, carried by the wind forming tunnels in the sky.

*POEMS / POEMAS*

# La maestra de los campesinos

Y fue en esa estación del año cuando el campo era la paleta del pintor de colores amarillos, rojos y carmesís cuando la conocí.

Ella caminaba con pasos firmes y suaves mientras los campesinos en pantalones manchados y sucios corrían de fila en fila cortando tallos, estirados por el peso de sus cargas, llenos de líquido del azúcar de las frutas. Instintivamente encontraban sólo las maduras.

Corte va.　　Corte va.　　Corte va.

Pero era el hábito de la maestra sonreír y hablar con la certeza de una tibia brisa, suave, gentil, callada, y resolver sin preguntas.

Ella tenía innumerable niños bajo su cargo, amando a cada uno como si fuera propio, animando a todos a alcanzar el anillo de cobre del carrusel de la vida.

Y los campesinos que nunca conocieron a una maestra así, continuaban su caminata arriba y abajo fila por fila, parcela tras parcela, acre tras acre interminable, haciendo su sueldo mientras pateaban el polvo en el aire, llevado por el viento formando túneles en el cielo.

*PROFILE / PERFIL*

"Save them from this," beckoned the men in sweat and dirt and juice-soaked shirts.

She smiled, embraced their offspring. "I shall," she guaranteed, speaking with the measured conviction of the self-assured.

And the *campesinos*, they smiled the smile of hope and waved to *La Maestra* displaying like trophies their fingers, scarred and sliced and bandaged from the errant swing of the hook that divides stem from branch.

"I shall," she vowed, and walked off in a deliberate pace with her youthful charges in tow.

"Sálvalos de esto", imploraban los hombres envueltos en sudor y tierra y con las camisas empapadas de jugo.

Ella sonreía, abrazando a sus hijos. "Lo haré", les aseguraba con la convicción medica por la seguridad en sí misma.

Y los campesinos, sonreían con risa de esperanza y saludaban a "La maestra" mostrando como trofeos sus dedos cicatrizados, rebanados y vendados del errante mover del gancho que divide el tallo de la rama.

"Lo haré", ella prometía, caminando con paso firme con su juventud en carga.

*PROFILE / PERFIL*

## *El Jardinero*

I think of the *señora* in the morning, her legs, her arms; the sound of her laughter is the music of a silver harp guiding the lonely king to forgotten smiles.

Her hair is a field of gleaming wheat waving in a harvest breeze.

*Señor* Peacock fans his shining blue and green feathers and dances his luring dance for her, but alas in vain, for she would not settle for someone who offers only handsome plumage.

I think of her in the morning when the sun shines through her hair, aglow like a halo in the cool dawn. I hear her singing with the birds, serenading and welcoming the world from the land of happy and sad dreams. I think of her graceful walk, barefoot on rose petals, causing not so much as a bruise on those delicate wafers of the blossom.

I stole a glimpse of her silhouette through her gown; sun rays hugged, then passed around her gentle curves that would frustrate the most skilled sculptor.

*POEMS / POEMAS*

# El jardinero

Pienso en la señora en la mañana, sus piernas, sus brazos. El sonido de su risa es música de un arpa de plata guiando al rey solitario hacia sonrisas olvidadas.

Su pelo es un campo de trigo reluciente ondeando en una brisa de primavera.

El señor pavorreal despliega sus brillantes plumas azules y verdes y baila su atrayente danza para ella, pero ¡ay! En vano, pues ella no se conformaría con alguien quien ofrece sólo plumaje atractivo.

Pienso en ella esta mañana, el sol brillando a través de su pelo en el alba fría. Yo fui tan afortunado de atrapar un destello de la luz del día de su pelo brillante como una aureola. Escuché su canto con los pájaros, dando serenata y recibiendo al mundo de la tierra de sueños felices y tristes. Pienso en su gracioso caminar, descalza en pétalos de rosa causando nada más que una raspada en esos panecillos delicados en flor.

Robé una copia de su silueta a través de su camisón; los rayos de sol la abrazaron, después pasaron alrededor de sus curvas delicadas que frustrarán el escultor más diestro.

*PROFILE / PERFIL*


I dream of touching, of embracing her, but what will she have of someone who is only hired to tend her garden? But that I could simply hold her smooth feet in my hands and wash them a hundred times, and when she naps, steal a kiss on each toe, on each heel, on each ankle, on each sole.

But that I could tell her of my love of her spirit. But that we could sit under the oak together, speaking only with our eyes.

This midday is hot, but I remember her in the cool morn, watering her garden and humming the hymn of the contented.

*POEMS / POEMAS*

Soñé con tocarla, con abrazarla ¿Pero tendrá ella algo
que le pertenece a quién es contratado sólo para cuidar
su jardín? Pero yo podría simplemente sostener sus pies
suaves en mis manos y lavarlos cien veces y cuando ella
duerme la siesta, robarle un beso en cada dedo, en cada
talón, en cada tobillo y en cada planta de sus pies.

Pero que podría yo decirle de mi amor por su espíritu.
Pero podríamos sentarnos juntos bajo el roble, hablando
sólo con nuestros ojos.
Este mediodía está caluroso, pero la recuerdo en esa
mañana fresca, regando su jardín mientras tarareaba el
himno de los contentos

.

*PROFILE / PERFIL*

## *El Paletero*

His fingers stop ringing the string of small brass bells as he peddles harder pulling out of a lazy neighborhood street and onto the avenue of honking horns and screeching tires. Cars speed past this mobile vendor, some a little too close for comfort drawing concerned or vexed glances from harried drivers.

He offers *paletas*: frozen fruit bars of coconut, strawberry, tamarind, watermelon. Can he earn enough today selling popsicles to feed his family? His shirt is dark with sweat, but one must do what one must to meet his obligations; *si no trabajes no comes* (if you don't work, you don't eat).

A sparrow living this adage pulls a worm from an area where cats are known to dwell – a risky business indeed. He flies up into a tree and eyes the man peddling the insulated box on bicycle wheels passing below him.

*El Paletero* slows his pace as he rides into another neighborhood and begins working his bells like a maestro hoping to lure those with a sweet tooth and a little extra to spend.

The sparrow bounces branch to branch until he is at his nest and puts bits of today's earnings into anxious little beaks as children line up at the curb hopping with excitement clutching coins in their little hands.

*POEMS / POEMAS*

# El paletero

Sus dedos paran de jalar la cuerda de las campanitas de cobre mientras pedalea más fuerte para salir del barrio dormilón y dándose paso hacia la avenida con cláxones ruidosos y llantas chillantes. Los carros pasan veloces dejando atrás su carrito de ventas, algunos demasiado cerca de él y otros motoristas con prisa lo miran molestos.

Vende paletas, barras de fruta congeladas, coco, fresa, tamarindo, sandía ¿Podrá ganar lo suficiente para mantener a su familia vendiendo paletas? Su camisa está obscurecida por el sudor, pero uno tiene que hacer lo que pueda para cumplir con sus obligaciones; si no trabajas no comes.

Un gorrión viviendo sabiamente jala un gusano del área donde se sabe los gatos viven – por supuesto es un movimiento arriesgado. Vuela hacia un árbol y mira al hombre que pasa pedaleando la bicicleta con la caja aislada.

El paletero baja la velocidad cuando se acerca a otro barrio y comienza a tocar las campanitas como si fuera un maestro esperando atraer a los que les gusta el dulce y tienen unos centavos para gastar.

El gorrión brinca de rama en rama hasta que llega a su nido y pone pedazos de sus ganancias en los pequeños picos mientras que los niños brincan con gusto formados en la banqueta apretando los centavos en sus manitas.

*PROFILE / PERFIL*

# *El Gran Viento*

A great wind blows from the south to the north.

A great wind blows, from the south, to the north, over mountain and valley, over desert and river, and under and over and through the hands of those who would try to stop it.

A great blowing wind a thousand miles long, bringing with it a language and a food, an accordion and a fiddle, and a song for each star in the heavens.

A great wind blows from the south to the north bringing hope and determination; the hope of a home, and the determination to earn it.

Coyote and hawk know this wind. Armadillo and antlered buck, rattlesnake, puma; and the ancient peoples of this land recognize this wind that blows from the south to the north.

They say.

"It is the grandchild of the cold wind that blew across the great waters that have no end. The wind, which brought a thousand huge canoes with sails."

*POEMS / POEMAS*

# El gran viento

Un gran viento sopla del sur al norte.

Un gran viento sopla, del sur al norte, sobre la montaña y el valle, sobre el desierto y el río, y por abajo y por arriba y a través de las manos de aquellos que tratarán de detenerlo.

Un gran viento sopla, del sur al norte, sobre la montaña y el valle, sobre el desierto y el río, y abajo y arriba y a través de las manos de aquellos que tratarán de pararlo.

Un gran viento que sopla mil kilómetros de largo, trayendo con él un lenguaje, una comida, un acordeón, un violín y una canción para cada estrella del cielo.

Un gran viento sopla del sur al norte trayendo determinación y esperanza, la esperanza de un hogar y la determinación de ganarlo.

El coyote y el gavilán conocen este viento. Armadillo y venado, víbora de cascabel, puma. Los ancianos de estas tierras reconocen a este viento, que sopla del sur al norte.

Ellos dicen.

"Es el nieto del viento frío que sopló y cruzó sobre las grandes aguas sin fin. El viento que trajo mil enormes canoas de velas grandes".

*PROFILE / PERFIL*

They say.

"It is the cousin of the wind that blew from the east to the west bringing people in wagons covered with cloth; people with a curious tongue and the curious songs of the accordion and the fiddle."

"Ah," they say, "this fickle wind will change its course one day, and then blow from the north to the south."

Ellos dice.

"Es el primo del viento que sopló del este al oeste
trayendo con la gente en carretas cubiertas con mantas;
gente con una lengua curiosa y las curiosas canciones del
acordeón y el violín".

"¡Ah!", ellos dicen, "este viento de mente voluble
cambiará un día su curso y volará del norte al sur".

*PROFILE / PERFIL*

# Monks of the Field

Now, cool, quiet, serene. Hills the green of Ireland.
Clear as glass, this February air.
And sun, glorious sun, against a sky so deep, so blue,
one forgets it has ever rained.

Faint sounds from the distant valley below:
a car engine on a road somewhere,
the caws of crows echo overhead.
A single engine airplane putters along an endless
horizon.

Snip, snap, clip-clip, snap, the rhythm of pruning shears
in the strong and calloused hands of field workers. A
laborer, the hood of his sweatshirt pulled over his head,
examines the dormant vine as if it is the only vine on
earth.

"Field workers," "farm workers," *"campesinos,"* from
Oaxaca, from Guanajuato, Michoacán, a hundred places
that one hears of. But monks they are, monks of the field,
observing an unspoken oath of silence, observing an
ancient and holy motto: *"laborare orare est"*— "to work
is to pray."

Each man living, working in the moment, in the second,
no tomorrow for him, no yesterday, no morning, or
evening; only the ever present now.

*POEMS / POEMAS*

# Los monjes del campo

Ahora frescas, calladas, serenas. Las colinas con el verde de Irlanda. Claro como cristal, este aire de febrero. Y el sol, el glorioso sol, contrapuesto al cielo tan profundo, tan azul, que uno se olvida que jamás ha llovido.

Sonidos apagados del lejano valle allá abajo, el motor de un carro en un camino en alguna parte, el eco del graznido de los cuervos se oye arriba. El motor de un avión chisporrotea por el horizonte infinito.

Cortar, romper, y recortar, cortar, romper, y recortar, el ritmo de las tijeras de poda en las manos fuertes y callosas de hombres del campo. Un trabajador, la gorra de su sudadera sobre de su cabeza, examina la viña durmiente como si fuera la única en el mundo.

"Trabajadores del campo", "trabajadores de los ranchos", "campesinos" de Oaxaca, de Guanajuato, de Michoacán y de cien lugares que uno se da cuenta. Pero monjes son, monjes del campo, observando un juramento silencioso sin palabras, observando un antiguo y santo lema: "laborare orare est" – "el trabajar es rezar".

Cada hombre viviendo, trabajando en el momento, en el segundo, no hay mañana para él, no hay ayer, no mañana, o tarde; solamente el presente.

*PROFILE / PERFIL*

Sixty-five acres—50,000 vines to prune over these hills and valley. Are there too many for this crew of Alejandro, Noè, Manuel, Crisando, and Gabriel? Only one vine in the here, in the now, for each silent man.

By-and-by each vine will be pruned and retied to the stake, to the galvanized wire. By-and-by all pruned branches tossed between the narrow rows will be disked and tilled into the vineyard to become soil. By-and-by each vine will be sulfured in spring, thinned in summer, its purple fruit gathered in a frantic fall harvest when the sugar content is exact.

But in this now, there is only an infinite blue heaven, and silent monks of the field, their pruning shears chattering in the silence.

*POEMS / POEMAS*

Sesenta y cinco parcelas – 50,000 viñas para podar en estas colinas y valle. ¿Serán muchas para la cuadrilla de Alejandro, Noé, Manuel, Crisando y Gabriel? Solamente una viña en este presente, para cada hombre silencioso.

Luego cada viña estará podada y amarrada de nuevo al poste, al alambre galvanizado. Luego todas las ramas podadas tiradas entre filas angostas estarán disecadas y cultivadas en el viñedo de la ladera para que se hagan tierra. Luego cada viña estará azufrada en la primavera, estará podada en el verano, su fruta morada recogida en una cosecha frenética en el otoño cuando el nivel del azúcar está exacto.

Pero ahora solamente hay un cielo azul infinito y monjes silenciosos del campo, sus tijeras de podar castañeando en el silencio.

PROFILE / PERFIL

# *El Otro Lado*

He stands at the river's edge. Wisps of clouds turn red in the coming dawn. Some flying insects escape the jaws of largemouth fish in the hovering mist. To his back the motherland with sad breasts deplete of milk. To his back his woman and offspring. Ah, but to his front the land of a foreign tongue and foreign ways, peopled with those who will hate or pity him. To his front, a chance to prove himself, a chance to provide for those dependent on his muscle and dreams. To his front, mountains of work in *El Norte* where there is labor for a million strong men.

On ranches, one must stoop and strain and lug and bend, and there are countless herds of sheep, and cattle, and horses to tend. There is work in factories, estates, kitchens, and in the fields, work pouring cement, driving nails, planting trees, and serving meals, there is labor by day, labor by night, labor on the day of rest, putting the stamina of legs, backs, and arms to the test. There is never ending work in orchard and in vineyard from horizon to endless horizon.

And the river, the great dividing river flows slowly, calmly, deliberately, as if no one has ever drowned while being pursued through its currents in the angry season of tumultuous waters, as if there were never a time

*POEMS / POEMAS*

# El otro lado

Él se para a la orilla del río. Jirones de nubes se cambian a color rojo al amanecer. Algunos insectos voladores escapan de las quijadas de peces de boca grande en la neblina flotante. Detrás de él, la madre tierra con pechos tristes, reducidos de leche. Detrás de él, había dejado a su mujer y sus hijos. ¡Ah!, pero a su frente la tierra de una lengua extranjera y modos extranjeros, poblada con aquellos que lo odiarán o se compadecerán de él. A su frente, una oportunidad de demostrarse, una oportunidad de proveer a aquellos que dependen de su fuerza y sueños. A su frente montañas de trabajo en "El norte" donde hay trabajo para un millón de hombres fuertes.

En los ranchos, uno tiene que agacharse, esforzarse, arrastrarse e inclinarse; hay incontables manadas de borregos, vacas y caballos para atender. Hay trabajo en las fincas, las fábricas, las cocinas y en los campos; trabajo vertiendo cemento, clavando clavos, plantando árboles y sirviendo comidas. Hay trabajo de día, trabajo de noche, trabajo en el día de descanso, haciendo la prueba de resistencia de las piernas, las espaldas y los brazos. Hay trabajo interminable en las huertas y en los viñedos de un horizonte a otro infinito.

Y el río, el gran río de separación corre lentamente, tranquilamente y pausadamente; como si jamás nadie se hubiera ahogado mientras fuera perseguido a través de sus corrientes en la estación feroz de aguas tumultuosas; como si allí nunca hubier

*PROFILE / PERFIL*

of a ravenous torrent with an insatiable appetite that consumes all things from the docile cow to the venomous viper, and any other man or beast or flower or tree that dares it.

The river, the river burdened with the task of dividing avarice-plagued nations. But on this day, and in this dawn, this river that perpetually moves from the yesterday to the tomorrow, and yet is perpetually in the here, seduces this man, lures him to ford its waters, invites him to look into his future.

He gazes into a pool to see not a man in tattered pants and a worn out sombrero, but the reflection of a *caballero*. A gentleman, a man of means who stands straight and pays his own way, and on Sundays takes his family to church in an automobile.

There, reflected in the baptismal water is a man in fine clothes, with hair that is combed and trimmed regularly.

*This* is what the big river offers, and it is all his to seize, if he simply crosses to *El otro lado* undetected by those who would keep him from his destiny.

un torrente con apetito insaciable que consume todas las cosas, desde la dócil vaca hasta la más venenosa víbora y cualquier otro hombre, o bestia, o flor, o árbol que lo desafíe.

El río, el río que está encargado de dividir las naciones plagadas de avaricia. Pero en este día y en esta alba, este río que recorre perpetuamente desde el ayer al mañana, y está aun perpetuamente en el presente, seduce a este hombre, lo atrae vadear sus aguas, invitándolo a mirar hacia su futuro.

Él fija su mirada en un charco para ver no a un hombre en pantalones desgarrados y sombrero de paja, sino el reflejo de un caballero. Un señor, un hombre de dinero, que paga sus servicios, que se para derecho y se sostiene, y los domingos lleva a su familia a la iglesia en un automóvil.

Allí reflejado en el agua bautismal, está un hombre en ropa fina y pelo que está peinado y recortado regularmente.

Esto es lo que el río grande ofrece, y está para que él lo obtenga, si él simplemente cruza al otro lado, sin ser descubierto por aquellos que podrían quitarle su destino.

*PROFILE / PERFIL*

## *Fresas*

One straight furrow follows another and another along a landscape that looks as if a colossal comb was run over it.

Ignacio spent most of his life preparing, planting, and harvesting this acreage.

His knees ache with rheumatism. "He spent too much time in the cold damp earth," Doña Flor, his wife says.

Strawberry shortcake, strawberry jam, strawberry ice cream; and see how lovely they look on the cereal box, deep red against white milk and flakes of grain; food for happy, healthy people.

Ignacio built a house in his native land after working and saving for most of 30 years in these fields. His house is solid: constructed of lumber, blocks, mortar, and wiring for electricity and plumbing for running water.

*POEMS / POEMAS*

# Fresas

Un surco derecho sigue a otro y a otro en el paisaje que se mira como si un peine colosal hubiera pasado por ahí.

Ignacio se ha pasado casi toda su vida preparando, plantando y cosechando estos acres.

Sus rodillas le duelen por el reumatismo. "Pasó demasiado tiempo en la tierra fría y húmeda", dice su esposa, Doña Flor.

Pan de fresa, mermelada de fresa, helado de fresa ¡Mira qué bonitas se ven en la caja del cereal! Rojo obscuro en contraste con la leche blanca y las hojuelas del grano; comida para la gente saludable y contenta.

Con el esfuerzo del trabajo en estos campos, y los ahorros de casi 30 años, Ignacio construyó una casa en su tierra natal. Su casa es sólida: construida de cemento, bloques, mortero, cables para la electricidad y drenaje interior para agua.

*PROFILE / PERFIL*

It is time to plant vegetables in his garden but his swollen joints do not allow him to do so, at least not today. Maybe tomorrow his body will feel up to it, and besides his son, Alejandro, leaves for *"El Norte"* today. The season for preparing the soil for planting strawberries has come.

Unknowingly, many will toast the labor of these men when they enjoy ice-cold strawberry daiquiris on warm summer afternoons.

Es el tiempo de plantar verduras en su jardín pero sus coyontunas hínchadas no se lo permiten, de menos no ahora. Quizas mañana su cuerpo se sienta mejor, ademas su hijo Alejandro, se va para "El Norte" hoy. La temporada para preparar la tierra para plantar fresas ha llegado.

Sin saberlo, en las calidas tardes de verano, muchos van a brindar por el trabajo de estos hombres cuando gozen de sus helados daiquiris de fresa.

*PROFILE / PERFIL*

# Which Foot?

My hands harvest fruit from tree and vine in this land of promise. I labor as an angry sun causes me to sweat rivers. I perform any job willingly: wash floors, remove the innards of butchered hens, construct homes so that the citizens of this nation may live in comfort.

Calloused hands I trade for a wage, for my children to have a chance. I live in the most modest of homes without complaint, only grateful for the opportunity of employment.

But my feet shall remain firmly planted in the land of the eagle and serpent. One day I will return to the town of my birth in a shining new vehicle. I will stroll the plaza each evening dressed in store-bought clothes. "*Hizo bien, hizo bien*, he did well!" they will whisper. "He worked decades and has returned to build his family a house!"

But alas, my children's feet are taking root here! I talk to them in our tongue; they answer me in this other! "Ju noh leeve heer," I tell them in this foreign language. They only hide their smiles and laugh.

## ¿Cual pie?

Mis manos cosechan la fruta del árbol y la parra en estas tierras de promisión. Trabajo mientras que un sol enojado me hace sudar ríos. Hago cualquier trabajo de buena voluntad; lavando suelos, quito las tripas de las gallinas, construyo casas en donde los ciudadanos de esta nación puedan vivir cómodamente.

Manos con callos como intercambio por un sueldo, para que mis hijos tengan una oportunidad de hacer algo. Vivo en casas modestas sin quejarme, solamente estoy agradecido por la oportunidad de tener empleo.

Pero los pies quedarán firmes en la tierra del águila y la serpiente. Un día volveré al pueblo de mi nacimiento en un nuevo coche brillante. Me pasearé por la plaza cada tarde vestido con ropa comprada de tienda "¡Hizo bien, hizo bien!" murmurarán. "¡Ha trabajado por muchos años y ha regresado a construir una casa para su familia!"

¡Pero finalmente los pies de mis hijos están tomando raíces aquí! ¡Yo les hablo en nuestra lengua; ellos me contestan en esta otra! "Ju no liv jir", les digo en esta lengua extranjera. Sólo esconden sus sonrisas y se ríen.

*PROFILE / PERFIL*

"*No somos de estos*, we are not of these people!" I remind them. "Here we only inhabit a house; our home, our hearts are over there; there can be no other way! Here we stoop; there we stand."

"Tell *Papá*, are there hamburgers in this land of yours?" My children ask, "Are there games to play on screens that flash green and white and red?"

One foot supports my body; one foot supports my soul; on which foot do I stand?

"¡No somos de éstos!" les recuerdo. "¡Aquí solamente habitamos una casa; nuestro hogar, nuestro corazón está allá; no puede ser de otro modo! Aquí nos agachamos; allá nos paramos".

"Diga papá ¿Hay hamburguesas en este país suyo?" mis hijos me preguntan. "¿Hay juegos para jugar en pantallas que proyectan rápidamente los colores verde y blanco y rojo?"

Un pie sostiene mi cuerpo, un pie sostiene mi alma; ¿en cuál pie me paro?

*PROFILE / PERFIL*

# Wild Flowers

They don't grow in greenhouses, nurseries, or tended gardens, and survive on but a single season of rain. Borne of hardship they are tempered and thrive where the less hardy wither away.

The wildflower seed migrates riding the wind, the wind that recognizes no borders. When in foul moods, the wind casts the seed onto barren rock or wetlands, fated to dry under a merciless sun or sink into the mire. When in good humor, the wind sets the seed onto arable land to germinate and rise tall and firm, but even here it may be consumed by grazing herds.

The migrant rides this angry or gentle wind to the land of opportunity. He makes his perilous odyssey leaving the barren ground of the homeland where his aspirations have long since been scattered by the arid storms of greed. He comes seeking those grueling labors that the less hardy are unable to do.

Desperate for a chance to sprout and grow, he pays smugglers to slip him into the land of eternal promise, but at times he is abandoned, and left to the fate of the wildflower drying in the desert under an unforgiving sun. At times he is swept away while attempting to cross the river of hope. And even when he succeeds at crossing, he often falls victim to the avarice of godless bosses.

## Flores silvestres

No crecen en invernaderos, viveros o en jardines bien cuidados y pueden sobrevivir nada más con una estación de lluvia. Nacidas de las penalidades y se han templado y sobrevivido donde otras no tan fuertes se marchitan.

La semilla de la flor silvestre emigra cabalgando el viento, el viento que no reconoce fronteras. Cuando el viento está de mal humor, lanza la semilla hacia tierra estéril o hacia pantanos, así su destino será secarse bajo el sol sin misericordia o se hundirá en el fango. Cuando está de buen humor, el viento deposita la semilla en tierra arable para que germine, crezca alta y firme, pero quizás todavía aquí, puede ser consumida por el ganado.

El inmigrante cabalga el enojado o gentil viento hacia la tierra de oportunidades. Hace su arriesgada odisea dejando la tierra infértil de su patria donde sus aspiraciones han sido regadas por las tormentas áridas de la ambición. Él viene buscando al trabajo agotador que los menos fuertes no pueden hacer.

Desesperado por la oportunidad de surgir y crecer, paga a contrabandistas para que lo pasen a la tierra de la promesa eterna, pero en ocasiones es abandonado y dejado a la suerte de la flor silvestre secándose en el desierto debajo del inclemente sol. En ocasiones, es arrastrado mientras que trata de cruzar el río de la esperanza. Y aun cuando tiene éxito cruzando, a menudo cae víctima de la avaricia de patrones sin dios.

*PROFILE / PERFIL*

But fueled by the dreams of earning a dignified life, he continues his arduous treks on, and on, and on. And the forever wind carries countless seeds of wildflowers to uncertain destinations, casting them onto barren rock or sowing them over fertile loam.

Behold, how their blossoms in every color grace the land.

Pero cargado de los sueños de alcanzar una vida digna,
él continúa su camino difícil y sigue, y sigue, y sigue.
Y el eterno viento lleva incontables semillas de flores
silvestres a destinos inciertos, fundiéndolas en tierra
árida o sembrándolas en tierra fértil.

Miren cómo sus flores de todos colores agracian la tierra.

*Stories*

*Cuentos*

*PROFILE / PERFIL*

# Bless Me Father for I Have Sinned

My twin, Fernando and I walked slowly down the aisle, each with his girl partner toward the altar to receive communion. We wore white shirts, black shoes, and the new navy blue slacks that our parents had tailor made in Tijuana, just south of where we lived in San Diego, California. The pants had pressed cuffs, creases, and were stylishly loose-fitting. Our older siblings never got such lavish items as tailored clothes. Pa's truck-driving salary didn't allow for such extravagances, but Ferd and I were Ma's little twin dolls.

The girls wore white lacy dresses, veils, and patent leather shoes. We all carried prayer books draped with rosaries and had been sitting in the pews, as still as second graders were able. When the time came to receive communion, we rose, formed couples, and slowly walked to the front of the church to kneel at the communion rail. I had seen my family and the bigger kids of my Catholic grammar school receive this blessed sacrament all of my life. At long last, this was *my* First Holy Communion.

In order to receive the body of Christ, we had to fast from all foods and drink, even water, since the night before. I felt light headed and my stomach growled like an angry cat.

*STORIES / CUENTOS*

## Bendíceme padre por pecador

MI CUATE GEMELO, Fernando y yo caminamos despacio por el pasillo hacia el altar para recibir la comunión. Cada uno al lado de una niña como pareja. Vestíamos camisas blancas, zapatos negros y los pantalones nuevos color azul marino que nuestros padres habían mandado hacer en Tijuana, al sur de San Diego, donde vivíamos. Los pantalones tenían presillas, estaban bien planchados con la raya en la mitad y eran de los más modernos, sueltos de las piernas. Nuestros hermanos y hermanas mayores nunca tuvieron esta ropa tan cara hecha a mano. El salario de mi papá como chofer de camión de carga no permitía ciertas extravagancias, pero Nando y yo éramos los gemelos muñecos de mi mamá.

Las niñas usaban vestidos hechos de encaje, velos y zapatos de charol. Todos llevábamos nuestros libros de oraciones envueltos en nuestros rosarios y habíamos estado sentados en las bancas, tan quietos como los niños de segundo año pueden estar. Cuando la hora de recibir la comunión llegó, nos levantamos, nos formamos en pareja y despacio caminamos hacia el frente de la iglesia para hincarnos en el podio. Yo había visto toda mi vida a mi familia y a los niños más grandes de mi escuela primaria católica recibir este bendito sacramento. Finalmente, ésta era mi primera y sagrada comunión.

Para poder recibir el cuerpo de Cristo, no pudimos comer alimento alguno desde la noche anterior, ni siquiera pudimos tomar agua. Me sentía mareado y mi estómago rugía como un gato enojado.

*PROFILE / PERFIL*

Father McGuinn walked along the communion rail, placing the sacred hosts on the new communicants tongues. An altar boy followed Father, holding a shiny brass paten under our chins to catch whatever minute scraps of the consecrated host that would otherwise fall to the floor and become desecrated. We were told to never ever touch the sacred host, but to swallow it immediately. Only a priest's consecrated hands were allowed to touch the shiny little wafer of unleavened bread that was now Jesus Christ.

The nuns did a fine job of preparing us for this profound moment in our religious lives. They taught us of the sacraments; baptism had cleansed our souls of Adam and Eve's "Original Sin." They disobeyed God by eating of the forbidden fruit in the Garden of Eden. Disobeying one's parents was one thing. But how could anyone even consider disobeying Almighty God? Anyhow, we had inherited their sin and we couldn't enter heaven until it was cleansed by the holy water of baptism.

Baptism was a ritual performed by an ordained priest. But when someone who wasn't baptized was hurt in a car accident or wounded on a battlefield and they were dying, then anyone could baptize them by pouring holy water over their head while saying, "I baptize thee in the name of the Father, and of the Son, and of the Holy Ghost."

El Padre McGuinn caminaba por el podio poniendo la sagrada hostia de la comunión en la lengua de los niños. Un monaguillo iba detrás del padre, poniendo un platito de bronce brillante debajo de nuestra barba para prevenir que cualquier pequeño pedacito de la hostia sagrada cayese al suelo y fuera profanada. Nos dijeron que ni siquiera podíamos tocar la sagrada hostia, la teníamos que tragar inmediatamente. Sólo se le permitía a las manos sagradas del padre tocar la pequeña y brillante hostia hecha de pan sin levadura, que era el cuerpo de Cristo.

Las monjas hicieron un buen trabajo al prepararnos para este momento profundo en nuestras vidas religiosas. Nos enseñaron todos los sacramentos; el bautismo limpia las almas de Adán y Eva del "pecado original". Ellos desobedecieron a Dios cuando comieron la fruta del árbol prohibido en el Jardín del Edén. Desobedecer a nuestros padres es una cosa, ¿Pero cómo se atreven a desobedecer al Dios Todopoderoso? De cualquier manera, nosotros heredamos sus pecados y no podemos entrar a la gloria sin antes limpiar nuestra alma con el agua bendita del bautismo.

El bautismo es un rito llevado a cabo por un sacerdote. Pero cuando alguien que no ha sido bautizado y es herido en un accidente de carro o herido en el campo de batalla y se está muriendo, entonces cualquier persona le puede realizar los ritos del bautismo al ponerle agua bendita en la cabeza al mismo tiempo que dice: "Yo te bautizo en el nombre del Padre, del Hijo y del Espíritu Santo".

Regular water would do if there wasn't holy water near by. I asked during a religion class, "What if the person has only seconds to live, and the water is far away? Could I use spit?" Sister didn't answer.

I worried about my little neighbor, Chris. He was a first grade public school kid whose family wasn't Catholic and never went to church. I didn't want him to miss out on going to heaven with me. I took him into the garage one afternoon and explained Baptism to him. I then poured water over his head and said the holy words. I felt great. I was in the second grade and had already saved my first soul.

Holy Eucharist (consuming the body of Christ) was the next sacrament. Sister Alvira Marie, our second grade teacher, told us that before receiving Holy Communion our souls had to be cleansed from the splotches of sin and be "white as a bottle of milk." She then told us the story of a girl who didn't confess a big sin, and when she went to communion, "the host singed her tongue!" I imagined the girl screaming and running from the church as steaming saliva billowed from her mouth.

Confession, the forgiveness of sins, was the next sacrament. Small sins were "venial," big ones "mortal." The punishment for a mortal sin was to be sent to hell and burn forever. Kids rarely committed mortal sins like murder, although I really wanted to kill my little sister, Carmen.

"¿Se puede usar agua regular cuando no hay agua bendita?", pregunté durante la clase de religión "¿Qué pasa si la persona solamente tiene unos segundos para vivir y el agua está lejos? ¿Podría usar saliva?", la hermana no respondió.

Me preocupaba por mi pequeño vecino, Chris. Era un niño de primer año que iba a la escuela pública y su familia no era católica y nunca iban a la iglesia. No quería que se perdiera la entrada al cielo junto conmigo. Una tarde lo llevé a la cochera y le expliqué el bautismo. Entonces le eché agua y dije las palabras sagradas "Te bautizo en el nombre del Padre, del Hijo y del Espíritu Santo". Me sentí muy bien. Estaba en segundo año y ya había salvado mi primera alma.

El segundo sacramento era la sagrada eucaristía (consumiendo el cuerpo de Cristo). La Hermana Elvira Marie, nuestra maestra de segundo año, nos dijo que antes de recibir la sagrada comunión nuestras almas tenían que ser limpiadas de las manchas del pecado y ser tan "blancas como la botella de la leche". Después nos contó la historia de una muchacha que no había confesado un gran pecado. Cuando fue a tomar la comunión "¡La hostia le quemó la lengua!" Me imaginé a la muchacha gritando y corriendo afuera de la iglesia mientras que la saliva hirviendo le brotaba como olas de la boca.

El siguiente sacramento es el de la confesión que perdona los pecados. Los pecados pequeños eran "veniales", los grandes eran "mortales". El castigo por un pecado mortal era el infierno para quemarse eternamente. Los niños raramente cometen pecados mortales como el matar, aunque de verdad, yo quería matar a mi hermana menor Carmen.

*PROFILE / PERFIL*

"No!" said Sister, answering another of my hypothetical questions during class, "If a person killed somebody by accident God wouldn't punish them, but He would know if they did it intentionally. Then he would punish them." So, I thought, if I killed my little sister and made it look like an accident, then the police would let me go and I wouldn't get the electric chair, but God would send me to hell. I could just see the little brat looking down at me and getting the last laugh. But if it really was an accident that only looked suspicious, then I'd get the chair, but go to heaven. What if she could be gotten rid of and it really *was* an accident? Then I wouldn't get it from anyone. I prayed for divine intervention.

There was a cold and heavy fog outdoors last Friday when we walked into the church to make our first confession. I was in mental anguish. Surely Father would recognize my voice and know that it was me who would confess to looking at one of my older sisters once when she was changing her clothes. Sins of the flesh were among the worst a person could commit. But if I didn't tell him of this great sin, then it wouldn't be forgiven, and I would receive Holy Communion with a mortal sin on my soul and I'd wind up in hell forever.

There were three doors in the wall: door number one, door number two, and door number three. Father waited for us behind door number two ready to hear of our sins.

"¡No!" dijo la Hermana en clase cuando respondió a otra de mis preguntas hipotéticas, "Si una persona mata por accidente a otra persona, Dios no lo castiga. Pero si Dios sabe que lo hizo intencionalmente, Dios si lo castiga". Entonces yo pensé, si mato a mi hermana menor y hago que parezca un accidente, la policía me soltará y no me pondrán en la silla eléctrica, pero Dios me mandará al infierno. Me imaginaba a la pequeña traviesa mirándome desde arriba y siendo la última en reírse. Pero si de veras era un accidente, que nada más despertara sospechas, me mandarían a la silla eléctrica pero me iba al cielo. ¿Qué tal si de veras me pudiera deshacer de ella, si de veras fuera un accidente? Entonces no tendría problemas con nadie ¡Cómo rezaba por una intervención divina!.

El viernes pasado cuando caminamos a la iglesia para confesarnos y hacer nuestra primera comunión había una neblina fría y pesada. Me sentía con una angustia mental. Seguramente el Padre reconocería mi voz y sabría que era yo el que confesaría que había espiado a una de mis hermanas mayores cuando se estaba cambiando de ropa. Los pecados de la carne eran los peores que una persona podía cometer. Pero si no me confesaba, no podría ser perdonado de este pecado y recibiría la primera comunión con el pecado mortal en mi alma y terminaría en el infierno para siempre.

Había tres puertas en la pared: la puerta número uno, la puerta número dos y la puerta número tres. El Padre nos esperaba detrás de la puerta número dos, listo para escuchar nuestros pecados.

*PROFILE / PERFIL*

Sister lined a few of us on either side of the confessional and sat the rest in pews to "examine our consciences" while we waited our turns. She opened door number one and pushed in the first little sinner, Ruth, and did the same at door three, making my friend Gerry go in. In a few minutes Ruth came out, walked to the front of the church, and knelt to say her penance prayers. Sister signaled the next little lamb to take her place. Door number three opened. Gerry stepped out and walked down the aisle to join Ruth in the penance pew. And the holy carwash began. Dirty little splotched souls entered, and shiny clean ones exited.

I knelt in the pew sweating it out. Father was about to learn that I was a lecher of the worst sort. How could I possibly convince him that I really wasn't, but a good Catholic boy who would like to be a saint someday? I hoped that there would be an earthquake or maybe Father would have a heart attack before I had to go in, but no luck. It was my turn. I hesitated to enter the confessional. Sister glared at me.

I hung my head, opened the door, and walked in. It was dark in the small cubicle. I knelt on the pad in front of the little screen in the wall. I heard mumbling; some kid on the other side was confessing. Hey, what if his sins were really big so mine wouldn't seem so bad. What if he murdered someone? There was a brief silence and then the little door across the screen slid open. I could see Father's silhouette against the wall behind him. My anxiousness erased months of preparation, and I forgot how to start my confession.

*STORIES / CUENTOS*

La hermana nos formó en ambos lados del confesionario y a los demás nos sentó en las bancas a "examinar nuestras consciencias" mientras que esperábamos nuestro turno. Abrió la puerta número uno y empujó hacia adentro a la primera pequeña pecadora, Ruth, hizo lo mismo en la puerta tres, empujando a mi amigo Gerry hacia adentro. Después de unos pocos minutos Ruth salió, caminó hacia el frente de la iglesia y se hincó para rezar su penitencia. Gerry salió después y caminó por el pasillo para unirse a Ruth en la banca de la penitencia. El sagrado lavadero de carros había comenzado a trabajar. Almas pequeñas manchadas entraban al confesionario y de ahí salían limpias y brillantesMe hinqué en la banca sudando y nervioso, el Padre estaba a punto de saber que era yo una sanguijuela de lo peor. ¿Cómo podría convencerlo que no era malo, sino un buen niño católico al que le gustaría convertirse en santo un día? Pedía que de pronto hubiera un temblor o que al padre le diera un ataque al corazón antes de que yo entrara al confesionario, pero no hubo tal suerte. Llegó mi turno. Dudé de entrar al confesionario pero la hermana me vio con malos ojos.

Bajé la cabeza, abrí la puerta y entré. El pequeño cubículo estaba obscuro. Me arrodillé en el reclinatorio acolchonado enfrente de la pequeña malla. Escuché un murmullo; un niño se confesaba del otro lado. ¿Qué tal si sus pecados eran más grandes que los míos y ya los míos no se verían tan malos? ¿Qué tal si mató a alguien? Hubo un pequeño silencio y la puertita del otro lado de la pequeña malla se abrió. Podía ver la silueta del Padre reflejada en la pared detrás de él. Mi ansiedad borró meses de preparación y se me olvidó cómo empezar mi confesión.

*PROFILE / PERFIL*

Father waited a bit then asked, "Are you here to confess?"

"Um, yes Father."

"You may start."

"I forgot how."

"Bless me Father..."

"Oh, yeah! Bless me Father for I have sinned. This is my first confession. Since I was born I've fought with my brothers and sisters a whole, whole bunch of times. If I told you a hundred but it was really a hundred and one, then could I go to hell for missing that one?" Father put his fist to his mouth and coughed to hide a chuckle.

"Just do the best you can, my son."

"And I disobeyed my parents a whole lot of times too. I wish I could tell you how many, um, maybe about a thousand?" More coughing.

*Quick! Make up some sins, so I won't have to tell him the whopper!* "And, and Father. I, I threw rocks at the neighbor's cat, but my mom told me to because it kept pooping in her garden. And once after I saw Moe poke Curly Joe in the eyes, I did it to my little sister and made her cry! And, and um..." I was in a tug-of-war, too ashamed to tell this holy man of my terrible sin, but if I didn't, then Jesus would host a barbeque in my mouth. There was no escape. My voice broke with emotion. "And, and Father I, I committed a real nasty sin." He leaned toward me.

"Yes, my son, tell me about it."

El Padre esperó unos momentos y finalmente me preguntó "¿Estás aquí para confesarte?".
"Mmm, si Padre".
"Empieza".
"Pero se me olvido como empezar".
"Bendigame Padre…"
"¡Ah, sí claro!" "Bendígame Padre porque he pecado. Ésta es mi primera confesión. Desde que nací he peleado muchas, muchas veces con mis hermanos y hermanas. Si le dijera cien, pero la verdad es que fueron ciento una veces ¿Me iré al infierno por no haber confesado esa vez?" El Padre se puso la mano en la boca y tosió para esconder la risa.

"Nada más haz lo que puedas, hijo mío".

"Y también muchas veces desobedezco a mis padres. ¿Me gustaría decirle cuántas veces, mmm, quizás mil?" Más tos.

*¡Rápido! Inventa algunos pecados, ¡Para que no le tenga que decir del embuste!* "Y, y padre. Yo, yo le tiré piedras al gato del vecino, pero mi mamá fue la que me dijo que lo hiciera porque el gato estaba haciendo sus necesidades en su jardín de flores. Y después una vez que vi a un payaso picarle el ojo a otro ¡Se lo hice a mi hermana menor y la hice llorar! Y, y mmm...". Estaba en el estira y afloja, muy avergonzado para decirle mis pecados terribles a este hombre sagrado, pero si no se los decía, Jesús haría una barbacoa en mi boca. No había escapatoria. Mi voz tembló de emoción. "Y, y Padre, yo, yo he cometido un pecado muy cochino". Se inclinó hacia mí.

"Sí hijo, dime qué pasó".

*PROFILE / PERFIL*

"Father I, I tried to look at one of my sisters when she was changing her clothes." I started to cry in humiliation and expected his fist to smash through the screen and smack me in the face, but he only sat silently for a moment.

"I see. Well, did you see anything?"

"No, Father. She knew I was in my bed and kept looking at me. I couldn't get the covers high enough to get a good look. I saw something that looked like my uncle's bald head; must've been her butt."

Father went into a coughing fit. I felt bad about making him so sick. He settled down.

"Well, God is proud of you for having had the fortitude to confess this, but you must understand that this is an invasion of privacy. Wouldn't you be embarrassed if people looked at you when you were dressing?"

"Yes, Father. I'll never ever do it again."

"Very good. For your penance say three Hail Mary's and three Our Fathers. Now say the Act of Contrition."

"Oh, my God, I am heartily sorry for having offended thee, and I detest my sins because of thy just punishments…" As I prayed, he recited the forgiveness prayer and ended by raising his hand and making the sign of the cross.

"I absolve thee in the name of the Father, and of the Son, and of the Holy Ghost. Amen. Go and sin no more. You're a good and brave boy."

"Gee, thanks Father!"

"Padre yo, yo traté de ver a una de mis hermanas cuando se estaba cambiando de ropa". Empecé a llorar de la humillación y esperaba que su puño cruzara la malla y se estrellara en mi cara, pero en cambio, se sentó en silencio por un momento.

"Ya veo. Bueno ¿viste algo?".

"No Padre. Ella sabía que yo estaba en mi cama y no me quito la vista de encima. No pude subir las cobijas lo suficiente para poder ver algo. Pero si vi algo que parecía como la cabeza calva de mi tío; a lo mejor fue una nalga".

El Padre tuvo un ataque de tos fuerte, me sentí mal por hacer que se enfermara tan feo. Por fin se calmó.

"Bueno, Dios está muy orgulloso de ti por haber tenido el valor de confesar esto. Tienes que entender que eso es una invasión a la privacidad personal. ¿Estarías apenado si la gente te mirara cuando te estas cambiando de ropa?"

"Sí, Padre. Nunca lo vuelvo a hacer".

"Muy bien, tienes que rezar tres ave marías y tres padre nuestros como tu penitencia. Ahora dime el acto de contrición".

"Oh Dios mío, de todo corazón pido perdón por haberte ofendido y rechazo todos mis pecados a cambio de tu justo castigo…". Mientras que yo rezaba, el recitaba el rezo del perdón y terminó al levantar su mano e hizo la señal de la cruz.

"Yo te absuelvo en el nombre del Padre, del Hijo, y del Espíritu Santo. Amén. Vete y no peques más. Tu eres un niño bueno y valiente".

"¡Ay, gracias Padre!".

*PROFILE / PERFIL*

I was absolved of my sins! I felt like skipping all the way down the aisle to the penance pew. The sun broke through the fog outdoors and shone through the stained glass windows, brilliantly lighting up the church. My soul, after saying my penance prayers, was white as a bottle of milk. What a feeling! I could be killed on the way home and go straight to heaven!

All I had to do was stay sin free at least until my first communion on Sunday. I'd have to obey my parents, not fight with my siblings, or sneak into my sister's bed to scare the hell out of her at night. I had barely managed to stay clean over the weekend except for when I flicked a booger at Carmen, but I missed so it probably wasn't a sin.

Sunday had finally come. I walked with my partner to the communion rail. Father McGuinn stopped in front of me. He put a hand into the golden chalice and took out a host. I closed my eyes, raised my head, and stuck out my tongue. The alter boy put the paten under my chin.

"Corpus Cristi," Father said placing Jesus on my tongue. I tried to swallow him as taught, but couldn't! He was stiff as cardboard, and my mouth was dry and pasty from not eating or drinking since dinner last night. I tried again and gagged, nearly coughing Him out onto the floor. Mercifully, Jesus finally softened to mush and slid down. I walked back to the pew.

¡Fui absuelto de mis pecados! Sentí que quería brincar de gusto por el pasillo cuando regresé a la banca de las penitencias. El sol se libró de la niebla y penetró por los vitrales de las ventanas, alumbrando la iglesia de una manera brillante. Después de rezar mi penitencia, mi alma estaba tan blanca como la botella de leche. ¡Que emoción! ¡Podría ser asesinado en mi camino a la casa e irme derechito al cielo!

Nada más tenía que mantenerme fuera de pecado hasta el día de mi primera comunión, el domingo. Tendría que obedecer a mis padres, no pelear con mis hermanos y hermanas, ni en la noche, meterme en la cama de mi hermana para espantarla. Con mucho trabajo quedé limpio de pecado durante el fin de semana con la excepción de cuando le eché un moco a Carmen, pero como fallé, a lo mejor no fue un pecado.

Por fin llegó el domingo. Caminé junto a mi pareja hacia la fila de la comunión. El Padre McGuinn puso una mano dentro del cáliz dorado y sacó una hostia. Cerré mis ojos, levanté la cabeza y saqué la lengua. El monaguillo puso el plato de bronce bajo de mi barba.

"Corpus Cristi", dijo el Padre al poner a Jesús en mi lengua. ¡Traté de tragarlo como me habían enseñado, pero no pude! Estaba tan duro como un cartón y mi boca estaba seca y pastosa porque no había comido ni tomado agua desde la noche anterior. Traté de tragarlo otra vez y sentí ahogarme, casi escupo en el suelo a Jesús todo misericordioso, finalmente se suavizó como papilla y se resbaló hacia mi garganta. Caminé de regreso a la banca.

*PROFILE / PERFIL*

It was done. Jesus was in me, but I didn't feel any different than I did before! I looked at my partner to see if she looked different somehow. She didn't. I caught my twin's eye and whispered over his partner sitting between us. "Feel anything?" He shrugged his shoulders. I gave him a "what the heck?" look. Sister, sitting behind me pinched my shoulder. I turned, closed my eyes, and lowered my head pretending to pray. Maybe there was something deep inside that I had to think about in order to feel Jesus' presence. I kept trying but nothing came.

Toward the end of mass I felt something on the roof of my mouth. I put my finger to it and drew out a small glob of a curious looking white paste. I stared at it for a second before the revelation came. IT'S JESUS! I shot my finger back in my mouth and swallowed His arm, or leg, or whatever body part. Holy smokes! Was this a sin? Did I need to confess it? I prayed my mouth wouldn't start burning.

Mass seemed to go on forever before we finally got to walk down the aisle with our partners, parading past our families, out of the church. Ma had Pa take a picture of my twin and me standing at the church wall in our new shirts and tailor-made pants.

Por fin, tenía a Jesús dentro de mí ¡Pero no sentí ninguna diferencia de cómo me sentía antes! Miré hacia mi pareja para ver si se veía diferente. Y no se vio diferente. Alcancé con la vista a mi gemelo y por encima de su pareja que estaba sentada entre los dos y le susurré. "¿Sientes algo?" Él levantó los hombros. Le eché una mirada de "¿qué demonios…?" La Hermana que estaba sentada detrás de mí me pellizcó el hombro. Me volteé, cerré los ojos, bajé la cabeza y pretendí rezar. Quizás dentro de mí, había algo bien profundo que tenía que pasar para que así sintiera la presencia de Jesús en mí. Seguí tratando pero nada pasó.

Casi al final de la misa sentí algo en el paladar. Lo saqué con mi dedo. Era una bolita de pastilla blanca. La miré por un segundo antes de que la revelación me llegara. ¡ES JESÚS! Puse mi dedo en la boca y tragué su brazo, o pierna, o cualquier parte de su cuerpo ¡La sagrada hostia! ¿Era esto un pecado? ¿Necesitaba confesarme? Recé para que la boca no se me quemara.

Parecía que la misa duraba una eternidad antes de que finalmente camináramos por el pasillo al lado de nuestras parejas. Desfilando enfrente de nuestras familias, hacia la salida de la iglesia. Mi papá y mi mamá nos tomaron fotos a mi gemelo y a mí, parados frente a la pared de la iglesia, vestidos con camisas nuevas y pantalones hechos a man.

*PROFILE / PERFIL*

From that day forward, on the first Friday of each month, we got to join the third through eighth graders to receive communion at mass before school. I got one of those cool cinnamon rolls and cartons of milk at my desk for breakfast just like the rest of the big kids. Boy, in the name of the Father, and of the Son, and of the Holy Ghost, this was great!

*STORIES / CUENTOS*

Desde aquel día, el primer viernes de cada mes, íbamos a misa y a recibir la comunión con los alumnos del tercero al octavo año. El desayuno en nuestro escritorio consistía de un rollo de canela y un cartón de leche igual que el resto de los niños más grandes. ¡Qué cosa! En el nombre del Padre, del Hijo y del Espíritu Santo. ¡Esto era fabuloso!

*PROFILE / PERFIL*

# Don't Fall Asleep

We had just seen *The Wolf Man* and I was lying in the dark with my twin brother, Ferd, and our sisters, Ana, Carolyn, and Martha. We were in the living room lying on olive-green army surplus cotton-stuffed mats. Ana and Carolyn were the oldest and in high school. They had allowed Ferd and me to stay up with them, and Martha who was in sixth grade, to watch the Friday night scary movie on TV. Ferd and I had been so excited! We got to stay up late, eat popcorn, drink soda, and watch a movie that didn't even start until 9:00 o'clock at night.

It was terribly dark and quiet after we turned in. I looked around the room and into the kitchen. There he was. I could see the Wolf Man's silhouette, lit by the faint moonlight. He was waiting for me to fall asleep before making his move to get me. He had been attacked and bitten by a wolf and was cursed to become a Wolf Man. I saw him turn into the monster that was half wolf and half man. He didn't want to be one, but that was the curse; on a full moon, the hair on his face and arms and legs grew longer and longer, and his teeth got big and sharp. He walked through the fog and found his first victim, a poor old man happily smoking his pipe and raking leaves. The old guy didn't stand a chance against the powerful Wolf Man.

## No te quedes dormido

ACABABAMOS DE VER LA PELÍCULA de *El hombre lobo* y estaba acostado en la obscuridad con mi gemelo Nando y con nuestras hermanas Ana, la Chata y Martha. Estábamos acostados en la sala, en los colchones de algodón del ejército. Ana y la Chata eran las más grandes y estaban en la preparatoria. Habían dejado que Nando y yo nos quedáramos con ellas, a ver la película de terror de los viernes en la tele. Nando y yo estábamos muy emocionados. Nos podíamos quedar despiertos hasta tarde, comer palomitas de maíz, tomar refresco y ver una película que no empezaba hasta las nueve de la noche.

Estaba terriblemente obscuro y muy silencioso cuando ya nos íbamos a dormir. Miré alrededor de la sala y luego a la cocina ¡Ay Dios mío, ahí estaba! Podía ver la silueta del hombre lobo, alumbrada con la tenue luz de la luna. Estaba esperando a que me quedara dormido para llevar a cabo su plan y atraparme. Él había sido atacado y mordido por un lobo y había sido maldecido a convertirse en el hombre lobo. Lo vi convertirse en el monstruo que era mitad lobo y mitad hombre. No quería convertirse en hombre lobo pero esa era la maldición. Durante la luna llena, el pelo de la cara, los brazos y las piernas crecía más y más largo, y sus dientes crecían y se hacían más filosos. Caminó entre la neblina y encontró su primera víctima, un pobre hombre viejo que estaba fumando su pipa contento mientras barría las hojas del árbol. El pobre hombre no tenía escapatoria del poderoso hombre lobo.

*PROFILE / PERFIL*

Carolyn's back was to me. I scooted closer and turned, putting my back against hers. She was hot, but I was hotter, especially with the blankets over me. Even so I kept my back, butt, and legs up against her.

She shifted half-asleep, "Back off," she said.

"I'm scared," I whispered. "I think he's in the kitchen."

"Who?"

"The Wolf Man."

"No he's not, *cuatito*. There's no such thing, now go to sleep," she said as she reached back and patted my hip. She pulled away. I heard deep breathing coming from my other sisters. They were lucky to be sleeping. I wished I could. I peered out from under my blankets. He was still in there. And he wasn't happy about my telling on him. I wanted to say I was sorry, but it'd only make things worse for me.

I broke out in a sweat and wanted to pull off the covers, but moving around might trigger his attack all the sooner. And me being exposed, he'd be able to tear straight into my skin. At least the covers protected me a little. My only hope was to scream when he came for me, then Carolyn would yank me back from him and we'd all fight him off until Pa came running down the hall to save us. No one was stronger or braver than our Pa.

I looked toward the kitchen. *Hijo!* He had sneaked behind the door and was peeking at me through the crack between the door and hinges. I had to do something. I tapped my sister's back.

"Carolyn," I whispered. "Carolyn."

La Chata me estaba dando la espalda. Yo me acerque más y puse mi espalda en contra de la suya. Junto a ella sentí mucho más calor, especialmente porque tenía completamente de bajo de mí la cobija. Aun así, mantuve mi espalda, trasero y piernas junto a ella.

Ella se movió medió dormida y dijo "Hazte para atrás".

"Tengo miedo", le murmuré. "Creo que está en la cocina".

"¿Quién?"

"El hombre lobo".

"No, no está cuatito. No existe algo así, ahora duérmete". La Chata se estiró hacia atrás y me dio una palmadita en la cadera. Se apartó de mí. Escuché la respiración rítmica de mis otros hermanos. Tenían suerte de estar dormidos. Yo deseé poder dormirme. Espié por debajo de mis cobijas. Él seguía ahí. Y no estaba nada contento de que lo había acusado. Le quería decir que lo sentía, pero eso haría las cosas peor para mí.

Empecé a sudar y quería quitarme las cobijas, pero el movimiento iba a causar su ataque más rápido. Y si estaba expuesto, él podría desgarrar mi piel. Al menos las cobijas me protegían, aunque era poca protección. Mi única esperanza era gritar cuando viniera por mí, entonces la Chata me jalaría de sus garras y así todos pelearíamos con él hasta que mi papá viniera corriendo por el pasillo para salvarnos a todos. No había nadie tan fuerte como mi papá.

Miré hacia la cocina ¡Híjole! Se había escondido detrás de la puerta y a través del espacio creado por las bisagras me estaba viendo. Tenía que hacer algo. Le toqué la espalda a mi hermana.

"Chata," le murmuré. "Oyé, Chata".

*PROFILE / PERFIL*

"Ayyy, what do you want?"

"Can I sleep between you and Ana?"

"I don't care, just settle down!"

I sprang to my knees and rolled over her, dragging my blanket with me, and landed between the two.

"Ayyy, what are you doing?" Ana said.

"Nothing," I said softly, covering myself with the blanket. I was safe at last. But it didn't take but a minute to realize that it was much hotter between my sisters. At least I couldn't see over their bodies into the kitchen. I lay quietly sweating and listening for the Wolf Man to come around from behind the door.

Somebody shuffling blankets broke the silence. Then I heard Ferd whisper, "Martha, Martha."

"Whaat?!"

"I'm scared."

"Go to sleep! I told you, Carolyn. We shouldn't have let them see the stupid movie!"

My good luck; Ferd and Martha had drawn the Wolf Man's attention away from me.

I felt something against my cheek and put my hand to it. It was a piece of popcorn. I stealthily picked it up and sneaked it into my mouth. I didn't dare chew it. The crunching would draw the Wolf Man's attention back to me. The popcorn had salt and butter and tasted good. It slowly dissolved in my mouth, and I slowly dissolved into sleep.

"¡Ayyy! ¿Qué quieres?"

"¿Puedo dormir en medio de ti y Ana?"

"¡Está bien, nomás quédate quieto!"

Me arrodillé de un brinco, rodé pasando sobre su cuerpo y me metí entre las dos mientras que jalaba mi cobija.

"¡Ayyy! ¿Qué estás haciendo?" dijo Ana.

"Nada", dije suavemente, mientras me cubría con la cobija. Al fin estaba seguro. Pero ni siquiera me toma un minuto para darme cuenta que hacía mucho más calor al estar entre las dos. Al menos sus cuerpos me tapaban la vista para ver qué había en la cocina. Me quedé bien quieto sudando y escuchando para ver si el hombre lobo que estaba detrás de la puerta venía por mí.

Alguien rompió el silencio al mover las cobijas. Entonces escuché a Nando murmurar, "Martha, Martha".

"¿Qué?"

"Tengo miedo".

"¡Vete a dormir! ¡Te dije Chata que no los deberíamos de haber dejado ver la estúpida película!"

Para mi buena suerte, Nando y Martha habían desviado la atención del hombre lobo lejos de mí.

Sentí algo en contra de mi mejilla y lo toqué con mi mano. Era una palomita de maíz. Con cautela la removí y me la comí rápidamente. Ni siquiera traté de masticarla. Lo crujiente atraería al hombre lobo hacia mí. La palomita sabía rico con el sabor de la sal y la mantequilla. Despacio se disolvió en mi boca y despacio me disolví en el sueño.

*PROFILE / PERFIL*

# *Chato's* Steal

In spring, Christ and baseball are risen. I never understood the importance of this hallowed sport until the day that my father voluntarily came out of the house and squatted like an umpire to call balls and strikes for my twin brother and me. We had signed up for Saint Rita's Grammar School baseball team and were practicing for tryouts. My father! The same man who never did much more than smoke cigarettes and drink beer when he wasn't eating, watching sports on television, or sleeping before working the graveyard shift at the trucking company from midnight to eight in the morning delivering freight. But he gave up his precious free time to coach us on playing baseball.

We made the team and got real uniforms. I put mine on and gazed at myself in the mirror. I looked just like a major leaguer! Pa drove us to practices and never missed a game. It became a part of our routine, like going to church on Sundays, except that Ma and my sisters weren't involved. They only heard about our coaches and teammates, and descriptions of the games that we always seemed to lose.

"It's only a game," Martha, one of my older sisters, said. But what did she know about competition?

*STORIES / CUENTOS*

## *El robo del Chato*

En la primavera, Cristo y el béisbol resucitan. Nunca entendí ese deporte tan reverenciado hasta que un día mi papá voluntariamente salió de la casa y se puso como ampáyer en cuclillas y empezó a dirigir a mi gemelo y a mí con las bolas y los strikes. Nos habíamos apuntado para las pruebas del equipo de béisbol de la Escuela Primaria Santa Rita y estábamos practicando. ¡Mi padre! El mismo hombre que nunca hizo más que fumar y tomar cerveza cuando no estaba comiendo, viendo deportes en la televisión, o durmiendo antes de trabajar el turno de la medianoche hasta las ocho de la mañana entregando carga para la compañía de camiones en la que trabajaba. Pero el dio su precioso tiempo de descanso para entrenarnos en béisbol.

Pasamos la prueba y nos hicimos parte del equipo y nos dieron uniformes de verdad. Yo me puse el mío y me contemplé en el espejo. ¡Me veía como alguien de la liga mayor! Mi papá nos llevaba a las prácticas y nunca se perdió un juego. Llegó a ser parte de nuestra rutina, como ir a misa todos los domingos. Con la excepción de mi mamá y mis hermanas que nunca iban a los juegos. Nada más escuchaban acerca de los entrenadores y los compañeros del juego y la descripción de los juegos, que parecía siempre perdíamos.

"Es solamente un juego", dijo Martha, una de mis hermanas más grandes. ¿Pero qué sabía ella de la competencia?

*PROFILE / PERFIL*

"Duck when a pitch is close. It can make an inside strike look like a ball," Pa yelled from the pitcher's mound he constructed in the backyard. "Ready? Here it comes. Oh jeeze, you're 'stepping in the bucket. You're backing away because you're afraid of getting hit by the ball. Don't be afraid. Stand closer to the plate and swing, *Chato.*" Chato. I hated that name. It was a Spanish term referencing a person's nose. I fell and broke it when I was little, and it remained a bit disfigured.

"It's okay to have that name," Pa explained. "In Mexico people call each other names like that all the time and think nothing of it. There was a man with one leg when I was kid in Mazatlán. Know what everybody called him?" Ferd and I shrugged our shoulders. "*Mocho*, Stump!" Ferd and I snickered.

"And I knew a man who had to have one of his balls cut off because it had cancer. We called him '*huevo,*' egg!" Ferd and I busted out laughing. "The gringos are ready to fight you if you find something unusual about them and then give 'em a nickname around it. Mexicans don't get mad. It's your street name and makes you one of the guys."

"I wasn't born in Mexico," I told Ferd when we lay in our bunk beds that night. "I still hate being called Chato." Pa called Ferd *"El Abuzado,"* the smart one. Ferd, a little bigger and stronger than me, outdid me at most everything: wrestling, running, even school work. But at baseball we were close to equals.

## STORIES / CUENTOS

"Agáchate cuando el lanzamiento está cerca. Puede ser que un strike parezca como una bola". Mi papá gritaba desde la loma de lanzamiento que él había hecho en el patio de atrás de la casa "¿Listo? Aquí va. Vamos, estás pisando en la cubeta. Te estás echando para atrás porque tienes miedo de que te pegue la pelota. No tengas miedo. Párate cerca del plato y batea, Chato". Chato, yo odiaba mi apodo. Era un apodo que se refería a la nariz. Cuando era chico me caí, la nariz se me quebró y me quedo un poco desfigurada.

"Está bien tener ese apodo", explicó mi papá. "En México la gente usa apodos todo el tiempo y no se ofenden por eso". Cuando yo era niño, en Mazatlán había un señor con una sola pierna en Mazatlán. ¿Saben cómo le decían?" Nando y yo nos encogimos los hombros. "¡Cojo mocho!" Nando y yo nos reímos.

"Y también conocí a un señor al que le tuvieron que cortar un testículo porque tenía cáncer. ¡Le decíamos el huevo!" Nando y yo explotamos a carcajadas. "Los gringos se ofenden y están listos para la pelea, si le ponen un apodo que no le gustan. Los mexicanos no se ofenden. Es el nombre de tu calle y te hace ser parte del grupo de muchachos".

"Yo no nací en México", le dije a Nando esa noche cuando estábamos acostados en nuestras literas. "Aún odio cuando me dicen Chato". Mi papá le decía a Nando "El Abusado". Nando era un poco más alto que yo y era más fuerte. Me ganaba en casi todo: luchas, carreras, hasta en las tareas de la escuela. Pero en el béisbol, estábamos casi parejos.

*PROFILE / PERFIL*

This was our team's rookie season, and it showed. Our coaches couldn't keep us from fooling around at practices. And once our manager, Mr. Rodriquez, was warming us up before a game by hitting ground balls to the infielders. He smacked a smoker to his son, Cruz, who was playing second base. The ball took a bad hop and hit him in the mouth. Cruz wailed as his father carried him off the field. We found chunks of his teeth lying on the ground by his position. He came to our next practice with a set of gleaming silver front teeth that reflected the sun.

We lost one game after another. I was bored in left field once and started making designs in the dirt with my cleats. I heard people screaming as the ball sped between my feet. I ran to the fence, picked it up, and threw it hard to the infielders. The batter got a triple and cleared the bases. If I'd been on my toes, he'd gotten a single and only one man would've scored.

"What the hell were you doing out there, Chato?" Pa said on our drive home. "You weren't paying attention to the damn game!" I sat quietly in the car looking down at the floor. "Not paying attention." It's what my teachers were always telling me.

We became the "doormats" of the league. St. Didicus got the best of us. St. Agnes pounded us. St. Anthony's gave us a holy beating, scoring 13 runs to our 3. Our coach, Mr. Aguilar, sat us in the dugout after that one.

Esa temporada era la primera para nuestro equipo y era obvio. Nuestros entrenadores no podían detener nuestros errores durante las prácticas. Una vez el gerente, el Señor Rodríguez, nos estaba calentado antes de un juego lanzando pelotas al suelo hacia los del campo. Le lanzó con fuerza una pelota a su hijo Cruz, quien estaba jugando en la segunda base. Al rebotar la pelota golpeó la boca de Cruz. Cruz gritaba llorando de dolor mientras que su padre lo llevaba cargando afuera del campo. Encontramos pedazos de sus dientes en el área donde él estaba jugando. Llegó a la siguiente práctica con un juego de dientes frontales de plata nuevos que reflejaban el sol.

Perdíamos juego tras juego. Yo me aburría mucho en mi posición de campo izquierdo y empecé a hacer diseños en la tierra con mis zapatos. Escuché a la gente gritar cuando la pelota pasó rodando entre mis pies. Corrí a la barda, la agarré y la lancé con fuerza a los de las otras bases. El bateador hizo un triple y limpió las bases. Si solamente hubiera estado atento, hubiera hecho un out y solamente un jugador hubiera llegado a home.

"¿Qué diablos estabas haciendo allá Chato?", me preguntó mi papá mientras manejaba a casa ¡No le estabas poniendo nada de atención al maldito juego!". Me quedé sentado, callado y mirando hacia el suelo. "No pones atención". Es lo que mis maestras siempre me estaban diciendo.

Nos convertimos en los "perdedores" de la liga. San Dídacus se llevó lo mejor de nosotros. Santa Agnes nos ganó. San Antonio nos dio una buena paliza, con resultados de 13 carreras y nosotros 3. Nuestro entrenador, el Señor Aguilar, nos sentó a todos después de ese juego.

*PROFILE / PERFIL*

"You guys couldn't beat a troop of girl scouts! You're playing like dead men out there! It's a goddamn embarrassment!"

Word got around the parish of his outburst and Monsignor Gallagher, the pastor, had a talk with Mr. Aguilar. "Now, Ramon, you mustn't set a bad example for these lads just because you've lost a few games."

Our team rose from the dead for one glorious moment. It was the final game of the season. Pa sat on the slope overlooking the field, where he got a better view than did the people who sat in the bleachers below. We went into the bottom of the last inning actually tied at three runs with Saint Jude's. There were two outs when I got my ups. I worked the count full, three balls and two strikes. The next pitch barely caught the inside of the plate, but I ducked away and fooled the umpire.

"Ball four!" he yelled. "Take your base batter." It should've been strike three and the end of the game. I jogged to first hiding my smile. I didn't dare let their pitcher, Frankie Santana, see me. I could feel his scowl. I was afraid of him. He was big for his age and was always picking on kids smaller than him. He threw rocks at me once on my way home from school. All I could do was run scared.

Pete Piedras, my closest friend on the team, came up next. He was our best player. He could hit, catch fly balls, snag grounders, and throw hard with accuracy. He hit a single and advanced me to second.

"¡Ustedes no podrían ganarle ni a un equipo de niñas! ¡Están jugando como si estuvieran muertos! ¡Es una pinche vergüenza!"

Por toda la parroquia se supo cómo explotó y Monseñor Gallagher, el Pastor, tuvo que hablar con el Señor Aguilar. "Vamos Ramón, no puedes poner el mal ejemplo entre estos muchachos simplemente porque han perdido unos cuantos juegos".

Nuestro equipo resucitó de la muerte por un glorioso momento. Era el juego final de la temporada. Mi papá se sentó en la loma viendo hacia la cancha, donde tenía una mejor vista que la gente que se sentaba abajo en las bancas. Al final de la última entrada, estábamos empatados con tres carreras con San Judas. Había dos outs cuando me tocó batear. Llegué a tres bolas y dos strikes. El siguiente tiro apenas llegó hacia dentro del plato pero yo me agaché y engañé al ampáyer.

"¡Cuarta bola!" Gritó. "Vete a la primera base". Debería de haber sido el tercer strike y el final del juego. Yo me emocioné escondiendo una sonrisa. No me atreví a dejar que el lanzador, Frankie Santana, me viera. Era grande para su edad y siempre estaba molestando a los más chicos que él. Podía sentir en mí su mirada fuerte. Una vez a la salida de la escuela, caminé a mi casa y Frankie me aventó piedras. Lo único que pude hacer fue correr espantado.

Pedro Piedras era mi mejor amigo y estábamos juntos en el equipo. Él era nuestro mejor jugador. Podía batear, volar pelotas y tirar fuerte con certeza. Con un tiro directo me avanzó a la segunda base.

*PROFILE / PERFIL*

Then scrawny little Felipe, whom we called *Perrito*, came to bat. It was a given that he'd be the final out of the game. He reached base only three times all year, and two of those came by way of throwing errors. Perrito was a bonafide "strikeout King." Everyone knew it including Frankie, who fired his first pitch over the plate.

"S-t-e-e-r-i-k-e one," the umpire yelled raising his arm. I stole third base and didn't even draw a throw from the catcher, Eddie. Eddie was one of Frankie's cronies.

Eddie wasn't paying attention to me and threw the ball back to Frankie. The strategy was obvious: "strike out the little *pendejo*." Frankie sneered and aimed his next pitch, a screaming fastball, right at Perrito. Perrito flung out of the batter's box and fell to the ground. His batting helmet went tumbling up the third base line.

"Back in the batter's box, son," the umpire said. Frankie's plan worked. Perrito got back into the box but stood as far away from home plate as possible, leaving it a wide-open target. He raised his bat into the air, trembling with fear.

Coach curled his fingers through the chain-link fencing of the dugout. He looked at the ground and shifted the dirt with his toe, waiting for the inevitable end of a miserable season for a bunch of rookies. The best he could hope for was to tie one lousy game.

I took a long lead from third and could have easily been thrown out, but Frankie threw the ball hard to the plate. Dust exploded from the catcher's mitt.

"S-t-e-e-r-i-k-e two!"

Entonces le tocó batear al flaquito Felipe, le decíamos "El Perrito", era su apodo. Estaba decidido que le tocaría hacer el out final. Durante todo el año, nada más llego a una base en tres ocasiones y dos de esas ocasiones fue porque hubo tiros erróneos. Se sabía que "El Perrito" era "el rey de los outs". Todo el mundo lo sabía, incluyendo a Frankie, quien lanzó su primer tiro sobre el plato.

"S-t-r-i-k-e", grito el ampáyer levantando su brazo. Yo robé la tercera base porque Eddie, el cácher, no me estaba poniendo atención. Eddie era el títere de Frankie.

Eddie ni siquiera estaba poniendo atención a lo que yo hacía y le lanzó la pelota a Frankie. La estrategia era obvia: "hacer un *strike* al menso". Frankie sonrió y tiró la pelota directamente a "El Perrito". "El Perrito" voló fuera del plato y cayó al suelo. Su casco rodó hacia la línea del tercera base.

"Regrésate a la caja del bateador hijo", dijo el ampáyer. El plan de Frankie funcionó. "El Perrito" se regresó a la caja pero se mantuvo alejado del plato de *home*, dejándola completamente abierta para un ataque. Levantó su bate en el aire temblando de miedo.

El entrenador enroscó los dedos en el alambre de la reja que lo separaba de la base. Miró hacia el suelo y movió la tierra con su pie, esperando por un empate en este mal juego en ese inevitable fin de una temporada de pérdidas.

Yo aproveché la tercera base y fácilmente me podrían haber hecho un *out*, pero Frankie lanzó con fuerza la pelota sobre el plato. El polvo explotó en el guante del cácher.

"¡Segundo s-t-r-i-k-e!"

## PROFILE / PERFIL

"Frankie's going in for the kill," I thought. Then it hit me. No one was paying attention to me. What if I tried stealing home? The catcher smiled wickedly as he brought his arm forward throwing the ball to Frankie for the final strike. *Now! Now! Now!* screamed a voice in my head. I broke for home. By the time Eddie noticed me it was too late; the ball was out of his hand and on its way to Frankie. Eddie jumped to his feet and landed between home plate and me. I slid feet first with my eyes closed. Eddie stretched his mitt high over his head reaching for Frankie's frantic throw. My cleats collided with Eddie's. His body flew sideways and landed on mine. The momentum took us both sliding over the plate. Everyone sprang to their feet, craning their necks witnessing the collision at home.

Did he catch the ball? Was I out? I opened my eyes to see through a cloud of dust the umpire bent over with his arms outstretched like a bird on the wing.

"S-a-a-a-f-e!"

Safe? Safe? I was raised from the earth as coach set me on his shoulder. Screams and cheers filled the air. He put me down to the back-slapping and head-slapping and shoving of my teammates. Frankie slammed his mitt to the ground. His lower lip quavered in anger and frustration.

I looked at him and narrowed my eyes. "I got you, *carbon*," I said softly.

Pa laughed and patted me on the knee several times on the drive home. "That was heads up ball, *Mijo*. That was heads up ball." He stopped at a liquor store for a can of ale and bought Ferd and me candy bars.

"Frankie iba al mate", pensé. Entonces me decidí. Nadie me estaba haciendo caso. ¿Qué tal si trato de robar el plato de home? ¡Ya! ¡Ya! ¡Ya! Gritó una voz dentro de mi cabeza. Corrí al plato. Cuando Eddie se dio cuenta, ya era muy tarde; la pelota estaba fuera de su mano y en camino a Frankie. Eddie brincó entre el plato y yo. Yo me deslicé con los pies primero y con los ojos cerrados. Eddie estiró su guante tan arriba como pudo esperando furioso el tiro de Frankie. Mis zapatos chocaron con los zapatos de Eddie. Su cuerpo voló de lado y cayó sobre mí. El episodio nos deslizó juntos sobre al plato. Todo el mundo se levantó a ver el resultado. Estirando el cuello para ser testigos del choque.

¿Agarró la pelota? ¿Fue out? Abrí mis ojos para sólo verme en medio de una nube de polvo. El ampáyer estaba agachado con los brazos estirados como un pájaro volando.

"¡Seif!"

¿Seif? ¿Seif? El entrenador me levanté de la tierra para cargarme en sus hombros. Gritos y porras llenaron el ambiente. Cuando me bajó me dio la rutinaria palmadita en la espalda y en la cabeza, mientras que empujaba a los demás chavos. Frankie aventó su guante al suelo. Su labio superior temblaba de rabia y frustración.

Yo lo miré intensamente. "Te agarre, cabrón", dije suavemente.

Mi apá se rio y me palmeó la rodilla varias veces mientras que manejaba camino a la casa. "Hiciste muy bien mijo, hiciste muy bien". Se detuvo en la licorería a comprarse una cerveza y a Nando y a mí nos compró dulces.

*PROFILE / PERFIL*

Later that afternoon I was sitting on the back porch with my little neighbor, Chris. I dropped my pants, showed him the large red burn on my hip from the slide home.

"It's what baseball players call a 'strawberry,'" I said proudly.

I heard Pa talking excitedly to Ma and my aunt and uncle in the house.

"And then he made for home and slid over the plate, and ha, ha, ha, he knocked the ball out of the catcher's mitt! And Armando won the game! Our Armando won the game!"

Esa tarde estaba sentado con mi vecinito Chris en el patio de atrás de la casa. Me bajé los pantalones y le enseñé el gran moretón que tenía en la cadera debido al robo de home que había hecho más temprano.

"Es lo que los beisbolistas llaman una 'fresa'", le dije con orgullo.

Mientras escuché a mi apá, dentro de la casa, que estaba diciéndole a mi amá, mi tía y mi tío, estaba muy contento.

¡Entonces se tiró al plato de home y se deslizó sobre el plato, y ja, ja, ja, se le cayó la pelota al cácher del guante! ¡Y Armando ganó el juego! ¡Nuestro Armando ganó el juego!".

*PROFILE / PERFIL*

# Voice Behind the Wall

My older brother, Tony, took me to meet a woman who lived behind a wall. He drove me after my Little League baseball practice to a neighborhood where hardly any houses needed painting and the lawns were green and mowed, the shrubs neatly trimmed.

"She lives up there," Tony said, pointing to the top of a hill where an old three-story house stood. It had long green fingers of ivy crawling up its walls and huge trees that kept it in shade. It reminded me of a house I'd seen in a Dracula movie.

"What does she do?" I asked.

"You'll see," he said, looking over his shoulder at me as we scaled the concrete stairs leading to the house.

"Will I be able to see her?" I asked, panting a little as we climbed the steps.

"No."

"Can't I just go back down and wait for you in the car?"

"No! Now keep going!"

I, like my Ma, Pa, and the rest of the family, had complete faith in Tony. He was in his fourth year studying to be a priest at Immaculate Heart Seminary in San Diego where we lived, but this time he was stretching the limits of my trust.

Why would he think that I'd want to meet some strange woman who lived behind a wall? And what if she had a way of snatching kids?

*STORIES / CUENTOS*

# La voz detrás de la pared

Toño, mi hermano más grande, me llevó a conocer a una mujer que vivía detrás de una pared. Después de la práctica de la liga de béisbol me llevó a un barrio donde las casas no necesitaban pintarse, el pasto estaba todo verde y parejo y los arbustos estaban bien cortados.

"Ella vive allá", dijo Toño mientras señalaba hacia la vieja casa de tres pisos en la punta de la colina. La casa tenía largos dedos verdes de hiedra que habían gateado por las paredes y árboles grandes que le hacían sombra a la casa. Me recordaba una casa que había visto en una película de Drácula.

"¿En qué trabaja?", le pregunté.

"Vas a ver", me dijo mirándome por encima del hombro mientras subíamos las escaleras de concreto que nos llevaban a la casa.

"¿La vamos a poder ver?", pregunté, jadeando un poco mientras subíamos las escaleras.

"No."

"¿Por qué no me regreso al carro y te espero ahí?"

Yo, como mi mamá, papá, y el resto de la familia, teníamos la fe completa en Toño. Él estaba en el cuarto año de sacerdocio en el Seminario del Corazón Inmaculado de San Diego, donde vivíamos. Pero en esta ocasión estaba sobrepasando los límites de mi confianza.

¿Por qué pensaría que yo quería conocer a una extraña mujer que vivía detrás de una pared? ¿Y qué tal si tenía la práctica de robarse a los niños?

*PROFILE / PERFIL*

"Will I be able to see her?"

"No, I told you! Now don't be afraid."

When we reached the porch, Tony grabbed the worn brass knocker and banged it against the door. I tried to take his hand, but he brushed mine away. I could hear faint shuffling inside as someone neared. The doorknob turned. The door opened with a creak. A thin, wrinkled woman dressed in a black nun's habit peered at us through a set of thick wire-rimmed glasses. She nodded at Tony, then with her bony finger, signaled us in. I followed Tony inside.

It took a moment for my eyes to adjust to the dimness in the entry hall. The old woman closed the door behind us. It echoed through the cavernous room.

"Sister Theresa," Tony said.

The old woman nodded, then walked across the room and disappeared out a door on the opposite side. I noticed a wooden cylinder the size of a small barrel that was constructed into the wall. Tony pointed to a chair by the cylinder. "Sit there," he said.

The room smelled musty, reminding me of the time my twin and I had crawled under our house, and everything, even the dirt, smelled old.

The wooden benches, chairs, and a tall chest of drawers gleamed. On the walls down the darkened hallway were rows of painted portraits of saints. It was still and calm like the sanctuary of my church, where I served Mass as an altar boy during the sunrise service.

I had brought my mitt with me and pressed it with both hands against my chest.

"¿La vamos a poder ver?"

"¡No, ya te dije! ¡Vamos! No tengas miedo".

Cuando llegamos al portal, Toño tomó la aldaba de cobre y tocó la puerta. Traté de agarrarlo de la mano, pero él me soltó bruscamente. Yo podía escuchar un movimiento tenue del otro lado. La manija de la puerta giró para ser abierta. La puerta se abrió con un rechinido. Una mujer delgada y arrugada, vestida en un hábito negro, nos observó detrás de unos lentes gruesos. Con una señal de la cabeza y con sus dedos largos y delgados, nos invitó a pasar. Yo seguí a Toño hacia adentro.

Me tomó un momento adaptar mis ojos a la obscuridad del recibidor. La mujer cerró la puerta detrás de nosotros. Haciendo eco en el cuarto cavernoso.

"Hermana Teresa," dijo Toño.

La mujer señaló con la cabeza, entonces caminó a través del cuarto y desapareció por una puerta ubicada al lado opuesto. Me di cuenta que en la pared había un cilindro incrustado hecho de madera, del mismo tamaño de un barril pequeño. Toño señaló hacia una silla junto al cilindro. "Siéntate ahí", me dij.

El cuarto olía a moho, me recordó el día que mi gemelo y yo nos metimos debajo de la casa y todo, incluyendo la tierra, olía a viejo.

Había un brillo en el armario alto, en las bancas y en las sillas de madera. En las paredes que conducían hacia el obscuro pasillo, había hileras de pinturas de santos. Estaba todo tan quieto y callado como el santuario de la iglesia, donde trabajaba como monaguillo durante la misa de la alborada.

Yo había traído mi guante de béisbol y lo apretaba fuertemente con ambas manos en contra de mi pecho.

*PROFILE / PERFIL*

It was the only thing that offered a sense of familiarity and comfort. The glove still had a new reddish-tan look, though I had used it all season and it was close to being broken in. I heard something move behind the wall next to me and pulled away.

"Sister Theresa?" Tony asked.

*What in the heck is he doing?* I wondered. *This is getting weird.*

"Hello!" said a woman's voice. "How are you, Antonio?"

*Holy smokes, there's a woman trapped behind the wall!*

"Doing fine, Sister. I know it's close to time for your midafternoon prayers. I thought I'd stop by for a quick visit."

*He's talking to a nun behind the wall!* I remembered a woman who had screamed at me when I hit a baseball through her window last year. I never saw her face, though she must have been ugly from the way her deep and raspy voice sounded. Maybe this nun was ugly and didn't want anybody to see her.

"Who have you and the sisters been praying for lately?" Tony said.

"The early morning Matin session was dedicated to death row prisoners and single mothers, the midmorning Prime was offered for the mentally ill and their families. The Laud will be devoted to peace in the Middle East, and we get so many prayer requests from people who drop in with personal petitions."

Era la única cosa que me ofrecía un sentimiento de familiaridad y comodidad. El guante tenía todavía el color café rojizo, como si aún fuera nuevo, a pesar de que lo había usado toda la temporada aunque todavía se veía y sentía como nuevo. Escuche que algo se movió en la pared detrás de mí y me alejé.

"¿Hermana Teresa?", preguntó Toño.

¿Qué demonios está haciendo? Me pregunté. Esto se está poniendo extraño.

"¡Hola!" Sonó la voz de la mujer. "¿Cómo estás Antonio?"

¡Bendito cielo, hay una monja atrapada detrás de la pared!

"Estoy bien Hermana. Sé que es tiempo de sus oraciones de la media tarde. Y decidí pasar a saludarla un momentito".

¡Está hablando con una monja que está atrapada detrás de la pared! Me acordé que el año pasado una mujer me había gritado cuando le pegué a una pelota de béisbol y rompió su ventana. No vi su cara pero me imagine que estaba bien fea por lo profunda y rasposa que sonó su voz. Quizás esta monja estaba muy fea y no quería que nadie la viera.

"¿Por quién han estado usted y sus hermanas orando últimamente?", preguntó Toño.

"La sesión de la mañana temprano fue dedicada a los que estaban destinados a la pena de muerte y a las madres solteras. La de la media mañana fue dedicada a los enfermos mentales y a sus familiares. La alabanza será dedicada para la paz en el Medio Oriente, también tenemos muchas peticiones personales de gente que viene aquí".

*PROFILE / PERFIL*

She sounded sad. "One poor soul asked us to pray for her son who had recently taken his own life."

"I know you are a busy group, Sister. By the way, Mrs. Grenno's cancer is in remission. I think your prayers had something to do with it. Sister Theresa, I brought one of my brothers, Armando, to meet you."

I cringed at the sound of my name. It was okay listening to my brother talk with this nun, but now I'd have to say something.

"Wonderful!" Her voice sounded excited.

I leaned further back.

"I'm so pleased to meet you!" she said. "How old are you?"

"Ten," I said, barely loud enough to be heard.

"I have a ten-year-old nephew. He's in the fifth grade. Are you in the fifth?"

"Yes, ma'am."

"Where do you go to school?"

"St. Rita's Grammar School, ma'am."

"Oh my! The School Sisters of Notre Dame teach there, right?"

"Yes, ma'am."

"I understand they're a bit strict. Do you find them that way?"

"Sometimes, um, what's your room like?"

"Excuse me?

"Your bedroom, what's it like?"

Se escuchaba triste. "Una pobre alma vino a pedir que rezáramos por el alma de su hijo que se había quitado su propia vida".

"Hermana, sé que son un grupo muy ocupado. Le quiero decir que el cáncer de la Señora Grenno está en remisión. Pienso que sus oraciones han tenido que ver mucho en su mejoría. Hermana Teresa, he traído a uno de mis hermanos, Armando, a conocerla".

Sentí que me encogía con el sonido de mi nombre. Estaba bien mientras que mi hermano y la monja platicaban, pero ahora yo tenía que decir algo.

"¡Qué hermoso!" Su voz sonó emocionada.

Yo me hize más para atrás.

"¡Estoy muy contenta de conocerte!", dijo ella. "¿Cuántos años tienes?".

"Diez", le dije, apenas lo suficientemente fuerte para que me escuchara.

"Yo tengo un sobrino que tiene diez años. Está en quinto año. ¿Estás en quinto año?"

"Así es Madre".

"¿A qué escuela vas?".

"A la escuela primaria de Santa Rita, Hermana".

"¡Ya veo! ¿La Orden de las Hermanas de Notre Dame enzeñan ahi verdad?"

"Si, Hermana."

"Entiendo que son un poco estrictas. ¿Tú crees que lo son?".

"Algunas veces, mmm ¿Cómo es su cuarto?".

"¿Disculpa?".

"Su cuarto ¿cómo es?".

*PROFILE / PERFIL*

"Well, there's not much. I have a crucifix hanging on the wall, a cot, and a small chest of drawers. I need little space for clothes, since I am given only two habits; one to wear while I the launder other. There's a table with a pen and paper, a chair, and my prayer book."

"Do you pray a lot?"

I heard her chuckle softly.

"I guess you could say that. Everything we do is prayer. The many jobs and tasks we perform are done for the glory of God, like when we bake the unleavened bread that is made into the communion wafers you take in church. We also have formal group prayer sessions from early morning into the late hours."

"Do you pray more than my mother?"

She laughed. I didn't understand what was so funny about my question?

"Well, I don't know. That's a good question. Maybe not! Your brother tells me your mother is good at praying. How about you? What do you like to do? Do you play sports?"

I sat up. "Yeah! I play baseball!"

"I love baseball. Do you play for a team?"

"My school. I pitch, catch, play right field, and second base."

"Wow, a good utility player. That's great!"

"Sister Theresa, he brought his mitt," Tony said.

"I'd love to see it if it's okay with you."

"Sure, I'd really like to show it to you. But how do I get in?"

"Bueno, no hay mucho. Tengo un crucifijo colgado en la pared, un camastro y un pequeño armario con cajones. Necesito muy poco espacio para mi ropa, porque nada más nos dan dos hábitos. Uno para usar mientras que lavo el otro. Hay una mesa con una pluma y papel, una silla y mi libro de oraciones".

"¿Usted reza mucho?".

Escuché una sonrisa callada.

"Creo que adivinas bien. Todo lo que hacemos es rezar. Todos los oficios y el trabajo que hacemos es para la gloria de Dios, como cuando horneamos el pan sin levadura que después se usa para la hostia que tú tomas en la iglesia. También tenemos grupos formales de oraciones desde muy temprano en la mañana hasta las altas horas de la noche".

"¿Usted reza más que mi mamá?"

Se rio. ¿No entendí que tenía mi pregunta de graciosa?

"Bueno no sé. Esa es una buena pregunta ¡Quizás no! Tu hermano me dice que tu mamá es muy buena para la oración. ¿Qué tal tú? ¿Qué es lo que te gusta hacer? ¿Juegas deportes?".

Me senté derecho. "¡Sí! ¡Juego béisbol!".

"Adoro el béisbol ¿Juegas en un equipo?".

"En el de la escuela. Yo tiro, cacho, juego campo derecho y segunda base".

"¡Ah! Entonces tienes muchas posiciones. ¡Eso es genial!".

"Hermana Teresa, él trajo su guante", dijo Toño.

"Me encantaría verlo, si no hay problema".

"Seguro, me gustaría mucho enseñárselo. ¿Pero cómo entro?".

She and Tony laughed.

"You can't go in," Tony said. "Put your mitt in the turn."

"In the what?"

Tony pointed to the wooden cylinder. "In there."

I set the glove in the center of it, and Tony gave it a slight push. It spun almost silently to the other side. I tried to catch a glimpse of her as it spun, but the design didn't allow even a peek.

"It's a Wilson," she said, "good make. And it's nearly broken-in. Have you oiled it yet?"

"No, Sister."

"Wash it with saddle soap and warm water, then wipe it with a rag. Then rub in leather oil really well. It'll stay malleable and keep it from drying out. Dryness weakens the leather."

I could hear her slapping leather. She must have put on the glove and was hitting it with her fist like I do when waiting to catch a fly ball.

The cylinder spun back around with the mitt in it. "It's a good mitt," she said. "Take good care of it, okay?"

I picked it up and put it on to see if I could feel the warmth of her hand. I smelled it to see if I could catch her scent. I noticed that my mitt was shaped to be round.

"See how I formed it?" she asked.

"Yeah, how'd you get it like that?"

Ella y Toño se rieron.

"No puedes entrar", dijo Toño. "Pon tu guante en el cilindro".

"¿En el que?".

Toño señaló al cilindro de madera. "Ahí".

Puse el guante en el centro del cilindro y Toño le dio un ligero empujón. Se fue calladamente hacia el otro lado. Yo traté de mirarla aunque fuera un poquito mientras que el cilindro se movía. Pero el diseño no dejaba ver.

"Es un Wilson", dijo ella, "buena marca. Y ya casi está blando. ¿Le haz untado aceite?".

"No, Hermana".

"Lávalo con jabón de alforja y agua tibia, entonces sécalo con una toalla vieja. Después úntale bastante aceite para cuero. Se va a poner más maleable, esto le va a ayudar a que no se seque, ni se agriete y ni se haga duro. La sequedad debilita el cuero".

La podía escuchar pegándole al guante. De seguro se lo habrá puesto y le estaba pegando con el puño como le pego yo cuando estoy esperando una pelota.

El cilindro dio la vuelta de regreso y ahí venía el guante. "Es un buen guante", dijo ella. "Cuídalo mucho ¿Está bien?".

Lo recogí y me lo puse para ver si podía sentir el calor de su mano. Lo olí para ver si podía oler su aroma. Me di cuenta que mi guante estaba más redondo.

"¿Viste la forma que le di?" Me preguntó.

"Sí ¿Qué hizo para que se pusiera así?".

*PROFILE / PERFIL*

"I loosened the laces and brought the wrist strap over to the tightest setting, like you'd tighten your belt. It'll help your hand fit snugly, and it gives the mitt that fan shape. Put your two middle fingers into the last finger of the glove with your index finger and pinkie at rest on the outside. Now the chances of a hard-hit ball hitting and hurting your hand is much less likely. Hit the middle fingers of the glove with your fist and catch like that. The mitt will trap the ball."

I hit the middle fingers of my mitt with my fist, and it nearly snapped shut around my hand. "Cool! How'd you know to do all of that?"

"I played a lot of baseball with my brothers when growing up. I also played for school and city teams. I was an all-star. My team even went to the state finals two seasons in a row."

I looked at Tony amazed. I set my mitt on the floor, leaned forward in my chair and put my hands and cheek against the wall. I wanted to get closer to her.

"And promise me you won't throw a ball hard until you've warmed up your arm. I have a brother who was a great baseball player. He was being scouted for the majors. But once on a dare, he threw a rock as hard as he could at a bottle that was far away. His arm muscles weren't warmed up. Something snapped in his shoulder. He never threw well again. You must warm up before throwing hard, okay?"

"Yes, Sister, I sure will."

"Le aflojé las correas y moví la cuerda de la muñeca al ojal de más arriba, como cuando tú te amarras el cinturón. Te va a ayudar a que tu mano quepa mejor y le dé al guante la forma de un abanico. Pon tus dos dedos de en medio dentro del último dedo del guante y tu dedo meñique y el índice en los dos extremos. Ahora verás que cuando te pegue fuerte una pelota te va a doler mucho menos. Pégale a los dedos de en medio con el puño de tu otra mano y agarra la pelota así. El guante va a atrapar la pelota".

Le pegué a los dedos de en medio con mi puño y el guante prácticamente se abrazó a él. "¡Qué suave! ¿Cómo supo todo eso?".

"Yo jugué mucho béisbol con mis hermanos cuando estaba creciendo. También jugué con la escuela y los equipos de la ciudad. Yo fui una estrella. Hasta mi equipo fue a las finales del estado dos veces seguidas".

Miré a Toño con asombro. Puse mi guante en el suelo, me incliné hacia el frente de mi silla y puse mi mejilla y mis manos en contra de la pared. Quería estar más cerca de ella.

"Y prométeme que no vas a tirar una bola fuerte a menos que hayas calentado el brazo. Tengo un hermano que era un gran jugador de béisbol. Lo iban a  reclutar en las ligas mayores. Pero una vez, tratando de presumir su fuerza, lanzó una roca tan fuerte como pudo, a una botella que estaba bien lejos. Los músculos de su brazo no estaban calientes. Algo tronó en su hombro. Nunca pudo tirar bien otra vez. Siempre tienes que calentar el brazo antes de tirar fuerte, ¿Está bien?".

"Si, Hermana, lo haré".

"Very good."

Tony leaned toward the wall. "Sister, we have to go now," he said.

I looked at him disappointed. I wanted to stay longer and tell her about me stealing home and winning a game for my team, but I knew better than to question Tony.

"Thank you so much for the visit. Will you come again?"

"Yeah, Sister, I'd really like to."

"Wonderful. I'll look forward to it."

I was filled with questions for Tony as we walked down the hillside stairs.

"Will she live in there for the rest of her life? Can she see her family? Can she watch TV?"

At the car I realized that I had forgotten my mitt.

Tony sent me back to fetch it with strict warning not to disturb anyone. I made my way to the glove. My worn tennis shoes were as quiet as a pair of old socks on the shiny wooden floor.

"There it is," I whispered, seeing my mitt lying by the chair.

I grabbed it and walked back to the door. I carefully turned the doorknob and took a step out but stopped and looked back in from the threshold; one foot was in the peace-filled house, the other out in the echoing din of cars and trucks racing up and down the avenue below.

"Muy bien."

Toño se inclinó hacia la pared. "Hermana, ahora nos tenemos que ir" dijo.

Yo lo miré decepcionado. Me quería quedar más tiempo para platicarle cómo me había robado el plato de home y eso había ayudado a mi equipo a ganar el juego, pero yo sabía que lo mejor era no cuestionar las órdenes de Toño.

"Muchas gracias por tu visita. ¿Regresarás otra vez?".

"Si Hermana, me gustaría mucho regresar".

"Maravilloso. Te esperaré con gusto".

Yo estaba lleno de preguntas para Toño cuando bajamos las escaleras de la colina.

"¿Va a vivir ahí por el resto de su vida? ¿Puede ver a su familia? ¿Puede ver la televisión?"

En el carro me di cuenta que se me olvidó mi guante.

Toño me mandó a recogerlo con la amenaza estricta de no molestar a nadie. Llegué a donde estaba mi guante. Mis gastados tenis no eran tan callados como un par de calcetines sobre del piso de madera.

"Ahí está", murmure, cuando vi mi guante en la silla.

Lo agarré y caminé de regreso hacia la puerta. Con mucho cuidado di vuelta a la manija y di un paso hacia afuera pero me detuve para mirar hacia atrás por la rendija de la puerta. Un pie estaba en la casa llena de paz, el otro afuera en el eco del estruendo ruido de carros y camiones corriendo de ida y regreso por la avenida.

*PROFILE / PERFIL*

It was so very still inside, a good still, a serene still. I wanted to sit on the floor to hear Sister's whispers and gentle walking on the other side of the wall, but Tony had the car running and waving me back down.

An emotion I didn't understand welled up in my chest. I felt like crying and whispered, "I want to stay with you, Sister Theresa."

Adentro estaba todo muy callado. Una quietud, una quietud serena. Yo quería sentarme en el suelo para escuchar los murmullos de la Hermana y su caminar gentil del otro lado de la pared, pero Toño tenía prendido el carro y me hacía señas de que regresara.

Una emoción que no entendí, llenó mi pecho. Sentí que quería llorar y murmuré, "Me quiero quedar con usted Hermana Teresa".

*PROFILE / PERFIL*

# Portrait of a Rose

Philip Kijawa, my best friend in the sixth grade, would be dead by the end of the day. He and his neighbor friend, Danny Cortez, would be crushed and suffocated under tons of rain-soaked earth. The police would pull their mud-slick bodies from the cave the two had been digging on weekends and after school. Philip's mother would not get his daily after-school phone call where she worked. She would call Danny's mother to see if the boys were together. But Danny wasn't home from school either, though he should have been.

It had rained for almost a week. Unusual in the semi-arid climate of San Diego where we lived. And it had been raining all that day.

The nuns didn't allow us to go out to the playground at recess time. They had a room monitor lead the class in an indoor game called Seven Up. The monitor chose seven kids to line up in the front of the room, while the rest of us laid our heads on our desktops and hid our eyes. The seven then walked around, touched someone's head, and returned to the front. We raised our heads and tried guessing which of the seven had touched us. If we guessed correctly, we got to take the kid's place. Lame!

*STORIES / CUENTOS*

# Retrato de una osa

PHILIP KIJAWA, MI MEJOR AMIGO en el sexto año, estaria muerto al final de ese día. Él y su amigo, Danny Cortez, serían atrapados y sofocados bajo toneladas de lodo debido a la lluvia. La policía sacaría los cuerpos inertes llenos de lodo de la cueva que habían estado cavando después de la escuela y los fines de semana. La mamá de Philip no recibiría en su trabajo la rutinaria llamada después de la escuela. Ella le llamaría a la mamá de Danny para saber si estaban juntos. Pero Danny no estaba en su casa tampoco, aunque ya debería de estar ahí.

Había llovido por casi una semana. Era inusual debido al clima semiárido de San Diego, donde vivíamos. Y había estado lloviendo todo el día.

Las monjas no nos dejaron salir al patio durante el recreo. El prefecto nos puso a jugar un juego llamado "*Seven up*". El prefecto escogía a siete niños para que se formaran enfrente del salón, mientras que el resto de la clase poníamos la cabeza en el escritorio y nos tapábamos los ojos. Los siete niños entonces caminaban hacia nosotros y tocaban la cabeza de alguien, después regresaban al frente. Nosotros levantábamos la cabeza y teníamos que adivinar quién de los siete niños nos había tocado la cabeza. Si adivinábamos correctamente, tomábamos el lugar del niño ¡Un juego tonto!

Philip and I agreed that they were fools with no imaginations. Games were supposed to be fun, and this one wasn't even close to being fun. It was a stupid teacher's game, not ours.

Every time it rained Sister would ask, "What would you like to play class?" She smiled self-assuredly knowing that the indoctrinated would shout, "Seven Up! Seven Up!" Teachers liked the game because it was quiet play.

It rained the day Philip died, and we were playing Seven Up at recess time. Philip and I decided to spice it up a little by tripping the kid who walked down the aisle between our desks. Making contact with a kid's foot was one point. Making him stumble was two, and a fall-down was a five-point bingo.

Matthew would have fallen to the floor, but he caught himself on Ruth's desk and almost took her and her desk with him. We scored it four points. Now we were having real fun with our heads lowered while tripping kids passing our desks and hiding our laughter.

Philip and I became best friends at the beginning of the year when we were assigned desks next to each other. We came to realize that we liked impish humor.

Philip y yo estábamos de acuerdo en que los maestros eran tontos, sin imaginación. Supuestamente los juegos deberían de ser divertidos, pero este estaba lejos de ser divertido. Era un juego estúpido de los maestros, no de nosotros.

Cada vez que llovía, la Hermana nos preguntaba, "¿Qué les gustaría jugar en el salón?" Sonreía segura de sí misma sabiendo que las cabezas indoctrinadas gritarían, "*¡Seven up! ¡Seven up!*" A las maestras les gustaba ese juego porque era muy callado y tranquilo.

Había llovido el día que Philip murió y habíamos jugado *seven up* durante el recreo. Philip y yo habíamos decidido hacer el juego divertido de ponerle el pie al niño que caminara entre los dos escritorios. El contacto con el pie era un punto. Hacerlo que se tropezará eran dos puntos y si se caía era una lotería de cinco puntos.

Mateo se cayó al suelo, pero se pudo detener del escritorio de Ruth y casi se la llevaba a ella y a su escritorio en la caída junto con él. Nos ganamos cuatro puntos. Ahora si nos estábamos divirtiendo de verdad con las cabezas bajas mientras que le metíamos el pie a los que pasaban por nuestros escritorios, al mismo tiempo que escondíamos las carcajadas.

Philip y yo nos hicimos los mejores amigos cuando nos asignaron nuestros escritorios uno junto al otro. Nos dimos cuenta que los dos éramos muy traviesos.

*PROFILE / PERFIL*

He had a wide and high forehead that gave him the appearance of being bald. And he loved pulling pranks. Once, before school, while our class was waiting to go into church, he slipped on a set of large flesh-colored ears. Those standing behind him started laughing. He looked around as if wondering what the laughter was about. Even humorless Mother Superior couldn't help herself and chuckled when she told him to put them away. On another occasion he came to school with a nail through his finger. It was wrapped in gauze that was stained with dry blood.

"The doctor couldn't pull it out, see!" Philip tugged on the nail. "I've got another appointment to see him again tomorrow." It was too much of a distraction during class, and Sister made him take off the bandage and nail that was curved around his finger.

Philip wasn't the best of students, but he did have a curiosity and love of the natural world. Last year in fifth grade, he was excited because our teacher, Mrs. Balisarrio, introduced us to the natural sciences. She regularly brought cool specimens to class, like live reptiles in glass cases.

Tenía una frente amplia y grande y le daba el aspecto de estar calvo. Cómo le gustaba hacer bromas pesadas. En una ocasión, antes de que las clases comenzaran, mientras que esperábamos formados para entrar a la iglesia, se puso unas orejas falsas, eran grandes y coloridas. Los que estaban formados detrás de él se empezaron a reír. Él volteo para atrás, como si estuviera preguntándose el porqué de las risas. Hasta la Madre Superior que no tenía nada de humor, se sonrió cuando le ordenó que se las quitara y las guardara. En otra ocasión vino a la escuela con un clavo enterrado en el dedo. El dedo estaba envuelto en gasa que estaba manchada de sangre ya seca.

"El doctor no me lo pudo sacar, ¡ven!" Philip jaló el clavo. "Tengo otra cita para verlo mañana otra vez". Era bastante la distracción durante la clase y la Hermana lo mandó a que le quitaran la gasa y el clavo sólo estaba enroscado alrededor de su dedo.

Philip no era el mejor de los estudiantes, pero si tenía una gran curiosidad y amor al mundo natural. Un año antes, cuando estábamos en quinto año, estaba muy emocionado porque la maestra, la Señora Balisarrio, nos introdujo a las Ciencias Naturales. Regularmente traía especímenes interesantes, como reptiles vivos en contenedores de vidrio.

Philip worked hard for her and outdid the rest of us when it came to science projects. He once brought to class a one by one-and-a-half foot piece of plywood. He had mounted a landscape on it with miniature trees on a hillside and a lake made of clear blue plastic. Roaming all about it were dinosaurs. His was voted the best project. After that rainy day, there would be no more projects from Philip, and no more pranks.

I knelt in a pew with my twin brother, Fernando, and a classmate, Keith, at the funeral parlor where a memorial rosary was held the night before the funeral. Philip lay so very still in the casket. It didn't look like him, but a lifeless flesh-colored mannequin dressed in a dark suit.

At the end of the service, Keith suggested we go to Philip's parents and say we were sorry. I felt nervous about going but followed Keith. Philip's parents were sitting in the front pew. His mother had been sobbing and moaning through the entire service. She was dressed in black and sat leaning against her husband. She looked haggard and drained to the point of being sick.

"We're sorry Philip had to die," Keith whispered to her. She looked at us for a moment then put a hand on Keith's cheek.

All she could muster in a weak and trembling voice was, "You're nice boys." I stood staring at the odd spectacle of a grown-up completely depleted and vulnerable. Her soul had been ripped away from her.

En una ocasión, trajo a clase una tabla de triplay de un pie y medio. La usó para montar un campo en miniatura, con árboles pequeños, una colina y un lago hecho de un plástico claro de color azul. Alrededor de todo el campo había dinosaurios. Todos votaron por este proyecto como el mejor. Después de ese día de lluvia, no iba a haber más proyectos de Philip y no más bromas pesadas.

Yo me hinqué en la banca junto a mi gemelo, Fernando y Keith, un compañero de clase, el velorio se estaba llevando a cabo en una funeraria donde el rosario se estaba rezando antes del entierro. Philip estaba en el ataúd, muy quieto. Ni siquiera se veía como era él, parecía un maniquí, sin vida, sin color natural y en un traje obscuro.

Al final del rosario del velorio, Keith sugirió que fuéramos a darle el pésame a los padres de Philip. Yo me puse muy nervioso pero decidí seguir a Keith. Los padres de Philip estaban sentados en la banca de enfrente. Su mamá había estado llorando y gimiendo durante todo el rosario. Estaba vestida de negro y estaba sentada recargada en su esposo. Se veía desencajada y acabada hasta el punto de verse enferma.

"Sentimos mucho que Philip haya muerto", Keith le murmuró. Ella nos vio a los tres por un momento, entonces le tomó la mejilla a Keith.

Todo lo que pudo decir en una voz débil y temblorosa fue "Ustedes son unos buenos niños". Yo estaba parado mirando el extraño espectáculo de un adulto completamente desahuciado y vulnerable. Parecía como si le hubieran arrancado el alma.

*PROFILE / PERFIL*

That night at dinner my sister Martha said she had heard that Philip's mother had cursed the nuns, blaming them and the church for Philip's death.

"But it wasn't their fault," I said.

"Sister Cynthia said that Mrs. Kijawa isn't well because of her grief," Martha said. "Philip was her only child and we need to pray for her. Danny Cortez's father said he wasn't going to question God's will and that if God wanted one of his children, then he must obey as Abraham did with his son Isaac."

Fernando and I talked that night, lying in our bedroom. "He never told those silly snot jokes or played silly games with the girls like some of the other boys do," Fernando said.

"How could God allow this to happen?" I said. Neither of us said anything more.

All the next day I was preoccupied with Philip's death. I went to my neighbor Chris's house to see if he wanted to play. His mother invited me in and gave us cookies.

"I heard one of your schoolmates died recently."

"Yes, ma'am, he was my best friend in school. I wonder why God took him."

Chris's mother cupped my face in her hands and looked me in the eye. "I know that your family has certain beliefs, sweetheart, but some people see things differently. Some people aren't so sure there is a God."

Esa noche durante la cena, mi hermana Martha dijo que había escuchado a la mamá de Philip maldecir a las monjas echándole la culpa a ellas y a la iglesia por la muerte de Philip.

"Pero no fue su culpa", yo dije.

"La Hermana Cynthia dijo que la Señora Kijawa no está bien porque está de luto", Martha dijo que "Philip era su único hijo y necesitábamos rezar por ella. El padre de Danny Cortez dijo que no iba a cuestionar los mandatos de Dios y que si Dios quería uno de sus hijos, él tenía que obedecer, como Abraham hizo con su hijo Isaac".

Fernando y yo platicamos esa noche mientras que estábamos acostados en nuestro cuarto. "Él nunca nos dijo esos chistes estúpidos ni tampoco participó en esos juegos tontos como lo hacen otros niños", dijo Fernando.

"¿Cómo pudo Dios dejar que algo así pasara?" Ninguno de nosotros dijo alguna otra cosa.

Durante todo el día siguiente, yo estaba preocupado por la muerte de Philip. Fui a la casa de mi amigo Chris para ver si quería jugar. Su mamá me invitó a entrar y nos dio galletas.

"Supe que uno de tus compañeros de clase murió recientemente".

"Si señora, él era mi mejor amigo en la escuela. Me pregunto por qué Dios se lo llevó".

La mamá de Chris tomó mi cara entre sus manos y me miró a los ojos. "Yo sé que tu familia tiene ciertas creencias, mi corazón, pero algunas personas ven las cosas de manera diferente. Algunas personas no están seguras de que existe Dios".

*PROFILE / PERFIL*

My head spun with the very idea of not believing in God. *Didn't everybody know that He made us, and the world, and the entire universe?*

Chris's mom continued. "Whether or not a person believes in God, the same things will happen to them. Your religion teaches that a god created the world. But I believe that no one knows how it all happened. No matter, the world is a place in which all living things are designed to reproduce: people, animals, even plants. Everything is born, matures to reproduce, and dies. The reason for being created is to procreate and keep the life cycle going. Your poor friend's mother procreated, but her offspring will not, and she is suffering the greatest loss. The reason for her existence, for having known the joy and pain of motherhood, was stolen from her. Was it God who did this, or was it just a tragic fateful event that no one is responsible for? Who knows? What we know is that she will anguish and yen for her child to the end of her life. I can't think of a crueler irony than becoming a childless mother. Her baby was stolen from her. How could a merciful and loving God allow this to happen? I wish I had an answer."

I kept thinking for the rest of the day about what Chris's mom had said and decided I needed to take it up with Father McGuinn. Didn't God give Philip his curiosity and love of science? And that's what caused him to die!

*Mi cabeza dio vueltas con la idea de que hubiera alguien que no creyera en Dios. ¿Qué no era conocimiento de todo el mundo que Dios nos hizo a todos, al mundo y al universo?*

La mamá de Chris continuó. "Independientemente que la persona crea o no en Dios, las mismas cosas les pasarán. Tu religión te enseña que un Dios creó el mundo. Pero yo pienso que nadie de veras sabe cómo pasó todo. No importa, el mundo es un lugar en el que todas las cosas vivientes están diseñadas para la reproducción: la gente, los animales, hasta las plantas. Todo nace, madura para reproducirse y muere. La razón por el que somos creados es para procrear y para mantener el ciclo moviéndose. La pobre madre de tu amigo procreó, pero su hijo no lo va a hacer y ella está sufriendo una gran pérdida. La razón de su existencia, por haber conocido el gusto y el dolor de ser madre. Eso fue robado de ella. ¿Fue Dios el que hizo eso, o fue una tragedia del destino de la cual nadie es responsable? ¿Quién sabe? Lo que sabemos es que ella vivirá en una angustia y deseará tener a su hijo vivo hasta al final de la vida. No puedo creer que haya una ironía más cruel para una madre que quedarse sin su hijo. Le robaron a su bebé. ¿Cómo es posible que un Dios amoroso y misericordioso permita que esto pase? Cómo deseo tener una respuesta".

Seguí pensando por el resto del día acerca de lo que la mamá de Chris había dicho y decidí que necesitaba hablar con el padre McGuinn. ¿No le había dado Dios a Philip la curiosidad y el amor por la Ciencia? ¡Y eso mismo fue lo que le causó la muerte!

Philip and Danny had been digging a cave in the canyon near their neighborhood. They were looking for rocks for a youth science fair. But their digging had produced few specimens and so they dug further in. Why did they crawl into the cave when it was raining? It would have been cold and damp. And how could a loving and merciful God allow this to happen? I lay haunted by the question while trying to sleep that night.

The next day during the funeral mass, Father McGuinn told the story of a gardener who took great pride in his work tending the grounds of an estate. One day he noticed that someone had stolen a perfect blossom from a prized rose bush. He became angry until he learned that the owner of the estate, so moved by the beauty of the flower, took it into the mansion to show it to his dinner guests. The gardener was pleased that the owner so appreciated his work.

We stood outside the church in the cold fog as the pallbearers loaded Philip's coffin onto the hearse after the funeral. The last image I had of him was when we were laughing after tripping kids during Seven Up. What was it going to be like without him sitting in the desk next to me ever again?

The hearse, followed by the black limousine with Philip's parents and a procession of cars, slowly pulled away and disappeared into the fog.

Philip y Danny habían estado cavando una cueva en el cañón, cerca de su barrio. Estaban buscando rocas para una feria de Ciencia de jóvenes. Pero sus excavaciones habían producido muy pocos especímenes y por eso seguían excavando más profundo. ¿Por qué se metieron a la cueva cuando estaba lloviendo? La cueva habría estado fría y húmeda. ¿Y cómo un Dios amoroso y misericordioso permitiría que algo así pasara? Permanecí acostado torturado por esa pregunta mientras trataba de dormir esa noche.

El próximo día mientras que el padre daba la misa en el funeral. El Padre McGuinn nos dijo un cuento de un jardinero que con mucho orgullo cuidaba los jardines en una hacienda. Un día se dio cuenta que alguien le había robado la rosa más preciosa de su rosal. Se quedó muy enojado hasta que supo que el dueño de la hacienda, conmovido por la belleza de la flor, la cortó y se la llevó a la mansión para enseñársela a sus invitados de la cena. El jardinero estaba contento de que el dueño apreciara su trabajo.

Después del funeral nos quedamos afuera de la iglesia en la neblina fría mientras que los sepultureros metían el ataúd de Philip en la carroza fúnebre. La última imagen que tenía de él fue cuando nos estábamos riendo después de que le habíamos metido el pie a los niños durante los juegos de seven up. ¿Cómo iba a ser todo de ahora en adelante si el ya nunca jamás iba a volver estar sentado junto a mí, en el escritorio junto al mío?

La carroza era seguida por una limosina negra en la que iban los padres de Philip y detrás iba una procesión de carros, avanzaban lentamente hasta que desaparecían en la neblina.

*PROFILE / PERFIL*

# Lord, Snow, and Dawn

Tino began thinking of Lola, and how good it felt when she sat on the back of his motorcycle with her arms wrapped around him and her soft breasts pressed against his back. He was sure that she was the love of his life and one day they'd marry. But how could he support her? He wasn't all that good at holding down a job. *What about making a career out of the Marines after I join up?* he thought. *Marines don't get fired. Or maybe I could learn to be a mechanic from Rex the biker who we rode with in New Mexico. Rex hired guys like me who have a hard time making it in the regular world. There's good money in mechanics, and I could let my hair grow and dress however I want, and then ride motorcycles with Rex and his biker friends. Of course! That's it! I'll join the Marines, learn discipline, and earn my Pa's respect, then marry Lola and become an ace mechanic with Rex.* Tino's day brightened.

He rode with his head held high. He would show his parents and the rest of the doubters that he would not only succeed, but he'd do it his own way. He would become a great mechanic with a shop, and be like Rex helping young guys who'd gotten into trouble and give them a second chance, and on top of everything else, he'd have a beautiful wife.

*STORIES / CUENTOS*

# "El Señor", Nieves, y Aurora

Tino se puzo a pensar en Lola, en lo bien que se sentía cuando ella se sentaba en la parte de atrás de la motocicleta con sus brazos alrededor de él y sus suaves pechos apretados en contra de su espalda. Él estaba seguro que ella era el amor de su vida y que un día se casarían. ¿Pero cómo la iba a mantener? *En realidad nunca he podido quedarme en un trabajo por mucho tiempo,* pensó Tino. *¿Quizás sería bueno hacer una carrera en la Marina después de que me incorpore? A los marinos no los corren. Hasta podría aprender el oficio de mecánico. Rex el motociclista, con el que viajé a Nuevo México, me podría enseñar. Rex contrata a chavos que les cuesta trabajo adaptarse a el mundo regular, como a mí. Hay buen dinero en la mecánica y hasta me podría dejar crecer el pelo y vestirme de la manera que yo quiera, entonces me puedo pasear en la motocicleta con Rex y sus amigos los motociclistas. ¡Por supuesto! Siempre y cuando entre a la Marina, puedo aprender a disciplinarme y a ganarme el respeto de mi papá, después me caso con Lola y me convierto en un mecánico de primera con Rex.* El día de Tino se alumbró.

Les demostraría a sus padres y al resto de los que dudaban de él, que él no sólo podría tener éxito, sino que lo obtendría a su propia manera. Se convertiría en un gran mecánico con su propio taller, sería como Rex, ayudándole a jóvenes que han tenido problemas, al darles una segunda oportunidad, además de todo, él tendría una esposa hermosa.

Tino began singing loudly, "Get your motor running, head out on the highway," when his bike began slowing on its own. He turned the accelerator grip and the tach needle jumped, but the bike didn't respond with its usual burst of speed. *Damn it! Now what?* It was as if the bike was in neutral. It kept slowing until it came to a stop. He looked on helplessly as Sal, his older brother, continued down the road. Tino dismounted and made a quick inspection. His bike's drive chain had disappeared.

Sal had ridden two miles before noticing that Tino wasn't behind him anymore. Sal pulled over and took a nervous look at his watch hoping Tino would soon appear. Sal waited a couple of minutes before he sighed and made a U-turn to head back. He found Tino leaning against his bike with his arms crossed.

"Lost my drive chain," Tino said. "It's gotta be lying on the road somewhere back there."

"*Hijo de la…*" Sal said, then gunned his engine and doubled back with a close eye on the asphalt. Tino saw him stop a few hundred feet up the road, lean over, pick up the snake-like drive chain.

"What're we gonna do now?" Tino said as Sal pulled up.

"The master link's gone. There's gotta be a Honda dealer in the town we passed a while ago where I can get a new one. Be back as soon as I can." Sal sped off. A school bus converted into a motorized home and painted the colors of the rainbow approached in Tino's direction. *Humph, hippies*, he thought.

## STORIES / CUENTOS

Tino empezó a cantar fuerte "Prepara tu motor, tenlo corriendo, hacia la carretera", cuando su moto empezó a detenerse. Apretó el acelerador y la aguja del odómetro brincó. Pero la moto no respondió con su usual brinco de velocidad *¡Diablos! ¿Ahora qué?* Parecía como si la moto estuviera en neutral. Continuó deteniéndose hasta que se paró por completo. Se vio sin esperanza mientras que Salvador, su hermano mayor seguía por el camino. Tino se bajó e inspeccionó la moto rápidamente. La cadena que hacía mover la llanta de la moto había desparecido.

Salvador había manejado dos millas antes de darse cuenta que Tino no estaba detrás de él. Salvador se detuvo y miró su reloj nervioso esperando que Tino apareciera pronto. Salvador esperó dos minutos más antes de que suspirara frustrado y diera una vuelta en U para regresar. Encontró a Tino recargado en su moto con los brazos cruzados.

"Perdí mi cadena de manejar", dijo Tino. "Tiene que estar tirada en algún lugar atrás en el camino".

"Hijo de la...". Salvador dijo, entonces aceleró su motor y dio la vuelta mirando fijamente el asfalto. Tino lo vio detenerse a unos cien metros, agacharse y recoger la cadena en forma de víbora.

"¿Qué vamos a hacer ahora?", dijo Tino mientras que Salvador se detenía.

"La conexión primaria se perdió. Debe haber un vendedor de motos Honda en el pueblo que pasamos hace un rato, creo que ahí puedo encontrar una nueva. Voy a regresar tan pronto como pueda". Salvador se fue a toda velocidad. Un autobús de escuela convertido en una casa móvil y pintada con los colores del arcoíris se aproximaba a la dirección de Tino. *Mmm, hippies*, pensó.

*PROFILE / PERFIL*

Tino stared at the bus as it drew near. "Peace and Love" was written in elaborate lettering in the space between the windshield and roof. The driver smiled and waved as he pulled over. His full, dark beard hung to the middle of his chest, and a thin leather strap, wrapped around his head, kept his shoulder-length hair from his face. Grace Slick's voice bellowed from an eight-track tape deck stereo system. "When the truth is found, to be lies…"

The hippie opened the door, slid out of the driver's seat, and landed on the ground with a bounce. "Having trouble, brother?" His bone-white collarless shirt with puffy sleeves hung over gray corduroy pants tucked into a pair of tan suede boots adorned with tassels that dangled as he walked.

"Nothing my brother and I can't fix," Tino said, feeling a little weird about talking with a guy who was dressed like some kind of wild gypsy. "He went to get a part for my bike. But thanks for stopping."

"We are called to serve," Tassels said. "Too bad about your ride, man."

The double doors of the bus swung open. A pretty young woman descended the steps. Her milk-white skin was a stark contrast to her shining black hair that hung long and straight past her waist. A tan leather vest fit snuggly over her silky deep blue blouse. Her moccasins were barely visible beneath a long, chocolate brown skirt that swept the earth as she walked.

Tino fijó la vista en el autobús mientras éste se aproximaba. En el espacio que había entre el parabrisas y el techo, estaba escrito "amor y paz" con letras muy elaboradas. El chofer sonrió y con la mano le mandó una señal de saludo mientras se estacionaba. Su larga y obscura barba le llegaba hasta la mitad del pecho, tenía una diadema de piel amarrada en la cabeza, le ayudaba a mantener el cabello fuera de la cara. La voz de la artista Grace Slick se escuchaba fuertemente del estéreo. "Cuando la verdad se encuentra, son mentiras...".

El hippie abrió la puerta, se deslizó del asiento del chofer y de un brinco bajó del autobús. "¿Tienes problemas hermano?". Su camisa color hueso sin cuello y con mangas bombachas caía sobre sus pantalones de pana gris que estaban dentro de unas botas de cuero decoradas con borlas que se movían cuando caminaba.

"No es nada que mi hermano y yo no podamos arreglar", dijo Tino, sintiéndose un poco extraño de hablar con un hombre que se vestía como un gitano salvaje. "Él fue a comprar una parte para mi moto. Pero gracias por pararte".

"Todos somos llamados para servir", dijo el de las borlas. "¡Qué mala onda de tu moto hombre!".

Las puertas dobles del autobús se abrieron para dar paso a una mujer bonita bajando las escaleras. Su piel blanca como la leche era un severo contraste con su brillante pelo negro y lacio que le caía hasta abajo de su cintura. Traía una blusa sedosa azul debajo de un chaleco de piel que le quedaba apretado. Los mocasines apenas se veían porque su falda de color chocolate los tapaba casi completamente, parecía como si barriera la tierra cuando caminaba.

A thin halo of silver ribbon entwined with tiny dried yellow flowers rested on the crown of her head. She appeared to hover over the ground like a saint Tino had seen in a religious movie. She floated toward Tassels, stopped next to him, and set her head against his shoulder.

"Been on the road long, brother?" Tassels asked.

"Since California."

"Far out, man! I can't imagine spending that much time with anyone in *my* family."

"It's got its ups and downs," Tino said. "But mostly ups." He nodded toward the bus. "How's it traveling in that thing?"

"It's groovy, man. We've got everything we need."

"Would you like to see it?" the Saint asked.

"Yeah, I really would," Tino said.

The Saint and Tino climbed the steps. Tassels walked around to the rear of the bus. The dull-sweet odor of burned incense greeted Tino as he entered. Sitting on a wooden rocking chair behind the driver's seat was a petite girl who couldn't have been much past fifteen.

"This is my baby sister, Dawn," the Saint said. The girl in the chair raised her head only long enough to give a cursory smile, then got back to sewing a brightly colored patch of a mushroom to the cuff of a pair of well-worn jeans.

En la cabeza tenía una aureola de listón plateado que estaEn la cabeza tenía una aureola de listón plateado que estaba entretejido con unas pequeñas flores amarillas. Se parecía a una santa que flotaba sobre la tierra y que Tino había visto en una película religiosa. Se movió flotando hacia el hombre de las borlas, se paró junto a él y recargó la cabeza en su hombro.

El hombre de las borlas le preguntó "Hermano ¿Haz estado en el camino por mucho tiempo?".

"Desde California".

"¡Hombre, qué buena onda!" No me puedo imaginar pasándome tanto tiempo con alguien de mi familia".

"Tiene sus cosas buenas y malas", dijo Tino. "Pero en general estamos bien". Señalando hacia el autobús preguntó. "¿Qué se siente viajar en esa cosa?".

"Hombre, buena onda. Tenemos todo lo que necesitamos".

"¿Te gustaría verlo?" Le preguntó la mujer que parecía una santa.

"Sí, me gustaría", dijo Tino.

La mujer que parecía una santa y Tino subieron las escaleras. El hombre de las borlas caminó hacia la parte trasera del autobús. Cuando subió al autobús, lo recibió un olor de incienso dulzón fuerte. Sentada en una mecedora detrás del asiento del chofer, estaba una muchacha joven que no pasaba de quince años.

"Ésta es Aurora, mi hermanita", dijo la mujer que parecía una santa. La muchacha apenas y levantó la cabeza para mostrarle una sonrisa amable. Después siguió bordando un colorido parche de hongo que iba a ser pegado al dobladillo de unos pantalones gastados.

"Dawn's sewing Lord's pants."

"Lord?" Tino asked.

"Our man."

"That's a pretty interesting name," Tino said thinking it funny and heretical.

"He's an interesting man," the Saint said.

The Saint took a step toward Tino so her face was inches from his. He felt uneasy and took a half step back. She shifted and pressed her hip to his. His heart started pounding. He felt as though her dark doe-like eyes were seeing through him.

She cooed, "I'm Snow."

"Snow! That's a cool name."

She then extended her hand in a broad stroke, inviting Tino to admire the world they had created inside the bus. He looked around trying to appear as if he was more interested in the décor than her advances.

A portable stove for camping sat on a narrow counter, its green paint was faded and chipping. Hand-thrown ceramic plates and cups filled a small sink. Tino noticed that they were standing on the hide of a large animal.

"Aurora está cosiendo los pantalones de 'El Señor'".
"¿El Señor?", preguntó Tino.
"Nuestro hombre".
"Ese es un nombre interesante", dijo Tino pensando que era divertido y hereje.
"Pues él es un hombre interesante", dijo la mujer que parecía una santa.

Ella dio un paso hacia Tino de tal manera que su cara estuviera a pulgadas de la de él. Él se sintió incómodo y dio un medio paso hacia atrás. Ella se movió hasta pegar su cadera con la de él. Su corazón latió apresurado. Sintió como si los ojos de paloma de ella estuvieran viendo a través de él.

Ella dijo, "Me llamo Nieves".
"¡Nieves! Es un nombre suave".

Entonces ella extendió la mano de una manera amplia, invitando a Tino para admirar el mundo que ellos habían creado dentro del autobús. Tino miró alrededor tratando de aparecer más interesado en la decoración que en los coqueteos de ella.

Una pequeña estufa de acampar estaba sobre una barra angosta, el color de la barra era verde desteñido y se estaba pelando por el uso. Platos y tazas de cerámica hechos a mano estaban acumulados en el pequeño fregadero. Tino se dio cuenta de que estaba parado en la piel de un gran animal.

Tino squatted and ran his fingers over it. It felt soft and smooth. Blankets and pillows in blue and green paisley patterns lay over a large mattress to the rear. A guitar case leaned against a wall beside a tambourine. On the ceiling in glittering gold and outlined in deep blue was a huge peace sign with "It is possible" written over it.

"This is really bitchen," Tino said.

Snow smiled warmly and looked into his eyes. "Life is beautiful."

Tino's heart jumped. Why was she coming on to him with her man Lord just outside?

Lord climbed the stairs and entered the bus with a leather pouch in his hand and set it on the counter. He ignored Tino and Snow as they looked on. He took a pack of cigarette rolling papers from his shirt pocket, pull one out, and set it flat on the counter. He opened the pouch and took out a pinch of a green leafy substance and spread it along the center of the paper.

*Holy shit!* Tino thought. "Is that marijuana?"

Lord looked up smiling. "Well, it sure ain't tobacco."

"I've heard of it but have never seen the stuff."

Lord then rolled a near perfect cigarette in seconds. He ran the edge of the paper across his tongue to seal it and twisted the ends. He held it up looking at Tino with raised eyebrows. "Care to partake?"

## STORIES / CUENTOS

Se agachó y le pasó los dedos por encima. Se sentía suave y lisa. Almohadas verdes y cobijas de flores verdosas y azules estaban sobre un gran colchón al final del autobús. Un estuche de guitarra y un pandero estaban recargados sobre la pared. El techo estaba decorado con un dorado brillante y había un símbolo de paz gigante de "Es posible" en la orilla, estaba pintado de azul obscuro.

"Esto está bien chingón", dijo Tino.

Nieves sonrió cariñosamente y lo miró a los ojos "La vida es hermosa".

El corazón de Tino dio un brinco. ¿Por qué lo estaba provocando sabiendo que su hombre, "El Señor", estaba afuera?

"El Señor" subió las escaleras con una bolsa en la mano y la puso en la barra. Ignorando a Tino y a Nieves, que lo estaban observando. Sacó de la bolsa de la camisa un paquete de papel para hacer cigarros, sacó uno y lo alisó sobre la barra. Abrió la bolsita y sacó un puñado de hojitas verdes y las extendió sobre el centro del papel.

*¡Me cago en la hostia!* Pensó Tino. "¿Es marihuana?".

"El Señor" levantó la vista sonriendo. "Bueno, de seguro no es tabaco".

"He escuchado de esta cosa pero nunca la había visto".

"El Señor" enrolló un cigarro casi perfecto en cuestión de segundos. Se pasó la orilla del papel por la lengua y selló el cigarro, después torció las orillas. Mirando a Tino con la ceja levantada, mantuvo el cigarro alzado "¿Quieres participar?".

"No, thanks. I'm not into dope."

"How do you know, man? Ever try it?"

"No."

"Then how do you know?"

"I guess I don't, but I'm afraid that it'll lead to harder stuff."

"Aw man, that's the man's propaganda. It just ain't so. How do you get high?"

"Beer, when I can get it."

"This ain't nearly as hard as that shit, man. That stuff'll kill you. I've tried just about every drug there is, and alcohol was the hardest on my body. I always felt like I got beat up after drinking." He lifted the joint and raised his eyebrows again, smiling impishly.

Tino was softening. *He's right. I don't know what it's like, and if I tried it who'd ever know?* He looked at Lord, then at Snow, "Oh, what the hell."

"Well alright, man!" Lord said. Snow giggled and clapped her hands.

"Why're you so happy about me getting high?"

"Because you're converting to the light," Snow said.

Tino looked at her askew.

Lord struck a stick match against the counter and lit the joint. He closed his eyes as he sucked on it, slow and hard. His face turned red. He handed the joint to Tino.

"No, gracias. No estoy en eso de la marihuana".
"Hombre, ¿cómo sabes? ¿La haz probado?".
"No".
"¿Entonces cómo sabes?".
"Adivino que no sé, pero tengo miedo que me lleve a cosas más fuertes".
"No hermano, esa es propaganda del hombre que manda a los demás. La verdad que no es así. ¿Qué usas para elevarte?".
"Cerveza, cuando tengo acceso".
"Hombre, ésta es mucho menos dañina que esa mierda. Esa cosa te va a matar. Yo he probado casi toda la droga que hay y el alcohol es el más dañino en mi cuerpo. Siempre sentí que me habían dado una paliza después que tomaba". Sonriendo traviesamente, levantó el cigarro y las cejas otra vez en señal de invitación.

Tino se estaba ablandando. *Tiene razón. No sé cómo es ¿Y si la pruebo? ¿Quién se va a enterar?* Miró a "El Señor", luego a Nieves "¡Ay, pues al diablo entonces!".

"¡Hombre, está muy bien!" dijo "El Señor". Nieves sonrió y aplaudió.

"¿Por qué se ponen tan contentos de que me ponga marihuano?"

"Porqué estas dejando que te entre la luz", dijo Nieves.

Tino la miró dudoso.

"El Señor" prendió el cerillo en la barra y después encendió el toque. Cerró los ojos e inhaló del toque, fuerte y despacio. La cara se le puso roja. Le pasó el toque a Tino.

*PROFILE / PERFIL*

Tino tentatively raised the joint to his lips. "What do you mean by 'converting to the light'?" He imitated Lord and took a deep hit, but the harsh smoke tore at his lungs and he broke out into a coughing fit. He hacked out every bit of what he had inhaled and then some. The hippies burst into laughter. He passed it to Snow, still coughing. She took a much smaller hit, held it in and handed the joint down to Dawn, in her chair. Snow exhaled. "Ever hear of Timothy Leary and his church?"

"Yeah, he's the guy who keeps getting busted for using drugs."

"First of all, Timothy Leary's a *researcher* in psychedelic therapy at Harvard University," Lord said, offended that someone would reduce his guru to an addict.

"Secondly, he's a teacher with a new and beautiful message, like Jesus. Timothy Leary has seen the light that all men..."

"And women," Snow added.

"...that all men *and* women seek. He founded a church called The League for Spiritual Discovery. We are living his mantra: turn on, tune in, and drop out. We're on our way to San Francisco. I've wanted to go there since I heard about the Summer of Love there last year. After that we're going to join up with Leary and his church. They've declared lysergic acid diethylamide as their sacrament."

"Declared what?"

"Lysergic acid diethylamide. L-S-D, man."

## STORIES / CUENTOS

Tino se puso, con cierta duda, el cigarro en los labios. "¿Qué quieres decir con eso de dejar que me llegue la luz?" Imitó a "El Señor" y fumó fuerte, pero el humo le destrozó los pulmones mandándolo a un ataque de tos. La tos seca sacó todo lo que había inhalado y todavía más. Los hippies se soltaron a carcajadas. Todavía tosiendo, le pasó el cigarro a Nieves. Ella inhaló más suavemente, detuvo el humo adentro y después le pasó el cigarro a Aurora que estaba sentada en la silla. Nieves sacó el humo. "¿Has escuchado alguna vez de Timothy Leary y su iglesia?".

"Sí, él es el hombre que siempre está en problemas por usar drogas".

"En primera, Timothy Leary es un investigador de terapia psicodélica de la Universidad de Harvard", dijo "El Señor", ofendido de que alguien redujera su gurú a un adicto.

"En segunda, él es un maestro con un mensaje hermoso, como Jesús. Timothy Leary ha sido la luz de todos los hombres…".

"Y mujeres", añadió Nieves.

"…que todos los hombres y mujeres buscan. Él estableció la iglesia llamada La Liga por el Descubrimiento Espiritual. Estamos viviendo bajo su influencia: entónate y te sales. Estamos en camino a San Francisco. He estado queriendo ir allá desde el año pasado que supe del verano de amor. Después de eso nos vamos a unir a la iglesia de Leary. Han declarado el ácido *lysergic diethylamide* como su sacramento".

"¿Declararon qué?".

"¡Hombre! Lysergic acid diethylamide ¡L-S-D!".

*PROFILE / PERFIL*

"You gotta be kidding. They're using a drug as a communion host?" Now, Tino was offended.

"You don't understand. LSD isn't just a drug, man. It's a portal. A portal to the other side, a way to see, you know? A way to really and truly see. Try some and you'll understand."

Lord stared at Tino, studying him for a second. He then stepped to the glove compartment of the bus and took out a box of Kodak film. He removed the small gray canister and peeled off the lid, and tapped out what appeared to be tiny square pieces of shiny black film. He picked up a copy of a *National Geographic* magazine, opened it, and tore out a page with a photograph of ancient Mayan glyphs. Lord took a single-edge razor blade and cut a three-inch square containing a glyph of a stylized snake.

He then carefully folded one of the flecks of film into the paper. He looked up at Tino. "God forbade Adam and Eve to eat of the forbidden fruit."

"Are you saying God didn't want Adam and Eve to trip-out on LSD?" Tino said.

Snow and Dawn giggled.

Lord ignored them. "I'm going to explain something to you, man." He motioned Tino to sit on a chair next to the driver's seat. Tino sat, feeling a little nervous. *What was this guy up to?* Lord sat in the driver's seat and turned to stare into Tino's eyes. He spoke slowly and deliberately. "LSD has the same effect as mushrooms."

"¡Me tienes que estar vacilando! ¿Están usando una droga como la hostia de comunión?". Ahora sí, Tino estaba ofendido.

"¡Hombre, tu no entiendes! El LSD no es nada más una droga. Es una puerta, una puerta al otro lado, una manera de ver, ¿tú sabes? Una manera de ver la verdad. Pruébalo y vas a entender".

"El Señor" vio a Tino fijamente, estudiándolo por un segundo. Entonces se acercó a la guantera del autobús y sacó algo de una caja para guardar rollos de cámara Kodak. Removió un pequeño bote de color gris, le quitó la tapa y sacó de un golpecito lo que parecía ser una pequeña pieza cuadrada hecho de un rollo de fotografía negro brillante. Levantó una copia de la revista *National Geographic*, la abrió y arrancó de la revista una página que tenía una foto de jeroglíficos de los antiguos mayas. "El Señor" agarró una navaja y cortó un cuadro de tres pulgadas que tenía un jeroglífico de una víbora estilizada.

Después con mucho cuidado envolvió uno de los puntos negros del rollo en el papel. Miró a Tino y dijo "Dios le prohibió a Adán y Eva comer del fruto del pecado".

Tino dijo, "¿Estás diciendo que Dios no quería que Adán y Eva se dieran un viaje en LSD?"

Nieves y Aurora se rieron.

"El Señor" las ignoró. "Hombre, te voy a explicar algo". Le indicó a Tino que se sentara en el asiento junto al chofer. Tino se sentó, sintiéndose un poco nervioso. *¿Qué es lo que este chavo está tratando de hacer?* "El Señor" se sentó en el asiento del chofer y fijó la mirada en los ojos de Tino. Habló despacio y deliberadamente. "El LSD tiene el mismo efecto que los hongos".

*PROFILE / PERFIL*

"Mushrooms?" Tino said. "What do mushrooms have to do with anything?"

"Not just mushrooms, man. I'm talking about sacred mushrooms, psilocybin mushrooms. They'll expand your mind in ways you could never imagine. For me, it was the first time in my life I could see, I mean really and truly see, man. It wasn't LSD Adam and Eve were not to eat. It was psilocybin mushrooms. They helped them to understand so much more than their mortal minds ever could on their own. LSD has the same effect. You'll get it when you use it." He held up the small packet. "Do it when you're in a mellow mood, and do it in a place where you feel safe. And don't let it get wet or it'll lose its power."

"You mean this isn't film, but LSD?"

"It's a beautiful thing, isn't it? The pigs never suspect."

Lord placed the packet into Tino's hand.

Tino was overcome with an ominous feeling that he should not accept the offering. A deep curiosity gnawed at him. He slipped it into his coin pocket. *I'll toss it when I get back on the road.* "Is it like getting drunk?"

"¿Hongos?" Dijo Tino. "¿Qué tienen que ver los hongos con esto?".

"Hombre, no cualquier tipo de hongo. Estoy hablando de los hongos sagrados, hongos *psilocybin*. Estos hongos van a expandir tu mente en tantas maneras que nunca te has imaginado. Para mí, esa fue la primera vez que de verdad pude ver, hombre, digo que de veras pude ver. No significa que Adán y Eva no pudieran consumir LSD. Eran los hongos *psilocybin*. Los hongos le ayudaron a Adán y Eva a entender mucho más que lo que sus mentes mortales pudieran entender. El LSD tiene el mismo efecto. Lo vas a entender cuando los pruebes". Elevó el pequeño paquete. "Tómatelo cuando estés de buen humor y calmado, hazlo en un lugar donde te sientas seguro. No dejes que se moje o perderá su poder".

"¿Quieres decir que esto no es rollo de fotografía, sino LSD?".

"¿Dime si no es algo bello? Los puercos nunca sospechan".

"El Señor" colocó el paquete en la mano de Tino.

Tino estaba muy incómodo, tenía el presentimiento de que no debería de recibir el regalo. Una curiosidad más grande lo forzó a aceptarlo. *Lo deslizó en su bolsa de monedas. Lo voy a tirar cuando ya estemos en camino.* "¿Es como ponerse borracho?".

*PROFILE / PERFIL*

"Naw, man, nothin' like that. There's an intense ride up, kind of jittery. Some people don't like it, but it's fun if you're head's in the right place. Next you'll peak, your mind will expand, and you'll see as you've never seen before. And then there's a peaceful ride down."

Tino rose from the chair. "It's cool how you can hide this from the cops, but how do you hide the pot? Don't you get stopped and pulled over and searched, especially riding around in this bus?"

Lord stood. "It's been a major hassle, man. It's another reason we're going to California. It's mellower out there. We've been on the road two weeks, and the heat's pulled us over three times! They look inside the bus, but never under it," he laughed. "And I've got stuff to sell in sealed cans with Campbell's soup labels. And it's mm, mm good!"

"It's going to be groovy when we get to California," Snow said. "Is it as cool as they say it is?"

"Heck, I don't know," Tino said. "It's just home to me. Maybe it's a little easier in San Francisco where the hippies are taking over." Tino felt relaxed from the marijuana. "I love it that you guys are so free. You're lucky. My folks would never allow me do this. Are your parents okay with it?"

"¡No hombre! No es nada como eso. Es como un viaje intenso, como de nervios. A algunas personas no les gusta, pero es divertido si tu cabeza está en el lugar adecuado. Después de elevarte, tu mente se va a expandir y vas a ver cosas que nunca has visto antes. Y después, cuando bajes será muy pacífico".

Tino se levantó de su silla. "¡Qué buena onda que lo puedas esconder de la policía! Pero ¿Cómo escondes la mota? ¿No te paran y te registran, especialmente manejando este autobús?".

"El Señor" se levantó. "Hombre, ha sido un gran hostigamiento, esa es otra razón por la que vamos a California. Es más tranquilo allá. Hemos estado en el camino durante dos semanas ¡y la policía nos ha parado tres veces! Siempre revisan adentro del autobús pero nunca abajo", se rió. Y tengo mota para vender en latas selladas de sopa Campbell. Y es ¡Mmm! ¡Mmm! ¡Buena!".

"Va a ser muy buena onda cuando lleguemos a California", dijo Nieves. "¿Es tan buena onda como dicen?".

"¡Diablos! No sé", dijo Tino. "Es simplemente el hogar para mí. Quizás está mejor en San Francisco donde los hippies están controlando todo". Tino se sintió relajado con la marihuana. "Me gusta ver cómo es que ustedes son muy libres. Tienen suerte, mis padres nunca me hubieran dejado hacer esto. ¿Están sus padres en acuerdo con esto?".

*PROFILE / PERFIL*

"My once self was called Jethro Cornelius Taylor III," Lord said. "And Jethro was born to a confused rich man who married a confused Southern belle. The rich man got into politics and now votes to keep 'the nigras in their place,' as he says, and he supports dropping napalm and Agent Orange in Vietnam."

Snow and Dawn smiled warmly as they looked up at him. Lord put an alligator clip on the shortened joint, took a drag. "And the government thinks I'm going to register for the draft. Ha! I reject that life, all of it, even to the name given to me by agents of an oppressive society. I am 'Lord.' And Lord has discovered that love and peace are the way. We need to make love, not war, man." He passed the joint to Tino.

Tino looked at Snow and Dawn. "What about you guys? Aren't your parents worried about you?" Dawn pursed her lips hiding pain.

"We're not even sure they even know we're gone," Snow said. "We're the last of their sixteen children what live in the West Virginie Mountains. Mama dances with snakes and drinks poison as her worship, and Pap drinks as much shine as he stills. A man who be drinkin' that devil water does regretful things to his people, an' even worse to them who would cross him. Most of his young-uns have gone off to live with neighbors or hitched up with somebody to our likin' or just done disappeared like me and Dawn."

"Mi persona pasada era llamada Jethro Cornelius Taylor III", dijo "El Señor". "Y Jethro nació de un hombre rico y confundido quien se casó con una dama del sur. El hombre rico se metió a la política y ahora vota por mantener a los 'negros en su lugar,' según dice él, además apoya el lanzamiento de *napalm* y el agente *orange* en Vietnam".

Nieves y Aurora sonrieron cariñosamente mientras lo miraban. "El Señor" puso un clip en el cigarro, fumó fuerte y dijo "Y el gobierno piensa que me voy a registrar para el servicio militar. ¿Cómo no? Yo rechazo ese tipo de vida, todo, hasta el nombre que me dieron los agentes opresivos del sistema social. Yo soy "El Señor". Y "El Señor" ha descubierto que el amor y la paz es el único camino. Hombre, necesitamos hacer el amor, no la guerra". Después le pasó el cigarro a Tino.

Tino miró a Nieves y Aurora. "¿Qué tal ustedes muchachas? ¿No están sus padres preocupados por ustedes?". Aurora hizo una mueca con los labios para esconder su dolor.

"No estamos seguras si se han dado cuenta que no estamos allá", dijo Nieves. "Somos las últimas de dieciséis hijos, vivíamos en las montañas del oeste de Virginia. Mi mamá baila con víboras y toma el veneno como su culto y mi papá toma tanto licor como el que hace. El hombre que toma esa agua del diablo le hace cosas imperdonables a su gente y mucho más a aquellos que se le atraviesan en el camino. Muchos de sus hijos se han ido a vivir con vecinos o han agarrado aventones con alguien como nosotras y se desaparecen como Aurora y yo".

*PROFILE / PERFIL*

"That's sad," Tino said thinking it strange how her person changed when she talked about her family. "It's very sad."

He held up the clip and studied what little there was left of the joint. "It's making me feel really relaxed. I wish I could always feel like this."

"You're a good dude," Lord said. "Come with us. There's no church, no hassle, just love, happiness, and insight."

Snow neared Tino again and spoke softly. "This life's a whole lot more to my likin'. It's a free life, a free life to live and do what I want, and when I want."

She leaned against him and brushed her breasts against his arm. She looked into his eyes. "Do y'all believe in free love?"

Tino's head spun. "Sounds wonderful."

"I think I'd surely like to fuck ya'll right now."

Naked lust overcame Tino. He felt an erection coming on.

"We can give you privacy," Lord said, "or the four of us can have a love fest."

"Qué tristeza", dijo Tino con extrañeza pensando en cómo cambió su personalidad cuando ella hablo de su familia. "Es muy triste".

Mantuvo el cigarro con el clip a la altura de la cara y se dio cuenta que quedaba poco del cigarro. "Me está haciendo sentir muy relajado ¡Cómo me gustaría sentirme siempre así!".

"Tú eres un buen muchacho", dijo "El Señor". "Ven con nosotros. No hay iglesia, no hay problemas, nada más amor, felicidad y desarrollo interno".

Nieves se le acercó a Tino otra vez y habló suavemente. "Esta vida es más completa y me gusta mucho más. Es una vida libre, una vida libre de vivir y de hacer lo que quiero y cuando lo quiero".

Se recargó en Tino y rozó con su pecho su brazo. Lo miró a los ojos. "¿Tú crees en el amor libre?".

La cabeza de Tino dio vueltas. "Suena maravilloso".

"Pienso que me gustaría cogerte ahorita mismo".

El deseo desnudo se apoderó de Tino. Sintió una erección.

"Les podemos dar privacidad", dijo "El Señor", o los cuatro podemos tener una fiesta de amor".

Tino shook his head. "I could never do it in a group."

"Say no more, brother," Lord said and reached for Dawn's hand, helping her from the rocker. "Everything in our world is free man, free in every way."

Snow, still gazing into Tino's eyes, put her hand on his crotch and rubbed it gently. "Let's have a beautiful time."

Tino trembled with want, but Lola came to his mind. "I'm in love with someone."

Snow's eyes flooded with tears. "And ya want to be true to her. That's a beautiful thing," she whispered, "a real beautiful thing."

Lord put his hand on Tino's shoulder. "No hassle, man. Why don't you come along with us? Shed your old life. Live free, truly free. Get high when you want and make beautiful love, if and when you want."

"I'd surely like that," Snow said.

*Make love anytime*, Tino thought. *Get high anytime, no school, no church, no hassles.* Movement toward the back of the bus caught Tino's eye. He looked out the rear window. A small dark-skinned man on a motorcycle in the distance was coming toward them fast. "Holy shit! My brother!"

Tino negó con la cabeza. "Creo que nunca podría hacerlo en grupo".

"No digas más hermano", dijo "El Señor" y tomando de la mano a Aurora, la ayudó a levantarse de la mecedora. "Todo en nuestro mundo es libre hermano, libre en todos los aspectos".

Nieves, seguía mirando a Tino a los ojos, le puso la mano en el área del pene y lo acarició suavemente. "Vamos a disfrutar de un rato hermoso".

Tino tembló de deseo, pero el pensamiento de Lola se le vino a la mente. "Estoy enamorado de alguien".

Los ojos de Nieves se llenaron de lágrimas. "Y quieres serle fiel ¡Qué cosa tan hermosa!", murmuró "Qué cosa tan hermosa".

"El Señor" le puso la mano a Tino en el hombro. "Hombre, no hay problema ¿Por qué no te vienes con nosotros? Deja tu vida vieja. Vive libre, de veras libre. Elévate cuando quieras y haz el amor, siempre y cuando tú quieras".

"Eso me gustaría mucho de verdad", dijo Nieves.

*Hacer el amor a cualquier hora,* pensó Tino. *Elevarme a cualquier hora, sin escuela, sin iglesia, sin problemas.* Un movimiento de atrás del autobús se detuvo en la mirada de Tino. Vio por la ventana trasera del autobús. Un hombre moreno pequeño en una motocicleta en la distancia se acercaba hacia ellos rápidamente. "¡Mierda bendita! ¡Mi hermano!".

The hippies looked out the window that framed Sal as he approached.

"Your brother wouldn't be cool with this?" Lord asked.

"Cool with this? He's a Catholic priest!"

"Wow. Major bummer, man."

"He accepts people, he's cool like that. But there's no way he'd be okay with me getting stoned."

The three hippies looked concerned for Tino and ushered him out of the bus. Lord smiled at Sal as he pulled up and stopped. Sal narrowed his eyes, assessing the situation.

"How're you folks doing? You've been visiting with my brother?" He scanned the hippies. *What could his little brother be up to now?*

"We're doing good, Sal," Tino said, trying to sound casual. He pointed to the bus. "You ought to see the inside, it's really cool."

Lord took a step forward. "Nice to meet you, man." He raised his palm, greeting Sal in the form of an American Indian. "I. Am. Lord."

"Lord?" Sal said amused. "Well, I've been wanting to meet you for a heck of a long time!"

"It's my enlightened name!"

"That's very interesting. Why Lord?"

"Because I Lord over myself. I am the 'I am, who am,' of my life, and of my destiny. I reject the culture of consumption that destroys the spirit of men."

"And women," said Snow.

"You're a deep thinker," Sal said.

Lord gave Sal a hard, cold stare. "I have learned to see."

Los hippies se asomaron por la ventana y Salvador se acercaba.

"¿Tu hermano no está en onda con esto?" preguntó "El Señor".

"¿En onda con esto? ¡Es un padre católico!".

"¡Ay hombre! ¡Qué mala onda!".

"Él acepta a la gente, es buena onda. Pero de ninguna manera aceptaría que me pusiera pacheco".

Los tres hippies se preocuparon y encaminaron a Tino abajo del autobús. El "El Señor" le sonrió a Salvador mientras que él se detenía y asesoraba la situación.

"¿Cómo se encuentran ustedes amigos? ¿Han estado platicando con mi hermano?" Revisó a los hippies. ¿En que se estaba metiendo ahora su hermano menor?

"Estamos bien Salvador", dijo Tino tratando de sonar casual. Apuntó hacia el autobús. "Deberías de ver cómo está adentro, está muy suave".

"El Señor" dio un paso hacia adelante. "Hombre, mucho gusto". Levantó la mano saludando a Salvador en la forma estereotípica de los indígenas. "Yo soy 'El Señor'".

"¿El Señor?" dijo Salvador asombrado. "Bueno, ¡he estado queriendo conocerte por mucho tiempo!".

"¡Es mi nombre de alumbramiento!".

"Eso es muy interesante. ¿Por qué 'El Señor'?".

"Porqué yo soy mi propio señor. Yo soy el 'que soy quien soy,' de mi vida, y de mi destino. Yo rechazo la cultura de consumo que destruye el espíritu del hombre".

"Y la mujer", dijo Nieves.

"Eres un pensador profundo", dijo Salvador.

"El Señor" vio a Salvador de una manera fría y dura. "He aprendido a ver".

*PROFILE / PERFIL*

Tino, sensing a pissing contest between alpha males, intervened. "Sal, they stopped to help when they saw me pulled over."

Sal glanced at Tino and then at the hippies, and took a conciliatory tone. "Well, it's much appreciated." He pulled a small plastic bag from his pocket. "Found a master link, *hermano*. The mechanic said it's not unusual for them to wear out and pop off."

Sal took the drive chain, a set of pliers from his tool kit, and knelt next to Tino's bike.

Lord turned and hugged Tino. "Have a safe trip, man. It was real meeting you." He turned to Sal. "You got a good brother, man."

Dawn smiled and nodded a goodbye at Tino. Snow stepped to him and kissed him on the cheek. "I hope I'll see you in California," she said sadly. She turned and followed Lord and Dawn onto the bus.

Lord started the engine, pulled onto the road, and waved as they passed. Tino waved back. A bumper sticker on the back of the bus read, "Make Love Not War."

Sal finished with the drive chain and stood. The brothers watched the bus get smaller as it headed down the road.

"Looks like you made quite an impression on them," Sal said."

Tino presintiendo una apuesta de machos alfa, intervino. "Salvador, ellos se detuvieron a ayudarme cuando me vieron en la orilla".

Salvador vio a Tino, después a los hippies, y adoptó una posición reconciliadora. "Bueno es bastante apreciado". Sacó una bolsa de plástico pequeña de su bolsillo. "Hermano, encontré la conexión primaria". El mecánico dijo que era común que se gastaran y explotaran".

Salvador tomó la cadena de manejar, un par de pinzas de su juego de herramientas y se hincó junto a la moto de Tino.

"El Señor" se volteó y le dio un abrazo a Tino. "Hombre ten un viaje seguro. Fue un gusto conocerte". Se volteó hacia Salvador y le dijo "Hombre, tienes un buen hermano".

Aurora sonrió e hizo un gesto de adiós a Tino. Nieves se le acerco y lo besó en la mejilla. "Espero verte en California", dijo tristemente. Se volteó y siguió a "El Señor" y Aurora.

"El Señor" prendió el motor, se encaminó hacia la carretera y les dijo adiós con la mano cuando los pasó. Tino les respondió con la mano. Una calcomanía en la parte de atrás del autobús decía, "Haz el amor no la guerra".

Salvador terminó con la cadena de manejo y se levantó. Los hermanos vieron el autobús hacerse pequeño mientras seguía por el camino.

"Se ve que los impresionaste mucho", dijo Salvador.

"I guess so. I wonder if they're really as happy as they're making out to be."

"Hard to say," Sal said. "My guess is that they're trying to convince themselves as much as the rest of us that they've found *the way*."

"Say," Tino said. "You wouldn't have something sweet to eat stashed in your gear, would you?"

"Hungry?"

"Kind of. I just feel like having something sweet and crunchy like Oreo cookies or rocky road ice cream. Know what I mean?"

"Yeah, that'd be great, but you can forget about eating right now. We've got a lot of time to make up." Sal fired up his bike, and hit the road with a vengeance.

Tino followed him, nursing a case of the munchies.

"Creo que sí. Me pregunto si de verdad son tan felices como aparentan ser".

"Está difícil saber", dijo Salvador. "Creo que están tratando de convencerse a ellos mismos como al resto de nosotros de que han encontrado la verdad".

"Oye", dijo Tino. "¿No tendrás algo dulce que comer guardado en tu moto?"

"¿Tienes hambre?"

"Más o menos. Siento que quiero comer algo dulce y crujiente como galletas o helado con nueces. ¿Sabes a lo que me refiero?".

"Sí claro, eso sería bueno, pero por ahorita te olvidas de comer. Tenemos mucho camino que ganar por el tiempo perdido". Salvador prendió su moto con fiereza y se encaminó con venganza.

Tino lo siguió deseando una chuchería que comer.

*PROFILE / PERFIL*

# Love at First Sight

"You don't have to tell me your name," he said, walking up to the bench where she sat. "You fit the description to a tee."

She smiled. "And so do you, except that you are even more handsome than I imagined."

"And you're more beautiful than I could have imagined."

"Why did you suggest we meet in the Healdsburg Plaza?" she asked.

"Because it's where one should fall in love."

Her eyes flooded with tears. Without a thought, she leapt to her feet, cupped his cheeks in her hands, and kissed his lips. "Oh my goodness!" she said. "I've never done such a thing. I'm just beside myself!"

He felt a powerful stir in his loins. "It's meant to be. Just let it happen," he said. "My heart is beating so hard it's scary."

"And so is mine."

Their hands met, connecting the strange, yet wonderful, electricity buzzing through them. Their fingers meshed, and they began a slow stroll unable to keep their eyes from gazing at each other. His voice quavered, "Do you believe in love at first sight?"

*STORIES / CUENTOS*

## Amor a vrimera Vista

"No me tienes que decir tu nombre", le dijo él caminando hacia la banca donde ella estaba sentada. "Tu llenas la descripción al punto".

Ella sonrió "Y tú también, con la excepción de que eres más guapo de lo que me imaginaba".

"Y tú eres más hermosa de lo que pudiera haber imaginado".

"¿Por qué sugeriste que nos conociéramos en la plaza de Healdsburg?", preguntó ella.

"Porqué es el lugar donde uno debería de enamorarse".

Los ojos de ella se llenaron de lágrimas. Sin siquiera pensarlo, se levantó de un tiro, tomó sus mejillas entre sus manos y lo besó en la boca "¡Ay Dios mío!", dijo ella. "Nunca en mi vida había hecho algo así ¡Estoy fuera de juicio!".

Él sintió un movimiento poderoso entre sus piernas. "Está destinado a ser así. Deja que se den las cosas", dijo él. "Mi corazón está latiendo muy fuerte, me da miedo".

"El mío también late".

Sus manos se juntaron, conectando lo extraño, pero con una hermosa electricidad que zumbaba entre ellos. Sus dedos se entrelazaron y comenzaron a caminar lentamente sin poder quitarse los ojos de encima. Su voz tembló "¿Crees en el amor a primera vista?".

*PROFILE / PERFIL*

"Yes, yes I do, but I fell more in love with you each time we spoke online. Your being so handsome is only the icing on such a delicious cake." He stopped in mid-stride, whirled her around, and pressed his lips to hers surprising himself. And she allowed it, a willing partner in this unabashed public display, so unlike her usually shy self.

She wrapped her arms around his neck and kissed him, drinking in his very soul. Fate was a wondrous gift that had come to them, straight from the quiver of Eros.

She drew back and purred, "I've never been more sure of myself; I, I love you Kirk."

"What?"

"I said. I love you, Kirk."

"Kirk? Who's Kirk?"

"Kirk! Kirk Armstrong! The man who loves to snuggle by a winter fire. The man who loves walks on the beach, and intelligent women and cats, same as me!"

"Cats? I hate cats! And my name is Bob! I'm getting a feeling that you're not Brandy. The chick who loves the Forty-Niners, Budweiser, and Sunday afternoons at the sports bar."

"Brandy? My name's Luna, thank you very much! And, football? It's brutal. I hate football!"

"No you don't."

"Yes, I do."

"Do not."

"Sí, sí creo, pero yo me enamoré más de ti cada vez que platicábamos en internet. El hecho de que seas tan guapo es solamente la crema de un delicioso pastel". Él se detuvo a medio camino, la volteó hacia él y la besó en los labios. Sorprendiéndose a sí mismo. Ella se lo permitió, una compañera dispuesta a esos despliegues públicos, no reflejando en absoluto su personalidad callada.

Ella enredó sus brazos alrededor de su cuello y lo beso, tomándose su propia alma. El destino le había dado un maravilloso regalo que había venido hacia ellos, un regalo directo de Eros.

Ella se hizo un poco para atrás y gimió "Nunca he estado más segura de mí. Yo, yo te amo Kirk".

"¿Qué?".

"Dije que te amo, Kirk".

"¿Kirk? ¿Quién es Kirk?".

"¡Kirk! ¡Kirk Armstrong! El hombre que ama abrazarse con alguien junto a una chimenea en invierno. El hombre que ama caminar en la playa, a una mujer inteligente y a los gatos. Así como yo".

"¿Gatos? ¡Yo odio a los gatos! ¡Y mi nombre es Bob! Tengo el presentimiento que tú no eres Brandy. La mujer que ama los jugadores de los *Forty Niners*, las *budweiser* y los domingos por la tarde en un cantina de deportes".

"¿Brandy? ¡Mi nombre es Luna, muchas gracias! ¿Y fútbol americano? Eso es brutal. ¡Odio el fútbol!".

"No, no lo odias".

"Sí lo odio".

"No lo odias".

*PROFILE / PERFIL*

"Do so. And Budweiser? Paleese! Do I look like a barfly to you?"

He glared at her. "Next thing you know you're going to tell me you're one of those Merlot-sipping wine snobs who sends money to public radio."

"But I love Terry Gross!"

"Oprah?"

"Even more!"

"Eat meat?"

"Vegetarian!"


It is said that to err is human but to really screw things up takes a computer. Who would have guessed that the two did wind up falling in love after such a rocky start? They decided it would have been a shame to waste a Saturday evening, and they should at least try to get to know each other. By the end of the night they had polished off a pitcher of beer at the local sports bar (or rather, he did; she couldn't finish half a glass). Afterward they shared a dinner al fresco. She had a glass of Merlot, he another two bottles of Bud.

They married the following year at the Catholic Church to comply with his parents' wishes. The wedding was soon followed by a seaside ceremony at the coast to satisfy Luna's pagan leanings. Bob hunts on weekends, as he always had. Luna continues to volunteer at the pet hospital.

"Sí lo odio ¿Y las *budweiser*? ¡Por favor! ¿Me ves como una mosca de cantina?".

Él la vio con una mirada fulminante. "No me digas que ahora me vas a decir que tú eres una de esas que le gusta tomar el vino Merlot y que le mandan dinero a las estaciones de radio pública".

"¡Pero yo amo a Terry Gross!".

"¿Oprah?".

"¡Mucho más!".

"¿Comes carne?".

"¡Soy vegetariana!".

Se dice que errar es de humanos pero deveras que para empeorar las cosas se necesita una computadora. ¿Quién podría haber adivinado que estos dos terminarían enamorándose después de un inicio tan difícil? Decidieron que sería vergonzoso echar a perder una noche de sábado y al menos podrían tratar de conocerse. Al final de la noche, se habían terminado una jarra de cerveza en el bar local de deportes (o más bien se la termino él porque ella nada más pudo terminarse medio vaso). Después compartieron una cena en el fresco de la noche. Ella se tomó un vaso de vino merlot, el otras dos cervezas *budweiser*.

Se casaron el próximo año en la iglesia católica para cumplir con los deseos de los padres de él. Después de la ceremonia católica, otra ceremonia se llevó a cabo en la costa para satisfacer las ideas paganas de Luna. Bob se va de caza los fines de semana, como siempre lo había hecho. Luna continúa de voluntaria en el hospital de animales.

*PROFILE / PERFIL*

Bob and Luna named their son Bob after Bob's father and mother, Bob and Bobette. The boy's middle name is River, after the Russian.

Luna secretly loved being with a man who had primal tendencies. Bob was grateful to have been relieved of trying to live up to playing the role of a super-macho.

Note:

A second couple, Norm and Norma, had found each other online as well and had managed to find each other on the same night, and on the same bench in the plaza, as Bob and Luna. Norma had been sitting on the opposite end. They shared common interests and tastes in food, music, and art and soon married, but divorced the following year citing irreconcilable differences.

Bob y Luna nombraron Bob a su hijo, como el padre y la madre de Bob, Bob y Bobette. El segundo nombre es Río como el Río Ruso del condado de Sonoma.

De una manera secreta Luna estaba contenta de estar con un hombre con tendencias primitivas. Bob estaba agradecido de que lo hubiera liberado de continuar con el juego de ser un supermacho.

Nota:

Una segunda pareja, Norm y Norma, también se encontraron uno al otro a través del internet y trataron de encontrarse esa misma noche y en la misma banca de la plaza, como Bob y Luna. Norma había estado sentada en el lado opuesto de la banca. Compartían intereses y gustos similares en comida, música y arte, muy pronto estarían casados. Pero se divorciaron el próximo año diciendo que eran irreconciliablemente diferentes.

# Acknowledgments

This book would not have come to pass had it not been for Waights Taylor. Not only was it his idea for me to put this collection together, his encouragement and patience were invaluable. *Muchas gracias, mi amigo.*

I also am indebted to the fine writers whose work I so respect and admire for taking time to review and comment on my work.

Al Young is an internationally acclaimed novelist and California Poet Laureate Emeritus.

David Beckman is a novelist, poet, and playwright. His plays have been staged in New York City, Los Angeles, and Santa Rosa. He also authored the novel *Under Pegasus*.

Ianthe Brautigan is the author of *You Can't Catch Death: A Daughter's Memoir*.

Jonah Raskin, prolific Sonoma County writer, has authored enough books to fill a shelf in my writing studio. In researching his book on Jack London, Jonah came across a London quote, "I have been writing like a tiger all day." Jonah must be descended from the same litter.

Susan Swartz, author of *Juicy Tomatoes, Ripe Living after 50*, is a radio commentator and columnist for *The Press Democrat*.

# Reconocimientos

Este libro no hubiera podido existir si no hubiera sido por Waights Taylor. No sólo fue su idea el que hiciera está colección, su ánimo y paciencia fueron invaluables. Muchas gracias, mi amigo.

También estoy en deuda con los finos escritores con los cuales trabajo, respeto y admiro por tomarse el tiempo de revisar mi trabajo y escribir sus comentarios.

Al Young, quien es un novelista internacionalmente aclamado y un poeta emérito laureado de California.

David Beckman, quien es un novelista, poeta y escritor de teatro. Sus obras han sido presentadas en la ciudad de New York, Los Ángeles y Santa Rosa. También es el autor de la novela *Bajo pegasus*.

Ianthe Brautigan, autora de *No puedes atrapar a la muerte: memorias de una hija*.

Jonah Raskin, un prolífero escritor del condado de Sonoma. Ha escrito tantos libros que pueden llenar un librero en mi estudio. Mientras conducía su investigación de Jack London, Jonah se encontró un escrito de London que decía: "He estado escribiendo todo el día como un tigre". Jonah debió de haber descendido de la misma cuna.

Susan Swartz, autora de *Tomates jugosos, viviendo después de los 50*, es comentarista en una estación de radio y es columnista del periódico *The Press Democrat*.

Thanks to my editor, Arlene Miller, for her editorial eye on my work to make it presentable.

And a final big thank you to Laura Larque, Maria Inez Oria Peña, Mónica Ledesma-Lugo, and Dina Lopez for their patience in translating the poems and short stories. They did not simply but captured the spirit of my verses. Good job!

Armando's biggest supporters are his wife, Kathy, his two grown children, Cecilia and Emilio, and his twin brother, Fernando.

# Acerca del autor

Armando García-Dávila irrumpió en el mundo literario del condado de Sonoma a finales de la década de 1990. Lo que empezó como una serie de opiniones educativas y escritos acerca de la primera guerra en el Golfo Pérsico, y la memoria de sus amigos muertos en la Guerra de Vietnam, se inclina hacia la poesía para expresar un amplio contenido de pensamientos arraigados en sus raíces méxico-americanas y su educación católica. Para clarificar sus raíces humildes, él se llama a sí mismo el poeta de "cuello azul", poeta del "pueblo trabajador".

El columnista Ray Holley escribió entonces "Asegúrate de leer a Armando... (mientras que) tienes la oportunidad de verlo en un lugar íntimo antes de que, con justicia, se haga famoso por su trabajo".

Sus poemas han sido ampliamente publicados y también han hallado su camino en los boletines de noticias de sindicatos y en los púlpitos de los domingos. Ha leído sus poemas a trabajadores inmigrantes de la uva y a los presos de la prisión de San Quintín. En el año de 2002, fue nombrado por la ciudad de Healdsburg como el Literario Laureado.

www.ingramcontent.com/pod-product-compliance
Lightning Source LLC
Chambersburg PA
CBHW071304110426
42743CB00042B/1166

Gracias a mi editora, Arlene Miller, por su colaboración editorial en mi trabajo y hacerlo presentable.

Y finalmente muchísimas gracias a las señoras Laura Larque, María Inés Oria Peña, Mónica Ledesma-Lugo, y Dina Lopez por su paciencia al traducir los poemas y los cuentos cortos. No sólo tradujeron palabras sino que también percibieron el espíritu del mis versos.

Los principales apoyos de Armando son su esposa Kathy, sus hijos Cecilia y Emilio y su gemelo Fernando (Nando).

# About the Author

Armando García-Dávila burst upon the Sonoma County literary world in the latter part of the 1990s. What started as a series of op. ed. pieces he wrote concerning the first Persian Gulf War and the memories of friends killed in the Vietnam War, turned to poetry to express wide ranging thoughts rooted in his Mexican-American/Catholic upbringing. To make clear his humble background, he called himself the "blue-collar" poet.

Newspaper columnist Ray Holley wrote at the time, "Be sure to check out Armando...(while) you still have a chance to see him in an intimate setting before he becomes justly famous for his work."

His poems have been widely published and also found their way into union newsletters and Sunday pulpits. He has read his poetry to immigrant laborers in the vineyards and prisoners in San Quentin. In 2002, he was chosen as the Healdsburg Literary Laureate.